*Also by Frank Jewett Mather, Jr.*

THE COLLECTORS
ESTIMATES IN ART
A HISTORY OF ITALIAN PAINTING
MODERN PAINTING: 1664-1914
VENETIAN PAINTERS

D0908542

WESTERN EUROPEAN PAINTING OF THE RENAISS

REMBRANDT. Jan Six.—Six Coll., Amsterdam.

Frontispiece.

FRANK JEWETT MATHER, Jr.

# WESTERN EUROPEAN PAINTING OF THE RENAISSANCE

TUDOR PUBLISHING COMPANY

New York 1948

REPRINTED 1948
BY TUDOR PUBLISHING COMPANY

PRINTED IN THE
UNITED STATES OF AMERICA

TO

HELEN CLAY FRICK

WITH HIGH PERSONAL REGARD AND IN RECOGNITION

OF HER WISE AND GENEROUS FURTHERANCE OF ART HISTORICAL STUDIES

THROUGH THE FOUNDATION OF

THE FRICK ART REFERENCE LIBRARY

# CONTENTS

# PREFACE

Encouraged by the success of my *History of Italian Painting*, I now survey in a similar spirit the wider and more difficult field of Western European Painting of the Renaissance. Again I have had to omit many minor painters, some of them charming, in order to treat the great painters with reasonable fullness; in short, I have avoided anything like an encyclopedic handling of my theme. Encyclopedias, after all, abound.

When right and left are used in describing pictures, spectator right and left are meant unless the context clearly indicates the contrary. Pictures in Spain are located as they were before the civil war. When, in locating a picture, nothing but the name of a city is used, the chief museum in that city is intended. Thus, New York means Metropolitan Museum; Madrid, the Prado.

While, as is my habit, this book is written rather from direct experience of pictures than from other books, I have not neglected the literature of the subject, and my obligations to many predecessors are expressed in the bibliography and notes.

Where so many photographs were reproduced, it seemed tedious to repeat the usual elaborate acknowledgments through hundreds of captions. Accordingly I have acknowledged only exceptional aid and courtesy in the captions, and here express in general but no less grateful terms my obligations to many European and American museums which have facilitated my study of their treasures and have permitted the reproduction of their photographs. Among many museums in America I have depended heavily on the Chicago Art Institute, the Detroit Art Institute, the Frick Collection, the Metropolitan Museum. The Frick Art Reference Library has often shortened the task of minute research for me. Rudolf Lesch, Inc., have been indefatigably helpful in procuring rare photographs from widely scattered sources.

A writer who feels his craft is chiefly a means of communication always has in mind a certain kind of reader. I have written primarily for a reader who loves pictures, has reached some appreciative understanding of them, and wishes to extend and enrich his experience. But I feel also this book may help that perhaps rare sort of beginner who, aspiring to new experience, is willing to pay the price thereof in attention.

F. J. M., JR.

Three Brooks,
Washington Crossing, Pa.
October 16, 1939.

# CHAPTER I

## ITALIAN INFLUENCE ON GOTHIC TRA-
## DITION; THE WESTERN NEGATION

A COMPLETE title for this book should read *Western European Painting of the Two Renaissances*, for there really were two—first a development of the Gothic style in the direction of analytical realism; and later an assimilation of Italian stylism. The order of time suggests that the Italianizing movement may have destroyed and superseded the native endeavor, and this yielding to Italy has been bewailed by critics from Ruskin to Strzygowoski. To me the case looks rather like this: Long before Western Europe had surrendered esthetically to Italy, the Gothic Renaissance style showed every sign of exhaustion. It had culminated splendidly in Massys, Dürer, Gruenewald and Holbein, and then declined sharply into mannerism, from what seem to be inner causes. It plainly needed a rest, and after a half-century of intermittent activity, and recuperation, it emerged with renewed strength in the seventeenth century. Accordingly, those Transalpine painters who turned from their native inheritance to Italy were really not traitors, but intelligent renovators. Without the reorganization of Northern realism under Italian auspices, there would possibly have been generally in the North such a long period of stagnation as we actually witness in the Germanies. But my discrimination of two Renaissances in the North must be weighed against the view that there was none.

Many scholars feel that the development of Gothic realism in the fifteenth and early sixteenth century should not be called a Renaissance, for it involved no revival of classical antiquity; the sixteenth century they dismiss as manneristic; the seventeenth century is covered by the broad term baroque. To discuss these general terms may seem unprofitable; yet they imply attitudes, and, in candor, I should avow mine. Since the zeal for more truthful representation was constant in the Italian Renaissance, and equally so in the North, I do not see how we can deny to the late Gothic painting of the North the quality of a Renaissance of realism.

While in the sixteenth century this native realistic endeavor was somewhat in abeyance, or perverted, it never died. It emerged splendidly in the familiar painting of the seventeenth century, energized with new resources largely drawn from Italy. Thus, while the subject matter of Vermeer of Delft is actual and contemporary, his construction of the figure owes some debt to Italy, while his conception of spatial effect merely brings up to date the feeling and practice of Campin and Scorel. In short, the native, realistic Renaissance, as it progressed fitfully, drew in what it needed from many sources, native and exotic.

As for the seventeenth century, I will not quarrel with those who wish to comprise most of its achievement under the term baroque. For me it is merely the tardy flowering of the classical Renaissance in the North, or, in Spain, a normal persistence of Gothic realism—facilitating the assimilation of Caravaggio's tenebrism alongside the Italianate baroque. Not to labor this matter of classification tediously, we should beware of forcing so complicated a period as the seventeenth century into any simple framework. No single word covers Rubens, Poussin, Rembrandt, Velasquez, Murillo collectively, or indeed any one of them singly.

However, the persistent tendencies in seventeenth century painting are throughout classicizing, as in Rubens and Poussin, or realistic as in Frans Hals and Velasquez. In short, the Western European Renaissance in the seventeenth century pretty well repeated the pattern of the Early Renaissance in Italy, where we find such various contemporaries as Mantegna, Castagno, Giovanni Bellini and Botticelli; but always in one fashion or another an endeavor to master the representation of natural appearances tempered by reverence for the solutions of the problem of representation already achieved by the Greeks and Romans. It was the balance of these two endeavors—now swinging towards naturalism, now towards classicism—that made the greatness of the Italian Renaissance.

The special character of the painting of the Western European Renaissance in late Gothic times—its at once morally simpler and materially more ornate character—rests upon a negation. Western Europe in the fifteenth century lacked the presence and the vision of classical antiquity. While the Italian ever had before him the evidences of a civilization grander and more urbane than his own, the Fleming, German, Frenchman or Spaniard lived unrebuked in his own world. In a country where the sculptures and the buildings of Rome still stood, there was always among superior spirits a nostalgia for what those monuments represented. Western Europe knew nothing about such homesickness.

Civilization rests mostly on memory, and the memory of Western Europe was short as compared with that of Italy. One may say that the superior Italian at all times found Antiquity looking over his shoulder and keeping him up to his manners. No such mentor was at the shoulders of the Western European man. Italy was immensely rich, but her Renaissance painters, with an antique stoicism, ordinarily kept display of mere finery subordinate in their pictures, as well as ornate and overcomplicated decoration. Exceptions to this rule usually mark an Italian painting as provincial. But the Flemish or Spanish primitive painter tricked out his figures with the most exaggerated display of ornament. The rich man of the North had no scruples as to personal display, and the painters found no incongruity in representing the saints as wealthy patricians.

For Western Europe this meant a greater freedom of expression and small restraint from precedent or taste. A concrete example or so will make the matter clear. If any Italian painter ever represented the Christchild in newborn skinniness and ungainliness, I have not seen his work. An Italian *Bambino* never looks less than six months old at birth, and often two years. But a Christchild by Jan van Eyck or Rogier de la Pasture looks just as scrawny as every baby looks when he or she enters the world. The Northerner accepts the look of things; the Italian changes or attenuates it in the interest of beauty as he conceives it. Again, a bloodstained or painfully contorted Christ you will hardly find in the Renaissance painting of Italy. But in Western Europe agonized and horribly bloodstained Christs abound. The Western European artist has stood on the facts; the Italian artist has transformed them so that his picture may not repel. Italian painting in its good estate tends to return to those simple and legible compositions of religious themes bequeathed by the Christian East. Northern and Western Europe had done the same until the fifteenth century. Then we find a tendency to amplify and often confuse the old compositional patterns, and as well to invent new ones. Such experimentalism was at once the strength and the weakness of the Gothic North in its early Renaissance.

All this implies that the Western European painter was ordinarily more curious and strenuous in observation than the Italian painter, less dependent on the mind's eye. In religious painting the Northerner was more likely to profit by such spectacles as the Mystery plays, while the Italian would remain within his pictorial tradition. Perhaps it all comes down to saying that the Italian painter worked for a world that had early achieved civilization, while the Western European painter worked for a world in which civilization was only incipient, but vigorous and aggressive. The Italian Renaissance, considered in its broadest aspect, may be regarded as the tardy afterglow of an epoch of Hellenizing culture; whereas the Northern Renaissance may be regarded as the presage of a new orientation of the human spirit towards science and away from art.

It may be noted also that this experimentalism of the Northern painter was fostered by a technical negation. He lacked the discipline, ever bearing upon the Italian painter, of the practice of painting in fresco. Fresco painting had abounded in the North and West during the Romanesque and Early Gothic periods, but as churches and public buildings from the fourteenth century on were virtually skeletonized, there was lessened opportunity for mural painting, and pictured windows took its place. Accordingly, the Northern painter was never schooled in an art where everything had to be thought out before beginning actual work. He was more free to create as he executed.

As the Renaissance wore on in the North, its task of assimilation from the antique and from Italy necessarily went through wasteful processes of trial and error which Italy was spared. And this was inevitable, for Italy was, after all, merely reclaiming and recovering her own, whereas Western Europe was emulating something alien to her native genius. Naturally then, the Western European Renaissance in its ultimate Hellenizing phase produced nothing comparable either in quantity or quality to the greatest Italian painting, offering us, rather than a school, isolated great figures—a Rubens, a Rembrandt, a Velasquez, a Poussin. And for the same reason the greatest achievements of Western European painting are generally in, or closely associated with the native naturalistic tradition, or with the kindred art in Italy of Caravaggio.

Notwithstanding the tendency of modern painting to disappear in the blue of abstraction and dialectic, the realistic Northern tradition is still that of most of us English-speaking folk, and probably that of unsophisticated folk everywhere. And the tradition of the Italian Renaissance still means to most of us what it meant to the great realistic painters of the Netherlands and Spain. It is a warning to see and work in a large, simple and clear manner, rather than a pattern to follow closely. Thus as we study in Western Europe the rise of minute realism, its broadening and chastening through trial and error and through reference to the great painting of Italy, we are, unless we happen to be surrealists or the like, really studying ourselves. In the Italian Renaissance we sojourn in a fairer and more coherent world, in which we are at best sympathetic tourists; in the Northern Renaissance we find ourselves in more accidental surroundings, but also at home.

Italy through elimination and sacrifice achieved supreme quality somewhat at the expense of variety and richness. Western Europe, declining to make such sacrifice, produced the richest and most various painting the world has seen, and somewhat at the expense of quality. Here naturally I am not thinking in terms of technique, in which Western Europe may seem to excel Italy, but in terms of the respective creative moods implied. It was a Northerner, Goethe, who wrote that "the master reveals himself in renunciation," but the sentiment is Latin. As compared with Italy, Western Europe did very little renouncing, and this again makes it a homeland for us.

## CHAPTER II

## THE GOTHIC BACKGROUND, THE SHIFT TOWARDS MINUTE REALISM; HUBERT VAN EYCK

Fig. 1.   Hubert van Eyck, finished by Jan.   Adoration of the Lamb.—St. Bavon, Ghent.

FIG. 3. SIMONE MARTINI. Madonna Annunciate.—Antwerp.

FIG. 2. Unknown Dutch Painter, 1363. Calvary with Donor.—Antwerp.

11

FIG. 4.  Franco-Flemish, Ms. Miniature, about
1410.  St. Christopher.—Art Market.

FIG. 5.  MELCHIOR BROEDERLAM.  Annunciation
and Visitation.—*Dijon.*

FIG. 6. Limbourg Miniaturists. The Month of August.—*Chantilly.*

13

Fig. 7.  Hubert van Eyck.  Miracle of Count William of Holland.—
Lost Turin Hours.

Fig. 8. (Upper left) HUBERT VAN EYCK. Birth of St. John the Baptist.—
Hours of Milan, Turin.

Fig. 9. (Upper right) HUBERT VAN EYCK. Voyage of St. Julian.—Lost
Turin Hours.

Fig. 10. (Lower) HUBERT VAN EYCK. The Three Marys at the Tomb.—
Coll. of Sir Robert Cook, Richmond.

FIG. 11. HUBERT VAN EYCK. Cal- FIG. 12. HUBERT VAN EYCK. Last
vary.—New York. Judgment.—New York.

16

FIG. 13. HUBERT VAN EYCK. Madonna with St. Michael, Donor, and St. Catherine.—Dresden.

17

Fig. 14. Hubert van Eyck. St. Anthony and Donor.—Copenhagen.

Fig. 15. Hubert van Eyck, figures by Jan(?). Madonna of Chancellor Nicolas Rolin.—Paris.

Fig. 16. Jan van Eyck. The Singing Angels.—*St. Bavon, Ghent.*

Fig. 17. Hubert van Eyck. The
Playing Angels.—*St. Bavon, Ghent.*

Fig. 18. Jan van
Eyck. Adam.—*St. Ba-*
*von, Ghent.*

Fig. 19. Hubert van
Eyck(?). Eve.—*St. Ba-*
*von, Ghent.*

THE CONTINUITY of Gothic, pictorial style north of the Alps is better shown in the manuscript miniatures than in the few surviving frescoes and panel paintings. In the illustrated manuscripts from the twelfth to the sixteenth century we find the exemplars for mural and panel painting, for design in stained glass, and even for sculptured figures and groups. From the Christian East, and probably mostly from Constantinople, the Occident had early borrowed a very complete repertory of Biblical and other religious compositions. Apart from trifling and exceptional innovations, it held faithfully to these traditional patterns until the fifteenth century, but it animated the originally static figures in a fashion of its own. The bodies sway, there is greater freedom of gesture and expression of emotion. Until well along in the fourteenth century, the figure groups usually have no local setting, but are profiled sharply on a mere base against a gilded or chequered background, with a few properties. This stylistic situation is shown in a panel of the Crucifixion, at Antwerp, which was painted at Haarlem in 1363 (Fig. 2).

Before the middle of the fourteenth century an odd change takes place. The figures tend to flatten out and lose substance; the edges of their drapery crisp and roll and flutter in a controlled tension; the figures become merely picturesque color spots which are arranged with fastidious taste; for individual expression is substituted an unspecific and generalized delicacy and refinement; a soundly illustrative is plainly yielding to a merely esthetic ideal, and this is a sign of that decadent grace which is generally assumed by any art when it is about to die. I have briefly described the main characteristics of that manner which, because it overran all Europe outside the domain of the Eastern Church, the great French critic, Count de la Borde, called the Cosmopolitan Style.

Its most distinguished practitioner was Simone Martini of Siena (Fig. 3), who worked as well at Naples and Avignon. From him and his disciples seems to have developed what we may call a Riviera style, which is traceable from Palermo and Naples to Valencia, and everywhere extended inland. Fifty years after Simone's death, the miniaturists of the "Très belles heures" for the Duke of Berri, before 1400, knew and imitated Simone's compositions. So it has been natural to credit him with the invention of the Cosmopolitan Style. Into so broad and difficult a theme I cannot enter, but I may at least express a conviction that Simone's influence was merely contributory to a style already actively in formation in the North.

Towards the end of the century, the chequered backgrounds of manuscript miniatures give a certain place to local setting, and the landscape forms assume the rippling and spiraling character of the figures (Fig. 4). No wholehearted realism is involved; the endeavor remains exclusively esthetic and stylistic. This stage is well represented in the Calvary and other scenes of the Passion represented in the famous Parement of Narbonne, at Paris (Fig. 91), and in the miniatures made for the Duke of Berri and Charles V. A number of the earlier miniatures of the so-called Hours of Turin and Milan are ascribed plausibly to the unknown master of the Parement. They show all the characteristics of the Cosmopolitan Style in its last estate. Elsewhere in this book many examples of this style are illustrated.

At the close of the century there is a move away from the Cosmopolitan Style in works now touched, now guided by Italian, probably Lombard, influence of a more realistic sort. Thus in 1398 the painter Melchior Broederlam of Ypres made big shutters for a sculptured wood altarpiece in the Carthusian monastery at Dijon. The subjects are The Annunciation and Visitation (Fig. 5), The Flight into Egypt and The Presentation in the Temple. The high-rising mountain setting is fully, if conventionally, realized after the fashion set in Siena by the Lorenzetti. The figures are natural, with only slight traces of the Cosmopolitan Style. There is little decorative color spotting for its own sake, and the general low tonality and distribution of light and dark evince a concern with form and perhaps even with atmospheric conditions. Everything recalls the gentler mood of the contemporary Lorenzo Monaco. We are not far from fully rationalized illustration, and the century-long decorative conventions are almost completely in abeyance.

About the same stage of development towards an analytical realism is shown in the famous miniatures which Pol von Limbourg and his brother made early in the fifteenth century for the Duke of Berri. Some of the earlier miniatures are still in the Cosmopolitan Style.

Those painted by the brothers Limbourg are in a new and less stylized manner, for example, the miniature for August, with a hawking party in the foreground and reapers and bathers in middle distance (Fig. 6). In the big illustrations for the months of the year, preserved at Chantilly, it seems as if the charming and animated bas-reliefs of the works of the months seen on the fronts of so many French cathedrals had assumed color, called in additional figures, developed suitable backgrounds. In the background of the occupations of the months always appears one of the many chateaux owned by the Duke. Since these miniatures were made for a wealthy potentate, the manner is properly courtly, with only residual traces of the decorative conventions of the Cosmopolitan Style. There is probably some influence from the courtly painting of Lombardy—indeed contemporaries called such painting Lombard work, *ouvraige de Lombardie*, but the precise Italian derivation has never been ascertained.

Throughout, the drawing and expression of the figures are masterly beyond anything the Gothic past had shown. In the setting the Limbourgs did not realize the full implications of their invention. While there are admirable bits, the bare trees in the pruning season, the wheat fields at harvest, on the whole the setting is in the nature of a backdrop. The figures are rather before it than in it. One feels that these painters should have done more or less. One can read the works of the months more easily in the Gothic bas-reliefs and in the medallions with gold grounds in the Kalendars of the older missals and books of hours. The very variety and richness of the Limbourg illustrators is in some degree their defect. They have neither renounced nor insisted enough, but it is a defect full of promise for the future.

So far, all the pictures we have been considering have been painted in tempera, that is, in colors laid on in an egg vehicle or some gelatinous equivalent. Such pigments set quickly and very hard, could not readily be manipulated, and in particular had little transparency. For a silhouette or linear treatment they were eminently suitable, and with such pigments the painter was bound to think primarily of a blond decorative effect. When he began to think in terms of constructive light and shade and of great elaboration of details, he would need colors of a more manageable sort. In short, the art of Broederlam and the Limbourgs had reached a stage where it really required painting in oil, and that need was soon to be supplied by the young Netherlandish master, Jan van Eyck.

More than a century after Jan van Eyck's death in 1441, the tradition still persisted that he had invented the art of painting in oil colors. In the absence of contemporary records we do not know exactly what his method was, and probably never shall. Something may be gathered from the look of his pictures. Their brilliance tells us that his vehicle was something other than ordinary linseed oil, which resinates and darkens with age. At least it is certain that the vehicle was in the nature of a very permanent and flexible varnish, and his paints rather like our enamel than our ordinary oil colors, so that no finishing coat of varnish was necessary.

The advantages of the method were manifold. The painted surfaces could be manipulated at will. Many of the colors were transparent and could be glazed over a foundation of another color. Such superimposed films of color yield a depth and translucency of tone that the opaque, tempera colors could not attain. Finally, the finished work was very durable. Ordinary wetting, which ruined a tempera painting, did an oil painting no harm, the crackle was smaller and the tendency to come away from the ground less. Few old pictures in our galleries compare in preservation with those painted in Jan van Eyck's method.

Just when Jan made his invention we do not know, but since there are many pictures in the new method by 1430—his own earliest dated picture being of 1432—and we must allow some time for the divulgation of the new method, 1420 or even earlier seems about the probable time. Guicciardini, writing about 1561, gives 1410 as the date of the invention, and may transmit a true tradition. It is to be assumed that Jan promptly gave his elder brother, Hubert, the benefit of his discovery.

Concerning Jan van Eyck we have abundant information for the nineteen years between 1422 and 1441. Of Hubert we know only that he was actively employed at Ghent in 1425, died there September 18, 1426, leaving the famous altarpiece of the Adoration of the Lamb to be finished six years later by his brother Jan. A metrical inscription on that altarpiece states that Hubert had no superior in painting and that Jan was second in that art, also that Jan finished the work at the instance of Jodoc Vyd, a prosperous fiscal agent of the Duke of Burgundy. Our reconstruction of Hubert's work then rests upon ascertaining his part in the Ghent altarpiece—a most difficult problem—

and grouping together whatever pictures seem stylistically identical with that part.

With Jan we are in better case. For the last nine years of his life we have eight portraits, mostly signed and dated, four Madonnas, and an admirable unfinished St. Barbara. There is as well a portrait of Christ and an Annunciation which may be of early date. I am omitting doubtful and merely attributed paintings. All these pictures yield a consistent impression of their maker. We have to do with a penetrating and most accurate eye, with a sure but rather rigid hand, with a modeling so tense that the skin seems stretched, with a color brilliant rather than rich and harmonious, with an obtuseness to niceties of illumination, for which are substituted merely sufficient formulas. On the negative side there is hardly a trace of the calligraphy of the Cosmopolitan Style, the draperies reproducing the angular forms of contemporary sculpture in wood. The whole suggestion is of an artist too young to have been trained in the Cosmopolitan Style, a stark realist of the minute sort, an objective observer with little feeling beyond curiosity for what he saw. Such seems to be a fair inference as to Jan's artistic character from the pictures that are surely his.

We have as well a group of pictures technically very close to Jan and sometimes ascribed to him which reveal an artist trained in the Cosmopolitan Style, a sensitive and emotional person, an enthusiast for landscape beauty, deeply interested in the subtleties and varieties of illumination, with a draughtsmanship and handling very flexible as compared with Jan's. And all these pictures are similar in handling and feeling to that portion of the Ghent altarpiece which most critics regard as Hubert's. Many respected scholars assign this group to Jan's early activity, but this is to suppose that he hardened amazingly in middle life. Now the rule is that artists, like human beings generally, mellow as they mature—grow more urbane. So while the ascription of what I shall call the Hubert Group to Jan may seem justified by minute analysis, all broader consideration of the problem makes such a solution too preposterous to be seriously entertained.

As a result of this preliminary survey we seem to have a great idealist painter, Hubert, trained in the Cosmopolitan Style—that is, born no later than 1370—an artist whose fame, attested by the inscription of the Ghent altarpiece, early faded because there was otherwise little documentary record of him, and, like his Gothic predecessors, he failed to sign his pictures. We have also an objective and

realistic artist, Jan, too young to have been influenced by the Cosmopolitan Style—that is, born no earlier than 1380—who has always been
famous because he invented oil painting, was attached to the court
of Philip the Good and exercised recorded activities, and, finally, had
the good habit of signing his pictures. Under these conditions it was
inevitable that all the Huberts should be credited to Jan. Since the
account of Hubert's work which I am about to give is merely an
opinion based on long and loving study—an opinion contested by
many able scholars—it has seemed fair to the reader to show in brief
the basis upon which the opinion is formed.

We have seen that the settings of Broederlam and the Limbourgs
were like a skillfully designed scenic backdrop or curtain. The curtain was suddenly and sensationally to be raised upon Nature herself.
In a big book of hours started about 1400 for the Duke of Berri we
pass sensationally from an early group of miniatures in the Cosmopolitan Style to a wholly new and beautiful manner. In nine manuscript miniatures made before 1417, for the second owner of the
manuscript, William, Count of Holland, we see wind-swept estuaries
with driving clouds (Fig. 7), the glory of sunset down a tranquil river,
storm-tossed boats in a mixed sea (Fig. 9). We also look into spacious
and handsomely illuminated interiors seen in terms of convincing
perspective—the room in which St. John is born (Fig. 8), the grand
interior of a Gothic church with a coffin awaiting the rite for the
dead. Never before or since has an art been born so full-grown. The
artist can do whatever he wants with the figure, with landscape, with
architecture, and he does so from his own observation and almost
without aid from his predecessors.

Who is the painter? In the alertness and tenderness with which
the human form is treated, in the spacious beauty of his carefully
arranged parklike landscape, he is closely related to the designer of
the Ghent altarpiece, Hubert van Eyck. Indeed this wonderful book
of hours has a striking anticipation of the central theme of that masterpiece in a group of celestial maidens gently approaching the Sacri-
ficial Lamb displayed on a hillock. It is the motive which we shall
find some ten years later greatly amplified in The Adoration of the
Lamb.

Now while it is not certain that the author of these amazing
miniatures is Hubert van Eyck, to think otherwise is to multiply
hypotheses gratuitously. It is hardly reasonable to suppose that along-

side Hubert flourished a painter equally great, who painted in a style resembling Hubert's, and concerning whom absolutely no tradition has been passed down to us. Reasons for denying these tender and idealizing inventions to the stolid Jan have already been given.

We may note that this great book of hours was started in the late fourteenth century for the Duke of Berri by the master of the Parement of Narbonne or one of his disciples, that the unpictured part of it came into the possession of Count William about 1414, and Hubert's miniatures were probably begun shortly thereafter. Count William died May 31, 1417. The manuscript passed into other hands, and its historiation was completed by the middle of the century. It was divided into three parts, of which one was long kept by the Turin Library, and only lately lost by fire, another, the latest part as regards miniatures, is in the collection of Maurice Rothschild at Paris, while the most important fragment has recently passed from the collection of Prince Trivulzio in Milan to the Library of Turin.

About these nine miniatures, on the basis of style and feeling may be grouped about half a dozen anonymous pictures of evidently early date. They all are in one way or other related to the Ghent altarpiece, and they suggest much about the artist who conceived them. He was trained in the Cosmopolitan Style; he was a lover of landscape and immensely skillful in compiling it out of rich memories; he was assiduous in studying the look of architecture and in searching the lovely mysteries of interior illumination; in treating the figure he is sympathetic, tender and alert. He had traveled, probably to Italy, for he loves to set snow-clad mountains against the sky, and introduces humble semi-tropical plants into his foregrounds. In all the figure drawing and composition there is a whiff of Italy, something reticent and distinguished—in Flanders absolutely exotic. All these characteristics recur in the Adoration of the Lamb, serving there a new dignity and stateliness—which again is a solitary note in the art of Flanders.

Of these pictures the Three Marys at the Tomb (Fig. 10), in the Sir Robert Cook Collection, Richmond, is probably the earliest. The sense of a cool and even misty morning twilight is admirably conveyed. Surprise, eagerness and hesitance in the holy women are well felt. The hulking forms of the sleeping armored guards are perhaps overemphasized. The nearby terrain is firmly realized both in its forms and in the half-light which sweeps its knolls, but the picturesque background of Jerusalem on its hilltop is composed after the manner of the Limbourgs as a backdrop and is spatially unsatisfying, which seems a reason for setting this fine picture rather early, say about 1415 at latest.

Next may come the pair of little shutters, for a lost Adoration of the Kings, now owned by the Metropolitan Museum. The Calvary (Fig. 11) in its tall panel does not seem to me extraordinary as a picture, but it is full of thrilling details, richly modulated emotionally, and it has a lovely landscape outlet looking towards snow-clad mountains. It is more elaborate and populous than any Calvary previously made north of the Alps, and one may imagine some influence from the late Gothic painting of Italy. The color shows the bold spotting of azure and crimson proper to an artist trained in miniature painting.

The Last Judgment (Fig. 12), on the dexter panel, is on the other hand a highly novel and imaginative invention. A foreshortened, skeleton Death spreads great bat wings as a kind of domical canopy over a land and sea giving up their dead. Above, a gorgeously armored St. Michael stands strongly, feet apart, ready to render judgment. At the top an enthroned Christ, flanked by apostles and saints displayed in a very formal symmetry, presides. This portion is conventional and even insipid, but it abounds in lovely faces. Death dominating the resurrection is one of the finest creations of its moment in the North. The date is probably not far from that of the miniatures, say 1417–1420.

The Giustiniani triptych at Dresden (Fig. 13) is, apart from the Ghent altarpiece, the most beautiful picture in the Hubert Group. The Madonna is enthroned in the nave of a Romanesque church, in the aisles of which, in the shutters, stand a lovely, meditative St. Catherine, and a burly and competent St. Michael, fantastically garbed in rich armor, with a kneeling donor, Giustiniani, beside him. Outside the shutters, in monochrome, are a Virgin and Gabriel annunciate as lovely in their sweet gracility and ease as any contemporary vision of Fra Angelico. Elaboration reaches a limit in this little picture, but it is an elaboration that is never confusing or indulged for its own sake. Everything plays into the pictorial unity. All forms, every particularity of lighting, are sensitively searched—the glint through bull's-eyes in the windows, the flash on the floor, the sweep of the light as it touches or caresses complicated moldings and capitals, or defines the textures of metals, stuffs, flesh, hair—all this is an exquisite celebration of things, but of things as they hallow and enrich the Mother of God, her companions and her abode. In the seventeenth century this picture still carried a traditional attribution to Hubert. Accordingly we may regard this as the surest ascription in the Hubert Group. It has been dated as early as 1410, but because of the perfection of its workmanship I am inclined to set it as late as 1420.

Hardly inferior to it is the little standing Madonna in a Church, known to us only through old copies—the best at Berlin. It retains the idyllic sweetness of the Dresden triptych, but is somewhat less elaborate, while the lighting is more simple, audacious and truthful. A date of 1422–1424 seems right for it.

St. Anthony with a Donor, at Copenhagen (Fig. 14), is apparently a shutter for a wooden figure of the saint ordered by Robert Poorter of Ghent, and mentioned in his will of May 9, 1426, as in the hands of "Meester Hubrechte." This has been contested by good authority, and the panel has been ascribed to a pupil of the Van Eycks, Petrus Christus. A little observation of the fine, rocky landscape, most sensitively worked out in fine gradations of light and dark, incidentally identical with the treatment of the crags behind the Holy Pilgrims in the Ghent altarpiece, a comparison of the head of St. Anthony with that of St. John at Ghent, speaks for the same mind and hand. If this view be right, the panel is very precious, because being painted at the same time as the masterpiece of Hubert, it assures us that the actual painting of the Ghent altarpiece must be mostly by his hand.

Other pictures, such as the admirable Stigmatization of St. Francis at Philadelphia, may be ascribed to Hubert with some plausibility, but upon this ambiguous ground, with a single exception, I shall not venture. The rather big panel of the Madonna with Nicolas Rolin, Chancellor of Burgundy, at Paris (Fig. 15), has been frequently ascribed to Hubert. Certainly the wide-spreading river landscape with cities and bridges and distant snow mountains is entirely in the manner of the miniatures, the Calvary and the Ghent altarpiece. The rather stiff portrait and somewhat perfunctory Madonna are more in Jan's style. It is possible that we have an unfinished Hubert with the figures finished by Jan, possible also that it is a work of Jan's early years. From the apparent age of the donor, who was born in 1376, the picture can hardly be dated later than 1425.

The masterpiece of Hubert van Eyck, perhaps of all Flemish painting, is the Adoration of the Lamb, which is still shown in the church for which it was painted, St. Bavon's, formerly St. John's, at Ghent. Before approaching the very difficult problem of authorship, we may briefly describe the piece, recalling that Hubert van Eyck died late in 1426, and that under pressure from the donor, Jodoc Vyd, Jan had the piece ready for exhibition in May of 1432 (Fig. 1). It consists of two orders, a lower order showing four processions converging upon the altar of the Lamb—the figures of small scale—and an upper order with Christ enthroned as King of Kings, the Virgin Mary, John the Baptist, singing angels, angels playing musical instruments, Adam and Eve—all these in varying but always large scale—serving as sponsors for the celestial ceremony below.

In the lower range of the open altarpiece are five panels; in the upper, seven. The uprights dividing the panels fail to meet, and the resulting effect is disorderly. For this and other reasons Professor Panofsky suggests persuasively that the altarpiece was put together by Jan from at least two works left in Hubert's shop. The upper order, he thinks, was made by adding to the three central figures the two panels of angels, perhaps intended for organ shutters; to these were added the Adam and Eve, by Jan. This was superimposed arbitrarily upon the oblong triptych of the Lamb, originally a separate work, the wings of which were subdivided to bring the composition of the two orders into reasonable relations. I cannot agree with this ingenious hypothesis in all its details, but it seems probable to me that the Ghent altarpiece was made up of at least two originally independent works.

Most critics ascribe the majestic group of the Enthroned Christ with Mary and John to Hubert. Being traditional figures, they show traces of the Cosmopolitan Style. The Christ is noble yet gentle, Mary is sweetly intent on reading her prayer book, St. John the Baptist has a suggestion of a magnificent savagery. The setting—in crowns, borders with seed pearls, backs of thrones with inscriptions on gold—is sumptuous, but not oppressive. It seems a fit accompaniment for the sacredness of the persons—a material symbol for the spiritual beauty of holiness.

The groups of angels, on a different pavement and in smaller scale, may be, as Professor Panofsky thinks, panels made for another purpose. The Singing Angels (Fig. 16) show that linear treatment, that harsh and schematic light and shade, that obtuseness to subtle effects of light which we find in all Jan's sure work. The Playing Angels (Fig. 17) show that softness and tenderness of touch, that thoughtful manipulation of the surfaces, that sensitiveness to subtleties of lighting which we have found in all the pictures of the Hubert Group. To make this clear one has only to study the handling of the cabinet work and the hair in the two panels. A reasonable conclusion from this difference, first worked out by the French critic, Durand-Gréville, is that Hubert painted the Playing Angels, while the Singing Angels were designed by him and actually painted by Jan. And this difference of style is the starting point for finding the respective parts of the brothers in the altarpiece.

The Adam (Fig. 18) and Eve (Fig. 19) offer a problem for which no ready solution lies at hand. It seems to me that Hubert may have designed them both. Certainly the painting of the Adam is Jan's—linear, harsh, most authoritative. The exaggerated reflected light along the contours is unexampled in Hubert and most characteristic for Jan. The Eve is the feature of the composition that Albrecht Dürer noted for praise in his diary, and it is the noblest detail of the great work. The large globularity of the modeling is one of the great achievements in all figure painting; the soft, transparent shadows and the lost contours are in Hubert's style. Jan's painting, doubtful attributions apart, shows nothing of this sort, So, against most of my colleagues, I venture to claim the Eve for Hubert. And if I am right, the Adam and Eve, which closed exactly over the figure of Christ, are part of the original composition, while the two panels of angels may have been fitted in to supply spaces for which no design had been made.

It is a pleasure to leave these highly controversial matters and proceed to the radiantly vivacious lower order representing the Adoration of the Lamb (Fig. 1). Nobody doubts that Hubert designed it, and if Jan may have finished more or less of it, the fact is of little esthetic significance. The picture is not merely a unit, but unique in its various loveliness. The motive is four processions converging upon the altar on which stands the Lamb. From the altar flows to a fountain the River of Life. About the altar kneel angels bearing the symbols of the Passion. From the groves in deep middle distance move converging processions of men and women who suffered martyrdom. All these groups move or stand on a greensward richly spangled with flowers. From the right march in the ecclesiastical orders, the apostles kneeling at the head, the Church doctors, the pilgrim and hermit saints. These pass before crags which catch the light mysteriously. Above the cliffs is a forest. From the left, mostly riding, advance pious laymen, towards a vanguard, kneeling, of pagan, Hebrew and Christian philosophers. Grave personages are easily identified, indeed plainly labeled Just Judges; gallant riders in armor are Good Knights. Behind the procession the landscape opens up across rolling hills and a river valley to a distant city, with architectural features recalling Utrecht and Cologne. In the distance under a slightly striated blue sky are the snow-clad serrations of an Alpine range. In general I feel that the two left-hand panels are executed by Jan on Hubert's design, and that most of the rest of the lower panels is by Hubert.

For serenity, dignity, picturesqueness, variety of character, profusion of landscape charm, above all for a pervading sense of devotion, this great picture hardly has an equal in the world. Something like two hundred and fifty crowded figures are held together without confusion. In its complicated harmony this seems the complete solution of the problem which Hubert set for himself over ten years earlier, but could not then solve, in the little Calvary (Fig. 11). Thinking in terms of the Netherlands, the Adoration of the Lamb completely justified the inscription added by Jan—that "No greater [than Hubert] had been found," *majorque nemo repertus.*

The altarpiece with the shutters closed (Fig. 23) offers rather little occasion for comment. Nothing is really notable in it except the formidably characterful kneeling portraits of Jodoc Vyd and his wife Elizabeth. In their large scale, nearly life size, they are exceptional at the moment. The woman's portrait is unmistakably by Jan; the man's may, I think, be by Hubert. Reasons for this opinion are the flexibility of the contour, unlike Jan's wiry outline, the softness of the modeling, a certain canniness, quietness and inwardness of expression. When Vyd commissioned so important and costly a picture, he would have been likely to speed up the painting of his own portrait; his wife's could wait.

Beyond this nothing need be said about the closed altarpiece. The work, and probably most of the invention, seem to be Jan's, while such features as the two St. Johns may well be executed by his assistants. The interior, with a window looking out over a street in Ghent, is an admirable example of Jan's meticulous realism, and incidentally, of the beautiful preciseness with which he painted still life.

This great panorama of a very human paradise had singularly little influence. Contemporary and later artists seem to have wisely felt that its perfections could not be repeated. Despite its sound theological core, in a certain blithe worldliness the Ghent altarpiece stands apart from that austere tradition of religious painting which had come down from the Middle Ages. The true succession was not in the Van Eycks, but in the more earnest and generally more provincial painters of Ghent, Tournai, Louvain and Haarlem.

# CHAPTER III

## JAN VAN EYCK AND PETRUS CHRISTUS

FIG. 20. JAN VAN EYCK. Arnolfini and Wife.—London.

36

Fig. 21. Jan van Eyck. Annunciation.—Washington.

Fig. 22. Jan van Eyck. Elizabeth
Vyd.—St. Bavon, Ghent.

37

Fig. 23. Jan and Hubert(?) van Eyck. Ghent Triptych (closed).—
St. Bavon, Ghent.

38

Fig. 24. Jan van Eyck. Madonna of Canon van der Paele.—*Bruges.*

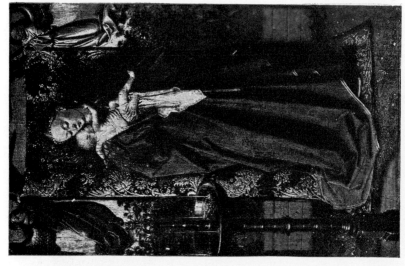

Fig. 26. Jan van Eyck. Madonna of the Fountain.—*Antwerp.*

Fig. 25. Jan van Eyck. St. Barbara (unfinished).—*Antwerp.*

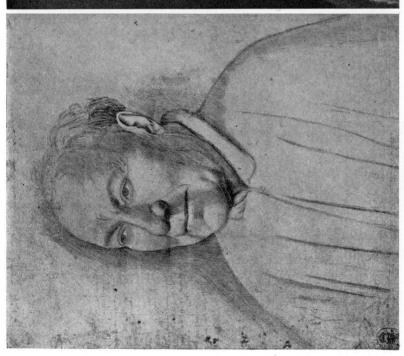

Fig. 27.  Jan van Eyck.  Cardinal Albergati (silverpoint).   Fig. 28.  Jan van Eyck.  Cardinal Albergati.—Vienna.
Dresden.

41

FIG. 30. JAN VAN EYCK. Margaret van Eyck.—Bruges.

FIG. 29. JAN VAN EYCK. Tymotheos.
—London.

42

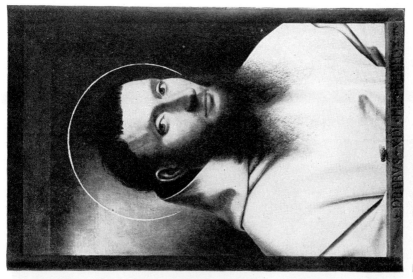

FIG. 32. Petrus Christus. A Carthusian.—Bache Collection, New York.

FIG. 31. Petrus Christus. Annunciation.—New York.

43

Fig. 33. Petrus Christus. St. Eligius and a Couple.—Robert Lehman
Collection, New York.

44

THE RANGE of Jan van Eyck's artistic interests and activities, when compared with Hubert's, seems singularly narrow. He was chiefly a portraitist. Much of the last sixteen years of his life was spent in travel as a confidential agent for the Duke of Burgundy. For these years we have twelve pictures, mostly tiny portraits and small altarpieces, with whatever he may have painted on the Ghent Adoration. It is a very scanty production, even allowing for pictures now lost, and it suggests that Jan had little creative urge, but depended on occasion.

In the same book of hours in which we feel we have found the glorious beginnings of Hubert are four miniatures which are often ascribed to Jan—God the Father Enthroned, the Lamentation, the Agony in the Garden and the Crucifixion. The reason for the attribution is a drastic and even vulgar realism, and a handling of drapery in angular folds based on wood sculpture. Such characteristics set these miniatures apart from the nine ascribed to Hubert. It is of course possible that he may have had an assistant, other than Jan, who did this work, but since the miniatures are of a technical excellence entirely worthy of Jan and of a feeling at least akin to his, to ascribe them to him seems the reasonable course. He was probably about twenty-five years old when they were painted.

In 1422 we find Jan working in the Castle of the Hague for John of Bavaria, Count of Holland. Since this mural decoration may have been on secular themes, its destruction is much to be regretted. We may only guess that Gothic tapestries of the moment give the general look of such work. Count John died early in 1425, and the decoration of the castle was already completed, for when in May of the same year Jan thriftily accepted a position as "varlet de chambre" for Philip the Good of Burgundy, the bargain included an allowance for moving Jan's effects from Lille to Bruges. From now on Jan was frequently employed on secret missions for the Duke, often to distant parts. He seems to have become a confidential agent, who (in Whistler's words) "also painted."

It seems to me that the very elaborate Annunciation (Fig. 21), in the National Gallery, Washington, may have been painted at Lille before 1425. The event takes place in a Gothic church which, while fantastic in design, recalls rather than Flemish churches the high naves of French churches of about 1300. Upon this interior Jan lavished work and attention. Everything is accounted for—stained glass, mural painting, pictured tiles, complicated stone carving. The details are marvelous, but the feeling of interior light is only feebly conveyed, the figures are badly out of scale with the architecture and in perfunctory relations to each other. The faint smirk on the archangel Gabriel's face forecasts the nervous grin of St. George in the Van der Paele Madonna (Fig. 24). It is a trait which suggests an artist trying to express a feeling which he does not really experience.

During the nearly six years between Hubert's death and the finishing of the Ghent altarpiece by Jan, Jan made three long trips for the Duke, including a sojourn of over a year in Spain and Portugal, where the Duke was seeking a bride. Except for the portrait of Cardinal Albergati, early in 1432, there are no signed pictures of Jan for these years, and it looks as if he were too busy to make them. During these years he was also far too deep in other matters to have painted or even finished any considerable portion of the Adoration of the Lamb, and whatever he did to it was probably done in the year or so preceding the unveiling on May 6, 1432. I have already tried to show that Jan painted the whole of the backs of the shutters (Fig. 23), excepting perhaps the portrait of Jodoc Vyd, which I hesitatingly give to Hubert, and of the open altarpiece surely carried to completion the Adam and the Singing Angels, and probably most of the figures on the left-hand panels. This amount of work could hardly have been finished within a twelvemonth, and we may reasonably imagine that Jan devoted much of the two years after his return from Spain at the end of 1429 to the pious task of completing his elder brother's masterpiece.

The portrait of Elizabeth Vyd in prayer (Fig. 22) is one of Jan's finer portraits, notable, as we have already remarked, for its large scale. It gives a formidable sense of presence, is unforgettable in its stark energy of character; for the rest, like most of Jan's portraits, it is seen like so much still life with no expenditure of sympathy on Jan's part. Now great portraiture sets one to wondering what the sitter thinks and does when not a sitter. In Jan's portraiture there is little enough of this overflow beyond and behind the frame. His men and women are eternally frozen in the aspect he caught in his studio. It is precisely because the companion portrait of Jodoc Vyd (Fig. 23) subtly and almost humorously blends the episodical humility of a devotee with the habitual cunning of a man of great affairs, that I think it not by Jan but by Hubert—a psychological difference which is confirmed by differences of physical construction. One feels that the attitude of Jodoc is prayerful, while Elizabeth is merely in an attitude of prayer. Most, not all, of Jan's portraits have this detached, still-life character. Before considering them it may be well to survey his few religious pictures.

The great technical mastery and the defects in invention of the early and comparatively large panel of the Annunciation we have already noted. The charming little Madonna at Melbourne, dated 1433, is entirely disarming in a richness which paradoxically expresses a homely domesticity. To make the Divine Mother simply a rich and youthful Flemish matron somewhat travestied as a noblewoman, to enthrone her richly and conventionally under a brocade canopy in her own home, while leaving her equally indifferent to its well-furnished cleanliness and to the Infant playing with her prayer book on her knee—this was surely a very novel and picturesque invention. To compare the housewifely impassivity of this Madonna with the tender solicitude of Italian Madonnas and Hubert's is to pass the frontier of two worlds. Yet there is something comfortable and even delightful about the assurance with which Jan insists that no better symbol of the Blessed Virgin can be found than a prosperous Flemish housewife who, without fuss or undue concern, keeps both her home and her babe in order. Incidentally, it is a bachelor's vision. While it is probable that Robert Campin may earlier have made Madonnas of this bourgeois type, none is finer than this little picture of Jan's. It is really a miniature, about nine by six inches, and the fastidiously elaborate rendering of the accessories is entirely proper to the scale. A little later Jan enlarged and changed the composition in the Madonna at Frankfurt-am-Main, and though a sumptuous picture, it is also a rather stiff and empty one.

The altarpiece of Our Lady and Child with St. Donatian, St. George and Canon van der Paele, at Bruges (Fig. 24), is generally regarded as Jan's masterpiece, and perhaps justly so. Of the larger panels of the moment no other is so profusely enriched. Stuffs, em-

broidered and jeweled borders, polished and curiously carved stone-
work, elaborately fashioned metal, translucent glass, are juxtaposed,
with hardly a gap to rest the eye or release the imagination. As painting, in a harsh and metallic way, it is magnificent. "It is painting,"
writes Fromentin, "that makes one forget everything beyond itself."
Yet if, as I believe, a test of a great picture is that one remembers it as
a whole, this, however masterly in mere execution, is not a great picture. Parts of it are stamped into my memory—the immovable gor-
geous mass of the Bishop saint, the porcine, furrowed mask of the
donor, and, disagreeable feature, the awkward gesture of St. George as
he doffs his fantastic helmet, and the nervous grin with which he
seems to accost the Mother of God. Beyond this, my memory begins
to fade. I recall vaguely a space which seems cramped in plane and
inadequate in depth. The tact with which Hubert made factually
impossible ratios of figure to architecture acceptable to the eye was
not vouchsafed to Jan. Of the ornateness required by the Burgundian
plutocracy of Church and State, this panel is perhaps the finest example. Before the Van der Paele Madonna, Fromentin is right, one
thinks of nothing but the painting. Before great pictures one thinks
of much else. The Van der Paele Madonna was signed in 1436,
shortly after Jan's marriage. He was in the middle forties and at the
height of his powers.

The little unfinished St. Barbara at Antwerp, dated 1437 (Fig.
25), is the only creation of Jan's that is gracious and charming. Had
he finished it, doubtless he would have painted out much of the
charm. The exceptional attractiveness of this little picture depended
on a very simple decision—to give St. Barbara an actual tower in
process of building instead of the usual tiny emblematic tower. She
sits meditatively over her book of hours, oblivious of the work going
on in her honor behind her. The elaborately lovely Gothic structure
rises lightly. Workmen are busy on ledges, on scaffolds and about
the base. Jan either had great talent for architectural design, or, as
is more likely, thriftily and tastefully used the sketch of an architect
friend. Beyond the tower there are receding, gently drooping and
rising lines of hills, punctuated by single trees and coppices. There
is much about this picture that makes one wish Jan had been an
engraver; the point rather than the brush seems the tool really congenial to him. As showing the way in which an early Flemish picture
was prepared, this little panel is indeed precious. When we think

of parts of the Adoration of the Lamb left unfinished by Hubert, we must imagine them like the St. Barbara, elaborately drawn out on the panels and needing only to be colored.

The tiny panel of Our Lady and Child by a Fountain, dated 1439 and at Antwerp (Fig. 26), has evident relation to the garden pictures of the Rhenish school. The closed garden, *hortus conclusus*, and sealed fountain, *fons sigillata*, are established symbols of Mary's virginity. Jan has worked out the details of vines, flowers and the latten fountain with the most loving care, and the very small scale of the picture, as always, has been favorable to him. For the Madonna he has chosen a type which is at once exceptional and wholly his own, in a Mary who is humble and tender without aristocratic pretensions, while he shows an unusual vivacity of observation in the naturally flung attitude of the active Christchild.

Of course Jan van Eyck must have painted portraits before he entered the service of the Duke of Burgundy, but those that have come down to us fall within the last ten years of the painter's life. In the Burgundian court he found magnificent sitters—visages shaped by character, often grotesquely. Merely to treat such masks as still life was to make very interesting pictures, and this in the main is what Jan did, simply animating the face by some trick of suggesting aggressive intentness in the eyes. Generally the faces he painted cannot be conceived as moving, as being other than they are. They hold the eye, but they do not enlist the imagination.

The earliest is that of Nicholas Albergati, saintly Cardinal of St. Cross, who was in Bruges on a peace mission from December eighth to eleventh, 1431. This learned and devout Carthusian would have preferred the quiet of his Roman cell, but his friendly tact and diplomatic ability made him a wanderer about Europe. At Bruges he stayed with his fellow Carthusians, and at the Charterhouse Jan van Eyck must have persuaded him to sit for a couple of hours. The result was one of the most precious relics of early Flemish art, the silverpoint drawing of the Cardinal with annotations of the colors, in the print room at Dresden (Fig. 27). It is of small scale, very sensitively caressed by the silver stylus, and it suggests much of the humility, benignity and shrewdness of the prelate whom the Pope described to Charles VII as "free from all passion," *ab omni passione remotum*.

In the oil painting at Vienna (Fig. 28), which a little later was made from this drawing, there is considerable loss of expression. The forms have hardened and frozen. One senses a man of moral dignity and force, but not the various gifts of the diplomat Cardinal. And this raises the issue already posed by the unfinished St. Barbara, whether all the portraits of Jan do not represent the loss of some drawing much finer than the painting we now see—whether, in short, his gift as a draughtsman was not superior to his gift as a painter.

However that be, the procedure of painting a portrait not from the sitter but from a carefully prepared drawing remained standard for Western Europe for over two centuries. It was the method of Holbein, of the Clouets and their successors. It had many advantages over the Italian fashion of painting from the sitter. The final character of the portrait was established in a single intent act of observation. To attain this character, the significant forms had to be sought strenuously, and eliminations and syncopations made unsparingly. On such intense initial observation the artist stood firmly. The painting was guided as to color by notes on the drawing and by memory. Consequently color and lighting were somewhat generalized. The painting went on confidently and one may imagine almost mechanically. There was no concern with small particularities of coloration, no confusion from change of mood or shifting of light. Such portraiture was not precisely true to any momentary appearance, but it had a timeless sort of truth of its own, taking the sitter out of a changing world into a realm that is changeless.

Simply as records, the portraits painted in this way seem to me the best and truest we have, if only because there is no division of interest in making them. The great portraiture of the later Renaissance—Titian's, Rembrandt's, Velasquez's—had to cope with the appearance, with actual illumination, with decorative fitness, with intimate interpretations, and while the harmonizing of these many endeavors produced much greater works of art than the late Gothic portraits, I doubt if it really produced, in the narrower sense, better portraits.

The portrait of a scholar labeled in Greek letters Tymotheos, at London (Fig. 29), is dated October 10, 1432. Its general stiffness is at once enhanced and relieved by the awkward but natural action of the hand holding a scroll. The expression is searching, withal a little worried and pathetic. There is an effort for intimate interpretation rare in Jan's portraits, which suggests that we have to do with someone dear to him. As an apparition it is astonishingly real, and the workmanship is of the finest. The tension of the modeling and the unpleasant bricky ruddiness of the hue are, for me, sufficient evidence that within a year of this work Jan could not have painted much on the Ghent altarpiece. Its easy modeling and the lightness of its carnations are of quite a different sort.

Dated about a year later, the portrait of a Man with a Turban, at London, differs only in being more linear and in the transparency of the shadows. It expresses an old age at once shrewd, wistful and defiant. Without good reason many critics regard this as a self-portrait. Despite, or perhaps because of a somewhat provincial and homemade look, it is one of the more pleasing of Jan's male portraits.

Sir Baldwin de Lannoy was one of Jan's companions on the Portuguese mission of 1428. He received the order of the Golden Fleece in 1431. Jan has searched all the concavities and convexities of the wasted face, omitting no wrinkle, with the result that the portrait is completely wooden and expressionless. It is a hard mask behind which there seems to be nothing. The collar of the Golden Fleece sits rather badly, which may suggest that the portrait was painted early before the award of the order, and that the insignia were added later. In that case it may be the earliest portrait by Jan that has come down to us. In any case it is one of the more esthetically negligible.

The portrait of the goldsmith, Jan de Leeuw, at Vienna, has more style than most of Jan's portraits. It is handsomely set in the frame, even if the hand holding a ring is awkwardly placed. The plastic effect is secured without overemphasizing the modeling. It is an attractive presentation of a capable and robust personality. It has nothing of the strenuously homemade look of many of Jan's portraits, rather a fairly Italian simplicity, concentration and elegance. All this may suggest either that in limning a fellow craftsman Jan worked with exceptional sympathy, or, as is more likely, that he had become conscious of his defects and was seeking a broader style. By this time he must have seen the admirable portraits of Rogier de la Pasture, sensitive, broadly conceived, distinguished for tactful elimination. He could not imitate them, his nature forbade that, but he could move their way. This was in 1436.

Perhaps the finest of Jan's portraits is that of his wife Margaret, at Bruges, painted June 17, 1439 (Fig. 30). Whether as sensitive characterization or simply as so much finely disposed material, Jan painted nothing more handsome. The pattern and the tinted whites of the headdress are perfect; the roseate carnations of the flesh have nothing of Jan's earlier unpleasant brickiness; the solid modeling is effected by infinitesimals of luminous shadow; the expression is of a patient and rather sad benignity and wisdom. Nothing is amiss save the ill-placed hand, which is a restorer's contribution. It is hard to realize that this is a woman in the early thirties. Seen by an eye respectful, one hopes loving, but also relentlessly observant, after five centuries she is tremendously alive in her fading comeliness.

For a similar rightness and beauty of workmanship the undated portrait at Berlin generally called John Arnolfini must have been painted about the same time. It seems to me that it bears only a casual resemblance to the famous Arnolfini portrait at London, and that the identification lacks a sound base. Of all Jan's portraits it is one of the best composed. The long horselike mask has an odd deadness, a relaxation which is perhaps only a sign of self-control. The fleshless eye sockets and tired eyes seem to me that of an ailing person. Traditionally this is a self-portrait, and such may very well be the case. It suggests the hard-won imperturbability of a man who had to double the function of painter with that of secret agent and courtier. However that be, and despite its considerably damaged condition, this seems to me one of Jan's latest portraits and one of his best. It has the elegance which seems to be an attainment of his last years.

If I am treating last, and out of its chronological order, the portrait of John Arnolfini and his Wife, at London (Fig. 20), it is because it is exceptional in Jan's activity, and his masterpiece. Fundamentally it is a portrait of a richly appointed room. Everything is included and defined—windows with bull's-eyes transmitting cool light, a most elaborate chandelier of yellow metal, a diminishing mirror with the reflection of two figures entering the room from the front, its tiny medallions of glass or enamel with passion scenes in the mirror frame. But there is no confusion or overemphasis, merely a harmony of great richness; everything keeps its place in a scene impregnated with an opulent restfulness. In many ways this picture anticipates later triumphs of portraiture of rooms by Jan Vermeer of Delft, but when we come to the figures the analogy fails. Vermeer's figures belong. One may regard them as a necessary emanation from the space, or the space as a sort of extension of the figures. Jan van Eyck's husband and wife have no air of being at home; they stand stiffly and awkwardly like visitors enduring the discomfort of being portrayed.

The portraits are admirable. One fairly hates the sanctimoniousness of the money-grubbing Italian merchant Arnolfini; one likes the doll-like comeliness of his youthful bride, who seems to be masquerading not very successfully as one of the St. Catherines or St. Barbaras of Hubert van Eyck. Husband and wife are unrelated to each other and by no means agreeably related to the space they occupy, but they imperiously hold the eye. Everything except the shaggy white terrier is conceived as so much splendid still life. No other picture reveals so impressively Jan van Eyck's marvelous technical resourcefulness and his spiritual limitations.

The panel bears the curious inscription "Jan van Eyck was here, 1434," *Johannes de Eyck fuit hic, 1434.* Certain critics, ignoring the apparently sound identification of the figures as John Arnolfini and his wife, interpret the inscription to mean Jan van Eyck lived here, and hold that the persons are Jan and his wife Margaret. It is unnecessary to contradict a far-fetched theory justified neither by the form of the inscription—anyone mentioning his home would have used not the perfect but the imperfect tense—nor by the age of the sitters, nor by any resemblance of the very young woman to the portrait of Margaret van Eyck painted only five years later. As a mere suggestion, the odd *fuit hic* may mean that Jan painted the picture on the spot, as distinguished from his general habit of painting in the work shop from a drawing. Indeed, it is hard to see how the picture could have reached its material perfection unless it were painted before the objects themselves. As painting it seems to me unqualifiedly Jan's greatest work, and on the technical side I know of no finer late Gothic picture.

On July 9, 1441, the Church of St. Donatian, at Bruges, received payment for burying Jan's body. About a month later the Duke made the substantial gratuity of 360 livres to the widow. Less than a year later Jan's brother, Lambert, arranged for moving the body from the churchyard to more honorable sepulture in the church itself, and the estate endowed an annual mass for the repose of his soul. They were taking notable pains after his death about a person who had been notable in life. Wherever we meet Jan in records it is as the employee of some potentate. He had met the great of the earth, had traveled widely. The Duke had stood godfather to his children, had used him for difficult and delicate missions. To the courtly, official world in which he moved Jan brought acceptance and a most accurate eye. Without criticism he gave the look of his world. The imagination goes forward two centuries to another painter and court chamberlain, Velasquez. With the difference imposed by the times, he was to do at Madrid what Jan had done at Bruges— give a dispassionate but amazingly truthful account of what he saw about him. From painters who are also chamberlains, official or un- official, no poetry is to be expected. Enough if they give us a veridi- cal prose. Jan's age at death we do not know, but it is unlikely that he had reached his sixties. Velasquez, too, barely reached that term. To be at once artist and courtier apparently does not make for lon- gevity.

I fear my survey of Jan's work has taken a debunking turn. Before any reader reproaches me for seeming to diminish a great fame, let him ask himself and answer the following questions:

Suppose Hubert had not been early forgotten and all his most gracious creations had not been attributed to Jan. Suppose we elimi- nate all contested attributions and make our estimate of Jan from the pictures which are surely his—would that estimate be very different from that which I have suggested?

Suppose Jan had not enjoyed for four centuries a great and favorable publicity as the inventor of oil painting, suppose we had just his signed and reasonably attributed works—would any sensible critic think him a great artist in the sense that, say, Rogier de la Pasture and Hugo van der Goes were great artists? I think not; I feel the judgment would be that Jan's lack of range and of spiritual vision emphatically excluded him from the class of great artists, while as surely he was a very great painter.

Though the brilliant innovations of the Van Eycks were widely imitated, they seem to have few direct pupils. Indeed Petrus Christus seems to be the only one whose discipleship is perfectly sure. He was born in eastern Holland, probably before 1420; we first meet him admitted as a master painter at Bruges in midsummer of 1444. It is reasonable to suppose that he had been an assistant of Jan van Eyck. But on the whole he seems rather influenced by the painting of Hubert, two of whose compositions he copied freely—the Last Judg- ment, and the Rothschild Madonna with a Canon. Both these pictures are at Berlin. Hubert's easier line and modeling reappear in Petrus Christus, as also his preoccupation with effects of light.

In his various religious pictures, represented at Madrid, Berlin, Antwerp, Washington and New York, Petrus is a good rather than a striking artist. He shows some tendency to increase the relative scale of the figures, is always thoughtful; as a colorist, rather adequate than distinguished. One delightfully romantic painting, at New York, an Annunciation before an ivy-clad Gothic portal (Fig. 31), is generally ascribed to him. If so, it must be regarded as a remarkable and probably quite early assimilation of the idealizing manner of Hubert. This entrancing little picture has been ascribed to Hubert van Eyck. I am inclined to see in it a copy or version of a lost picture by Hubert. For me the slack quality of the figure painting hardly justifies an attribution to any great painter.

Petrus Christus was an excellent portraitist. His portraits are related to the observer, have a certain vivacity rare at the time. None of them seem highly distinguished to me except the grim and amazingly vivid likeness of a Carthusian (Fig. 32), in the collection of Mr. Jules Bache, at New York. In the facility of the execution and relatively large scale it marks a progress. Indeed at long range one might pardonably indulge the momentary error of seeing a very hard and early Rubens. It is dated 1466, and is far more modern in accent than the contemporary portraiture of Rogier de la Pasture and Dirck Bouts.

Petrus Christus's most inventive picture is the St. Eligius with a Bridal Pair, dated 1449, in the collection of Mr. Robert Lehman, New York (Fig. 33). It is conceived entirely as a genre piece, for St. Eligius is merely a goldsmith in his shop, shrewdly dealing with a cautious young husband and wife. The picture is quite beautifully painted and the lighting of a roofed but open space very carefully studied. It is perhaps the better that there is no emphasis of the shopping motive, the attraction resting on the assemblage and refined representation of materials. It stands at the head of a long line of genre subjects in half length, notably those of Quentin Massys and his imitators.

Our last notice of Petrus Christus is in 1473 and we know that by 1477 he was dead. He had followed with humility and intelligence the best models, and had made his own modest contribution to the progress of his art. Of rather few minor painters can as much be said.

The art of the Van Eycks is an episode and not in the direct line of Gothic realism. Just as the Burgundian dependencies in which they lived managed to keep out of the tragic events of the Hundred Years' War, so the art of Jan and Hubert evaded the harsher religious emotions of the time. Their art has always a courtly and moderated character, and this they passed on to the later school of Bruges. But it fell to painters farther from the court and closer to the church to continue the tragic religious tradition of the Middle Ages while embodying it in new and more appealing forms. Thus the great inventions were to be made rather in French than in Teutonic Flanders, in such cities as Brussels, Louvain and Tournai.

# CHAPTER IV

## THE SCHOOLS OF TOURNAI, GHENT, LOUVAIN, ETC.

Fig. 34. Rogier de la Pasture. St. Luke Painting the Virgin.—
Boston.

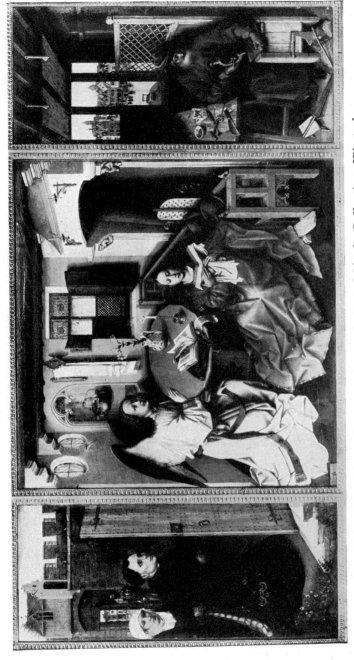

Fig. 35. Robert Campin. Annunciation.—Mérode Collection, Westerloo.

FIG. 36. (Lower left) ROBERT CAMPIN. Canon Werl with St. John Baptist.—Madrid.

FIG. 37. (Upper) ROBERT CAMPIN. Calvary (old copy).—Liverpool.

FIG. 38. (Lower right) ROBERT CAMPIN. St. Veronica.—Frankfurt-am-Main.

Fig. 40.  ROGIER DE LA PASTURE.  Christ Appearing to His Mother after the Resurrection.—New York.

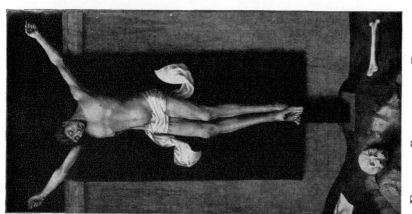

Fig. 39.  ROGIER DE LA PASTURE. Crucifixion.—Philadelphia.

61

FIG. 41. ROGIER DE LA PASTURE. Deposition.—Escorial.

FIG. 42. (Upper) ROGIER DE LA PASTURE. Bladelin Nativity.—*Berlin.*
FIG. 43. (Lower left) ROGIER DE LA PASTURE. Portrait of a Woman.—
*Washington.*
FIG. 44. (Lower right) ROGIER DE LA PASTURE. Portrait of an Este.—
*New York.*

Fig. 46. Geertgen tot Sint Jans. Family of the Virgin.—Amsterdam.

Fig. 45. Aalbert van Oudewater. Resurrection of Lazarus.—Berlin.

Fig. 47.   Dirck Bouts.   Last Supper.—St. Peter's, Louvain.

Fig. 48. Dirck Bouts. Gathering Manna; Elijah and the
Angel.—St. Peter's, Louvain.

Fig. 49. Dirck Bouts. Beheading of the Innocent Knight.—Brussels.

IN CONTRAST with the courtly idealism of Hubert and the courtly realism of Jan van Eyck, both innovations, the painting of the Walloon-French city of Tournai preserves a traditional character, is less fully pictorial, less colorful, more derivative from sculpture—at once more popular and more conventionally religious. It was also more widely influential, lending much to the popular schools of Ghent, Haarlem and Louvain, and later shaping the character of the emotional and dramatic painting of Antwerp. It has little pride of workmanship and great interest in subject matter—in persons, in emotional relations. Thus it is in the succession of the noble Gothic sculpture of France.

The earliest painter of Tournai who concerns us is Robert Campin, born probably before 1380, died in 1444, being a slightly older contemporary of Jan van Eyck. He was probably, like his wife, a Hollander, but he appears at Tournai as early as 1406. From then on we have fairly frequent notices of him at Tournai, sometimes concerning guild honors, sometimes regarding his dissipations. The reconstruction of his artistic personality rests on relating a group of pictures to the records on one hand and to the style of his historically recorded pupil, Jacques Daret, on the other. It is an inferential reconstruction, but though it has been sharply contested, I feel it is convincing. No pictures of Campin can be surely dated much earlier than 1420 or so, and these reveal the influence of Hubert van Eyck and are in the new oil technique. The chances are that in the early years of the fifteenth century Campin had studied with Hubert in Holland.

Possibly his earliest picture is the Marriage of the Virgin with Other Episodes, at Madrid. It is a vivacious and disorderly narrative, perhaps implying knowledge of pictures like Hubert van Eyck's Calvary, perhaps derivative from sculpture. In any case it shows nothing new except a careful study of such details as denote emotion, and certain critics regard it as too poor for Campin. To me it is about what an early venture in his popular style should be. The great archaeologist, James Weale, from the architectural forms, dated it before 1425.

Campin's art appears full grown in the Annunciation generally called the Madonna of the Mousetrap (Fig. 35), in the Mérode Collection, at Westerloo.  What is spiritually new and remarkable is the placid and domestic character of the picture.  It is as far from the tender ideality of Hubert as from the sumptuousness and emphasis of Jan.  Campin tries to make the scene continuous across the three panels of the triptych, setting the donors in a courtyard outdoors, and St. Joseph busy making his mousetrap in a workshop adjoining the Madonna's room.  Campin opens street scenes, after Jan van Eyck's fashion, behind the shutters.  The central subject, the Annunciation, is handled very tranquilly and with no sense of a solemn rite.  The three panels are well held together in silvery tones which sufficiently suggest the actual illumination.  The abundant household furniture and utensils are carefully and charmingly painted, but only fairly well placed as regards composition.  The figures are indifferently drawn and set, but their tender modeling is attractive.  The perspective is inferior to that of the Van Eycks.

In its way, however, the picture makes as great an innovation as any of Hubert's or Jan's.  We are here at the fountainhead of the popular realism of the Low Countries, and St. Joseph so contentedly concentrated upon his work is the promise of all the little masters of two centuries ahead.  The big beaver hat of the donor seems to date the picture about 1430.  Of the Cosmopolitan Style there is no trace.  Campin, who was both sculptor and painter, must have received his training in painting after the Cosmopolitan Style had passed out of vogue.

Other characteristic works of Campin are the portly maternal Madonna before a wicker fire screen, at London, and the little Madonna at Leningrad patting the back of the nude Child as she warms Him before a fire.  In these themes there is some disharmony between the formal Gothic oval of the face and the intimate feeling implied. Jan van Eyck's short-faced, homely Madonnas were really better.

In 1438, being about fifty, Robert Campin painted a triptych for the prelate, Heinrich von Werl, of Cologne.  Only the wings have come down to us, and they are at Madrid.  One represents St. Barbara seated intent on her prayer book.  The sweet and meditative sentiment recalls Hubert van Eyck. In the other wing we see the kneeling donor supported by St. John the Baptist (Fig. 36). All the handling of the two simple interior settings is of the finest. Everything is much better drawn than in the earlier pictures. The silvery lighting is charming, and in its way symbolical of the religious quietism of the mood. "For a quiet unadvertising excellence," writes Sir Martin Conway, "these are perhaps Campin's best paintings."

Certainly the most delightful of the pictures ascribed to Campin is the animated Nativity at Dijon. The figures are instinct with a sensitive reverence, the suggestion of a spacious winter landscape quite masterly. Its ecstatic character transcends Campin's habitual tranquillity.

He attempted such an ambitious theme as the Crucifixion with poor success. The great triptych with the three crosses included as prelude the Crossbearing and as postlude the Entombment. The only remaining fragment, the Repentant Thief, at Frankfurt, tells us that the mood was emphatic to violence—the effort probably of a gentle nature to be strong. An old and apparently faithful copy at Liverpool (Fig. 37) and a close imitation in the Church of St. Sauveur at Bruges, tell us that the composition was crowded and confused, and the painter's powers inadequate to the tragic theme.

Campin, like the Flemish painters generally, was a good portraitist, as the Werl picture attests (Fig. 36). Usually the manner is linear and somewhat dry. The massive face of an obese man at Berlin is delineated with great plastic effect and with full appreciation of the robust character.

So far we have been dealing with a good but by no means great talent, of a temper at once experimental and hesitating. Three panels at Frankfurt from larger works give a surprising impression of greatness. A standing Madonna and an austere St. Veronica (Fig. 38) yield both a monumental and sculptural effect, and are also infused with a deeply devotional spirit. A Trinity adapting Gothic sculptural models is of great loveliness of color and is profoundly tragic in feeling. The Madonna and the St. Veronica show a positiveness and brilliance of color which we find in no other works of Campin's.

So great is the qualitative difference between these fragments and Campin's other paintings, that one might be inclined to question the attribution. Yet the forms are unmistakably his. Campin was a sculptor, and possibly a much better sculptor than painter. We may guess that these exceptionally grand paintings may have had sculptural precedents. In any case, some such explanation for their unique excellence must be sought. Robert Campin is highly important as fixing at the outset the swing of the school of Tournai between the familiar and the tragic mood.

Campin's influence spread widely through the Low Countries and even up the Rhine and into Spain. Of his many imitators, only Jacques Daret need detain us, and that chiefly because we can give him a name and local designation. He was born at Tournai about 1403, studied fourteen years with Campin, became a master of the painter's guild in 1432 and shortly thereafter provost. Between 1433 and 1435 he painted four panels as wings for a sculptured altarpiece for the monastery of St. Vaast, at Arras. A Nativity is in an American private collection, the Epiphany and Visitation at Berlin, while the Presentation in the Temple is in the Petit Palais, at Paris. The touch is very heavy-handed, the forms a coarsening of Campin's, the mood quite stolid, even dead, in all these little pictures. There is rather a stupid profusion of superfluous ornament. We have to do with an artist quite without taste.

Daret may have shone chiefly as an executive. He held the most important guild offices, in 1464 directed the work of the group of painters called to Bruges to plan the decoration and pageantry for the marriage of Charles the Bold and Margaret of York. He must have been respected for something beyond the four rather poor pictures that have come down to us.

If one may judge by the influence he exerted, Rogier de la Pasture of Tournai was regarded by his contemporaries as their greatest painter, and modern criticism generally accepts that verdict. He was great despite certain marked deficiencies. He was an indifferent landscapist; as a colorist he was often merely adequate. His greatness lay on the spiritual side—in his capacity for realizing the standard religious themes with insight and power, in his understanding of the gentleness and dignity of the persons whose portraits he made, in the gravity and massiveness of figures based rather on sculpture than on painting. Beyond this, unlike his fellow painters who often worked on a small scale, Rogier painted many big pictures. These stood in churches and town halls, were seen and admired by everybody, whereas much of the work of the Van Eycks had promptly disappeared in collectors' cabinets. Thus Rogier's influence spread well up the Rhine and into northern France and is traceable as far as Castile and the Neapolitan region.

Rogier was born at Tournai a little before 1400. The fifth day after Easter, 1426, most surprisingly, we find him registered as an apprentice of Campin. About six months later the magistrates of Tournai, calling him "Master" Roger, made him a compliment of eight casks of wine, double the quantity they had voted to so celebrated a visiting painter as Jan van Eyck. On August 1, 1433, Rogier was inscribed as a master of the guild. This tangle of records has never been satisfactorily unsnarled. It is clear that the apprenticeship was purely perfunctory, that he was already a famous master at the time. It was possibly a necessary formality in order to gain guild membership after an absence, or to qualify himself for studying the new technique recently invented by Jan van Eyck. Or we may have to do with two Rogiers.

To establish the order of Rogier's painting is very difficult, for until his maturity documents fail us, and we can only work from small differences in a style that for all the early years is pretty uniform. So the chronology here given is offered subject to correction. I know of no Rogier which looks earlier than the noble Crucifixion (Fig. 39) with a wing representing Mary and John in agony of grief, in the Johnson Collection, Philadelphia. The gold background, the flash of scarlet in the hanging cloth, the delicately modulated whites and ineffable pale rose tints recall vaguely the decorative accent of the late Gothic painters of Italy, such as Lorenzo Monaco. I know nothing just like it in the North at any time. It has that unusual incisiveness of line which is often the mark of a young artist trying very hard. So, while this may be a unique experiment of his maturity, I am inclined to set it as early as anything so masterly can be dated, say about 1425. It has the highest emotional reality, the peculiar and lucid concentration of a well-staged scene or a hallucination. Rogier, though he was to exceed it in richness and complication, was never to surpass it in tragic intensity and nobility.

A little triptych, once in the convent of Miraflores, near Burgos, according to a not very credible tradition, came from Pope Martin V, who died in 1431. It may well be ten years later. The central panel depicts the Lamentation over Christ's Body, the right-hand panel the Nativity—these are in the cathedral at Granada—the left-hand panel, in the Metropolitan Museum, represents Christ appearing to His Mother after the Resurrection (Fig. 40). A contemporary copy of the entire composition is at Berlin. The whole altarpiece is not pictorially impressive, being overweighted by the Gothic accessories, exquisite in themselves, such as the stone arches with elaborately carved groups in the voussoirs which frame the stories. The color is rather cold and negative. The mood is pathetic almost to dolefulness, but there is always a saving nobility of a homely kind. There are superbly realized features, the body of the dead Christ, the response of the whole body of Mary to the amazement, fear and joy awakened by the sudden apparition of her Son. In short, we must think rather in terms of the parts than of the whole.

Almost a companion piece, and possibly an old copy, is the triptych of St. John at Berlin. The subjects are the Birth, Baptism and Decapitation. It has similar Gothic accessories, and again has not achieved formal unity.

There is no more complete and characteristic achievement of Rogier than the Deposition made for the Crossbowmen's Guild of Louvain in the early 1430's and now in the Escorial (Fig. 41). Against a gold background and a lower wall the group occupies a shallow space, like a piece of polychromed sculpture. The arrangement is highly studied and complicated. The guiding motive is the drooping curve of the body of Christ. It is most variously countered, repeated and continued by the curves of the other figures. In a tonal way the color is lovely. The pervading mood of sorrow is sincere, thoughtfully modulated, and above all restrained. We have to do with a solemn ceremony seen in some eternal aspect, and not with so many personal expressions of grief. The forms are chosen for delicacy—very long feet, very refined hands. The oval faces are of a similar fineness and sensitiveness. Everywhere the endeavor is for delicacy: note the hands of the swooning Madonna, the gentle, almost hesitating character of all movements.

There is little attempt to represent the scene as a happening—as it would have seemed to the actual participants—but rather to express the reverence with which all devout souls must recall it. Rogier follows not the way of fact, but that of legend, as his great Sienese predecessors had done. Fierens-Gevaert writes aptly that in such work Rogier must not be classed with the innovating painter realists of his time, but should be regarded as the continuer in painting of the idealistic Gothic sculpture of the thirteenth century.

Soon Rogier had a favorable change of fortune in an appointment as official *portrater* of the City of Brussels. In 1436 it voted to discontinue the office after his death—which is evidence of the value they set on his services. His task was to paint four panels of examples of Justice for the courtroom. It already contained a Last Judgment painted in 1420. One must greatly regret its loss, for it might have told us much about a period concerning which we are ill-informed. Rogier painted Trajan giving Justice to the Widow, Pope Gregory praying for Trajan's Soul, Count Herkenwald condemning to Death his Nephew guilty of a Rape, the Host and with it Absolution miraculously administered to the Guilty Nephew. For a couple of centuries these compositions were admired by visitors, among them Albrecht Dürer, only to be discarded and lost some two hundred years ago.

The subjects still exist in Gothic tapestries at Berne, which were part of the booty from the rout and death of Charles the Bold at Granson, and certain critics ask us to find here copies of Rogier's stories. It seems to me that the tapestries may echo Rogier's work, but with little exactness, and that from them we can gain no satisfactory idea of the look of the decorations at Brussels.

We shall again meet such examples of Justice painted for courtrooms in the works of Dirck Bouts and Gerard David. They are of a very curious sort, for usually they merely announce in a civic tribunal the vanity of all earthly justice. It needed the Latin optimism of a Giotto or an Ambrogio Lorenzetti to conceive justice as normally and successfully administered on earth. The late Gothic painters of the North rarely celebrated actual official jurisprudence. For them justice came exceptionally and miraculously from heaven. The prayers of a Pope release a just Emperor's soul from hell; the Host descends from heaven in time to save the soul of a condemned rapist. Possibly these Northern painters were in this matter more realistic and less fantastic than they seem. In the fifteenth century official justice may as a rule have deserved no more respect than they gave it.

In the years following 1443 Rogier painted a big picture of the Last Judgment for Nicolas Rolin, Chancellor of Philip the Good. It is still in the beautiful hospital, the Hôtel Dieu, which he built at Beaune. It shows the usual arrangement of the apostles and saints to right and left of Christ, as a sort of celestial bench of judges, with angels in the air and the naked dead struggling out of their graves below. A vestured St. Michael is director of the ceremony. On this vast scale the rather negative character of Rogier's color becomes unpleasantly apparent. The surface abounds in vivid and telling details, but there is no unity of effect. The large proportions of the apostles dwarf the other figures. After all, a Last Judgment is primarily a challenge to make a fine and complicated decoration. Failing that, it will fall apart into episodes, as Michelangelo's came perilously near doing. Giotto realized the decorative possibilities of the theme superbly in the big entrance wall of the Arena Chapel, and Hubert van Eyck very adequately in the tiny panel at New York. Rogier was a great painter, but his decorative sense was slight, and what should have been his masterpiece suffers sorely from that defect.

In 1450 Rogier made the pilgrimage to Rome for the Jubilee. He admired the sumptuous (now lost) frescoes of Gentile da Fabriano at the Lateran, made profitable connections with such ruling houses as the Estes and Sforzas. As a painter he seems to have learned little from the trip, and no wonder. He was a visiting celebrity and not a student. To have tried to learn from Mantegna or Masaccio was to be undone. It is just possible that something of Italian urbanity transpires from his later portraits, with their quiet, unaggressive distinction.

The Seven Sacraments, at Antwerp, is often dated before the Italian journey. The gentleness and ease of the mood are that of Rogier's last phase, and suggest a date in the 1450's. To paint the interior of a Gothic church, to make it spacious, cool, silvery, was well within Rogier's powers, and his church is one of the best in an art that produced many of great excellence. The little groups enacting the sacraments—baptism, confirmation, confession, communion, marriage, ordination, supreme unction—are so many jewels of narrative painting. But in the great church they have an accidental, scattered and almost intrusive look. Moreover, they are so nearly in true scale that their being after all too large, jars upon a sensitive eye. The Van Eycks really did better when they ignored the actual ratios so completely that the question did not arise. So while these little groups show Rogier in his most ingratiating aspect, the picture misses unity and adds little to his fame.

In the triptych of a Nativity (Fig. 42), at Berlin, made for

Pierre Bladelin of Middelburg after 1455, we find Rogier in his sweetest vein. While the panels are not notably well composed as units, nor yet carefully articulated to make a whole, the perfection of the workmanship and the fully realized devotion of the figures go to make an entirely delightful if not a great picture.

The ecstatic *Meditations on the Life of Christ*, ascribed to St. Bonaventura, gave Rogier the traits of the central panel, the Nativity. One sees the column against which Mary leaned in painless childbirth. One finds her kneeling and praying ardently to the Divine Babe. "She who bore Him adored Him"—*quae genuit adoravit*. The accessories, the ruined building, etc., are of much picturesque charm. The wings represent the Magi seeing the Christchild in the clouds, and the Sibyl telling the Emperor Augustus of the coming Advent of Jesus. These are loosely knit, romantic compositions, unlike the general tenseness and density of religious pictures of the time. In short, what makes the Bladelin triptych so winsome is precisely a sort of ease and irresponsibility. It has the artless, folksong charm of an old Christmas carol.

St. Luke painting the Virgin (Fig. 34), at Boston, of about the same time, is much more carefully arranged. The somewhat stolidly sweet Virgin and St. Luke with his craftsman's concentration on his job are well related to the deep central vista, where between rows of houses and quays a broad canal is whipped rough by a stiff breeze. Two people, backs turned to the spectator, look down this waterway, and that carries the eye of the beholder along in the same direction. All the details of this seaport background are painted with an uncommon harmony of blond color, the pale blue of the canal with its sharp little chop being the dominant tone.

An antiquarian will observe that St. Luke is not painting the Madonna, but drawing her with the silver point. That is, he is following the fixed procedure of late Gothic portrait making as we have described it under Jan van Eyck (p. 50). There are no less than three versions of this picture—at Leningrad, Munich, and Boston. The last is finest in quality and pretty certainly the original.

From the end of Rogier's busy life we have a picture which singularly combines sweetness and dignity with material richness. It is the Adoration of the Kings, at Munich. The arrangement, with the girlish Madonna enthroned like a queen in the central position, is very rare in the North, while beginning to be common in Italy. In

choosing this symmetrical composition rather than the usual processional arrangement, Rogier may have had Italian precedents in mind.
Fra Angelico had done something like this in a lunette at S. Marco,
and so had Filippo Lippi in a round picture of the most fantastic richness.   Rogier well expresses the worshipful fervor of the kings and
their attendants, gives it something of the old chivalric quality as directed towards a queen who rules only through her gentleness.   At
this time a young German apprentice, Hans Memling, from Mainz
up the Rhine, was in Rogier's shop.   His execution here and there
may have given this great pageant picture a lightness of touch which
Rogier did not command.

There are from these last years many half-lengths of the Madonna and Child.   Most of them derive from the Madonnas of the
great panels, and to draw the line between what Rogier painted for
himself and what was painted for him on his design is by no means
easy.   There is no great variety about these pictures, but they are
uniformly excellent in expressing without overemphasis a somewhat
tragic maternal solicitude.   They were popular long after Rogier's
death and multiplied indefinitely in small copies.   They even served
for tomb pictures, as an example in the Fogg Museum shows.   These
half-length Madonnas again were common in Italy well before they
appeared in the North, and in this case we may be sure that Rogier
is profiting by his Italian reminiscences.

Here perhaps it should be said that these gentle and sweet creations of Rogier's last years differ so much from the strenuous creations of his prime that certain critics have set up two Rogiers to account for the discrepancy.   The difference is not so sharp as to call
for so drastic an explanation.   It seems to rest partly on the influence
of subject matter.   There are few if any Madonnas in Rogier's early
period; these early pictures, his masterpieces, are almost without exception on tragic themes.   There is no reason to suppose that Rogier
would ever have agonized over a Nativity as he did over a Deposition
or a Last Judgment.   Apart from that, a high-strung temperament,
on penalty of reaching a breaking point, normally relaxes as it ma-
tures, so I see no need for inventing on stylistic grounds a Rogier
of Bruges for whom there is not a whit of documentary or traditional
evidence.

Rogier's portraits are larger and easier in modeling, less searched
in minute facial topography, than those of Jan van Eyck.   They are

somewhat generalized and not so aggressive in assertion of character. The color, if conventional, is cooler and more pleasant. All this means that while Rogier's portraits are perhaps not so thoroughgoing in a descriptive way, they have a pictorial distinction which Jan's lack. They are larger in scale and more decoratively set in the frame. Without pretentiousness of any sort, their feeling is aristocratic. From a few one may judge the quality of all. Take the strong and placid likeness of Philip de Croy, at Antwerp, the more ardent and forceful visage of the Man with an Arrow, at Brussels, the demure and nunlike equanimity of the woman in the National Gallery, Washington (Fig. 43), above all, the hawklike mask of a grandee of the Este family in the Metropolitan Museum (Fig. 44). These will tell sufficiently of the modest greatness of Rogier as a portraitist. It may be noted that only the faces are studied from nature. The hands follow Rogier's usual formula.

Rogier died June 18, 1464, at Brussels and was buried in the Cathedral of St. Gudule. His epitaph, with a truthfulness unusual in lapidary inscriptions, said that "Brussels feared never again to see so great a master. Art grieved at being deprived of a master whom none has equaled." Despite the unevenness of his accomplishment, which I have perhaps conscientiously overstressed, this praise, certainly as regards such tragic masterpieces as his Crucifixion and Deposition, seems well justified. Rogier had followed the way of progress without sacrificing the precious heritage of the Gothic past.

His successors had no doubt as to his pre-eminence, for his influence was felt widely in Europe for fifty years after his death. Aside from such direct successors as his nephew, Gosson de la Pasture, and Colin de Coter, he bequeathed much of his chivalric idealism to Hans Memling. The number of his obscure or nameless imitators is great. Of no other Flemish painter up to Rubens have we so clear an instance of the work living long after the worker.

The early painters of the Haarlem school seem to me rather detached from the general ongoing of things. We have notices of an Aalbert van Oudewater, between 1450 and 1480, one accredited picture, a Resurrection of Lazarus, at Berlin (Fig. 45), and a considerable batch of merely plausible attributions. Aalbert seems to have been, to judge from the Berlin panel, of a quietistic temper, a very competent narrator, interested in problems of interior lighting. The breadth of the distribution of light and dark is simple and fine, otherwise unexampled at this early period.

Concerning his successor and probable pupil, Geertgen tot Sint Jans, we have paucity of information. It is merely a good guess that he was born about 1460 and died rather young about 1495. He is an odd and baffling phenomenon. Often a mere compiler, lifting figures bodily from Rogier de la Pasture, he develops types of an exquisite sort which are wholly his own, and now and then rises to the stature of a great tragic painter. He was a brilliant colorist and resourceful as a landscapist.

Perhaps we remember best of Geertgen his young feminine types —nunlike maidens immovably posed, with pure, impassive oval faces within fantastically lofty headgear. We find them in such a picture as the Relatives of the Virgin (Fig. 46), at Amsterdam, the group being oddly disposed in a church. These young devotees are most unlike the meditative princesses of Memling; they never relax, are always severely on duty like a nun who is also a trained nurse. They have a high degree of puritanical charm.

In the Deposition at Vienna—a smaller and better-composed version is at Princeton—Geertgen falls little short of tragic greatness. The rigid, warped body of the Christ is an invention of the first order, superb whether as evocative of Christian sympathy, or merely as a marvelous material object. The detached grieving women are almost equally notable, the fine inclosure of the group within the skull-like contour of Calvary, in the Princeton version, is an admirable compositional device, as is the small outlet to a trim town and a pleasant landscape. Blemishes are the intrusion of figures borrowed from Rogier, and some vacillation as to scale. On the whole Geertgen seems an intense and lucid temperament without being quite a first-rate judgment.

The last important figure of these younger contemporaries of Jan van Eyck whom we have been considering is Dirck Bouts. Old tradition tells that he was born at Haarlem where he would have come under the influence of the very static art of Aalbert van Oudewater and Geertgen tot Sint Jans. For his early activity we are reduced to attributions. On the basis of a coherent group, including a Crucifixion, Descent from the Cross, and Resurrection, in the Chapel Royal, Granada; an Annunciation, Visitation, Nativity and Epiphany, at Madrid; and an Entombment in tempera, at London, it has been suggested that Bouts was an assistant of Rogier de la Pasture. All this is plausible rather than proved.

Dirck Bouts married with equal tardiness and prudence, in 1447, an heiress of Louvain, and made the remainder of his career in that city, becoming official painter, *portrater*, in 1468.

Since there is really little variety in Bouts's accomplishment, it will be sufficient to study a few of his more famous works. St. Luke painting the Virgin, in Lord Penrhyn's collection, is interesting chiefly for comparison with Rogier's picture on the same theme. In Bouts's version everything is at once stiffer and less balanced. Instead of the water vista we have simple lines of overlapping hills, oddly antici-patory of Perugino. The stilted postures, the frozen gesture of the Christchild, a general bourgeois stolidity, are pure Bouts. For a stu-dent of technique it is interesting that both the silverpoint drawing on the easel and the panel to be painted from it are in sight. If, as is likely, the long-faced quizzical artist is Bouts himself, we may think of him as in the middle fifties and date the picture about 1455. The specific note of the picture is imperturbability without ease, and that is the mark of Bouts's painting generally.

Far the most famous of Dirck Bouts's pictures is the triptych of the Last Supper (Fig. 47), painted after 1468 for the Church of St. Peter at Louvain. Where the Italian painters had conceived the theme monumentally, as a spectacle, with the Apostles, except Judas, spread to right and left of Christ behind the table—an arrangement found in the North in a fourteenth-century fresco in the Bilocque, Ghent—Bouts rejected or ignored such considerations of decorative fitness and religious dignity, offering instead all the particularities of a group of friends at supper in an inn. And at that, the friends are very little interested either in their leader or in each other. There is no hint that the most touching of memorial rites is being enacted. The mood being casual and familiar, it seems to me it is not casual and familiar enough. The woebegone Apostles in their robes look out of place in a public house. Nobody is really at ease except the cook and the host, seen through a service opening in the back wall. While I cannot agree with Fierens-Gevaert that the Last Supper would have to be included in any list of the six or seven greatest pictures of the early Flemish school, that seems to have been the feeling of Bouts's younger contemporaries and successors. For many years after his death Flemish painters of Last Suppers merely rung the changes upon the type he had established.

For me the real interest of this work lies in the little subjects in the shutters. Here, without decorative relation of any sort to the central panel, we see four little outdoor subjects in two rows. These are the feasts which foreshadowed the Last Supper—Abraham and Melchisedek, Gathering the Manna (Fig. 48), Elijah Waked and Fed by an Angel (Fig. 48), the Feast of the Passover.

In these subjects there is nothing that asks deep emotional response, and Bouts's dispassionate handling of the narratives actually achieves a certain value of idylism. Thus, while the narratives are completely undramatic, they have, perhaps almost accidentally, a quiet psychological rightness of their own. For example, the Gathering of the Manna, which in a realist would have evoked the grasping eagerness of hunger, in an idealist, some ecstasy of gratitude, becomes in Bouts's mind merely a cautious and precise physical act. The famine-stricken gatherers of the heaven-sent food might just as well be picnickers gathering up chestnuts. And yet the phlegmatic reading of the theme is of a satisfying charm. Highly romantic both in figures and landscape is the scene of Elijah and the Angel (Fig. 48), but it is a romance inherent in the subject and not in the painter's mind.

The landscape with well-ordered, overlapping hills, behind a rounded hillock in the foreground, is a novelty. It is simple and spacious. The contrasts of light and dark are unusual—as unlike the diffused afternoon sunniness of the Van Eycks as the linear coldness of Rogier. While this larger feeling for landscape may begin with painters of Haarlem older than Bouts, at least he developed it so far that it was left for Gerard David and Patenier only to enrich it by more precisely studied and carefully selected details. It seems to me that Bouts may have gained his honorable place as a renovator of landscape painting from a lucky effect of the negative quality of disinterestedness. Where in Hubert van Eyck there was always some idea of making an earthly paradise and in Rogier de la Pasture some intention of reinforcing a religious impression, Bouts seems to have cared so little about landscape painting that he actually looked at landscapes and painted them about as they looked to him. In short, he was moving from the mental richness of contemporary landscape painting towards the innocence of the eye.

In 1472, being over seventy himself, Dirck Bouts finished a Last Judgment for the courtroom of the Hôtel de Ville of Louvain. It has perished. He undertook to add four big wall panels, of which he lived to execute two. These are at Brussels. They represent a grisly legend of miscarriage of justice and Divine intervention under the Emperor Otho. An innocent knight, falsely accused by the Empress of soliciting her adulterously—he had really repelled her advances—has been condemned to death. We see him resolutely marching to the block accompanied by his intrepidly impassive wife and an agitated Franciscan confessor (Fig. 49). The arrangement of the figures is in rigid verticals and all expression is fixed in the long, set and highly refined masks of the husband and wife. The picture is in several episodes. The chief note of a gentle, self-contained awkwardness is struck by the complete impassivity of the judge, and by the central figure, the headsman, courteously and carefully lowering the severed head into the cloth held by the bereaved wife. Her face and posture seem frozen in place, and less with grief than with complete resignation. In short, this extraordinary picture may be thought of as variations on the theme of self-restraint. There are compositional novelties, such as the two men in the foreground facing different ways, their figures cut by the frame. It is a setting-back and space-making device which could be paralleled in more skillful fashion in such contemporary Italian painters as Mantegna and Piero della Francesca. The construction is strangely uneven. The small drawing, faces, hands, etc., is generally fine and often exquisite; the large drawing, involving bulk and balance of figures, is feeble in the extreme. Bouts lacked the technical equipment of a really great artist.

While this is not a deeply felt picture, it is all the same very thoughtfully conceived, and given the inherent horror of the subject, Bouts's lack of poignant sympathy may be regarded as merciful to the beholder, and advantageous to his own art.

In the second panel Divine justice has intervened. Before the Emperor the widow stands holding in one hand a white-hot iron ingot, and on the other arm her husband's head. The ordeal has proved his innocence. In the background is a busy scene where the guilty Empress is being burned at the stake. Again, impassivity is the chief note and a curious evasion of relations. No eye meets eye. The Emperor looks rather mildly disgusted than deeply shocked. The composition is built out of rigid, unharmonized verticals. Nothing is salient except the set and very tragic masks of the wife and the severed head. The color is deep and rich in details but generally of a somber and neutral effect. All the same, if only for their curiousness and the problems they raise, these are among the more notable creations of the early Flemish painters. Again, as in the case of Rogier de la Pasture's examples of justice, we may remark the strange complacency with which the judges of the time were willing to advertise in the courtroom the bankruptcy of their procedure, while counseling all pleaders to look for justice only in heaven.

While the problem of Bouts's phlegmatism is very alluring, I cannot, for reasons of space, go into it elaborately. The real issue is—was he an unfeeling artist who now and then accidentally capitalized his defect? Or was understatement a conscious professional policy with him? The answer I leave to the thoughtful reader. As an innovator in breadth of landscape and possessor of a more correct practice of linear perspective, Dirck Bouts was of considerable evolutionary importance. He was pretty widely imitated and his manner was continued into the sixteenth century by his pupils, including his son, Aalbert. He died at the good old age of seventy-five, being the longest-lived Flemish painter we have yet met. No zeal for technical perfection, no reckless expenditure of sympathy had worn him out prematurely. With him closes that generation of painters who were contemporaries of Jan van Eyck and active early in the second half of the fifteenth century.

CHAPTER V

THIRD GENERATION OF GOTHIC
PAINTERS IN FLANDERS, HUGO
VAN DER GOES, HANS MEMLING

FIG. 50. HUGO VAN DER GOES. Nativity (central panel).—Florence.

Fig. 51.   (Upper) Hugo van der Goes.   David and Abigail (old
copy).—*Novak Collection, Prague.*
Fig. 52.   (Lower) Hugo van der Goes.   Nativity.—*Berlin.*

85

FIG. 53. HUGO VAN DER GOES. Death of the Virgin.—Bruges.

FIG. 54.  HANS MEMLING.  Triptych of Sir John Donne.—Chatsworth.

87

FIG. 55. HANS MEMLING. Marriage of St. Catherine (central panel).—*Bruges.*

FIG. 56. HANS MEMLING. Floreins Epiphany.—*Bruges.*

89

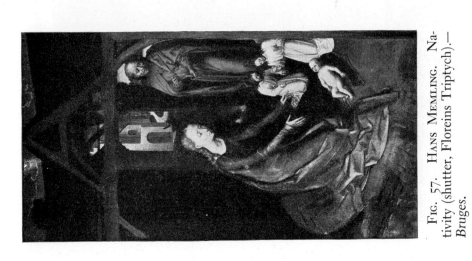

Fig. 58. Hans Memling. Presentation (shutter, Floreins Triptych).—Bruges.

Fig. 57. Hans Memling. Nativity (shutter, Floreins Triptych).—Bruges.

Fig. 59.   Hans Memling.   Shrine of St. Ursula.   Landing at Cologne, at Basle; Reception by the Pope.—*Bruges.*

FIG. 61. HANS MEMLING. Martin Nieuwenhoven.—Bruges.

FIG. 60. HANS MEMLING. Madonna of Martin
Nieuwenhoven.—Bruges.

Between 1465 and 1480 the early Flemish school reached a new and double orientation under two great masters of the third generation—Hugo van der Goes and Hans Memling. Hugo van der Goes broke with the tradition of idealism and courtly decorum of Hubert van Eyck and as well with the pietistic medievalism of Rogier de la Pasture, experimenting boldly in the direction of individual expression, emotional intensity, everyday psychology, and seeking a color no longer chiefly decorative but dramatically various and more realistic. Campin and Dirck Bouts may be regarded as his predecessors, Quentin Massys as the fulfiller of his great but broken endeavor. Hans Memling further refined upon the idealism of his master, Rogier, and of Hubert van Eyck, bringing the old, decorative, medieval color to its ultimate perfection and at once sublimating and completing the old aristocratic ideality in a note of fastidious personal mysticism. His art has no important sequel and closes an era.

Hugo van der Goes was probably a Hollander, from Zeeland, and born about 1430, but his career was mostly made at Ghent. We first meet him there registering as a master in the painters' guild in 1467. Since he was elected vice-dean the next year, he must have been already highly considered. In 1468 he was one of the group of painters who, under Jacques Daret, planned the pageantry for the marriage of Charles the Bold and Margaret of York. The festivities lasted ten and a half days and there were pantomimes between the courses of the banquets. Whatever the painters contributed by way of decoration and scenery was necessarily ephemeral and surely of a secular and allegorical character. The same year at Ghent, for an official entry, Hugo was paid for "certain figures on cloth placed along the streets and elsewhere." The preservation of such work would have relieved the generally religious impression we gain from early Flemish painting, and would have given a truer idea of its scope. We may measurably fill this gap in the record by studying Gothic tapestries of the moment.

In Hugo's case we fortunately have better evidence in old copies of his lost picture of David and Abigail (Fig. 51). The lost original stood over a chimney piece at Ghent. It was really an idyl, and put together with the charming informality proper to the theme. In the First Book of Samuel, Chapter XXV, we read that Nabal, the churlish husband of Abigail, repulsed the messengers of King David, who planned an exemplary punishment. But Abigail received the second mission with courtesy and hospitality, interceded for her hus band, and won the favor of the king, whom, on the prompt and op portune death of her husband, she married. Hugo represented sev eral incidents within one frame—in the background, center, David confronts Nabal, for whom Abigail pleads; in the right foreground Abigail pays homage to the king's envoys; in the left foreground we see the betrothal of David and Abigail.

It would need only a slight transformation to make the story over into a contemporary, chivalric idyl, with richness of episodes, graciousness of landscape setting, a sense of coming and going of gallant folk. The whole thing is full of the often hesitant poetry of youth, and while the original cannot have been a great picture, it must have been a very delightful one. It bears witness to the versa tility and even more to the sensitiveness of its creator. Its date we do not know, but surely so blithe a thing must have been painted well before the cloud of religious melancholia settled upon Hugo.

About 1476 the Italian merchant, Tommaso Portinari, commis sioned a Nativity from Hugo for the church of the Florentine hos pital of Sta. Maria Nuova, which the Portinari family had founded a couple of centuries earlier. In this picture, to be sent to a famous city of art, Hugo naturally outdid himself. First of all he planned what was to be the largest Nativity made before the High Renais sance (Fig. 50). The Romanesque architecture seemed of practi cable scale and the figures were nearly life size. Everything was done to give largeness of effect.

For the time the arrangement is informal, being built on an ir regular diagonal with compensating and supporting thrusts. In prin ciple it is not far from the system which Titian was to introduce about fifty years later in the Pesaro Madonna. The heavier group of the shepherds at the right is equipoised by a massive Romanesque column, by the portal in the middle distance and the weighty figure of kneeling St. Joseph. The single outlet at the right comes unex pectedly, like an unconscious sigh of relief, and the airiness of the covered space is emphasized by angels hovering among the beams of the shed.

The figures, whether that of the sad and stolid Madonna, of the prim kneeling angels, or of the animated drolls who have rushed in from the field, are plastic, strongly balanced, highly existent. Just in this technical capacity to evoke the sense of mass, Hugo at his best seems to me superior to all the other late Gothic painters of the North, and not far behind such great Italian contemporaries as Piero della Francesca and Signorelli.

Ornate features are strictly economized, a novelty. Only the brocaded cope of the angel kneeling in the foreground and the beautifully painted Florentine *albarello* are at all sumptuous.

In lighting, Hugo indulges sharper contrasts of bright and dark than his contemporaries. In color he is soberly rich rather than blithely decorative. All the brighter colors have been reduced to hues by tempering with black.

The mood is very quiet, solemn and almost sullen, with fine contrast notes in the clumsy eagerness of the worshiping shepherds and the prim, hieratic loveliness of the two angels kneeling between them and the Madonna. The other angels share the somewhat stolid melancholy of which Mary's long, oval mask is the focus.

Hugo feels the Nativity as joyous only to unthinking folk like the shepherds, and their joy is qualified by mere curiosity. Otherwise the tragic gravity of the event is emphasized. The picture completely lacks that blithe character of a Christmas carol which the late Gothic painters generally found proper to a Nativity. Joseph seems tense and oppressed at the prospect opened by the miraculous birth. This heavy and apprehensive mood is also that of Tommaso Portinari and his very plain wife and family, with their attendant saints, in the shutters.

I doubt if so unsparing and truth-telling a Nativity would have been liked, had it remained in the North, at the moment when most people thought of the theme in terms of the tenderness of Rogier de la Pasture, Hans Memling and the painters of Cologne. In going to Florence, where technical research in the construction of the figure was intense, it went to the place where nothing much would be thought of its lack of obviously ingratiating quality—where much would be thought of its mastery in realizing and disposing masses on several planes. It was admired for over seventy years, was a notable influence on such experimental masters as Ghirlandaio, Piero di Cosimo, and probably Signorelli. It made the hospital of Sta. Maria Nuova for more than four hundred years a goal of esthetic pilgrimage, and when that venerable institution generously deposited it in the Uffizi, it became immediately and beyond dispute the greatest Northern primitive work in that rich collection.

In a Nativity (Fig. 52), and an Epiphany, at Berlin, Hugo introduced a novelty in composition which was never followed up. The oblongs are very wide and low so that the figures are effectively cramped within the short headroom, after a fashion anticipatory of the compositional norms of the Italian Renaissance. It seems possible that Hugo, who was in touch with Italian patronage, may have seen predella panels disposed in this manner. The Nativity repeats that onrush of eager, grotesque shepherds from the left, which we have seen in the Portinari triptych, but the motive gains a more urgent and drastic character, without monumentality of any kind, from the odd, low dimension of the panel. The whole scene achieves a certain aloofness, from the odd feature of two impassive prophets in the lower corners drawing a curtain aside as if to discover a mystery play. The picture is one of the most ingenious and agreeable of Hugo's creations.

The Adoration of the Magi, on the contrary, is completely anomalous. The elegance of the Madonna, the ceremonial rigidity of the Kings are quite unlike Hugo as we see him elsewhere.

Brother Ofhuys, Hugo's cloister mate, tells us that the painter on his death had commissions and pictures which it would have taken nine years to finish. Here is a field that deserves more investigation than it has enlisted, for surely we must expect to find many pictures draw in or started by Hugo and finished by others. It seems to me that the Berlin Epiphany may be one of these, and completed by a good painter of the school of Bruges. A similar thought occurs in connection with a much finer Epiphany at Princeton which will be later considered.

Hugo's incidental portraiture shows him a master in that branch for character, gravity and plastic value. Apparently he was not a professional portraitist, for we have virtually no separate portraits surely his. His impressiveness in this branch may be gathered from portraits of a male donor and patron saint, in the Walters Gallery, Baltimore. Through the accident of having been cut out of a larger composition these powerfully rendered busts have the quality of separate portraiture and testify to Hugo's potential greatness in that field.

Probably Hugo's latest picture is the Death of the Virgin (Fig. 53), at Bruges. In a certain disequilibrium and in a morose sort of restlessness it seems to me to betray the symptoms of that melancholia which darkened the end of Hugo's career. The highly concentrated figure composition, with many heads close together, shows new audacities in sharply diagonal disposition of the forms, with the prone and dying woman much foreshortened. The bleak whitey-blue tonality, with a sense of chill in it, oddly forecasts the colder Vermeers, as does the large and simple modeling of the Virgin's face. The faces of the Apostles reveal as much bewilderment as grief. Their gestures are hesitating and almost automatic, as if from impaired nervous control.

The sparse accessories of the interior and consequent crowding of the figures up to the picture plane again anticipate the compositional problems of the Italian Renaissance. The entirely unrelated character of the glances—no eye, save the Virgin's and Christ's, meeting eye—is perhaps compositionally a defect, but Hugo may have intended to imply a bereavement too deep to be shared. The drawing of everything is the finest, the Madonna's face a marvel of construction without palpable shadow. The whole effect is paradoxically quiet and distracted, very homely and entirely noble. We have in this legacy of Hugo's the promise of Quentin Massys' more consciously dramatic pathos.

About the time he finished the Portinari Nativity, 1476 or 1477, Hugo sought rest and recuperation in the Red Cloister near Brussels. He was only forty-seven or so, but he had used himself up. Unluckily he was a much spoiled novice. He met and feasted with the numerous visiting celebrities, indulged harmful excess in eating and drinking. After five or six years, on his return from a trip to Cologne, he fell into a dreadful religious melancholia from which he never rallied, dying in 1482, in his early fifties.

His comrade in the Cloister, Brother Gaspar Ofhuys, describes and moralizes the case in a way that would do credit to a modern psychiatrist:

"Hugo was excessively preoccupied with the problem of contriving to finish the pictures he had to paint, which he could have finished with difficulty, as they thought, in nine years."

This not merely tells of the overstrain that hastened, if it did not cause Hugo's breakdown, but, as I have observed, suggests that many pictures started by him must have been finished by others. We probably have such a picture in an Adoration of the Magi, at Princeton, where four portraits, including two superb portraits of Moors, and the St. Joseph, seem of Hugo's finest, while the Madonna and the remaining figures have all the characteristics of the idealizing school of Bruges; indeed may well be by Gerard David.

Brother Ofhuys's final comment on Hugo's mental collapse is of general application:

"In order not to fall into a danger so fatal and irremediable, we should then check our dreams and imaginations, our suspicions and the other vain and useless thoughts which could trouble our brains. We are men, and what happened to that monk as a result of his reveries and hallucinations, might it not also befall us?"

Hugo seems a great genius and a consummate technician, undertaking problems for which the time was not ripe, at once aided and ultimately undone by the intensity of his emotions. Of the Northern painters of his century he is at once the most Northern, modern and romantic.

While Hugo was a considerable influence in the Netherlands and further afield, his direct pupils seem to have been few and of small importance. Justus of Ghent, Joost van Wassenhoeve, deserves a paragraph chiefly because he worked in Italy, and through Vasari's praise has become perhaps unduly notable in the history of art. We meet him as a master in the guild at Antwerp in 1460. He was working at Ghent in 1464. Ten years later he went to Urbino at the call of Federigo da Montefeltro, humanist, tyrant and captain-general of the Pope. There is still at Urbino a Last Supper by Justus. It is on the whole a gloomy and ill-arranged picture. The chief influence is Hugo, but Dirck Bouts may have counted for something. Beyond this picture, nothing much is certain about Justus. He seems to have modified his style in an Italian direction, while he was an influence upon such Umbro-Florentine painters as Melozzo da Forlì.

The attainment of a fastidious refinement is usually the sign that an art has passed the stage of healthy growth and has passed into that of decline. The exquisite art of Hans Memling seems to mark this moment in early Flemish painting. He carried the tender idealism of Hubert van Eyck and Rogier de la Pasture to a perfection beyond which no progress was possible. Indeed the sweetness of his art can be cloying, and Sir Martin Conway's remark that the Memlings should be seen one at a time is profoundly just.

Hans Memling was born at Mainz somewhere about 1433, and his early influences must have been those of the idealizing school of Cologne and the Middle Rhine. One may perhaps find some trace of Stephan Lochner, head of the school of Cologne, about 1450, in Memling's feminine types, but Lochner himself had drawn much from the Van Eycks and Rogier. We first meet Memling registered as a master painter at Brussels in 1454. He apparently served Rogier as an assistant, for in a document of June 16, 1454, a "Hanse jone"— young Hans—is mentioned as painter of the frame of a picture by Rogier. The German Christian name, and the palpable influence of Rogier throughout Memling's work permit us to identify this "young Hans" with our Memling. The two mentions in documents agree in calling for a birth date about 1430, or perhaps a little later. Since, despite certain ingenious surmises of Sir Martin Conway, we have no accredited early pictures by Memling, we may fairly assume that he remained Rogier's assistant at Brussels until the master's death in 1464, probably moving shortly thereafter to Bruges. He may have done some painting on such late works of Rogier as the Seven Sacraments, St. Luke painting the Virgin, the Middelburg Nativity and the Adoration of the Kings, but it would be hopeless to try to trace his handiwork. What is really much more important is that the gently pensive mood of these late Rogiers left an unforgettable impression on young Hans.

Memling was not one of that group of painters who in 1468 made the decorations for the wedding festivities of Charles the Bold and Margaret of York, but he must have been already settled at Bruges and well known there, for he painted the portrait of the Duke's Italian medalist, Niccolò Spinelli, and also made a triptych for a member of Margaret's English escort, Sir John Donne of Kidwelly. Painted in Memling's prime, when he was nearing forty, these two pictures pretty well represent the range and excellence of his art. He was to ring many changes upon their quality, but not really to excel them.

Thus the portrait of Spinelli, at Antwerp, tells us pretty nearly what we need to know about Memling's portraits generally. The heavy, thoughtful face of the medalist is closely set in its frame and backed by a wide stretch of landscape with a winding river, after the contemporary Italian fashion. Spinelli may well have ordered this himself. As compared with the portraits of the Van Eycks, Rogier, and Bouts, the method is more picturesque, less assertive. It is also more painterlike. The modeling is no longer rigid, but flexible; there is more breaking of light into the structural shadow; there is less tenacity of observation, but so far as it goes, the observation is very fine. Without knowing the contemporary Italians, Memling has divined their secret, that good portraiture must also be good picture-making. His many later portraits show the same characteristic of a gentleness that is sufficiently robust and the same sense of carefully studied proportions.

In the little triptych painted for Sir John Donne in 1468 (Fig. 54), and now at Chatsworth, Memling, as Sir Martin Conway has well remarked, fully reveals the charm of his devout traditionalism. The girlish, frontal Madonna, symmetrically flanked by the donors, their patron saints and angels, with a river view glimpsed through Romanesque columns behind, and a Turkish rug below and in front —all this follows the consecrated formulas of the Van Eycks. The two St. Johns in archaic interiors with openings sharply defined against the incoming light are in the pure tradition of Rogier. From him the gaunt Baptist, with his great, gnarled feet, is lifted bodily.

Memling's personal contribution is the demurely charming meditativeness of it all; such natural, hesitant, maidenly postures as those of attendant St. Catherine and St. Barbara—celestial maids of honor such as only Memling's fancy conceived. The fine, tranquil ovals of their faces are repeated in the Madonna and St. John the Evangelist. Purest Memling are the childish, fumbling action of the two angels, the patient yet easy devotion of the kneeling donors, the glooming of stately columns and walls against a distant blue sky, and above all a sort of sumptuous humility pervading the whole composition. In color everything is as radiant as a Hubert van Eyck—who in this regard was Memling's exemplar, rather than Rogier, but the splendor is tranquilizing, not exciting.

Repeatedly, Memling played charming variations upon this theme, in a little triptych at Madrid; in two shutters in the J. P.

Morgan Library, in New York; in the Virgin among Virgins, at Paris
—simply as painting one of his loveliest works; in the famous Marriage of St. Catherine at Bruges; and he frequently developed the
theme with fewer figures, but was never to surpass or even greatly
alter the perfection of this his earliest known masterpiece. Again one
must agree with Sir Martin Conway that, like even the choicest
sweetmeats, the Memlings should be savored at long intervals.

Some time before 1473 Jacopo Tani, representative of Lorenzo
de' Medici at Bruges, commissioned from Memling a big Last Judgment, with the intention of sending it to Florence. It is interesting
to recall that this was a few years before Hugo van der Goes painted
his Nativity destined for Florence. So Memling's Last Judgment was
probably the most important commission yet given by an Italian patron to a non-Italian artist. Any hope of international fame, sup-
posing Memling's gentle spirit to have been capable of such an ambition, was dashed by the capture of the ship bearing the big altarpiece by a Baltic freebooter, Peter Benecke. In pious gratitude for
his piratical success he bestowed the Last Judgment upon his favorite Church of St. Mary at Danzig, where it still hangs.

It is Memling's most ambitious performance, and his least successful. Better in general composition than Rogier's Last Judgment,
there remains a sense of confusion and exaggeration. Even in the delightful episode of the ascent of the eager nude forms of the just to
receive their ascension robes before the splendid Gothic gate of
heaven, Memling falls below the simplicity of arrangement and
earnestness of sentiment of his exemplars of the Cologne school. Individual figures are ingeniously but not convincingly invented. There
is no horror and little joy in the picture. One feels a gentle talent
doing the best with refractory subject matter. Indeed, save Hubert
van Eyck, in that stupendous little panel at New York (Fig. 12), no
Northerner up to Rubens brought adequate force of imagination to
the theme. The Italians have done better with it because, omitting
smaller details, they have generalized it as a sublime and ultimate
assize, claiming attention rather for the Divine Judge and his celestial associates than for the throng of mortals awaiting judgment.
Not a Northern but an Italian poet wrote that sublimest of hymns,
"Day of wrath, that dreadful day"—Dies irae, dies illa.

Before leaving the altarpiece, it should be noted that the little-
known portraits of Tani and his wife on the backs of the shutters are

perhaps the best Memling ever painted—his only portraits favorably comparable for force of character to those of the Van Eycks, rendered with a new alertness and sensitiveness beyond the Van Eycks' somewhat static vision.

Surely the richest of all the Memlings is the Mystic Marriage of St. Catherine (Fig. 55), in the Hospital of St. John, at Bruges. Here the strict symmetry of all such compositions of the master is subtly varied by various directions of glance, by the slight tilt of the Virgin's head, by the free posture of the Christchild athwart the upright compositional lines. Four saintly handmaids of the Virgin sit in mystical contemplation. They are arrayed like so many princesses, but the sheer sumptuousness of the beautifully painted stuffs and jewels is after all dominated by the radiant pearliness of the flesh, by the exquisitely languid hands, and even more by the mood of virginal revery which pervades the whole picture. It is at once very courtly and very devout. The fine critic, Eugène Fromentin, has written of Memling's sainted ladies in this picture:

"He creates a feminine type, an elect being unknown before, and disappearing with him. These are women, but seen as he loves them and according to the tender predilections of a spirit fixing upon grace, nobility and beauty. Of this unique sort of woman he has made at once a real person and a symbol. . . . He arrays her both morally and physically. While he paints the lovely face of a woman, he also paints a charming soul."

The shutters representing, right, St. John's Vision on Patmos and, left, the Decapitation of St. John the Baptist, are in themselves rather negligible, the mood of ecstasy and tragedy being forced and relatively unfelt, but compositionally, with their picturesque diagonal arrangements and deep vistas, which enhance the formality of the central panel, they successfully vary and complete the decorative effect. The Marriage of St. Catherine is undoubtedly Memling's show piece, but many will prefer, with me, the little triptych made in the same year, 1479, for Jan Floreins.

This little Adoration of the Magi, at Bruges (Fig. 56), is in many ways a tactfully diminished echo of Rogier's big triptych at Munich, but the effect is such as Rogier never attained—more personal, more appealing. There is a freedom and unexpectedness about all the postures of the worshiping kings and their train which rests upon a closer observation of the behavior of men than Rogier ever indulged. The prevailing central symmetry is delightfully varied by changes of direction and level. Nothing could have better emphasized the tranquillity of the Virgin's face than to set it against the serrated line of the fence and the horns of the cattle. All devices of this sort are of the choicest. The color is rather quiet, but also rich and harmonious.

The Nativity, on the left shutter (Fig. 57), is merely as an illustration one of the most delicious morsels in Memling's work, while the realization of a dusky, romantic interior is novel and experimental. The Presentation in the Temple (Fig. 58), on the other shutter, leans very heavily on Rogier, and is confusingly cut up by the lights, but its gently ceremonious mood is entirely winning.

One does not think of Memling as a narrative painter, but apart from the famous shrine of St. Ursula, stories of the Passion, at Turin, and of the Life of Mary, at Munich, prove that he was skillful in that branch. Both panels suffer much from the inclusion of many actions in the same landscape setting, with an effect naturally confusing. The little stories are alertly conceived and gracious in mood, but hardly superior to the hundreds of such narratives in contemporary miniatured manuscripts. Indeed Memling saved himself extreme pains of invention by freely consulting such miniatures. The two panels are chiefly interesting as proving that he could easily have made himself a good, but not a great illustrator.

Where Memling emphatically shines as a painter-in-little is in his most famous, if not his best work, the shrine (Fig. 59) at Bruges, in the Hospital of St. John, containing relics of the martyr princess, St. Ursula. The six narrative panels are in the most delicious vein of make believe. Memling tells his charmingly absurd tale with an entirely straight face. The eager bride, Princess Ursula, with her complaisant fiancé and a pictorially practicable quota of her eleven thousand virgins, resolutely pursues her quest of martyrdom up the Rhine and over the Alps to Italy, where she enlists a kindly pope. The party, returning down the Rhine to Cologne, find the opportunely arrived heathen Huns, who provide the desired martyrdom with their crossbows. The six episodes offer a lovely series of embarkations, debarkations, receptions—a celestial pleasure tour. There are fantastic ships, picturesque architecture, splendidly clad young Christians and pagans—equally of highest breeding. Everything is in the best vein of the fairy tale—everything mattering esthetically, and nothing otherwise mattering—save as youth, beauty, ardor, adventure, always matter. There is no effort at imaginative insight—indeed such an effort would have left the legend shattered and discredited, but there is a most lively and tactful play of fancy throughout—a fancy served by all the resources of a great technician's craft. Now this fairy-tale business is never quite great business, whether in letters or in art, but of its sort and for its purpose the Shrine of St. Ursula is entirely perfect. Faith demands fantastic jewel boxes, and has none lovelier than this. When on October 21, 1489, Bishop Burdemaker solemnly inaugurated the reliquary, the Hospital of St. John was proud of it, and has been proud ever since.

A collector privileged to select just one of the many Memlings would do well to consider very seriously the diptych in the Hospital of St. John which represents Martin Nieuwenhoven in his young manhood, half facing the Virgin and Child. Apart from her adolescent loveliness the Madonna (Fig. 60) has all the accessories one would want in a fine Memling—a bit of a Turkish rug and of a cut velvet cushion, stained glass and plain, a diminishing mirror, a glimpse of a road curving from distant hills and turning about a grove. The Madonna herself is less aloof from us than the many with veiled eyes, but I find her half-open eyes, hesitating perhaps between the Christchild and the advancing couple reflected in the mirror, completely captivating. The substance is of jewel-like brilliancy, and the complicated play of light upon nacreous flesh and through cold and colored glass is extraordinarily beautiful.

In the companion panel (Fig. 61), the lucky owner would have one of the finest example of Memling's portraiture. The stolid face, with its suggestion of fullness of sensuous life, suggests that the young patrician may need the Virgin's good offices with the recording angel. Again the attraction is largely that of exquisite arrangement and consummate painting. Traces of the preparation which have come up with time show that Memling laid the composition out on an elaborate geometrical scheme based on the golden section. That is, Memling must have been aware of the studies in artistic proportion which were being conducted in Italy by Fra Luca Pacioli and others. In the Nieuwenhoven portrait, all angles, the half-opened shutters—catching the incoming light so charmingly, after Campin's fashion—all this has its carefully studied reason. Hence we must suppose that the fastidious proportioning of the traditional arrangements throughout Memling's work rests not only upon happy intention, but also upon conscious study and choice.

The latest Madonnas by Memling are mostly regally enthroned with attendant angels, and ensconced fantastically in more or less Italianate pavilions, often decorated with swags of flowers. Familiar examples are at New York, Vienna and Madrid. In general these add little to Memling's artistic stature, indeed their sweetness is somewhat cloying, and the display of material richness seems exaggerated. Every painter as he ages tends to fall back upon formulas and to apply them increasingly rather from habit than from reflection. This is particularly true of artists narrow in intellectual range and dependent largely on sentiment. We may reasonably imagine that in the four or five years before his death in 1494 Hans Memling's art was in gradual and benign decline. He had, after all, given abundant gauges to immortality—why multiply them unduly?

It is easy to underrate or overrate Hans Memling. The greatness of his technical gift is obvious, but so is the narrowness of his imagination. His attractiveness within his range has never needed and never lacked celebration. As the culminating figure of late Gothic painting both in a material and spiritual way he is highly important. A full generation before he was born the Van Eycks were trying to give oil painting a splendor which the Northern world had earlier seen only in stained glass and enamels. It remained for Memling to bring that splendor to a radiance beyond which no merely coloristic progress was possible. On the spiritual side Memling made for the first time visible all those tendernesses towards the Virgin and the virgin saints which the Middle Ages had expressed lyrically in Latin and vernacular poetry. After Memling, everyone could see what had been the private, chivalric ardor of a few mystics who were also poets. Others made the attempt, notably his immediate predecessors of the Cologne school, but no one struck the note so lovingly and with such richness of overtones. To have created an enduring symbolism for this exquisite phase of the beauty of holiness, is surely distinction enough for any artist.

CHAPTER VI

THE LAST PHASE OF GOTHIC PAINTING
IN FLANDERS

FIG. 62. QUENTIN MASSYS. Madonna Enthroned.—Berlin.

108

FIG. 63. (Upper) GERARD DAVID. Marriage of St. Catherine.—
London.
FIG. 64. (Lower) GERARD DAVID. The Virgin among Virgins.—Rouen.

Fig. 66. Gerard David. Baptism of Christ.—Bruges.

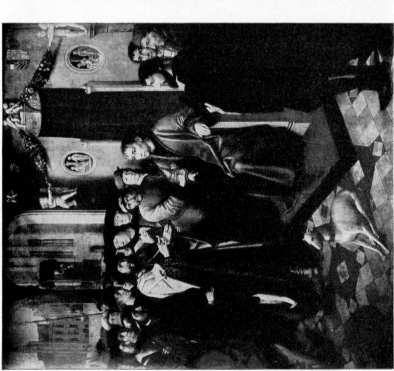

Fig. 65. Gerard David. Judge Sisamnes Accused.—Bruges.

Fig. 67. Joachim Patenier. Landscape with St. Jerome.—New York.

111

FIG. 68.  QUENTIN MASSYS.  Death of St. Ann (l.).  An Angel Appears to
St. Joachim (r.).—*Brussels.*

FIG. 69. QUENTIN MASSYS. A Choirmaster.—Liechtenstein Collection, Vienna.

FIG. 70. QUENTIN MASSYS. Aegidius.—Earl of
Radnor's Collection, England.

113

FIG. 71. QUENTIN MASSYS. Deposition, Salome's Dance, Martyrdom of St. John the Evangelist.—Antwerp.

114

Fig. 72. (Upper left) Quentin Massys. Banker and Wife.—Paris.
Fig. 73. (Upper right) Antwerp Mannerist. Mary Magdalen Anointing
Christ's Feet.—Brussels.
Fig. 74. (Lower left) Jan Gossart. Epiphany.—London.
Fig. 75. (Lower right) Jan Gossart. Madonna and Child.—New York.

115

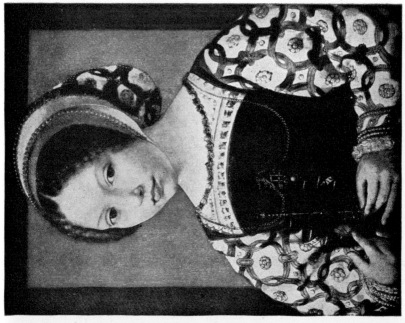

FIG. 77. JAN GOSSART. Princess Jacqueline of Burgundy.—London.

FIG. 76. JAN GOSSART. Adam and Eve.—Berlin.

116

Fig. 78. Jan Gossart. Jean Carondelet.—Coll. M. van der Veken, Brussels.

117

FIG. 79. JAN GOSSART. The Agony in the Garden.—Berlin.

Fig. 80. (Upper left) LUCAS VAN LEYDEN. The Chess Players.—*Berlin.*
Fig. 81. (Upper right) LUCAS VAN LEYDEN. Lot and His Daughters.—*Paris.*
Fig. 82. (Lower) JEROME BOSCH. Epiphany with Saints and Donors.—*Madrid.*

FIG. 83. (Upper left) JEROME BOSCH. Nativity.—Cologne.
FIG. 84. (Lower) JEROME BOSCH. Christ before Pilate.—Princeton.
FIG. 85. (Upper right) JEROME BOSCH. The Prodigal Son.—Ex-Figdor Collection, Vienna.

120

Fig. 86.  Jerome Bosch.  The Hay Wain.—*Escorial.*

121

FIG. 87. JEROME BOSCH. Earthly Delights, or Lust.—Escorial.

FIG. 88. JEROME BOSCH. Temptation of St. Anthony.—*Lisbon*.

Fig. 88a. (Upper) Jerome Bosch. Temptation of St. Anthony (detail).—
Lisbon.

Fig. 88b. (Lower) Jerome Bosch. Temptation of St. Anthony (detail).—
Lisbon.

W E ARE to deal in this chapter with painters of the third and
fourth generation of Gothic realists, with men to whom the
Van Eycks, Rogier, and Dirck Bouts were legendary, while
Van der Goes and Memling were transient, youthful impressions.
Few of these transitional painters escaped the influence of Italy, which
ultimately was to stifle the native manner. In Gerard David we shall
study the decorous continuation and end of the Gothic style; in
Quentin Massys, the successful endeavor to animate the style through
a more emotional utterance; in Jan Mabuse, the vain attempt to borrow Italian graciousness and monumentality without abandoning the
old technique; in Joachim Patenier, the emergence of landscape painting as a specialty; in Jerome Bosch, the tardy exploitation of the vein
of sorcery and diabolism, and initiation of a new interest in common
folk.

Hans Memling left a number of pupils or imitators. Their names
we rarely know, and we name them from their best-known picture—
Master of St. Lucy, Master of St. Barbara, Master of the Magdalen
Legend, etc. They are all mildly attractive, but cannot be reckoned
with in a general survey. Superficially the most faithful follower of
Memling was Gerard David; actually, he was much more than that.

Gerard David was born in Holland, at Oudewater, about 1460,
and his earliest influences were presumably from the prominent painters of Haarlem, Aalbert van Oudewater and Geertgen tot Sint Jans.
Little passed from their art to David's except a certain composure.
Hugo van der Goes may have been a stronger influence, for Gerard
David copied or more probably adapted one of his great compositions
in Epiphanies at Berlin and Munich. In 1485 Gerard David was
registered in the painters' guild at Bruges, and became its dean in
1501. Memling was of course the leading influence, and something
of his sweetness and quietism passed with his favorite compositional
forms into much of Gerard David's work.

But even where Gerard David is closest to Memling, as in the delightful early Madonna with two female saints, in the New York His-

torical Society, he preserves his own difference. There is less aloofness, more intimacy, more humanity in the work. This is true not only of his numerous half-length Madonnas, which are often in a familiar, almost domestic vein—but also of those more monumental groups in which the reference to Memling seems clearest.

Perhaps the loveliest of these is the Marriage of St. Catherine, at London (Fig. 63). We are in a definite place and among people like ourselves. The touching ceremony takes the participants out of the world only for a moment; they will go back to their usual gracious and serviceable pursuits. The pious cantor, Richard de Visch, who gave the picture, will take his staff in one hand and his pet dog in the other and return to the study of his choir books in the sacristy of St. Donatian's. While the composition has much of the formality of Memling, that formality oddly assumes an accidental character. The figures might move and make a different picture.

Gerard David's most elaborate composition of this symmetrical sort is the Virgin among Virgins, at Rouen (Fig. 64), and it is also one of his most accomplished works. It was the painter's gift, in 1509, to the Carmelite nuns of Bruges, and in this pious offering he gave all he had as an artist. While the relation to Memling is obvious, it is also superficial. The feminine types are not etherealized; they have moral and physical gravity, are more like Rogier than Memling. And the familiar central composition is developed with surprising novelty. Gerard David eliminates the customary accessories and fills his oblong closely with the figures, partly because the contemporary Italians were doing this, more because he feels his flower bed of saintly maidens would lose from an elaborate border. Some postures are Memling-like, but no mask is really like his. The expressions are more homely, the acts more specific. Everything is on a mundane plane, expressing the reasonable and sufficient piety of every day.

The six faces in the background may be saints or portraits. Gerard David's own wistful, relaxed face is in the left-hand corner. As to the rather moody woman below him with flowers in a basket—is she St. Dorothy, St. Elizabeth of Hungary, or simply Cornelia Cnoop, the painter's wife, with her offering to Our Lady of Mount Carmel? Such questions do not arise in a Memling.

The group is beautifully composed, of a dense orderliness; the symmetry is subtly relieved by varying the glances; the triple division is nobly punctuated by the massive and gracious forms of the playing angels in the background, and the whole is at once well united and eased up by the splendid swirl of draperies across the bottom.

In such tragic themes as the Crucifixion and Deposition Gerard David avoids exaggerated expression and seeks and achieves a measured pathos and a fine dignity. It is the attitude rather of a self-respecting believer than that of a pietistic visionary. Indeed the sense for decorum allies Gerard David with his great Italian contemporaries. Like them he is always a little in danger of seeming heavy and unfeeling. But such aspersions are groundless. The socially religious painter of whatever race naturally and properly subordinates his merely personal expression to that of the whole body of the faithful. He and they wish sacred themes, however poignant, to be interpreted with sobriety and nobility.

For one of his most stilted compositions, the Madonna with St. Ann, in the Widener Collection, Gerard David, following an Italian precedent, provided little arched predella panels, which are now in the collection of Lady Wantage, England. These reveal him as one of the most accomplished narrative painters of his school, and make us regret that he so rarely followed this vein. The subjects are miracles of St. Nicholas and St. Anthony of Padua. Particularly delightful are the three panels dealing with St. Nicholas, protector of children. We see him a new-born babe precociously praying in his bath; reviving three boys who had been cut up and pickled in brine; slyly dropping the purses which will save three girls from a life of sin. We are not in Memling's fairyland, but in a world kindly and a little matter-of-fact, where a saint goes about his business with as much discretion as enthusiasm. One thinks of the little groups with children in Rogier's Seven Sacraments. The figures in these predellas are rather large for their frames, the lighting is calm and equable, the accessories few but expressive of the matter in hand. Certain Italian contemporaries, for example Montagna, would have conceived these subjects very much in this manner.

In 1498 Gerard David painted two examples of Justice for the town hall of Bruges, and it is significant that whether by choice or under orders, he chose not such fantastic miracles as had pleased Rogier and Bouts, but instead a solid example from ancient history—the venal Judge Sisamnes accused by King Cambyses and by his orders flayed alive. It was an incident calculated to give pause to any

Flemish judge considering a bribe, and such practicality is consonant with Gerard David's art in general. There is perhaps a trace of Bouts in the types and phlegmatic conception of the Accusation of Sisamnes (Fig. 65), but there are also psychological touches quite Gerard's own. The tense, despairing dignity of the doomed judge is admirably caught. The throwing back of the whole group from the picture plane is an innovation. There are superficial Italianisms, in the vaguely Renaissance type of the architecture, in the sculptured classical medallions, in the little nude geniuses holding swags of fruit and flowers. It is in no sense a great work, but it is very thoughtfully conceived, with a desire for gravity and style. One thinks a little of such contemporary traditional painters at Florence—the Franciabigios and Granaccis—who essayed without complete success the passage from a merely picturesque to a monumental style.

In the field of landscape Gerard David was a notable progressive. Where all the earlier landscapes had tended to eliminate the foreground and spread out the middle distance and distance as a sort of curtain behind the figures, Gerard insisted on the foreground and spent himself in studying the details. The trees are of reasonable scale, rocks are rendered in their character, running or rippling water is studied with the most delicate accuracy. All this might be verified in many paintings of Gerard's, but I prefer to rest the case on his most carefully studied picture, The Baptism, for Jean de Trompes (Fig. 66), which was in hand for the eight years between 1502 and 1510. It is in the Museum at Bruges.

The landscape, very minutely yet very nobly treated, is the remarkable feature of this picture. The scene, with its pleasant overlappings of leafage, tree trunks, crags, cities and distant castles, is far better ordered than in earlier Flemish pictures. The blue pool with its extraordinarily studied concentric ripples about the ankles of Christ and the Baptist is of jewel-like effect. Throughout, the minute detail is fastidiously studied from nature. Something like this had been done by the best Lombard painters of the time, and Gerard may have profited by their example. In the construction of the figures there are new depths of shadow that again may betray an Italian influence. The chief group is a little stolid and set, unelegant, one may think, but the theme perhaps calls only for composure and simple truthtelling.

The shutters of this fine work, especially that depicting the wife of Jean de Trompes, Magdalena Cordier, presented by the Magdalene to the Virgin, show a new concentration, and without sacrifice of intimacy, a real monumentality.

Bruges, owing to the silting up of the canal to the sea, was rapidly sinking as a city of commerce and artistic patronage, so not long after finishing the Baptism Gerard David moved to the very prosperous city of Antwerp, where in 1515 we find him inscribed as a master in the painters' guild. In a city which had already seen Quentin Massys' most important works Gerard David must have seemed something of an old fogey. Happily there are compensations for old fogeydom in the esteem of one's surviving contemporaries, and that Gerard David seems to have had, for he was productive in these last years. From this time comes the most Italianate page in his work, the Trans-figuration. There is strain in the attempt for expression of ecstatic surprise in the three Apostles, but the whole has its touch of sublimity. The simple relation of landscape and sky to the figure of Christ is extraordinarily fine. One is reminded of greater things—of the Trans-figuration of Giovanni Bellini, for example. This picture has re-mained in the Church of Notre Dame, where on August 15, 1523, in his sixty-second year, Gerard David's body was honorably laid to rest.

It is easy to make too much of Gerard David's composure and obvious limitations of temperament. He has many claims to distinc-tion, and seems to me generally underestimated. I can hardly think of another artist who brought a style to an end without exhibiting a trace of mannerism or of decadence. This soundness seems to rest on exceptional open-mindedness and good judgment. Refusing to abandon what seemed valid in the inherited style, he seems to have weighed very carefully such suggestions as came up from Italy, adopt-ing only those that he could reasonably assimilate. And he was aware not merely of alluring new materials, but also of new principles of monumental design, and these he adopted so far as the old technique and feeling permitted. It seems possible that a successor of his ju-dicious temper might actually have achieved that assimilation of the Italian manner, which actually had to wait, across a century of the very wasteful efforts of the Romanizers, until the advent of Rubens. But the task of innovation was to be in the hands of such more pas-sionate and volatile men as Quentin Massys and Jan Mabuse.

Gerard David's influence was strong, especially upon the minia-ture painters of Bruges. We have a few miniatures of exquisite execution which are plausibly attributed to him or to his wife Cornelia. The famous Grimani breviary and its class draw heavily upon his forms and arrangements. Among his direct followers none but Adriaen Isenbrandt claims notice. The group of little pictures, reasonably but not certainly attributed to him, show in the figure compositions Gerard David's leading, while the landscapes are of a depth and saturation of color which suggests an influence from Italy. The effect is intimate and romantic. Isenbrandt has his own small, sweet note. The tiny triptych at New York, in which the Nativity is flanked by an Epiphany and a Flight into Egypt, tells sufficiently of his limited gift as an inventor and of his great charm as a mere painter. We do not know Isenbrandt's birthplace. He came to Bruges in 1510 and apparently worked there until his death in 1551.

We have seen that landscape seemed ready to emerge as an independent art in such highly elaborated landscape backgrounds as that for Gerard David's Baptism of 1510. It actually emerges only a little later under the auspices of a young imitator and probably friend of Gerard's, Joachim Patenier. He was born at Bouvignies on the Meuse, about 1475, and is likely to have seen the panoramic landscapes of Jerome Bosch with the figure interest subordinated, but Patenier was to work rather with the landscape materials of Gerard David. We find Patenier registered as a master at Antwerp in 1514. Seven years later his name appears frequently in Dürer's diary, and always in friendly and helpful guise. He lent Dürer colors, invited him frequently to his table, bought prints of him. It is hard to imagine the role of colleague being played more courteously and generously. Even without Dürer's evidence, we should imagine such open-heartedness and amiability in the painter of Patenier's landscapes. Without much pretension to originality, he compiles the rich materials which had come down from Hubert van Eyck to Gerard David—compiles them lovingly and modestly, brings the very various local color of the superabundant forms into reasonable harmony, employs good painters to put in those little figure groups in foreground which assert that this is not merely a landscape, but a subject picture. There is not much strenuous observation in these pleasantly devised panoramas. In the main we simply have the old parklike paradise backgrounds, with richer punctuation of picturesque copses and crags.

Of these average landscapes of Patenier we may say that while they are very carefully modulated there is much of a sameness of esthetic effect. The Repose on the Flight to Egypt, at Brussels, with a fine natural arch behind the Madonna happily nursing the Child, is characteristic in its modest idylism. There is a reassuringly fine luncheon basket. The dense, well-formed trees are like those of Gerard David.

It was a theme that pleased Joachim and he repeated it often with variations. For example, the version in the New York Historical Society is more animated, with angels shaking the fig tree for foraging St. Joseph, and a well-grown, solicitous angel offering figs to Mary. While these figures were generally painted by friends of Patenier, doubtless he directed what was to be done, and the figures in his pictures should be credited, if not to his hand, at least to his genial invention.

While Patenier is an ingratiating personality, we cannot think of him as a great landscape painter, as Hubert van Eyck had been and Pieter Bruegel was soon to be, yet Patenier had moments in which he transcended himself, forgot the charming particularities of nature, and contemplated its grander and austere simplicities. The spaciousness of the river valley behind St. Jerome, in the admirable Patenier at New York (Fig. 67), has its hint of sublimity. It is felt very largely, and seen as so many Chinese landscapes are, from a high point whence a liberated spirit may expand to the breadth of the scene. Of course we cannot imagine, as we must with a Far-Eastern painter, any mystical fusion of Joachim Patenier with his landscape vision. At least in this picture he fully realizes the simple and natural elation that comes of taking account of the run of a great water course and its relations to the encompassing earth.

Patenier is even grander in that extraordinary picture, Charon's Barque, at Madrid, with its blue estuary rising and broadening towards a distant sea. Save Hubert van Eyck, no European painter before him had ever seen such a thing with interest, and few European painters since have done any better with a theme usually, and wrongly, regarded as pictorially impossible. Had Joachim had any gift for abstraction, what might he not have achieved? But this is of course to ask unreasonably for quite another Joachim than the companionable nature lover whom history has vouchsafed to us. He was probably the first painter to establish a taste and patronage for landscape as an independent art, hence is important in an evolutionary way.

In 1494, the year Memling died, the Zwyn canal finally silted up, and Bruges ceased to be a port of consequence. Unemployment set in. Her more energetic merchants moved to Antwerp, which was clearing five hundred ships a day. By marrying the daughter of Charles the Bold, the imperial adventurer Maximilian of Austria, after some difficulties including a mild imprisonment at Bruges, fell heir to what is now Belgium, and Antwerp became the western capital and outpost of the Empire of the Hapsburgs. This associated the Southern Netherlands with Austria, Spain, and Italy, and tended to substitute a European for a provincial culture. It also alienated the Imperial Netherlands from such persistently Gothic countries as those foes of the Empire, France and England. But for this political and cultural change, the entire Netherlands might have joined in the Protestant revolt, and there might have been no fit place for a Rubens to make that assimilation of the Venetian Renaissance which was largely to guide the painting of Western Europe for two centuries. Instead, the leadership would have fallen to some painter like Frans Hals, with a much restricted effect. Antwerp, like most cities of wealth, was rather to attract great painters than produce them. The first and one of the greatest was Quentin Massys, the first modern mind and heart to seek expression in painting in the Low Countries.

He was born in Louvain about 1460, possibly trained under Aalbert Bouts, son of Dirck, intelligently consulted the older masters, especially Rogier de la Pasture and Hugo van der Goes. His earlier works, notably a Calvary, at London, suggest in their emotional emphasis an influence from Hugo. Later he was to temper this manner by consulting the great Italian painters, Raphael and Leonardo da Vinci, whose works he knew only in copies or drawings. Massys' particular contribution to painting was a color no longer conventional and merely decorative, but specifically dramatic; a composition more dense, complicated and energetic; a more lyrical pathos and more popular humor; a greater sensitiveness to characteristic or passing mood in portraiture; finally, a larger and almost monumental scale for the altarpiece. An innovator on all main issues, in the mere handling of brushes and pigments he held to the traditional manner, and this was perhaps unfortunate, for what he had to express required a freer technique than that of the Gothic North.

The legend that he began in his father's and brother's trade as an ironsmith is credible enough, but the sequel that he became a painter in order to improve his social standing and win a bride is a silly bit of romanticism. No Antwerp girl and no Antwerp parents of the time would have thought a painter more eligible than a smith.

In 1491 Quentin Massys was received as a master in the Guild of St. Luke, at Antwerp, without the usual probation, which means that he brought credentials as a painter. Though soon the most famous of Antwerp's painters, he never held office in the guild nor enjoyed imperial patronage. One imagines a self-centered individualist, perhaps of a solitary disposition. He throve, however, on the favor of the trade guilds and the merchants, men of great affairs and generous manner of life, to whom the candid emotionalism of Massys may have been a welcome change from the rigidity and reserve of the old Gothic style.

In 1509 the Confraternity of St. Ann, of Louvain, unveiled in their chapel, in St. Peter's, Massys' first great altarpiece, the Family of the Virgin. It is now at Brussels. Despite the superficial familiarity of the theme—Germany had supplied many examples of the cousins, uncles and aunts, symmetrically grouped about Mary and Jesus—the Confraternity must have felt a certain novelty in Massys' work. The central panel is planned with the old symmetry, but the poses are more natural and momentary. Mischievous children, the Saviour's cousins, crowd about their mothers' knees; the Saviour's bearded uncles, relegated to the background, have that hungry, neurotic eagerness which we have noticed in the men of Hugo van der Goes. The stately, rather classical architecture, based vaguely on Florentine forms, frames the group without cramping it, and behind it vaporous, blue hills overlap till they reach a pale sky, after the fashion of Leonardo da Vinci.

New also is the large scale of the figures and their free swing in diagonals. New and more important is the rose, pearl, and azure transparency of the color—in treble, one might say, as compared with the sonorous middle register of the older schools. New, too, are the delicate, unshadowed ovals of the young women's faces, vaguely recalling the early Raphaels.

The new manner asserts itself even more emphatically in the shutters. In two of them—St. Joachim's Offering rejected by the High Priest, and the Parents of the Virgin giving Alms to the Poor— the richness of the architectural setting and the variety of expression are somewhat confusing. But in these less successful compositions there are signal beauties. Such a sensitive face as that of the acolyte watching the spurned offering is unexampled in earlier Northern art, while the heartbroken humiliation of St. Joachim, somewhat exaggerated, in operatic fashion, is a new note fully sounded.

Better as a whole is the Appearance of the Angel to Joachim (Fig. 68), where the setting of the figures on air and on earth is admirable, and the expression of a hallucinated awe and ecstasy is fully realized. Best of all is the concentration of hushed awe, love and grief in the Death of St. Ann (Fig. 68). Massys, in imagining this, his first masterpiece, must have had in mind Hugo van der Goes' Death of the Virgin, at Bruges, but Quentin is quieter, more orderly, more reverent, pathetic and natural, while in his use of the broadly streaming cool light, with an effect at once liberating and ennobling, he moves to a parity with some of his great Italian contemporaries, Carpaccio, for example.

The Family of the Virgin is a transitional work, and the artist is at times oppressed and overburdened with his own emotions. We have to do with the work of a man who had lived and felt much. He had married twice, had been father and friend to seven children like those winsome cousins of Jesus whom we see in this picture. He was yet to see seven children come and go. He had contemplated everyday men and women and children in their essential humanity as no other early Flemish painter had done. So the art of Quentin Massys represents the invasion of the decorum of the older painting by some ardor from common living, and this ardor is kept short of extravagance by a remote but sound divination of the monumental compositional laws of the Italians.

The Madonnas of Massys vaguely recall the sentimental schools of contemporary Italy, notably that of Umbria, but they have hardly a trace of that dignity which no Italian painter wholly sacrificed. Where the earlier Madonnas of the Flemish school had remained objects of worship—idols in a good sense—those of Massys excite rather sympathy than devotion. He spent himself in studying the always somewhat uneasy and poignant relation of a young mother to her first child, conceived it simply as a human experience (Fig. 62). Its various phases of solicitude, tenderness and anxiety deeply engaged both his curiosity and his sympathy, and he made them visible with a truthfulness which is occasionally qualified by exaggeration. The result is that the Madonnas of Massys have little religious or traditional character, are in a high degree appealing—sometimes too overtly so. They vary within strict limits, the accessories gradually becoming more Italianate, the pathos more emphasized, as he grew older. The common and adequate merit of them all consists in a fragile kind of charm.

Without exception the early Flemish painters were excellent portraitists, but Massys' portraits have the difference that one expects from his sensitive and mobile sympathy. Jan van Eyck, Rogier, Bouts, Memling, paint a man as a sort of abstraction of the way he would always look. With difficulty one imagines the sitter as ever looking different from the portrait. Waiving this sense of permanent aspect, Massys studies momentary and changing expression. Under other conditions, one feels, his sitter might look quite otherwise. That is, in portraiture he pursues the particularizing and unconventionally psychological way which we have just noted in his Madonnas. This means some gain in human interest, with some loss of distinction. The artist, like the mere layman, cannot have it both ways.

Thoroughly characteristic is the Man with the Spectacles, at Frankfurt. Massys has caught him at the moment when his wide cap cuts the double window and the landscape most picturesquely, has arrested the moving hands where they best break the monotony of the robe, has made the figure turn a little askew, as through the impact of a surprise or a perplexity. This overlaying of the fugitive and picturesque upon the enduring fact of character is Massys' peculiar contribution, and, at the moment, it is unique.

Less salient in these respects is the almost aggressive Portrait of a Choirmaster, in the Liechtenstein Collection (Fig. 69), Vienna. But here too the posture is transitional, and it seems as if the strong, self-contained mask must either brighten or sink into deeper repose. The relation of the figure to the landscape is in the contemporary Italian feeling.

Massys is most thoroughly himself in the portraits of the humanist, Erasmus, and his friend the able and learned Aegidius, town clerk of Antwerp (Fig. 70). In both the note is that of a beneficent alertness and shrewdness, which is qualified in the Erasmus by a guarded and kindly irony. Originally united within one frame as a gift to Sir Thomas More, these portraits are now respectively in the National Gallery, Rome, and in Longford Castle, England. These likenesses of two amiable, learned and wise men are literally so speaking that Erasmus in his letter of presentation by no means exaggerated when he wrote: "We send these portraits to you so that we shall be still with you, even when we shall have passed on." Little Erasmus guessed how prompt and tragic was to be the passing of his great English friend and patron.

Unquestionably Quentin Massys' masterpiece is the triptych of the Deposition (Fig. 71), painted in 1511 for the Chapel of the Carpenters' Guild in the Cathedral of Antwerp, and now in the Museum of that city. On the merely compositional side this is perhaps the densest and best-organized group that the North had yet seen, and even Italy, the Sistine ceiling being still veiled, had rarely seen a figure arrangement of such complicated perfection. The composition is laid out in easy yet energetic zigzags culminating in the crags of Calvary, and these diagonals work both in plane, as pattern, and in depth, as a factor in space. Massys' characteristic flushed pallors are nowhere more transparent and beautiful than in this picture, and they are varied by warm and luminous passages of shadow which are never empty or imprecise. The actions are specific, feelingful, and yet restrained and noble. Within my knowledge, no other painter has dared so drastic an incident as St. Joseph of Arimathea plucking away the bloodclots from the dead Christ's hair.

The actions are vehement, as that of St. John catching the swooning form of the Virgin, but also appropriate and compositionally balanced. The reverent, hesitating touch of the Marys who tend the pierced hands and feet of their Lord is especially lovely. Very effective is the contrast of the oval, wistful faces of saintly women with the rugged visages of the men. In the whole picture everything is driven to that perilous brink where sincere emotionalism plunges into sentimentalism, but that brink is never quite reached. The pervading reverence, the keeping of a keen human curiosity within religious bounds, is a heritage from the old school. The energy and suppleness of the expressive forms, on the contrary, look forward to the baroque and Rubens.

The wings of this altarpiece are far more novel in conception than the central panel. In the right wing the preparations for the martyrdom of St. John the Evangelist are depicted (Fig. 71). What has interested Massys is the contrast between the imperturbability of the physically frail apostle, the official ferocity of the soldiery, the honest sweaty toil of the hangmen feeding the fire under the huge caldron. The picture might equally well be labeled Spiritual Fortitude or Futile Toil—for the boiling oil did no harm to St. John.  A very sensitive person is often an ironist, and Massys may have felt humoristically the discrepancy between the toil involved in heating the caldron and the small result in torture.

Until our own times, with Gustave Moreau, Oscar Wilde, and Richard Strauss, no one but Quentin Massys had glimpsed that atmosphere of elegant sadism in which the drama of St. John the Baptist found its dénouement (Fig. 71).  Depravity and cruelty first achieve esthetic birth in this masterpiece.  Everybody is fitly bestialized, from the magnificent, sensual Herod to the almost imbecile courtier in the background, and the musicians in the balcony gloating over so refreshingly bizarre an event at court.  And the luxurious setting enhances the action.  One feels the room is hot and perfumed. Dancing Salome, with the pearly pallor of a poisonous fungus, winces in her measure, as Herod winces while Herodias calmly probes John's severed head with a table knife.  The perceptions implied in such a work are both penetrating and sinister.  We have left the conventional decencies of legend behind and are fully launched into morbid psychology.  What makes the work a masterpiece is the refinement with which its ruthless insight is invested.  For the first time since classical antiquity we have revealed the strange and disquieting beauty that haunts the moral nether depths.

When I recall this masterpiece, I seem to understand why Albrecht Dürer, though promptly paying his visit of courtesy to Quentin Massys, never repeated it through the months he passed at Antwerp. The two masters could not have been congenial.  I fancy Quentin may have fully appreciated Dürer's sturdy, cerebral art, but Dürer must have divined in the master of Antwerp intense and introverted curiosities and sensibilities of a sort perilous to a Christian painter.

It would be tactful to leave Quentin Massys here at the climax of his creative activity, but to do so would be to ignore minor phases of his talent which had their influence and also to oversimplify the analysis of a very complicated character.  We have seen that in the most elevated creations of Massys there is often some intrusion of the familiar, satirical and grotesque.  In some of his later pictures these usually incidental interests become dominant.  Some fifteen years later than the Deposition, in 1526, falls an Epiphany, at New York, which is highly instructive because it exposes unsparingly pretty much all the defects of a great talent.  It is practically an overempha-

sized study in physiognomy, a cluster of heads characterful to caricature, such as Leonardo da Vinci, Jerome Bosch and Albrecht Dürer
had already drawn or painted. The ignoble grotesque predominates.
What eager, ugly, intentionally gnarled mugs the Magi and their
bizarre train present to the almost simpering Virgin Mother! The
picture consists in this contrast; the rest is mere enrichment with
stuffs, galloon, superb metal work, Italian arabesque pilasters. The
whole effect is overcharged, ambiguous and unsatisfying, without the
meaning that so clearly transpires from the other works of Massys,
and it is pictorially far less accomplished.

It is for that reason a problem, and psychologically most interesting. Here the master waives his ideality and taste in favor of character study; here he admits the brute pressure of those costly objects
in which Antwerp abounded; here he abandons the old formal arrangements; here in the chubby, well-grown Babe—months old at birth
—he pays fleeting homage to the Italian canon of physical beauty.
The intensity that had earlier concentrated upon the great simplicities
of faith now wreaks itself upon the shifting mundane spectacle, with
its inconscient interblending of the lovely and the hateful, the noble
and the grotesque. It is a sharp shift in moral and esthetic orientation, but it should surprise no one who has outgrown the bad habit of
regarding the people of remote times, artists particularly, as much
more simple and consistent than ourselves.

The mundane or libertine pictures of Massys are after all few—
many attributed to him are by his plagiarists, and they find their
explanation in the readiness of his sympathy and the volatility of his
talent. And the few common or raw episodes which engage him are
treated with great refinement. Such is certainly the case with the
Banker and his Wife, of 1514, at Paris (Fig. 72). The money changer
with careful phlegmatism weighs and judges a gold coin, while his
young wife listlessly turns her eyes from a splendid prayer book, regarding an habitual act with that condescending tolerance which any
wife bears towards the professional ritual of any husband. We seem
to have a gentle bit of social satire, and, to attenuate it, the picture is
cast in the ornate manner of the older schools. The rich accessories
are multiplied, and tell much about a tranquil and perhaps somewhat
tedious prosperity. One may guess that Massys had shrewdly scanned
Petrus Christus' St. Eligius (Fig. 33), or one of the lost genre pictures

of Jan van Eyck. The picture, and others similar, set a fashion for character pieces in half-lengths with elaborately studied interiors.

If the wisest of kings was amazed at the way of a man with a maid, he would have experienced a more emphatic shock over the way of an old man with a wench. It is this permanent, ugly social fact that Massys has celebrated in the painting Unequal Love, in the Pourtalès Collection, at Paris. It is a character study of heads against a plain background, a fashion Giorgione and his immediate followers seem to have set in Italy. The masks are admirably expressive. Even without the significant incident of the filched purse, the base comedy of the situation is evident. The courtesan has appropriately the precise toss of the head of dancing Salome (Fig. 71), and paradoxically, the choice features of the Madonnas. Here may be an allegory of the very various contents of the alluring female shell. Not an agreeable picture, for the theme is the ugliest, it is most honestly and intently observed and excellently painted. With it the moralist can have no issue. To senile lust and the gold-digging wiles of courtesanship it lends no attractions.

Perhaps Sir Thomas More's seemingly perfunctory eulogy of Quentin Massys: "O Quentin! renovator of an old art!" (Quintine! O veteris novator artis!) really sums up his accomplishment in a broad sense. Without radically departing from traditional methods, he vivified them by a new color, by more energetic compositional forms, by a new and more sensitive feeling, and finally, by the assimilation of all that could be drawn from contemporary Italy without violating the Flemish genius. He at once marks the brilliant conclusion of an old style, and presages the necessity of a new. He had numerous imitators, but nothing they did had significance save in so far as multiplying genre pictures, generally with a religious pretext; they kept alive and growing the taste that was to demand and support in the next century the delightful familiar art of the Dutch little masters.

When Quentin Massys died in 1530, he left late Gothic painting in the condition of an outdated fortress which was crumbling rapidly inside while under attack from without. Which is a long, but I hope interesting way of saying that there were really two destructive forces undermining the old school—the replacement of the old sincerity by the mere dexterities of mannerism, and the turning of the more intelligent painters towards the superior art of Italy, a choice which had its good reasons, produced unhappy results for a couple of generations, but carried promise with it and eventuated ultimately in the glorious synthesis of Rubens.

The Gothic mannerists deserve little attention; the reader is referred to Dr. Max Friedländer's admirable pages on them. One and all they cultivate tricks—preposterous complications of flamboyant architecture, minute rendering of the refinements of chased gems or chiseled metal, pretentious deployments of the new lore of linear perspective, sensational but also superficial assertions of oddities in interior or artificial illuminators. The accessories eat up the figures. Fantastic stage settings are invented, but the actors are virtually missing. Nothing really happens, or can happen—the artist is merely showing off, and often he does so with a skill that is both amazing and despicable.

A little triptych at Palermo, a good contemporary copy of the central panel in the New York Historical Society, is generally ascribed without complete certainty to Jan Mabuse. It has a fantastic sort of charm, but it is really a flamboyant Gothic tabernacle in which a Madonna occurs incidentally rather than a Madonna in a tabernacle. It represents the new mannerism in its more amiable aspect.

Upon the unfortunate observer, Christ in the House of Martha, at Brussels (Fig. 73), imposes a tediously ornate setting and a confusing multiplication of spaces, in or before which the tiny figures pretend to be interested in the action. A much better picture is a Ceremony in an Unfinished Church, at New York. It has been ascribed without good reason to Herri met de Bles. The necessity of thinking out a late Romanesque interior has sobered the artist. He has treated his theme with much picturesqueness, the lighting is sensitively studied, and the accessories are appropriate and charmingly painted. Probably by the same hand is a more pretentious and much poorer Adoration of the Kings, at Madrid. Here the glamour of a courtly legend is well realized at the sacrifice of all religious feeling and truthfulness. The towering shadowy interior inclosing tiny figures anticipates certain of the Romantic effects, and the cheaper ones, of Rembrandt's early pictures.

One and all these late Gothic mannerists ignored the law that the good picture involves simplification, selection and elimination; instead they made appearances much more complicated than they are, impoverished meanings by burying them under vain enrichments. One turns with relief from these fussily ingenious spirits to the far more serious, if perplexed and not quite integral, figure of Jan Gossart van Mabuse, the first Flemish painter to give himself wholeheartedly to the Italian manner. But Jan Gossart's tardy conversion to Italianism was more sincere than discriminating, and, broadly speaking, he may be regarded as a good Flemish painter gone wrong. All the same he pointed out a course that had to be followed, and if he was hardly to be a leader, he succeeded in being a herald.

Jan Gossart was born at Maubeuge, in Hainault, before 1480, and possibly was trained under Gerard David. We have very few pictures from his youthful years. Two, the little triptych at Palermo, and another, its main theme a Rest on the Flight to Egypt, show Gossart transiently leaning towards the Antwerp mannerists. He was soon to develop under Italian guidance a mannerism at least his own. By the early years of the sixteenth century he had followed the drift to wealthy and generous Antwerp. Before that time he had begun and carried far forward his largest and most imposing picture, the Epiphany (Fig. 74), at London. A credible tradition tells that he worked seven years at it, and in 1504 it was still in the making, for Sir Martin Conway has shown that there are borrowings from Dürer's print of the Nativity of that year. The fairly monumental effect of the picture rests on the relation of the stately Romanesque ruin to the well-composed group which it incloses. The layout is entirely traditional, with some such exemplar as Hugo van der Goes' Nativity—doubtless available in copies—in mind. Indeed, while the prevailing gravity and immobility recall Gerard David, the picture is a skillful composite of many older Flemish traditions. It is a product rather of taste and intelligence than of any deep insight, yet a painter in his early thirties could hardly give a better gauge of his studiousness.

Posterity chiefly remembered Jan Gossart as a boon companion, a wag, an ingenious practical joker. It was probably quite as much these qualities as his painting that got him appointed to the court of Philip of Burgundy about 1507. The Duke's travels in Italy in 1508 and 1509 were Jan Gossart's great esthetic adventure. One of his traveling companions was that strange cosmopolitan figure, Jacopo de' Barbari. A Venetian, he had early sojourned in the North, had traveled widely, and had transmuted the naïve Venetian poetry into an ambiguous and disquieting eroticism of his own. That tinge of decadence which is in all Mabuse's Italianate painting could easily have rubbed off from such a mate as Jacopo.

From a first pilgrimage to Italy a Northerner often comes back equally enthralled and confused. It was probably so in Mabuse's case. One should recall that the great Raphaels, Michelangelos and Titians were not yet painted. Mabuse's admiration seems to have gone out to the transitional painters of the second order, not to Fra Bartolommeo, for example, but to the facile Milanese imitators of Leonardo da Vinci, possibly to such Central Italian semi-primitives as Bacchiacca, Aspertini, Peruzzi. His Italianism then was built not on the grand style, but on the decline of the primitive mode. The results are seldom pleasing. A Madonna of 1518, at Madrid—a similar picture is at New York (Fig. 75)—is Leonardesque in its construction with graded shadow, mildly maternal, very elegant in execution and rather empty in effect. The artist has hesitated between the queenly and the motherly motive. A Danae at Munich is an atrociously bad picture, cluttered with meaningless Renaissance architecture, ensconcing a plain little maid who raises her skirt above her unsightly shins to entrap the falling gold pieces which are an embodiment of amorous Jove. An even more offensive business is the Adam and Eve, at Berlin (Fig. 76). Beside the tree of knowledge our first parents hunch and twist themselves to show off their anatomy and their charms. The nudes and mythologies of Gossart are all of this mincing sort. First class as a craftsman, nearly so as a portraitist, Gossart's crippling deficiency was in taste.

The Florentine historian, Guicciardini, tells us in his invaluable description of the Low Countries that Mabuse "was the first who brought from Italy into those countries the art of painting stories and poesies with nude figures." Except that he was unconsciously preparing the way for Rubens, one could wish that Mabuse had not made this importation. Such character studies involving the nude as Christ at the Column, and Job visited by his Friends, at Antwerp, are hardly better, but at least more sincerely conceived in their drastic exaggeration of emotion and character. In their love for the horrible and repulsive these pictures parallel much greater creations of the same order by Jerome Bosch, and to name him is to give a measure for Mabuse's inferiority.

In portraiture, however, Mabuse gained much from his Italian studies. His improvement was chiefly technical. His linear drawing became more tense and searching, his constructive shadow became diaphanous without sacrifice of modeling power. What he chiefly pondered is clearly the excellent portraiture of the Leonardesques of Milan. From them he learned to cut loose from the outworn decorative conventions of Flanders, and to master new refinements of construction in light and dark which made for character. The character is no longer generalized; idiosyncrasy is sought for. The sitters are no longer tranquil in some no-man's land, but tense and often worried in a world that is ours.

Admirable portraits of this searched and studied kind abound. One of the finest is that of the Prelate Jean Carondelet in Old Age (Fig. 78), a very late work. Apart from the solidly constructed and characterful mask, the silhouette is highly impressive, and the arrangement in the odd oblong, which Holbein was soon to use effectively, is impeccably right. When one is forced, as often, to cavil at Gossart's lapses in taste, one should not forget that he ranks high among those few painters who are constructors.

None is more intensely asserted than the sinister Man with the Beautiful Hands, Governor Lehman's Collection, New York. Of course, the delightful group of the Three Children of Christian of Denmark, at Hampton Court, is widely known and justly loved. That sensitivity which was so often neurotic and exhibitionistic was a passkey to the understanding of children. Similar in charm is the young Jacqueline of Burgundy (Fig. 77), at London. More ornate and singularly accomplished and lovely as mere workmanship is the richly jeweled effigy of a gentlewoman, at New York. In general such portraiture is important, because it helped to fix the character of an official or international manner for a full century. There was to be clarity of technique, a construction primarily linear, a candid and if possible rather blond decorative effect, flat modeling preserving a positive sense of pattern, in fine, a crystal clarity throughout. All this constituted a bulwark against the poetizing portraiture of Giorgione and Titian which hardly got its foothold beyond the Alps till a hundred years later, with Van Dyck. One may say that Massys and Mabuse saved what was valid in the old method of portraiture at a time when it might have perished.

Apart from the portraits not much can be said favorably of Gossart's pictures in the Italianate manner. But in the Agony in the Garden at Berlin (Fig. 79), he achieved a work of novel and surprising excellence. In it he conveys the mystery of moonlight with a skill for which the world otherwise had to wait more than a century.

By making Jesus a haggard and beardless stripling he emphasizes rather pathos than agony. The consoling angel in the air is of great elegance, and the contrast of the burly, deeply sleeping forms of the apostles with these variously alert adolescent figures is most effective. In this picture the cold intelligence of Jan Gossart achieves an exceptional triumph.

Mabuse was never without noble patronage, and was generally a wanderer. With Duke Philip he visited Denmark, and resided for a time at Utrecht. When Philip died in 1524, Mabuse passed into the service of Adolf of Burgundy, Admiral of Zeeland, with whom he habitually lived at Zeeland. He died about 1554 in his early sixties, and with him passed one of the earliest examples of a type that was to be now tragically, now comically numerous—that of the uprooted, nostalgic artist. Across the centuries Jan Gossart, perhaps wistfully, greets such uprooted talents as Henry James and John Sargent, James Joyce and Ezra Pound.

Of these transitional painters, Lucas van Leyden, better known as an engraver, is one of the more interesting. According to Van Mander, Lucas was born in 1494, and, although this involves an almost incredible precocity, it seems to be the truth. As an engraver Lucas ran a consecutive course, working in his own fashion, while somewhat guided by prints after Mantegna and Raphael. In painting his course was highly erratic. He was successively influenced by his father, by his fellow townsman, Engelbrecht, by Dürer, Gossart and Scorel. The result is such a difference of styles that, but for genuine monograms, one would hardly think of the group as by the same hand.

The Chess Players (Fig. 80), Berlin, is a group of well-characterized heads, unrelated and crowded painfully together. There is no sense of space. This badly compiled picture must be a youthful effort. Considerably later, in the Card Players, at Wilton House, England, Lucas did a similar subject with delightful freedom and geniality. These and other half-length groups in oblong form are important in the history of genre painting. They are somewhat earlier than the genre pictures of Massys and his imitators.

In 1521 Lucas met Dürer at Antwerp. Dürer drew his portrait and noted in his diary that Lucas was a very little man. The little man was about to undertake a masterpiece, in the Last Judgment, Leyden. Meanwhile he had made a round of Ghent, Mechlin and

Antwerp, and had admired Gossart's proficiency in the nude. The feebly tinted Last Judgment is essentially a showpiece and as such a failure. All one can say is that the nudes are treated with better taste than Gossart's.

Lucas' most striking and original invention is the rather early picture, Lot and his Daughters, Paris (Fig. 81). The fire falling from heaven and from the burning city of Sodom sweeps forward over a river with sunken ships, catches the faces of castellated crags, silhouettes a tree, and faintly illumines the foreground group of three figures. The inherently revolting theme of the seduction of a drunken father by his own daughters is handled with reticence and discretion. Yet it yields its effect as an awful moral disaster culminating a horrible physical catastrophe. Few pictures anywhere and at any time have attained an effect at once so romantic and so sinister.

Lucas' most accomplished picture is Christ healing the Blind, at Leningrad. The populous group is handsomely organized, dense but not crowded. The glimpse of a craggy landscape beyond lush trees in middle distance is romantically effective, in Scorel's manner. The postures and expressions of the amazed bystanders are sensitively studied, and without exaggeration. The date is 1531. Two years later Lucas died.

His career is chiefly interesting as revealing vividly that disquietude and hesitation which affected all the more intelligent Northern painters as they perceived the bankruptcy of the old Gothic style and faced the new wonder of Italy.

Unique in his aspect as a sinister visionary, Jerome Bosch as a narrative painter of religious subjects merely continues the drastic and popular manner of Van der Goes, and by subordinating actions to the places in which they occur, prepares the way for the plebeian and landscape art of Old Bruegel.

In the records of Our Illustrious Lady's Brotherhood of Heertogenbosch in Brabant, Jerome of Aaken, called Bosch, appears as a member, and his death is noted in 1516. This bare information is after all valuable, for it tells us that that strange, sardonic, life-denying spirit which was Jerome Bosch was nevertheless a Catholic in good standing. Between 1493 and 1512 we have some half-dozen notices of payments or contracts for pictures, designs for stained glass, and sculptures at Heertogenbosch; the works themselves have perished. A self-portrait in pen and ink at Arras shows a very haggard and unkempt old man, surely beyond sixty. So counting back from his death in 1516, he was born somewhere about 1450, and was considerably older than Massys and Mabuse.

In Jerome Bosch's complicated yet lucid art certain underground shudders of the late Middle Ages reach the surface and produce visible results. He is the spokesman of the terrifying belief in sorcery, witchcraft and all manner of diabolism which in a century of frequent pestilence and constant wars had become the plague of Western Europe. As the old protecting faith waned, these superstitions became tortures, and developed their own malign fascinations. It is the century of dances of death in words or in paint, of hideous cadavers under stately tombs. This murky realm of fear, obsession and nightmare had been below the ken of painters indoctrinated in the dignity of the central Catholic tradition. You merely glimpse it in early Last Judgments, in which after all it is kept in the future and out of the here and now. Jerome Bosch made this nether world of the troubled soul peculiarly his own, and save for the work of a few inferior imitators completely exhausted it.

During his early activity Jerome Bosch painted the traditional religious subjects. Many have been lost, and of such as have come down to us the attribution is often unsure. But the surviving group has common characteristics which tell of Bosch's origins and of the very original bent of his mind. The various Epiphanies at New York, Philadelphia and Madrid all reveal a connection with the school of Haarlem in the pale tonality of the landscape and in the types. His originality evinces itself in his religious pictures. To borrow a useful term from the theater, he completely changed the distance—either increasing it greatly, as in the Epiphanies, or decreasing it as much as possible in such pictures as Christ bearing His Cross, at Ghent, or Christ before Pilate, at Princeton.

The older Flemish painters had adopted a conventional and effective distance. The main group and action are well forward, pretty well filling the frame, but never crowded up to the picture plane. Only Massys in his genre pictures seriously broke with this convention. Bosch often sets the main group well back, thus diminishing the scale of the figures, and, far from isolating the group, provides it with a spacious and somewhat competitive setting. Thus he minimizes the dramatic importance of his subject, making it merely an interesting happening in a world where other things are happening or might happen. In his tragic subjects, on the contrary, he pushes his group to the picture plane, isolates it with a plain background, often reduces it to a cluster of heads, presaging the close-up of the modern cinema. These are the greatest Bosches, and the art of painting offers few parallels for them.

A little picture of the Epiphany, at New York, is probably very early. It illustrates long before Patenier a tendency to subordinate the action to the landscape. The scene takes place before a ruined castle well away from us. There is little suggestion of devotion. Indeed, but for the inquisitive shepherds who peer in from an upper window, there would be little clue to the importance of the event. The tints are pale, even a little washed out. Everything looks cool, quiet and picturesque. Beyond placing the action in the center, there is little staging, one's eye catches the scene almost accidentally, and this element of discovery and surprise is one of the charms of a very charming picture.

In other versions of the Epiphany, at Madrid (Fig. 82), and Philadelphia, Bosch brings the group near, but he still keeps the scale of the figures small and builds up enough landscape background to keep the beholder reminded of the smallness of any event in so big a world. The facial types tend to be grotesque and peasantlike; inquisitive shepherds are in the tradition of Van der Goes. The Epiphany at Madrid has an exceptionally statuesque negro king, and, in the wings, very sensitive portraits of the donors. Their patron saints, Peter and Agnes, are of a graciousness and dignity which recalls contemporary Venetian types. The picture well represents the wide range of Bosch's sympathy and observation. Had he chosen, he could have competed with such painters as Massys on their own ground, but he was to choose otherwise. In general, Bosch's tendency in these idyllic religious themes is decentralizing, depoetizing, moving from a higher to a lower social level. It is the expression of a mind which thinks less in terms of legend and worship than in terms of historic probability.

Just once in such themes Bosch adopted his later device of a close-up. The Adoration of the Shepherds (Fig. 83), at Cologne, good contemporary copy at Brussels, is really a cluster of five heads of which the most prominent are those of the ox and the ass. The Child in the manger is stark but comfortable under the warmth of the breath of the friendly beasts; Mary almost simpers with tenderness as she folds work-worn hands in prayer; one shepherd hangs awkwardly over the stone rim of the manger while he regards the skinny Babe with wistful tenderness; the other shepherd smirks in a fashion which would seem sinister, were it not merely nervously awkward. The endeavor is simply to represent the event as a fact, as it might have happened. There are none of the overtones of solemn ecstasy which most painters have wished to evoke as they recall the first Christmas Eve.

This device of a close-up presentation finds its most memorable expression in two great pictures, the Crossbearing, Ghent, and Christ before Pilate, Princeton. They perhaps imply some knowledge of Leonardo da Vinci's caricature drawings, hence should be dated rather after than before 1500. In both pictures the theme is really the same, a resigned sufferer among faces distorted by hatred and malice and cruelty. We have an eternal epitome of the persecuting frenzy of the mob with a victim in sight—a universal symbol.

In the picture at Ghent the Christ is more noble and pathetic, other faces are more distorted and frightful, but there is little orderly arrangement. It is more vehement and heartrending and also far less skillfully modulated than the greater signed masterpiece at Princeton (Fig. 84), which I think may represent Bosch in his latest phase.

Unlike the noble and dignified Italian Christs who always dominate the situation, Bosch's Christ is just a dogged little preacher, hopelessly trapped, and resigned to His fate. The character of the heads is extraordinarily modulated. Pilate is bored and somewhat peevish at finding himself compelled, for reasons of state, to give over an innocent man to death. The close-shaven and the heavily bearded Jew are quietly and grimly efficient, as they make sure of their prey. They probably work with a clear conscience. The two guards who have dragged Christ in are merely warped and seasoned soldiers, their cruelty merely professional. The extraordinary painting of their armor with lunar blues and dull incandescent reds tells us once for all that while Bosch holds to the old technique he wrings new and romantic effects from it. The cruel and howling mob that filled the picture at Ghent is here represented by four grotesque masks relegated to the background. It is secondary, would have no power, had not the Christ first been caught in the toils of a malign and a calculating organization, to wit, the Church and State.

I have lived with this great picture for nearly thirty years, and oddly, I am even now not sure where Bosch's sympathy lay. Does he want us to pity the Christ? to admire the potent guile of the Pharisees? the efficient professional cruelty of the guards? the bestial energy of the mob? or does he want to remind us that all these rational and insensate defenders of things as they are, will, world without end, reduce such perceptive gentlemen as Pilate to silence, and bring whoever seeks radically to change things as they are to an appropriate Calvary? On the whole I am inclined to feel that Bosch's vision in this matter is impartially clear and cold, and that therein may lie its value. If we have really understood the picture, we know the world better, are perhaps less likely to be scheming Pharisees, hesitant Pilates, military automata or bloodthirsty mobsters.

The Flemish yokel had been celebrated in painting as early as Hugo van der Goes, but only incidentally. It remained for Jerome Bosch to promote the peasant to a central point of interest, thus inaugurating that genre painting which the Netherlands were to exploit superbly for a couple of hundred years. But unlike the later celebrants of peasant life and humors, Bosch's attitude towards the peasant is neither benevolent nor condescending. In the grotesqueness, deformities, and follies of poor folk he takes at best a wholly disinterested, at worst a somewhat malign interest. Folly is universal, but this fact is more easily proved from the poor, who promptly suffer the consequences of their folly, than from the rich, who often seem able to buy an escape. Such seems to me Bosch's attitude towards the bent and vicious and often crippled forms which he constantly saw toiling in the fields about Heertogenbosch or swarming the streets of the cities he occasionally visited.

The accuracy and gusto of Bosch's observation of toiler, beggar, and wastrel appears better in the numerous popular engravings than it does in his pictures. In general he limits his genre pieces to a few figures, often giving them a satirical or allegorical implication. Among the best are the single figures of the Prodigal Son, prematurely aged and shifty, striding like a tramp through a characteristic Dutch landscape. He liked the theme, for he did it twice, in a little round panel formerly in the Figdor Collection, at Vienna (Fig. 85), and on the backs of the shutters of his most famous picture, the Hay Wain, at the Escorial. Similarly there are two versions of the Cure of Madness, in which a quack pretends to relieve an insane person by excising an imaginary stone from his head, while a credulous group gapes about. These pictures are at Amsterdam and at Madrid. Even more amusing as recording multiform phases of curiosity and credulity is the Quack, at St. Germain-en-Laye, in which a roving charlatan exhibits and extols his all-curing bolus before his gaping hearers.

More subtly satirical are the two Water Concerts, in the Pontalba Collection, at Senlis, and in that of C. Benoit, at Paris. Here gross, ribald men and women—lay and monastic—huddle together in a boat as they sing and play raucously. We have to do probably with a symbolism of the insensate clamor of mankind. It is pictures like this which make one sure that Bosch was primarily a satirist and only exceptionally a practical moralist. He rejoices in the intellectual lucidity that enables him to see the topsy-turviness of the world, and I imagine he entertained little hope or even desire of setting it in order.

In a number of pictures of this sort, as in his Epiphanies, Bosch paints a rural landscape which a traveler in the Low Countries can still recognize. Here is nothing of that park-like scenery which had ruled from Hubert van Eyck to Joachim Patenier, but one which, with its thatched, half-timbered hovels, gates and ditches, fairly smells of the good, alluvial soil. Pieter Bruegel and three subsequent generations of Dutch landscapists were to profit handsomely by this example.

A generation or more after Jerome Bosch's death the Florentine historian, Guicciardini, made notes in Flanders and wrote that Bosch "was a noble and amazing inventor of fantastic and bizarre things." The Italian recorded faithfully the memory that Bosch had left. It concerned not his religious or rustic pictures, but what his immediate posterity called his "dreams" and what a modern might be inclined to call his nightmares. It is in this unique phase of his expression that he is the satirist and moralist which most of his critics acclaim. Considerations of space force me to represent this important class of pictures by a few outstanding examples.

Sometime or other Jerome Bosch read or heard the solemn words of Isaiah, xl, 6, "All flesh is grass." Sharply a vision shaped itself before him, and since his eminently symbolizing mind was also singularly concrete, he saw perished grass in the form of a great hay cart (Fig. 86), moving heavily by itself before a receding stretch of pleasant river lowlands. On the load was a curious party. A seated youth strummed the viol for a girl who sang from a sheet of music. Behind them two lovers, standing, shared a kiss. Behind them knelt on the hay a disregarded angel; before them danced an elfin winged creature with a pope's tiara fingering his nose extended in the form of a flageolet. Behind the hay wain rode a pope with other dignitaries. Between the wheels and before the wagon nuns, priests and laymen strove to get aboard. Nearer a man held down his foe while inserting a dagger just above the collar bone. In the foreground a procuress whispered to a girl, a quack advertised his wares, a fat priest received gifts from four nuns. As the wheels crushed an unfortunate, a throng partly human, partly grotesque combinations of fish and animals, led the way to the mouth of hell, half concealed by a trap door.

Not precisely a great picture, because too complicated and unclear, we have at least a great thought pictorially expressed. All flesh is grass, but men given to their pleasures and vices hasten blindly to the bourne where flesh-grass burns eternally.

The picture needed shutters and these give the prologue and epilogue of mankind's urgent march towards the eternal burning. At the left is the Garden of Eden, with the creation, sin and expulsion of our first parents. It is their sin that has made all flesh as weak and transient as grass. High in the clouds is the Creator. Below Him is an obscene flight of tiny fiends, and poisonous insects, probably symbolizing Satan and his fallen angels. Above the hay wain in the central panel Christ stands unregarded below a rainbow of promise with beseeching outstretched hands. On the right shutter the torments of hell are depicted. The fiends, travestied as animals, go quietly about their dreadful business. There are fantastic towers, with apes serving as workmen, reeking chimneys, and below a dark stream coming through an arched bridge. Everything is particularized, and the scheme is that, or nearly that, of the very popular *Vision of Tyndale*.

The closed shutters take us out of the world of religious legend and allegory into the world in which we live. A vagabond with eyes suspiciously askance, followed by his skinny dog, shambles towards a foot bridge. The countryside is pleasant with fertile meads and shallow ponds—a true bit of the Low Countries, but there is a gallows against the sky on a distant hill, while in middle distance robbers plunder a victim tied to a tree and a soldier drags a nun along, as a shepherd pipes unconcernedly behind. In left foreground the bleached skull and bones of a horse suggest one destination of grass and the transiency common to beasts and human animals. Here Bosch meditated an effective and well-organized picture, easily seen and easily read.

The picture is in Philip II's gloomy palace of the Escorial, with its memories of past and forgotten glory. Surely Bosch's painted homily is worthy of its text from Isaiah: "All flesh is grass, and all the goodliness thereof is as the flower of the field. The grass withereth, the flower fadeth: because the Spirit of the Lord bloweth upon it: surely the people is grass."

In the Escorial is an even stranger picture, so strange that some critics, I think without good reason, deny it to Bosch. Officially it is called Earthly Delights (Fig. 87). The Spaniards, more concretely, call it Lust, and indeed lust is the prevailing theme. But the picture is really a sort of saturnalia of the seven deadly sins, as enumerated by the Roman Catholic Church—Pride, Envy, Lust, Sloth, Gluttony, Anger, Greed. The picture swarms with tiny nude figures, lithe and impudent. Almost no sky is seen. The horizon is cut by strange pinnacles, bristling like thorns or like the spiked tails of such marine creatures as the skate. These pinnacles rise from globes, some opaque, some transparent, inclosing nude couples in outlandish postures. Below these globes, in a circle foreshortened as an oval, ride round and round the naked perpetrators of the capital sins. Their mounts are symbolic beasts—pigs, lions, stags, griffins, camels. Inside the riding ring is a pool in which naked folk, two of them blackamoors, dally. The foreground is occupied again by naked people, mostly in pairs. Some are within transparent balls, some caught in what look like octopus coils, others posing in defiant or provocative fashion. Generally the picture is hard to read, but here and there the meaning is heavily underlined—that huddle of the gluttonous under a huge strawberry, that gigantic purse standing like an idol for the covetous to adore. Any complete description of this picture would require rather a chapter than a paragraph.

Unlike the Hay Wain this picture is of great decorative effect, but of a bizarre and almost unexampled order. The repeating of the varied nude forms, the intermingling with strange animal shapes, the repeating of geometrical elements, the bristling termination above in spiky pinnacles and ships as of sprung steel—all this composes a tense and nervous decorative ensemble of a remarkable order. I can recall nothing even remotely similar, except certain crowded Persian miniatures where the figures are so many thrusts and spots in a loose but dynamic pattern. Some such thing Bosch may have seen.

The shutters show the creation of Eve, which Bosch with orthodox lack of gallantry, presents as the origin of the seven deadly sins. In the Garden of Eden we find those same sinister pinnacled globes which we saw in the playground of the sinful. The other shutter shows the humiliation and tortures of hell as described in the vision literature of the Middle Ages, which records the foul imaginings or actual hallucinations of hag-ridden ascetics seeking salvation in solitudes horribly peopled by their own overwrought religious imaginations. In this case the source is the very popular *Vision of Tyndale, Visio Tungdali,* which was printed in Bosch's city in 1484. The paraphernalia of this hell are obvious—a human stomach ruptured to reveal the gluttonous folk within, a lustful man repelling the advances of a sow coiffed like a nun. These are the mildest symbols; those more intolerably drastic I leave the curious reader to discover for himself. One has to shake himself hard to realize that men actually believed that a merciful God had planned such a cesspool eternity for most of mankind, that the deranged monk Tungdalus had been privileged to receive a divine revelation. Of course no appreciation of this infernal phantasmagoria is possible until we recall that Bosch and those who saw this picture believed it all, and shuddered.

Of the various productions of Jerome Bosch in the diabolic vein there is space to consider only one more, the triptych of the Temptation of St. Anthony of Egypt (Fig. 88), at Lisbon. Well in the middle distance, by the steps of a ruined castle, the harassed desert saint kneels in prayer. Before him an armless dwarf, whose legs grow from his shoulders, mocks. Behind him, fashionably dressed courtesans have set up a table at which they invite him to drink. In the distance, left, the flames of hell flash before thick smoke rising from a gigantic furnace. Across the sky, at the right, floats a crane whose body behind develops into a well-rigged airship. To the scene of temptation there are the strangest witnesses—a bird with the legs of a goat; a minstrel, whose head is a bleached horse skull, playing a harp; a big jug dripping from the neck and provided with the legs of a cow; near it a huge rat, on its back a witch mother and child. The scene of the temptation is above a culvert from which issues a murky stream. Upon it swims a huge carp, back covered with the frontal armor of a horse, tail developing into a boat from which a witch fishes while a naked Moor plies the landing net. A mere enumeration of such details, some of which are illustrated here (Figs. 88a and 88b), gives an impression of the wholly insensate yet also wholly logical, completely nightmarish character of the whole. One reads with greater sympathy and understanding the words the author of *The Golden Legend* puts in St. Anthony's mouth: "O Lord, I want salvation, but my thoughts prevent."

Whence did Bosch derive his grotesquely childlike and yet most sinister zoology? Mostly from his own imagination, we may be sure, but also from those ingenious caricatures in stone and wood, exhibited in capitals or hidden under choristers' seats, in which the medieval artisan asserted amidst the serene order and security of the cathedral the presence and the potency of the disorder and ambiguity of the great world outside. How far the carver was playful in such creations, how far tragically serious, we can never know, and such, as we shall see, is our case with regard to Jerome Bosch. This unnatural blending of forms, and implicitly such hallucinatory thinking as St. Anthony deplored, a far greater saint than St. Anthony was to ridicule and deplore. Almost four centuries before Jerome Bosch ceased to paint, St. Bernard had noted with displeasure those monstrous imaginings which, for him, disfigured the cloisters designed for holy meditation. So he wrote:

"You see under one head many bodies, and on one body many heads. One sees on a quadruped a serpent's tail, and again on a fish the head of a quadruped. There a beast is a horse in front, dragging his rear parts as a goat. . . . In short, there is such a marvelous diversity of forms, if they prefer rather to read in stone cuttings than in books, to spend the whole day gazing at these singularities rather than meditating the law of God. God save us! If one is not ashamed of such ineptitudes, at least let him deplore their expensiveness."

I hope St. Bernard in heaven has no inkling of the expensiveness of any picture by Jerome Bosch in the present art market.

Bosch's pictures were not numerous, but his diabolism in diluted form was widely disseminated by his imitators. It was they, not he, who childishly filled their pictures with a sort of animated hollow ware—jugs and kettles with heads and practicable legs. The engravers, Alart van Hameel and Jerome Cock, gave to his designs an enormous circulation. And right here the critical problem arises—how serious was the cult of Bosch's art? how serious was he himself? Was he a moralist seeking to convert his fellow men? as most of his critics insist, or was he rather a dilettante of the diabolical, indulging his sinister imaginings chiefly for the pleasure he took therein?

Obviously no dogmatic answer to these questions is possible. As a practicing Catholic, Jerome Bosch in a broad sense painted just what he believed. Everything he painted had sound Catholic warrant, even if rather from the baser folklore of Catholicism than from its higher authoritative tradition. That he painted to do anyone good I much doubt. In all his pictures I divine not an evangelical, but a coldly intellectual character. I doubt if he ever shuddered or wept at the horrors he evoked. Rather he rejoiced in his own capacity for evoking them. I imagine him, as Edgar Allan Poe described his creative self in the famous "Essay on Poetry," as detached from the emotions he meant to cause in others, calmly planning and elaborating his effects with an artist's skill. I fancy that Jerome Bosch, seeing the immensely rich and almost unused raw material for pictures in current superstition, eagerly and most intelligently seized upon it and exploited it magnificently for his private artistic purposes. That his pictures might incidentally do good perhaps pleased him, but, I believe, mattered little to him. Indeed, the gusto and lucidity with which he conceived his symbols of depravity, vice and cruelty, strongly suggest that he was fascinated to obsession by the spectacle of the evil in the world. In the great Christ before Pilate, at Princeton (Fig. 84), one justly suspects that his sympathy tips towards the bestial captors and accusers. In short, so able a celebrant of the powers of darkness, may, as an artist, and unconsciously, have been somewhat on their side. Pictorially, at least, the spectacle offered by the powers of light may have seemed relatively insipid.

If this reading of Jerome Bosch's genius be correct, we must regard him both as the last of the old and the first of the new. With him our chapter on late Gothic painting in Flanders reaches no happy ending, for the epilogue which he painted for the Middle Ages brought out a baser substratum of feeling and thinking which other painters had merely scanned passingly and, perhaps charitably, had declined to explore. If not happily, at least the painting of the dying Middle Ages when it ended with Bosch ended with a promise and a prophecy. Something more racy, less limited by religious and courtly convention, was to come. The people were to become subjects for the painter. Bosch had brought their follies and inner fears into visibility. Others were to make charmingly visible their ordinary walk and conversation.

# CHAPTER VII

## LATE GOTHIC PAINTING IN FRANCE

Fig. 89. Maître de Moulins. Assumption (central panel).—Moulins.

FIG. 90.  (Upper) Unknown Master.  Crucifixion, with Martyrdom of St.
Denis.—*Paris.*
FIG. 91.  (Lower left) Unknown Master.  Parement of Narbonne.  Calvary
(detail).—*Paris.*
FIG. 92.  (Lower right) JACQUEMART OF HESDIN(?).  Dormition of the
Virgin.—*Paris.*

Fig. 94. Jean Foucquet. Juvénal des Ursins.—Paris.

Fig. 93. Jean Foucquet. Madonna of Étienne Chevalier.—Antwerp.

160

FIG. 95. (Lower) MAÎTRE DE MOULINS. Nativity.—Archbishop's Palace, Autun.

FIG. 96. (Upper) Unknown Master. Calvary with Four Male Saints.— Paris.

Fig. 97. Unknown Master. Descent of the Holy Spirit.—*Chicago.*

Fig. 98. Unknown Master. Jeremiah (right shutter).—*Brussels.*

FIG. 99.   Unknown  Master.   Annunciation.—Aix.

163

FIG. 100.   Unknown Master.   Pietà of Villeneuve.—*Paris.*

164

FIG. 101. ENGUERRAND CHARONTON. The Virgin Crowned by the Trinity.—
*Avignon.*

165

Fig. 102.  Nicolas Froment.  The Burning Bush.—Aix.

166

Until our own times the history of art knew nothing about a primitive French school of panel painting. But in 1904 a loan exhibition of real and alleged French primitives was held at Paris, and ever since, through the zeal of collectors and dealers and through the patriotism of critics, the list of French primitive panels has swollen. The material thus gathered hastily together is of most disparate character, and entirely lacking that coherence which normally marks a national school. Perhaps this is to be expected, for there could hardly be a French painting until there was a France, and, in a political sense, France emerged well after the middle of the fifteenth century through the nationalistic activities of Louis XI. Our only sure evidence for painting in the Gallic regions in the late fourteenth and the fifteenth century is the admirable miniature painting which, as we have already noted, probably at times guided, and was influenced by, the new Gothic realism of the Van Eycks and their Flemish followers. Well before the end of the fifteenth century, we may confidently speak of a Franco-Flemish style of miniature painting which seems to give the patterns for panel painting, tapestry weaving and stained glass. This Franco-Flemish, with the allied Burgundian manner, is about the only fixed point in our study. The rest is mostly conjectural, for we really seldom know where the early panels claimed for France were painted, or whether the painters were rather French than foreigners.

Take, for example, the famous profile portrait of King John of France, in the Bibliothèque Nationale, Paris. Its date should be not far from 1360. Being completely in the Sienese tradition, only patriotism has brought French critics to hail it as one of the earliest panels of the French school. For me it is more likely to be Italian; one senses the work of a man who habitually painted in fresco.

The crude and gaudy Martyrdom of St. Denis, on the same panel with a Crucifixion, at Paris (Fig. 90), is unquestionably French and of about 1390. It is customary to credit it to Jean Malouel, a painter mentioned in documents, but there is no certainty in the matter.

The coarse profiling, the sharp contrast of the color areas, the open spacing of the figures, seem to me to rest upon a misunderstanding of the Sienese manner. The work has no precedent in French miniature painting. The painter, Malouel or another, probably had his training in southern France.

The only artistically fine work of the early Italianate class is the famous Parement of Narbonne (Fig. 91), at Paris. On a cloth is simulated in an admirably handled monochrome an elaborate Gothic polytych of five compartments, the center being a Crucifixion, the side pieces Passion scenes. The forms are energetic and austere; the line is hard yet expressive; the shading is sparing yet sufficient, as in old Chinese pictures; effective decorative use is made of the swirling calligraphic formulas of the Cosmopolitan Style. It seems to me to be datable somewhere near 1390, and it is one of the earliest pictures that has, with notable esthetic value, an unmistakably French accent. Though it comes from Narbonne in southern France, the marked Italianism of the treatment seems to me not to imply Sienese influence from Avignon, but rather the study of fine French miniature painting which had assimilated much from Siena. I am thinking of that exquisite silverpoint of an Assumption attributed to Jacquemart of Hesdin (Fig. 92), at Paris, and of the miniatures of the Très Belles Heures, at Brussels. This supposition gains weight from a series of miniatures in the older part of the Hours of Milan, which offer a style very like that of the painter of the Parement, and may be his work. At least they show a similar moderate Italianism which evinces rather selective study than slavish imitation. Many critics classify with the above pictures the famous panel of Richard II with his Patron Saints, at London. The general decorative feeling, though finer, is about that of the Martyrdom of St. Denis, already mentioned, and the style seems French, though the actual painting may be that of an English artist.

The appearance of a new Italian influence, from Lombardy, about 1400 and a little later, we have already noted in Melchior Broederlam and the Limbourg miniaturists (Figs. 5, 6). Existing manuscripts in this style seem pretty well confined to the two Burgundies, yet it must have been known also in France proper. But the manuscript miniatures, which in this matter are barometric, retain a soundly French Gothic character till 1460 or thereabouts. Indeed, for the first sixty years of the fifteenth century we have a singu-

lar lack of panel paintings that are surely French. Then comes a
formidable invasion of the Gothic realism of Flanders, conquering
most of northern France, Picardy and Upper Normandy, and ex-
tending to Paris itself, perhaps even further south, to the Loire and
Tours.

It would seem no difficult matter to pass from miniature to panel
painting, or vice versa, but singularly few painters have actually made
the change. Among them is Jean Foucquet of Tours, who was born
about 1420. He is chiefly a miniaturist, and his designs for the Hours
of Étienne Chevalier and for a translation of Josephus are triumphs
of the transition from a Gothic to a Renaissance manner. To him
are attributed certain panels, mostly portraits. On the whole, his
best painting is a diptych, of which the Madonna is at Antwerp
(Fig. 93), the donor, Étienne Chevalier and St. Stephen, his patron,
at Berlin. The new note is a great sensitiveness, otherwise the mere
workmanship is not remarkable. The Madonna is merely a French
lady, cruelly tight-laced, with a breast bulging out towards a nude and
stolid Christchild. Mary wears a crown, a diaphanous veil and a mantle of ermine. Chevalier and his patron look neither at Mary nor at
each other; there is a suggestion of an easy, silent relation between
friends. We have to do with a definitely courtly picture. No one
else at this time had carried so far the secularization of a sacred theme.
Behind the Madonna are chubby nude cherubs strongly picked out
with gold lights, after the fashion of miniature painting.

Foucquet had traveled in Italy sometime about 1450. Incidental
echoes of Italian decoration and architecture enliven his later miniatures and some of the portraits generally ascribed to him. The earliest
of these may be the stupid, suspicious face of Charles VII, at Paris.
It was probably painted before Foucquet's Italian journey, perhaps
about 1445. Also at Paris is Foucquet's most decorative and famous
portrait, that of Juvénal des Ursins (Fig. 94). The praying posture
tells us that it was half of a diptych, the Madonna being lost. The
wainscoting is carved in a vaguely Renaissance fashion; the realization of the form under the puffy robe is inadequate; the portraiture
is vigorous, but also somewhat inert. There is a more vital quality
in the melancholy Man with a Wineglass, at Paris, and in the Young
Man with a Cup in the Liechtenstein Collection, Vienna. In both,
the modeling of the face and hands is labored. The character comes
with an effort, but still it comes. Beside the contemporary por-

traiture of Memling and Antonello da Messina, Foucquet's seems
tentative and almost amateurish, yet on the main issue of asserting
character it fairly holds its own.  He died about 1485, having served
Louis XI, and having witnessed the emergence of a real France.  To
it he had contributed something, for the secular quality of his art, a
certain cool judgment and absence of sympathy in it, are perhaps
the first expression of the French spirit in panel painting.  These
characteristics fit the dour and offish man whose self-portrait we have
in an enameled medallion, at Paris.

Hardly so much can be said for his younger contemporary, and
probably fellow citizen of Touraine, the Maître de Moulins.  Such is
the name which, for want of other information, we give to a French
painter whose best picture is at Moulins, and who worked in the last
quarter of the fifteenth century for the Bourbons.  The art of the
Maître de Moulins seems to me to grow out of Franco-Flemish miniature painting.  He merely repeats on a large scale the somewhat
saccharine ideality of the late Gothic miniaturists of the Franco-
Flemish school.  Within his limitations he is charming, has the grace
of real devoutness, a sense of maidenly beauty.  Such a picture as
the Nativity with a donor, in the Archbishop's palace, at Autun (Fig.
95), is captivating in its eagerness.  The artist has retained the old
tender ideality while rejecting the old formulas for drapery, studying
such details on his own account.  The date of this picture may be
about 1480, contemporary, that is, with the late Memlings and early
Gerard Davids.  The mention of such names relegates our French
master to at best a secondary place.

At least he was inventive, for his Madonna (Fig. 89), in the
Cathedral of Moulins, is as a composition quite novel in the North.
The Madonna is in the air before a nimbus and upon the crescent
moon.  Somewhat illogically she sits in mid-air upon her light throne.
With veiled eyes she looks lovingly towards the vivacious nude Christchild.  He waves a salutation to angels who hover in graceful festoon-
ing curves about the glory which encompasses the Mother and Child.
The sweet, upturned faces of the angels, the varying direction of their
glances, the softness of floating drapery modestly suggesting adolescent forms below—all this recalls distantly such contemporary
Italian sentimentalists as Francia and Perugino, but there is something gentler and less professional in the touch.  There is less concern with structure than in the contemporary Flemings and Italians,

the light and dark being rather the result of a caress than of study of appearances. In short, we have a successful adaptation to panel painting of graces long familiar to lovers of manuscript miniatures. The portraits of the donor, the Duke of Bourbon, and his wife are in the Franco-Flemish tradition, and highly competent.

To Jean Bourdichon, well known as a miniaturist about 1500, several panels are attributed, at best plausibly. The most important, if indeed it be his, is a triptych in the Church of St. Andrew, at Loches, in which we see a populous Calvary, flanked by a Crossbearing and a Deposition. It is rather an imposing than a fine picture, while the handling of the landscape and figures is, as in Bourdichon's miniatures, moderately Italianate. Beyond him, we have from central France a number of early sixteenth century pictures which betray a slavish and unskillful imitation of the last generation of Italian primitives. It is a style badly belated from its beginnings, without promise, and without outcome.

In general, the painters of Touraine and the Île de France seem to have grown out of the native miniature painting, with a tendency to borrow from Flanders and increasingly, and ultimately disastrously, from Italy.

So far we have been considering only religious painting. There are abundant records of military and other secular decoration long ago lost. The miniatured histories and romances of chivalry furnished excellent precedents for this work; from them and from the late Gothic tapestries of Arras we may still get a fair notion of a kind of painting that must have been completely native.

From the last quarter of the fifteenth century, for some fifty years, there are plenty of paintings of a generally Flemish style which were certainly made in northern or central France. Since most of them are of slight esthetic importance, I need only mention a few typical examples. Perhaps the most famous is the handsome panel of a Calvary, with St. Charlemagne, at Paris (Fig. 96). It seems to me to reveal the influence of Bouts, perhaps filtered through Massys. If so, the date should not be much earlier than 1500, and the work a retarded one. The same hand in a slightly softer and Italianate mood seems to me to reveal itself in a Deposition, at Chicago, which suggests that the painter in his later years was subjected to some influence from Avignon.

More significant are seven panels of Passion scenes and figures of the Madonna and saints, at Chicago. Here in the stiffness of the figures and the verticality of the patterning the manner of Dirck Bouts plainly betrays itself. The work is in no way inferior to his, indeed is more strenuously conducted, and the bleak, rather acid coloring, is entirely appropriate and original. The panel representing Pentecost (Fig. 97) may represent the series. The saints, Honoré and Hugo, point to Amiens as the place of origin, and the panels came from a monastery in that vicinity. The date is late fifteenth century. Amiens was near Lille, where Jan van Eyck had lived, and not far from Louvain, where most of Bouts' career was made. Whether we have to do with a Flemish painter working in Picardy, or, as I feel, with a French painter trained in the Flemish style, must remain uncertain. Doubtless much Franco-Flemish painting of this fine quality has most regrettably perished through war or simple neglect. In general, most of northern France in the last half of the fifteenth century was artistically dependent on Flanders and Burgundy, while Lorraine and Alsace merely borrowed from adjacent Germany.

It is customary to speak of an Avignon School, deriving chiefly from the Italian painters called to the papal court by the exiled popes, and later developing under various, chiefly Flemish, influences, but under close examination the term "Avignon School" pretty well loses specific content. It has been freely used as a dumping ground for puzzle pictures which we cannot locate. Many of these are Spanish, others provincial extensions of Northern Italian painting. What seems to be the case is that southern France, in the fourteenth century under the popes, who were of Italian taste, and in the fifteenth century under King René, whose taste was Flemish, was a center of patronage. Without creating a style of its own, it called in painters from many quarters and encouraged its own painters to study abroad. In most instances it is difficult to tell whether we are dealing with a foreign painter or with a Frenchman who has assimilated a foreign manner. So, while we may cautiously speak of a School of Central France, we cannot accurately use the word "school" of that very miscellaneous painting which flourished on the Riviera and the region behind it.

Among the really great pictures made in southern France we have already considered the Parement of Narbonne (Fig. 91). The only pictures comparable to it, indeed superior to it, are the Annunciation in the Church of St. Mary Magdalen, at Aix, and the famous Pietà from Villeneuve, now at Paris.

The Annunciation (Fig. 99), with its admirably drawn and carefully painted figures and its fine interior of a church in a difficult diagonal perspective, has, offhand, an entirely Flemish look, yet there is a difference from any Flemish painting we know. The mood is more familiar, one might say more secular. The rich architecture is felt not in terms of stateliness and religious effect, but rather as a festive setting for an interesting social ceremony. The grand prophets in the wings (Fig. 98) with admirable still life of books and writing gear on shelves above, are of great plastic force and beautiful in their illumination. About this picture critics hold widely different views. A Neapolitan convert to the Flemish manner has been suggested, with little good reason. Another attribution is to the Swiss master, Conrad Witz, and indeed the massiveness of the construction and the sense of cool, ambient air and light in this picture does recall the master of Basel, and suggests vaguely a painter influenced by him. It has recently been reasonably suggested that we are dealing with an excellent French mystic who was profoundly influenced by the sculpture of Claus Sluter at Dijon. The superbly massive character of the saints in the shutters gives weight to such a hypothesis (Fig. 98). There we simply have to leave the problem. We may merely hope that what is cited as one of the finest French primitives is French at all.

Happily less doubt gathers around the stupendous Pietà of Villeneuve, now at Paris (Fig. 100), which is the only great masterpiece of painting by a French artist before Poussin. In the nervous and highly competent construction of the figures, as in the face of the kneeling donor, the work remotely recalls Mantegna, and implies, I feel, study of some good Milanese admirer of his style—perhaps Zenale, or Bramante in an early phase. Somewhat Milanese, too, is the general dulled silvery effect. But in larger matters there are no Italian precedents. The beautifully spaced open, clear-cut pattern of the group of four against a cool, yellow gold is entirely original. The reticence with which an atrocious sorrow is expressed is highly personal to the artist; a certain vitality in the stark curve of the dead body, like a strong bow unstrung, is a very distinguished and unique invention. The hands are amazingly expressive. On the merely decorative side, the border tooled in the gold, a survival of the Sienese manner, is exquisitely designed and proportioned. In the creator of such a masterpiece we have to do with an artist whose unmistakable power is tempered by most intelligent self-criticism and a fastidious taste. In its measured intensity, its orderliness and lucidity, and even in a kind of fit preciosity, this seems to me not merely a very great picture, but also one of a greatness peculiarly French. Who painted it we probably shall never know. Whoever he was he was the real pioneer of that ardent yet discreet assimilation of the great style of Italy which was to feed the genius of France in the Renaissance. This picture has been very variously dated. To me it seems quite of the end of the fifteenth century.

With Enguerrand Charonton (more correctly, Quarton) we come upon that reassuring phenomenon, an Early French painter with a real name and a few sure dates. He was born at Laon in northern France, probably as early as 1420. We have records of him at Aix, 1444; Arles, 1446; and Avignon, 1447; and contracts for pictures, mostly lost, between 1441 and 1464. The earliest picture we have from him, a Madonna of Pity with a Male and Female Donor, and the two St. Johns, at Chantilly, was paid for in February–May, 1453 (new style) and its types and feeling are disconcertingly advanced for that year. There is virtually nothing that can be traced to Flanders, though it was near his birthplace. Possibly the flanking saints have drawn something from the monumental tenderness of Hubert van Eyck. The Madonna and the group, all portraits or portraitlike, seem definitely Italianate. In this work Charonton had the assistance of a Frenchman, Pierre Villaté. The very long panel is a gracious thing, well spaced and highly decorative. Its considerable difference from the Coronation of the Virgin, at Villeneuve, dated only two years later, 1454, indicate that Villaté may have had a large hand in the work.

The famous panel of 1454 at Villeneuve (Fig. 101), across the Rhone from Avignon, represents the Madonna in a rich brocade, piously kneeling with crossed hands in cloudland, while God the Father and Christ, depicted with identical features, place a splendid crown upon her head, assisted by the Dove of the Holy Ghost, as big as an eagle. To right and left are angels and the sanctified souls, these very portraitlike, as in the earlier picture at Chantilly. Below opens up a vast prospect ending with the sea and what seems to be smoking Vesuvius. Between two walled cities, Rome and Jerusalem, is a crucified Christ, conceived in a wholly Sienese manner, with the body pulling the arms down into a Y and the knees bent sideways. In the foreground is a Last Judgment with many tiny nude figures.

The break of the draperies of God and Christ is very angular, quite Flemish. The color is of a somber richness. The general relation of the celestial group to the landscape below is decorative, and while the piling up of detail at the bottom is confusing, the details themselves are carried off with spirit and picturesqueness. In general, the parts of the picture are most ingeniously invented, and rather better than the whole.

I hardly know a picture more baffling or more difficult to reconcile with its assured date. In a kind of desperation I am inclined to guess that Charonton may have made his studies at Naples during the reign of René of Anjou, which ended in 1442, and possibly later under the Aragonese sovereignty. At Naples there was represented almost every style. The Sienese had left notable frescoes and panels; there were faithful followers of the Van Eycks; sculptors like the Gagini and Laurana had created an oval Madonna type very like Charonton's; painters from Catalonia and Aragon abounded; Antonello da Messina pretty certainly made his early studies there; finally, Naples was the only place where one could make such a recognizable sketch of Vesuvius as we seem to find in the picture at Villeneuve. Such evidence is merely circumstantial, and perhaps I should not impose it on the reader, but it is also the part of simple honesty to avow the difficulty of such a problem and the uncertainty of anybody's solution, including naturally my own. Our last notice of Charonton is of 1464, and it is probable that he died rather young.

Between the Villeneuve Pietà and the documented pictures of Charonton there is such similarity of forms, especially hands and facial types, that it is possible we have in the Pietà a Charonton in an exceptional moment of inspiration. The alternative theory would be a pupil of greater genius than his master. Only the group of pictures stylistically associated with Charonton seem to me to deserve the designation Avignon School.

With Nicolas Froment, Charonton's younger contemporary, we are happily on firmer ground. He was born probably about 1440 at Uzès, north of Nîmes. Oddly, we first find him in Tuscany, in 1461, signing a Gothic triptych for the Franciscan Observants of the Mugello. The central panel depicts the Resurrection of Lazarus, the wings, Christ pardoning Mary Magdalen, and Mary anointing Christ's feet. The picture is in the Uffizi. At first glance the style seems completely Flemish, but on closer study the rather grisly insistence of certain expressions—that of the patrician sniffing as Lazarus rises, that of Lazarus, that of Peter and Judas in the Supper at Bethany, and also the brocade background of the central panel, suggest the drastic mode of Catalonia copying Flanders. So it seems likely that before going to Italy, Froment had been trained thoroughly under some Hispano-Flemish master. For all of its vulgar insistency and tendency towards caricature, the work is highly competent and commands respect.

By 1465 Froment was settled at Avignon. There we may trace a various activity. He designed for stained glass and made the windows, painted processional banners, and planned decorations for the entries of visiting dignitaries. By 1476 he had gained the favor of the art-loving King René of Anjou, for that year he was paid for the extraordinary triptych of the Burning Bush, in the Church of St. Sauveur, at Aix. Vigorous portraits of King René and his wife, with their patron saints, occupy the shutters. The central panel (Fig. 102), incidentally the most charming primitive painting in southern France, offers, in a very curious symbolism, the Burning Bush as antetype of Mary's fertile yet inviolate virginity. The Middle Ages spent itself in discovering in the Old Testament prophecies of the virgin birth. Among these was the burning bush unconsumed, from which God spoke to the prophet Moses. We read in a twelfth-century German manuscript:

> "Namque rubus incombustus
>    Moysen qui terruit
> haec est virgo, quae pudore
>    salvo deum genuit."

> "So the bush that burned unwasted
>    At which Moses was a-feared
> Is the Virgin who bore God,
>    Her own modesty unimpaired."

A number of painters have represented the Burning Bush with Moses taking off his shoes. It is an inexpressive symbolism, which needs a verbal label. Nicolas Froment has, in order to make a picture, compromised between history and symbolism. High in the center he has perched the Virgin and Child very comfortably on the leafy and flowery roof of a tiny grove on a hillock. You know, though the flames are barely visible, that this is the Burning Bush, for below, a graceful, solicitous angel, mouth opened with precision to warn Moses that he is on holy ground, addresses a stalwart old man who raises his right hand as if to protect his face from heat or light, while with his left hand he strips off his shoe. A flock of sheep with a fine dog is set between the figures with delightful casualness. To left and right of the hillocks one looks upon feathery trees, winding roads and streams, walled cities and distant hills—precisely such a panorama as we find in such contemporary Italian painters as Baldovinetti and Piero della Francesca.

And, in general, the mood is Italianate, though in the drapery of Mary and the angel the angular Flemish formulas persist. The fine oval of Mary's face daintily turned away from the Child, the Child's head turned in the other direction, his chubby, agile form— all this is in the Italian taste, and curiously anticipates considerably later painting in Italy—say that of Piero di Cosimo. But the panel asserts its Northern derivation in a frame simulating sculpture, with prophets in elaborate Gothic niches, while in the spandrels above the Hunt of the Unicorn, again a symbol of Mary's virginity, is depicted with much spirit.

Obviously the picture is of mixed and eclectic inspiration. All the same, it achieves esthetic unity of a sort that is both idyllic and realistic. The distribution of light and shade is broad and picturesque. Except for Masaccio, hardly a European painter had achieved anything so skillful in this branch of design. Indeed, both on the side of technique and taste, Froment seems to me surpassed only by the greater Italians of the moment.

He must have painted many pictures of this quality, for we have notices of him till 1482, six years after his Burning Bush. But these pictures either are lost or, passing under false attributions, await identification. In 1482, at Avignon, Nicolas Froment drew up his last will and testament, and probably died soon thereafter. With him passed an artist who had in a high degree the Gallic virtues of selective assimilation and intelligent self-criticism.

The later history of painting in southern France is of too little importance to detain us here. In general there was a destructive invasion of Italian taste misunderstood by French painters, or represented on an inferior level by incoming Italian painters. Here one need only glance at the very elaborate Renaissance Calvary, at St. Maximin's, Marseilles, which was finished in 1520 by the Venetian, Antonio Ronzen. It seems a coarsened echo of Carpaccio, or even of some Venetian of the third order, like Mansueti. Indeed, from 1500 almost to our own time, southern France has produced great painting only sporadically, the leadership having from the seventeenth century passed to Paris.

Reviewing this chapter, we come to the following conclusions: Apparently only a few really fine panel paintings were made in France in the fifteenth century; these generally are not superior to the admirable manuscript miniatures with which lovers of graphic design in France seem to have been contented; we may hardly speak confidently of a French school of primitive painting, and still less of a school of Avignon. If our theme were not painting, but pictorial design, there would remain to be made a study of picture-making in enamels, stained glass and tapestry. Such a study would be very interesting in itself, and it would enlarge an idea of primitive French pictorial design here necessarily limited by pictures on panels. To undertake such a study, which would be as necessary in the case of the Netherlands, England and Germany, would swell this handbook beyond tolerable proportions.

CHAPTER VIII

LATE GOTHIC PAINTING IN GERMANY

Fig. 103. Stephan Lochner. Virgin of the Rose Trellis.—Cologne.

Fig. 104. (Upper left) Bohemian School, Late XIV Century. Madonna.—
Vienna.

Fig. 105. (Upper right) Meister Bertram. Angels Announcing the Passion
to the Infant Jesus.—Hamburg.

Fig. 106. (Lower left) Meister Francke. Nativity.—Hamburg.

Fig. 107. (Lower right) Meister Francke. The Crossbearing.—Hamburg.

181

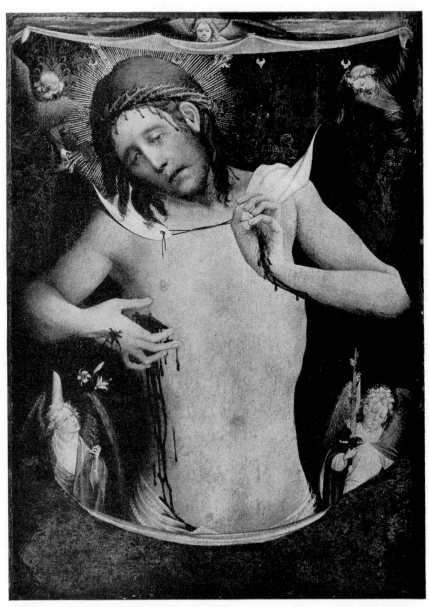

FIG. 108. MEISTER FRANCKE. The Man of Sorrows.—Hamburg.

Fig. 109. (Upper) Cologne School, late XIV Century. Calvary with
Four Narratives.—*Cologne.*
Fig. 110. (Lower left) The Veronica Master. Madonna of the Bean
Blossom.—*Cologne.*
Fig. 111. (Lower right) Stephan Lochner. Madonna of the Violet.—
*Archbishop's Palace, Cologne.*

FIG. 112. STEPHAN LOCHNER. Epiphany (central panel).—Cathedral, Cologne.

FIG. 114. Master of St. Bartholomew. Descent from the Cross.—Paris.

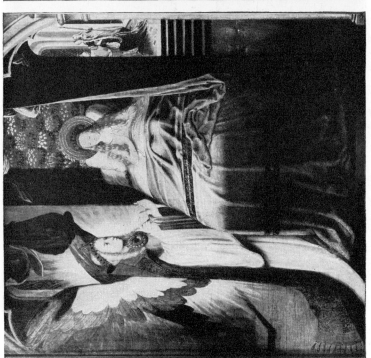

FIG. 113. Master of St. Ursula. An Angel Tells St. Ursula of Her Martyrdom.—Cologne.

185

Fig. 115. (Upper) Barthel Bruyn. Nativity.—*Frankfurt-am-Main*.
Fig. 116. (Lower left) Lucas Moser. Voyage of St. Mary Magdalen.—
*Tiefenbronn*.
Fig. 117. (Lower right) Lucas Moser. The Magdalene Heals a Sick
Man.—*Tiefenbronn*.

Fig. 118.  Conrad Witz.  St. Mary Magdalen and St. Catherine.—
Strasbourg.

FIG. 119. (Upper) CONRAD WITZ. Christ Walking on the
Water.—Geneva.
FIG. 120. (Lower) CONRAD WITZ. An Angel Delivering Peter
from Prison.—Basel.

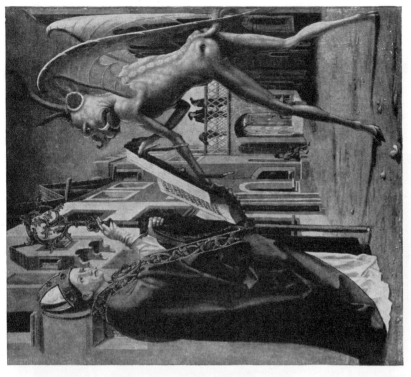

Fig. 122. Michael Pacher. St. Wolfgang and the Devil.—Munich.

Fig. 121. Michael Pacher. St. Gregory and Trajan.—Munich.

189

FIG. 123. MICHAEL PACHER. Last Communion of St. Wolfgang.—
Munich.

190

Since in nearly five centuries the German regions have produced only three or four great painters, it is clear that the German genius works uncongenially in that field. Oddly, within the same period and almost uninterruptedly Germany has produced at least fifty engravers and illustrators of the first order, or nearly so. The racial deficiency, then, is not in the arts, but in what are technically called the fine arts—those that represent a high degree of culture. This the Germanies, for of course there was no Germany until our grandfathers' time, were only beginning to attain at the time we are considering.

To borrow a useful if none too popular British classification, the early painting of Italy may be thought of as aristocratic in temper; that of Flanders, as upper middle class; that of Germany, as lower middle class. That is, the primitive German painter had to meet the taste of people of very limited outlook—small tradesmen, prosperous mechanics, a rather ignorant clergy. Indeed this small-town character seems to have prevailed at all levels of German society.

Out of the taste of such people no great art has ever grown, and that was the case in the Germanies. On the other hand, a very lively and interesting art of painting did grow up under these auspices. The aristocrat wants an art finer and better than himself, and so does the educated and successful man of affairs. But the small-town man wants an art just like himself—an art without difficulties or finesses, an art forthright, hearty, drastic. And this kind of painting we have in abundance from the Germanic countries. For its homely shrewdness it is often very attractive, but only in very exceptional instances, a Dürer, a Gruenewald, a Holbein, does it rise to greatness, and even then, with qualifications. About 1500 the general cultural standing of the Germanic countries was markedly improving, and that was the opportunity for the great painters just mentioned, but the belated humanistic movement had no permanent effect so far as the visual arts were concerned.

The heroic episode of the Protestant Reformation actually

worked against the arts. By splitting the Germanic region into a Northern, Protestant, and a Southern, Catholic, zone, it postponed indefinitely that national unity out of which a great art normally grows. Moreover, a sincerely Protestant civilization, because of its inveterate Hebraism, is unfavorable for the visual arts. Such a civilization is less concerned with seeing than with hearing and reading. It is not accidental that printing was invented in Germany and that for more than a century she led the world in book illustration.

Since on any European standard nearly all of Early German painting is of negligible value, I must treat it very briefly, confining myself mostly to the study of the few great painters, and merely sketching the antecedents of their art. As elsewhere in Europe the background is the miniatured manuscript. In Germany, which had had admirable Romanesque schools of miniature painting, there was no such Gothic development in that art as there had been in England, Flanders and France. The preciosities of the Cosmopolitan Style had touched Germany rather lightly, as had the influences from Italy. There developed a rather coarse, but also sincerely emotional, style of narrative design. The color was strong, with few pigments and no fine gradations. We often find that heavy outline which survives in the early woodcut illustrations. Much of Early German painting is merely an enlargement of the old manuscript designs. These had been good and legible illustration without much pictorial accomplishment, and their offshoot was true to the parent stock.

I must hasten to add that while what I have written is, broadly speaking, true for Eastern and Central Germany—the North at this time being an esthetic vacuum—it is at best a half truth for such Germanic regions as the Tyrol, Switzerland, and the Lower Rhine. These districts, either because of location on the trans-European trade routes or through contact with Italy or Flanders, achieved an art of painting more European and more distinguished. In particular the art of the Lower Rhine, centering at Cologne, ran more slowly a course somewhat similar to that of the painting of the neighboring Netherlands and Burgundy. Since the school of Cologne assumes prominence almost a century earlier than the other German schools, with it and nearby Hamburg we shall begin our study.

For a great trading city, Cologne was singularly tender-minded. This was due to a pervading atmosphere of religious legend. At Cologne St. Gereon's legion and St. Ursula's eleven thousand saintly maids of honor had joyously achieved martyrdom. And if anyone doubted it, he could count their browned skulls in their pigeonholes in St. Gereon's and St. Ursula's church. Cologne too had bred mystics in abundance, whose meditations rose to hallucination, and who taught others how to put the body to sleep and free the soul for union with God. These guided ardors, though often directed towards the mysteries of Christ's redemptive grace, were more often centered upon the maidenly and queenly perfections of the Virgin Mary. The poems which mystics wrote to her are a kind of reverent love-making. They cover her with flowers of rhetoric, spend themselves in search of endearing diminutives and similes, often farfetched, but always with something of the fragrance of flowers. A Netherlandish poem of this period calls Mary "sweetheart" and compares her with a dozen flowers, including the violet, and the bean blossom which we shall see in her hand in paintings by Lochner and the Veronica Master. A Latin poem finds similitudes for her in as many precious stones. Such poetry finds visibility in a painting tender and feminine in quality, in a fine sense sentimental. Even such tragic subjects as the horror of Calvary are attenuated, and, waiving the harsh reality, seem to make visible the measured and pathetic cadences of Good Friday chants. A Memling could emerge from such an atmosphere, but not a Jan van Eyck, a Rogier de la Pasture, or a Hugo van der Goes. In short, the old rule of the impossibility of having it both ways held, and what the Lower Rhine gained in tender ideality she naturally had to forego in sound realism.

A Renaissance style of painting first makes an exotic and transient appearance in the second quarter of the fourteenth century in Prague, whither the broad-minded King of Bohemia, Karl IV, called many foreign painters and architects. In particular he employed gifted French miniaturists versed in the Cosmopolitan Style, and an Italian fresco painter of talent, Tommaso da Modena. Tommaso was settled at Prague by 1357, and there developed two pupils, Dietrich of Prague and Nicholas Wurmser from the Rhineland. Time has pretty well effaced whatever was done at this outpost of Franco-Italian culture, and it is probable that little of great consequence has been lost. But the only brilliant court west of the Rhine was naturally admired and its taste imitated in less-cultured regions. King Wenzel, Karl IV's successor, continued a generous patronage of foreign, mostly French artists, but the Hussite wars brought all prosperity in Bohemia to an end and arrested prematurely what had promised to be a notable artistic movement. The fantastic charm of this Italianate painting may be sensed in a little Madonna, Byzantine in composition and sincere in feeling (Fig. 104). The paintings of the school of Prague remained possible sources of an influence which became effective a little later at Nürnberg and Hamburg.

From ancient records we learn that Meister Bertram van Byrde, in 1397, painted very elaborate shutters for a carved altarpiece in the Church of St. Peter at Grabow, near Hamburg. These oblong wings, now in the Hamburg Museum, contain in two registers eighteen Old Testament subjects, from the Creation to the Deception of Isaac; and six from the New, from the Annunciation to the Flight to Egypt. The figures are big-headed, alert, attractive—somewhat crowded in their narrow, upright panels. The background is gold, often mostly hidden by accessories. Fantastic Gothic canopies, symbolizing buildings, are such as we see in Lombard miniatures of the moment, and, like the rippling Cosmopolitan Style of the draperies, probably are an extension of the influence of the Franco-Italian school of Prague. The color is gay and well harmonized. Picturesqueness and animation are the rather modest merits of the work. For the rest, affectations and exaggerations betray a tender and feeble spirit moving out of its depth.

In a will drawn in 1390 in favor of his wife and the churches of Hamburg, Meister Bertram writes, "I purpose to make a pilgrimage to Rome for my soul's comfort." Shutters for two carved altarpieces were painted after this journey. Of these only the Buxtehude altar, with eighteen scenes depicting the entire Life of the Virgin, need detain us. The setting is a little more elaborate than in the presumably earlier Grabow altar. The general look is rather like that of rustic Sienese work. On his way to Rome, Meister Bertram pretty certainly passed through Siena, yet all one is safe in asserting is that some influence has made the figure drawing a little larger and softer than it had been. Throughout, Meister Bertram is inventive as an illustrator—take the extraordinary scene where God warns our First Parents against eating the apple (Grabow altar); the Nativity (Grabow), where Joseph dandles the Child as he hands it to Mary; or (Buxtehude), where he empties his flask, regardless of Mary and the Child; or the unique scene where the boyish Christ, prone and reading on the grass, glances with curiosity at two angels approaching with prophetic emblems of His Passion (Fig. 105). Such inventions show that Meister Bertram brought a fresh mind and a vivid fancy to his hackneyed themes, and make him one of the most ingratiating of minor artists. Disarming as such work is, its lack of consistency leaves an aftertaste of dissatisfaction. Bertram is trying to express through inherited aristocratic forms that familiar folksy feeling which was to be proper to German narrative painting. His successor, and probably his pupil, Meister Francke of Hamburg, was to effect a more satisfying blend of the old and the new.

In sharpest contrast to the easy-going geniality of Meister Bertram is the neurotic intensity of his successor. Meister Francke is a sophisticate—about the only one old Germany produced; he cultivates strong and strange emotions and exploits them in his art. In 1424 he undertook to paint the shutters of a carved Crucifixion for the English Trading Company of Hamburg. Of the many stories of the Life of the Virgin and of Christ and of the patron saint of the Company, the Martyr, Thomas à Becket, nine are now in the Hamburg Kunsthalle. They show hardly a trace of the Cosmopolitan Style and in setting they mark a considerable advance upon Meister Bertram. The architectural and landscape features are more numerous and more reasonable. There is a new regard for perspective relations; the figures are cut by mounds or hedges or overlap each other; they diminish in distance with approximate correctness. The emotional range moves between the tender, the grotesque and the gruesome. Perhaps no other Early German painter has plucked so many and so various strings. The highly self-conscious talents not seldom command such an apparently contradictory variety of moods. A Poe writes an "Annabelle Lee" and also a "Murder in the Rue Morgue." In Meister Francke's case nothing could be more sweet and tender than the Nativity (Fig. 106), with its worshiping girl-mother attended by shy little boy angels, its realization of a picturesque, tree-decked skyline against a heaven with big stars, its suggestion of the herald angel diving down towards the distant shepherds and their flocks. It is one of the lovelier Christmas Eve pictures.

Compare this with the Crossbearing (Fig. 107), the Christ with face nearly hidden by his shoulder so that the painful buckling of his body may be more apparent, the executioners brutally prodding and dragging him along, the whole composition a dense tangle of cruel actions; compare this again with the chivalric nonchalance of Thomas à Becket as he waves a greeting to the pursuing assassins who have got near enough to cut off the tail of his white charger; and finally compare all this with the quiet solicitude of the group that bends over the tomb into which Jesus' outraged body descends.   In this scene is a most extraordinary invention; the crushing grief of Mary is fully suggested by the mere profile of her cloaked head and shoulders seen beyond a ledge in the foreground.   Evidently in Meister Francke we are dealing with a subtlety and intensity of imagination rarely exampled among the late Gothic painters anywhere.

At Helsingfors is a carved altar with painted wings representing the Legend of St. Barbara.   Here the note is of an opulent, ornate orientalism in the Romans, of an alert elegance and self-confidence in the virgin doomed to martyrdom.   To find anything so distinguished as a maidenly type one must go forward fifty years or more to Memling, and his type is far less vital.   In all these pictures the color is of pearl-like transparency and delicacy.   In this regard few Gothic paintings equal Meister Francke's.

A temperament as mobile and sensitive as this almost always has its morbid side.   Such morbidness is latent in the pictures we have been considering; it comes into full bloom in the two pictures of the Man of Sorrows, at Hamburg (Fig. 108) and Leipzig.   The nude, pale body is shown at half length before a brocade which three tiny angels bring forward at the top as a sort of canopy.   Below, an angel with a lily and one with a flaming sword hold a crimson curtain before the loins of the Christ.   They are presumably the archangel Gabriel of the Annunciation, and the archangel who guarded the gate of Eden, now reopened, with a fiery sword.   The smooth torso of the Christ is not marred by scourging, but bleeds profusely from its wounds and under the crown of thorns.   The eyes are half veiled by the eyelids and unfocused, as if the Saviour were in a trance.   Then, strangest of motives, the fingers of the right hand feel delicately for the wound in the side, as if, like a doubting Thomas, to make sure it is really there.   The contours of the body against the dark background are drawn with the greatest suppleness and expressiveness, with a hand never for a second inert or inattentive.   Overcharged with emotion, oversubtilized in expression, morbid in a high degree, this is in many ways a disagreeable picture.   A healthy mind resists its effect.   It is also a noteworthy picture, if only because it teaches us that the proverbial artistic temperament and its attendant neuroses are by no means modern inventions.

For the rest of the fifteenth century there were painters at Hamburg, enough to form a guild in 1490, but there were none of any importance. Meanwhile the painter's art was thriving mightily at neighboring Cologne.

That tender mysticism which at once directed and sharply limited the painting of Cologne, we have already considered. We should note that the mysticism influencing the painters was not that of Tauler and Suso—highly individualistic and strenuous—but rather a much popularized and attenuated mysticism, of common folk, a sentimentalized pietism. It remains to sketch briefly the story of a school that for nearly a century, if far less various in interest, was as fecund as that of the Netherlands. Cologne, one of the greatest trading cities of Europe, was as prosperous as she was pietistic, affording to the painter a generous patronage. From the anonymous early fourteenth-century pictures at Cologne we may reasonably infer that the new panel painting was based on manuscript miniatures, and on a miniature painting which had avoided the heavy-handedness of Central Germany and had wisely borrowed from the nervous elegance of the miniaturists of France. A triptych of a Calvary, with four smaller scenes, at Cologne (Fig. 109), though dated in the middle of the fourteenth century, recalls the energy of French miniature painting of a full generation earlier, and suggests, what is usually the case in Germany, that the Cosmopolitan Style had established itself only partially and transiently.

About the middle of the fourteenth century we have several laudatory notices of a Meister Wilhelm who was regarded as a great realist. He is now generally identified with the so-called Veronica Master, who was probably Herman Wynrich, first mentioned in Cologne in 1387 and dying there in 1414. In the Veronica Master we have a substantial figure and the true founder of the school. His note, in whatever subject, is a rather bloodless prettiness and tenderness. Of his considerable list of paintings, mostly at Cologne, we need consider only the St. Clara altar, in the Cathedral, in which twelve scenes from the life of Christ vary from a rather saccharine prettiness in the early stories to ineffective caricature in the stories of the Passion. A Calvary in the Cologne Museum is a better business, having with its sweetness something of contemplative dignity. The established conventions for the theme were a safeguard for a feeble artist. The most famous picture of this group is the little triptych of a half-length Madonna with the Bean Blossom (Fig. 110), with full-lengths of St. Barbara and St. Catherine on the shutters. It is handsome in Gothic decorative color, and otherwise quite negligible. Fortunately that prettiness which was to be at once the quality and the defect of the school of Cologne was rarely to present itself in so empty a form.

To the prettiness of the Veronica Master his successor, Stephan Lochner, added the necessary touch of gaiety and reserve, thus making himself, if but a fair third-rater on any European standard, the best painter that Cologne produced. He was born at Meersburg, on Lake Constance. The relative authority of his figure drawing suggests to me that before moving to Cologne he may have come into passing profitable contact with such highly competent Upper-Rhenish painters as Lucas Moser or Conrad Witz. Lochner had probably been some years in Cologne before our first notice of him as a married man and buyer of a house, in 1442. Before his death in 1451, his guild had twice elected him as its senator in the city council.

Lochner may have come to Cologne about 1430, when Hubert van Eyck's great altarpiece was awaiting completion by his brother Jan and Rogier de la Pasture was painting his earliest pictures. A few years later he painted the Last Judgment, of which the central panel is at Cologne, the shutters at Frankfurt and Munich. Now a Last Judgment with a populous resurrection of the dead is a trying subject for any painter, but few have made such a mess of it as Lochner. It is hard to imagine anything more confused and unbalanced, and even the individual episodes, horrific or humoristic, are of a far-fetched and mannered sort. They exhibit, however, much ingenuity and suggest a master who with a more congenial theme might do much better.

Some ten years later, probably towards 1450, the more congenial theme offered itself in a commission to do a triptych of the Adoration of the Kings (Fig. 112), for the Chapel of the City Council in the Cathedral. Lochner adopted the then unusual composition of the Madonna enthroned in the center with the Magi and her favorite saints arranged more or less symmetrically at the sides, and on the shutters the patrons of Cologne, St. Ursula and St. Gereon, with an escort of their martyr followers. As pure decoration this famous altarpiece, with its radiant colors, its variety of gracious postures and faces and its elaborate frieze of gilded Gothic tracery, is one of the more appealing primitive pictures. I doubt if the severe Albrecht Dürer fully approved it when he saw it in October of 1520, but he did not waste his money when he paid "two white pfenning" to have it opened. Between it and the Last Judgment lies a story of re-education. Lochner must have visited the Netherlands and seen the works of the Van Eycks and of Rogier de la Pasture. Too old and well-established to copy details, he was young enough in spirit to ponder new principles. The heads are now more strongly constructed, the faces more sweet, dignified and significant. The figures are still built rather weakly, but they now stand well in space, keeping their positions as they overlap in depth. More technically, Lochner now is highly resourceful in weaving his linear patterns, as in assembling richly draped or decorated areas without losing clarity. In short, Lochner is now a very competent stage manager of a courtly spectacle from which emanates a tender piety.

In handling curvilinear compositional patterns Lochner is really more facile than his far greater Flemish contemporaries, in a sense more modern. Or is this merely a survival of the gracefulness of Gothic miniature painting? The generally medieval character of this charming picture as compared with similar things in Flanders should not pass unnoticed. Unlike the Van Eycks, Campin and Rogier, Lochner does not locate his story. Everything, including the Annunciation on the outside of the shutters, takes place before a gold background or a brocade. There is no practicable stage-setting such as was required in Flanders, and perhaps this rich and ornate no-man's land really better served the purpose of devotion, as practiced at tender-minded Cologne, than any scenic realism could have done. It should also be noted that, despite the ostensibly courtly and extremely sumptuous character of this work, its mood is simple and popular. The Madonna is just a plump and pretty Fräulein; the saints are rather amiable than dignified in aspect. All this is in the spirit of the city for which the picture was painted.

Perhaps Lochner's masterpiece, a rather big word for anything of his, is the Madonna of the Violet (Fig. 111), in the archbishop's palace at Cologne. In this full-length figure he greatly enlarges his usual scale without loss of substantiality, and while multiplying casual and personal features and insisting on his wistful prettiness, he achieves

an effect wholly dignified and almost monumental. While the judgment says that this is far inferior to similar figures of the great Flemish
painters, it also must admit that it is far more charming. Merely as
an arrangement in flat pattern it is an extraordinarily accomplished
thing.

Less able in this regard, the little Madonna with a Rose Trellis
(Fig. 103), at Cologne, is quintessential Lochner. To realize its vast
superiority to an earlier and similar experiment in prettification, the
Veronica Master's Madonna of the Bean Blossom (Fig. 110), is to
advance in esthetic education.

While Lochner left a considerable number of imitators, they
were much his inferiors, and the school of Cologne was unhappily
and tardily transforming itself along lines of Flemish realism. There
is much tranquil pleasure in strolling through the rich museums of
Cologne and surveying the works of the painters of the last third of
the fifteenth century. For lack of documented names their works are
grouped stylistically about some key picture—the Master of the Life
of Mary, the Master of the Glorification of Mary, of St. George, of
the Lyversberg Passion, etc. In their works is much that is pretty,
graceful, curious and ingenious. But after such a visit, one feels that
nothing has taken hard hold upon attention or sympathy, and that
what have been viewed are technically well managed, but after all
rather muffled echoes of greater things seen in Flanders. So, on the
whole, I feel I do the reader a service in merely reminding him of the
existence of these *Meister*, and in leaving him to his own devices.
None of them seems to me of any general consequence, with the
possible exception of the Master of St. Ursula, who had the sense,
otherwise unexampled among his fellow painters, of hieratic and
aristocratic dignity.

About 1500 he painted the Legend of St. Ursula, at Cologne.
The series is of unequal merit, but it has the merit of taking its theme
seriously. In comparison, what Memling had already made of the
legend seems the work of a fastidious playboy; what Carpaccio had
produced, the expression of a delightful chatterbox. In short, the
good faith of the Master of St. Ursula permits him to stand advan-
tageously beside much superior painters. Perhaps the finest of his
pictures is the Visit of the Angel to St. Ursula (Fig. 113). The earnest form of the angel, carrying a glory of light with him, fills the
whole left side of the picture. St. Ursula in her bed is seen fore-

shortened and well back at the center. At the right is a glimpse up a flight of steps into an adjoining room. This stepping back in distance from left to right is compositionally novel and effective, as is the bold distribution of light and dark. More important is the sense of a supernatural event, of a true vision. There may be, as has been suggested, some influence from the school of Haarlem, but the admirable compositional arrangement of the picture can be credited only to its unknown master. He represents at its best such painting of Cologne as was made in the Flemish manner.

From the moment when the painters of Cologne began to emulate the minute realism of the Netherlanders, the school of Cologne was doomed. Her painters had no capacity to assimilate any kind of realism, and their endeavor therefore, being half-hearted, naturally failed. The end of the school came with a belated and more serious attempt to catch up with Quentin Massys and his Flemish contemporaries. The oddest and most interesting figure of this last phase is the Master of St. Bartholomew. He is the first and really only pretentious artist that Cologne produced. He models the figure with energy, pushing its bulk with rather exaggerated emphasis towards the spectator. He carries off difficult foreshortenings, breaks his Gothic draperies into the most complicated folds, invents rhetorical postures and positions of the hands. On the decorative side he is reactionary, designing in the shallow space afforded by gold or brocade backgrounds. Without taste or restraint, he practices ably a highly exhibitionistic art. One may imagine him complacently competing with the new marvels of Massys and Dürer—in his own eyes successfully. A glance at any of his pictures, say the Calvary, at Cologne; or the Deposition, at Paris (Fig. 114), will show that he was well fitted to be the sacristan-undertaker of the school he felt he was adorning.

Beyond him it is hardly necessary to go. Barthel Bruyn, a Hollander by birth, for the first half of the sixteenth century continued the religious painting of Cologne in a direction parallel with the broader emotionalism of Massys. He painted at least one charming picture, a Nativity, at Frankfurt (Fig. 115), conceived as a nocturne with adoring angels. Whether representing donors on the shutters of altarpieces, or in independent portraiture, he was entirely competent, so much so that in viewing his portraits, in order to realize their essential mediocrity, one must recall those of Massys, Dürer and Holbein. Probably indirectly, through Dürer's engravings, he received, rather disadvantageously, a modicum of Italian influence—a taste which led to sheer plagiarism in his son, Barthel the Younger. Cologne could hardly escape the pitfall that lay in the path of every late Gothic painter of the North.

When the Cologne school faded out there was nothing tragic in its extinction. In a rather small but often quite winsome way it had served its times. When the new times of the Reformation and Catholic reaction ensued, Cologne seemed to have outgrown or perhaps forgotten her need of visualized expression through the painter's art. After all, one could look at the towering apse of the Cathedral, stroll through the solemn Romanesque churches and see the browned skulls of St. Gereon's legion and of St. Ursula's eleven thousand martyred virgins shadowy in their pigeonholes. And if anything more still needed to be seen, the fifteenth-century pictures, mostly in their original places till a century or so ago, seem to have sufficed both for the few art lovers of Cologne and for her many devotees.

To treat even in outline the local schools of the German region would require a book rather than a chapter. So at the sacrifice of much that is charming and of more that is merely quaint, I pass to the few remaining painters of the fifteenth century who seem to me still of artistic importance.

Far more advanced than anything painted so early on the Lower Rhine, or for that matter in Flanders, are the works of two painters who flourished at the headwaters, Lucas Moser and Conrad Witz. By Lucas we have in the village church of Tiefenbronn, near Lake Constance, a painted tabernacle, dated 1431, inclosing a carved Assumption of St. Mary Magdalen. The gable shows the supper at Bethany, with the Magdalene anointing Jesus' feet, and Judas deploring the waste to Peter. The scene is in the open air before a vine trellis; the construction of the forms is firm yet urbane, the actions amazingly easy and natural. At first glance one would feel the work seventy years later and of Massys' time.

The three stories of the Magdalene, in tall panels on the front, are again, for the ease and specific character of the figure drawing and for the excellent realization of spatial conditions, far in advance of anything painted at the time north of the Alps, and fairly abreast, excepting only Masaccio's art, of anything then painted in Italy. In the voyage to Marseilles (Fig. 116), a choppy sea is represented by spirited formulas, while the looming of distant mountains against the sky evinces a genuine observation such as we shall not find elsewhere in the North for a couple of generations, nor even in Italy for twenty years or so.

The central panel (Fig. 117) represents the saint working a miracle of healing in an upper pavilion, while in the court below her three male companions and St. Martha are asleep in the most natural positions. The compositional features of both these pictures are calculated to bring the onlooker very near or even into the action, and are quite novel. In the remaining panel we see the last communion administered to the Magdalene, clothed only in her long hair, and upheld by angels. The scene is a Romanesque church, of which the interior has a singularly Italian look. There is a predella with Jesus and the wise and foolish virgins, all half-lengths. Here there is much fine modulation of the feelings and characters involved in the parable.

While this is, after all, not a great painting, it is of exceptional charm and competence for its date. One is inclined to suspect Italian influence, but it would be very difficult to specify it. In fact, the likeliest explanation is one abhorrent to art historians of evolutionary bent—that the whole thing rests on Lucas Moser's own observation and experimentation. After all, such unexpected emergences do occur—think of Hubert van Eyck, Masaccio and Caravaggio. We merely are not used to thinking of them as occurring in the country. Evidently Lucas was right prematurely, and suffered the usual penalty of neglect, for the inscription reads, in translation:

"Cry aloud, Art, and mourn bitterly, for no one now desires you! Alas! Alas! 1431. Lucas Moser of Weil, Master of this work; pray God for him."

This outcry is of considerable historical importance, for, so far as I know, it is the earliest expression of an artist embittered from lack of appreciation and patronage. It is a despairing note that was to become tragically frequent only in the nineteenth century.

In acute observation of larger appearances no Northern painter of the early fifteenth century equals Conrad Witz. Beside his carefully studied effects of actual lighting, the very skillful expedients of the Van Eycks and Campin seem merely conventional. Save for the surviving angular formulas of the draperies—an inheritance from wood carving—Conrad Witz's pictures are as accomplished as Italian works fifty years later. His figure construction yields a surprisingly plastic effect: the homeliness of his squat types, with their discreet suggestion of actual portraiture, gives credibility to his narratives. With such people, it might all have happened so. Thus in technical equipment Conrad Witz was superior to all his painter contemporaries, and if he, after all, does not seem a great painter, it is because he lacked qualities of poetic imagination which his rivals possessed.

He was born at Constance, and after working in Swabia, came to Basel, where in 1434 he is registered as a master painter. For two years after 1444 he was at Geneva, whence he returned to Basel to die in 1448. We may then think of him as a contemporary of Jan van Eyck, whose work he apparently never saw.

A typical Conrad Witz is St. Mary Magdalen and St. Catherine in a Church, at Strasbourg (Fig. 118). The theme of youthful contemplative female saints in holy contemplation looks forward to Memling, and the comparison tells much about Conrad Witz's temperament. Here are no meditative maids of honor, but two strong young women of the people, whose thinking is resolutely guided. The Magdalene holds out her alabaster box of precious ointment, but gazes intently above it, as if trying hard to summon up the supreme occasion on which it was used. Her plain face, with a pug nose, her actively maintained sitting posture, suggest, not the visionary, but the experienced woman of good sense and disciplined will. And St. Catherine, though her crown and the wide borders of her voluminous robe gleam with pearls, has no air of a princess in celestial revery over a neglected book. Instead she seems hard at study, verifying or memorizing something from her book of hours. It is this voluntary character of all Conrad Witz's figures that allies them strangely with those of Signorelli.

But the remarkable innovation is the lighting. Everything is observed and accounted for—in few contemporary pictures is there so truthful a complication of cast shadows. All the columns, half columns, moldings, even St. Catherine's wheel on the floor, produce the just depth of shadow. Fine, too, is the dark frame of the door and traceried doorhead against the light, making a picture of a square with people and a house beyond. With all this elaboration the decorative effect, rather frosted-silvery, is unified and handsome. The proportions of the figures and architecture are much more reasonable than in similar compositions by the Van Eycks. The figures come nearer to us; they are not in a tabernacle from which we are excluded, but in a place we might enter ourselves.

Christ walking on the Water (Fig. 119), at Geneva, is chiefly remarkable for its reasonably correct perspective relation of figures to each other and to the landscape. The scene is a whole, and not, as in Conrad Witz's Flemish contemporaries, a backdrop far away. Especially broad and successful in treatment is the countryside beyond the water, rising from farm lands to high hill pastures with hedgerows, with a very faint distant gleam of a snow-clad range of mountains under a marbled sky. The date 1444 tells that the scene is on the Lake of Geneva. This is possibly the first truthfully elaborated portrait of a place in the art of painting. Everything is admirable, the eager apostles drawing the net, terrified sinking St. Peter—except the main figure of Jesus, artificially posed, and expressionless. No pictures could better illustrate Conrad Witz's probity and seriousness and, withal, his lack of imagination.

On a lower level of invention, he was a remarkable narrative painter. In this phase the Deliverance of St. Peter (Fig. 120), at Basel, may represent him. There are two episodes in one picture. At the right before the miraculously opened prison door a sturdy angel is removing the neck shackle from St. Peter, sound asleep in a sitting posture. At the left the angel is leading the bewildered apostle away. The scene is a courtyard with sharp contrasts of dark and light areas caused by artificial lighting. Of four guards, one sleeps in a corner while three vainly prepare to use their weapons. Their forms cast picturesque shadows, their armor glooms and gleams with palpable roundness. The face of the guard with a halberd at the left, open-mouthed and rigid with indignation and fear, is worthy of a Mantegna. Few pictures at any time give so much as this the sense of an actual happening.

With the achievement of Conrad Witz, the foundation was laid on which a great school of realistic and humanistic painting might have been built. That he died leaving no trace of influence indicates that he was self-made and had the bad luck to live in a community which, while perhaps appreciating his skill, could inspire him with no great feelings or ideas, for it is these, after all, rather than technical accomplishment, which go to the making of any great art.

The last quarter of the fifteenth century in the Germanies offers us a confusion of names and of painters, few of whom, on any general scale of values, are of other than antiquarian importance. In the West one may note a gradual invasion of the Flemish manner; in the East

and Danube Valley an indigenous, vehement style of narrative painting, with curious analogies with the contemporary art of Catalonia,
the chief figure being Wolf Huber. His art represents an odd mixture of progressive study of nature, with illogical retention of the old
decorative effects and gold backgrounds. Like many early German
artists his designs in black and white for woodcuts, which he made
himself, are superior to his painting. Central Germany chiefly developed a rather plebeian type of narrative painting, tempered at Nürnberg by a refining influence from the Italianate school of Prague.
Augsburg produced in Hans Holbein the Elder an excellent artist of a
minor sort. Born in 1460, he probably worked for a couple of years
in Italy. In any case intelligent study of Italian models taught him
to simplify and clarify his compositions, made him curious of picturesque effects of light and shade, initiated him in Italian forms of
decoration, and helped him to create types of a new graciousness and
urbanity. His paintings are so charming that to realize their after all
retarded character we must recall that before he died most of the best
painting of Quentin Massys and Dürer had been done. The Elder
Holbein drew sensitive and characterful portraits, which was prophetic
of the gift of a greater son of a worthy father.

The only Early German painter who could compete with the
Italian primitives on their own ground was Michael Pacher of Bruneck
in the Tyrol. He was born before 1440 of an artist family, two of his
brothers being painters. Michael Pacher practiced with equal power
and dignity wood sculpture and painting. Perhaps his masterpiece
is the sculptured and painted altarpiece for the Church of St. Wolfgang near Salzburg, which on double wings displays four stories of
the Virgin, eight of the Life of Christ, and four from the Legend of
St. Wolfgang. This shrine, one of the most impressive of the century,
was executed between 1477 and 1481. It represents Pacher in his
early prime. While the painted and sculptured ornament is flamboyant Gothic, and the feeling of the figures native, their dignity,
with certain expedients in lighting and perspective, tell us that Pacher
must have made the trip over the Brenner to Padua, where Mantegna's
frescoes in the Ermitani were a new marvel, and a schoolroom for all
progressive painters of Lombardy and Emilia. I think Pacher must
have pursued his Italian journey as far as Ferrara, where Mantegna's
scientific discoveries were being applied less archaeologically, and in
a manner more Italian than his own. Something in the stately pose

of the figures and the cellular cast of the draperies in Pacher's later works remotely, but I feel distinctly, recalls the austere dignity of Francesco Cossa and Cosimo Tura.

The greatness of Michael Pacher is shown by the fact that before the bewildering spectacle of a new and unprecedently resourceful art he borrowed not patterns but principles. He cannot be thought of as an Italianate; he rather worked out an art essentially his own with the aid of principles learned in Italy.

His most accessible work, an altarpiece dedicated to St. Wolfgang, and finished for the Cathedral at Brixen, is now at Munich in incomplete form. Four panels display eight subjects, the Four Latin Doctors, and four scenes from the Legend of St. Wolfgang. The four leading theologians of Latin Christianity, in their rich vestments, sit with sculpturesque dignity, yet with ease, in elaborate canopied niches of the most ornate Gothic sort. Some reminder of a signal miracle wrought by him accompanies each saint. Thus St. Gregory (Fig. 121), at Munich, looks down at the nude crowned form of the Emperor Trajan, whose raised arm he holds firmly, for because of Trajan's self-sacrificing act of justice in condemning his own son for a rape, St. Gregory prayed Trajan's soul out of hell. The broad, correct and authoritative construction of the nude in light and shade implies direct study of Mantegna, while the type of St. Gregory and the tortured cast of his robe suggests the style of Ferrara.

St. Wolfgang compelling the Devil to hold his Bible (Fig. 122), is a bizarre masterpiece in plastic realization and effective emotional understatement. The setting, with a bridge and passers-by in middle distance and town buildings correctly foreshortened away, as also the even and accurate distribution of light and shade, tell of fundamental studies in Padua. The gentle, unreproachful gesture with which St. Wolfgang converts Satan into a living lectern is very telling. A real saint, the patron saint of a decent Tyrolese town, would take only the minimum trouble in handling so usual an affair as a visit from the Devil. Dr. Martin Luther, who later in such an emergency threw a heavy inkstand, really showed a deplorable lack of self-control. What is especially remarkable in this picture is the real handsomeness of the obviously compiled Satan. The general motive is that of a desiccated cadaver, which still seems athletically competent, which has developed cloven hoofs, bat wings, and an incredible tusked and horned head. All this fanciful nonsense, for it is hardly better than that, gains a sort of dignity and even beauty from the strength and suppleness of the modeling in light and dark.

The Last Communion of St. Wolfgang (Fig. 123), is even more masterly, in the constructing play of light in a Gothic chapel, in the despairing posture of the saint prone on the steps of an unfurnished altar, in the birdlike swoop of the foreshortened angel who with one hand sets the ciborium on the vacant altar, while with the other gently touching the saint on the shoulder to remind him that the bread which is Christ's body is miraculously vouchsafed. Few pictures of the time were so clearly imagined and so cleanly executed. Such intuition of the economy of picture making evinces in Michael Pacher an intellectual superiority over most of his contemporaries.

He seems to have understood and practiced that balance between representation and convention which goes to the making of a great work of art in any medium. Generally there was no such understanding in the Germanies in the fifteenth century. Cologne, feeble in representation, will make a good use of convention; the Danube Valley will push forward in drastic representation untempered by convention. The general mediocre quality of fifteenth-century painting in Germany rests on the failure to develop and utilize suitable conventions, and that, of course, implies a low degree of culture in the Germanies, for the business of culture is largely to supply helpful conventions and avoid the wastefulness of merely individual experimentation. It is, of course, memory that conserves and sifts the conventions. A cultured people is merely one that has a retentive and projective memory. This the Germanies, as compared with France, Flanders and Italy, lacked, hence the discontinuity of their early painting, and its lack of style. Since these necessary observations may seem unsympathetic, I am glad to take leave of the subject with Michael Pacher, whose greatness seems to me indisputable. Such an art as his should have produced a school, but the Tyrol was of short memory and promptly forgot or took for granted the only great artist it ever produced.

# CHAPTER IX

## LATE GOTHIC PAINTING IN SPAIN

Fig. 124. School of Borassá. Retable of St. Michael.—Cruilles.

FIG. 125. Valencian Madonna, about 1425.—Walters' Collection, Baltimore.

FIG. 126. (Upper) LUIS BORASSÁ. Christ Enthroned.—*Soler y March*
*Collection, Barcelona.*
FIG. 127. (Lower left) JACOMART. St. Martin and the Beggar.—*Segorbe.*
FIG. 128. (Lower right) Master of St. George. St. George and the
Dragon.—*Chicago.*

FIG. 130. JAIME HUGUET. Conseration of St. Augustine.—Monastery of St. Augustine, Barcelona.

FIG. 129. LUIS DALMÁU. Madonna of the Councilors.—Museum of Catalan Art, Barcelona.

FIG. 132. FERNANDO GALLEGO. Pietà.—Weibel Collection, Madrid.

FIG. 131. JAIME HUGUET. St. George and the Princess.—Museo de la Ciudadela, Barcelona.

214

Fig. 133. Bartolomeo Bermejo. Santo Domingo de Silos.—Madrid.

Fig. 134. Bartolomeo Ber-
mejo. Santa Engracia.—Elizabeth
Stewart Gardner Museum, Boston.

Fig. 135. Bartolomeo Bermejo.
St. Michael.—Coll. Lady Ludlow,
London.

Fig. 136. Bartolomeo Bermejo. Pietà.—*Cathedral, Barcelona.*

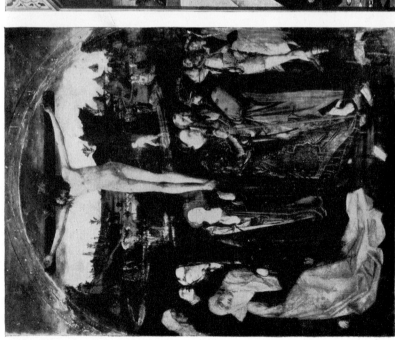

Fig. 137.  Rodrigo de Osona.  Calvary.—S. Nicolàs, Valencia.    Fig. 138.  Pedro Berruguete.  St. Peter Martyr in Prayer.—Madrid.

218

To CHARACTERIZE the Early Renaissance in Spain is a task so difficult and unrewarding that I undertake it most grudgingly. To begin with, the primitive painting of Spain in the fifteenth and early sixteenth century is of inferior quality, as compared with that of Italy and Flanders, even with that of France and the Germanies. Next, it is most difficult to locate the beginning of anything that can properly be called a Renaissance in Spain. Spanish art was backward-looking and retarded, with no such landmark figures as Masaccio, the Van Eycks, Dürer, Pieter Bruegel. Indeed, there is an all-overishness about Early Spanish painting which may seem to justify a similar all-overishness in its treatment, and all the more that the material is accessible in detail to such as are interested in Professor Chandler R. Post's standard *History of Spanish Painting*.

In most of the period we shall consider, Spain was divided into independent provinces, and without national unity. The regions most productive of painting were Catalonia and Valencia, the western end of a Riviera, the eastern end of which was Naples. These two provinces faced Italian seaports which were outlets for Italian art and its influence. Catalonia, speaking a language more akin to Provençal than to Spanish, was especially susceptible to influences from beyond the Pyrenees.

As early as the middle of the fourteenth century Ferrer Bassa of Barcelona made mural paintings and panels in a style ultimately derived from Siena. This manner was continued through the century, in Catalonia, by members of the Serra family. But since the movement failed to take root, it needs only passing mention.

If we must locate the beginning of a Spanish Renaissance, our criterion can only be that moderate move from a purely decorative basis towards analytical realism which took place in Catalonia about 1400, the pioneer, if indeed he deserves so large a name, being Luis Borassá. The stylistic fashion for half a century earlier had been the decorative calligraphy of the Cosmopolitan Style, which we have already described. It seems to have filtered into Spain from several sources. Simone Martini and his Italian and French followers had established it firmly in the Mediterranean littoral from Avignon to Narbonne. Naples, in active trade relations with Spain, and after 1442 a dependency of Aragon, was esthetically an outpost of the Cosmopolitan Style as practiced at Siena. So, in a lesser degree, was Pisa. From any of these sources, or from all combined, the style reached Spain. There it was interpreted in the rather heavy-handed manner which is excellently represented in a Valencian Madonna of about 1425, in the Walters' Collection, Baltimore (Fig. 125). One may note a discrepancy between the heavy and profuse ornament and the real sensitiveness of the faces and hands. Such inconsistencies, as we shall see, are characteristic of primitive Spanish painting generally.

This Madonna was the central panel of a great retable, which originally illustrated the story of her life in many small panels. The taste for these big compartmental retables set severe limitations upon pictorial design in Spain. The only possible unity was supplied by the frame maker, and these great carved and gilded structures have an impressive decorative existence of their own, quite apart from the painted panels, which in the gloom of a Spanish Gothic church often become mere color areas. Thus while the big retables are immensely decorative, their simple ornateness often defeats their purpose of devotional appeal (Fig. 124), by reducing the sacred narratives to virtual illegibility. And when the move towards analytical realism and a sounder construction came, it was seriously retarded and hampered by the requirement that the new realism should respect the old decorative profuseness. This was to demand the incompatible. One often sees a face modeled with the sculptural tension of a Florentine realist caught in a swirl of embossed and gilded scrolls and borders—a strange cage for such a bird. And again, beneath so real a head, the robes will hang slackly as if from a peg, because the projection of shoulders, elbows and knees, and the resulting folds, must not be allowed to impair or confuse the rich pattern of the stuff. So the Spanish Renaissance began with contradictory ideals, demanding with a maximum of decorative effect a maximum of realistic emotional expression. To liberate Spanish realism, decoration must give way, and it took nearly a century and a half to make its too long-delayed abdication.

The retable of Guardiola, painted after 1404 by Luis Borassá, and now in the Soler y March Collection, Barcelona, seems to mark the first very moderate step towards realism (Fig. 126). It represents an enthroned Christ with five passion scenes. The reader will wonder why I find a Renaissance character in such a work. Well, the decorative are subordinated to the pictorial elements, the gold background has given way to blue; the drapery is on the whole studied in its natural hang and folds, with only slightest reminiscences of the calligraphy of the Cosmopolitan Style; the larger construction of the figures is truthful and even vigorous; there is an attempt to state and realize the spatial relations. Taken broadly, the work, if infinitely less able, has advanced along the lines of realism about to the stage reached by the Giottesques.

The background of Borassá's art, as seen in this retable, seems to be entirely medieval. One can imagine him knowing vaguely the Sienese painters of the Lorenzettian schools, or more probably some belated Florentine exemplar of the manner of Orcagna. The transmission might have been through the miniatures of a Tuscan choir book. However that be, there is in Borassá no trace of that Franco-Flemish influence which was soon to dominate the painting of Spain.

Valencia, like Catalonia, practiced the Riviera style, but in a gentler and more idealistic spirit. Refining and restraining influences from Italy are more apparent. For example, Valencian paintings of the fifteenth century eschew that exaggeration of embossed and gilded decoration which is so characteristic of Catalonia. The Valencians, with greater taste and discretion, painted or incised their ornament, with the result that the pictorial interest dominates. As a class, Valencian paintings vaguely recall those ingratiating minor masters of Siena and Umbria which one always sees with pleasure, but remembers with difficulty.

Among the many Valencian painters whom recent research has piously disentombed, I can, for reasons of space, mention only Jacomart. Son of a French father, he flourished greatly as a contractor for retables, and while it is most difficult to disengage his personal work from that of his many assistants, still his influence clearly dominated Valencia in the middle of the fifteenth century, and we have a certain number of paintings which seem mostly by his hand. He was born early in the century and by 1442 was at Naples as court painter to its conqueror, Alfonso of Aragon. He spent several years in Italy, and we can trace him at Tivoli, so he must have visited Rome. He returned to Valencia by 1451 or earlier, and died there in 1461.

From the new Flemish influence his work is almost free, and

it is hard to see in it any very specific imitation of Italian painting. Yet I feel the delightful Madonna of the Portiuncula, a celestial vision of St. Francis at Segorbe, may imply some knowledge of the little masters of Camerino, who inherited something of the ornate graciousness of Gentile da Fabriano and of the more distant Venetians. In any case, though rather feebly executed, it is as sentiment and as decoration entirely captivating. A truer poetry is in the even feebler St. Martin and the Beggar (Fig. 127), Segorbe. Its schematized but also happily disposed landscape again suggests to me some influence from Umbria beyond the Apennines. In those enthroned effigies of austere saints, which are often the best products of the Spanish primitives, Jacomart has a modest superiority over his contemporaries. Examples are St. Ildefonso, at Jativa, and St. Martin, at Segorbe. It seems a pity that the gentle idealism of Jacomart had no further development. Valencia, always at its best when most Italianate, was like the rest of Spain, dominated for a couple of generations following Jacomart by the compelling influence of the Gothic realism of Flanders.

We have perhaps the earliest hint of it in the work of the Master of St. George, who flourished in Catalonia after 1430. His most interesting picture is St. George and the Dragon, at Chicago (Fig. 128). There is a new energy of representation, a reasonable concern with perspective and spatial relations, a new, careful minuteness in the painting of rocks. Finally, the princess, with her high, bulging forehead and elaborate crown, might have been lifted from some picture by a modest follower of Hubert van Eyck, while the technique shows the new varnish mediums of the Flemish school. Later works of the Master of St. George, such as St. Lucy's Distribution of her Dowry, in a private collection at Barcelona, are even closer in feeling to good Flemish pictures, and suggest to me acquaintance with works of Rogier de la Pasture's school.

To abridge a really complicated matter, we must imagine the Franco-Flemish manner quickly gaining against the old Riviera style and recurrent but transient new influences from Italy. Before the year 1500 there were many fine Flemish pictures in Spain. Many Spaniards had studied in Flanders, and Spanish painters generally were imitating with reasonable skill, if with little sensitiveness, such Northern masters as the Van Eycks, Rogier and Dirck Bouts. It appears too that some of the best pictures of Hugo van der Goes went to Spain directly, as did many of those of his younger contemporary, Jerome Bosch. Such pictures satisfied that desire for a somewhat minute and drastic realism towards which Spanish taste had for centuries obscurely aspired.

It was Luis Dalmáu (ca. 1400–ca. 1463) who made the fullest assimilation of the new Flemish style. By him we have only one surely identified picture, the Madonna of the Councilors, in the Museum of Catalan Art, Barcelona (Fig. 129). The figures of the Madonna, saints and councilors show the closest study of the mature art of the Van Eycks, the architectural setting in an elaborate and contemporary Gothic style is more in the taste of the Tournai School. Though plainly derivative, the picture with its severe symmetry and excellent figure construction is one of the more impressive Spanish productions of the moment. We can trace Dalmáu from 1428, when he was already a court painter of Alfonso V at Valencia. In 1431 he was sent to Flanders where he probably spent several years. It is clear that he must have profited by the study of the art of the Van Eycks in such rare monumental expressions as the Ghent altarpiece, and probably the Van der Paele Madonna. In 1443 at Barcelona he received the commission for the Madonna of the Councilors, and it was signed in 1445. For the remaining eighteen years or so of Dalmáu's life we have a few attributed pictures, and records of artistic activity of a quite minor sort. Though possibly a Valencian, his career was made in Catalonia. It is possible that his considerable accomplishment was too exotic to hold its popularity either against the imported Flemish pictures or the more alert and racy inventions of such followers of the Master of St. George as Jaime Huguet, the dominant figure in Catalan painting after the middle of the fifteenth century.

Our first notice of Jaime Huguet is 1448, our last, 1489, and in 1494 his wife was a widow. His art grows out of that of the Master of St. George but is less touched by Flemish influences. Until recent discovery of documents and closer stylistic scrutiny, most of the pictures now surely known to be his were ascribed to various members of the Vergos family, minor painters who occasionally served Huguet as assistants. Huguet handles the old decorative expedients with taste, commands a gentle ideality, which condones his rather feeble and conventional figure construction. He is perhaps to be taken most seriously in such massive rich and ornate compositions as the Consecration of St. Augustine (Fig. 130), in the church of the monastery of St. Augustine, at Barcelona; or in the dour enthroned St. Anthony of Egypt, which the confraternity of "the racers of animals" of Barcelona ordered in 1454. But in this statuesque vein Huguet meets a damaging competition, and he is perhaps most original in whimsically tender inventions such as St. Anthony directing the Exorcism of a Queen, or St. Michael's rescue of a Woman and Child, at the House of the Guild, Barcelona. In this charmingly fanciful vein Jaime Huguet, though manifestly inferior both in power and in delicacy, shows himself of the same spiritual family as his older Italian contemporary, Francesco Sassetta. An excellent example of this fantastic and delicate vein is the Meeting of St. George and the Princess (Fig. 131), in the Museo de la Ciudadela, Barcelona. The incident is handled with an enchanting sense of chivalric decorum and youthful reticence.

Jaime Huguet really represents a moment of hesitation when the old sumptuous Catalan manner was carrying on with some difficulty against competing alien influences. That moment of hesitation he graced with an unpretentious poetry. A greater contribution was to be made by more tenacious talents which set themselves to mastering the new marvels of the Flemish style.

A typical representative of the Hispano-Flemish style is Fernando Gallego, who may, as his name suggests, be a Galician, but worked mostly at or about Salamanca. His activity falls into the last quarter of the fifteenth century. He knew and imitated the prints of Schongauer; had probably studied in the Low Countries. His mood is more emotional and plebeian than that of his Flemish models. As a true Spaniard he cares too much for facial expression. He can be almost comically insistent, as in the picture of the piecemeal decapitation of St. Catherine, in the Old Cathedral, Salamanca, and he can be very alert and refined, as in the Madonna and Child, at Salamanca, New Cathedral, or in the signed Pietà in the Weibel Collection, Madrid (Fig. 132). His landscapes favor the broader and larger features of Bouts, but there are fine crags, which suggest contemporary Florentine painting, though in both cases only interest in similar objects in nature may be involved, and the sweep of his cold lighting across his landscapes is emphatically his own. His originality may be judged from the Pietà mentioned above. It recalls the masterpieces of Rogier de la Pasture, but is more intimate and human, and less austere.

The very schematic handling of the lights on the nude body gives emphasis and pathos at the expense of truthfulness to appearance.

At all times Gallego studies expression with much thoughtfulness, and he deserves a distinguished place among minor painters of sentiment. Other Hispano-Flemish painters have their interest; the Master of Burgos, for example, with the singular starkness of his forms and expressions, which at times yield a genuinely tragic effect; but in a handbook of this sort we must turn directly to the single Hispano-Flemish painter who has any claim to greatness, Bartolomeo Bermejo.

Our knowledge of him is based on a few dated pictures, and inferences from their style. I follow here the ingenious analysis carefully worked out by Professor Chandler R. Post. Bermejo was born at Cordova. The date is uncertain, but we may reasonably set it between 1440 and 1450. His mastery of the new technique of oil painting and the clear influence of the Van Eycks, Rogier de la Pasture, and other Flemish and Dutch painters in his early works make it highly probable that he got his training in the Netherlands and was there for several of his impressionable years.

It has been suggested that perhaps we first meet Bermejo in a Dormition of the Virgin, at Berlin. It is so Northern in feeling that until lately it was catalogued as Flemish or Lower Rhenish. Yet it is Spanish and by Bermejo, as the elaborate and rather inappropriate accessories attest, and even more that glum fixity of expression which characterizes all of Bermejo's masks. Apart from such considerations, the drastic portraitlike visages are wholly Spanish. The composition is striking and unusual. It is a very tall oblong containing a barrel-vaulted room lighted by an open door and a window. The dying Mary and her bed are foreshortened, her face set. The apostles are represented as composed and resigned; St. Peter even reads his prayer book intently—or is he reading the Office for the Dead, in Mary's behalf? Above, like a carved wood group suspended in air, God the Father and four angels receive Mary's soul. The skill of the painter is shown in the broad and effective sweep of the light, and in the strong and characterful construction of the figures.

But in its qualities and defects—it is completely static and emotionally unconcentrated—this seems to me a sort of diploma piece, and I agree with Professor Post in setting it in Bermejo's early years. But I differ from him in seeing any marked influence from the Van Eycks. I feel that Bermejo had profoundly studied Hugo van der Goes' masterpiece at Bruges, or more likely an earlier lost version of the Dormition which is represented by copies. If this be so, we can hardly date Bermejo's Dormition before 1480, and perhaps we may reasonably think of it as the product of a second visit to Flanders.

For we must concede that when Bermejo painted the solemn effigy of Santo Domingo de Silos, at Madrid (Fig. 133), as early as 1474, he had already visited Flanders. It is his greatest work, and perhaps the finest picture among Spanish primitives. The saint sits solidly and frontally upon a Gothic throne as elaborately turreted as Cologne Cathedral. His hands hold carefully open a devotional book, but his fixed eyes above the long nose and square jaws stare eternally over our heads at nothing. He is clothed with the richness of any idol, but one feels his solid body under the stiff embroideries and brocades. The general elaboration is charmingly varied by small figures representing the virtues ensconced in Gothic niches in the arms of the throne. Illogically but delightfully the virtues are conceived not as polychrome sculpture, but as richly clad women in courtly garb and attitude. These great ladies who impersonate Faith, Hope, Charity, Prudence, etc., are freely invented. Bermejo rejects the conventional symbols of the virtues. And these stalwart, gracious and reliable figures are among his most characteristic creations.

Technically this panel is a great advance on its predecessors. Bermejo does not mold and emboss his ornament; however elaborate, he paints it, surmounting the difficulties of the new task with a more than Flemish skill and pertinacity. Only a little later than this masterpiece may be the Santa Engracia, Elizabeth Stewart Gardner Museum, Boston (Fig. 134). Essentially she is the Prudence just mentioned, enlarged, more sumptuously clad, more withdrawn from the business and clamor of the world. In the set, oval, passionless face there is some hint of the virginal masks of Geertgen of Haarlem, but it may be merely a coincidence. There is a paradox in the picture, that a woman decked with every splendor the world can desire gives an impression of complete other-worldliness. On the technical side superb—the breaking of the general verticality by the slightly bent head, by the curve of the martyr's palm and the fall of the robe, its borders stiffened by heavy gold embroidery and pearls, the value of the crisp linear spots and lines in the inlay of the throne—all this is of the most fastidious selection. For the first and almost for the only time, as Professor Post has justly remarked, we meet a Spanish painter whose temper is primarily esthetic.

No picture of Bermejo's reveals the esthete and sophisticate more thoroughly than the famous St. Michael, in the collection of Lady Ludlow, London (Fig. 135). The lengthy, gracile form is borrowed from Rogier de la Pasture, but he would never have bent it so coyly, have cast the cloak in so effective a diagonal, which the sword repeats. Nor would Rogier have made St. Michael while conquering Satan not merely superior and indifferent, but also somewhat peevish and bored. Merely to list the elaborations in this picture—the reflections of buildings in the corselet and buckler, the favorite oak leaf pattern in the border—would need rather a chapter than a paragraph. Upon such details Bermejo fairly squandered the new and hard-won skill he had brought back from Flanders. The only interested person in the picture is the little donor—the mechanized Satan is far from convincing—and even the donor expresses merely a mild curiosity.

Within ten years of the pictures we have been considering an amazing change came over Bermejo's art. The Pietà in the Cathedral of Barcelona (Fig. 136), dated 1490, is technically almost as advanced as Florentine painting of the same period. Survivals of primitive features, such as the angular break of the draperies and the International swirl of the embroidered hem of Mary's robe, are singularly few. A broad landscape, with a harbor and ship, is treated with a beautiful minuteness recalling such Florentine backgrounds as those of Piero di Cosimo. The lift of clouds is strongly indicated, and there is even a skillful suggestion of a passing rain squall. The four figures are still wholly Hispano-Flemish. Notable for a worried, drastic realism is an unshaven St. Jerome with horn spectacles, bending over his Bible. Balancing him at the right is a stolidly woebegone donor. The landscape details—flowers, ledges swept by the light, tiny idyllic figures— are exquisite and, as Professor Post rightly suggests, recall similar idyllic features in the backgrounds of Giovanni Bellini's and Giorgione's pictures. The Pietà represents a complete and intelligent surrender to the last and most accomplished phase of Early Renaissance painting in Italy. It is only on close scrutiny that, despite a satisfactory documentation, we convince ourselves on stylistic grounds that we have to do with the creator of such primitive masterpieces as the Santo Domingo, the St. Michael, and the Santa Engracia.

For this jump of a generation in style within a few years, some explanation must be sought. Professor Post finds it in a trip to Naples, then under Aragonese rule, where, while the Flemish style dominated, pictures of a more Italian sort, and blends of the two styles were to be seen. Certainly some experience of this sort must have befallen Bermejo shortly before he painted the Pietà of 1490, and it is so far advanced beyond any Neapolitan work of the moment that I am inclined to think his Italian trip included Florence also.

It is a temptation to follow Bermejo's career further, to analyze the gracious and most patrician Madonna with a Donor, at Acqui, perhaps a little earlier than the Pietà, to study the richly modulated Epiphany in the Cathedral of Granada. But if my sketch induces the reader to carry further his study of this strange esthete before esthetics was known, it will have served its purpose.

Bermejo, to recapitulate, introduced into dying primitive painting in Spain certain refinements distinctly his own, the subordination of his most elaborate decoration to the general design, fastidious taste in thinking out the design itself, exquisiteness in handling difficult details—diaphanous veils, light-smitten ledges, reflections in metal and glass. These stylistic and formal perfections required a holding down of specific and urgent expression. Bermejo willingly made the sacrifice. Professor Post brilliantly sums up Bermejo's contribution as follows:

"One of the ways in which he obtained monumentality was the casting each of his pictures in a formal pattern; and he brought Spanish medieval painting to its culmination by matchlessly fulfilling the supreme purpose of the whole peninsular school of the Middle Ages, the strange fusion of this general, highly conventionalized design with the utmost realism in the rendering of the human countenance and its expression. Thus it was that he and other Spanish masters reconciled two opposing tendencies of the race, the realistic and the ritualistic conceptions of the function of art."

With this illuminating generalization I differ to this extent: I feel that in Spanish painting generally, and even in Bermejo, the fusion and reconciliation were never fully achieved, never in the nature of the case could be achieved. What Bermejo and the greatest of his Spanish colleagues attained was, for me, not harmony but dissonance of an exciting and magnificent kind. In this they may be said to anticipate certain esthetic effects which the unhistorically minded credit to modern music. Bermejo thus may be regarded as a remote spiritual ancestor of Stravinsky, Reger and Richard Strauss.

Bermejo's surrender to the Italian Renaissance was prophetic. It was in the air in Spain even before the High Renaissance had dawned in Italy itself. When you step from the nave of the Cathedral of Toledo to the Chapter House, and see the frescoes ascribed to Juan de Borgona, you have a perplexed feeling of being transported to Florence. Other Spanish painters of the end of the fifteenth century hold their Flemish allegiance lightly, and seem like exiled Italian primitives. The best of this mixed sort is Rodrigo de Osona, the Elder, who probably studied both in Flanders and at such Flemish outposts in Italy as Urbino and Naples. His Calvary (Fig. 137), the upper panel of a retable in S. Nicolàs, Valencia, shows in its rugged portraiture the influence of Hugo van der Goes, but the fantastic landscape, with groups and figures in middle distance, suggests Northern Italy, and more particularly the work of Ferrarese masters whose style had been slightly influenced by Mantegna and Piero della Francesca. The faces of the young women are Italian in feeling, and the whole picture balances successfully between the Flemish and Italian manner. But there is no feeling of casual eclecticism. It is a serious work, and generally, saving always Bermejo, Rodrigo seems to be about the only Spanish primitive who can safely be confronted with his exotic models. Rodrigo worked chiefly in the Valencian region and trained many pupils who paved the way for the delightful semi-primitivism of Juan de Juanes.

With the exception of Toledo, the Castiles through the fifteenth and most of the sixteenth century were artistically barren regions. Here flourished abundantly the usual mediocre sort of Hispano-Flemish painting. But towards the end of the fifteenth century there appeared a very competent synthesizing spirit in Pedro Berruguete. Rather little is known about him, but the pictures ascribed to him have a quite extraordinary technical authority for Spain in the moment. Such a work as St. Peter Martyr in Prayer, at Madrid (Fig. 138), for its incisiveness and plastic emphasis would do no discredit to a Melozzo da Forlì. Indeed, the painter must have fortified himself by long and sound study of Italian painters who had profited by the austerity of Mantegna and by the strenuousness of good Flemish masters. Such influences prevailed in Italy only in Ferrara and Urbino, and we may safely assume that Berruguete had worked in either or both of these cities. Indeed he is almost certainly the "Pietro

Spagnuolo" who is recorded as an assistant of Melozzo at Urbino. His considerable ability in creating effects of space and constructing the figure did not reach to the composition of crowded groups. He remains then a sort of isolated academic apparition among the primitive painters of Spain. With better luck he might have been a pioneer, but the spell of the Early Italian Renaissance was soon broken, and the new Renaissance movement in Spain was to be a forced growth under less favorable auspices. Things were moving fast in Italy and this influence of the last phase of the Early Italian Renaissance was transient. Leonardo da Vinci had a Spanish disciple: Michelangelo, a Portuguese. Spain was soon to follow all Northern and Western Europe in obeisance and mimicry of what it took to be the grand style of Italy. And this is matter for another chapter.

CHAPTER X

PAINTING IN THE GERMANIES, SIX-
TEENTH CENTURY

FIG. 139. DÜRER. Four Apostles: John, Peter, Mark, Paul.—*Munich.*

Fig. 140. (Upper left) Dürer.  Self-Portrait (aet. 22).—*Paris.*
Fig. 141. (Upper right) Dürer.  Self-Portrait (aet. 27).—*Madrid.*
Fig. 142. (Lower left) Dürer.  A Young Woman.—*Berlin.*
Fig. 143. (Lower right) Dürer.  Hieronymus Holzschuher.—*Berlin.*

FIG. 144. DÜRER. Madonna of the Rose Crowns (old copy).—*Vienna.*

FIG. 145.  DÜRER.  Adoration of the Trinity.—Vienna.

FIG. 146. GRUENEWALD. Temptation of St. Anthony (l.). Visit of St. Anthony
and St. Paul (r.).—Colmar.

FIG. 147. GRUENEWALD. Annunciation and Nativity.—Colmar.

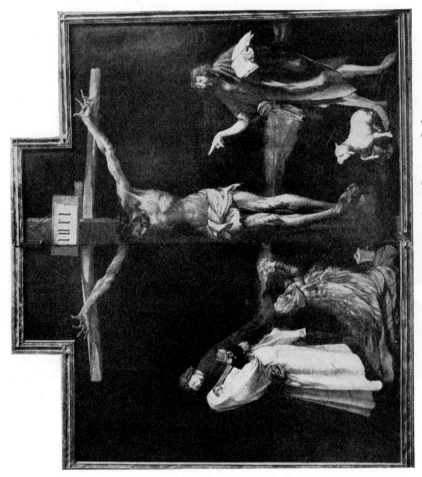

FIG. 148.   GRUENEWALD.   Crucifixion.—Colmar.

238

Fig. 149.  Holbein.  Benedikt von Hertenstein.—New York.

Fig. 150.  Holbein.  Bonifacius Amerbach.—Basel.

239

Fig. 151. Holbein. Madonna of the Meyer Family.—Darmstadt.

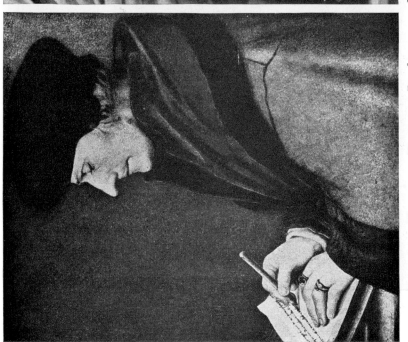

FIG. 152.   HOLBEIN.   Erasmus.—*Basel.*      FIG. 153.   HOLBEIN.   Sir Thomas More.—*Frick Collection, New York.*

FIG. 155. HOLBEIN. Christina
of Denmark.—London.

FIG. 154. HOLBEIN. Nicholas Kratzer.—Paris.

FIG. 156. HOLBEIN. Anne of Cleves.—Paris.

Fig. 157.   Holbein.   Catherine Howard.—
Toledo.

Fig. 158.   Holbein.   Catherine Howard (chalk
drawing reversed).—Windsor.

Fig. 159. Hans Baldung Grün. Nativity.—Frankfurt-am-Main.

Fig. 160. Altdorfer. Satyr Family.—Berlin.

245

FIG. 162. CRANACH. Rest on the Flight to Egypt.—Berlin.

FIG. 161. ALTDORFER. Rest on the Flight to Egypt.—Berlin.

246

FIG. 164. CRANACH. Judgment of Paris.— Karlsruhe.

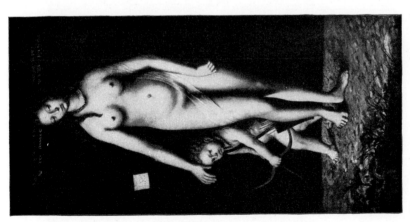

FIG. 163. CRANACH. Venus and Amor.—Leningrad.

247

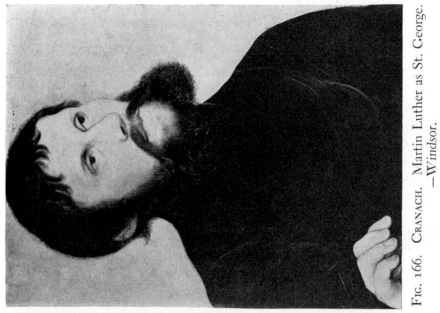

Fig. 166. Cranach. Martin Luther as St. George.
—Windsor.

Fig. 165. Cranach. Dr. Cuspinian.—Rinehart
Collection, Winterthur, Switzerland.

THE GERMANIES, on the whole a backward region in painting, in the first third of the sixteenth century suddenly took the lead among the transalpine nations. Only Italy at the moment could boast a trio comparable to Dürer, Holbein, Gruenewald. This lead was transient. After Holbein's death in 1543 the Germanies, so far as the art of painting was concerned, sank as abruptly into insignificance. To account for this historic fact is difficult, perhaps impossible. The usual simple explanations—the ferment of the Reformation, growing prosperity, etc.—do not serve us here. The great and the charming painters of the Germanies of this period worked far apart and under widely different conditions. As for the Reformation, if devotion thereto furthered the art of Dürer, so apparently did complete indifference thereto further the art of Holbein. In short, the usual explanations and correlations fail us, and we are driven reluctantly to Whistler's conclusion that art simply happens. Very often it happens in relation to environment. In the present case there is nothing in the environment of Colmar that accounts for such a miracle as Mathias Gruenewald, while even Nürnberg in the heyday of the new learning fails to explain why the son of a poor Hungarian goldsmith is remembered after four centuries as Albrecht Dürer.

To judge the artist, Albrecht Dürer, solely from his painting would be to get a fractional and quite false impression of his real greatness. His best, indeed practically all of his work of the first order, is in his drawings and engravings. To leave them out would be like judging Goethe, ignoring all his poetry, from his works in prose. There would emerge an impressive figure, but not Goethe. So in considering Dürer as a painter I must give some attention to his far greater accomplishment in the graphic arts.

For an artist who worked unflaggingly for some thirty-five years, the output of painting is surprisingly small. There are only about fifty pictures by Dürer, most of them bust portraits, and only three or four paintings that are either very large or very elaborate. Since he never lacked patronage, this lack of fecundity suggests some sort of temperamental inhibition. Possibly he belonged to that rare type of painter to whom the mechanical procedures of the art are distasteful. His great contemporary, Leonardo da Vinci, was like that. That this may have been Dürer's case is suggested by the famous letters concerning the Heller altarpiece, in which, under the artist's pride in his thorough workmanship, may be sensed both resentment at the toil involved and at the poor reward it received. But there is no hint that he found in any way irksome the long drawn out, meticulous and strenuous labor of engraving such plates as the Melancholia and the St. Jerome.

It was a formidable handicap to his career as a painter that he was born at the wrong time—about ten years too early or too late. Had he been born in 1461 instead of 1471, he might have worked out a massively German style entirely unperturbed either by pictorial influences from Italy or by that budding humanism at Nürnberg, which was to be as much a hindrance as a help to him. Had he been born in 1481, and studied in Italy in his flexible years, he might have effected some marvelous synthesis of the German and Italian styles, anticipating in some respects the service of Rubens. Dürer had the genius to do such a thing, but lacked opportunity. His long sojourn in Venice found him thirty-five years old, occurred at the moment of hesitation before such young geniuses as Giorgione and Titian had fairly announced themselves, found Dürer in a justifiably unteachable attitude of pride in his own matured workmanship, yet sufficiently sensitive to be perturbed for his remaining years by the glimpse of a serene beauty which he neither commanded nor even understood. In short, Father Time stacked the cards from the outset against Albrecht Dürer of Nürnberg.

He came up in a small way, the eldest son of an immigrant Hungarian goldsmith. The father was a shrinking, pious man, of small speech and companionableness. He unflinchingly begat sixteen children, most of whom mercifully perished in infancy. Albrecht was sent to school, but taken back into the shop as soon as he could read and write. How he looked in the shop we may gather from the careful silverpoint drawing at Vienna, which shows a doggedly serious little boy of thirteen, with forefinger extended, whether in exposition or rebuke. Young Albrecht turned towards painting, and his father reluctantly articled the boy to the eminently popular and prosperous middleman of painting and book illustration, Michael Wohlgemuth.

There, Dürer writes, "I had to suffer much from his 'prentice boys." Evidently the dogged little boy of the silverpoint sketch was sensitive, and a shining mark for Wohlgemuth's rowdy gang. From shrewd and probably friendly Wohlgemuth, of whom Dürer painted an amiable portrait many years later, nothing was to be learned but industry—a lesson Dürer never needed—and a sound Gothic technique. There followed, 1490–1494, the four *Wanderjahre* which qualified for the mastery. Recent investigation gives good reason to believe that he passed much of this time at Basel, where he drew for such woodcut books as *The Epistles of St. Jerome*, *The Ship of Fools*, by Sebastian Brandt, and *The Comedies of Terence*. Basel was on the direct route over the Brenner to Italy, and I believe Dürer must have slipped down to Venice during this period, though the dates do not tally with his statement of 1507 that what pleased him eleven years earlier no longer did so. I believe his "eleven years" was a mistake made in hasty writing to a friend. Late in 1493 or early in 1494 he may easily have been in Venice. He brought back what an inexperienced young man from the Gothic North might have gathered at random in a short trip to Northern Italy—some of the engraved Tarot cards, a print or two by Mantegna, a print or a copy of a drawing by Antonio Pollaiuolo—also a disturbing conviction that all was not well with the painting in which he had been bred at Nürnberg and Basel.

Returning to Nürnberg in the spring of 1494, Dürer found a marriage arranged with Agnes Frey, who brought him a much-needed dowry of two hundred florins, and apparently made him a good if not very understanding wife.

We may see the prospective bridegroom in a portrait at Paris (Fig. 140). The young man, richly dressed, clean shaven, with long hair, capped and disposed after a fashion that seems to me Italian, looks askance and somewhat mistrustfully, his strong, delicate hands hold the flower called in German *Mannestreue* (man's troth) and an inscription reads, "My affairs are as you see them below." It is a sad but also a most characterful portrait.

And here we may properly consider Dürer's portraiture as a whole. It begins with the pathetic and truthful likeness of his father, dated 1490, at Florence. The bust quite beautifully set in the frame, with fine spotting of the darks of the cap and partially exposed jerkin, is surmounted by a timid, patient face like that of a mild and resigned old woman. The shadows are slight and transparent, after good

Gothic precedent; the hands, unduly swollen by work or disease, fumble the big conversation beads—a Levantine solace for nervous fingers, brought from distant Hungary. The next portrait that deeply interests us is of Dürer himself, 1498, at Madrid (Fig. 141). He is finely dressed, with a striped, tasseled cap. The curled hair has grown down to the shoulders, a silky mustache and beard hardly conceal the fine mouth and chin. The construction is strongly linear, without palpable shadow. The right forearm rests easily on a window ledge, the hand nearly covered by the sensitively modeled fingers of the left hand. At the upper right another window gives upon a hilly landscape much simplified, not highly elaborated as in Dürer's later fashion. Here, possibly, is an influence from Italy. The expression is no longer mistrustful, as in his portrait as a bridegroom, but reserved and self-confident. The young husband has completed, or is about to complete, the most astounding woodcut book of a decade that produced many, the Apocalypse of St. John.

The portraits of succeeding years, such as those of Hans Tucher and his wife, at Weimar, and Oswolt Krell, at Munich, are handled in a similarly shadowless and linear fashion, are skillfully placed; all are too overinsistent and haggard in expression and without pleasing relations to the outlooks on minutely detailed landscapes. The young master is not yet at his ease in such work, and the strain of his effort is apparent.

On the wholly repainted background of Dürer's famous front-face portrait of himself, at Munich, we read the date 1500, and the age twenty-eight. But this is nonsense of some restorer, or possibly trickery of the copyist who long ago stole the portrait from Nürnberg. Such a change as we have from the jaunty self-portrait of 1498, at Madrid, implies the lapse of many well-filled years. The critics generally agree that this noble work has qualities of dignity, reserve and monumentality which date it either during or just after Dürer's Venetian sojourn of 1506. The rich costume may well be that of which he humorously brags in the Venetian letters to his friend Pirckheimer.

For the composition and graciously serene mood there can be little doubt that Dürer has reverently drawn his inspiration from some frontal bust portrait of Christ, by Giovanni Bellini, but even Bellini never painted so thoughtful a face. We feel an extraordinary power and composure—a mind which shirks nothing, but thinks things through. Such a man would create the great engraved allegories, would cope with fairness and without bitterness with the impending passions and fanaticisms of the Reformation. The clever, fantastically garbed young artist whom we saw in the self-portrait of 1498 has become the master; the artisan has become a gentleman, as Dürer wrote to Pirckheimer he had become, at Venice. It is one of the earliest Northern portraits that has an aristocratic accent, and on the technical side, which, since the interest of character preponderates, I neglect, it is the first Northern portrait that in style, and despite its exquisitely minute detail, in breadth, also, competes successfully with Italian portraiture on its own ground.

It is unnecessary to call the roll of the later portraits. They are well known, and their merits are obvious. With great emphasis of characterization they combine delicacy of feeling and workmanship. Perhaps the most attractive is that of a Young Woman, at Berlin (Fig. 142), which shows a remarkable assimilation of influences from Venice, perhaps was actually painted there. The mere make of it is of the utmost loveliness—firm linear construction, with broadly disposed and transparent shadows, beyond this, a sense of alertness, of shrewdness, of a sort of moral nobility without losing something that is merely dear and housewifely. Up to this time nobody but Leonardo da Vinci, not even the marvelous young Raphael, had made anything so distinguished, so pictorially accomplished.

Excellent for its gaunt shrewdness is Dürer's head of his master, Michael Wohlgemuth, at Munich. It shows, still very formidable at eighty-two, that sturdy artisan who had established a virtual monopoly of the profitable book-illustrating business of Nürnberg.

The last portrait I shall mention, that of the burgomaster, Hieronymus Holzschuher, 1516, at Berlin (Fig. 143), has a fairly startling vividness of character and an almost assertive picturesqueness. The fine, ruddy face is handsomely lined rather than disfigured by wrinkles; the eyes turned severely, even suspiciously, askance are bluer than the sky-blue background; the mask is framed by silvery hair and beard tinglingly crisp and alive; the general aspect is consciously stern, yet suggesting reserves of kindliness and good humor—all in all an admirable visualization not merely of this particular city magnate, but of that synthesis of qualities of physical and mental balance which goes to make a man of great affairs.

In the fifteen big woodcuts for the Apocalypse, 1498, designs which uniquely combined with sublimity a certain idiomatic homeliness, Dürer had made a magnificent beginning as a book illustrator. Such woodcuts were executed by others from his drawings on the block. His copperplate designs he entrusted to no others. For twenty years, from his twenty-fourth to his forty-fifth year, master-piece followed masterpiece, and while there is much gain in insight, there is singularly little in mere skill. The Holy Family with the Grasshopper, of 1495, probably his first copperplate, echoes the sweet-ness of his predecessor Schongauer and his delicate, open, linear workmanship, but it is as complete and masterly in its way as the in-effably luminous and silvery St. Jerome in his Study, of 1514, or as that incomparably precise and tonally subtle print, St. Anthony be-fore Nürnberg, of 1519. Between these extremes there lies rich ma-terial for a book, and good books on the prints abound. Here I need only remark the precosity of Dürer's development as an engraver, as compared with his slow development as a painter. Before 1500 he had engraved that marvel of fantastic alertness, the Little Courier, that fastidiously elegant nude, the Little Fortune. His phantasy also expressed itself early, in such mysteriously enigmatic symbols as the Dream, the Sea Monster, and the Nemesis.

In the years from 1500 on he was systematically making those drawings of the Life of Christ and of the Virgin which were to con-stitute his famous woodcut series—the Great and the Little Passion of Christ, the Life of the Virgin, and he was engraving on copper the Little Passion. All this effort came to a head in the marvelous year, his fortieth, 1511, when he reprinted the Apocalypse and pub-lished the Great and the Little Passion and the Life of the Virgin. Two years later followed the little copperplate Passion. The same year he finished that admirable allegory of Christian fortitude, the Knight, Death and the Devil, and was doubtless working on the great plates to be published in 1514, the Melancholia and the St. Jerome. Few artists have launched so many masterpieces in so short a time. From now on Dürer, who had known much hardship and the humiliation of chronic indebtedness, gained reasonable prosper-ity and enjoyed international acclaim. For a generation his prints were being pirated or forged or honestly copied in Germany, Flan-ders and Italy. Great Italian painters, such as Andrea del Sarto, Lorenzo Lotto, and Pontormo, were studying the style of his prints or borrowing details from them. A century and a half after Dürer's death a classically inclined painter, Nicolas Poussin, collected no less than 357 prints by Dürer.

As for the religious pictures of Dürer, I wish someone else would write the two or three following paragraphs. I simply lack the sense for this elaborate, often frozen, generally overemphatic art, and what in honesty I must write about it the reader should correct by consulting the works of more orthodox Dürerists. I never have been able to look long at the famous Paumgartner Nativity, at Munich, with its foreshortenings carrying the eye away from the group, its confusing throng of miniature donors and angels—details which, to the great improvement of the picture, a restorer promptly painted out, only to have his charitable effort undone in our own day. Nor do I like much better the brothers Paumgartner consciously and stiffly posing on the shutters as St. Eustace and St. George.

The unquestionable richness of the Epiphany, at Florence, leaves me completely cold. Everything seems to me separately felt and unrelated; the ornament bewildering and not expressive. The picture seems rather compiled than organized.

Much more interest attaches to the Madonna of the Rose Crowns, which Dürer painted for the German Trading Company, at Venice, in 1506. The repainted and ruined ghost of the original is in the Convent of Strahow, at Prague; an old copy at Vienna gives a better idea of this nearly departed glory (Fig. 144). Dürer, painting at Venice, was working among jealous rivals, in magnanimous competition with his friend, Venice's best painter, Giovanni Bellini—working for the honor of his race and for his own fame. His model for the great altarback was pretty surely Giovanni Bellini's idyllic yet monumental Madonna with Doge Barbarigo, at Murano. The oblong form, the landscape outlets beside a central cloth of honor, the symmetrical arrangement of the kneeling emperor and prelate—all this seems to come from the Murano altarpiece. Other Venetian features are the tree trunks dark against the sky and the winsome lute-playing angel at the foot of the throne. Everything is carried off with fairly Venetian balance and urbanity while retaining a not quite compatible homeliness of the North. The flanks of the picture are badly crowded by donors and supernumeraries. Here Dürer, to the detriment of his composition, probably had to obey the orders of his German patrons. All in all it is a highly intelligent example of quick assimilation—a variously charming rather than a great picture. The best details are the massively kneeling kaiser and the prelate; nearly all the other figures are a little too conscious of observation, particularly the angel with head sentimentally bent sidewise in appreciation of his own music.

The picture was carried through in the incredibly short space of five months, and Dürer was justifiably proud of it. He writes to Pirckheimer that people pay a ducat to see it, that he has gained great praise but little profit from it. But he has silenced the rival painters who declared him good as an engraver, but a poor colorist in painting. Now everyone says he has never seen more beautiful colors. In the ruined state of the picture we cannot say whether or not Dürer was self-flattering in this estimate of himself as a colorist. At least he had backers for his opinion.

Dürer returned to Nürnberg and a broader way of life. He had lifted a load of debt, had been treated for the first time as a gentleman, had even taken, at thirty-five, a couple of dancing lessons, had secured redress for the piracy of his engravings, had had the friendship of the greatest Venetian painter, Giovanni Bellini. He had missed a contact which might have been most useful to him, for Leonardo da Vinci, in many respects a kindred mind, was at Florence. Yet I feel he must at least have seen a sheet of Leonardo's caricatures, for Dürer's Christ among the Doctors, Barberini Gallery, at Rome, is a cluster of grotesque faces—a study in pure physiognomy, such as occupied Leonardo's leisure moments. Indeed this thoughtfully conceived work, with its sinister masks and central tangle of exquisitely expressive hands, may be regarded as a middle term between Leonardo da Vinci and Jerome Bosch.

Returning to Nürnberg, Dürer accelerated his work for the woodblock and his copperplate designs, with small concessions to his recent Italian admirations. We must remember that he thought himself superior to the Italian painters whose works he actually saw. But while his graphic art happily pursued its wonted course, his painting suffered from some uneasy feeling of the superior urbanity and monumentality of the great pictures he had seen at Venice. He undertook a great altarpiece of the Assumption of the Virgin for Jacob Heller, conducting it with infinite pains described in his letters, and at a financial loss. It has perished, but the old copy at Frankfurt shows the same hesitations that we have noted in the Madonna of the Rose Crowns. Almost everywhere there seems to have been lack of ease, overemphasis. The broadly treated classical draperies do not belong on the bodies they cover.

The beauty of the nude, perhaps glimpsed through Hellenistic marbles seen at Venice, for Venetian painting had not yet conquered this realm, haunted him. As study pieces he made an Adam and Eve. Dürer painted the forms with strenuous care, but achieved only far-fetched and even insipid pictorial expression. The engraving, which he had made three years earlier, in 1504, while too obviously a study piece, was really more pictorially attractive and significant.

Dürer's most ambitious and successful emulation of the grand style of Italy may be studied in the Adoration of the Trinity, at Vienna (Fig. 145), painted in 1511. The compositional form, a celestial circle of saints dominated by a divine figure in the center, had haunted Italian imagination from Giotto and Orcagna, through Fra Angelico, to Fra Bartolommeo, only thirteen years before Dürer's Trinity was painted. Probably Dante's celestial architecture, in the Paradiso, underlies such arrangements. Dürer has poised his ring of saints above a realistic lake scene, God the Father holding the crucified Christ is high in the center, separated by clouds from the worshiping martyrs, confessors, and saints. The severe symmetry of the composition is skillfully varied by showing the bodies in various aspects, by different directions of glances, by costumes of many sorts. For the picture Dürer designed an ornate frame in the style of the Florentine Renaissance. In the lower left of the panel he proudly painted himself, in tiny scale, standing garbed with a patrician's robes beside the inscribed tablet. It is hard to imagine anything at once more ornate, dignified and carefully considered. But, alas! a great picture needs more than this.

With the sort of composition Dürer chose it is hard to go wholly wrong. One asks of such a composition, do the figures hover lightly in air, seeming to belong there? are the saints at ease in heaven or merely posed there like plausible actors? is there a sense of that measured blitheness and ecstasy which Christian teaching associates with paradise? To all these questions, as regards Dürer's picture, I fear the answer is no.

In 1526 Dürer, though but fifty-five years old, was failing. There is a drawing at Bremen, in which he points to his liver, with an inscription: "Where the yellow spot is, where my finger rests, there is my disease." Wishing to leave a permanent memorial of himself to his native city, he painted on two panels the four apostles, St. John with St. Peter, St. Paul with St. Mark (Fig. 139), and in a modest letter of presentation gave them to the city council.

The stately figures, which most ungratefully Nürnberg promptly sold to the emperor, are now at Munich. Dürer has, so far as possible, sought the grandeur of such contemporary Italians as Fra Bartolommeo, Raphael, Andrea del Sarto, and adopts their formulas, setting the figures against a dark background and filling the space with them, insisting on the mass and weight and stability of the forms, casting the drapery in large classical folds. But from no saints imagined by Italian painters ever transpired the racy, individual character of Dürer's four apostles. This formidably personal character is both their quality and their defect. It makes them unforgettable, it also makes their classical garb artificial and inappropriate. They should either be more consistently stately and idealized in a generalizing way or more completely personal and idiosyncratic.

I feel some shame in caviling at these noble and powerful impersonations. These are almost the only convincing Protestant saints, simple folk with the smell of the fishing net and the tentmaker's wax still upon them. They are a world away from those idealized figures, creation of immemorial legend, which Italy loved. They are of the kidney of Dürer's friend and religious leader, the robust and somewhat gross Dr. Martin Luther. Dürer meant them to teach a lesson, and lest they should fail, provided an inscription bidding all secular potentates to avoid being deceived concerning God's word and will—"Therefore listen to these four admirable men: Peter, John, Paul and Mark; give ear to their Warning." Their warning was of the deceits of false prophets, of the coming of that Antichrist which Dürer had so graphically visualized twenty-eight years earlier in the Apocalypse, of the imminence of the awful day of judgment. In order not to offend the Catholics of Munich, the emperor, when he bought the picture, left the inscriptions behind at Nürnberg, where they still are.

A few years before these pictures were painted there was a pleasant interlude in Dürer's generally sober life in a trip to the Netherlands. The object was to sell his prints, and his wife Agnes served as a sort of secretary, while as usual providing for her great man's comfort. They visited Cologne, Ghent, Bruges, Antwerp, and other centers of art, always selling the prints well, painting or drawing a portrait occasionally, exchanging drawings with the local artists.

Dürer, to the least copper, duly sets down everything he spent on this journey. Apart from such thrifty entries, there is much of general interest in Dürer's diary. He was treated by the artists like a visiting prince. On St. Oswald's day the painters of Antwerp invited him to dinner with his wife and maid, their wives gracing the feast. The silverware and food were extravagantly fine. "As I was led to table, the people on both sides stood up, as if a great lord were being escorted." The counselors of Antwerp presented four cans of wine and offered their services.

Erasmus gave him a Spanish cloak and three portraits. He saw a magnificent procession for the Feast of the Assumption, the Three Kings riding on camels. At Antwerp he saw the bones of a giant, magnificent metal work and stuffs from Mexico; at Mechlin a Portuguese gave him three pieces of that unheard of rarity, porcelain. He manages to trade his prints for some of deceased Raphael's things, through a Polish assistant of Raphael. At Aachen, in Charlemagne's cathedral, he notes the columns were brought from Rome and proportioned according to Vitruvius. At Cologne he bought a small ivory death's head for a florin. Off Middelburg he was nearly shipwrecked, but when the mainsail blew away, manfully helped haul up the storm sail. At Antwerp again, he made a mummer's mask for an English gold crown, and saw a walrus.

At Bruges the painters dined him, the burgomaster presented twelve cans of wine, and the whole company of sixty saw him home by torchlight.

To Antwerp came a false report of Luther's death, and Dürer writes five pages of wailing and prayer to God, exhorts Erasmus to become the champion and leader of pure Christianity.

I have cited enough, I hope, to make the reader wish to look up this diary, which amusingly reveals the shrewd tradesman in the great artist. It records joys and honors that it must have been pleasant for Dürer to recall as premature old age fell upon him. The last four or five years were largely given to writing on mensuration and perspective, books which were reprinted for the use of artists in many languages and for many years. He died in early spring of 1528, in his sixtieth year.

Reviewing this extraordinary career, the creative period lies between 1497 and 1515, from his twenty-sixth to his forty-sixth year. Very little work of great significance falls outside of this span, and the work that has lived on was in engraving. His painting was an episodical and probably an uncongenial activity. For its seriousness and probity one must deeply respect it, but one can admire it only with reservations, and one cannot love it at all. As one of the keys to a very noble and solidly German character one must study the paintings, just as one must study those thoughts which Dürer jotted down about his art. We may well take leave of him with a selection from these thoughts which cast light upon the greatness and limitations of the man:

"Never, never imagine thou canst or willst make anything better than God has given his creature, nature, power to make."

*        *        *

"No powerful artist will give himself exclusively to one art, but he must be practiced and competent in many directions and in the arts all and sundry."

A few years earlier Leonardo da Vinci had insisted that the artist must be universal.

*        *        *

Again: "Verily art hides in nature; who can pull art out, he it is who has her."

This is about the principle of selective imitation preached from Leonardo da Vinci to Poussin.

*        *        *

Our last quotation is of pathetic sort and suggests at least one cause of the great engraver's frustration as a painter:

"Alas! How often I see great art and good things in sleep, the like of which do not present themselves to me waking. But as soon as I awake, their memory slips away from me."

Happily Dürer's graver recalled and held fast many a great dream which escaped his diligent brush.

Plato has written that the poet creates in a divine madness, but common sense tells us that this frenzy is not the whole of the process. Alone it will produce only disorderly and confused ejaculation and not poetry. Poets occasionally go mad, but madmen never emerge as poets.  It seems then that poetry requires that the expansive emotion indispensable to it should be accompanied by some shaping principle of discipline.  It is the critical judgment—that *giudizio* so highly extolled by Leonardo da Vinci, which ultimately imposes upon the poet's most passionate expression that fitness of form which assures it permanency.  If this close alliance of a kind of excitement with serene judgment be necessary in an art that involves no more technical or manual difficulties than are implied in speaking or writing, then it should be doubly true in the case of such arts as demand a prolonged and difficult training of the eye and hand.  The painter may well need selective judgment more than the poet.  His synthesis of feeling and form is more complicated; his mistakes more irreparable.  And this means that the good and even the great picture are made at much lower pressure and temperature than the layman, with his always romantic misconception of the artist, imagines.

But now and then we find a painter who seems to be able to create at frenzied tension while avoiding confusion and remaining articulate.  His divine madness seems to carry with it the necessary organizing discipline, the whole creative act seeming to rest on a sort of possession by a higher power.  With such painters it is foolish to think of passion and judgment as separate factors in creation; at every moment and every point they interact, as upward explosive force and the downward pull of gravitation interact to adorn an erupting volcano with its sublime smoke tree.  Such painters are so rare that criticism generally classes them as abnormal, which is right enough if the term be used descriptively and not, as too often, disparagingly.  Among these fiery spirits one thinks of El Greco, and then of Vincent van Gogh.  Such also was Mathias Gruenewald of Aschaffenburg, whose passionate Christian lyricism allies him to El Greco as his amazing color orchestration to Van Gogh.  He seems to me the greatest artist that the North produced before Rubens and Rembrandt.  And here I am not thinking in terms of technical greatness, in which the North ever abounded, but in terms of greatness of the imagination.

When we consider just the make of any picture by Gruenewald, we find that, unlike all the Gothic work we have been considering, it is entirely painterlike.  About it there is no sense of a colored drawing; it is felt in color.  Then it will seem that Gruenewald has about four times the technical resources of his ablest contemporaries, say

Dürer and Massys. Gruenewald's line is never thought of separately; it is an edge where one form meets another. These edges are of the utmost strength and subtlety; they change direction and meaning incessantly; they tell of mass, of anatomy, of lighting, and above all, of feeling. They model with the authority of bronze and disappear in blurs which tell of the forms of landscape, of the natural or miraculous movement of clouds. And these quivering, form-making, emotionally expressive contours which seem so spontaneous really rest upon severe studies, for there are numerous chalk drawings by Gruenewald, some of them closely observed records of appearances, others warped and tortured in the tense spirit of the paintings. His figure construction runs from sculptural massiveness to the flat spectral indications that denote a risen Christ.

Where the older and contemporary pictures had a more or less fixed and decorative color scheme, usually based on the immemorial Gothic balance of azure and crimson, the pictures of Gruenewald have each its own color scheme, which is a special language or symbolism expressing, as it may be, dignity, awe, ecstasy, contemplation, measured grief, consternation, or horror unmitigated. In short, the color, which materially is often the most splendid, is not just an attribute of the forms, but an eloquent symbol of the dominating emotion. Where an obscure lad from the Middle Rhine got the idea of such a color is mysterious, and our ordinary search for master and influence utterly fails. Strictly speaking, such affluence of meaningful color had its sole existence in Mathias Gruenewald's eye, but it is permitted to guess that study of the ever-shifting glories of stained glass may have suggested such an extension and enrichment of the inherently poorer resources of painting.

We have nothing of Gruenewald earlier than his late thirties, and the two monumental pictures of male saints at Munich merely tell us of the audacity and entire novelty of his construction and coloring, while the half-dozen or so pictures at Aschaffenburg, Karlsruhe, Basel and Munich, which follow his masterpiece of 1511, hint of exhaustion in their creator and really add nothing to his stature. We find him complete in the altarpiece, now at Colmar, painted between 1509 and 1511 for the Church of the Antonine Convent of Isenheim. To the Isenheim altarpiece we may then confine our studies.

It is really a very elaborate painted tabernacle with ten panels, depicting eight subjects, and folding as a double layer over a central panel in which a St. Anthony Abbot, a St. Jerome and a St. Anthony, with a predella of a blessing Christ with the apostles, are represented in polychromed woodcarving of great monumentality. This work is by a Savoyard sculptor. Since the painted wings have pictures on both sides, as they are successively closed three separate compositions are revealed, and while it is not quite certain that the arrangement by Dr. H. U. Schmid, which I follow, corresponds to the original, still it provides an unfolding of the great work which is as varied as that of a symphony, and as impressive.*

When the altarpiece is fully opened, the double shutters turned back, the mood is *andante*. We see the three majestically arranged figures in an open symmetry, and above the central figure of St. Anthony, like grace notes playing about a solemn theme, a most complicated lace-like Gothic tracery, which at once enhances and relieves the static majesty of the carved figures.

The two flanking shutters are mostly in modulated grays which do not compete with the gilding and polychromy of the sculptured forms. Topically they are in the nature of commentary, explaining how agony of temptation and austerity of solitary contemplation preceded Anthony's apotheosis as a saint. In the Temptation (Fig. 146), on the left, St. Anthony, still grasping his rosary, is buffeted, pinched, and tossed about in a confusing welter of the most hideous and malignant devils. Horrid yet fascinating detail, a bloated and pustulent leper, though almost unable to move himself, has managed to filch the hermit's holy and consoling books. Those sensual temptations of which the legend tells, Gruenewald eliminates. He presents not those lesser allurements of the flesh to which, merely as human animals, we are all subject, but rather those more grisly and destructive phantoms which are evoked by and frightfully haunt the unsanctified and even the sanctified mind.

In the right-hand panel the ordeal is over, and Anthony, decorously clad and seated in a pleasant wilderness, consults his fellow hermit, St. Paul (Fig. 146). He is gaunt and horribly wasted; two shy fawns crowd to his knees. With outstretched, contorted hand and eagerly raised face he bids Anthony seek peace by becoming as selfless as these innocent beasts. The setting is crags and dead trees

---

* It is regrettable that this arrangement has recently been changed, apparently only to avoid opening and closing the shutters.

with drooping moss; the color ranges from cool gray to violet in a manner strangely anticipating Velasquez's treatment of the same subject nearly two centuries and a half later. This whole aspect is a kind of solemn prelude to the lyrical outburst which follows as we turn the painted shutters inward and reveal their backs.

Here the mood is the most vivacious *allegro*, slowed in the Annunciation, rising to a solemn shrillness in the Resurrection. The central panels offer two subjects. At the left Mary awaits the Annunciation in prayer, in a rich Gothic chapel, while attendant angels play a trio on stringed instruments, and tiny, expectant cherubs hover in the dusk under the vaults (Fig. 147). The peasantlike faces of the playing angels are glorified by a flamelike adoration. The robe of the angel who kneels in the foreground while playing a kind of cello is of cherry red shot with pale yellow—perhaps the most blithe and audacious passage of color in all painting.

At the right, Mary, the roseate reflections of her blue robe echoing the keen tints of that of the playing angel, sits in the open while she dandles her naked Child (Fig. 147). Her robe is cast in large, powerful folds, which one is tempted to call, by anticipation, baroque, quite unlike the contemporary angular formulas based on wood sculpture, and equally unlike the tranquil arrangements of the contemporary Italians. In the contrast of colorful darks with most luminous lights one is reminded of El Greco. Behind is a hint of landscape with castellated crags and distant serrated mountains. From a kind of storm cloud, above which one divines the gigantic spectral mask of God the Father, distant herald angels shoot down with the velocity of reversed rockets to deliver their glad tidings to the shepherds. Though the face of Mary is radiant with worship and love, she has not forgotten the maternal essentials. They are there—in the form of the tub with its neatly disposed towel, the well-tended crib and the quite beautifully shaped and decorated chamber pot. A crisply painted rose tree and a garden gate tell us that Mary is the rose of roses and, for her intact virginity, a closed garden. These two pictures built around a gamut of reds like those of sunrise offer one of the strangest and most captivating color arrangements existent.

In the outside left-hand panel, the Annunciation, sparkling *allegro* yields to a graver tempo. While the ecstatic scene of the preparation for the Annunciation takes place in a fantastic, flamboyant interior, the tremendous rite of the Annunciation itself is in a simple Gothic interior of older style. Mary recoils in fear from the celestial messenger—"she was sore afraid," we read in St. Luke's Gospel—and her fingers, which had been joined in prayer, begin to clasp each other in trepidation. The archangel Gabriel, nearly descended to the pavement, is so earnest in his message that his sign of blessing becomes an ungainly pointing gesture. The flying folds of his mantle seem at once to ease his descent and in their flamelike forms to carry his message towards Mary.

The Resurrection, outside right-hand panel, is presented as a kind of second birth. Of the many interpretations of the theme, it is the most theatrically effective. The Christ before a circular glory of prismatic hues is a wraith anchored to earth only by the cerements heavier than his body which still connect him with the open tomb. The mailed guards are contorted in helpless consternation. The light snaps with almost painful sharpness from the bosses of their plate armor. The Resurrection is a fact, but Gruenewald sees it like the Roman soldiers, as an appalling apparition. The impassioned utterance and the blue-black murkiness of the night form the transition to the final revelation, the Calvary, which, to pursue our symphonic analogy, is conducted as a tremendous *maestoso*—in a mood of intensest tragedy. It appears as the two outside panels are turned inward.

The five figures constituting the Calvary (Fig. 148) are forced out violently from the gloom by a light which fairly smashes upon them from the front. It is the effect of a stage with a group picked out by a spotlight in the gallery. Against and within the blackness, white areas gleam sensationally, all faces and hands, the ample robe of Mary, the book of St. John the Baptist, the downward curved crosspiece of the cross, while in the distance on the horizon a bleak light of the most tragic of dawns slightly invades the lower murkiness of the sky and steals forward over barren hills. The central, but not quite the strongest light, is reflected from the tortured body of Jesus. No detail of horror is spared. Lips, hands and feet are swollen and distorted, spines from the crown of thorns stick everywhere in a body which sweats blood from every pore. The head sinks far down against the breast; the weight of the body spreads the arms upward in a sort of Y. With all these unsparingly horrible details, the merely visual effect is singularly noble and even monumentally serene. And the artist has deliberately calculated this effect. While the sinking

down of the heavy body would inevitably have spread the legs wide
apart in an ugly fashion, Gruenewald has, defying facts and logic,
kept the knees together, giving to the whole body of Christ that sense
of growing actively upward from the joined feet which we get from
any good Crucified Christ of Italian make. The strongly and most
variously modulated contours of Christ's body give it at once tremendous plastic effect, and a singularly life-communicating force. One
shares the controlled tremor with which these edges were painted.
Much of the dignity of the Christ depends on the careful arrangement of the loin cloth—a detail which Gruenewald himself neglected
in his later Crucifixions, much to their detriment. In expressing utmost horror within the bounds of beauty Gruenewald finds few peers
among painters, finding his fellows rather among the tragic dramatists
of Greece.

Apart from such stylistic attenuations of the horror of the scene,
there are fine balances of a spiritual order. The group at the left,
Mary, St. John and the Magdalene, do not oppress us with their
grief, for however shattering to them, it imposes itself less than the
insensate torture of the Man-God. One may say that this group sorrows for us vicariously, and thus drains off our own excessive emotion so that we may view the mere spectacle with the detachment
necessary to discern its strange beauty. Incidentally this group gives
strongest evidence of the painterlike methods of Gruenewald. Unlike his contemporaries, he refused to be bound by his working drawing or the panel, and made changes and corrections as the painting
proceeded. The form of Mary was originally upright with eyes open.
The more poignant and decorative position we now see was a second
thought.

Another attenuation of what is merely horrible in this great picture is the unflinching detachment of St. John the Baptist on the
left. Of course his presence is merely symbolical, indeed he seems
rather a wraith than a man, and his feeling transcends human pity, for
as he points fixedly at the Christ, and repeats his own words, "He
must increase, and I must decrease," he has before him the whole
new vista of the ever-continuing drama of redemption.

Returning to decorative issues, which in Gruenewald, for all his
mental and emotional appeal, are never to be ignored, the general
spotting of white on murky, dun blacks is punctuated by only two
areas of pure color, the small display of scarlet in the robe of the

apostle John, and the large, shimmering expanse of a fairly incandescent reddish orange in the dress of the Magdalene. It is at once the resplendent focus of a calculated color effect, and a symbol for a consuming grief.

The sonorous and tragic chords of the Calvary diminish into a quietly pathetic finale in the Deposition of the predella. It is unexpectedly composed, Christ's limp body and the heads of the three mourners at the right, finding their balance only in the rigid block of the open tomb, at the left, with an outlook above it towards bare crags, and a barren river valley. Christ's body has not yet assumed the rigidity of a corpse; the head and shoulders supported by John, it forms a gracious curve which is variously repeated or opposed in the bent heads and shoulders of the three attendants, and in the splayed spreading sides of the panel. The outrage done to the body by scourging and by the nails is still apparent, but no longer painfully so. The grief expressed in the faces runs from solicitude in John to resignation in Mary and wailing in the Magdalene, but nothing of this is emphasized, and the whole impression is both noble and serene. As in the Calvary, the spotting of light spots against a dark background is positively calculated and most picturesque, but the contrasts are less sharp. The symphony moves to a close in an *andante*, as it began, now impassioned, but not too much.

We have ignored the flanking panels, a St. Anthony Abbot, and a St. Sebastian, and indeed, although they are very characterful, one hardly notices them. They seem to belong not to the world of the picture, but to our world, merely as very distinguished members of that cloud of witnesses which through the centuries has attested the saving efficacy of the sacrifice on Calvary. They may be said to indicate the two ways to sainthood—the short road through martyrdom, the long road through contemplation and endurance of tribulation. To the monastery which commissioned the work they meant more: St. Anthony was their patron, St. Sebastian their guarantor against pestilence. For us he has the great interest of representing the moody, melancholy face of Mathias Gruenewald himself.

Merely looking at this pictorial symphony involves that high emotional tension with which we listen to the sublimest music—say, Bach's St. Matthew's Passion. We turn from it with a sigh of relief which lets us down to the level of our ordinary living. To find any true analogy for the expenditure of creative energy required to make such a work one may not think in terms of single pictures but rather in terms of famous ensembles—Signorelli's Chapel of the Last Judgment; Michelangelo's ceiling for the Sistine.

Reviewing one's most general impressions of this great masterpiece, what sets it apart not only from the painting of its time but from almost all painting in Europe is its most various and equally sustained vitality. There is no quiet spot—everything is dynamic, the sculptured prophets as much as the demons, the flowers and shy animals as much as the shattered Mary, the clouds as much as the Gothic vaultings. In this pervading dynamism Gruenewald either surpasses or transgresses the bounds of European painting, which usually requires a balance of active and inert objects. In Gruenewald, as in the great painters of China and Japan, the balance is of force with force. European painting was rarely to seek this dynamic balance. There is much of it in Tintoretto and perhaps more in Rubens, but to seek a real European analogy for the richness and variety of such complete energizing of a picture surface, one must come about sixty years down the ages to El Greco.

Concerning Mathias Gruenewald's life we know almost nothing. He was born at Aschaffenburg, on the Middle Rhine, about 1468, and we begin to have notices of his works only when he was past fifty. More than a century after his death an admirer, the German painter and art historian, Joachim Sandrart, bemoaned the fact that so great an artist had wholly passed out of memory. He adds, from what source he does not tell us, that Gruenewald "lived, mostly in Mayence, a solitary and melancholy life and was wretchedly unhappy in his marriage." This may be true, but it sounds like a reverberation of the legend that ever since Socrates' Xantippe has tended to pillory the wives of geniuses. In fairness it should be said that no corresponding roster of geniuses who were inadequate husbands has ever been drawn up.

Of Mathias Gruenewald we have no notices after 1529 and by 1531 he is mentioned as dead. He had lived only a couple of years beyond sixty, a long life, for one lived at perilously high pressure. Since his works were in remote, provincial cities, and when seen offended the classicized taste of the sixteenth century, he was soon forgotten. It has remained for rather recent criticism to restore to him that pre-eminence as an artist equally passionate and thoughtful which he had so arduously earned.

The most famous, on the whole, of German painters was a man of very different type from Dürer and Gruenewald. That Hans Holbein was born at Augsburg seems a kind of accident. One hardly thinks of him as German. He passed from country to country as interest dictated. A sojourn in France taught him a better way of preparing a portrait and gave him a profitable relation with the publishers of Lyons. His entire working career was only about twenty-five years, of which eleven were passed in distant England. We have no intimation that he ever indulged a strong emotion. There is no such episode in his scant biography as Dürer's prostrating grief over his aged mother's death or the outcry of despair when word came that Luther was gone. No word of Holbein concerning the principles of his art or the bases of morality has been preserved; there is no record of scientific curiosity. As to his religion, we do not know if he professed any faith with conviction. His morality was no better than that of the average sensual man. While we should not argue dogmatically from the absence of evidence, there is every reason to believe that Hans Holbein lacked the soul of a great artist, being merely a great painter, and one of the first of cosmopolitan type.

We think of him as a portrait painter, and he was one of the greatest, but his book decorations and illustrations, and his mural painting at Basel and Lucerne, destroyed, but dimly known to us through copies, would constitute alone a notable career for most painters. There never was a more placid and efficient diligence. Of discontent with the difficulties of his art, Dürer's constant note— not a word. His icy perfection was apparently achieved without effort.

He was born at Augsburg in 1497, and trained there as a painter by his father, with his elder brother, Ambrose. His general education must have been of the slightest, for from seventeen he was busily occupied as a painter. The imperial city of Augsburg was a center of Italian influence. Those international bankers, the Fuggers, were, like international bankers of all times, good patrons of painting. They were in constant touch with Italy, especially with Lombardy and Venice. Hans Burgkmair, most prominent painter of Augsburg, settled there after an Italian trip, bringing with him a repertory of Italian ornamental patterns, the heavy chiaroscuro and rather sentimental forms of the Milanese painters. He was the leading influence as the boy Hans Holbein grew into young manhood. No wonder

then that Holbein's first datable picture, a feeble little Madonna at
Basel, rests vaguely upon Mantegna for its forms, and offers a painted
border with nude geniuses clambering among Renaissance candelabra
and paired dolphins.

The next year Holbein painted the large Crossbearing, now at
Karlsruhe.  It is a drastic, crowded and sensational piece, of smallest
artistic merit, but it shows an amazing technical power for a lad of
eighteen.  Everything is forced out by heavy shadow after the correct
Italian fashion.  A little later he painted a big serving tray for Hans
Baer.  Hard use has ruined the original, as we still see it at Basel,
but good line copies tell us that it already evinced the fine decorative sense that never deserted Holbein.  The jolly jousts, hunting and
fishing scenes about the wide border, the odd forms of animals,
flowers and implements, light against the dark central oblong, are
spotted in with the vivacity, and have the brittle harmony, of contemporary Indo-Persian miniature painting.  Much could be expected from the youngster who, not yet out of his teens, could paint
the Crossbearing and this tray.

Already the good portrait painter that his father's son was bound
to be was asserting himself.  To be sure, the busts of Jakob Meyer
and his wife, at Basel, are pretty inert, and overloaded with Italianate
architectural accessories, but the character is there and the details
are exquisitely realized.  Again, the half-length of Benedikt von
Hertenstein, at New York (Fig. 149), painted when Holbein was
twenty, has something of that unpleasing aggressiveness which characterizes much Early-German portraiture.  Apparently the Early-
German sitter carried a chip on his shoulder, wanted to be taken for
upper-middle and not lower-middle class.  But all the same, the
Hertenstein, for its pellucid color, its delicate modulation of lights
and darks, its eminently decorative pattern—is a very distinguished
work.

In the absence of documentary evidence, frequent reminiscences
of actual buildings in Lombardy and clear echoes of Lombard painting in Holbein's work assure us that at twenty-one he crossed the
Alps and studied in Northern Italy.  Thereafter the Mantegnesque
perspective was a constant, while the sweetness of such imitators of
Leonardo da Vinci as Luini and Gaudenzio Ferrari was an occasional
influence upon him.

It is probable that his frescoes for the house front of his friends, the Hertensteins, at Lucerne, were begun before and finished after the Italian journey. The fashion of decorating façades elaborately came up from the Venetic region. Time and weather play havoc with such decoration, and of Holbein's we have only a figure or two, some of his own drawings, and sketch copies made from the ruined frescoes a century ago. These tell us that the simple Gothic front was converted into a three-story framework by painted pilasters of classical type, the resulting oblongs being pictured with such subjects as a stag hunt, a battue of partridges, a coursing of hares by grey-hounds, a wagon crowded with noisy beggars, a fountain of youth well filled with nude bathers, the old folk being brought along in litter or wheelbarrow. There were friezes of playing nude geniuses, plentiful swags of laurel in good Italian style. The whole effect must have been more playful and charming than really decorative, and we glimpse here and there the sardonic humor that was later to leave its eternal monument in the woodcuts of the Dance of Death.

Within a year or two, at Basel, Holbein frescoed the front of the house which was to receive the name, the House of the Dance. Here his new lore in perspective was given full swing. The Gothic front was painted away into an elaborate pavilion of the Roman Corinthian order, seemingly open to the air on both sides. Figures strolled behind the balconies; statues crowned the projecting capitals; a foreshortened horse and rider reared perilously over the portal; the long lower frieze was occupied by peasants madly dancing. What had been a façade became an animated world. Ultimately the exemplar for this illusionistic decoration was Mantegna. It was an amazing expression both of inventiveness and technical resourcefulness, and while its taste might be challenged, Holbein was modest when he declared it "fairly good," *ein wenig gut.*

To complete this sketch of Holbein's mural painting at Basel, in 1523 he decorated the assembly hall of the town council with stories from classical antiquity and the Bible. Happily Basel still treasures Holbein's composition sketches, from which it is easy to see that these designs had force and dignity, with stately architectural features. Evidently these were the first mural paintings in the Renaissance manner that had yet been produced north of the Alps, and it is doubtful if they have been greatly surpassed by any later artist of the North.

Meanwhile Holbein had been busy designing title pages and

making models for those sheets of stained glass (*Scheibe*), which it was the fashion to hang in windows. He had painted a sensational Passion series—Christ in the Garden, His Arrest, His Scourging, Pilate washing his Hands. The types are drastic and sinister to grotesqueness—a young man's overemphasis. The light flashes about effectively in most theatrical fashion. These panels at Basel attest a visit of Holbein to his father, at neighboring Isenheim, where Gruenewald's masterpiece had lately been unveiled. As compared with the ecstasy and terror of his exemplar, Holbein's emotion seems forced and not instinctive, but it is forced with great ability, if also with just a touch of vulgarity.

In October of 1519 Holbein signed his first great portrait, that of the humanist, Bonifacius Amerbach (Fig. 150). It is hardly more than a miniature, but it is very large in feeling. The handsome, bearded face is presented in lost profile; the spotting of the cap and fur-collared robe is highly picturesque; just the bole of an oak bearing an inscribed tablet and the gnarled twigs with their leaves against a blue sky give a sufficient sense of out-of-doors. The mood is gentle and thoughtful, the handling easy and painterlike, with little dependence on the contour. Seeing it from afar in the gallery at Basel, one might be excused for thinking it a fine North-Italian portrait, of the sensitive type which we associate with Lorenzo Lotto or Moretto of Brescia. Nothing could be more unlike those nervously linear and austere portraits which Holbein was before long to make in England.

Two years later he finished that grim masterpiece, at Basel, the Dead Christ in His Tomb. For greater effect of emaciation he has stretched the prone stark body to the impossible proportions of nearly ten heads. The grisliness of the theme is much attenuated by the exquisite drawing of the extremities, by the subtle modulation of the fine contours, by the breadth and tenderness with which the light is made to model the rigid forms. An artist who can create such a thing is limited only by his own heart and head. His eye and hand are infallible, at twenty-four.

Other Passion pictures of this period at Basel and at Münster we must pass with bare mention. Behind them in their picturesque backgrounds of towering ruins lies admiration of the painters of Piedmont, possibly Defendente and Gaudenzio Ferrari. Worthy of more particular mention is the Nativity, at Münster, with the light emanating from the Child and picking out the faces of pilasters and soffits of broken arches, while high above a veiled moon is about to break through the clouds it illumines. Here is something of Gruenewald and even more of the eminently picturesque Hans Baldung Grün.

Having succeeded in the picturesque, Holbein turned to the monumental. In the Madonna with a Bishop and Military Saint, at Solothurn, Holbein adopted the most usual of Italian symmetrical compositions, setting the group under a fine arch tied together with iron rods and open to the sky. The sweet and rather insipid Madonna and the well-grown, lively Child recall Gaudenzio Ferrari. The color is inharmonious. Holbein's innovation lies in keeping the Madonna massive and lower than the flanking figures, in the chivalric pose of steel-clad St. Ursus and his banner bright against the sky, in the compassionate gentleness of the bishop saint giving alms. It is the creation of an independent spirit seeking Italian monumentality, but seeking it on the artist's own terms.

About four years later was painted his greatest religious picture, the Madonna of the Meyer Family, at Darmstadt (Fig. 151). It completes the effort nearly achieved in the Solothurn Madonna—to gain a real monumentality without waiver of homely and idiomatic character. The motive, the Madonna in a niche, with lateral outlets to the sky varied by tree fronds, may hark back to Giovanni Bellini or to some altarpiece of his school. The Madonna herself is not Italianate, but a substantial Swabian mother, and the Child is not a Christian symbol, but a chubby German infant gesturing at random in baby fashion to the people below. Characteristic for Holbein is the density of the pyramidal group, with no sense of crowding, and the physical and moral weight with which they bear upon the rug and pavement. The motive is that of the Madonna of Pity, covering and protecting her worshipers with her mantle. Three of the worshipers have already received this benefit in heaven—the two boys before the kneeling father, Meyer's deceased wife with her chin bound like a corpse. The plain little girl kneeling in front is the sole heir.

The ardor of Jakob Meyer's prayer seems to fill the picture, and he prays not ceremoniously, like an Italian donor, but huddled down in humility, as one who sorely needed and confidently expected an answer to his prayer. The color is more rich and contrasted than in Italian altarpieces of this time and type. Decorative effect is achieved not as an end in itself, but through exquisite truth telling. Nearly a century before Caravaggio, Holbein attempted to depoetize a religious theme, to make it contemporary and near us, and, in my opinion, did it much better. I have suggested that Holbein's own religious experience may have been perfunctory; at least the man who created the Madonna of the Meyer Family had an imagination that understood sympathetically that expansion of the soul towards some higher power which we call prayer.

Holbein was about twenty-nine when he finished this great picture, and had he died that year, all historians of art would outdo themselves in extolling his extraordinary versatility. As a painter he had vied with Gruenewald and left Dürer clearly behind. In view of these facts there is something disconcerting in his declension into an official portrait painter, who occasionally was a good mural painter and an admirable illustrator.

In 1523 and 1524 the most interesting man in Europe, Erasmus, sat no less than three times to Holbein. The gentlest and wittiest of liberals—the harsh word reformer does not suit Erasmus—had been living at Basel with his publisher, Froben, since 1521. Probably the first portrait of Erasmus is the little half-length in profile at Basel (Fig. 152). The great scholar is represented as intent on his writing, the beginning of his paraphrase of the Gospel of Mark. The prevailing mood is that of patience—and indeed patience in that age of raw passions was a difficult virtue to maintain. The famous profile at Paris is merely the Basel study elaborated into a picture, by providing an easier and more spacious composition and rich accessories in the form of a pilaster and a brocaded wall hanging. This background, prevailingly green, gives warmth to the pallid face and to the cool brown of the fur collar. The many verticals in the background give liveliness to the contours of the profile and make the head seem to bend more positively towards the well-fleshed, busy hands. The irregular spot of white formed by the paper echoes the rather angular pattern of the fine face. The whole handling is less linear than that of the study at Basel. Indeed, one may say there is nothing specifically local or Northern about the effect. Depicting a notable cosmopolitan, the artist has appropriately cosmopolitanized his own handiwork. While the picture is treated factually, choosing such a variety of facts as will please the eye, it is also a kind of symbol of the laborious tranquillity of the true scholar's life.

Probably only a few months later is the half-length, three-quarter face portrait at Longford Castle, England. Here the accessories count for much; a curtain, a shelf with books and a carafe, a Renaissance pilaster with a siren in the capital. Erasmus, in a velvet robe with magnificent fur linings well exposed, is here represented as a sort of prince of scholars, quietly awaiting the homage that had never failed him. The eyes are unfocused, the fine, worn face impassive. No work is in progress. The delicate hands finger, almost caress, one of his books, the title of which, *The Labors of Hercules*, you may read in Greek letters on the gilt edge. The beautiful contours do the work of modeling, colors are kept in large, flat areas as a sort of pattern. Compositional refinements abound—the slight rake of the curtain pole, answering the diagonal perspective of the big book, and the slant of the book on the shelf. The bracket of the shelf repeats the volutes of the capital, the verticals stabilize these diagonal elements and the subtle curvilinear contours of the cap, head, shoulders and hands. It is a work of impeccable taste and selectiveness, and again the feeling is cosmopolitan, not Northern.

We may note here that when Holbein painted a European he generally produced what is technically called a *portrait d'apparat*, that is, with abundant appropriate accessories. When, later, he painted an Englishman, he generally eschewed accessories and preferred a background of uniform hue. This difference perhaps merely represents the respective taste of the two patronages. But there may be another reason. From a letter of Erasmus dated July 3, 1524, we learn that Holbein, who is with some understatement described as "a by no means unskilled artist," had gone to France. There he surely saw the portraits of the Clouets, and their summary and delightful preparations for portraits in colored chalks. Holbein himself promptly adopted colored chalks in drawing from the life, as a material yielding quicker pictorial effect and more tractable than the pen, silver point or wash, which he had previously used. Doubtless he also noted the happy decorative effect which the well-chosen green, blue, or red backgrounds of the Clouets lent to their small portraits. In any case, such simple and effective backgrounds are the rule in the portraits which Holbein was later to paint in England. During the trip he must have made the acquaintance of the printers Tretzel, at Lyons, who later published his most famous illustrations.

Until his first venture in England, in 1526, there are now few portraits. He must have been largely occupied with religious pictures, and mural decoration, not to mention his constant designing

for stained glass and book ornamentation. The gap as regards portraiture is unsatisfactorily filled by the two half-lengths of a notable
light-o'-love of Basel, Magdalena Offenburg, according to tradition
Holbein's mistress. At Basel you may still see her, once explicitly
labeled Lais Corinthiaca, after a famous Greek courtesan, and again
more kindly presented as Venus. Neither picture is worth much of
your attention, the workmanship being soft and at best merely pretty,
the bulging curtain in the background confusingly and ineffectively
disposed. Such pictures I mention at all only because they mark
Holbein's final homage to Italy. In their affectedness they could as
well be by some third-hand Milanese imitator of Leonardo da Vinci
as by the greatest of German painters. If, as may be, they were
painted *con amore*, then love was not an asset for an artist of Holbein's pragmatic kind.

In spring of 1526 Holbein, leaving his wife and children at Basel,
journeyed down the Rhine and through the Low Countries towards
England, bearing a letter of recommendation from the most charming man of letters in Europe, Erasmus, to the most charming in England, Sir Thomas More, Lord Chancellor. Holbein must have lived
much at Sir Thomas More's pleasant suburban place at Chelsea, for
he immediately began a family group of no less than ten Mores and
in-laws. Long ago this picture was destroyed, but Holbein's composition sketch at Basel gives at least his first intention and some general notion of the general disposition of the group. It was skillfully
arranged, with postures varying from standing to sitting in chairs or
on the floor. The interior was handsomely appointed and provided
with attractive still life. Up to this time European painting had seen
no portrait group so populous and well conducted. Its early destruction must be regarded as a major calamity for all historically minded
art lovers.

Happily we still have, in the Frick Collection, a noble half-length
portrait of Sir Thomas More (Fig. 153). The fine, slightly melancholy face is set off picturesquely against such green curtain as we
have seen in the Offenburg portraits. The face is mobile, but one
feels strength and conscience in it. The pose is assured, but something foreboding in the look tells of surrounding insecurity. To be
Henry VIII's chancellor was as hazardous as to be Henry's queen.
Except for the official chain nothing is handled in a linear, that is, a
German, manner, and most of the painting is as broad as that of the

contemporary Italians. Another admirable portrait of this year is that of William Wareham, Archbishop of Canterbury, again a friend of Erasmus. There are versions at Lambeth and at Paris. Whether as characterization or as decoration it is one of the finest Holbeins. The accessories, a bronze archbishop's staff with a crucifix, a miter contoured with pearls, an open book, are prominent and highly picturesque, but the stern, honest face of the great prelate easily dominates them. The hands are arranged precisely like those of Erasmus in the portrait at Longford Castle. Surely the Archbishop knew that picture, indeed it is likely he owned it. The handling, as befitting the materials and the hard, bony face of the sitter, is now distinctly linear, the whole look Northern. At Windsor one may study the chalk sketch of the Archbishop's face from which this picture was painted. It is clear that the elaboration with the brush has brought some loss in liveliness, with of course a compensating addition of decorative richness.

Of the handful of portraits that fall within Holbein's first visit to England only that of Henry VIII's German astronomer, Nicholas Kratzer, at Paris, need detain us (Fig. 154). It is the first of many admirable likenesses that Holbein made of his fellow countrymen in England, and for its fastidiously elegant pattern one of the best. Despite the subtle modeling of the face and hands, the contour is the main means of expression. The scanty gear then needed by an astronomer—we are in the days before the telescope—is laid out or hung up with utmost effectiveness. Indeed, before this picture one inevitably recalls later Japanese triumphs in assembling refractory material into a consummately harmonious pattern, and this, unlike the Japanese, Holbein effects without sacrificing mass and spatiality.

Holbein's first visit to England seems to have been in the nature of a reconnaissance, and his patronage pretty well limited to that obtained through Erasmus and More or from his own expatriate countrymen. In 1528 he returned to Basel, where he was mostly occupied with completing the decoration of the Town Hall. From a few fragments and some composition sketches one gathers that these murals were stately and entirely Italianate. One of the most striking was that representing the Prophet Samuel cursing victorious King Saul. The strongly gesticulating old figure of Samuel checks and fairly balances the whole escort, horse and foot, of the hesitant and amazed King; the flames of burning cities in the background carries on and enhances the processional movement, which is slowed by the evenly slanting lances seen against the sky. The overlapping of figures three or four deep is very skillfully handled, and the varying of the aspect of the bodies is easy and resourceful. So much Holbein's composition sketch at Basel tells us. At thirty-five, Holbein seems on a parity with his Italian contemporaries so far as competence in classical composition is concerned.

But the most substantial, and a somewhat pathetic record of his last stay in Basel, is the portrait of his Wife and Two Children. It was his farewell to them. Nothing of Holbein's is more tenderly modeled or less dependent on the line. The broad masses of light— the mask and bosom of the mother, the aspiring boy's face in profile, the almost casual pattern of the girl baby's balancing head and arms active at random—all this represents the most intense and accurate observation and, one ventures to hope, a degree of affection. Sexual vagabonds, such as Holbein seems to have been, have managed to retain a kind of love for wives no more intellectually or sexually attractive than Frau Holbein. Incidentally this is the last and perhaps the greatest of the portraits which Holbein painted in the Italian fashion.

To these last years in Basel belong several small portraits of the old Erasmus, at Parma, New York, Basel and elsewhere. The six years between these and Holbein's earlier portraits had treated the liberal theologian harshly. The brutality of the religious wars and the sack of Rome had shattered his dream of reform within the Church. The fine face is now haggard and listless, the generous mouth droops at the corners, there is no longer any hint of the internationally famous wit who only some fifteen years earlier had set Europe to chuckling over his *Praise of Folly*. Much history and much tragedy Holbein has written into this face of the old Erasmus.

By September of 1532, at thirty-five, Hans Holbein found himself once more in London. His old patron, Archbishop Wareham, was dead, Sir Thomas More in retirement, deposed from his chancellorship and before long destined for the scaffold. But the German Hansa merchants of the Steelyard knew Holbein's worth and gave him generous patronage. The high type of such portraits is that of Georg Gisze, at Berlin. The fine decorative contrast of the cherry-red sleeves and green background dominates. Everything of the exquisite paraphernalia of a business office of the Renaissance is present

—books, seals, inkstands, quill pens, balances, a beautifully wrought brass ball to hold the string, a Venetian glass vase holding carnations, a yellow and scarlet Turkish rug as tablecloth—yet with all this elaboration there is no crowding or confusion, everything is held together pictorially. One has only to compare this masterpiece with the numerous pictures of St. Jerome in his Study painted about the same time at Antwerp by followers of Massys to realize Holbein's superior control of his material. Next year, 1533, he finished the famous and variously interpreted picture, at London, called the Ambassadors. The large scale was unfavorable to him, and while it is a very rich picture, the detail remains unassimilated. Worse defect, and very rare in a Holbein, the noble layman and the prelate have the air of posing, while the gigantic, foreshortened skull, out of all possible balance in the center, is a distracting element.

About this time he painted Chancellor Thomas Cromwell, More's unworthy successor. The picture is in the Frick Collection. The porcine, shifty face is one of the meanest ever painted by a great artist. The revelation of the low wiliness of the plebeian place hunter is unsparing. But we must not suppose Holbein cared about this, or worked as a moralist. He simply painted what he saw—the visible baseness of Cromwell, as he had earlier painted the visible nobility of More. Among other admirable portraits of the early thirties may be mentioned the alert effigy of the king's falconer, Robert Cheseman, at Dresden, and in the same gallery the massive, gentle and sagacious Charles de Solier, Sieur de Morette, French Ambassador to the court of Henry VIII. In these portraits it is interesting to note how the mere format effects the meaning. The falconer in his easy oblong has the elbow room his occupation requires; the diplomat, almost crowded into an upright rectangle, lives in narrow quarters dense with calculations, perhaps with machinations.

For the dining hall of the Steelyard Holbein painted the first murals made in the North, which compared favorably with those of contemporary Italy. The subjects, the Triumphs of Wealth and of Poverty, were executed in tempera on linen, went astray in the seventeenth century, and today are represented only by prints and careful old copies. These tell us sufficiently of the energy, richness, dignity and characterfulness of the originals. Even in the copies there is an extraordinary feeling of mass and movement. The difficult placing of the figures several rows deep is easily and agreeably handled. The motive of symbolic figures proceeding triumphantly in their chariots and attended by allied symbols and by historical characters illustrating the central idea—all this mummery was made popular by Petrarch in his Triumphs of Love, Death, Time, Fame, Chastity, Divinity. Petrarch's elaborate descriptions afforded excellent material for the numerous illustrators of the Triumphs, and the processional theme appealed widely to the minor Italian painters. More recently Andrea Mantegna had splendidly decorated the ducal palace of Mantua with painted cloths representing in classical fashion the Triumphs of Caesar. This famous series was engraved and widely copied. Holbein had it quite definitely in mind as he designed his murals for the Steelyard.

The prosperous Hansa merchants of London agreed with rich people of all times and places in emphasizing the disadvantages of wealth and the attractions of poverty. So Holbein's allegories took on an ironic tinge. The lead horses of Wealth's chariot are Avarice and Imposture; an outrider is Usury. Blind and fickle Fortune sits before Wealth in the car; Nemesis hovers in the air behind. Did the German merchants think this out? It looks more like Holbein's already prepared designs for the Triumphs of Death. But it surely was the merchants who chose the Latin inscription which may be translated:

"Gold is father of deceits and son of grief.
Who lacks it grieves; who has it fears."

An effective, pompous quality in the design is offset by its vigorous processional movement and by a fantastic quality in the figures.

Wealthy people have seldom failed in the duty of reminding the poor of their blessings, so the Latin inscription in Holbein's allegory of Poverty tells the poor man that he is free from vicissitudes and fear; he has nothing to lose and may live joyfully and hopefully as he piously worships God. History does not record any unusual exaltation of spirit among the poor of London when this extraordinary canvas was unveiled. The chariot is drawn by an unequal team—the ox, Negligence; the ass, Stupidity and Laziness. On the chariot before the hag Poverty sit Hope, Craftsmanship, Employment, Memory—the moral, industry leads to poverty. Holbein is here at odds with Benjamin Franklin, and possibly nearer the facts. Paupers and laborers walk beside the car. In picturesque variety this decoration is even more remarkable than its companion piece.

The very competent Italian painter, Federigo Zuccaro, declared these panels to be equal to Raphael's decorations in the Vatican. While the compliment is greatly exaggerated, it justifies us in giving a certain attention to a phase of Holbein's genius which is generally ignored.

Holbein's woodcut illustrations for the Dance of Death, 1538, and the Old Testament, 1539, lie apart from our theme, yet no account of him could omit them. The drawings were probably made from 1523 to 1526. The tiny woodcuts of the Dance of Death give final expression to a motive that had obsessed that century of plague and slaughter, the fifteenth. The energy, the largeness of these tiny woodcuts, defy verbal description. The skeleton, Death, works with a mischievous zest, seems exultant rather than malign, acts according to his nature. Whether crowning an emperor, breaking the mast of a foundering ship, drumming before a bride and groom, throttling a successful gambler, lashing the forspent plowman's horses—Death is a sort of macabre Figaro, always active and on the spot. Avoiding the more hideous traits with which his many predecessors invested the theme, Holbein conceives Death as gay, if to sinister ends. Such a vision of the inevitability of death seems that of a man of the world and a cynic more interested in describing than in moralizing our common mortality. There is no curiosity, no hope, no tears, in Holbein's Dance of Death. He does not ask with François Villon,

"Where is Helen, fair dame of Troy?"

and he accepts without a qualm the inevitable disappearance of "the snows of yesteryear." The people who bought the *Imagines Mortis* for any moral lesson it contained were simply badly fooled.

It was a princess who sensibly declined to marry the much-marrying Henry VIII, Christina of Denmark (Fig. 155), who inspired Holbein to make his loveliest portrait of a woman, and, for me, the loveliest portrait of a gentlewoman in existence. Holbein, at Brussels, in March of 1538, made probably within three hours the sketch on which this masterpiece is based. The extraordinary beauty of this portrait defies analysis. One may talk of the exquisite blue-blacks of the gown, of the choice relations of the standing figure to the tall panel, of the tranquil oval of the face, contrasting with the uneasy pattern of the casually joined, nervous hands—all these technical merits can be clearly stated, but to do so tells little about the irresistible charm of the picture. It lies hardly in the child-widow herself. She is no more appealing than the average patrician girl. The mere lines of her face are singularly like those of the impassive Anne of Cleves. I give it up. It is one of the most moving portraits in the world, and possibly what moves is its impeccable perfection as so much pattern, tone, and placing. At the risk of incurring the reproach of sentimentality, a part of the appeal of this great picture may also lie in one's joy over Christina's escape from the bed and block of bluff King Hal, but of course nothing of this can have been in Holbein's mind. He had every reason to suppose his portrait would make a new queen, and he took greatest pains with it.

Naturally Holbein painted his royal patron many times. Several wall paintings including the burly figure of the King have perished, some are represented by copies. Of portraits in the narrow sense singularly few of Henry VIII have come down to us. The best is the long bust with a face in three-quarters aspect in Earl Spencer's Collection. It is choice in composition, most crisp and authoritative in linear notation, while on the side of character it suggests at least a bodily attractiveness in a monarch who was incidentally something of a poet and musician. The more elaborate half-length in the National Gallery, Rome, perhaps because it is presented in full face, hints more at Henry's grossness and cruelty. It is extraordinarily sumptuous, and, if it be, as many think, only an old copy, it gives a true account of its original.

Of the many portraits made in these last years none is finer than that of Jane Seymour, at Vienna. It shows that consummate taste and scrupulously fine workmanship which suffice to make a masterpiece, for there are no overtones of sympathetic imagination. You see the stolid and somewhat stubborn great lady precisely as everybody saw her.

Among the latest male portraits that of the Duke of Norfolk, at Windsor, dominates. The Marshal and Treasurer of the realm was a melancholy survivor from the happier days of Henry VII. He had been an unwilling witness of the English Reformation; had seen the heads of queens and lord chancellors fall, kept his own head on his shoulders perhaps chiefly because he had married the king's stepmother. All this Time had written on the haggard, composed mask, and Holbein had merely to transcribe it. Hardly inferior is the half-length of Dr. John Chambers, at Vienna, titular physician to a king now ailing, and dangerous when he ailed. It needed such determination as one reads on the hard face of this eighty-eight-year-old physician to cope with such a patient.

But the best and completest record of the portraits of Holbein's Gothic prime is not the paintings, but that extraordinary series of chalk drawings at Windsor. These are the standard preparations for Holbein's painted portraits—swift studies in two or three chalks representing each hardly more than an hour or two of intensest observation. From these sketches, with the aid of memory, the famous official portraits were painted. The method, as we have already noted (p. 50), came down from the Gothic past through the Van Eycks.

We need only mention the miniatures of Holbein, which are really little pictures. The most noteworthy of them are the few that represent himself, square-bearded, solid, imperturbable, perhaps a little suspicious. The best example is in the collection of Dr. G. H. A. Clowes, Indianapolis, Ind. It is the likeness of a man who saw clearly, knew what he wanted, was free from nonsense and probably from sentiment. There is nothing of the sensitiveness we associate with the artist. One feels a personality, but it could be that of a great banker or merchant.

By 1536 Holbein had become the king's painter, and the remaining seven years of his activity were devoted chiefly to portraiture of the court. The fashion in England was for the older Gothic manner and its continuation in Flemish miniature painting. The face was to be painted without perceptible shadow, the background was to be of some plain, sharp color, there were to be no distracting accessories. The Englishman wished his counterfeit presentment to be taken neat. For Holbein this meant a long step backward, but he made of these reactionary restrictions a positive merit. Since the method was to be linear, he made it as linear as possible, and since the line must do the modeling, he gave it a new severity and a more subtle modulation.

The Gothic, last manner of Holbein is best studied in the portraits which he made of three English queens, Jane Seymour, at Vienna; Anne of Cleves, at Paris; and Catherine Howard, at Toledo. In the Jane Seymour and Anne of Cleves (Fig. 156) we have rather great decoration of the most ornate kind than great portraiture. The brush works with the accuracy of a graver, a chisel or a needle, creating without smallness or overemphasis jewelry, brocades, gold webs. The effect is of a gorgeously bedizened idol, hardly of a particular woman. Doubtless this was what was wanted, and out of what was wanted Holbein made something most distinguished and wholly his own. Anne of Cleves is almost as impassive as a queen of cards, and hardly less conventional, but the picture is unforgettable. Having not much beyond decorative fitness, it has that exquisitely and consummately.

Catherine Howard (Fig. 157), at Toledo, on the contrary, is a personage. Partly because she is more soberly clad than her fellow victims, the mind in her betrays itself under her apparent demureness, and her firm, oval, self-willed mask is, even for Holbein, a triumph of plastic effect secured mostly by contour. To find anything as skillful in this line one must look forward three hundred years to Ingres. To show Holbein's method of workmanship, I reproduce the life study in chalks at Windsor (Fig. 158).

On October 7, 1543, Holbein signed his will. His wife and two children at Basel were provided for through a legacy from her brother. He saves the words usually given to explaining such a situation, not even mentioning his legitimate wife and family. His horse and other effects are to be sold to pay debts owed to friends. A reasonable provision is made for the little family of bastards whom he had begotten in London. He died about six weeks later, being only forty-six years old, presumably of the prevailing pest.

To estimate a genius such as Holbein's was is by no means easy. He lacked most of the graces of the artist temperament—sympathy, discursive imagination, instinctive creativeness. In his abundant and versatile production everything speaks of exquisite calculation. Everything that a good intelligence can think out he did superbly. He undertook nothing too great for his powers, hence risked and incurred no failures. From Dürer's far less accomplished painting one senses that the man was greater than his work. Holbein's painting yields no hint that he had in reserve anything beyond what the picture tells. His mural painting represents a high type of academism, is what can be intelligently planned, with no daemon whispering in the ear.

His portraiture, apart from its highly decorative character and admirable craftsmanship, is based on the closest study of those physical traits which identify us as individuals. His inerrant hand catches what is personal in features; beyond that is not much but fine manufacture. Nothing is elaborated beyond the requirements of identification. His sitters raise no questions and ask no questions, have ordinarily aroused no admiration in him, nor even a sympathetic curiosity. His portraiture is one of face values. Of course, there are exceptions to such sweeping generalizations. There is affection in the profile of his friend Amerbach; deep respect in the early portraits of Erasmus; warm understanding in the portrait of Sir Thomas More. But this was a transient mood of his young manhood which soon passed. Possibly he scorned his fellows.

Perhaps the simplest definition of his gift would be that with extraordinary taste and judgment he commanded about the finest eye and hand known in the art of painting. There was no music in his soul, and of course no poetry. If only for the coarser stories, Holbein had probably read *The Canterbury Tales*. If so, he had probably read the Man of Law's disclaimer of any relation with the Muses and, in particular, with the poet Ovid. The Man of Law finally boasts:

> "I speke in prose, and lat hym rymès make."

If Holbein read these words, I imagine he indulged the, for him, rare indulgence of an approving chuckle.

In the first half of the sixteenth century the Germanies had many painters of competence and a certain interest, yet when I recall my impressions of Hans Sebald Beham, Heinrich Aldegraver, Georg Pencz, I find nothing that I should impose upon the reader. Hans Baldung Grün, of Strasbourg, tempts to delay. His homesickness for Italy was so pathetic, his endeavor for a more intense and picturesque expression so ardent. His frustrated accomplishment does him personal credit and offers much of interest to the amateur of artist psychology. But like all the artists just mentioned he was a better engraver and designer for woodcutting than he was a painter. A handful of his best woodcut designs, such as the herd of wild horses and the two or three woodcuts of nude witches, outweigh, for their bizarre and sinister fancy, all his paintings. His Nativity, at Frankfurt (Fig. 159), though not free from his mannerisms, achieves a highly picturesque expression, largely through the strangeness of the illumination, but also through such inventions as the donkey answering the song of the angel, and the faces dazzled by the sudden light.

Like Baldung, the other little masters knew thoroughly what they were about when they handled the graver or the quill pen, but were confused when they handled the brush. Their compromises with the invading Italian style were often charming on the small scale of graphics, but inadequate on the larger scale of painting.

The single exception to this general rule seems to me to be Albrecht Altdorfer, who in engraving, woodcut design or painting evinced a sensitive and penetrating fancy of a most romantic sort. He worked in the delightful and rather irresponsible spirit of those German folk tales which, already current in his day, were collected some three centuries later by the Brothers Grimm. And however exotic the subject matter, it left his hands imbued with the tender sprightliness and instinctive sympathy of the best household tales of Germany.

In 1505 he acquired citizenship in Ratisbon in Southern Bavaria, where probably he was born; he soon prospered as architect, engraver and painter; he rose to high civic office. Though a devout Lutheran, and delegate to important Protestant councils, he continued to paint the old Biblical subjects required by the Catholic Church. But he divested them alike of the residual Gothic monumentality, and of the plebeian everyday character which they were fast acquiring. Everything happens "once upon a time" and in an enchanted fairyland which is Altdorfer's personal discovery. He knew Dürer and studied his work respectfully, but drew rather little from it except the notion of keeping fairyland true to the natural appearances in the forested valleys of the Upper Danube. Altdorfer's novel and poetical use of color and illumination tempts one to guess that in his *Wanderjahr* he had seen the great Gruenewalds in Alsace.

Considerations of space force me to leave Altdorfer in these general terms, and to cite a few where I would gladly cite many pictures. Most of the pictures keep a certain distance from the beholder, are virtually intimate landscapes or broad panoramas. So the Satyr Family, at Berlin (Fig. 160), are perfectly at home in their Danube landscape. One happens upon them; they are not exhibited. Again, dragon-slaying St. George, at Munich, is almost lost in a dense and lofty forest. One feels it is the kind of place where one might come upon a knight, a princess, and a dragon. The little Rest on the Flight to Egypt, at Berlin (Fig. 161), is delightfully casual. Nothing tells of the saintliness of the characters. The young Mother reaches for fruit offered by the aged father, the vigorous Christchild dabbles in a fountain surmounted by a pagan statue. Little angels paddle and play in the basin or on its brim. Beyond a building, half farm-house, half castle, the eye goes back to hills overlapping along a lake front, the lake deepest blue, the equally blue heaven partly veiled by easily floating clouds. It is a lyric of pleasant wayfaring. The Holy Family might easily be a nicer and cleaner sort of gypsies.

In Altdorfer generally, the usual formal arrangements are es-chewed. You happen into the picture. Take the Nativity, at Berlin. You see a gigantic moon making a globular lantern of the clouds, jubilant angels above a complicated ruined barn, before you see the newborn Babe supported in a cloth as in a hammock by two sturdy little angels, and the father and Mother devoutly praying.

Perhaps the greatest Altdorfer is the Calvary, at Nürnberg. You see it as if you were passing at some distance. The group of apostles and holy women are seated about the despairing Virgin, not aligned operatically and standing, as in nearly all Crucifixions. The three crosses are so far away that one feels not horror, but a gentle pathos. A splendid blue sky, slightly marbled with creamy clouds, is the back-ground. The action of the soldiers about to take Christ's body down is respectful and official. Fine fir trees catch the light. A sonorous chord of rose, azure and deep green tranquillizes the effect.

Even the battle pieces, at Munich, absurd for their multiplica-tion of tiny figures, are amazing as panoramas of earth, water and air. From the moon a warring world might look like that.

I may seem to be describing an unserious character, and I hasten in justice to say that on the technical side Altdorfer is entirely serious. His numerous drawings attest his searching study of the human form and of landscape. In his pictures everything is well understood and accounted for. His handling of light is amazingly skillful, he achieves otherwise unknown effects of color, effects full of poetical suggestion. And on the spiritual side I feel Altdorfer has his own sort of serious-ness. He is the ideal story teller, believing his legends so thoroughly that he spares no pains to make others believe—shapes his narrative, caresses his phrases, modulates his delivery. This is a tribute both to his legend and to his hearer. Of all painters of legend, Altdorfer is one of the most charming and persuasive, and his persuasiveness rests largely upon his nonchalance. He loves his theme and so fully believes in it that he never imposes it upon you, but sets it in a path where you may happen upon it yourself.

He died in 1538, probably in his prime. He had witnessed the bitterness of the religious wars, but since there was no bitterness in him, he had kept the peacefulness of his own spirit.

Writing in 1531, the Protestant reformer Melanchthon remarked, omitting Holbein, that the three greatest painters of Germany were the recently deceased Mathias Gruenewald and Albrecht Dürer—and his own friend, Lucas Cranach, which merely goes to show that Melanchthon's judgment in art was no better than that of reformers generally. Since Cranach was perhaps the most popular German painter of his time and lived through the glory and prompt decline of the German Renaissance, we may well close with him our survey of Renaissance painting in the Germanies.

He was born at Cronach, in Franconia, in 1472, and we have no inkling of his artistic education, except for certain of his studies from Pollaiuolo and other contemporary Florentines and a few early pictures with some suggestion of Italian urbanity. By 1504 he must have become famous, for then he was called to Wittenberg as court painter by Frederick the Wise, Elector of Saxony. Him Cranach served for nearly fifty years, first at Wittenberg and later at Weimar. He must have developed qualities as a courtier, for in 1509 he was sent to the Netherlands as special commissioner to represent Saxony in the festivities for the young Emperor, Charles of Hapsburg. The whole glory of Flemish painting from the Van Eycks to Massys was spread before him, but it produced no impression upon his imperturbably German soul. In his early forties he married above his station, and as time went on, not satisfied with his considerable gains as a painter, he added to his activities those of apothecary and bookseller.

Luther, whose reform Cranach warmly espoused and, as an illustrator, aided, was his friend, being a witness at his marriage and standing godfather to one of his children. In 1547, after Frederick's defeat at Mühlberg, Cranach accompanied his master to mild internment at Augsburg. There he met the great Titian, and they painted each

other's portraits. Both have vanished. One would give much to recover Cranach's, for it surely would reveal a wholly unidealized aspect
of the patrician master of Venice.

Cranach, his output increased by aid from his sons and assistants,
painted on till his death at eighty-one, in 1553. His production was
enormous and of very uneven quality. We can treat it only by representative examples. With exceptions, which shall be dutifully noted,
it reveals the taste of the small shopkeeper in Cranach. Significantly,
such was also the taste of his noble and wealthy patrons.

The pictures of Cranach's early period generally show much
thoughtfulness and grace of invention. The earliest Cranach, so far
as we know, St. Jerome in Penitence, dated 1502, at Vienna, shows a
solid and learned construction of the nude, a sentiment theatrical, but
also sincere, a finely romantic elaboration of the lightly forested, craggy
background, and above all, a really beautiful interplay of lights and
darks. The artist clearly has all the qualifications needful for the production of fine pictures of the illustrative sort. These characteristics
recur in the Rest on the Flight to Egypt, dated 1504, at Berlin (Fig.
162). As a romantic illustration it is delicious. Charmingly felt is
the relation of Joseph and Mary and the eager posture of the well-
grown Italianate Babe. Delightful, too, is the various solicitude of
the cluster of ministering angels and cherubs. The setting is a fine
bit of Franconian scenery in its most intimate charm—overlapping
bushy crags, a serrated fir and birch wood against the sky, in the foreground wild flowers painted with an exquisite, fairly botanical precision. A painter who could make such pictures for a lifetime would
be sure of a minor immortality, but Cranach was to achieve his minor
immortality rather by reason of the quantity than of the quality of his
production.

The first of many mythological pictures is Venus and Amor,
dated 1509, at Leningrad (Fig. 163). It is executed with an exquisite
enamel, and the loom of the homely body against the dark background
is of an appealing awkwardness. Perhaps this is one of the best of his
mythologies, being seriously studied and free from the forced archness
of most of his nudes. There are many gracious Madonnas of this
period, but we may sufficiently sense their quality in the Flight to
Egypt.

The early portraits, too, are sensitive in execution and vivacious
in effect. One of the best is that of Doctor Cuspinian, with the in-

spired look of a poet, in the Rinehart Collection, at Winterthur (Fig. 165). It should be dated about 1503. For its energy of expression and romantic landscape setting it compares very favorably with portraits by Piero di Cosimo painted at about the same time. The companion piece, Frau Cuspinian, fails to hold together its far more elaborate accessories, and suggests that the tasteful arrangement of the portrait of the doctor may be in the nature of a happy accident. But the effigy of Frau Cuspinian, if not unified, at least has sound plastic effect and tells of a formidably dour character. She is a woman to hold her imaginative spouse down to earth.

Before his fiftieth year, under the strain perhaps of quantity production, Cranach's work begins to go off sadly. There is no longer sound construction, just human shapes against a background; details of landscape are no longer exquisitely studied, but carelessly improvised. We have now only an art of pattern, and of rather inferior pattern. What remains is the illegitimate attraction of quaintness, which only means that we take unseriously what the artist took seriously—the attitude of a heckling gallery to players doing their best with a melodrama. There are still good moments, like that in which Cranach painted the Hunt of Charles V, Madrid. A pool bristles with the antlers of noble stags pressed by drivers and hounds towards the crossbows of the emperor and his friends. One is inclined to make much of so picturesque a document until one recalls that it has at best the quality of a second-rate Persian hunting piece.

The numerous mythologies with nudes of Cranach's later years suggest not quite pleasantly that his dangerous age was painfully prolonged. About them all there is a sort of arch and covert libidinousness. One feels how he loved to strip the little white bodies and gloat over the small, hard breasts, the globular, protruding bellies and the big hips. To enhance these attractions, he poses them affectedly and often emphasizes nakedness by leaving it still adorned by heavy jewelry or big plumed hats. The most elaborate effort to express a small shopkeeper's erotic imagining is the Fountain of Youth, with its swarming nudes, at Berlin. A more characteristic example is the Judgment of Paris, at Karlsruhe (Fig. 164). The youthful shepherd, Paris, is travestied as a Landesknecht with full plate-armor and a big hat. He sits in delighted ease while he weighs the charms of the three nude girls who pose provocatively before him. All wear massive necklaces and one a huge picture hat. Paris' white steed champs foolishly behind, and the carelessly arranged and executed landscape merely cheapens an effect already cheap enough.

As for those many Lucretias who, while retaining their picture hats, expose more than necessary of their white torso and prod it feebly with an oversize dagger, I gladly pass them without looking.

Cranach's later portraits share the defects of his religious and mythological composition. He remains an accurate topographer of lineaments, but there is next to nothing behind the mask. More's the pity, for great men sat to him repeatedly, the Elector of Saxony, Melanchthon, Luther (Fig. 166). From him we know how they looked to one who envisaged them with a tepid accuracy, but without intellectual curiosity or real sympathy. So while these historical portraits of Cranach's are within their limits dependable documents, esthetically they are documents of the third or fourth order.

This declension of Cranach's considerable talent is all the more strange that he was nearly first class as an engraver and designer for woodcuts—in both fields, probably, second only to Dürer. Such sensitively invented and executed engravings as the St. Hubert, St. Genovesa and St. Jerome give Cranach a permanently high place among engravers, while his dramatically energetic and sincere woodcut designs for the Passion of Christ, often made for his friend Luther's books, seem the work of a great artist. Possibly this discrepancy is to be explained by the fact that nearly all of Cranach's work in black and white falls in his good early period, and is probably furthered and stimulated by the contemporary triumphs of Dürer in the graphic arts. Again Cranach's defect may have consisted not so much in lack of inventiveness—in this to the end he was fertile and ingenious—but of that brooding patience and tenacity, that capacity to retain an initial creative mood through long processes of execution which is the unique gift of the great artist. As representing and fully satisfying the average German taste of his time, Cranach is important beyond the value of any or all of his works. He shows how difficult it was for any sort of great art to emerge from a small-shopkeeping culture, and he emphasizes the achievement of an Albrecht Dürer who within this culture did produce a great art.

Well before Cranach died, the Germanies had ceased to be important in the art of painting, and they never have been important since in this branch. For the generation of Dürer, Gruenewald and Holbein, Germany had led Western Europe and had measurably vied with Italy—then sudden obscurity again. To account for this short and sharp rise and fall is difficult, indeed the real problem is why Germany had its group of great artists at all, and we have no way of knowing what produces great artists. To account for the lack of continuity in German painting seems possible. While the other transalpine nations were developing a culture of their own, Germany was merely bickering and pottering with the débris of culture and falling behind in essentials. No literature of any account was created in the Germanies, while France and England were vocal with the new poetry. No fruitful ideas of statecraft were developed. The Germanies had largely lost the charm of provincialism without attaining the grace of civilization. A kind of historic good luck had given the great generation of painters, and that kind of luck is never repeated. Anything like continuity in an artistic tradition rests upon an achieved culture of some sort, and this the Germanies in the sixteenth century had perhaps sought, but failed of attaining.

CHAPTER XI

ITALIANISM IN FLANDERS, SIXTEENTH
CENTURY, THE NEW POPULAR STYLE

FIG. 167. OLD BRUEGEL. February.—Vienna.

FIG. 168.   SCOREL.   Baptism of Christ.—*Berlin*.        FIG. 169.   VAN ORLEY.   Madonna.—*New York*.

FIG. 170. VAN ORLEY. Last Judgment (central panel).—Antwerp.

FIG. 172. FRANS FLORIS. Fall of the Rebel Angels.—
Antwerp.

FIG. 171. FRANS FLORIS. Man with a Falcon.—Braun-
sweig.

297

FIG. 173.   MARTEN DE VOS.   The Tribute Money.—Antwerp.

FIG. 174. MORO. Bloody Mary.—Madrid.　　FIG. 175. PIETER AERTSEN. The Cook.—Brussels.

299

Fig. 176. (Upper) HEMESSEN. The Prodigal Son among Harlots.—*Brussels*.
Fig. 177. (Lower) HEMESSEN(?). Feeding of the Five Thousand.—*Braun-sweig*.

FIG. 178. (Upper) OLD BRUEGEL. Triumph of Death.—*Madrid.*
FIG. 179. (Lower) OLD BRUEGEL. Carnival and Lent.—*Vienna.*

Fig. 180. (Upper) Old Bruegel. The Bird Nesters.—Vienna.
Fig. 181. (Lower) Old Bruegel. The Blind Leading the Blind.—Naples.

Fig. 182. (Upper) OLD BRUEGEL. Peasant Dance.—Vienna.
Fig. 183. (Lower) OLD BRUEGEL. The Crossbearing to Calvary.—Vienna.

Fig. 184. (Upper) OLD BRUEGEL. Return of the Herd.—Vienna.
Fig. 185. (Lower) OLD BRUEGEL. The Wheat Harvest.—New York.

I N GENERAL, the Gothic manner expired in the Low Countries by the middle of the sixteenth century, to be replaced by an Italianate manner which already had the impetus given by a previous generation of endeavor. No nation of Western Europe, not even conservative England, was exempt from this alien enthusiasm. Here painting merely followed tardily the example of the other arts. Poetry was making the discovery of the dulcet lyricism of Petrarch, Poliziano and Bembo, with the result that such springtime talents as Ronsard and Du Bellay and Surrey and Wyatt came into splendid flowering. Criticism in Sidney and Du Bellay and Montaigne emerged from renewed study of the classics and of their interpretation by the Italians. The drama again arose, earliest in England, from Greek and Roman precedents recovered by Italy and often seen through Italian eyes. A prodigious activity in editing and translating the classics made their lesson of measure and nobility more or less common property. New feelings and new thoughts demanded new forms of visual expression.

Italian artists, mostly of the second order, were called by the French, English and Spanish courts as a sort of missionaries of taste. The sculptors Torregiano and Benedetto da Majano worked in England at the dawn of the century; later Leone Leoni went to Spain; Benvenuto Cellini to France. Such great Italian painters as Andrea del Sarto and Leonardo da Vinci entered the service of Francis I, who also called Rosso and Primaticcio to fresco the corridors of the new palace of Fontainebleau. From Vienna to Antwerp and from Antwerp to Madrid princes of the blood and princes of mere wealth vied with each other in collecting Italian pictures.

It was the vision of the antique that captured the imagination of the painter of the North. In some confused but ardent fashion he felt, and rightly, that what we now know to be the dregs of the Greek manner represented a graciousness and a nobility of conception which the Northern Gothic painters had not even glimpsed, and unhappily in this new enthusiasm the compensating merits of the old Gothic painters were denied or ignored. At the end of the century the Flem-

ish art historian, Carel van Mander, himself a fair painter, wrote that
owing to the presence of the antique statues "the Italians early arrived
at the just understanding of true nature, while we Flemish set ourselves to seeking progress by rule of thumb work, without any other
model than vulgar nature." By "true nature" Van Mander meant
selected and ennobled aspects of nature—what criticism had already
called "beautiful nature," *belle nature*. To discover this beautiful
nature one had to go to Rome. Van Mander writes confidently:

"The painters who have made a considerable sojourn abroad, particularly in Italy, generally bring back a style to us which surpasses
in beauty as in excellence the ancient Flemish manner." What actually came of the program was a mannered art far inferior to "the
ancient Flemish manner." Why?

For one reason, because the Northern painters had no background for understanding and putting in practice their sudden vision
of antique beauty. It was in the blood of Italy, while merely external
to Flanders, France and Germany. Next, the Northern painters had
rather slight direct experience of the antique; they tended to see it at
second hand through the works of contemporary Italian painters.
Finally, the Northern Renaissance came when Italian painting was
declining. The Northerners drew not from Raphael and Titian, but
from the mannerists who succeeded these giants. Thus the Northern
Italianates imitated, not classical antiquity, but certain fashionable
Italian misinterpretations thereof. From such a process no great nor
even pleasing art could come, and this is why the Italianate painting of
the sixteenth century is far inferior to the contemporary poetry, sculpture and architecture.

Nevertheless, this Italianate painting should not be regarded as
so much wasted effort. It rested on sincere, if confused, perception
of real superiorities. It prepared the way for the great syntheses of
the following century. Paradoxically, in the ongoing of art, the giants
have to be carried on the shoulders of the dwarfs, without whom
there would be no giants. One may feel that but for the unrealized
ideals of a Marten de Vos or a Frans Floris, we should not today
rejoice in the fully realized ideals of a Rubens and Poussin. We often
have to start plants in the cramped and artificial conditions of the
cold frame in order to see their splendid ultimate growth in the open
air.

It was in Flanders that the impact of the Italian Renaissance was soonest and most deeply felt. For this there were many reasons. Flanders was a part of the Empire, which had the overlordship of such art centers in Italy as Tuscany and Lombardy. The cosmopolitan city of Antwerp was in close commercial relations with Italy, and these led to artistic relations in the form of buying Italian pictures and sculpture and imitating Italian architecture. All this caused well before the middle of the sixteenth century the complete domination of that Italian influence which we have seen gradually increasing from Gerard David, through Quentin Massys to Jan Mabuse.

The external marks of the new style were the general increase in the scale of figures and pictures, substitution of various and more naturalistic color schemes for the old decorative Gothic balance of scarlet and azure, a heavier constructional shadow, looser and more animated compositional arrangements, a new interest in anatomy, foreshortening and perspective, with a rejection of the Gothic ornateness. For two generations these new resources were employed with much ingenuity but with very little taste. They were appropriate to that grandeur which the Italian painters naturally sought. In the hands of the Flemish Italianate who had no grandeur of feeling these new resources became mere affectations. He was like a country fiddler suddenly called upon to compose for and conduct an orchestra—with the result of more noise than music. When the Italianates, or, as they called themselves, the Romanists, painted portraits, they retained much of their native simplicity and probity; in religious subjects and mythology they were playing a part, and their work showed it.

Carel van Mander, who, as an arch-Romanist himself, was likely to be well informed in this matter, regarded Jan van Scorel, of Utrecht, as the pioneer in mastering the Italian style. Unhappily, nearly all the works upon which Van Mander based this opinion were destroyed in the religious wars, and critics differ greatly as to what pictures may be ascribed to Scorel. In these circumstances I must do my brief best with a difficult problem. On the biographical side we have almost a superfluity of information about Scorel. Born in Alkmaar, in 1495, he was from the first a roving and versatile spirit. He worked transiently under many masters, including Dürer, traveled as far as Jerusalem, spent a couple of years in Italy, mostly at Rome, about 1520. He was a canon of Utrecht Cathedral, but produced and acknowledged a nice little family of illegitimate children—withal a learned man, a linguist, an excellent musician and a good shot with the crossbow.

His pictures are singularly various, but all agree in a general, almost colorless blondness, in the oval, rather insipid faces of the women, in the studied and highly artificial picturesqueness of the landscape backgrounds.

The Baptism of Christ (Fig. 168), at Berlin, is sufficiently characteristic of Scorel's mature style. The figures seem to me vaguely Raphaelesque, while the highly composite landscape with fine tree masses, a river vista, and distant mountains, suggests intelligent consultation of Titian's landscape drawings and woodcuts. The relations of the figures to the landscape forms are carefully studied, and on the whole, happy. Everything is idylically felt, alive, if rather too consciously, and gracefully carried off. It surely is this sort of picture which made Van Mander claim pioneer honors for Scorel.

He died at sixty-seven, in 1562, after a premature and gouty old age.

About the end of August, 1521, the great Albrecht Dürer was guest of honor to the young painter of Antwerp, Bernard van Orley. Dürer wrote in his journal: "He gave me so expensive a dinner that I think ten florins would not cover it." Van Orley considerately invited members of good society—the treasurer of the Regent Margaret, the high chamberlain of the king, the treasurer of Antwerp, all possible patrons. Dürer made a charcoal portrait of the hospitable Van Orley and later from it made the painted portrait now at Dresden. In it we see the ardent and sensitive face of a man in the middle twenties. So Bernard van Orley was born about 1493. He must have been prosperous or lucky, for he had already made his studies at Rome, being there when the marvels of Raphael and Michelangelo were novelties, or actually in the doing, in the Vatican. Over a century after his death tradition held that Van Orley had had the friendship of Raphael, and while this is unproved, it is likely enough that two such friendly artists of fairly equal age should have got together in the relatively small artist group at Rome. Tradition also holds that Van Orley was entrusted by Raphael with arranging for the weaving of the famous cartoons of the Deeds of the Apostles, and this, though unconfirmed by documents, is probable.

By 1515, at twenty-two, Van Orley was already working for the empress-regent, and three years later he was regularly appointed as a court painter. Much of his work for the regent was in portraiture of the imperial children. Unhappily it is lost. Without becoming anything like a great painter, Van Orley developed an amazing skill, industry and versatility. His stained-glass windows in St. Gudule, at Brussels (1537), are still a joy for a sensitive visitor. For the famous tapestry looms of Brussels he made scores of designs, of a charming and appropriate sort. It is perhaps rather in these activities than in painting that he is really important. Nobody more thoroughly advertised the technical superiority of Italian draughtsmanship or made the cause of Romanism more persuasive.

Like all Flemish painters he was an accomplished portraitist. One of his best is that of Dr. Georg Zelle, at Brussels. It has much dignity and character. The date is 1519. Equally notable is the youthful Charles V, at Budapest. It was painted towards 1520, when the Emperor was in his late teens. His accession, in 1519, fell upon the troublous times of the religious wars. He must maintain by craft and force the empire which his ancestors had won on the easy terms of prudent marriage. One feels that he is bearing up with a peevish aggressiveness which hardening experience was to convert into a shrewd forcefulness.

Van Orley sensibly kept away from mythology, and saved himself and us a repetition of the vulgarities of Jan Mabuse and Jan Massys. The best of Van Orley's religious pictures veer between the sweetness of Quentin Massys and the ampler beauty of Raphael. Characteristic is the Lamentation over the Dead Christ, at Brussels. It is really a cluster of heads against a gold ground, and if it has little dramatic intensity and concentration, it at least offers a bouquet of charming faces. His Madonnas, the one at New York (Fig. 169), is typical, are sweet and somewhat insipid in a Raphaelesque fashion, and generally show Italian influence in landscape and architectural accessories. His more elaborate religious pictures say little to us now. The triptych of Job, at Brussels, 1514, merely superimposes upon the vivacity of Massys alien features from Raphael and Michelangelo, and however intelligently studied as illustration, gives a crowded, confused and wholly unpleasing effect.

The Last Judgment, at Antwerp, 1519 (Fig. 170), is Van Orley's challenge to Italy—his most ambitious venture in the sublime. In a theatrical way this picture is still effective. Its geometry, consisting in the great symmetrical curves and circles favored by Raphael, is thoughtful, if stilted and unconvincing. An obvious but also fetching melodramatic touch is to make the resurrection overtake an actual burial. The nude forms are learnedly constructed, and, while most of them strike poses, a few are sensitively felt. In the whole work one feels a real talent striving with a task beyond its capacities. The wings, representing the Giving of Alms and the Parable of the Beggar Lazarus, again continue the manner of Massys with Italian trappings. The crowding and confusion of the whole nullifies the profusion of really admirable parts.

Save for an unpleasant session with the Holy Inquisition, for alleged Protestant leanings, Van Orley's career seems to have been one of unclouded prosperity. Even the Inquisition imposed upon him only the mild penalty of attending a soundly Catholic sermon. He married twice and had nine children, of whom four were sons. They became painters, as did certain of the grandsons. Van Orley died in 1542, just short of fifty. A picture of the Nativity by his hand adorned his tomb in St. Sebastian. One read, in French, that he had been court painter to two queens. All in all, he seems to belong to the class of enterprising and delightful men of the world who pursue art chiefly as a lucrative business.

The mention of the Van Orley succession recalls those painter families who flourished generation by generation in Flanders—the Franckens, De Voses, Bruegels, etc. Painting was still regarded as a trade, and a painter's son, as naturally as a mechanic's or shopkeeper's, followed his father's calling.

I must abridge this somewhat tedious list of well-meaning Romanists. The most famous, and on the whole the ablest, was Frans Floris, "the Flemish Raphael." He was born about 1516, studied under the dismal Romanist, Lambert Lombard, and made a considerable stay in Rome in the early 1540's, when Michelangelo's Last Judgment was a new sensation. Floris handily learned all the tricks of foreshortening and sensational workmanship. These he brought back with him to Antwerp in 1546, and with them he promptly dazzled the citizenry. He was a portraitist of great power of characterization, as the Man with a Falcon, at Braunsweig, attests (Fig. 171). His allegories and mythologies, such as the Feast of the Sea Gods, at Stockholm, are distressing for their insistent mannerism. It seems as if he had studied rather Michelangelo's basest imitators than the master himself. Though a toper and burdened with a domineering and extravagant wife, he was a prodigy of productiveness. Nothing came amiss to him—planning the decorations for imperial entries, painting great altarpieces for the new baroque churches; without genius, he had all the ways thereof. Money came and went freely, and at last he ruined himself building a sort of palace. He died in 1570, at a little past sixty, and was shabbily buried.

All the same there was, what most of the Romanists lacked, abundant power in the man. His Fall of the Rebel Angels (Fig. 172), at Antwerp, has a competent and fetching sensationalism which anticipates by three centuries the illustrations of Gustave Doré. The archangels thrust down the dragon Satan and the insurgent angels with athletic zest and ease. The fiends have beasts' heads on well-muscled Michelangelesque bodies. The picture is an incredible tangle of foreshortenings, yet all is carried off with vigor and even a sort of reasonableness. What hopelessly mars an ably executed picture is the coarseness and obviousness of the conception. Floris insists that you believe in his devils wearing the heads of beasts, but he doesn't believe in them himself. For the bitter tragedy of his exemplar, Michelangelo's Last Judgment, Frans Floris substitutes mere physical exuberance and bugaboo. All the same, in his tasteless energy he won something for Flanders by which Rubens was soon to profit.

Marten de Vos was born at Antwerp about 1531 and died past seventy in 1603. He studied with Floris, later went to Rome and at Venice actually served as studio assistant to Tintoretto. From these experiences he gained a mild competence in picture making, and if among the scores of his pictures extant there are none very good there are also none very bad. One may fairly judge him by the Tribute Money, at Antwerp (Fig. 173). The dense groups are intelligently put together after Tintoretto's fashion, and well set before architectural backgrounds; the heads have a certain sweetness and character, but the color is negative and poor and the construction of the figures barely adequate.

At least Antwerp owes him two substantial debts. He patriotically spoiled the deal, in 1577, by which Queen Elizabeth, exceptionally gone artistic, tried to buy the great Deposition by Quentin Massys, and he started a dynasty of a score of painter De Voses, two or three of whom were excellent artists. Which goes to show that the mediocre painter may after all have his social and biological uses.

By the end of the sixteenth century the younger Romanists had fairly assimilated the Renaissance style and culture, if in a somewhat attenuated and provincial form. A Carel van Mander effects an extraordinary work of self-education, becomes something of a humanist while retaining much of his Flemish raciness. His big altarpieces often have a gentle charm. Their color is tender rather than fine. We have a tasteful but somewhat debilitated offshoot of the eclecticism of the Carracci. Van Mander saved in his *Painter's Book* the scanty and disappearing traditions of Flemish painting, set down interesting anecdotes of his artist contemporaries, wrote a poem on how to paint, and digested classical mythology for the use of students— all in all a very queer mixture of wag, chronicler, and sheer pedant. He probably had a little to do with the elementary training of Frans Hals.

Otho van Veen, or Vaenius, as he preferred to call himself, had more solid learning, composed books of emblems, made his studies for five years in Italy under Federigo Zuccaro, became a court painter, achieved a somewhat insipid sprightliness in his painting. He seems to have been something of a snob, but was of generous disposition. His Antwerp studio seemed a center of culture to the younger painters, and his greatest pupil, Peter Paul Rubens, was on the whole merely to carry out the program of Vaenius with gusto, resourcefulness, power and creative taste. There are others whom one is sorry to ignore—Hendrik Goltzius, who despite a hand crippled in childhood became more than a fair painter in the Italian fashion and perhaps the best engraver of his time; that odd talent, Cornelis van Ketel, excellent in portraiture, affected in allegory and mythology, who varied the monotony of painting with brushes by applying and manipulating his paint with his fingers or his toes. He may seem the symbol of two generations of painters who had pursued an exotic dexterity to express borrowed and half-understood ideals. The future of art in the Low Countries lay with men of more resistant native fiber.

Having considered those Italianizing painters who prepared the way for Rubens and Van Dyck, we may now take up a far more interesting group who either retained much of the rectitude of the old Gothic realism or undertook new popular and native themes, and thus broke the path towards the Dutch genre painting of the seventeenth century.

Such pictures of common life as Massys' Banker and his Wife

(Fig. 72), and Unequal Love, mark the beginning of a new patronage. Up to this time the painter had depended upon the church, the monasteries, the court, and officialdom, and when the private patron appeared, it was, apart from portraiture, usually in a religious mood. But the great accumulation of new wealth, largely due to the recently opened trade with the Indias, was quietly doing its work of social transformation. The rich traders and bankers of Antwerp soon set the tone for their class ever since. They were energetic people of limited education and small culture, chiefly concerned with their own affairs and belongings. All their activities, whether in business, recreation or dissipation, looked good to them, and fit to be portrayed. The doings of poorer people they viewed with humorous interest and condescension. Of all this they wanted true portraiture, and this the younger painter contemporaries or successors of Massys, such as Pieter Aertsen, Jan Hemessen and Pieter Bruegel, were to supply in ample measure. Here we find the beginnings of that genre painting which, when Protestantism had banished religious painting from Holland and given her national independence, was to be the characteristic art of the Netherlands. These pioneer genre painters did many pictures on the old religious themes, but they conceived them in the new familiar manner, without that dignity and reserve which was the expiring legacy of the Middle Ages. Such pictures are generally of small importance save in so far as they prepared the taste which a century later would accept the lowly Biblical art of Rembrandt.

Among these painters of native mood Antonio Moro occupies a place apart. He was almost exclusively a portrait painter, and at once the first and ablest specialist in this class. Born at Utrecht about 1512, or a little later, he studied with the Italianate Scorel, but developed along his own lines through penetrating observation of men's faces and character. One of his earlier masterpieces, the massive bust portraits of two Ecclesiastical Pilgrims, at Berlin, is in the sound and drastic tradition of Massys, or at least of the best late-Gothic portraiture. One realizes primarily the brawn and bone and bulk of these two devotees—their formidable masculine quality, their strength of will whether in affairs or in prayer. They are such as, according to the apostle Paul, take the kingdom of heaven by storm. And the picture, with its white surplices in the form of truncated cones over the strong shoulders, the varied turn of the heads, the graceful relief afforded by the curving palms, has a decorative quality rare in Moro.

In general we must not look to him for portraiture of the poetized and decorative sort—that was the specialty of his great Venetian contemporary, Titian. Instead one expects from Moro a most accurate and emphatic expression of the greater and smaller forms of his sitters, and through these forms a most lucid and powerful expression of the essential character. Here I am reminded of an admirable saying, I think by the American painter, Philip L. Hale. He said, I paraphrase: "When we say a painter expresses character we may merely mean that he sees and renders the forms before him with exceptional fineness and accuracy."

Moro was to be one of the first itinerant, cosmopolitan portraitists. His wanderings we cannot trace completely, but we know that in 1552 he was in Portugal, in 1553 in England, in 1559 in Spain. He painted chiefly the great of the earth in tragic times, and his gallery consists of men and women oppressed by the burden of power. Through him we know the hard, fanatical, suspicious mask of Bloody Mary, Madrid (Fig. 174); the inscrutable ruthlessness of the Duke of Alba, Brussels; the weak arrogance of Philip II; the urbane, foxlike astuteness of his chancellor, Granvelle, Vienna. One marvels that these potentates let themselves be painted, really be betrayed, with such unsparing truthfulness. It evinces a fine scorn of opinion. One feels that when they ordered wholesale burning at the stake and military massacres, they did so with a clear conscience.

The technical methods of Moro are resolute, the effect metallic, almost sculptural; there is rarely beauty of color or studied arrangement. Moro was not making pictures; he was making true records of what he saw, and he saw much that was physically and morally ugly. This seems not to have mattered to him. Without his cool and resolute intelligence and his unflinching scrutiny, the history of the sixteenth century would be singularly impoverished for all eye-minded people. His own attitude seems to have been amoral and wholly professional. He lived on friendly terms with three of the cruelest figures in history, Mary Tudor, Philip II, the Duke of Alba. For the rest, he was a good citizen and father. He died at Antwerp in 1575, probably in his early sixties. He painted a few religious pictures of which only a St. Sebastian, virtually a portrait, has come down to us. It shows that the loss of the rest is not too deplorable.

Since virtually no drawings by Moro are preserved, it seems probable that, departing from the traditional practice, he painted with the sitter present. Indeed the extraordinary vitality of his portraits could hardly have been attained in any other way.

Pieter Aertsen, nicknamed Long Peter, is chiefly important for his interest in the life of the people. Kitchens, taphouses, dancing halls—these are his favorite themes. He attacks and executes them with energy and gusto, but without selection or taste. He adopts the large scale of the Italian painters, but otherwise is only superficially influenced by them. His more important genre pictures are the Egg Dance, Amsterdam; the half-length of a stalwart cook holding an oddly Michelangelesque pose as she surveys her viands (Fig. 175), Brussels; a Kitchen Scene, Copenhagen; a Peasants' Revel, Antwerp. In all these pictures there is a surplusage of still life and accessories which forecasts what was the characteristic of later Dutch painting—a somewhat indiscriminate love of things. In this vein, for his energy and good nature, Aertsen points forward to Jacob Jordaens.

His religious paintings are almost negligible, though again the tendency to treat the sacred themes as actual events, and without glamour of convention or legend, reveals a new and completely secular point of view which is prophetic. Such a picture as Christ with Mary and Martha, Brussels, shows an unexpected psychological insight, but also a lack of capacity to turn this gift to artistic ends.

In his Crossbearing, 1552, at Berlin, Aertsen was one of the first Netherlandish artists to paint a crowd. The tragic march to Calvary is very fully described, so much so that the figure of Christ, beaten as He sinks under the weight of His cross, is pretty well lost among the straggling throng that moves towards the treat of a Crucifixion. There is some lack of clarity in the picture, but also much energy and variety of character. It is likely that Aertsen's younger contemporary, Pieter Bruegel, profited by such pictures as this, and was moved to create them with greater power and lucidity.

Biographical details for Pieter Aertsen are few and unimportant. Born somewhere about 1508, at Amsterdam, he soon moved to the capital of the Low Countries, Antwerp, where he registered with the painters' guild in 1535. He died in 1575. His character is written plainly in his pictures. He loved life in its ordinary, including its grosser, aspects. He accepted common people and things without selection or criticism. Thus, a genial and sympathetic figure, he lacked the fineness of judgment essential to greatness in any artist.

Jan Sanders, usually called from his village birthplace near Antwerp, Hemessen, ran a course similar to Aertsen's, but ran it with greater care and skill. He better understood the economy of picture making, studied physiognomy and expression with more insight and subtlety. He was born about 1504 and studied with a painter, Hendrik van Cleve, by whom we have no extant pictures. But the main influence on Hemessen was undoubtedly the familiar pictures of Massys and his imitators. Unhappily the magic of Massys' coloring entirely escaped young Hemessen, who painted in those slatey tones which the younger generation imagined to be Italian chiaroscuro.

Hemessen was precocious. At twenty, in 1524, he was admitted as a master at Antwerp and had already set up as a teacher. He soon married, but was certainly no exemplary husband, for at fifty, when he was old enough to know better, a maidservant, Bethe, had a child by him. He painted religious subjects which required understanding of usual situations, the Calling of Matthew, 1536, Munich; the Prodigal Son, of the same year, Brussels (Fig. 176); St. Jerome doing Penance in his Cell, 1536, New York Art Market. All these pictures are ably constructed and retain much of the old charm in still life and landscape features, and on the side of expression all are too insistent.

If we are to identify him with the painter called the Monogrammist of Brunswick, and I think we should do so, Hemessen was among the first Northern painters to make a crowd in action clearly visible to an observer. The Miraculous Feeding of the Five Thousand, at Braunsweig (Fig. 177), is immensely picturesque for the contrast of the eager, active throng with the stability of the castle in the near background. The scores of little figures are carefully and sensitively studied with regard to action and expression. There is none of the grimace that often mars the larger pictures. Another picture of similar merit is Christ's Entry into Jerusalem, a larger and more populous version at Stuttgart, a smaller version in the Graefe Collection, at Weimar. Since Van Mander, who, writing only fifty years later, should be well informed, mentions a picture on this theme by Hemessen, our identification of Hemessen with the Monogrammist seems justified.

If not Hemessen, the Monogrammist was an assistant of his who painted the landscapes and background figures of certain of his pictures. Whoever did this group of pictures of crowds, which we may date, with Dr. Friedländer, about 1540, entered the path which Pieter Bruegel was to tread more vigorously, and it does not really matter whether this pioneer of the portraiture of throngs be Hemessen himself or one of his many pupils.

Both honors and adversities befell Hemessen.  In 1539 he bought a house at Antwerp and next year went bankrupt.  In 1548 he was elected dean of the painters' guild.  Two years later he was in financial difficulties, sold his house and moved to Haarlem.  His last dated picture is of 1556, and sometime before 1563 he died.  From the later years there are two remarkable pictures, one representing the reception room of a bawdyhouse, at Frankfurt, the other with half-lengths of a solid citizen being beguiled by a pretty wench while the old procuress rejoices.  The picture is at Karlsruhe.  It was a life which Hemessen thoroughly understood, and nothing is to be said against these pictures except that Hemessen, as usual, rubs it in too much.

In some of the later religious pictures, such as Tobias and his Father, Paris, and Abraham's Sacrifice, Nürnberg, Hemessen yields to the Italian fashion to the extent of crowding his figures in the frame, exaggerating the postures and fussing the draperies.  They are the poorest expression of his considerable talent.

The Operation for the Stone, Madrid, is a masterpiece, if of the grisly kind.  A quack is pretending to excise a stone from a man's forehead to cure him of madness.  Physiognomy can hardly go farther.  The gusto of the surgeon quack, the agonized expression of the patient, the professional imperturbability of the two attendant nuns, the stark frenzy of the madman awaiting his turn—all this is handled with an energy hardly inferior to Bosch's, who, the reader will recall, had treated the same subject rather humorously.  If this picture be indeed a Hemessen, as I feel it is, his importance as a link between Jerome Bosch and Pieter Bruegel is indisputable.

Those intimations of a popular art which we have seen in Massys, Aertsen and Hemessen were to be fully realized by Pieter Bruegel— the true pioneer of the great genre and landscape art of Flanders in the next century.  He was born about 1530 and took his name from his native village of Bruegel, near Bois-le-Duc.  His parents, according to Van Mander, were peasants, and Pieter's work often celebrates the festive, humble doings of peasants, their work and play, their follies, their drastic folk wit and wisdom. Thus he brings into painting the mood which had earlier found a voice in literature in the *Proverbs of Hendyng* and *Le Dit du Laboureur*. This note may be regarded as an appeal from the conventional morality of church and aristocracy to the common-sense morality and mother wit of working people. But in Pieter Bruegel any feeling of protest is surely slight. Negations of any sort were alien to him; he worked from direct observation and positive sympathy, usually without critical preoccupation, and herein lies his novelty and his greatness.

His native village was within a half-day's walk of Bois-le-Duc, Jerome Bosch's town, and it is likely that from an early age he was acquainted with Bosch's diableries. In any case, these influenced him directly. For that matter, he came up in the atmosphere of religious persecution, cruel dragonnades, pestilence, imminence of death which pervaded the greatest and perhaps the unhappiest of centuries. It is even possible that he had some training under a disciple of Bosch, before about 1545, when he went to Antwerp and was regularly articled as an apprentice to the Italianate painter, Pieter Coecke. From him young Pieter Bruegel had little to learn, but after all, Coecke, as the backgrounds of his woodcuts on Turkish subjects show, was a very competent composer of picturesque mountainous landscapes. These may have furthered Pieter Bruegel's latent ambition to make landscapes of a grand and spacious sort.

Coecke died in 1550, leaving behind, among other children, a four- or five-year-old daughter, Maria, whom young Pieter had carried in his arms and who some twelve years later was to be his wife. In 1551 Pieter was registered as a master in the Antwerp guild. About the time Pieter Coecke died a young painter, Jerome Cock, returned from Italy, and modestly set up a print business at the sign of the Four Winds. For ten years Pieter Bruegel's chief activity was to be drawing for Cock's engravers. Cock's brother, Matthias, was an excellent landscapist, and the engravings after his designs probably prepared a patronage for Pieter Bruegel's much more important landscape prints.

In 1552 Pieter Bruegel made the customary pilgrimage to Italy, going down through France and the Rhone, and coming back over the Brenner. Oddly, what impressed him on this trip was not the grandeur of Italian art and the authority of the antique, but simply the scenery through which he passed. He sketched it with a rapid and accurate pen, using nervous little strokes which made the surface twinkle with light and air. Here was a new resource which he was to exploit in many ways. Before following the brief fifteen or sixteen years of his activity as a painter it may be well to classify his work and define its scope.

He continued the religious, allegorical and moralistic vein of Jerome Bosch, but with more sobriety and completeness and, on the whole, more genially.

He studied and represented incomparably the feeling and actions of crowds of common people, and did this with the greatest vivacity, sympathy and variety. No one since has equaled him in this branch of painting. Apart from this he painted the doings of the individual peasant and of small groups with truthfulness and raciness.

He was the first painter to make noble and spacious landscapes, without either slurring or overemphasizing details, and without sacrificing optical to decorative effect. Thus his great landscapes, his latest and ripest work, are the fountainhead of all landscape of a realistic sort ever since.

Now it will be seen that all these classes of subjects required much detail and suggestion of motion. Pieter Bruegel's genius as a technician provided a new method to meet the new themes. Avoiding the error of Massys and his followers of painting genre subjects on too large scale, and freezing them by continuing the linear Gothic handling—a handling suitable for static religious subjects—Pieter Bruegel invented a method of indication which left the contour free and mobile. Like his predecessors, he made the line tell as much as possible about mass and motion, but he handled it far more variously and applied it to more difficult subject matter. And when he painted, the line became the edge of a color spot. Such carefully made edges did the work of suggesting mass without much inner modeling, while the edge never hardened into a boundary, but left the form apparently free to move. It was a sort of flat painting much more akin to the contemporary practice of Venice than to anything in the North. Possibly on his way to the Tyrol Pieter Bruegel made the short detour to Venice and saw the Carpaccios and the early Tintorettos. One is tempted to think so. When he saw fit, he could model as roundly as Hugo van der Goes, but this is done rarely and for particular emphasis. Generally the painting is flat, and it looks forward to Frans Hals. It is this unity of touch and handling which brings into harmony crowded compositions which otherwise would be merely confusing and almost illegible.

Why did Pieter Bruegel want to go to Italy? Surely not for the usual reason of learning the secret of the grand style. I guess it may have been a shrewd business move of the print maker, Jerome Cock. He doubtless saw the possibility of profit in engraving his own brother's landscape drawings, and probably realized the much superior talent of Bruegel, and his value to an engraver's shop. If so, Bruegel went to Italy to gather material for prints. Everything looks like that, for on his return Bruegel soon became Cock's mainstay as a designer, largely for landscape prints that show unmistakable reminiscences of Italy's Northern Alpine rim.

The Expulsion of the Rebel Angels, Brussels, 1562, is in many ways in Bosch's manner, and not one of Bruegel's good pictures. A lanky St. Michael in armor, accompanied by white-robed archangels and angels, beats down a flight of demons in reptilian and insect forms. Bruegel spends himself in devising obscene, ophidian forms for the rebels, but one feels rather a ready inventiveness than seriousness, and the picture, a welter of hovering and falling shapes, is confusing.

The Triumph of Death, Madrid (Fig. 178), on the contrary, is a great invention. The theme is simple and concrete. Upon terrified people, caught at their usual occupations, some attempting a vain defense, platoons of skeletons move inexorably, concentrating towards the center in good military order. Across the front a skeleton Death, on a lean horse, swings his scythe. Nearly three and a half centuries later Albert Ryder will borrow this motive and in his Death on the Race Track will make excellent use of it. The background of the Triumph of Death is a quiet sea with sinking ships, and burning buildings on the headlands. Everything in this most elaborate picture is concrete, even obvious, but the whole effect is grimly impressive. One can hardly speak of composition. It cannot be grasped at a glance; there is no clear pattern; it has to be read bit by bit, like a page of proverbs or epigrams, and it is worth reading.

More cryptic is the picture Dulle Griet, 1564, Mayer van den Bergh Collection, Antwerp. Yet it is not hard to grasp Furious Meg's meaning. She is the spirit of insensate wrath, of violence and discord, a woman moving towards hell mouth, having already made a hell on earth. Once the motive is sensed, the extraordinary complication of attributes and symbols falls into place, yet it possibly is more of a visible essay on the formidableness of a harridan than a picture.

Of a similar sort is the Battle between Carnival and Lent, Vienna (Fig. 179). Lent, a lean old woman, tilts with a long toaster on which are two smoked herring, against Carnival, an obese man mounted on a wine cask who tilts with a spit which transfixes a roasted pig. They are about to clash. Behind the champions are the votaries of the abstinent and the abundant life. The grotesque scene is domesticated and made even plausible by placing it in a village square upon which little groups and pairs continue the debate. Here Bruegel is merely visualizing, perhaps parodying, the pedantic exercises of the chambers of rhetoric and colleges of his time. A hundred years earlier the students of some Italian university gave a dramatic interlude on this theme. Lent, represented as a widow with three daughters, broke in on and dispersed the singers and dancers of Carnival.

There must be a similar literary background for the Battle between the Penny Banks and the Strong Boxes, one of Bruegel's most genial inventions represented by a painting, and more strongly and concisely by an engraving. The penny banks and strong boxes are conceived as men at arms engaged in a hand-to-hand fight. They become a sort of mechanized soldiery without ceasing to be money boxes. We have thus a sort of rebus for the eternal strife between the haves and have nots, labor and capital, little and big business— what you will. Are such creations pictures, or verbal debates pretending to be pictures? I feel the liberal answer is that they are, after all, pictures, but pictures of a special and unusual sort to which, in view of their energy of fancy and ability, we must learn to accustom ourselves.

This proverbial vein of Bruegel is perhaps his most characteristic, if not his best. We may follow it indefinitely and with pleasure in his prints. There one finds the greatest richness of fancy, a mind saturated with immemorial folk wit and wisdom. One must seek these prints in Bastelaer's standard work. They are far too many to enumerate. Yet I cannot refrain from mentioning such masterpieces of good-natured caricature as the Fat and the Lean Kitchen, or that marvelous sleeping peddler with monkeys pilfering from his pack and gloating over his gewgaws.

Before treating Bruegel's portraiture of crowds, just a word on his pictures of peasants, single, or in small groups. Here are some of his masterpieces, such as the Bird Nesters, Vienna; the Bad Shepherd, Johnson Collection, Philadelphia; the Wooden Leggers, Paris; the Peasant Dance, Vienna.  The artist's extraordinary technical ability is at its best in these simpler compositions—his power to suggest bulky form and to make it seem ready to move.  And the simple Flemish landscapes in these pictures are again of the best, for solidity, for spaciousness, for cunning alternation of broadest and most detailed representation, for sense of shifting light and enveloping air.  It is easy to dismiss Pieter Bruegel as merely a resourceful illustrator, but the view is only half the truth.  On the material side of his art he was a constructor second to none.  It is no wonder that such a constructor as Peter Paul Rubens owned and even copied Bruegel's pictures, nor yet that that great constructor almost of yesterday, Jean François Millet, always kept prints of Bruegel pinned to his cottage walls at Barbizon.

Many of Bruegel's pictures of peasants, though they look like things seen, and are, carry a secondary meaning, and others continue the moralistic and emblematic vein which we have already discussed. Thus the admirable Bird Nesters, Vienna (Fig. 180), which seems remarkable only for its luminous landscape, for the hulking ease of the grinning peasant, the agility of the climbing boy, for the strong sense of growth of the oak tree—really illustrates the proverb:

> "He who knows where the nest is knows it,
> But he who takes it, shows it."

One may say that the picture is complete without the motto, but since the motto interested Bruegel, it properly interests us.  Certainly the picture has not suffered from its proverbial reference; it could not be more strongly and agreeably asserted merely as a thing seen.

Similarly the bulky peasant who almost hurtles out of the picture in the Johnson Collection, while the wolf harries his sheep in the distance, is the bad shepherd of the Gospels, who deserts his sheep, while the shepherd knocked down with the wolf at his throat, at Princeton, is, despite the grotesqueness and even horror of the mood, the good shepherd who gives his life for the sheep.  In both pictures the landscape backgrounds are of singular breadth, delicacy and beauty—and purely Flemish.  The Princeton picture is possibly a copy by the younger Pieter Bruegel.

One of the most terrible of Bruegel's creations, the Blind leading the Blind (Fig. 181), Naples, again illustrates a saying of Christ, "If the blind lead the blind both shall fall into the ditch." Christ thought in terms of two persons, Bruegel, characteristically, of more— five. They are of various degrees of blindness. Empty eye sockets mark the beggar tottering at the brink of the ditch. One winces and draws a short breath as he seems about to fall upon his comrade, already down with his bass viol. Towards the rear of the single file with grasped hands the beggars see dimly and sense the trouble ahead. It is a picture of ghastly truthfulness, with an almost cruel impact upon the nerves of the beholder, and its grim and sordid terror is much enhanced by the quiet scene with its trees, greensward, and modest village church. Few painters have been able to turn so taut the screw of pathos and horror, and we doubtless have here not merely a devastating event, but also a universal symbol of human blindness.

There are peasant and pauper pictures without ulterior meaning. An extraordinary drawing of Epileptics out for a Walk, and a print of a Picnic of Mad People, are here highly characteristic. It is said that the great psychiatrist, Dr. Charcot, asserted the minute truthfulness of the observation embodied in these designs. Of pictures of this sort none is more remarkable than the Wooden Leggers, *Les Culs des Jattes*, Paris. Here is not only cruelly complete observation of physical deformity, but a tragic sense of corresponding moral deformity. These cripples seem huddled together not to share their misery and lighten it, but to pool their misery in some sort of sinister reprisal against the more fortunate. Here is direct and concrete diabolism as compared with the indirect diabolism of Bosch.

If Bruegel could be sinister, he was habitually genial. The sheer jollity of the Peasant Dance (Fig. 182), at Vienna, and of the several Wedding Feasts which show peasants celebrating holy matrimony by the joys of gluttony—the sheer jollity of such pictures is so captivating that one overlooks their technical mastery and their beauty of a sharply contrasted coloring that remains harmonious. The superiority of such pictures lies largely in their tremendous vitality. Bruegel accepted the human animal, and celebrated uncritically his prowess in work and play. Thus Bruegel stands at the head of a great line which was soon to include Jordaens, Brouwer, and, exceptionally, Rubens.

Bruegel's most diligent and enthusiastic biographer and critic,

M. Bastelaer, sees in such pictures the sign of a turnover from allegory and proverb to direct observation.   And this is the general truth
of Bruegel's last years.   It should be recalled, however, that he never
abandoned symbolism entirely and to the end loved to give his pictures some moral or at least literary reference.   What is important,
after all, in these peasant pictures is their skillful use of direct observation.   They amply bear out Van Mander's testimony that Pieter
Bruegel and his employer, Jerome Cock, had the habit of going about
disguised as peasants, talking and drinking with the real workers in
the little shops and broad fields.   It is a procedure that undoubtedly
furthered Bruegel's art, and probably shortened his life, for it is still
hazardous for any man of sedentary habit to eat and drink on equal
terms with the peasants of the Low Countries.

Bruegel's famous pictures of crowds should be looked at as peopled panoramas which have to be explored.   This crosses the habit of
most picture lovers, who expect to grasp the look and the meaning
of a picture at a glance.   But after all, the appreciation of these works
is of a sort which we all accept in the case of architecture.   We take
in the whole of a building from several aspects, we walk about it and
study its structure and details and ornament.   Keeping all these observations in mind, by a constructive process of memory we attain to
the sense of the building.   Because we rarely go through so long a
process, nor yet tax memory so much, in appreciating pictures, is no
reason why we should decline to do so in the case of these anomalous
masterpieces of Pieter Bruegel.   The effort to read them will always
be richly rewarded.

Of this class we may first study the Massacre of the Innocents,
Vienna, if only because it ties up with Bruegel's peasant art.   Everything is contemporary and actual.   Down a snow-covered village street
of Flanders moves inexorably a platoon of mounted men at arms,
their lances bristling upright in military order.   Before them a crowd
of peasants in groups scatters and yields, while frightened dogs run
about.   The general grimness of the theme, the sacking of a peaceful
village, appears at a glance.   Everybody in Flanders had heard of, or
even seen, just this sort of thing in the religious wars.   It would have
interested everyone, without much shocking anybody.

The specific horror of the theme appears only on closer inspection.   Dismounted horsemen are seizing and killing the little children of the village with a cool and businesslike efficiency.   The help-

less parents and relatives resist feebly and not much. There is no use. Bruegel rings the changes on these despairing family groups. At the left a father tries in vain to barter the life of a well-grown little girl against that of an infant son, whom a soldier holds head downward by the feet. Everything is dispersed, yet the dispersion is of the emotional essence, and through this particularizing method step by step a cumulative effect of pitifulness is gradually built up. Nothing could be more unlike the Italian method of selection, dramatization and concentration.

An Italian artist would limit himself to a few figures, give them carefully chosen, even noble attitudes of terror, perhaps introduce King Herod symbolically as the planner of the massacre. Poussin will make a great picture of the theme by focusing it in the hopeless struggle of a single mother with one soldier. Bruegel treats everything as it might have happened, indeed as it again might happen if the Duke of Alba's dragoons should get out of hand when seizing a rebellious village. Bruegel accepts the fact that in life tragedy is not arranged and staged. The terrible event happens among other happenings, relevant to it or not. Jacopo and Gentile Bellini and Carpaccio in Venice had already treated pictorial themes, without much central emphasis or isolation, as merely circumstances amid other circumstances, and to this extent these Venetian masters lack true Italian accent. One could argue at length as to which is the better method. Evidently Bruegel's, even if it be thought to lack some fealty to art, is far truer to life, and our purpose is not to raise and solve broad problems in esthetics, but rather to understand the art of Pieter Bruegel.

Perhaps his handling of crowds is best studied in the Crossbearing, Vienna (Fig. 183). We have a plunging view of a grassy slope that leads to a hill upon which is a gallows. Beyond, in the center, is a fantastic, spiky butte absurdly surmounted by a windmill. It shows that Bruegel must have gone to Italy by way of Le Puy and the Rhone. A thin crowd with a few horsemen straggles towards the hilltop at the right. In the foreground is a seated group of St. John and the Holy Women comforting the Virgin Mary. Dressed in the traditional robes, they are like an excerpt from something of Quentin Massys. But this alien feature after all tells what causes the movement of the throng. Beside it is a favorite accessory of Jerome Bosch,

the bleached skull of a horse.  Beyond the group, Christ, barely distinguishable, sinks under the weight of the cross.

The eye now moves along with the crowd to its objective, the
crowded circle of enterprising early comers awaiting the rare spectacle of a triple crucifixion.  Except for the concession to tradition in
the group of the Marys, Pieter Bruegel thinks in terms of a Flemish
crowd of all sorts going out to see a hanging.  There is no attempt to
emphasize the particular meaning of this execution.  It is hardly a
Christian picture, but it is a singularly truthful account of antecedents and the surroundings of the death on Calvary, in terms of
Bruegel's day.  There is no space to describe the variety and interest
of the figures, of the groups so desultory yet so resolute in their direction.  There could be no finer example of Bruegel's keen and perceptive enthusiasm for the collective human spectacle.

Equally remarkable, and somewhat more legible, is the picture,
Children's Games, at Vienna.  One looks across a village square
which opens at the left upon a rural vista and is extended at the
right by a street.  The irregular quadrangle swarms with little boys
and girls.  Even before one realizes that they are engaged with the
intentness of childhood upon ritual games, one feels an agreeable
picture of a busy village.  There is a toy shop at the lower left, and
the some two hundred children are playing some fifty games, many
of which will be familiar to readers who have not forgotten their
own childhood joys.  Merely as a document, the picture is an extraordinary compendium of child folklore, and it is interesting to realize
the duration and perennial attractiveness of these exercises of youthful muscles and wits.  While each group is skillfully and vivaciously
composed, so that the picture would cut up into forty complete pictures, one can hardly speak of composition.  The groups are simply
polka dotted about the irregular quadrangle.  Care in composition
has been limited to the setting, which is usually the case of the pictures in which Bruegel celebrates crowds.  The animation and good-
natured sympathy with which the children and their acts are touched
in makes the picture uniquely refreshing.

Before passing to Pieter Bruegel's ultimate achievement as a pioneer landscape painter, we may go backward a little and pick up the
thread of his life.  Much of 1552 he spent in Italy, returning by winter of the next year, for his print of skaters is dated in 1553, and the
original drawing can hardly have been made before December.

Rather few Italian sketches are preserved, but many either in drawings or prints which recall his impressions of the river valleys of France and the crags of the Alpine passes. After his return he drew for Jerome Cock's engravers and painted assiduously, on the whole moving away from his early symbolic and moralistic vein towards such studies of the life of the people as we have considered above. For ten years he remained a bachelor, consoled by a mistress who, according to Van Mander, was an inveterate liar. She naturally wished to be a wife and Pieter promised to marry her if she would stop lying. He tallied her lies on a long stick, and when it was notched from end to end he naturally withdrew the conditional promise.

In 1563 he married his first master's daughter, Maria Coecke, whom he had dandled as an infant. He was in the middle thirties, she probably only half his age. Perhaps he settled down. One hopes so. In any case, through their sons Pieter II and Jan was established for three generations a remarkable dynasty of successful painters. Perhaps to detach himself from his lying mistress, the marriage took place at Brussels where Pieter was to live for the six remaining years of his life. This meant breaking of relations with boon companions, also with the various chambers of rhetoric who, through their pedantic debates and adventures in set allegorical themes, had fostered his early vein. It was a moment of new responsibilities and an opportunity for reflection. One may imagine him turning over his well-filled portfolios of landscape drawings and planning a grander and more truthful landscape painting than Northern Europe had yet seen.

Pieter Bruegel's most diligent and recent critic, Professor Jedlicka, divides the painter's activity into two phases—the first devoted to exploitation and implicit condemnation of human folly, the second guided by a consolatory vision of the vastness and orderliness of nature. This analysis, if not pushed too far, has much to commend it. Unquestionably Bruegel explored with zest the spectacle of a cockeyed world, conceived human relations as essentially irrational, as if not human will, but some insensate automatism were involved. Professor Jedlicka remarks acutely that in Pieter Bruegel's figures we deal not with persons, in individuals, but with types, almost with abstractions. Even his children have nothing youthful about them, but are merely an urgent sort of dwarf. So far we may go with the strenuous Swiss critic.

The larger issue whether Pieter Bruegel shifted from an intolerably tragic attitude to one of wise passiveness in the face of nature remains to be considered.  Unquestionably Bruegel painted a handful of pictures so appalling in their moral implications that one might justly regard their creator as an unqualified pessimist.  The Blind leading the Blind (Fig. 181) may be taken as a terrifying allegory for universal human blindness; the Men with Wooden Legs draws the eternal and very dreadful analogy between crippled bodies and maimed souls.  In short, such black visions of the hopeless incapacity of mankind to lead any sort of life of reason were evidently within Pieter Bruegel's range.  They do not seem to me characteristic.  I find his customary mood, on the contrary, genial and life-accepting. His attitude towards a deranged world seems to me rather one of amusement than of censorship.  I imagine him not so much deploring as rejoicing in the unfailing spectacle of the follies and vagaries of the human animal—fascinated by the vision of folly as Jerome Bosch had been by that of sin, and perhaps the smaller intellectual and moral stature of Pieter Bruegel is shown precisely in the fact that he was content to specialize on folly, whereas Jerome Bosch fathomed the far deeper abyss of iniquity.

If this view of Pieter Bruegel's attitude towards his fellows be correct, we may feel that he may have turned to landscape for the prosaic reason that he had fully exhausted his earlier vein.  Indeed in his drawings he had for years been preparing for his ultimate triumphs as a landscape painter.  In short, we do not need to suppose that he became a landscape painter in order to shake off a nightmare.

The last three or four years of Pieter Bruegel's short life were devoted chiefly to landscape painting, and he made an art peculiarly his own.  He could be as minute as Patenier or as broad as Rubens. In any of his great pictures you will find these seemingly opposed ideals harmonized.  While really using rather few colors—so that the tonal landscape of Hercules Segers and Jan van Goyen really grows out of his practice—he gives a sense of rich color.  Everything in his landscapes is alive—the trees twist and fork strongly, the slopes seem active, the rivers run, the crags and mountains rise dynamically from the level.  Then he rejects the quiet, afternoon lighting of his predecessors.  He deals with sunset and sunrise, with the gray chill of winter.  His cumulus clouds float lightly; his slaty storm clouds threaten.

He paints undauntedly in the face of changing nature, or rather he remembers its moods so well that he can reproduce them at will.

An artist thus gifted can never have been indifferent to the variety and nobility of natural appearances, but this native bent seems to have been much emphasized and concentrated by the impressions and recollections of the trip to Italy made in his young manhood. Possibly it needed the sharp sensations which the grandiose scenery of the Alps awoke to make him fully realize the intimate charm of the fields, copses and villages of the Low Countries. Both in the grandiose and familiar vein he excels. He paints with equal felicity and conviction the towering crags under which King Saul fights his last battle, Vienna; the village common and church behind the Blind leading the Blind, Naples (Fig. 181); or the broad acres of golden, ripe wheat across which one glimpses the distant sea, New York.

But, assuming this native bent for landscape, it is likely enough that it was his Alpine impressions which released the great landscape painter in him. These experiences of mountain grandeur haunted the rest of his activity. In the fantastic words of Van Mander, Bruegel "in passing the Alps swallowed the mountains and crags to vomit them up on his return on his canvas and panels." Indeed the peaks and ranges which so often rise beyond the Flemish foregrounds and middle distances of his landscapes seem, as Van Mander felt, to be disgorged from some inexhaustible inner store, for there are singularly few pen sketches made on the spot.

At this point I might simply advise the reader to look up the various excellent reproductions of the incomplete series of the Months, at Vienna, and the stray member of the series at New York. Yet a word on the art involved in making these great panoramas of the changing seasons may not seem superfluous. One of the richest in mood is Winter, Somber Day. Much of its effectiveness depends on the contrast of the exquisitely and nervously felt tracery of the bare treetops and fallen branches with the broad masses of the landscape. The lighting, too, is admirably calculated. The crisped pewtery gleam of the river bend is repeated in the silvery bole of a fallen beech tree in right foreground, in the white masses of the shirts and hose of the group of wood choppers, in unexpected flashes of light on clay banks and cottage roofs, in the ominous bright swirl of the sky at the left and even in the tiny fleck of a seagull flying across the sooty sky at the right.   Everything is so modulated as to produce and relieve an effect of noble dreariness.

February (Fig. 167), on the contrary, has a bleak charm.   Three hunters with their hounds stride into the picture from the left.   From the hillock rise sharp and dark against the sunny landscape the trunks and lower forking of three trees.   In the center a tangle of brush forms a delicate arabesque against the snow.   Looking with the eyes of the hunters—it is as if we plodded with them through the snow— we look over two square skating ponds, enlivened by skaters and bordered by willows already russet with presage of spring, to a gently rising farming country which ends where Alpine crags push up against the sky.   The sky itself, in order not to compete with the numerous interesting forms below—snow-covered roofs of cottages, files of trees and the like—is held to a uniform tone of veiled, grayish blue.   About this picture there is something welcoming, something of elation, as there was something of doom in the January.   Whoever has known the thrill of work or play in great snowfields will be perfectly at home in Bruegel's February.

Return of the Herd, probably November, at Vienna (Fig. 184), is a marvelous pageant of the dying year.   Everything is filled with the threat of coming winter.   Crags, bare trees, the sharply bent river, the hard, gleaming edges of the clouds, are felt with a cruel lucidity. As a contrast to the precise, almost geometrical pattern of the landscape, the hesitant, round forms of the casually moving cattle are singularly effective.   No one before Bruegel, and few since, have felt so deeply and truly the varying moods evoked by nature as the months achieve the cycle of the year.

It may be noted that all these landscapes have a structure of pronounced diagonals which counterpoise each other actively, and are varied and relieved by the easier upright forms of the trees.   As a system of composition it is precisely Titian's in figure design and Bruegel's accomplished use of a distinctly Renaissance formula makes one feel that he had profited more than is usually admitted by his Italian sojourn.

Less romantic and immediately attractive than its fellows, the Wheat Harvest, July, at New York (Fig. 185), is for me one of the greatest of the series.   The great, irregular, cubical block of golden wheat is shoulder high in near middle distance.   The reapers have worked at the edge near us, and now are eating the noonday meal under a tree, beside which in sprawling sleep lies an exhausted work-man.  Beyond the wheat is a church tower and grove, a quiet stretch of farm lands, the gleam of an inlet from a distant veiled sea which loses itself without a perceptible horizon in a misty sky.  There is something honest, foursquare and Wordsworthian about this picture.  It represents the greatness of its painter in his twofold aspect, as the vigorous celebrant of everyday work and play of common folk, and as the first searching observer of the actual look of landscape and interpreter of its characteristic moods.  We may well take leave of Pieter Bruegel with a masterpiece that is completely Flemish and with-out any alien and borrowed embellishment.

Early in September of 1569 Pieter Bruegel died, being not much past forty.  He charged his young wife to destroy his allegorical and moralistic designs.  In those troubled times they might bring down political or religious persecution upon his young family.  Through the prints after his drawings, his own pictures, and the numerous able copies thereof made by his son Pieter II, Old Bruegel's art became a marked influence on the landscape and genre painting of the next century.  No less than twenty-six of his descendants were to be paint-ers.  Few painter lives have been at once so short and have carried so far.

CHAPTER XII

FRENCH AND GERMAN PAINTING IN
THE SIXTEENTH CENTURY

FIG. 186. (Upper) FRANÇOIS CLOUET. Diane of Poitiers in Her Bath.—
Coll. Sir Robert Cook, Richmond.

FIG. 187. (Lower) PRIMATICCIO. Panel from Gallery of Francis I.—Fontainebleau.

Fig. 188. (Upper) JEAN CLOUET. Francis I.—Paris.
Fig. 189. (Lower) Fontainebleau School, about 1550. Toilette of Venus.—
Paris.

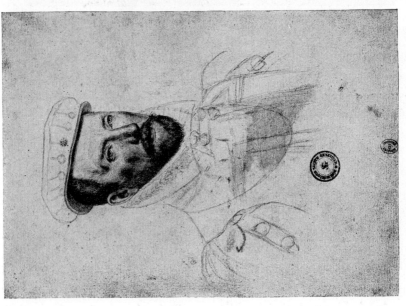

FIG. 191. FRANÇOIS CLOUET. Elizabeth of Austria.—*Paris.*

FIG. 190. FRANÇOIS CLOUET. Admiral Coligny.—*Paris.*

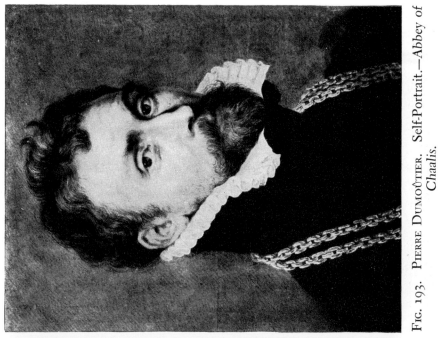

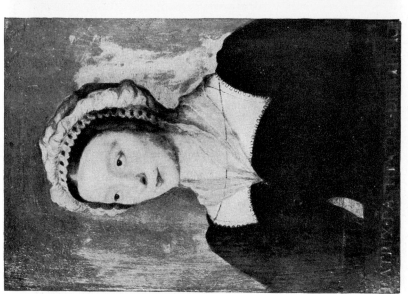

Fig. 192. Cornelle de Lyon. Beatrice Pacheco.—Versailles.

Fig. 193. Pierre Dumoûtier. Self-Portrait.—Abbey of Chaalis.

337

FIG. 195.   FRANÇOIS POURBUS THE YOUNGER.
Henri IV.—Chantilly.

FIG. 194.   FRANÇOIS POURBUS THE YOUNGER.   Louis
XIII.—Florence.

Tʜᴀᴛ constant trickle of Italian influence into France which had
begun in the late fourteenth century swelled to a flood before
the middle of the sixteenth. Its permanent results were the
poetry of the Pléiade, the exquisite sculpture of Jean Goujon and
Germain Pilon, an admirably alert and sensitive ornamentation of
Renaissance inspiration, the new Louvre and the great châteaux. As
compared with these gains in literature, sculpture, decoration and
architecture, the new achievement in painting was almost negligible.
Why were the few and poor painters of the so-called Fontainebleau
School so far inferior to their contemporaries in the other arts?

Partly because they were of less intelligence; partly because the
Italian painters brought to France by Francis I and Henry II were
themselves of the second order and unfit exemplars; partly because
of the difficulty of exchanging a smooth late-Gothic technique for
one appropriate to the new Italian themes. The shift towards Italy,
in short, so far as French painting was concerned, came too suddenly.
The new style was studied in its externals, as a fashion, and not in its
principles, from which, even in the decadence of the Italian manner,
much might still have been learned.

The simplest expression for the Fontainebleau School is that it
was a sort of ill-born and undernourished love child of Francis I by
the Gonzaga palaces at Mantua. To the general rule that Italy ever
conquered her actual or would-be conquerors, the vainglorious but
sensitive Francis I was no exception. On his return from imprisonment at Madrid, for the rest of his life he employed the most able
Italian artists that could be tempted to France. In particular he drastically remodeled and enlarged the old hunting lodge at Fontainebleau into something like the stately pile which we still see. He tried
to draw Giulio Romano from Mantua, but instead had to satisfy himself with Giulio's able young Bolognese assistant, Primaticcio, and
with the veteran Florentine, Il Rosso. They proceeded to design interiors fairly comparable to those at Mantua. Ornamental and figure sculpture framed the spaces reserved for frescoed pictures, the

sculpture on the whole predominating (Fig. 187). In these spaces the two Italian masters painted the accepted subjects—mostly mythological, sometimes allegorical, painted these already hackneyed themes with a vigor and versatility which the North had not yet seen. What remains on the walls today is wreck, or worse, drastic restoration, but fortunately many of the preliminary sketches, and even some working drawings, have been preserved. From them we may infer the character of these famous decorations.

Both Rosso and Primaticcio were mannerists, deliberately seeking novelty and elegance by elongated forms and artificial postures; both liked to solve the difficult problem of densely arranged groups of figures without relieving interspaces or steadying background. Both were resourceful and ingenious in invention and technically able in execution. The general quality of this art may be represented by Primaticcio's spandrel design for Apollo and the Muses, in the British Museum. One may note the consciously willed elegance of the small joints, the graceful feet, the calculated twists of the tall bodies. This sort of thing seemed marvelous to young French artists with a deep inferiority complex and eager to paint as elegantly as these masters from fabled Italy.

After Rosso's death in 1544, Primaticcio succeeded to control of the works. He not merely superintended the new construction and decoration of Fontainebleau, but became a self-appointed chief of works for all royal artistic projects, designed for stucco reliefs, stonecutting, enamels and tapestry. Gradually many able Italians joined him and assured the continuation of his work—Niccolò d'Abate, Luca Penni, once Raphael's assistant, and Pellegrino Daniele. Naturally dozens of French assistants were at one time or another employed, and Fontainebleau became a center from which the Italian and manneristic taste radiated throughout France and even to Flanders and the Germanies.

On architecture, decoration, and sculpture the new influence was beneficial. In these branches the borrowings from Italy soon took a lighter and more fanciful Gallic cast. In painting the new enthusiasm evoked only a heavy-handed imitation of the superficial features of Italian mannerism. The architects could steady themselves by reading Vitruvius and Leon Battista Alberti; the poets who imitated Petrarch and Bembo knew thoroughly the classical exemplars of these celebrated Italians. Had not Pierre Ronsard read Homer through in three days? We have his sonnet for it. But the painters seem to have been mere journeymen without critical capacity, and the painting of the Fontainebleau School that is French, and not Italian, is of abject inferiority.

In the new Italianate manner there are many nudes and semi-nudes, mostly ideal portraits of the mistresses of Henri II, Gabrielle d'Estrées and Diane de Poitiers, at least tolerable as pictures, though generally of feeble construction and execution. One of the best of this sort, in the collection of Sir Robert Cook, Richmond, is Diane de Poitiers in her bath, by François Clouet (Fig. 186), with servants and a vista of her living room, where very oddly, a unicorn, symbol of chastity, is embroidered on a chair back. In mythology some French painters of the Fontainebleau School acquired a passable proficiency. Characteristic here are such pictures as the Judgment of Paris, and the Toilette of Venus (Fig. 189), Louvre. On any general standard, these sophisticated and mildly agreeable pictures are at best fourth rate.

It is unnecessary to trace the few known and named painters who carried the style of Fontainebleau to the end of the century. The two Cousins, father and son, and Martin Fréminet had a certain ability and power undirected by anything like taste. The best paintings of the Fontainebleau School sink into insignificance beside some tiny engraving by Jean Gourmont or Étienne Delaune. What is admirable in sixteenth-century painting in France is the continuation of the Gothic style in portraiture from Jean Clouet through his son François and his imitators Corneille de Lyon and the Dumoûtiers to François Pourbus. In short, the attempted assimilation of the Renaissance manner by the Fontainebleau School was a flash in the pan. The whole task had to be undertaken anew in the next century by such intelligent painters as Simon Vouet and his rivals. It was they who prepared the way for the tardy flowering of the Northern Renaissance in the grave and noble art of Nicolas Poussin.

All the same, Fontainebleau as a halfway house to Italy was of considerable importance. Netherlanders and Germans whose lack of time, funds or inclination kept them out of Italy, found a working substitute in the frescoes of Il Rosso, Primaticcio and Niccolò d'Abate. Thus Fontainebleau became a secondary center of promulgation of Italian mannerism through much of Europe. And if the artistic results were on the whole trivial and unpleasing, the process was of a certain historical importance. Fontainebleau gave the death blow to the feebly surviving Gothic style and cleared a field upon which something new might be built. Country by country the new building was quite various, as we shall see.

It was in portraiture that France maintained her dwindling loyalty to the Gothic past, but to do so she had to borrow her portraitists from Flanders. Under the name of Clouet we have scores of paintings and hundreds of chalk drawings of French celebrities of the Renaissance—a documentation unique in its richness. Considerable differences of style and greater differences of quality tell us that we have to do with an industry of portrait making, probably managed by a couple of leading spirits but actually conducted by many hands. The Clouets, to use the term generically, served their times about as a photographer of celebrities serves us today. The chalk portraits of the Clouets were multiplied by copyists, could be sold at a reasonable price. There are entire collections at Chantilly and Paris and few print rooms lack their group of these drawings. This produces a difficult problem for the connoisseur. For example, at the beginning of the seventeenth century Marie de Médicis had a set of such crayon portraits of great personages of the two generations before her and down to her own time. She wrote the names on the sheets in her own firm hand. But was her retrospective collection made up of originals from life, from good old copies from such originals, or from copies made expressly for her? It would be a bold critic who would answer these questions dogmatically drawing by drawing. Hence a writer who is not at all a specialist in this field seems to be justified in treating the work of the Clouets and their successors in very general terms.

What is certain is only that a certain Jean Clouet, called Janet, whose training was Flemish, was settled in Paris as early as 1522, was soon appointed *valet de chambre* to François I, and worked for him and Henri II till about 1540. We reasonably associate him with a great mass of chalk portraits of the Court, mostly at Chantilly, and with a mere handful of painted portraits. Beyond this is a large number of portrait drawings and paintings, which may be from his shop, or may be later copies. Such relatively certain Jean Clouets, as the portrait of the dauphin, later Henri II, at Antwerp; that of the Duke of Guise, at Florence; the Equestrian Francis I, in the Pitti and the half-length, at Paris (Fig. 188), give the impression of a merely competent portraitist. The work has neither power nor finesse. One is sure, however, that it is resemblant. For the rest, the decorative effect of these carefully finished and almost shadowless busts on their well-chosen backgrounds of green or blue is pleasing if not exciting.

Janet's son, François Clouet, who in 1541 succeeded his father as *peintre du roi*, is a more substantial and accomplished figure. Without great power or penetration, finesse he commanded in a high degree. All his portraits, especially his chalk drawings, have an elegance truly Gallic. Whether with the brush or with the chalks, his touch was light and yet precise. He worked from about 1530 to 1572, serving four kings at one of the most interesting moments of French history. From his portraits we know the very look of those hard-fighting and hard-loving noblemen concerning whose amours Brantôme has fully informed us. As vivid, are François Clouet's portraits of those gentlewomen who inspired valiant deeds of arms and ardent enterprises of love. Indeed the historical and documentary value of the portraiture of François Clouet and his assistants is so great that it is difficult to treat the work merely as art.

On this score François Clouet's paintings and especially the drawings in black and colored chalk should be credited with the French virtues of neatness, precision, economy and taste. Beyond this there is really not much to say about them on the esthetic side. It is perhaps unfair to compare this work with the contemporary and stylistically similar portraiture of Holbein. To do so will show sharply the difference between consummately fine observation and execution and that which is merely good and competent.

François Clouet's sensitiveness as a draughtsman with the chalks is sufficiently represented by the portrait drawing of Admiral Coligny, at Paris (Fig. 190), while his grasp of character is well exemplified in the bust portrait of the vain and vacillating king, Charles IX, as his delicacy is in the portrait of Elizabeth of Austria (Fig. 191), both at Paris.

François Clouet's contemporary and rival, Corneille de Lyon, offers the same problem as the Clouets—namely, that of disengaging from a great number of portraits made in his style and often under his direction, the few that he painted himself. We shall never be able to draw this line exactly. Enough to say that at his best, in such a portrait as that of Beatrice Pacheco, at Versailles (Fig. 192), Corneille has made a little masterpiece of characterization such as neither of the Clouets ever equaled. The hundreds of excellent little portraits attributed to Corneille de Lyon in public and private collections are presumably products of his shop made under his supervision. Their quality is surprisingly uniform and high.

Corneille came from the Hague, was at Lyon by 1534, appointed painter to the dauphin, later Henri II, in 1541 and died in 1574. No chalk drawings by him have come down to us, which suggests that he may have abridged the usual process of painting from a drawing, by making the drawing on the panel itself.

The ingenuity of French enthusiasts has worked out groups of anonymous portraitists of this time, some of whom are of great excellence. But since nothing in the field is really first rate, these interesting classifications can merely be mentioned in a general survey.

About the time François Clouet and Corneille de Lyon died, the brothers Étienne (fl. 1560–1603) and Pierre Dumoùtier (fl. 1570?–1589) succeeded under Catherine de Médicis to the court functions of their predecessors. They seem to have worked exclusively in chalks, and to give the chalk portrait greater dignity they tended to enlarge its scale and to add new colors to the old black, red and white. Their drawing is more free and urbane, perhaps influenced by Italy. The chalk portrait under their hand becomes less of a sketch and more of a finished picture, looking towards portraiture in pastel.

Pierre Dumoùtier in his most serious vein may be represented by a male portrait probably of himself in the Abbey of Chaalis (Fig. 193). Étienne is seen at his best in the head of the Prince of Mayenne, ill-fated chief of the League, which is in the Cabinet des Estampes, Paris. The fact that this carefully studied head is squared for copying, shows the intention of making a highly finished portrait of the champion of the Church.

The activity of the Dumoùtiers reached beyond the end of the century and covered the reign of Henri IV. They left sons to continue their style.

But by the beginning of the seventeenth century the fashion of the chalk portrait waned. A host of competent Flemish portrait painters in oil flourished at Paris and enjoyed most of the patronage. The only one of these who retains any present importance is François Pourbus the younger. He was born at Antwerp about 1570, free of the guild in 1594. He worked in Italy, was for ten years employed by Vincenzo, Grand Duke of Mantua. He came to settle in Paris in

1610 about the time Henri IV was assassinated. Pourbus painted the dead king on his bier, and was appointed court painter to the Queen Dowager, Marie de Médicis. Despite his Italian years, his style remains Northern. He paints in the minute linear fashion and with that objectivity which had persisted in the Gothic North from the Van Eycks down. We may regard him as an adoptive member of the French school. He died in 1622 when Rubens was already working on the designs for the Luxembourg. He was more fortunate than the last of the old usually are, for he enjoyed both opulence and prestige. For the unvarying soundness and probity of his official portraiture he deserved his good luck. He painted no great picture, but he painted many carefully studied portraits of the men and women who for better or for worse shaped the modern nations out of the débris of medieval Europe. We may fittingly represent François Pourbus' really quite versatile art by his sensitive portrait of the Dauphin Louis XIII (Fig. 194) and by his portrait of Henri IV (Fig. 195) who, aside from making France a nation, cherished visions of a federated Europe. Pourbus had the merit of painting the figure competently, whereas his predecessors from the Clouets to the Dumoûtiers were merely face painters, who rarely undertook the representation of the whole figure, and when they did so did it badly.

In reviewing this century of official portraiture in France, much of it made by painters of alien birth, we must be struck by its general high level and its absence of masterpieces. This meritorious equality is in striking contrast with the ups and downs and general inferiority of the Fontainebleau School. What is remarkable about this portraiture from Jean Clouet to François Pourbus is its fine imperviousness to Italian influence, its avoidance of anything like mannerism or pretentiousness. It confidently carries on the native Gothic tradition, while the poets of the Pléiade and the painters of Fontainebleau were aping Italy. Apart then from the rather modest esthetic and the very high historic importance of this portraiture, it served a useful evolutionary purpose, in retarding the full invasion of France by the Renaissance style until the time had come when a reasonable and national assimilation of that style was possible.

The second half of the sixteenth century in Germany saw a little good architecture in the Renaissance manner and an abundance of good engraving and book illustration which continued decently well, if on a declining basis, the great tradition established by Dürer and his contemporaries. In painting there is virtually nothing to claim the attention of a modern art lover. The religious wars, the provincial courts, were inauspicious for art of any sort. The few gifted German painters fled for their esthetic salvation to Italy and a few distinguished themselves there, much as our American expatriates of the black-walnut era sought a refuge and a career in Paris, London, Rome or Munich.

The list of pioneer German expatriates is neither long nor bright, and its members belong in the main in the early seventeenth century. Rottenhammer made himself a mild echo of Tintoretto; Adam Elsheimer of Frankfurt became a delicate idylist and landscape painter at Rome. His tiny pictures still charm, and his work was widely influential. Matthew and Paul Bril, spirits akin to Elsheimer, if less fine, made of Germany a stepping stone to Rome, where they flourished worthily and mightily. Jan Liss early moved from Holstein to Venice and there made himself a distinguished member of that brilliant group which gathered about Fetti and Strozzi. Such excellent expatriate German painters seem to illustrate once more the melancholy truth that, German soil being the poorest possible for his development, the German painter does best when transplanted.

On the whole the Italian Renaissance imposed itself successfully in Germany only in architecture, ornamentation and the graphic arts, while the native Renaissance in painting, marked chiefly by analytical realism, exhausted itself early in the works of Dürer, Holbein and their contemporaries. From about 1550 on, the student of Western European painting of the Renaissance need not much concern himself with Germany.

CHAPTER XIII

SPANISH PAINTING IN THE SIXTEENTH
CENTURY

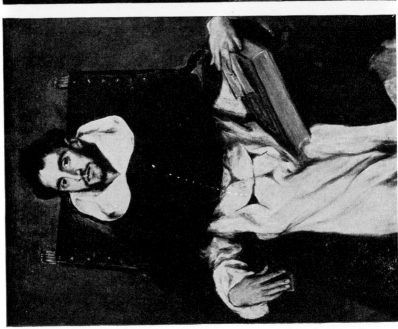

FIG. 196. EL GRECO. Fray Feliz Hortensio Pallavicino.—Boston.

FIG. 197. SANCHEZ COELLO. The Infanta Isabella Claudia
Eugenia.—Madrid.

348

FIG. 199.  VARGAS.  The Ancestors of Christ.—
Seville.

FIG.  198.  PEDRO CAMPAÑA.  Descent
from the Cross.—Seville.

FIG. 201.  ROELAS.  Martyrdom of St. Andrew.
—Seville.

FIG. 200.  FRANCISCO HERRERA THE ELDER.  St. Bonaventura Received as a Franciscan.—Coll. Earl of Clarendon, England.

350

Fig. 203. Ribalta. Vision of St. Francis.—
Valencia.

Fig. 202. Juanes. Visitation.—Madrid.

351

FIG. 204. (Upper left) MORALES. Madonna and Child.—Madrid.
FIG. 205. (Upper right) EL GRECO. Martyrdom of St. Mauritius's Legion.
—Escorial.
FIG. 206. (Lower) EL GRECO. Portrait of Giulio Clovio.—Naples.

Fig. 207. (Upper) EL GRECO. Christ Expelling the Money Changers.—
Coll. Sir Robert Cook, Richmond.
Fig. 208. (Lower) EL GRECO. Christ Expelling the Money Changers.—
London.

Fig. 210. El Greco. Assumption. —S. Vicente, Toledo.

Fig. 209. El Greco. Assumption.— Chicago.

354

FIG. 211. EL GRECO. Burial of Count Orgaz.—S. Tomé, Toledo.

355

FIG. 213. EL GRECO. Salutation.—Dumbarton Oaks Collection, Washington.

FIG. 212. EL GRECO. Resurrection.—Madrid.

Fig. 214. El Greco. Repentant St. Peter.—Phillips
Memorial. Washington.

Fig. 215. El Greco. Self-Portrait(?).—New York.

357

Fig. 216. El Greco. View of Toledo.—New York.

On a declining basis the old Hispano-Flemish style lasted well into the sixteenth century, only gradually yielding to Renaissance influences from Italy and, less auspiciously, from the Antwerp Romanists. In portraiture the old style persisted well beyond the sixteenth century, being reinforced and modernized by such court painting as that of Moro, Bronzino and the Pourbuses. The best Spanish practitioner of such portraiture was Sanchez Coello, born in the Valencian region in 1515. He had copied Titian, and in 1552 accompanied Antonio Moro to Portugal. On his return he became court painter to Philip II at Madrid, enjoyed the friendship of that gloomy and dissolute monarch, and probably painted more royal portraits than any artist known to history. Like all the court portraiture of the period, Coello's portraits are of extraordinary neatness and precision. The method is linear; no pains are spared in representing the sheen of silk and velvet, the deep gleam of gold embroidery, the glitter of pearls and jewels.

On the side of character all these official portraits have a uniform goodness without achieving anything like greatness. Generally they are not deeply individualized. All seem of one aristocratic family. In short, Coello never, or at least very rarely, goes beyond a most painstaking superficiality. In the portrait of the ill-fated Prince Carlos, Madrid, perhaps one feels that something more—a sense of moral maladjustment and of doom. Or are we merely reading into the picture recollections of Goethe's tragedy? At any rate it is an exceptionally fine Coello, and the odd composition gives a sense of loneliness. Coello is better known for his many pictures of richly bedizened princesses, such as that of the Infanta Isabella Claudia Eugenia (Fig. 197), at Madrid. It is only on close inspection of such portraits that their defects appear—in mechanical expedients for rendering the difficult details, in flaccid, patrician hands all of a pattern. In this very fine manufacture there is after all only a modicum of real observation. Everything is done by formula, and the whole work stands a little apart from the sound tradition of Spanish realism.

As a court painter Coello was much occupied with temporary decoration—the settings for pageants or for royal entries. He worked on till 1590 and died universally honored. His best pupil and successor at the court, Pantoja de la Cruz, on the whole showed the master's qualities and defects, but at his best had a more penetrating sense of character.

This may give, by sample, a fair notion of Spanish portraiture before Velasquez. It will be noted that, despite the numerous portraits by Titian at Madrid, there is no hint of his influence. The Spaniards preferred the older and more explicit methods, so their portraiture depended on procedures already exhausted, and it transmitted the minuteness of primitive portraiture—but without the primitive grace of intense and loving scrutiny.

The Renaissance entered Seville in 1537 in the person of the Fleming, Peter de Kempener. He was born at Brussels, probably trained with Bernard van Orley, is said to have studied ten years in Italy, where he is traceable at Bologna and Venice in the 1530's. He made a brilliant career at Seville as Pedro de Campaña. His style did not greatly progress beyond that of Van Orley, but certain graceful figures make one feel he had studied the early paintings of the pioneer mannerist, Parmigiano. Campaña's famous Descent from the Cross, in the Cathedral of Seville (Fig. 198), may for our purposes sufficiently represent him. The great scene is conceived with much picturesqueness, and, despite minor affectations, with real feeling. There is an ease and grace about the carefully studied arrangement, the like of which Spain had not seen. After some twenty-three years of success at Seville, the jealousy and machinations of the local painters drove him back to his native Brussels, where he was still to have some twenty years of acclaim as painter and director of the tapestry industry. He died after 1580 at an advanced age. While he was essentially an eclectic and compiler, drawing now upon the sweetness of Raphael, now upon the sublimity of Michelangelo, his borrowings seem to rest rather on real enthusiasm than on self-interest, so that among the Flemish Romanists he is one of the more original. His importance for Spanish painting is the introduction of the curvilinear, dynamic compositional schemes of the Italians; the attempt to express pathos with reserve and nobility; the simplification and concentration of design along lines of monumentality. In short, Seville and Spain were fortunate in having an *ad interim* missionary of the Renaissance of the capacity of Pedro Campaña.

The first native Sevillian to import the Italian manner was Luis de Vargas. Though he was older than Campaña and abler, his long studies in Italy brought his influence to Seville long after Campaña had made his mark. After a long probation in painting banners and such ephemeral work, Vargas found his way to Italy where he spent many years. His pictures are tediously plentiful in Seville, but they reward analysis, for something of honest Spanish realism intrudes oddly in works generally deeply infected by the fake grace and grandeur of Italian mannerism. His show piece and perhaps his most remarkable work is the Ancestors of Christ, ·in the Cathedral of Seville (Fig. 199). From a skillfully painted and prominent feature it is called "The Leg"—*La Gamba*. The Madonna and Child are poised high among clouds, and are of a vaguely Raphaelesque type. They look down upon a dense group of venerable persons—the ancestors. Only a few could be shown, but there is a sense of a multitude gradually lost in the shadowed background. Two women and a nude man flung across the group in vigorous foreshortenings are a sensational and effective element in the design. The sharp contrast of light and dark is not quite Italian. In this respect even the Italian mannerists were less overtly theatrical. However Vargas carries it off well, and establishes his composition in balance of active thrusts, having probably caught the trick from study of Michelangelo in the Sistine Chapel. But there is something solidly Spanish in the heavy, serious masks of Christ's bearded ancestors, while the skeleton emerging behind the exhibitor of the famous leg—I take him to be St. John the Baptist—is a macabre feature entirely in the Spanish taste.

Now if you will imagine the sensationalism of Vargas toned down, sweetened and refined, and his emphatic contrasts of light and dark fused into a harmonious tonality, you would have something very much like Murillo. It is this ancestral potentiality of Vargas that gives him an importance that his actual accomplishment might hardly justify.

The only important successors of Campaña and Vargas at Seville were Juan de las Roelas (1558–1625) and Francisco de Herrera (1576–1656). In them the Italian manner begins to speak Spanish, indeed in Herrera it is ultimately discarded in favor of a drastic method through which the native extravagant emotion could be expressed. While Herrera had assimilated the Italian teaching, in the sense that he knew his anatomy, his constructive light and dark, a reasonable fashion of crowding large figures into a unified composition, he utterly rejected the Italian taste for gracefulness and conventional elegance. He painted his rugged Spanish models as they looked to him, and to express that look he invented a coarsely effective handling, loading the paint on and pulling it about so that the light splintered from it as it does in nature. Thus his pictures are very much alive, not to say agitated. Herrera must be credited with the invention of this new technique, for there were no Italian precedents, and his style was well established before he could have seen anything by his much younger contemporary, Ribera. As a pioneer he is here treated, though most of his career falls in the seventeenth century.

Herrera is the first Renaissance painter of Spain who unflinchingly called a spade a spade. His pictures are full of the savage dignity and fanatical ardor of the national character. Herrera's most accessible and best known picture is St. Basil dictating his Book, at Paris. The whole thing is most emphatically expressed in mass. These monks and clerics have blood and bones, formidable digestions, and an equally impressive concentration on the inspired utterance of the saint. The relicf is almost unpleasantly realized—you could handle the edge of any robe, pull any nose. All the same the rugged integrity of the vision and execution commands respect and sticks in the memory.

We may represent Herrera by a less familiar picture, St. Bonaventura received as a Franciscan, one of a series in the collection of the Earl of Clarendon, England (Fig. 200). Everything is conceived as taking place in a contemporary chapter of Friars Minor in Spain. We see the sort of men who were heroic missionaries in the New World and in the recently opened regions of Asia.

Now again if you can imagine the handling of Herrera subtilized, his preoccupation with illumination refined by a more delicate and strenuous observation, his love of the look of things tempered by reflection and analysis—then you would have something very like Velasquez. In short, whatever the judgment of Herrera's painting, his value as an ancestor is beyond cavil.

Juan de las Roelas was born in 1558 of a distinguished family, well educated and ultimately attached to the Cathedral of Seville.

He studied in Italy and sensibly took rather the Venetian painters than the Roman as his models. Under his hands the altarpiece grows in size, includes more figures, offers more energetic and complicated arrangements and a greater fusion of color. About his best work there is something grandiose. The Crucifixion of St. Andrew, at Seville (Fig. 201), is in most respects a disagreeable picture, but in its superimposition of figures several rows deep, in its skillful handling of half-tones, in its selected contrasts of light and dark, it is highly effective. Again, the Death of St. Hermenijildo, in the Cathedral, shows a merely professional accomplishment equal to that of the contemporary Italian mannerists, and a greater sincerity. It is like so many late-Renaissance pictures divided into a celestial and terrestrial order. Above, the Madonna, supported on clouds among angel choirs, receives the soul of the saint, while below mourners gesticulate with grief and amazement. It is somewhat overcrowded and overstated, but the overstatement is that of a believer, and it achieves an effect of real ecstasy. Even finer is St. James in Battle, in the Cathedral, a picture full of romantic ardor.

The fortunes of Roelas were various. For a time he was a prebendary at the little church at Olivares. Later he vainly sought the patronage of Philip IV in the new capital, Madrid, and received instead promotion to a canonry at Olivares. This position he held for only a year, for he died in 1625, but in his last months he painted for his church two of his best pictures. Roelas, like Vargas, was somewhat hampered by his Italianism, but he was probably helped more. The century of the great religious mystics, Juan de la Cruz, Santa Teresa, Ignatius Loyola, demanded a more oratorical utterance of its faith than the older painting could supply, and only Italy could teach the needed pictorial rhetoric. Accordingly it is foolish to ask of these transitional men that they should do the impossible—invent a style (it has remained for our times to commit that folly). They had to learn the best style available, and they did, and in so doing they well served their time.

For two centuries Valencia had been Italy's stepping stone to Spain, and such she was to be both for the declining Renaissance style and for the vigorous new realism of Caravaggio. Here the pioneer of the Renaissance is Juan de Juanes. He was born in 1523, and when studying in Italy modestly drew from the early manner of Raphael, or perhaps from belated Italian imitators of this style. Thus the pic-

tures which he painted after 1550 have the look of being good provincial Italian work of some forty years earlier. They are agreeable
enough, and of small importance. A Madonna with two Male and
two Female Saints, at Valencia, has the general quiet idylism of a
Venetian sacred conversation without the beauty of Venetian coloring, and with unassimilated Spanish features such as St. Agnes' lively
lamb and the nude babes struggling to catch the Christchild's attention. The circular panel representing the Visitation, Madrid (Fig.
202), has greater seriousness. St. Elizabeth's anxious genuflexion is
Spanish in feeling, so is it Spanish to introduce a secondary salutation
between St. Joseph and St. Zachariah. The picturesquely generalized
landscapes might have come out of an Italian picture. There is much
that is charming in Juanes' modest art, but perhaps the real importance of such work as his and Campaña's is rather negative than
positive. It brings about a new taste, it kills off older styles which
cannot express the new feeling. Thus it clears a site upon which
something may be built. Juanes died in 1579, and with him went,
not a great painter, but perhaps the most ingratiating Spanish artist
of Italianate mood.

His younger contemporary, Francisco de Ribalta (1551–1628),
had the intelligence to imitate not the forms but the principles of the
Italians. In Italy he studied especially such chiaroscurists as Correggio and Schidone. Thus he brought back to Valencia a new means
of realistic expression and became a true harbinger of what was to
come through his pupil, Ribera. Ribalta's Vision of St. Francis, at
Valencia (Fig. 203), is a thoroughly Spanish picture, in the unrestrained ardor of its religiosity. The sensationally concentrated and
sinister lighting is of a melodramatic intensity which his exemplars,
the Italian chiaroscurists, still somewhat influenced by Renaissance
decorum, would have disapproved.

The Castiles, as we have already noted, were relatively unpro-
ductive regions in all the arts until Philip II built the Escorial well
along in the sixteenth century and prepared to make the little city
of Madrid his capital. Morales was born at Badajoz about 1509.
Nothing substantial is known about his training, but since his work
shows a strangely sentimentalized Michelangelism, we may guess
either that he studied prints or drawings after that master, or possibly
studied the manner in Flemish dilution in the paintings of the Antwerp mannerists.

In Morales' work there is little variety—always the same gracile contours, the same diaphanous bleached-out carnations, the same exaggerated and woebegone pathos, always the same pallid dead Christs and sentimental Madonnas (Fig. 204). All this the Spaniards loved, and they called Morales "the Divine," *El Divino*. To me he seems merely the precursor of such insufferable sentimentalists as Carlo Dolce and Ary Scheffer, and I know of no other painter who has got so great a name from so slender an accomplishment.

In advanced middle age, about 1564, he was called to the Escorial by Philip II, and later received a handsome pension from that monarch. Morales died in 1588, nearly ninety and full of honors. I wish we knew just what Spaniards adored his pictures, for nothing more unlike the forthright realism proper to Spain could be imagined. I fancy his popularity was launched by an influential and highly sentimental class of gentlewomen immured in convents.

Fulfilling a vow made during the battle of St. Quentin, in 1564, Philip II began to build on the Sierra Guadarrama guarding the northern approach to his future capital, Madrid, the gloomy granite pile of the Monastery of the Escorial. It was designed rather heavily by Spanish architects, but there were no Spanish painters who seemed worthy to undertake the altarpieces and mural paintings. So Philip called in Italian artists, Carducci, Pellegrino Tibaldi, Federigo Zuccaro, Luca Cambiaso—mannerists all. Soon the king placed his collections in the Escorial. These included dozens of Titians purchased from the artist. The construction and decoration of the Escorial occupied about twenty years, and in this time certain of the Spanish painters employed as assistants had the sense to prefer Titian to the mannerists. Among these more intelligent Spanish painters was a deaf mute, Fernandez Navarrete, called, from his affliction, "the Deaf Mute," *El Mudo*. He studied and copied the Titians to such effect that he was called the "Spanish Titian." He was an admirable portraitist and a sincere and dignified composer of religious pictures. He died at Toledo in 1579, having made a satisfactory confession by the sign language, and left an entirely legal will conveying seven bequests in nine lines and thirty-seven words.

In 1580 there appeared at the Escorial a Greek painter of Venetian training, named Domenikos Theotokoupolos. The name being most unhandy, they called him "the Greek," El Greco. He had a commission from the king to paint the Martyrdom of St. Mauritius

(Fig. 205). The theme was refractory. In the foreground the Roman general, Mauritius, consults his Christian officers, while a multitude of his soldiers in middle distance await martyrdom or already lie headless before the executioner. A glory of angels, above, applauds the martyrs and prepares to receive their souls. It is a most impressive picture, but it has holes and confused passages. El Greco had probably seen Pontormo's picture of St. Maurice in the Pitti, at Florence, for he forces the horror and pathos in much the same way. Philip II disliked the picture, in fact a nearly contemporary writer tells us it pleased few, and relegated it to a more obscure altar than had been originally intended. El Greco went back to Toledo where for some five years he had been well established. One can hardly blame Philip II for disliking the picture—it is, as Padre Siguenza, already cited, remarked, more able than likable, but the art-loving king failed signally in perception when he saw only eccentricity in the work and failed to see that this alien Greek was the only man who had made or could make the long-sought grand style of the Italian Renaissance serve a Spanish use.

Before coming to Toledo about 1575, this Greek had had a varied and cosmopolitan career. He was born at Candia in 1541. The capital city of Crete was then a Venetian possession, and a boy growing up there in the 1550's would have had three kinds of painting before him—Byzantine painting of the severe traditional style, Byzantine painting much influenced compositionally by the Italian manner, and Venetian painting of developed Renaissance type. One may imagine some hesitation in the youth, and possibly a hope of adapting the new Renaissance technique to express more vividly and passionately the static solemnity of the ikons.

In 1570 the famous Croatian miniaturist, Giulio Clovio, recommended El Greco to Cardinal Farnese as a young and able disciple of Titian. We may reasonably suppose that El Greco, as pupil or assistant, had been with Titian for the seven or eight previous years. Whether he came to Venice to study with Titian, or whether his parents earlier joined the colony of four thousand Greeks at Venice, we do not know. We may be sure, however, that the young Cretan remained an exotic, and yielded little to the voluptuous urbanity of his civic and artistic surroundings.

We have a few portraits and perhaps a score of early pictures, mostly small, and since most of them have been attributed to such painters as Titian, Tintoretto, Veronese, and Francesco Bassano, we can be sure that the young Greek kept his eyes open and educated himself by critical study of his elders and betters. It should be recalled that the Titian whom El Greco served was a bereaved and lonely man in the late eighties, worried about the misconduct of a son, and about his financial relations with Philip II. Most of his great pagan mythologies had been painted, perhaps forgotten, and he was engaged in devout and tragic mood on such harrowing subjects as the Crowning with Thorns, the Agony in the Garden, the Crucifixion, the Entombment. And these painful themes which he had earlier attenuated, he now paints drastically with the most Christian sympathy. To interpret them he now seeks tone, eschews the old gay polychromy, employs a lighting no longer chiefly descriptive and defining, but chosen for its emotional potency.

Thus Titian's shop was calculated to enhance any tragic and mystical bent which may have been native to the young Greek who ground the paints and cleaned the brushes. But there are indications that the influence of Titian worked tardily, and only after the move to Toledo had furthered detached reflection. For the Italian Grecos have nothing of Titian's tragic profundity. They suggest rather the forthright athleticism of Tintoretto and the rather overt stage management of the Bassani. The swollen muscles and pinched-in joints are entirely in Tintoretto's manner, and where the critics see a trace of Michelangelism I believe we really have chiefly a reflection of Tintoretto's constant homage to Michelangelo.

Probably only a small fraction of what Greco painted in Italy has come down to us, and that remnant merely announces a good talent, giving very slight hint of the future genius. The sound and dignified half-length portrait of a Venetian patrician, at Copenhagen, generally passed for an average Tintoretto, before cleaning disclosed the signature. The better-known portrait of Giulio Clovio, at Naples (Fig. 206), but for the signature would probably be catalogued as a Francesco Bassano. The long oblong is a favorite shape in his portraiture as is the outlook to a landscape through a window. It is a worthy, quite literal, rather dull performance. We are far indeed from those strangely stylized portraits with their suggestion of fanaticism and exaltation which Greco was soon to be painting in Spain.

In the religious pictures of this early period appears the habit, which was to be lifelong, of repeating his compositions with constant changes. We have about a dozen pictures on two themes, Christ healing a Blind Man, and Christ driving the Money Changers from the Temple. It is as if Greco were deliberately experimenting with a tranquil and an agitated theme.

The progress from picture to picture is always in the direction of simplification and concentration. Greco begins in the spectacular and static vein of Paolo Veronese and moves towards the dramatic mood of Tintoretto. And the color follows the same course—from a rather blond polychromy to a limited tonality and sharper contrasts of light and dark. The process is most easily traced in the Expulsion of the Money Changers, which begins with the dispersed arrangement and superfluity of accessories and figures which we find in the example in the Cook Collection, Richmond, England (Fig. 207). The action is almost lost in the general heaping up of agreeable details. But all that is soon swept away. The action is brought forward, unexpressive features are eliminated, the architecture becomes merely a frame. The figures are more elongated, sharp contrasts of light and dark assert the forms and suggest vehement action. Indeed the later examples of the Expulsion have so much of Greco's Spanish fire and energy, not to mention the elongated forms, that it is customary to suppose them, for example, the picture at London (Fig. 208), painted in Toledo. Be this as it may be, Greco, while remaining within the bounds of Venetian realism, was already seeking that more passionate utterance which, to find maximum expressiveness, must find fit symbolisms of color and suitable distortions of form.

It is customary to place in the Italian years the strange and thrilling genre picture, Man is Love, Woman is Fire, the Devil blows it. The proverb is Spanish, but it may have been current elsewhere. There are several versions of this picture, and a study at Naples for the central figure. The picture has the strangest fascination. A woman carefully touches a bunch of tow or tinder with a candle while she puffs carefully with pursed lips; a man in profile at the right observes the act fatuously. At the left a big ape, apparently an amiable embodiment of the devil, leans over the woman's hand and gives an aiding puff. One sees only the busts in shadow and the faces spectrally glowing from the light thrown up by the candle. It is an odd picture even to have been conceived in Italy. Only Savoldo and Correggio at this time had played with such theatrical effects of illumination, and they in more conventional mood. The workmanship of the several versions of this picture seems to me of Greco's early Spanish period. This issue is relatively unimportant. What is important is that Greco could create such a masterpiece of sardonic romanticism, and decline to follow up the vein. It is the single playful episode in the most serious of careers, and its playfulness is of a sinister sort.

Just how life at Toledo developed in El Greco these new capacities for emotion and this new pictorial language we may only guess. One may imagine that the mere loneliness of a proud, irritable, pleasure-loving alien would have exaggerated a natural introversion. It is not a happy painter who needed to hire musicians to play during his meals. Perhaps the move from the most compromising people in the world to the most uncompromising may have fostered the intransigent mood with which El Greco was born. In Italy the desire for grandeur and decorum set limits to expression in all the arts. Not so in Spain, where a humanistic moderation in expression would have seemed absurdly and gratuitously insincere, and where nerves were ever braced to welcome any attack the artist might make upon them. Into this absolutism of the emotions El Greco readily fell, with the result that he became more Spanish than any of his painter contemporaries in Spain.

He came to Toledo in 1575 or 1576, being about thirty-four years old. The strange intensification of his emotional life and pictorial manner did not come about suddenly. Indeed his earliest work at Toledo was really a respectful farewell to his Venetian training, as if he wished, before moving on to new conquests, to consolidate the position he had gained. So the great retable of the Ascension of Mary painted for S. Domingo el Antiguo, and the Stripping of Christ, in the Cathedral, are not merely the most accomplished Venetian pictures from Greco's hand, but also the most Titianesque. It is as if the consummate greatness of the master had dawned upon the pupil only after the master had died, as if only then had been felt the need of paying a worthy tribute to a great memory.

The central panel of the retable of S. Domingo, an Assumption of the Virgin, now at Chicago, and dated 1577 (Fig. 209), is, save for a few very sharp edges of the draperies and some very heavy and edgy darks, without Spanish features. There is no distortion; the dense groups about the empty tomb and the flight of angels about the

Virgin, perilously balanced on her crescent moon, are composed in Titian's fashion with an active equipoise of opposing diagonal thrusts. The color is both brilliant and cool, with rather little of the Venetian crimsons, green and yellow dominating. It is as if Greco had had in mind the rather equable, cool coloring of Veronese, whose superb adolescent angels he surely imitated, or the rare blond pictures of the Bassani, which avoid the obvious color harmonies. Otherwise it is a typical masterpiece of what we may with entire respect call the operatic mood of the Venetian Renaissance. The poses and gestures are carefully chosen for compositional effectiveness. The fundamental contrast between the masculine ardor of the group of apostles in the lower order and the feminine ecstasy of the Virgin and her celestial attendants is strongly asserted and constitutes much of the emotional appeal of the picture. It is a very fine Greco, but also a Greco of calculated and academic sort.

The future master reveals himself more clearly in the Trinity, Madrid, which once surmounted the Assumption, and in the magnificent figures of St. John the Baptist and the Evangelist, still in Santo Domingo. There is still much of Titian in all these pictures, not merely in their urbane linear pattern but also in their sobriety and measured emotionalism. But the coming style is presaged in clouds bulging and billowing as if storm-driven, in hard, luminous edges, in brows raised and distorted with grief. As for the beautifully modeled and disposed Dead Christ in His Father's arms, the nude forms seem to be skillfully adapted from Michelangelo.

To realize the difference between this admirable Assumption in the Venetian manner and one in Greco's own idiom one need only walk a short distance from Santo Domingo to San Vicente, where is an Assumption (Fig. 210), which Greco finished thirty-five years later, in 1613, only a few years before he died. The Madonna, elongated and distorted, sways to the right; from below a strong angel, hovering to the left, supports her. Two angels at her right draw away in ecstatic observation, at her left is an incandescence which resolves itself into angelic forms. The only link with earth is a few flowers which grow up from the bottom of the frame towards the delicately drooping feet of the supporting angel. And the guarantee that this angel can furnish the needed support is given only by one strong wing that fills the right center of the canvas. Harmonizing with the elongation of the figures, the tall rectangle, as is usual in the later Grecos, is no less than two squares high. This would ordinarily be regarded as an ugly and refractory proportion. But before such a picture no one thinks about proportions. It is simply a surface tremendously alive, alive through slashes of color and contrasts of light and dark, with no arresting contours anywhere. One might say that the forms are swept energetically by light, or better, that the coruscation of the pigment incidentally creates form. One may again think of the composition as a progress from left to right, from the gloom of the lower left corner to the ineffable gleam of the upper right. Before it one feels an awe, an ecstasy, a bewilderment. Everything is most powerfully suggested, almost nothing is explicitly stated. We are worlds away, in a wild and irresistible poetry, from the noble prose of the Assumption of Santo Domingo.

In 1577 El Greco agreed to do for the Cathedral a large canvas of Christ led to Calvary, or, as the people called it, Christ stripped of his Raiment—*El Espolio*. The processional forward advance with the pathetically resigned Christ, and the throng with such fine contrasting elements as brutal executioners, dignified captains in armor and the holy women—these elements would have delighted Tintoretto, and in essentials El Greco handled the group much as Tintoretto would have done, in terms of drama and energy. But the cooler color, with certain illogically incandescent areas, is tending strongly towards the Spanish style. The picture still keeps something of that unmistakable, if also fine, melodramatic character which we have noted in the several versions of the Expulsion of the Money Changers. This is practically El Greco's farewell to the Venetian style.

The Espolio was the occasion of the first of many lawsuits. The chapter wished to cut down the price and to make the artist paint out the holy women, who were thought to be improperly crowded by the rabble. A referee honored Greco's claim for pay. Indeed, in such frequent quarrels the courts usually bore him out. It seems there may have been a tendency to put upon him as a foreigner, and that in his numerous litigations he was merely protecting his rights. In this case he agreed to paint out the holy women, but apparently the chapter was satisfied with a surrender in principle and did not press matters, for happily the four holy women, a most effective feature of the great picture, are still there.

During the hearing about payment for El Espolio, El Greco, being asked if he had come to Toledo to paint for Santo Domingo, declined to answer. One may reasonably guess that he was drawn to Spain by the report of the painting of the Escorial. When he was actually called there in 1580 he probably went with high hopes, expecting from Philip II that constant patronage which his own master, Titian, had enjoyed. But El Greco either failed to divine or completely disregarded what was in the king's mind. Philip in summoning a disciple of Titian, who had died about four years earlier, wanted a series of Titianesque paintings. Instead he got the Martyrdom of St. Maurice (Fig. 205), perhaps the first important picture in El Greco's individual style, disliked it, and El Greco went back somewhat disappointed and discredited to Toledo.

But the lonely stay in the gloomy mountain monastery had given El Greco the vision of his own gift. He spoke little Spanish, probably despised both the work and the personality of the facile Italian painters and that of their Spanish imitators. At Venice he had seen the Renaissance style in vigor; at the Escorial he saw its pitiful and pretentious liquidation in mannerism. Such reflection may have loosened finally his already wavering allegiance to his adored Venetians, may have quickened a latent purpose to do something quite different, and his own. Some such intense reconsideration of his aims, amid the chill and winds of the Guadarrama, with the warning of the manneristic frescoes ever before him, must underlie the St. Maurice. It is probable also that he restudied such drastic and uncompromising Titians in the Escorial as the two versions of the Agony in the Garden and the Martyrdom of St. Laurence. Here decorative color was in abeyance, the light played about sensationally for emotional effect. Pretty surely El Greco had seen Titian paint these pictures, perhaps had painted on them himself, but then he had not fully understood them. Now, without imitating them, he could build on them.

Even to a convinced admirer of El Greco, the St. Maurice is a disconcerting masterpiece. No wonder it baffled a mere king. Gone is the sound athleticism derived from Tintoretto—or rather, it lingers only partially in the superb adolescent angels hovering in the glory above. The numerous bare legs have no wholesome Venetian or masculine brawniness, and they serve only approximately the purpose of support. They are pallid, with little muscular suggestion. With the bodies they serve ambiguously, they have taken on an incorporeal character. Hands and fingers no longer look capable of grasping weapons; fingers flicker in distraught fashion. Eye rarely meets eye;

the martyrs elect are united only in a common mood of devout resignation. As for color, the usual martial reds are absent, the balance
is between cold yellows and spectral blues. We are dealing with a
grisly fact—a military massacre, and the treatment is completely other-
worldly. The martyrdom is viewed in some eternal aspect, as a vision
or hallucination common to all Christians who meditate intently on
the legend.

The new manner which had offended the king found favor among
El Greco's passionately fanatical Toledan neighbors. He throve
mightily. Probably he already owned the big house in which he was
to die, and had already the mistress, Doña Geronima, and the son,
George Manuel, who was to carry on his style. Whatever his first
Spanish manner had to give was given in full measure in his masterpiece, the Burial of Count Orgaz (Fig. 211). The commission for it
was drawn in March, 1586 (old style), and the picture was to be ready
by Christmas.

To say that a picture defies words is a most hackneyed evasion
for a critic, but it is perfectly true of the Burial, *El Entierro*. In September of 1904 I had the good luck to stumble upon the great picture
at nightfall in the little Church of S. Tomé. I did not know of its
existence. Only a few adepts then knew of the greatness of El Greco;
he was entirely unadvertised. The shock and ecstasy of surprise rendered a journalist wordless. There was no thought of what might be
written, just a complete acceptation of two solemn rites, on earth and
in heaven, in the spirit of those possessed Spanish gentlemen who
witness the rite. I did not know precisely what was happening, and
it did not seem to matter. Something very strange and thrilling was
happening, and it was enough. Like all art lovers of the moment I
reveled in sumptuous painting, and in the moss green and crimson
vestments of the two saints I was seeing the most sumptuous painting, merely as touch and color, I had ever experienced. What drew
one into the picture and made one part of it was the devotional or
fanatical intentness of all the faces, modulated from a ceremonial
composure to an ecstatic awareness of the scene of reception in
heaven, for such I soon saw the celestial glory must be. I strolled
back to the inn dazed, happy, completely enthralled.

I must apologize to the serious reader for this Proustian attempt
to recover a now far-away bit of my esthetic past. And yet it may
shorten my treatment of a masterpiece of painting which now is only

less familiar than Titian's Assumption, or Rubens' Descent from the Cross. I need perhaps only point out in a marginal way that while El Greco has pushed the expression of awe and amazement nearly to a breaking point, his terms of expression are men of a heroic type, if fantastically so, who cannot break, while he has actually attenuated the central theme in a fashion that an ancient Greek, nourished on Aristotle's criticism, would have approved. The legend tells that nearly three hundred years before this picture was painted Don Gonzales Ruiz, governor of Orgaz, abounded in piety and rebuilt the Church of S. Tomé. When, in 1323, they planned to move his body to that church, St. Stephen and St. Augustine came down from heaven and carried the body to its new sepulcher "where they placed it in the presence of all, saying: 'Such reward receive those who serve God and His saints.'" The contract required that St. Augustine and St. Stephen must hold the head and the feet, "with many people," and that "above this should be a heaven open in all glory." So much and no more guidance the rector of the Church of S. Tomé gave to El Greco's genius.

Another painter than El Greco would have been justified in emphasizing the fact that a corpse is being translated, or even a corpse that has been many years in its cerements. This would have made a very different picture, and perhaps a more Spanish picture. El Greco declined to paint it, and in eliminating all sharp and disagreeable mortuary features justified by the legend, he merely followed his own master, Titian, who in such subjects evoked pathos without reference to the uglier aspects of death. Since criticism must always emphasize the extravagance and vehemence of El Greco, it is a duty also to note his discretion.

Promised for Christmas of 1586, the picture was not finished till May of 1588. There followed the usual dispute about the price. Estimates of appraisers varying between twelve hundred and sixteen hundred ducats, El Greco took the drastic step of attaching the revenues of the church, and finally got his twelve hundred ducats only on condition that he should desist from the troublesome habit of appealing to the pope on such matters. Unquestionably El Greco was of a litigious temperament, but he generally seems to be right. Eight years earlier he had received nine hundred ducats for the Espolio. Surely the Burial was worth, merely considered as work, twice as much, and in having to accept a settlement at twelve hundred ducats El Greco was very hardly used.

After the Entierro, El Greco's pictures generally show those distortions which troubled his contemporaries and still trouble many of us. The figures now are often ten heads high; hands and feet are generally too small; tilted faces are often out of symmetry through the swelling of one cheek, or the setting of the line of eyes or mouth off perpendicular to the axis. Draperies seem to bind the figure arbitrarily with great folds that have little relation to the points of strain and support. The line has pretty well given away as a means of construction to the color area, light or dark, and much of the surface is inundated by a spectral gray. The lighting follows no system. Light falls where there is need of defining an expression or realizing a projection. Dark contours are cut out and detached by a light border which no logic explains. The general effect of these pictures is apparitional, yet they have extraordinary plastic quality. It was this insistent relief that forced the learned Pacheco reluctantly to class El Greco with the great Italians.

Among the pictures of this second period, the St. Martin of the Widener Collection is especially fine and characteristic. The horse and rider are audaciously set across the tall canvas. The horse is a mere wraith, so is the lanky, nude beggar receiving his half of St. Martin's cloak. His look and attitude are more or less idiotic. What, after all, makes the picture is the fastidious delicacy and accuracy of the gesture of the knightly saint as he divides his mantle with his Toledo blade. The picture suggests both surprise and calculation, a springtime outing of a noble youth and a sudden act of consecration. It skirts the ridiculous perilously, much of the construction is merely approximate, but the picture has, all the same, very high existence both on the material and on the spiritual plane.

The numerous Crucifixions and the scenes of Christ's passion show the new manner at its best. Take the Calvary, at Madrid, with the light from despairing hands and angels' wings slashing the gloom about the almost incandescent body of the Christ. The aims of tragic expression are attained by technical means as sensational as those of the electric spotlight of the modern stage, but the result is noble and dignified. Incidentally, in the figures of the women desperately clasping the foot of the cross, El Greco has consulted that master of pathos and light and dark expressive thereof—Federico Baroccio. It is the most elaborate Crucifixion by El Greco. There is perhaps a more concentrated pathos and compositional unity in the several Crucifixions with patrons, or with glimpses upon landscapes and strange skies.

The Resurrection, at Madrid (Fig. 212), shows the extravagance of El Greco's invention at its height. The nude Christ rises with His swelling banner above a welter of nude bodies tossed as if by a whirlwind—the Roman soldiers. All this is fantastic. The Roman guards were armored, not nude; they were few in number. The distortions are extreme. But the general sense of triumph is completely realized. Christ seems risen from a stormy human sea, which He dominates. Fear and admiration alternate in such faces as the light thrusts upon our view. The constructional elements in this picture are flamelike flashes of light which, while they mark the position and action of limbs, also have a sort of independent existence. These flamelike elements are in active balance. These upward flashes seem to sustain the body of the Christ. Even the strangely bent back hands, entirely ambiguous as emotion, serve a necessary function of support. Much in the picture is reminiscent of Michelangelo's Last Judgment, but the forms are in process of dissolution, and the balance is not of mass or movement but of dark and light. Everything has an extraordinary reality, but reality of dream or hallucination, not that of observation.

For the distortions which are usual in Greco's pictures after 1588 various explanations have been offered. Pacheco complained that Greco painted very carefully and at the last retouched roughly "to make the colors distinct and discordant, and to slash them cruelly with brush strokes to affect strength. And this I call working in order to be poor."

An ingenious Spanish oculist has diagnosed Greco's astigmatism, backwards—that is, he has made lenses through which, to a normal eye, a Rubens will seem to have the distortions proper to El Greco. At first blush such experiments are persuasive, but against the theory of abnormal eyesight we must set the fact that from beginning to end of his career El Greco could and did paint portraits in their true proportions and without distortion of any sort. He once wrote on the elongation of his figures that the distant lights seemed taller than they are. In short, there is every reason to suppose that he knew perfectly well what he was about, and simply found in the elongations, asymmetries, and arbitrary impact of light, a language in which he could express himself. In one way or another the expression was tragic, and El Greco may be thought of as applying pictorially that rhetoric of calculated hyperbole, of suspense, and purple patches which tragedy has always employed, and without reproach. In short, in passing beyond that air of good society with which Titian and the Italians generally had envisaged the ecstasies and the terrors of the Christian legend, El Greco was merely coming closer to his theme, so that it lives with his own tender or ferocious living. One may feel that such pictures are lived from the inside out rather than painted planfully from outside. And here El Greco's habit of constant repetition or of variation upon his theme is significant. He no more demands novelty of emotion, but only of the means of expressing it. No one tires of the Te Deum, or the Dies Irae, because there are many ways of chanting those sublime hymns.

The single figures of the second period show little distortion. Such half-lengths as the Magdalene, Worcester, Mass., and Repentant St. Peter, Phillips Memorial, Washington, D. C. (Fig. 214), represent the class at its best. The St. Peter, in particular, is executed with alternations of harshness and urbanity which keep the mood of repentance, while poignant, also noble and restrained. The superb physical presence of the saint seems to make our sympathy superfluous. One is not sorry for him; he is not of our world. One may say that El Greco in such pictures has almost abolished distance, while insisting on detachment. Technically it comes to a form of staging which produces in us tremendous awareness of figures completely unaware of us. Most imposing and portentous of these half-length saints is perhaps the idealized portrait of a Cardinal impersonating St. Jerome, in the Frick Collection. It is a true symbol for the tragic fanaticism of Spanish religiosity, and full of sinister beauty.

As a portraitist El Greco is consistently good, and now and then great. About the dozens of hidalgos with pointed beards and eyes deeply imbedded in their sockets there is a certain monotony, if one of excellence. Nor do the various female portraits of Greco, picturesque as they are as a class, deeply thrill me. They are neither impersonally sumptuous in the Venetian fashion, nor yet persuasively personal. Many of these portraits of the early Spanish years are overgeneralized in the direction of formal dignity. Doubtless the sitters were like that, but I fancy they were something more. The alien tended to reduce them to a type. Evidently he liked the type. One may doubt if he read the greatest of contemporary romances, *Don Quixote* (1598), or he read it too late to interest himself in the greatest variety of human idiosyncrasies that Spain has ever offered.

But there are great portraits by El Greco. The bust, full face, in the Metropolitan Museum (Fig. 215), which may represent the painter himself, is entirely unforgettable for its fairly plastic emphasis of the ravaged forms and also for its stately melancholy. It would have been easy to make such a face merely pitiful, but pity is the last feeling one admits as he views this half-burnt-out hero. The actual handling draws much from Titian and Tintoretto, but it is more direct, simple, and drastic in construction. The eyes are those of a possessed person—wide open, but illumined from within.

If I could own just one portrait by El Greco it would be the Fray Feliz Hortensio Pallavicino (Fig. 196), at Boston. I prefer it to the obviously more salient and decorative Cardinal Guevara, at New York. Both are consummately fine pictures. If I like the Fray Hortensio better, it is because of his look of a magnificent half-tamed human animal, and because it was more difficult to make something out of the blacks and creamy whites of his robes than it was to make something out of Guevara's crimson vestments. The Fray Hortensio is at once most reserved in its effect, with a sense of passion smoldering under the general discretion. It is hard to realize that it is dated in 1609, at the moment when Greco had in favor of vehemence cast discretion aside. Evidently there was something about these great prelates that sobered El Greco, made him, exceptionally, look outward. At his moment of extreme introversion, he becomes once more an extrovert on the impact of personalities which he felt to be greater than his own.

The Guevara is Greco's show piece. The sheer sumptuousness of the crimson satins, laces, stamped and gilded leather, merely enhances the fine, autocratic face. He is the Grand Inquisitor, pledged to honest and relentless persecution and to merciless punishment. You feel his probity and his necessary cruelty as less appalling than one would expect. It is a sumptuous picture, with a strange iciness about it. Everything is observed with a strenuousness that precludes comment or sympathy. It is tremendously seen. Velasquez at his greatest is already implicit in the Guevara, as Van Dyck at his most romantic is forecast in the Fray Hortensio.

In the last ten years of El Greco's life, 1604–1614, the style still broadens. What Pacheco calls the "cruel slashes" spread a sea of light and dark waves across the surface, and though these broad flecks of light have no obvious relation to familiar shapes, yet the eye sufficiently infers the shapes from the undulating pattern of light and dark. Ashen, sepulchral grays, phosphorescently luminous, are the dominating tones, but there are often fine contrasting areas of moss green, cold yellow, pale azure. It is a dematerialized art, but also one of tremendous reality.

The Salutation (Fig. 213), in the Dumbarton Oaks Collection, Washington, shows the method in epitome. The rugged forms of Mary and Elizabeth are summarily suggested by the folds and light and dark of the drapery. The contours have no human character, are like the edges of a cliff. Little of the broad drawing of the draperies can be referred closely to the underlying forms, yet the construction has a most imposing and convincing character, a portentous reality which looks forward some three hundred years to a similar paradoxical reality in Rodin's Balzac. The forms would hardly be interpreted as human were it not for the curved base and the little door—concessions to the ordinary observational experience of the spectator.

There is often one such feature in El Greco's most volatilized pictures. In the Agony in the Garden, London, one of many versions, the link with ordinary experience is simply the carefully rendered olive branches, which tell us the scene is the Garden of Olives. Otherwise there is no difference in touch and texture between the clouds, the boulder behind the kneeling Christ, the draperies of the figures, while the cavern that encloses the sleeping disciples like a womb and supports the angel with the chalice—is it made of cloud, or stone, or earth? It does not seem to matter. The eye and the mind accept it without analysis or misgiving. Indeed it seems fitting that these solemn, tragic, or ecstatic events should take place in their own tempestuous world of light, where forms come to life only as the impact of light drives back an invading gloom.

Of these latest Grecos nothing is finer or more characteristic than the Adoration of the Shepherds, at New York. The surface is tumultuous, like a broken sea. The light shoots out radially from the nude body of the Christchild—a motive borrowed from Correggio or Baroccio, but asserted with a furious energy which they neither commanded nor approved. Everywhere flashes of light—profiles, flickering hands, gracile feet, edges of robes, frayed edges of distant clouds—

just one stable point of identification—the illumined soffit of an arch in the upper center—and it gives way to a hurtling trio of nude angels, whirling against the gloom like a human Catherine wheel. Everywhere distortions at will—heads without occiputs, features slewed off axis, limbs almost detached from their bodies. The whole effect is of a cosmic rapture, orgiastic, a little terrible in its accent. According to your capacity for emotion and your patience, it is a thrilling masterpiece or a disagreeable puzzle.

It is plain that pictures of this sort must have been painted in creative fury, remote memory supplying the scanty observational features. In making such pictures with a brush which applies rather phosphorescences than mere pigments, Greco perhaps had in mind certain remarkable tempera drawings of Tintoretto and some of the latest paintings by his master, Titian, but the method is El Greco's own. No Venetian so much cut loose from average appearances and dealt so audaciously in color symbolism.

When considering what may seem a pure romantic subjectivism, we should recall that El Greco was leading the life of a patrician, that he was reading Vitruvius and all the contemporary Italian writers on architecture, that his own architectural designs for retables and his sculpture are in a very conservative Renaissance taste, finally that while his religious compositions were apparently dissolving in pyrotechnics in some murky void, he was also painting those exquisitely seen and minutely studied portraits which were to give lessons to Velasquez.

We may appropriately take leave of El Greco with the view of his beloved Toledo under impending storm (Fig. 216), New York. It is only an epitome of a city that straggles from the towered castles at the left, across the spectral bridge to the little group of buildings from which the tower of the cathedral and the mass of the Alcazar rise bleakly against a slaty sky. Whirling clouds are broken by light that struggles down and smites the contour of hills, the curve of roads, the crisp foliation of little trees. Any moment the storm may break and efface the vision. But you will never forget the apparition of the cruel and lovely city seen at hazard. It is one of the greatest romantic landscapes in Amiel's sense, that it is really just the exteriorization of an apocalyptic state of mind. To endue the most intense and tragic emotions with a kind of eternal value—such was the secret of El Greco's always troubled, always triumphant art.

CHAPTER XIV

THE SEVENTEENTH CENTURY, RU-
BENS AND THE FLEMISH SCHOOL

FIG. 217. RUBENS. Holy Family, with St. George and St. Matthew.--
St. Jacques, Antwerp.

FIG. 219. RUBENS. The Raising of the Cross (central panel).—Cathedral, Antwerp.

FIG. 218. RUBENS. The Artist and His Wife Isabella.—Munich.

FIG. 220.   RUBENS.   The Descent from the Cross.—Cathedral, Antwerp.

384

FIG. 222. RUBENS. Debarkation of Marie at Marseilles.—Paris.

FIG. 221. RUBENS. Last Communion of St. Francis.—Antwerp.

Fig. 223. (Upper) Rubens. Death of Adonis (sketch).—*Princeton*.
Fig. 224. (Lower) Rubens. Garden of Love.—*Madrid*.

FIG. 225. RUBENS. Landscape with a Rainbow.—*Paris.*

FIG. 226. (Upper) JORDAENS. The King Drinks.—Vienna.
FIG. 227. (Lower) JORDAENS. Allegory of Fertility.—Brussels.

388

FIG. 228. VAN DYCK. Frans Snyders.—Frick Collection, New York.

FIG. 229. VAN DYCK. Cardinal Bentivoglio.—Pitti, Florence.

389

Fig. 231. Van Dyck. Charles I.—Paris.

Fig. 230. Van Dyck. Marchesa Cattaneo.—
Coll. Joseph Widener, Esq., Elkins Park, Pa.

FIG. 233. VAN DYCK. Anna Wake.—The Hague.

FIG. 232. VAN DYCK. Marchese Cattaneo.—London.

391

Fig. 235. Van Dyck. James Stuart, Duke of Lenox.—New York.

Fig. 234. Van Dyck. Queen Henrietta Maria.—Windsor.

THOSE progressive painters of Western Europe who had emulated the Italian style, on the whole produced only a negative result. They failed to effect that assimilation of the Italian manner which they sought, and they brought to naught any promise which still may have feebly inhered in the old Gothic style. It remained then for the seventeenth century to witness the creation of new and idiomatic styles in Holland, Belgium, France and Spain. And here the critical date is 1630, which saw the perfection of Rubens' transformation of the Venetian manner, the full flowering of the art of Frans Hals, the beginnings of Velasquez and Rembrandt in that "dark manner" which spread through Europe from Caravaggio and his tenebrist disciples. It will be noted that, with the partial exception of Frans Hals, we still have to do with Italianism, but at last with an Italianism critically studied by first-class painter intelligences who could admire without copying, holding fast to their own native and racial ideals.

The reader need not be reminded that in the first quarter of the seventeenth century Italy offered to the Transalpine painter two competitive styles—that of Titian and his later Venetian contemporaries; that of Caravaggio. A man of painterlike spirit would reject the synthesis of the Italian eclectics. They were draughtsmen rather than painters. So the influence of the Carracci and their followers remained in abeyance till a great artist who was not a painterlike spirit, Nicolas Poussin, utilized it to the full. The radical difference between the Venetian style and that of Caravaggio may be expressed in a few antitheses. The former valued aristocracy and nobility of sentiment; the latter, character and the expression of the drastic emotions of common folk. Similarly the Venetians emphasized richness and variety of color and used it most decoratively; the tenebrists reduced color to light and dark and half-tones, cared little for decorative effect, sought, above all, powerful construction and emphatic rendering of character. Now a fully decorative and colorful manner has to surrender something of character and construction, while a manner that

393

insists on construction and character must forego something of color and decorative effect. Such a style will tend to be a sort of strenuous draughtsmanship in light and dark. Such was the early manner even of Rubens, and even more notably that of Velasquez and Rembrandt. The good painter will naturally seek to minimize the sacrifice involved in his choice of styles. Thus a Rubens, whose propensity is chiefly for color and decoration, will also seek to express all the character that is compatible with his aims, and a Rembrandt and a Velasquez will sublimate the once harsh means with which they achieved character and construction, so that their later work will be, as you choose to put it, completely decorative, while rejecting the usual decorative conventions, or perhaps something that transcends decoration entirely.

The great movement in painting briefly sketched above was merely one chapter in that chronicle of high adventure which was lived in the early years of the seventeenth century. It was a moment of extravagance and expansion in many directions. The English were settling America, the Dutch the East Indies; American gold was enriching Spain. A Francis Bacon discovers the true method of experimental science; a Kepler solves the riddle of the solar system; a Grotius lays the foundations of international law; a Descartes plays havoc with the traditional philosophies; a French gentleman keeps fit with a duel a week. The lives of a Shakspere, Cyrano de Bergerac and Corneille overlap, as do those of Queen Elizabeth, Henri IV and Giordano Bruno. Genius of all sorts was in the air, and a prophetic spirit a generation earlier might have read what was impending in the writings of such free spirits as Rabelais and Montaigne and in the winged music of Palestrina.

In art this moment of elation and hopefulness is most fully expressed in the painting of Peter Paul Rubens. He represents the conservative and social aspect of the new movement as Rembrandt may be said to represent its radical and individual aspect. While Rubens was a cosmopolitan person, painting in France, Spain and England, most of his career was made in the imperial city of Antwerp. When Holland had become Protestant and France was torn by religious wars, what is now Belgium remained Catholic and an isolated outpost of the Holy Roman Empire. It had commercial and cultural relations with all Europe, but the leading influence was from Italy. Its art was much colored by that Neo-Catholic style which is rather vaguely comprised under the term baroque.

Primarily baroque means extravagant, and the extravagance of the new style was enlisted to bolster up the shaken authority of the Roman Catholic Church and to glorify its champions, the emperor and a host of mere royalties. The style originated in Italy, drawing its precedents widely from such painters as Mantegna, Correggio, Michelangelo, Tintoretto, and the later mannerists. Surprise, unexpectedness, an operatic expansiveness, were its leading characteristics. The architect, retaining the old fundamental symmetries, plays audaciously with the details. Pediments are interrupted in the center; heavy moldings unexpectedly break the line; the surfaces are crowded with decorative high reliefs or with figure sculpture. The normal limitations of materials are ignored. Rushing, marble figures balance perilously or even take wing; we have curtains cut in stone or more thriftily modeled in plaster. In easel painting the old closed compositions calculated with regard to the geometry of the frame tend to lead past the frame into the air. In mural design the wall and the roof are often painted away under the same principle of overflow. Clouds bearing alluring angelic or saintly figures hover above the astonished worshiper; he no longer looks up to a structural vault, but into a fantastic cloudland. Foreshortening, which for the Renaissance painters had been functional, is now used for its own sake as a mere display of supreme technical skill. Compositional lines are no longer a balance of right lines and easy curves but become taut, spiraling curves of short radius. The equilibrium, formerly one of mass with mass, changes to one of thrust and counterthrust. A good baroque picture is often merely a successfully planned collision of such thrusts. Nothing is very personal or specific in this art. Its mood is generalized, animated, operatic, conventionally joyous and energetic.

It is this tinge of the theatric in the baroque which made the older puristic critics, such as John Ruskin, read it out of court for insincerity. These same qualities make it seem exemplary to the present generation of critics, mostly German, who are carried away by its sheer ingenuity. The true judgment, as is usually the case, lies between these extreme opinions. It is absurd to deny the energy and resourcefulness of the baroque; equally absurd to give it equal value with the grand style of the Renaissance. The gain from the new criticism has been to free the baroque from the unjust reproach of being merely the Renaissance style in decadence. It must be regarded as a new style, with its own ideals, and as very much alive.

I have written the above with some reluctance, for the subject really lies apart from our present study. In the seventeenth century the baroque is important and regnant only in Italy. Its impact on the North, particularly in the German kingdoms, is felt strongly only in the eighteenth century. Rather little in Flanders, England, France or Spain in the seventeenth century can properly be called baroque. On the other hand the operatic spirit of the baroque was far more pervasive than its forms. When below their best, Shakspere and Corneille may be regarded as baroque writers. But for the diffused influence of the baroque, the art of Rubens would have been quite different, though his art is only superficially baroque and formally is in the straight tradition of the Venetian Renaissance. So much explanation and definition is due the bewildered student who reads that Caravaggio, Frans Hals, Rembrandt, Rubens, Velasquez and Murillo are all baroque painters.

The baroque is often equated with the Jesuit style, and there is some kinship here. As a result of the Protestant Reformation, the authority of the Roman Catholic Church was sorely shaken. The passive defense of the Church was the considerable reforms worked out in the Council of Trent, 1545; the active defense was largely conducted by the Jesuits. They were good psychologists and saw that an institution which had lost authority could thrive only through persuasion, and of persuasiveness they made a very fine art. Such recommendation of Roman Christianity through persuasion varied from heroic missionary enterprise at the ends of the earth to politic condonation of the favorite vices of the great of the earth. As teachers of youth the Jesuits were and are the most effective and best beloved of the modern world. Unquestionably the Jesuit policy was a factor in the creation of the baroque. But when we recall that Ignatius Loyola founded the order in 1534, while the baroque as a style emerged some seventy-five years later, it will be plain that we should not overemphasize the relation between the two. Let it go at this—that the air which Rubens breathed was charged with Jesuitry and with the ampullosity of the baroque style. This fact conditioned him and somewhat limited him, but it did not make him, and it only partly explains him.

Though born in obscurity in the little city of Siegen, in 1577, Peter Paul Rubens was born to be a courtier. His father, a Doctor of Laws of Padua, was in disgrace for a foolish love affair with the dull-witted Princess Anne of Orange. When the philandering parent died, the boy was only ten years old. His faithful and wise mother moved to Antwerp, where the lad received an early education in the ways of the great world as a page in the household of Princess Margaret of Ligne, while in a Jesuit college he was so well grounded in the classical tongues that the mastery of the modern languages was easy for him. His vocation as a painter early manifested itself. He worked transiently with the Italianizing painters, Tobias Verhaeght and Adam van Noort, passing at eighteen to the studio of Otho Vaenius, mediocre poet, good humanist, convinced Romanist, practitioner of a certain taste and mild charm. In this congenial atmosphere of cosmopolitan culture, young Rubens progressed rapidly and at twenty-one, in 1598, was admitted as a free master of St. Luke's Guild. We have no pictures of this time.

In May of 1600, now twenty-three years old, he left Antwerp for Italy, not to return for eight years. A couple of months later he was working for Marquis Vincenzo Gonzaga of Mantua. In the Gonzaga gallery were the finest Titians, Correggios, Tintorettos, Carraccis, Caravaggios, not to mention the tiny blond landscapes of Adam Elsheimer and excellent antique statuary. By the study of these masterpieces young Rubens greatly profited—there are experimental works which show the dramatic tension of Tintoretto and the hard edges and sooty shadows of Caravaggio, but the young painter's allegiance was already for Titian in the midday splendor of his richest coloring and energetic, off-center compositional patterns.

Rubens was soon what he was often to be later, a confidential agent and diplomat, making in Marquis Vincenzo's behalf, in 1603, a trip to Spain with a gift of paintings and thoroughbred horses for Philip III. The much damaged but still magnificent Baptism of Christ, at Antwerp, was painted for Vincenzo on Rubens' return. In its strongly emotional accent and audacities of dramatic lighting it stems directly from Tintoretto. Secure in his Mantuan patronage, young Rubens painted at Rome, Genoa and Venice, being everywhere received as a master. In late autumn of 1608 word came that his mother was dying, and he got leave to return to Antwerp. There he was promptly appointed court painter at a big salary to the Regents

Archduke Albert and Isabella. At the prudent age of thirty-two, 1609, he married a bonnie and amiable young woman, Isabella Brandt, and started a quantity production of big pictures on the most varied themes.

The portrait of himself and his wife, at Munich (Fig. 218), shows his accomplishment at the time. Everything is strongly and knowingly asserted, but the method is unpleasantly linear, and the color lacks fineness. What makes a somewhat literal and heavy-handed picture after all important is its candor, character and vitality. Not much more than this can be said for the many official portraits which he painted before 1520. Their merit is that of vividness, clarity and an unaffected probity. Even in the technical triumphs of his later portraiture he was, as Fromentin justly remarks, a good, not a great portraitist.

His early figure compositions are obviously and harshly composed; the writhing, wiry contour (based, I think, on misunderstanding of Michelangelo) is positively ugly; so is the construction in swarthy shadow; the mood is undeniably energetic, but melodramatically and too obviously so. In short, we find the exaggerations of a strong spirit which has not yet achieved taste and discipline.

What seem to us defects were merits for a patronage that still admired the Frans Florises and was buying the early Riberas. And the development of Rubens himself shows that he was critical of his own success. Money and fame simply poured in automatically. The demand for his great canvases was such that he had to set up what was virtually a factory. He himself rapidly supplied small color sketches. These were converted into big pictures by his assistants. He personally supervised the work, and often added the slashing retouches which gave the picture its character. The factory never stopped during his lifetime, functioned almost as well in his absence as when he was present. Young painters applied eagerly for this employment. He refused a hundred of them. A Danish doctor, Otto Sperling, visited the factory in 1621 and found Rubens painting, dictating a letter, listening to the reading aloud of Tacitus, but nevertheless ready to answer questions. The anecdote well suggests the extraordinary capacity of the master for untroubled receptive and creative activity.

It is obvious that we know not the intimate Rubens but merely the great executive in these too numerous products of his studio. We must seek him in his autographic sketches and in the rather few large pictures which are wholly or mostly by his own hand. Yet the general puristic scorn of these delegated pictures is exaggerated, and due chiefly to their superabundance in the great galleries. If these canvases were rare they would seem masterly, for Rubens imposed his will and practice on his assistants, and if they never painted as well as he, they painted well enough. Perhaps to facilitate this quantity production, Rubens invented a new and beautiful technique. Where the Venetians, his models, had laid the design in in solid colors and finished it with transparent glazes, Rubens reversed the process. The picture was laid in in transparent colors. When these were not quite dry the preparation was crisped up by heavy accents of solid color. It was an expeditious method, involving hours where the Venetian method had required days, and the final touches which really established the picture could be quickly made or corrected by the master himself. Incidentally, it was a most durable method. Where all other contemporary canvases have darkened badly, we see the Rubenses, delegated or his own, virtually as they were originally.

Here and there in the generally displeasing early pictures a prophetic eye might have discerned the future mastery. The finest for me is the Hero and Leander, painted before 1505 in Italy, and now in Dresden. It is melodramatic, but magnificently so. The arabesque of small nude figures tossed in a murky sea, the huge curling breaker— we shall see it again years later in the Battle of the Amazons, at Munich—the cruel glint of the lightning and its reflection from the edges of clouds and surges of the sea—all this is of a fine romantic intensity. The literary inspiration is, of course, the late Greek poem ascribed to Musaeus. Only a little earlier Christopher Marlowe had translated it. I quote a passage, the original of which gave Rubens his main motive:

> "And now the cruel Fates with 'Ate hasted
> To all the Winds, and made them battle fight
> Upon the Hellespont. . . .
>
> .        .        .        .        .
>
> And forth they brake, the seas mix'd with the sky
> And toss'd distressed Leander. . . ."

In the contorted forms of this picture there is a reminiscence of Michelangelo, but the mood and the pictorial effect are Rubens' own.

It was a subject to which the exaggerations of his early manner lent themselves admirably.

By 1615 and his thirty-seventh year his experimental period was over, and he had found himself. The sharpness of the transition may be vividly felt by comparing the two famous triptychs that flank the choir of the Cathedral of Antwerp. The Raising of the Cross, at the left, is still in the early manner (Fig. 219). Learnedly and powerfully composed along the asymmetrical lines invented by Titian, it is restless, full of bumps and holes, exaggerated in light and shade, undistinguished and inharmonious in color. The eye is repelled by it. Immediately on its completion in 1610 the Descent from the Cross (Fig. 220) was begun. It was finished in 1614, and it witnesses to a complete re-education in taste. The color is still not rich or really fine, but it is reasonably harmonious and dramatically appropriate. The design is made in line, mass, dark and light. Here everything is powerful, reserved, expressive, concordant. A carping critic could only observe that discordance between the almost sculptural treatment of the central panel and the very pictorial handling of the wings. But, perhaps wrongly, nobody really looks at the glorious part of this masterpiece as mere painting. Considered as a colored sculptural group, the Descent is magnificent. Everything reinforces by contrast or parallelism the dominant diagonally disposed curve of the suspended body. From the point of view of narrative, everybody is about his tragic business—with extraordinary modulations, from the athletes above steadying the body, to the St. John strongly curved back as he supports the weight, to senile Joseph of Arimathea trying fumblingly to be of aid, finally to the superbly attentive and lovely Magdalene tenderly receiving the pierced feet. One can imagine the thing more exquisitely painted, but hardly more fully and sensitively felt.

From now on masterpiece followed masterpiece—so many that one is reduced to mere enumeration. Superb the blend of sheer athleticism and ardent devotion in the Miraculous Draught of Fishes, at Mechlin. Nothing greater here than the Last Communion of St. Francis, Antwerp (Fig. 221), in which the dying saint seems a stricken runner, while the assiduous priest and attendant Franciscans might almost be his competent trainers. Everything is felt most corporeally, but at the point of universal pathos, for how transient is the body's power and glory! One has the work of a most energetic, red-haired and red-bearded man, as we see Rubens in his self-portraits, whose mind and body are merely a two-track road to sympathy and understanding. Here is a temper that rejects whatever is unwhole or weak, at the expense of veracity heroizes all themes, perhaps as a higher truth.

Everything is of the same optimism—the Assumptions and Enthroned Madonnas building up ornately in the diagonal off-center balances of the Venetians; the ordered welter of such technical marvels as the various Last Judgments and the Battle of the Amazons, 1620, Munich; the great Hunts of Lions, Wolves, densely and intricately composed, hurtling yet rhythmical; most memorable perhaps, the Lance Thrust, Antwerp, where materially the staccato balance of diagonals is like a superb military march, while the merciful cruelty of the soldiers piercing Christ's side and breaking the legs of a crucified thief seem part of some grim necessary business of the world that goes on regardless of the feelings of the Marys and Magdalenes. Indeed the whole picture is more an apotheosis of the police power than of the theological meaning of the crucifixion. The Christ is a forspent athlete, worthy of being dispatched by so kindred a spirit as the knightly centurion.

I hear a tender-minded reader protest at this material, even political reading of the profoundest of personal tragedies, and I can only say that Rubens must be enjoyed on his own basis of exalting the collective and physical values of endurance, strength, splendor, even pomp. Rubens is a yes-sayer. He believes in kings and saints, in church and state, in health, wealth, bodily efficiency of men and women. Besides believing unflinchingly in things as they are, he believes in things as they were when the gods and goddesses of Olympus lived near, even among us. To him it seems natural that they should share with the saints the oversight and protection of kings. The gods and goddesses of antiquity are as much alive and contemporary to him as his own noble and royal patrons. In fine, his values are worldly, but they are also the authentic worldly values, and he so magnifies and exalts them that they reach a spiritual value of their own. His obliviousness to the misery and sordidness that abound in this world may seem a spiritual blindness; it was nevertheless his essential esthetic quality, his personal form of idealization. And here he merely extended and generalized his own superb optimism and efficiency. Doubts and hesitations never transpire in his work. Of all great artists he is the most extrovert. Naturally his art is pretty hard going for sensitive and introverted persons. It is also medicinal for such tender-mindedness.

Rubens' pictorial forms correspond perfectly to his deepest feelings. The color is morning freshness, the straw-yellow and rose of fields and gardens associating itself with the pale azure of the sky. There is no mystery in a Rubens—just magnificent plain statement. The compositional patterns derive from the off-center balances of Titian and the Venetians, but the tension is greater, the balance more dynamic, the curves of shorter radius. Where the curves of Titian were arrested by the frame those of Rubens rebound and come back into the picture. His plump, nude women have outraged generations of overrefined art lovers. His apologists have ruefully explained that Flemish women were like that, and the master had to do the best he could with such models as he could get. Such superfluous whitewashing ignores the fact that the good artist transforms the model to his own taste, and the far more important fact that to realize his compositional ideals Rubens would have had to invent such plump and rosy women even if Antwerp had not bred them in abundance. For the rest, Rubens, like his Venetian exemplars, habitually composes in shallow space, indeed is very slightly interested in space as an esthetic factor. The space is what the painted shapes require, and it is always enough.

It will be noted that in all these compositional preferences he differs radically from the baroque painters, who liked a sense of overflow beyond the frame, and played joyously and audaciously with the problem of deep space. As a constructor of the figure Rubens has no superior. Its bulk, poise, balance, weight, he renders faultlessly and with supreme ease. His expressiveness, dependent primarily on wholesome knowledge and sympathy, depends technically largely on the just and delicate distribution of lights and darks which are always colors. Such distribution is not realistic and based on optical appearances, but dramatic and emotional. It is the persisting element of refinement in methods which may seem exaggeratedly robust and almost crude. In his latest phase his always constructive use of color will be of ineffable delicacy with no loss of strength. What has been written should show that when Sir Joshua Reynolds found a simple formula for Rubens as founder of the ornamental manner, he expressed only a half truth, and an obvious one at that. The pictures of Rubens, to be sure, rarely lack a gay, decorative quality, and they always offer much more.

To make this analytical and perhaps tedious study concrete and vivid, let me simply advise the reader to study a reproduction of the Rape of the Daughters of Leucippus, at Munich. In favor of the dense dynamic balance, its massiveness, its oddly picturesque pattern, its validity in space, we must overlook something a little far-fetched and operatic in the poses and expressions of the women. Very characteristic of Rubens is the determined decency with which Castor and Pollux go about marriage by capture. It is a residuum of the Renaissance decorum, and alien to the cleverness and exaggerated vivacity of the baroque.

A production involving in the ten years we are considering, 1615 to 1625, scores of great pictures a year, cartoons for several series of tapestries (notably one devoted to the life of Achilles), a vast correspondence, exacting social relations, required orderly habits. Rubens rose early in the stately Chateau of Steen which he had built for himself near Antwerp. Before he began to work, he rode for his health, strolled about his collection of classical marbles while a secretary read aloud from a Latin author. His body and mind stimulated, he knocked off one of those marvelous sketches; finally he went to the factory, criticized what was going on and retouched what was ready for delivery. Here is nothing of mood or nerves, just a steady, determined, journalistic output, all of it at least tinged with his genius, the best of it with his genius unalloyed.

A man so engrossed with the city, court and business would seem disqualified for landscape painting. Indeed in most of his earlier pictures he seemed to care nothing for landscape, letting his mediocre assistants touch in such landscape backgrounds as were required. So it must have been a surprise when in 1618, his forty-first year, Rubens began to paint a series of little landscapes (you will find them at Dresden, London, Munich, Paris) of an amazing freshness and sympathy. There was no such strenuous dealing with difficult forms as Pieter Bruegel had undertaken and Jakob Ruysdael was soon to attempt. The method was loose, sketchy, improvised. But it yielded amazingly what no one earlier, save Titian, had divined—the sense of lushness, moisture, interplay of light and shadow, movement of clouds, wind in the trees. All this was effected with lively tints, sharp contrasts being avoided. This new phase must occupy us more in detail when we consider the still more animated and sensitive landscapes of Rubens' last years. Meanwhile these first landscapes may show that Rubens, wholesaler of big canvases, never got into a rut—maintained to the end his capacity for surprise and wonder.

It was characteristic of the luck that ever attended Rubens' steps that his greatest and most lasting commission, the decoration of the great gallery of the Luxembourg, came to him when he was at the height of his powers. In 1621, Rubens' forty-fourth year, the Italian-born Queen-Regent Marie de Médicis called Rubens to Paris to adorn her new palace. Doubtless the twenty-one subjects were then arranged. To a modern painter the themes would seem hopeless: Henri IV falls in love with the picture of Marie; Marie disembarks at Marseilles; Marie bears Louis XII; Henri IV leaves Marie for the Dutch Wars; Marie's Reign is Beneficent; Louis XII comes of Age; Marie, in Disfavor with the New King, leaves Paris—this was the sort of thing with which Rubens had to wrestle.

He made the series rich, thrilling, immensely picturesque and decorative by the conventional expedient of enlisting the gods and goddesses. They are generally present: the Fates predicting Marie's fame; the Graces presiding over her education; the Virtues supporting her beneficent sway; Minerva prompting Henri IV to fall in love with Marie's picture; and again sustaining Marie as she goes into exile. Now this interweaving of human and Olympian interests has been attempted a thousand times in painting and poetry, and generally with very qualified success or at the cost of artificiality and insincerity. The only hope of carrying it off at all is that the artist believes in his gods and goddesses, kings and queens. Rubens did so believe, and the result in painting is a robust and veridical fairyland with a hint of real persons involved and of great issues at stake.

Peter Paul Rubens was no critic of the great of the earth, nor yet of existing institutions. He accepted and enthusiastically approved them. He loved their power and pomp, was really part of it himself, and proudly so, and the Médicis series is really a confession of his mundane faith. It is easy for modern radicalism to tax him with lack of imagination or even with sycophancy. But this is wisdom of hind-sight and grossly unfair. In Rubens' cult of royalty was more than self-interest. His imagination was really very broad and, given the moment, profoundly just. Increasing dynastic power seemed to promise the ending of the disorders that had troubled the sixteenth century, the composing of religious feuds, the rise of strong and wise nations, the creation of a European solidarity. Such visions had hovered before Marie de Médicis' husband, Henri IV, and the cosmopolitan painter doubtless saw something prophetic in the continuation of the work of a great French king by an Italian queen-regent. In short, whoever feels there is any lack of imaginative vision and fervor in the apparent artificialities of the Médicis series ignorantly misreads these pictures.

On the technical and decorative side this introduction of the Olympians into the French court offered distinct opportunities. A great designer and colorist could play at will with ornate costumes, rosy nudity, slight draperies, sound portraiture, generalized types. Moreover, his use of these ingredients is tactfully varied. We have pure mythology and the heroic nude in the tall panels with which the series begins and ends—the Destiny of Marie, the Triumph of Truth. In the long panels near the center—the Apotheosis and Marie's Reign, we have almost pure symbolism and mythology. And the usual rather even distribution of real and mythological figures in these great canvases is punctuated effectively by pure narratives, recalls to earth as it were. Such are Marie's Marriage by Proxy, Henri IV's Departure for the Dutch Wars, and even in the Flight of Marie, what counts is not the escorting Minerva and geniuses, but rather the sad dignity of Marie, the assiduous courtesy of her fantastic champion, the Duke of Eperon, and the agitation of his soldiery. Rubens has been most skillful and sensitive in creating not only in many variations of compositional elements, but also on many levels of emotional interest.

Not much can be suggested about the Médicis series in words. Ten minutes with a set of fair reproductions will tell more than any amount of reading. So I have confined myself to such general consideration as may remove prejudice and make for sympathy, and I limit particular notice to the analysis of a single canvas in which mythology and courtly ceremony seem to me to be blended with magnificent success—the Debarkation of Marie at Marseilles (Fig. 222).

Behind the stern of the ship and below the gangplank, five lusty sea creatures rejoice that the sea has safely delivered the new queen to her destination. Superb, the three exulting Nereids entirely painted, or overpainted, by Rubens' hand! Above, the graceful figure of the queen holds its own amid a romantic welter of canopies, billowing flags, knights, ladies, welcoming divinities. Everything here is strange and aerial and, however specifically courtly, almost other-worldly. It seems as if the air, with the sea, vibrated powerfully in sympathy with the event. In all the history of painting the eye will rarely meet anything so nobly festive, so blithe in color, of so strangely conceived a beauty. Surely, as he designed and painted this masterpiece, Rubens believed to the bottom of his courtier heart that the landing of Marie in France was a profoundly important and auspicious event, and, while history has recorded its reservations, it has not wholly belied him.

Naturally there is some unevenness of invention and execution in these twenty-one great panels, but it is unfair to confuse them with the average output of the factory. Rubens gave uncommon care to their composition and superintendence, moving from Antwerp to Paris as the work proceeded. He retouched the canvases as they were being finished in the studio, and again after they were in place. So, while they inevitably lack the integral exquisiteness of the small autographic pictures of his later years, they reveal as a whole what one may call the public and civic merits of his art at their high point. They virtually mark the culmination and end of this phase of his creation. I imagine the three years between 1622 and 1625, when this work was in progress, were the years he liked best to remember as old age fell prematurely upon him. He was still to do public work of a notable sort, but in his last years it is exceptional. His ultimate painter perfection was attained in working for himself, in a kind of sublimated amateurism. The great hall adorned and ennobled by these pictures was formally opened in May of 1625, on what turned out to be an inauspicious occasion—the marriage of Marie's daughter, Henrietta Maria, to the ill-fated Charles I of England.

About a year later Rubens' wife died. His letters about her speak of respect and honor. Her vitality and good sense had been the support of his great effort. There were well-grown children to keep the Chateau of Steen from utter loneliness. For three years Rubens produced little, and that little chiefly on religious themes. Characteristic are the Assumption, in the Cathedral at Antwerp, and the Enthroned Madonna with Saints, in St. Augustine's. Here the diagonal compositions of Titian are the model, but these are elaborated in a florid and spectacular sense which is Rubens' own. Something of that generalized glamour which we noted in the Landing of Marie carries over without much change into these sacred themes. The lighting is theatrical, withal most sensitively expressive. Some going off in his art is suggested by the unevenness of the fifteen designs for tapestry, on the history and efficacy of the Eucharist, 1625–1628. Here the refractoriness of many of the subjects rather than failing inspiration may be to blame. But, on the whole, it looked as if Rubens at fifty had reached a limit, and could now only repeat himself, unless indeed some lucky event should inspire him to a fresh start. The renovation promptly offered itself in the form of, first, a diplomatic mission to Spain, and then, remarriage, to a charming and amiable young woman.

In midsummer the Duke of Buckingham, able if unscrupulous favorite of Charles I, appointed Rubens as a special envoy to Madrid to make peace between England and Spain. He spent some nine months at Madrid and while he accomplished his diplomatic mission painted many pictures. In particular he studied and even copied with intelligent admiration the light and atmospheric painting of Titian's latest manner. Their technical and spiritual unity, qualities far beyond the wholesome brilliancy of his own painting, he sought to emulate. Doubtless he shared such studies with a promising young court painter, Diego Velasquez, who in his turn was to assimilate the diaphanous strength of aged Titian.

The full flavor of Rubens' Spanish studies we may catch in the composition sketch at Princeton representing the Death of Adonis (Fig. 223). Since the big picture by a mediocre assistant is, or recently was, at Madrid, we may assume that there the sketch was made, and the style of this little masterpiece suggests this period for it. It is dashed off in muted tints of pale yellow, rose, azure, which seem rather sap of flowers than more material pigments, painted with nothing, yet it renders with truth and vigor the swing of trees and clouds and the most vehement actions of men and beasts, and the inextricable hurly-burly about the corpse of Adonis is knit into a stable and lovely order.

In April, 1629, Rubens sailed for England with a title of nobility from Philip IV in his portfolio and an honorary degree in prospect from Cambridge. For some seven months he continued with decreasing success his peacemaking activities, was welcomed at the court, and returned to the lonely Chateau of Steen with a commission to decorate the great ceiling of Inigo Jones' new Palladian palace of

Whitehall. In midwinter of 1630, being fifty-two, he married a buxom and amiable girl whom he had known since her infancy, Helène Fourment. There is a picture at Munich, painted a few months after the marriage, which tells much of his new happiness. The knightly and well-preserved artist is strolling on the shadowy parterre before the loggia of his country mansion. Helène, with a big picture hat and a huge feather fan, looks smilingly out at us as she moves along confidingly with her famous man. There is a suggestion of all the amenities: young trees cast a pleasant dappling shade; a maid-servant feeds the peacocks; a page, perhaps her stepson, attends Helène deferentially; a fine setter dog rushes in to join his master; through a wicket gate one senses cooler and more secluded joys under the trees and between the well-kept hedges of a formal plaisance. What a vision of the Indian summer of a great genius!

Hereafter Helène often appears in his painting—in every variety of sumptuous attire, lightly draped as a symbol of this or that, occasionally in her glorious nudity. One feels Rubens' passion for her beautiful form, but feels it sublimated and ennobled in a Lucretian sense. There is no mawkishness or innuendo about this old lover of a young thing who chronologically might have been a youngest daughter. He will still achieve great public commissions—the ceiling decoration for Whitehall, after 1630, by no means his best but after three hundred years still the most noteworthy decorative series in England; the scenery for the triumphal entry of the Cardinal, Prince Ferdinand; the decorations for the palace of William of Orange at The Hague— but his characteristic work is now private, portraits of Helène, mythologies that celebrate her nude beauty, peasant dances, garden parties of patricians, and above all, landscapes of the most fresh and ethereal charm. The method is now sublimated; what I have written about the sketch for the Death of Adonis covers it all generically. A transparent tone which is neither gray nor yellow here and there cools into azure and flushes into pale rose. It no longer seems painting, but like the shifting tints and textures of a gently moving cloud, at dawn.

Most famous of these pictures of his premature old age is Helène with her Two Children, at Paris. It combines with the casual veracity of a snapshot the most exquisite handling of blond tints, while behind it is the pride and joy of an aged husband and father in an unexpected and borrowed felicity. Admirable in this time are the two versions of the Judgment of Paris. A comparison of the earlier version at London, about 1633, with the later version at Madrid, about 1635, will show how his art grew in ardor and grandeur as his strength declined. Nothing is lovelier among the mythologies of this ripe sort than the little sketch for a Diana and Endymion, at London. In it is fully presaged the ardent and innocent sensuousness of Fragonard a century and a half away.

There is a new note in the two pictures of the Garden of Love, at Madrid (Fig. 224), and in the collection of Baron Edmund Rothschild, at Paris. Richly dressed women loll at their ease, but expectantly, while a few great gentlemen dally with the fair women whose expectation has been fulfilled. Above, before a stately, rusticated portal, little winged loves hover and offer flowers. Rubens and his young wife, Helène, are seen embracing at the right. All this merely needs to be sublimated in a wistful sense, and you will have the Fêtes Galantes of Antoine Watteau.

In contrast with these social joys qualified by courtly etiquette are the energetic and racy Peasant Kermesse, at Paris, and the even finer, because simpler and more lucid, version at Madrid. It is as if the weary courtier found vicarious zest in these very bodily transports of simple folk at uninhibited play. In his years of strength such themes made no appeal to him, and are absent.

How choose among the dozen great landscapes with which Rubens solaced his tired eyes! The promise in the landscapes of fifteen years earlier is more than fulfilled. These are not portraits of places, but spaces pulsating with air, light, and sense of growing things. Some will prefer the grave simplicity of the little Moonlight Landscape in the Mond Collection, London. Corot is already implicit in it. Personally I love the Landscape with Château Steen, at London, with its amazingly rich and alertly handled detail, its sense of work and habitation—like an Old Bruegel distilled into a subtler essence. But if anyone chose rather the Sunset, at London, or the Landscape with a Windmill or the Landscape with a Rainbow, at Paris (Fig. 225), or the more overtly romantic Shipwreck of Aeneas, at Berlin, I could have no quarrel with him. These improvisations of Rubens' failing years will give vital formulas to Watteau and Gainsborough, will dazzle and instruct Turner and Constable.

The belated idyl at the Chateau of Steen was to be brief. In 1635 Rubens retired. He was only fifty-eight, which has been merely the late prime of many a painter, but his various and incessant activity had told on him. There is a half-length self-portrait at Vienna, painted a year or two before he died. Rubens holds himself erect, but with difficulty; the gout had ravaged him. The face has set with suffering; the eyes are dull; the fine hand rests slackly on the hilt of the rapier. Rubens was eminently a Christian, and he prepared sumptuously for his last rest by painting an altarpiece for his chapel in the Church of St. James, in which he planned to be buried. The Madonna, an idealization of Helène, in the Venetian fashion, is enthroned among attendant saints (Fig. 217). Her Child is a portrait of her infant son. The saints are magnificent. A half-nude and fiercely ecstatic St. Matthew glares over his shoulder at the spectator as he brandishes his arm towards Mary. The dark-haired woman with exposed breast and lovely bare feet, who modestly approaches the Madonna, seems to be the Magdalene, and is probably drawn from one of Helène's sisters. Behind her Rubens himself, in splendid plate armor, assumes the role of the chivalric St. George, holding upright his victor's banner, while the pierced dragon lies limp at his feet. The dedication of such a picture is to the valor and moral strength of men and to the gentleness and devotion of women. This may seem to be Rubens' credo, and by it he chose to be remembered.

He has never been forgotten. The sanity and animation of his character have remained exemplary. The candor and skill of his handling had nothing recondite about it. It could be, and was, imitated with fruitful results. What Sir Joshua Reynolds was somewhat deprecatingly to call the ornamental style was to be helpful and normative generation by generation for painters of extrovert and life-accepting type. Till yesterday the influence of Rubens was very much alive in the great master Renoir, and there will be successors to Renoir who will see that so precious a tradition shall not die. Titian and Rubens are the pillars of modern painting, in so far as it seeks balance between observation, decoration, and content. This is the central tradition, with various types of classicism at the Right and various types of optical realism at the Left. It is no slight service to art to have marked out that broad middle road which the average artist, as the average human being, may most profitably tread. In Rubens we find that even balance between manual skill and fine judgment which Leonardo da Vinci regarded as the quality of the artist truly great. Such instinctive judiciousness, not without ardor, is the very basis of what Sir Joshua Reynolds calls Rubens' "eloquence."

If anyone doubt Rubens' greatness, let him study the works of his two most prominent younger contemporaries, both Flamands—Anthony van Dyck and Jakob Jordaens. Lack of taste limited the immensely long and able activity of Jordaens; lack of character left Van Dyck, with every opportunity, going off in his art in his prime, and snuffed out at forty-two. Indeed, the careers of these two artists are a very parable of the part of taste and character in forming a great painter. For both had a crafstman's gift hardly inferior to that of Rubens, while, at least in portraiture, Van Dyck's perceptions were actually superior.

Jakob Jordaens was born of prosperous merchant folk at Antwerp, in 1593. His vocation was early apparent, and as an urchin of ten we find him an apprentice of the half-Italianate painter, Adam van Noort. Van Noort had a reputation for brutality, but young Jordaens was no sensitive plant. He throve on strict instruction; in 1615, at twenty-two, was admitted to the painters' guild as a water colorist—probably as a maker of big temporary decorations—and a year later acted the good apprentice in marrying his master's daughter, Catarina.

Popular and prosperous, honors followed him. In 1621, well short of thirty, he was elected dean of the guild. He gave Antwerp what it wanted—big pictures of family revels; big mythologies in which the goddesses looked more satisfactorily like nude citizenesses of Antwerp than ever did those of Rubens; character studies of sad or glad philosophers apparently as truthful and expressive as those of that marvelous young Spaniard at Naples, Ribera, and naturally Jordaens supplied also the big religious paintings which were wanted in so Catholic a city as Antwerp. These various themes he invested with a construction energetic rather than fine, with a color rather immediately attractive than precious, with a drastic characterization and a genial humor which delighted the tired business men of Antwerp. On the whole the defect of so vigorous and wholesome an art is lack of stylization and sense for composition. Here the comparison with Jan Steen, who was painting on a smaller and more appropriate scale Jordaens' favorite domestic feasts, is most instructive.

Jordaens may be thought of as appealing to the Flemish love of Gargantuan eating and drinking. The mere records of the civic and private feasting of that day simply appall the half-hearted eater and drinker of this feeble time. For hours, nay, for days, they systematically gorged and swilled, and the men and women of Jordaens prove that the Flemish digestion was not inferior to the Flemish appetite. It is because Jakob Jordaens took all this seriously, and loved the look of it, that he is an important artist. No art is worth while, save as it rests on some sort of faith. Such faith may be centered on the court, on some bygone Olympus, on heaven, on the kitchen. Any one of these faiths will go far towards forming a great artist, if it be strong enough.

As a matter of record, Jakob Jordaens, genial improviser though he seem, had no lack of conviction. In his early sixties he took the hazardous step of associating himself with the Calvinists, held prayer meetings at his house, and paid a heavy fine for "scandalous writing," doubtless the expression of his new religious views—a foursquare man, if not quite a great artist.

He began early with religious painting, which he continued through his long activity. The class may be represented by the rather early Holy Family, at New York. It has a most pleasing simplicity, warmth and vitality. The eight figures are well concentrated, all drawn from actual models. It is a very happy picture, and it makes one happy to look at it. The dense composition suggests a study of Italian Renaissance pictures, which existed at Antwerp, and were readily available in engravings. The picture is everything he intended it to be, and everything it should be. Had Jordaens made it more precious in color and subtle in composition, he would have spoiled a masterpiece of domestic sympathy.

The geniality of Jordaens tends to be boisterous; he loves laughter and surprise—chooses his themes accordingly. Thus there must be half a dozen versions of Aesop's Fable of the Peasant and Satyr, none better than that in the Cassel Gallery. The bewilderment of the visiting satyr at the peasant, who blows hot to warm his hands and cold to cool his soup, is admirably rendered, as is the friendly interest of the peasant family in their odd guest. Again the closeness and massiveness of the figure group and the elimination of details betray sound Italian influence. The broad and form-making distribution of light and dark is very handsome and no more harsh than the subject matter requires.

Jordaens' power of characterization is favorably exhibited by the Four Evangelists, in the Louvre. He follows Ribera and possibly Rembrandt in making these major apostles earnest peasants. An Italian painter, saving only Caravaggio and his followers, would have given these Gospelers a Roman dignity. Jordaens wishes to make us feel a unity of devout contemplation among men of different ages and training. He has admirably succeeded. As mere painting, this is one of the finest pictures from his hand.

But he is perhaps more himself when he celebrates family merry-making—the grandfather leading the singing, while the young join heartily. These pictures, there are many of them, illustrate the local proverb:

"As the old cock crows
So peep the young."

The simplest version, at Paris, is perhaps also the best, though as a composition it has empty and untelling spaces. Jordaens tends to stop when his topical motive is complete, evading, or perhaps not understanding, the task of transforming his narrative into a pictorial and formal unity.

The Twelfth-night feast naturally attracted him. A family group follows the drinking of the night's king, an aged and capable toper distinguished by a gilded pasteboard crown. In the many versions of this theme there is usually some overcrowding and exaggeration. But Jordaens never fails to convey the rapture of innocent convivial-ity. The rollicking mood of the version at Vienna, painted in the 1650's, when Jordaens was nearing sixty, is simply irresistible (Fig. 226). It is well modulated by contrasts—the prim loveliness of the entirely sober queen, and the exuberant tipsiness of the maid-of-honor at her right. Fine, too, are the upraised hands holding bumpers against the gloom. Despite a most elaborate and skillful handling of the lighting, the picture is here and there confused, but it abounds in individual beauties and makes its point joyously. Oddly enough, Jor-daens inscribed a moralistic and deterrent motto upon the picture in good Latin—*Nil similius insano quam ebrius*, "Nothing is more like a crazy man than a drunken man." Just why is not clear. His Cal-vinistic phase was still ten years or more ahead, and he may have meant no more than that this bean feast was to remain within the bounds of decent conviviality.

With regard to these family feasts painted on the scale of life, the question arises whether the scale is not too large for the subjects, whether little pictures, like Jan Steen's on these themes, would not

have been more agreeable and more amenable to artistic development. Jordaens gives only a hint of place, or space; the figures crowd
both out. It might be argued that this generalizes the motive, gives
it more universality. But this seems to me a very sophisticated plea
for so straightforward a character as that of Jordaens. It is plain that
he always meant to particularize. He probably simply liked to exercise his skill in what he considered the most conspicuous way, and it
would probably never have occurred to him that the scale which was
right for a Bacchanal by Rubens might be wrong for a family carouse
by himself.

As for his numerous mythologies, they are more carnal—I intend
no slur by the word—than those of Rubens. With Rubens one feels
that he is looking at beautiful painting which incidentally has to do
with flesh; in Jordaens one feels something like real flesh which is
beautifully painted. In Jordaens' mythologies there is no esthetic
distance. You could walk into his groups of nude deities and slap
them on the shoulder—or elsewhere. He is a powerful painter of the
nude and has an eye for its casually charming poses. Since his taste
in composition is uncertain, perhaps his best mythologies are those
which involve few figures; for example, the various versions of the Infant Jupiter with the Goat Amalthea. The theme calls only for one
portly, maternal nymph, and he always paints her superbly.

Perhaps the Allegory of Fertility, at Brussels (Fig. 227), may best
express this phase of Jordaens' great talent. It is a noble picture,
with a sense of cosmic vitality about it—a true symbol of the universal
principle of growth. All the forms fairly sing with health. The individual passages are of great beauty—the crouching, easy postures of
the nymph and faun in the foreground, the profile of the little girl,
the tense and vivid elation of the fine face of a Moor at the right.
All this is fine selection, and painting of the first order. Even the
grapes and melons, touched in by the friendly hand of Frans Snyders,
add to the luscious effect. An imperfect note is the too personal and
matronly Pomona, with bowed head. She is not a symbol, but a
woman. Again the fine, stalwart boy on the satyr's back is just a
little distracting. I am a little ashamed of stressing, or even mentioning, such slight blemishes. They are, all the same, significant in
showing the limitations of Jordaens' genius. His energy was never
delicately balanced by taste. It is possible to like him better than

Rubens, precisely for his powerful spontaneity, but it is not possible to admire him as much.

Success ever attended Jordaens. He was asked to do decorations for England and for Holland; he made many designs for tapestry; was an excellent etcher. It must have been a singularly happy life that ended at eighty-five in 1678, and its happiness survives in scores of pictures before which the heart always beats more freely.

It is significant that though we never speak of Count Titian or Sir Peter Paul Rubens, we do habitually speak of Sir Anthony van Dyck. For his great predecessors titles seem to mean nothing; for him, deprive him of his romantic association with the court of Charles I, and his fame would immediately fall. Which suggests that, though he had nearly all the gifts of a great artist, his total accomplishment was less than great and needs to be bolstered up by his knightly prestige.

Anton van Dyck was born of a prosperous merchant family at Antwerp, near the end of 1599. At ten years old he was working with the Italianate painter, Hendrik van Balen, who followed Rubens' general course at a modest distance. At sixteen, young Van Dyck was living in his own house with the amiable and popular painter, Jan Bruegel, and doing business in his own right. At nineteen he was a free member of the painters' guild. His was an amazing precocity.

We have, in the Academy at Vienna, his own bust portrait of himself at fifteen. He is too handsome and well-grown for his age, has a roving, sensual eye, an air of distrust and arrogance.

Never a pupil of Rubens, Van Dyck profited much by the study of Rubens' early masterpieces at Antwerp. There is a similar athleticism, a swift and rich handling of the brush, a deeper and less stylized color, a tendency to sensationalism, in every way premonitions of extraordinary power and versatility. Rubens employed Van Dyck to make copies for the engravers, and in 1620 used him as a collaborator in the important decoration of the Church of the Jesuits. Unluckily, none of that early work has come down to us. A few early pictures show the exaggerations proper to a young talent that has not yet found itself. The Drunken Silenus, Brussels, is just beastly drunk,

whereas the Silenuses and Bacchuses of Rubens are superbly ex-
hilarated. The Crossbearing, 1617, in St. Paul's, Antwerp, emphasizes the pathos of Christ crushed low beneath the cross, while the
soldiers try to drag Him forward and Peter and Mary bend in sympathy behind. The picture is a flashing tumult of light and dark, with
storm flashes from nude torsos and nude or armored limbs. It is
theatrically effective, though not entirely clear in arrangement. There
are holes and bosses. Nevertheless, it is an entirely extraordinary
work for a youth of eighteen. Much better unified is St. Martin
dividing his Cloak with a Beggar, in the Parish Church of Saventhem,
a version also at Windsor. What is felt is the sudden chivalric gesture of the horseman, the amazingly developed anatomy of the beggar's back being for show and little expressive. In the face of St.
Martin is as much scorn as pity. What he does he does for his own
self-respect, which is incidentally the motive for much charity. It is
a strong and forthright picture, alertly rather than finely composed.
All the same, it says clearly and strongly what it wants to say.

His high point in this vein is the Betrayal of Christ, at Madrid.
It was painted in 1622, as a present to Rubens, with whom Van Dyck
had lived for months in 1620. Here the thearicalism of early Van
Dyck seems fully to justify itself. Against the gentle, yielding form
of Christ bursts a human wave, of which the impinging crest is the
sinister profile of Judas about to betray his Lord with a kiss. Except
for the Christ, everything moves in a common agitation; brandishing
arms, flickering hands, branches of a tree writhing in the light cast
from a cresset and against moonlit clouds. So skillful a use of pictorial and emotional illumination was without precedent in the
North. Even Rubens had not yet attained to it. Nothing would
seem impossible to a painter who at twenty-three could make a picture like that. Looking forward a little it is disconcerting to realize
that religious painting was merely an exercise and a means of making
money with Van Dyck, a branch which he quit as soon as he could.

Naturally a popular young artist was asked to do the customary
mythologies and poetical narratives. Van Dyck's production in this
field is significantly scanty, some eighteen canvases in his twenty-five
working years. To say nothing about them is the part of charity, for
they are at once frigid and vulgar. To do this sort of thing accept-
ably the spirit must be nourished on the great poets, as was Rubens'.

Presumably Van Dyck now and then read, but there is no trace of real reading in his pictures.

The fine portraiture of Van Dyck's early years must be carefully winnowed from his abundant hack work and from the numerous merely clever character studies—heads of apostles and the like—in which he is only practicing. I mean such double portraits—Van Dyck excelled in the specialty—as the landscape painter, Jan Wildens and his Wife, Detroit, and the animal painter, Frans Snyders and his Wife, Cassel. These painters were mainstays of Rubens' factory, many years older than Van Dyck, and doubtless they welcomed his amazing talent with friendly admiration. This he handsomely reciprocated in these two oblong half-length canvases. The method is the blond and candid one of Rubens. But the effect is quite different. Everything is more specific and personal. One feels deeply the fine sensitiveness and human dignity, the admirable humility of these two skillful craftsmen who modestly took the wages of their great superior. One feels strongly the bond between men of this tractable gentleness and their wholesome housewives. All this is stated with entire simplicity and understanding and without gratuitous emphasis.

Even more impressive are the single three-quarter lengths of Frans (Fig. 228) and Margeretha Snyders, in the Frick Collection, New York. Here the arrangement is more picturesque and distinguished, with a hint of Titian's influence, but there is no waiver of character. If anything, it is even more intensely felt. The color is deeper and more saturated, somewhere between that of Rubens and Titian. From Van Dyck's early years there are no finer portraits than these, indeed, in what we may roughly call straightforward portraiture, there are few finer in the world.

A close scrutiny of the fifty or more portraits painted before Van Dyck's Italian journey would warrant certain misgivings. Few canvases are carried through like those in the Frick Collection. It is evident that this rising young genius can paint whatever he wishes to paint, equally evident that he often concentrates all interest on the face and scamps the rest. There are heads ill-articulated with the bodies, bodies that have no convincing existence under the garments, a trick of showing off the hands by artificial arrangements of the fingers—this, even in the very early picture at Detroit—hands that are painted with exquisite observation and painstaking, hands again quite slackly felt and unrealized in their character.

Then there is already a tendency to conceive the portrait, not in terms of the human particularity of the sitter, but on terms of an aristocratic and picturesque formula which, without Titian's generalizing power, seems borrowed from Titian. Here the capital example is the immensely rich and picturesque portrait of the Flemish expatriate, at Venice, Lucas van Uffel, amateur scientist and art patron. It is at New York. One hates to take small exceptions to so vivid and accomplished a work. If it indeed antedates Van Dyck's trip to Italy—and I suspect it may be a little later—it is the diploma piece for his first period. Yet being painted so amazingly well, it could at points have been painted better. A Van Dyck did not need the expedient of emphasizing his contours with an illogical, creeping highlight. Rubens would not have done it. Again, a more substantial exception, this superb portrait possibly bears too heavily on the motive of interruption and surprise. Given the motive, it could hardly be more spiritedly carried through. As a composition this is one of the finest of Van Dyck's numerous show pieces, admirable in the relations between the face, the strong, fastidious hands, and the globes on the Oriental rug which serves as tablecloth.

The final impression of Van Dyck at this moment would be that of a stupendous natural gift supported only by an intermittent seriousness. What would the vision of Italian and classical art do to a genius of this as yet unintegrated sort? The answer is that classical art was to do nothing for Van Dyck, while contemporary painting and that of the glorious yesterday of the Renaissance was to impose less of its spirit than of its superficial decorative formulas.

Van Dyck went to Italy by way of London, being called there in 1620 through the efforts of Rubens' great friend and patron, the art-loving Earl of Arundel. Van Dyck settled with a Flamand and fellow painter whose house "was reckoned convenient for the intrigues of people of fashion," received a pension of one hundred pounds from the frugal James I, and was put at the unworthy business of copying and modernizing old royal portraits. To escape this servitude he got, through Arundel's influence, a leave of absence for eight months, which actually stretched to ten years, made decent provision for a mistress and an illegitimate baby daughter at Antwerp, painted the swagger St. Martin, which we have already studied, for Saventhem, and by the end of 1621 was in Italy. There he found abundant patronage. In repeated sojourns he painted many of the nobles of

Genoa, was at Venice (with the Arundels), Turin, Bologna, Florence, Rome, and as far as Palermo. To Italy Van Dyck did not bring the humility and teachableness which two generations of Flemish Romanists had handed on to Rubens. The young master of twenty-four was already a great painter in his own eyes, and was accepted as such. He influenced the contemporary Italian painters rather than receiving influence from them. But he did bring intelligent habits of study. His notebooks are full of memoranda of the compositions of the great Renaissance painters, and in particular he grasped the exemplary character of Titian's mature art. His color deepens into a range which, if it lack the preciousness and simplicity of Titian's, is yet rich, various and Van Dyck's own. He studies the stately arrangements of Titian's rare full-length portraits and enriches and modulates these arrangements to his own end. He studies Titian's habit of somewhat simplifying and generalizing the structure of a face so that it tells more about the social class than about the individual.

The outcome of such restudy was portraits, at their best perfectly balancing interest of character with that of decoration; at their average, sacrificing character to stately decorative effect. The seated portrait of Cardinal Bentivoglio, historian of the Flemish Wars, in the Pitti (Fig. 229), is the finest Van Dyck of this period. It was painted in the summer of 1623, when Van Dyck was a guest in the cardinal's house, finding there a refuge from the rough mockery and threatened violence of his fellow Flamands making their studies at Rome. For them his courtly manner meant only snobbishness, which they resented by dubbing him "the gentleman painter," *il pittore cavalleresco*. They made things so unpleasant for him that he shortened his sojourn at Rome. At least he was at home with his noble and learned host, author and diplomat, and the portrait of Cardinal Bentivoglio gives as strong an impression of thoughtfulness and moral dignity as it does of ecclesiastical and mundane splendor. About the great prelate there is something at once clear-cut and a little formidable, and yet perceptive and kindly. Van Dyck was rarely to equal and never to excel this superb portrait.

At Genoa Van Dyck found his most generous and congenial patronage, and collectors now tend to prefer these stately full-lengths of Genoese noblemen, who were incidentally great merchants, and their wives, to the more famous and formerly more popular portraits of

the Stuart court. This recent preference for the Genoese Van Dycks
is sound in so far as these are more beautifully and thoroughly
painted, and almost equal in romantic appeal. The stately picturesqueness of such a portrait as that of Marchesa Elena Grimaldi-
Cattaneo, in the Widener Collection (Fig. 230), is irresistible, and
small criticism of it would be unpardonable. The great gentlewoman
walks out from a stately portal to a terrace. She holds a sprig of
flower in her right hand as she looks askance out of the picture towards a probable admirer or a possible intruder. A cringing Moor-
ish slave from behind holds a crimson parasol over her proud head.
It glows with sunlight like a huge nimbus; behind it is a marbled sky
and a sense of open, hilly country. Van Dyck never did anything
more sumptuously effective.

If all the Genoese portraits were at this level, criticism would be
reduced to silence. But run through a series of reproductions, and
you will be surprised, if not distressed, at their elegant monotony.
They are not really very personal, but of a single aristocratic effect.
All the women are from eight to nine heads high. Now even so
slight an acquaintance as the writer has had with the nobly born
young Italian matron, is enough to prove that her proportions are
not those of a Hellenistic Artemis. There is no reason to suppose
the situation was otherwise three hundred years ago. Van Dyck simply did not paint these noble ladies from life, or at least only their
faces; he elongated their forms, as he painted their frocks over a
dummy, in the interest of elegance. But such elegance is far-fetched,
false, and superfluous. A study of the, on the whole superior, if less
sumptuous, portraits of the noble spouses of these ladies, produces
about the same results. These great gentlemen strike poses, show off
their well-kept hands. As for his popular and always winsome portraits of children, their winsomeness is egregiously played up; they,
too, are showing off.

Now it might be argued that these exaggerations yield the poetic
effect which Van Dyck and his Italian sitters reasonably desired, and
that is true. But there are deeper defects which concern the very
probity of the picture-maker's art. These men, women, and children
often stand in uncertain balance, give no sense of mass or weight;
under their rich garments often is no feeling of a valid body. And
this comes out of negligence and by no means from lack of skill or
knowledge. There are rare masterpieces of these five Italian years

which judge the rest. Take the superb half-lengths of Marchese G. B. Cattaneo (Fig. 232) and his Wife, at London. How strong and masculine they are in construction of form and reading of character, incidentally how perfectly they are set in the quadrangle; how present and vital they are in their own right and without the need of any special pleading by the painter. Here is the true Van Dyck, who, alas!, rarely reveals himself.

On the whole he had not gained much but fame and money during his five Italian years, had merely popularized the poetizing mood of Titian in portraiture without assimilating Titian's seriousness and nobility. Able young Italian contemporaries, Domenico Fetti and Bernardo Strozzi, oddly both admirers and imitators of Van Dyck's facile handling, were trying to lead Venetian portraiture, while retaining its dignity, in a more intimate and individualizing direction. A glance at any of their good portraits will give sad testimony as to the physical and moral flimsiness of most of the contemporary production of Van Dyck. He was, while on the wavetop of fame and popularity, on the down grade artistically. Happily his descent was arrested by an opportune return, in 1627, to the more wholesome air of his native city of Antwerp.

At Antwerp he faced a patronage trained to the highest professional standards—those of Rubens and Jordaens. Here nothing slack or false would be tolerated. The moment was one to sting a newcomer to his highest endeavor. Rubens, with the great task of the Médicis series completed, was already ailing, gradually drawing out of active practice, and soon to be absent. Jordaens had hardly come to his own. Under these conditions there is a toning up of Van Dyck's art. His numerous religious pictures are still conceived theatrically in the interest of sweetness or pathos, but they now reveal a more robust and manly sensationalism, are strongly constructed and even thoughtfully composed. The arrangements vary between the closed patterns of the Renaissance and the looser overflowing patterns of the baroque. These latter arrangements are his best. Since the merit of this work is chiefly professional, and none of it of first importance, I must treat it in general terms. Notably telling in a somewhat operatic way is the Lamentation over Christ, at Antwerp. It lacks nobility and tragic poignancy, but it has much tenderness and it is staged with power and dignity. Other notable compositions of a somewhat baroque type are the Crucifixion with the Thieves, Mechlin, St. Rombaut's; the Enthroned Madonna with Saints, Vienna. Mary with an Adoring Husband and Wife, at Paris, is a sound and handsome composition in the Venetian tradition. The old latent tinge of insincerity in these religious themes is generally absent. I feel it only in the numerous Madonnas and Holy Families which are all too sweet for my taste, and here I may be too severe with works that many find captivating. In this religious painting it seems to me Van Dyck honestly gave everything he had—no profound insight or sympathy, but a very alert and sensitive intelligence.

Even the mythologies and idyls of this time are of more substance and meaning. But the merit of such paintings as the Forge of Vulcan, Paris and Vienna, and Rinaldo and Armida, Baltimore, is not such as to arrest the course of a general survey.

It is in portraiture that the benefit of his home-coming is most apparent. In Flemish portraiture there was a long and fine tradition of simple truth-telling. That is what the prosperous burghers of Antwerp expected; they wanted to be painted as they saw themselves, didn't wish to be poetized. With amazing adaptableness the seemingly effete flatterer of the Genoese aristocracy accepted this tradition, and the portraits which he painted during this five-year sojourn at Antwerp individually and as a group are perhaps the finest descriptive portraits made in Northern Europe in the seventeenth century. Frans Hals did not excel them, nor even Rembrandt in his realistic phase, while the austere and characterful portraiture of Philippe de Champaigne, as less painterlike, was of quite a different order. And as Van Dyck paints his fellow citizens and these womenfolk he reverts to a Flemish manner akin to Rubens'. The Venetian depth and mystery of the Genoese period yield to a blonder and clearer manner. Daylight supersedes poetical twilight.

Here is an embarrassment of riches which makes selection difficult. The robust effigy of the medalist, Jan van Monfort, Vienna, would seem to me the finest thing possible of its sort, were it not for the sensitive and ingratiating likeness of the Jesuit Father, Carolus Scribani, in the same gallery, or that of the engraver, Karel van Mallery, in a private collection at Oslo, were it not for the stupendous double portrait of the mediocre painter, Jan de Wael and his Wife, at Munich, or the richly melancholy interpretation of the landscape painter, Marten Rijckaert, Madrid. As for portraits of women, could anything be finer than that of Maria Louise de Tassis, at Vienna—

nothing, surely, unless it be the Anna Wake, Hague (Fig. 233), or the Isabella Waerbeke, of the Wallace Collection, London. In all the portraiture of these years there is something sound, workmanlike and eminently truth-telling. Hands are no longer artificially disposed, but take the unconscious positions the hands of strong men assume when at ease, or the self-conscious positions that the hands of over-rich and overdressed women assume when, not quite at their ease, they face the portrait painter. Rich stuffs, elaborate costumes, are brilliantly represented, but nothing of this secondary sort is obtruded. Everything enhances the character and the pictorial effect. It is what Rubens might have done had God made him not merely a good, but a great portrait painter. The portraits of these five Antwerp years are Van Dyck's surest gauges to immortality. The best, as usual, are half-lengths. The full-lengths are relatively free from the Italian tricks, but many of them show the inevitable defects of the show piece. Oddly enough, it was precisely the enhancement of such defects that was to make Van Dyck's permanent fame in England.

Probably the worst luck that ever befell Van Dyck, both as an artist and as a man, was the call in 1632 to be court painter of Charles I. Ostensibly the invitation looked good. Charles was notably generous and an eager collector of paintings—the only British monarch ever so strangely disposed. He offered two hundred pounds a year, at least the equivalent of two thousand pounds now, and separate payment for all portraits. All this was unhappily irresistible to Van Dyck's restless, cosmopolitan spirit. He was doing magnificent work at Antwerp. In its sound, sensible air there was hope of moderating his wantonness and maintaining his health. To be transferred to the fantastic and sophisticated court of the Stuarts was to exaggerate his old vices and add new ones. Of course, the spoilt child of fortune could not see it that way. He went to London; the king gave him a winter house at Blackfriars and a summer house at Eltham, and within three months dubbed him knight.

The two houses were soon full of revelers. Between thoroughbreds, equipages, musicians and mistresses, Van Dyck lived at a pace which made his fairly princely gains merely the prey of his creditors. He also painted—in his nine remaining years nearly two hundred portraits were made, mostly full-lengths. These include, with many of his weakest performances, a mere handful of his best. He scamped his work. The Parisian banker and picture dealer, Jabach, writes that

Van Dyck ordinarily put in only one hour on a portrait. The faces and hands were finished from professional models, the costumes were painted by his numerous assistants from garments hung on the lay figure. To one who really understands fine painting there is nothing more distressing than to look over a series of reproductions of the famous Stuart Van Dycks—so much repetition of stilted posture and artificial gesture, so much ostentation of mere things, so many hollow figures rather hanging against the background than established in the picture. Yet individually these much-loved portraits have an aristocratic charm, and it has sufficed.

Very interestingly, whenever Van Dyck returns to Antwerp he paints with his old probity—such religious pictures as the two Pietàs, Antwerp, or the portraits of Justus van Meerstraten and his Wife, at Cassel. It is as if he were ashamed to practice at home the wiles he habitually employed at London.

Obviously, if Van Dyck paints without conscience and flimsily for the English market, it is not because his powers are declining, but because he gives the English market what it likes and deserves. From 1636, in his hour of apparent decadence, he is painting those admirable little black and white sketches of artists, men of affairs and of letters, which, in his own etchings, too often finished up by collaborators, will remain to make the best sheets of his "Iconography" so many masterpieces of the portrait-etcher's art.

The sum of the matter is that to realize the greatness of Van Dyck in his last phase, one must first eliminate nine out of ten of the famous courtly full-lengths as so much merely hollow, specious and sentimentalized society portraiture. The remainder are masterpieces, not of sound and well-felt construction, but all the same great masterpieces of the poetizing and romantic sort. A few among these are masterpieces of characterization. In the main, the reader must look these up for himself. All I can hope to do within reasonable space is to start him in the right direction.

Naturally the many portraits of Charles I are here of major interest. For Van Dyck he was always a figure of romance, and the posthumous romance of the unfortunate king is based rather on these portraits by Van Dyck than on serious historical documentation. Probably the only closely resemblant one is the head in three aspects, Windsor, which Van Dyck must have made in order to familiarize himself thoroughly with the royal features. One divines a soft and gentle stubbornness, without real force of character or clearness of thinking. The eyes are those of a poet and dreamer, and, though more literal portraits may suggest that Van Dyck may have contributed this grace to an actually sour and stolid visage—see Pot's portrait of Charles, in the Louvre—yet there must have been something of the poet and hero in the eminently foolish monarch who so gallantly offered his neck to the ax at Whitehall. More determined and stately, and probably less truth-telling, is the frontal half-length in armor at Arundel Castle. It has great melancholy distinction and occupies its space very grandly. The most broadly picturesque and dramatic of all the portraits of Charles is the famous canvas at Paris (Fig. 231), in which the king, leaving his champing steed with a gentleman in waiting, halts with arm akimbo and face haughtily turned outward as he prepares to walk away. The accessories are compositionally effective, and there is a freshness, even a breeziness, in the handling and conception, which in this period of Van Dyck's activity is rare and precious. The equestrian portraits of Charles seem to me merely effectively pompous and only fair second rate as compared with Titian's Charles V and the finer equestrian portraits of Velasquez.

The queen, the morally empty and mischief-making daughter of Marie de Médicis offered little to any painter but her somewhat doll-like comeliness. This Van Dyck exploited variously and skillfully, never better than in the full-face and profile at Windsor (Fig. 234), which suggest a soft and unintelligent determination, akin to that of her ill-starred husband. There was nothing here to excite a born portrait painter, and there is nothing exciting in Van Dyck's portraits of the queen, though among them there are some of a very decorative and sumptuous attractiveness, as the seated three-quarter length of the queen in blue satin, in the collection of the late Lord Duveen.

The much-loved groups of the royal children, at Turin and Windsor, are skillfully and sensitively felt as individual portraiture, but rather flimsy in construction, and composed as casually as any bad photograph. The full-length portrait of James, Duke of Lenox, at New York (Fig. 235), is primarily a show picture, but it is hard to imagine a finer one. The painting of the satin and velvet costume is superbly light and telling, as is that of the affectionate greyhound. In harmony of low tones the picture is exemplary and almost as modern in accent as a superlative Whistler. While there is no emphatic suggestion of specific character—rather of a generalized aristocratic mood—this Stuart duke really had rather little specific character, and there is a sufficient hint of that flabby Stuart obstinacy which was to cause his cousin James the unnecessary loss of a crown, as it had earlier caused his cousin Charles the unnecessary loss both of a crown and a head.

Not quite a great picture, but an extraordinary human document is the willfully picturesque full-length portrait of Sir John Suckling, in the Frick Collection, New York. This extravagant minor poet had fought among Gustavus Adolphus's mercenaries, had led the rosy life in the court of Charles, wrote alluring ballads and songs, raised his own troop of horse to fight for King Charles, conspired to release Strafford from the Tower, fled to Paris, where in poverty he took poison. He stands red-headed, highly self-conscious and with a somewhat worried complacency, fantastically garbed in blue and scarlet, while he fingers a huge folio which rests on a rock on which is graven: *Ne te quaesivers extra,* "Look not beyond thyself." Everything is fantastic and even a little foolish, but it is all of full-flavored romantic effect, and a fine and truthful document for that blend of volatile talent with moral instability which characterized the cavalier songsters as a class. Personally I should like the picture much better if Sir John bore more weight on his legs and feet.

We have been dealing with the fine English Van Dycks, pictures which, enlisting his talent and taste, perhaps did not draw heavily upon his genius. Such portraits are now few. High among them is that of the quack and mystic, Sir Kenelm Digby, at Knole. It perfectly expresses the furtive self-confidence of the charlatan, is strongly constructed and fastidiously composed—probably a labor of love, for the shifty and eccentric knight was the painter's close friend and the husband of a complaisant wife whom Van Dyck transiently adored. Less subtle, but equally clear-cut, is the double portrait of the cavalier poets, Thomas Killegrew and Thomas Carew, at Windsor. It is perfectly composed, both in plane and in depth, beautiful in the flashes of white linen and paper against the prevailing middle tone, while the distinction between the moody superiority of Killegrew and the more likeable eagerness of Carew is delicately asserted. The placing of the figures in the air is accurate and gives both true physical and esthetic distance. As fine in its way is the tiny canvas at Leningrad which shows the upturned, inspired face of the architect,

Inigo Jones, first English artist to feel the glow from the Italian Renaissance. Superb again in character, if not so impeccably made as the Killegrew and Carew, is the double portrait, in Earl Fitzwilliams' collection, representing the brave but ill-fated Count of Strafford, reflecting deeply some difficult thought and phrase, while his secretary waits admiringly. No less fine is the confident effigy of Van Dyck's mistress, Margaret Lemon, Hampton Court. Her posture, with an alluring breast half exposed, parodies that of Titian's Magdalenes, but the hard, sensual arrogance of the pose and expression mark the successful and entirely unrepentant courtesan. A comparison of this masterpiece with other portraits in which Van Dyck has charitably softened and prettified his light-o'-love will better than many words reveal its greatness. There are a few others, perhaps half a dozen or so, late Van Dycks of this quality. To find and appreciate them not merely betrays the agreeable mediocrity of the popular Van Dycks, but incidentally is a strenuous and instructive exercise in the practice of taste.

Immensely picturesque as it is, Van Dyck's bust portrait of himself with a sunflower, Duke of Westminster's collection, hardly deserves inclusion among his masterpieces, but it tells much about his declining years. He is just nearing forty, but the fine, unwrinkled face has an unwholesome delicacy, seems here and there flabby and sinking in. The left hand lifts and fingers listlessly the gold chain of a knight, the right hand points upward to a gigantic sunflower which balances the face, as a second head does in the numerous double portraits. Here may be a sardonic symbol for his own career. Like the sunflower he had ever turned towards the warmth and light of courtly favor, and it was withering him. Van Dyck, though hopelessly wayward and undisciplined, was highly intelligent, and must have had moments of bitterly true introspection. Of one of these moments this picture seems to be a pathetic record.

It was perhaps a sense of shortening years that made him apply for great mural commissions. With all his fame, he had done little mural painting, and this he knew was the surest guarantee of remembrance. Such ambition rising as his bodily powers failed, he asked to paint the walls of Whitehall, the ceiling of which Rubens had decorated magnificently. His exorbitant demands, and the first grumblings of the Civil War, brought this project to naught. He hastened to Paris to secure the commission for the new Long Gallery of the

Louvre. But Poussin had already been drawn reluctantly from Rome to undertake this work. Van Dyck lingered at Paris in feeble health. For this reason he had to decline to paint the portrait of Cardinal Richelieu. In 1639 his friends, in order to steady him, had arranged a marriage with a nice Scotch girl, Mary Ruthven. She was soon to witness the flight of the queen to France and the beginning of the king's futile counterattack on the Cromwellians from the North. Mary Ruthven's gifted and mostly absent husband returned to London virtually dying. About a week before he died, she bore him a daughter. Amid the confusion of the Civil War, his friends and boon companions dead or scattered, Van Dyck ceased to breathe. He was not yet forty-two. They buried him honorably in Old St. Paul's, and soon the great fire obliterated all traces of his tomb. His fame lasted. As his older friend Rubens had invented an ornamental style available for all purposes, so Van Dyck had worked out an ornamental style proper for aristocratic portraiture. Since his death no fashionable portrait painter has been unmindful of Van Dyck's elegance and charm. As a Sir Joshua Reynolds finally closes his dimmed eyes he will express the unlikely hope of meeting Van Dyck in heaven.

With the premature death of Van Dyck, what little remained of the glory of the Flemish school of painting was the robust and genial art of Jakob Jordaens and that of the best assistants of Rubens. There are isolated, charming figures which in a rapid survey must unhappily be passed with mere mention. Cornelis de Vos (1585–1661), worthy member of a dynasty of painters, sincere and sympathetic portraitist whose works are often sold as Van Dycks; his namesake and pupil, but not kinsman, Simon de Vos (1603–1676), who has left an unforgettably vivid and sympathetic portrait of himself, at Amsterdam, and otherwise only a name. Such artists maintained the prestige of the Antwerp school for a generation after Rubens' death against an ultimately losing fight with French influence.

Among the scores of pupils and assistants of Rubens only the two animal painters, Frans Snyders and Jan Fyt, seem to deserve special mention. Snyders had no children, and much of the curiosity and affection that normally go to the doings of children was turned to those of animals. It was he who painted the wolves, lions and magnificent hounds in the famous hunting pieces of Rubens. Ultimately he painted such pictures on his own account, with success. Their energy and truthful animal portraiture is disarming—in particular a dog lover and dog knower will recognize a kindred spirit in Snyders. To be sure, the issue of scale arises with him, as it has for us already with Jordaens. Does anybody reasonably want life-sized stags, wolves, hunting dogs, on his walls? At least the Antwerpers had no misgivings on this point. The sensitive artist in Frans Snyders, which may be divined in Van Dyck's portraits of him (Fig. 228), is revealed, better than in the celebrated hunts and piles of dead game, in some fantastic panels at Madrid. Here we have happy families of birds and beasts active in their own habitat. The characterfulness and instinctively right decorative feeling of such assemblies looks forward to two centuries and the birds and animals depicted in their homes by Audubon.

Jan Fyt (1611–1661) studied with many masters, among these, Snyders; worked for a time successfully in Italy, and built up a great fame as a brilliant executant. That he is, emphatically, but really little more. He probably cared much less about animals than Snyders and more about his own amazing skill. But a painter who does only one thing very well is pretty sure to be remembered, and a Fyt is, or at least recently was, a necessary item in the catalogue of any well appointed gallery.

With Rubens and Van Dyck the Flemish school, having imposed its ornamental style on all Western Europe, had spent itself. France was to invade Flanders with her armies, and more successfully still with her academic painting and art criticism. Flanders had had the lucidity to draw on the Italian Renaissance at its most available and exemplary fountainhead, the art of Titian and his great contemporaries. This precious heritage Rubens and Van Dyck had conserved, so that, amid temporary confusion, we are still profiting by it today. Flemish painting had done its work. The further task of a more analytical consideration of the various phases of Italian painting was to be taken up in France, and before the death of Van Dyck such reconsideration of the Italian examples was in vigorous progress under the lead of Simon Vouet. But because for many reasons our French chapters must be our last, we shall move North instead of South, and study the emergence of a new realistic art in Holland.

### CHAPTER XV

# DUTCH PAINTING OF THE SEVEN-TEENTH CENTURY: FRANS HALS AND THE SCHOOL OF HAARLEM

FIG. 236. FRANS HALS. The Sand Runner.—Antwerp.

Fig. 237.  (Upper) Frans Hals.  Officers of St. George's Doelen.—
Haarlem.
Fig. 238.  (Lower left) Frans Hals.  Nurse and Child.—Berlin.
Fig. 239.  (Lower right) Frans Hals.  An Officer.—London.

433

FIG. 240.  FRANS HALS.  The Merry Company.— New York.        FIG. 241.  FRANS HALS.  Junker Ramp and His Girl.— New York.

434

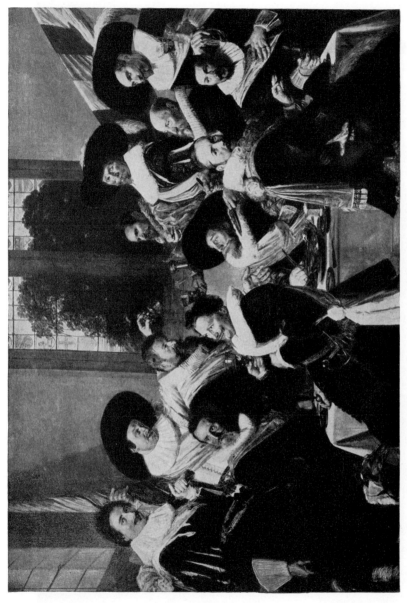

FIG. 242. FRANS HALS. First St. Adriaen's Doelen.—Haarlem.

435

FIG. 243. FRANS HALS. Second St. Adriaen's Doelen.—*Haarlem.*

FIG. 245. FRANS HALS. Balthazar Coymans.—Washington.

FIG. 244. FRANS HALS. Willem van Heythuysen.—*Liechtenstein Collection, Vienna.*

437

FIG. 247. FRANS HALS. René Descartes (sketch).—
Copenhagen.

FIG. 246. FRANS HALS. Portrait of a Man.—New York.

438

FIG. 248. FRANS HALS. Female Regents of St. Elizabeth's Hospital.—*Haarlem.*

439

Fig. 249. (Upper) Judith Leyster. The Smiling Man.
—Amsterdam.
Fig. 250. (Lower) Jan Miense Molenaer. Jan Miense
and Judith Leyster.—Coll. Henry Pfungst, Esq., London.

THE EMERGENCE of a Protestant and independent Dutch Republic meant for the art of painting that it suddenly lost the immemorial patronage of church and state, becoming a private concern. One may date the beginning of this process from the image-breaking of 1566. But for still a generation the Romanist style lived on from sheer momentum. By 1609, when the twelve-year truce with the King of Spain was signed, the Romanist style was waning, and Frans Hals was a very young student of painting. By 1648 and the Treaty of Münster, which gave legal sanction to Dutch independence, Frans Hals and Rembrandt were in their glorious prime. Within twenty years more the glory had passed.

We have to do then with a sudden, intense and singularly coherent impulse which produced within the lifetime of artists like Frans Hals and Rembrandt the most important mass of realistic painting that the world has seen, created a style, perfected it, abandoned it. Compare this situation with the gradual development of the style of the Italian Renaissance through two centuries and a half. What a striking suggestion of the swift tempo and instability of all individualisms as compared with the massive duration of the great classical and religious traditions! In Holland, so far as painting was concerned, the Catholic and classical tradition went down together. It was as hard to interest a Dutch art lover in the gods of Olympus as it was to interest him in the lives of the saints, or, for that matter, in the personages about whom he read in his Bible.

It was, of course, the character of the new patronage that shaped and limited the new art. The Dutch art patron was a city dweller and a man of affairs. Military service and the complications of growing overseas commerce had sharpened his wits and given him a rare self-confidence. The Dutch art lover is a patriot and knows the heroic tradition of his land, but he is singularly little interested in the past, or indeed in anything that does not minister to his present dignity and comfort. He has literally made the neat and snug world in which he thrives, and he is justly proud of his creation. He will have

441

little use for an other-worldly art, and a Rembrandt, providing it magnificently, will die in poverty.

The Dutchman will display a curious blend of thrift and lavishness. No costume is too gay or costly for his body, no food or wine too dear for his stomach. He is socially minded and serviceable—an inveterate joiner of trade and merchant guilds, chambers of rhetoric, crossbow companies, directorates of charities. He marries prudently and takes a keen pride in the neatness with which his city house is kept. To adorn it he is ready to lavish money on fine potteries and porcelains and on pictures. He likes to clothe his womenfolk and children sumptuously. While he is proud of his home or homes—for there is likely to be a tidy country place as well as the city house—his social life is elsewhere, at the tavern where the company may be mixed enough, or in the sessions of his societies and committees.

Such a man asks of the painter—as Fromentin has ably pointed out—just one service; portraiture of himself, and in a broad sense, of his belongings. All of Dutch art in its best estate may be regarded as sensitive and veracious portraiture of persons and things. Only Rembrandt at his greatest escapes the definition.

The world the Dutch painter has to deal with is emphatically a man's world. Women have little or nothing to do with setting standards of taste. Here is a marked difference from the conditions in the Renaissance and today, when the social and artistic tone was and is largely set by women. In the Holland we are considering there was no society in which women freely shared. Whether as housekeeper or chief ornament, her place was in the home, and the home was not a place of social resort.

When we say the Dutch art lover demanded only portraiture, we must take the word broadly. First he wants to be painted himself in all his manly bravery; he gladly pays also for his portrait in the groups of the corporations to which he belongs. Next he wants his women to be portrayed, and his children. He likes the tranquillity of his home, and welcomes pictures of the rooms in which his women prink or work. He is also willing to be painted in other women's rooms—women who prink but do not work. He cares much for his city and his street, and will pay for good painting on these themes. He loves feasting and merriment and will order impartially his own family celebrating Twelfth-night, or a carouse with boon companions at his favorite tavern. He is proud of his kitchen and tableware, and so is an excellent client for the still-life painter. As a prosperous person, he enjoys condescendingly the whimsical foibles of the poor. In business and in art he keeps on terms with them, with the superior person's relish for their raciness. Oddly, war pictures do not attract him—probably for the good reason that he has served. For landscape beauty his taste is limited. He prefers it with his own country house or cattle in evidence. Painters who, like Jakob van Ruysdael, love wild nature, will fare badly. The Hollander is enough of a sailor and gentleman-adventurer to like studies of the quiet or angry sea and of the fates of boats and ships.

In untechnical language we have described the chief branches of Dutch painting. Its scale was dictated by its destination. The good Dutch homes were modest mansions. Big pictures, such as were wanted in Catholic Flanders, were unavailable. Besides, the picture itself had come to be regarded, not as a fixture, but as a portable object, even as an object of speculation. There are now dealers, agents, and auctioneers—a commercial art market very like our own. A successful painter still works mostly on orders, but also makes pictures for stock in hope of private sale.

Though some critics have sought to find a public and monumental intention in the corporation groups, it seems to me that to speak of a public art in Holland is misleading. At most there is, beside the art made for the individual, that made for a small group. When the Stadthouders wanted a really public and monumental painting for their palaces they rarely employed a fellow countryman, but sensibly applied to Rubens and Jordaens at Antwerp. The Doelen (military) and Regenten (director) groups are, to be sure, often very large, and to that extent monumental; so are the anatomy lessons, but these were all hung in places relatively private. They were never seen by throngs, as were the earlier pictures painted for churches, town halls, and the public rooms of palaces. It should further be noted that the Dutch picture was never treated as a decoration, with relation to a particular setting. It could be hung anywhere, on any wall, and served in the quiet dusk of a Dutch house as a sort of conveniently portable window by simply rehanging, so you might enjoy your favorite view in a new place.

What was really the strength of the Dutch School was the confident narrowness of the taste upon which it rested. The Hollander had no misgivings concerning his own interest as subject matter of

art. And, indeed, there was wherewithal to occupy any artist in the
look of a strong and disciplined man, in the record of such persons
and things as his will to live and will to power had brought together.
The moment this self-confidence was shaken—and shaken it soon
was by the vision of a more cultured France—Dutch painting swiftly
declined in a smooth, meaningless and borrowed elegance. Dutch
painting had truthfully celebrated a period of personal and national
pride that had its warrant in achievement. When that pride passed,
there was really nothing left to celebrate.

The chapter opens brilliantly with the pioneer of the new style,
Frans Hals. As to the date and place of Frans Hals' birth, we are in
doubt. But the date must be in the early 1580's and the place Catholic Flanders, probably Antwerp or Mechlin. Throughout his activity
Frans Hals often showed rather the flamboyant character of Flanders
than the deliberation proper to Holland. But since his education was
at Haarlem, and he made himself one of the greatest Dutch masters,
we should not overstress any residuum of Flemish exuberance in him.
In Haarlem at the end of the sixteenth century there were many respectable painters of Italianizing sort. Mannered and rather negligible in religious subjects and mythology, they retained much of the
old Gothic probity in portraiture, and any of them would have been
a useful mentor to a young painter who was to be almost exclusively
a portraitist. Carel van Mander, who, writing at the time, should
have known, says Cornelis Cornelisz, of Haarlem, was Hals' master.
Moes thinks the painter-engraver, Hendrik Goltzius, also helped shape
the young genius. Van Mander's son and biographer, who should
have known the facts, mentions Hals as his father's pupil. In any
case, Frans Hals, who lived in Haarlem from early boyhood, must
have seen the carefully executed portraits of these three masters, and
also those of Van Ketel and Key. The style which he thus inherited
was still fundamentally native. The basis was careful linear design,
with a cautious approach to the more painterlike methods of the
Italians. This only meant a more elaborate and specific modeling
than that of the old Gothic style, multiplication of half-tones and
high lights; in general, a somewhat pedantic overemphasis of plas-

tic effect. Out of this rather small and timid procedure Frans Hals was to build the freest and most genial method of portrait-making that the world has seen. Such a transformation takes time. Frans Hals seems to have been nearly twenty years about it, not coming to his own as a technician until he had passed forty.

He was a casual person—apparently always poor, despite a constant patronage. Most of our records of him come from the police court of Haarlem or the overseers of the poor. He married rather early and begat many children, who came up at loose ends. In 1616, the year he painted his first famous picture—St. George's Doelen—the magistrates put him under heavy bonds to abstain from drunkenness, and abuse of his wife, Anneke. She could not long profit by any resulting reform, for seven months later she died, and within four months more the bans were cried for a new wife, Lysbeth Reyniers. She was married on January 15th, 1617, and within five weeks presented her husband with a daughter, Sara. What is really important in this shabby business is that during these months of moral disorder Frans Hals was carrying to completion, in the first Doelen of St. George's, a most strenuously executed masterpiece of an entirely original order. It gave promise of the best eye and hand of the moment. It is one more of those curious cases in which artistic gift seems isolated from personal character, as if the artist created from a better self.

Before considering this first Doelen group, of 1616, we should consider a few earlier portraits which recent research has identified. The earliest, 1610, is a bust-portrait of a bald-headed, bearded man in a great ruff, at Frankfurt. On a casual glance it could be just a good portrait of semi-Italianate type. It is massive and characterful, somewhat coarsely conceived in heavy contrast of light and dark, harshly linear, yet meticulous in the minor modeling. But a paradox—the little flicks of light and patches of shadow, which look so painstaking, are dashed in simply, audaciously, and without retouch. The brush has simply danced in making what looks like a pedantically minute finish. Here the fine eye of Dr. Valentiner recognizes the germ of the future handwriting of Frans Hals. Whoever could make as good a portrait as this must have been making good portraits for years. In this picture we meet Frans Hals certainly not younger than twenty-six. What he did earlier is probably irretrievably lost. We may note that this arbitrary compromise between a linear and a painterlike method will remain Hals' method for twenty years more. His growth seems to rest not on reflection, but on incessant practice—one may feel that the hand and eye almost automatically and very gradually perfect their own operations without much co-operation from the intelligence.

Other portraits assigned to this early period hardly call for mention, excepting perhaps a little oval of a melancholy young man with right arm akimbo and left hand daintily holding a glove. It reveals for the first time Frans Hals' gift of catching his sitters in momentary and revealing poses. Beyond this the method, though it forces the contrasts of light and dark, is more unified and painterlike and less linear than the method of the portrait of 1610. For this reason Dr. Valentiner dates this little half-length in 1615, the year before the first Doelen of St. George's.

For nearly a century before that picture, the corporation group had been developing as an important branch of Dutch painting. One may trace progress in Haarlem itself. In 1530 Jan van Scorel had painted processionally, in pairs, Twelve Pilgrims of the Confraternity of the Holy Land. Excellent in portraiture, one can hardly think of it as a composition. In 1562 Dirck Barentz had painted Fourteen Members of the City Guard, at Amsterdam. In 1583 Cornelis, probably one of Hals' masters, had painted with excellent color the Feast of a Crossbow Company. These groups are all at Haarlem. Well before 1600 we find anatomy lessons. Although these early groups show a tendency to develop unity of composition, none really achieve it. They remain at best assemblages of fine portraits seeking artistic arrangement. Topically these groups, by Hals' time, fall into three classes: Doelen (military), Regenten (directors or trustees) and anatomy lessons.

Today it is customary to pass rather slightingly the Doelen of St. George's (Fig. 237), which, as we have seen, was painted in months of family strife and moral disorder. Yet it is only fair to say that but for the later Doelen of Hals himself, this would universally be hailed as one of the finest group pictures in the world. Merely its solidity, veracity and character would without other merits give it this high standing, and it has many other merits. It represents a battalion staff at a dinner, which is also a conference. These are veterans who had served in many battles. They are doughty men, big-paunched, hard-muscled, determined, intelligent—human symbols of that constancy, resourcefulness and valor against which the military power of Spain was repeatedly hurled in vain.

The color is rich and various rather than harmonious, but the cherry-red and azure of the banner at the center sufficiently brings everything to a focus. The table, hardly big enough for four of the thirteen feasters, is a subterfuge, but the varied sheen of its damask cloth balances handsomely the spotting of the faces and the irregular patch of veiled sky at the top. Certain admirably painted details, such as the tableware, hardly count in the effect. The crumpled, drawn curtain at the upper left is boldly slashed in, and distractingly ugly. The general arrangement in a segment of a circle, with relieving figures inside and outside the curve, is adequate if a little obvious, but the stern yet kindly face of the colonel is admirably held in focus, chiefly through its vertical frontality, all the other heads being in easier presentation and generally tilted. On the negative side, there are very hard and relatively inexpressive edges, the figures in the foreground; there are considerable areas which are inert, functioning neither as color nor as design; there is no satisfying sense of the space occupied by the figures; some hands are too artificially disposed; the beautifully painted ruffs are too similarly treated, forming a sort of irregular pattern which tends to isolate the fine heads. On the other hand, Frans Hals has conveyed such a sense of a common, resolute purpose that these minor shortcomings are apparent only on cold analysis, and will disturb no uncritical spectator. If Hals himself had not wrought such refractory ingredients into decorative unity in the later Doelen, I am sure very few beholders would find anything amiss with so living and characterful a masterpiece.

The portraits should be individually studied. At least half are masterly. The method is still the compromise between construction in line and in light and dark, which Hals took from his immediate predecessors, but the line is less evident than in the portrait of 1610, and the tendency is towards construction in light and dark in gradations which vary inconsistently between tenderness and harshness. Where red is introduced into the flesh tone, the effect is hot and even unpleasantly bricky. That was the price at the moment of emphatic and vital construction. Later he will admirably achieve construction on more sensitive terms.

Frans Hals was about thirty when he painted the first St. George's, and he had given his best. It would seem that the novelty and worth of his contribution passed unnoticed, for it was eight years before he got a similar commission. Parson Samuel Ampsing, who in 1621 wrote *The Praise of the City of Haarlem*, merely mentions Frans Hals and his younger brother, Dirck, alongside of such various names as Van Dyck, Pot, Molyn and Bray.

For the next ten or twelve years, the professional portraiture of Frans Hals, without essential change in method, steadily gains in incisiveness, character, and fine tonality. Very fine pictures of this time are Nurse and Child, about 1620, Berlin (Fig. 238), a marvel of genial and sympathetic interpretation, a picture the mere seeing of which is happiness, marvelously crisp in the rendering of difficult textures, well set in the space, and exquisite in its cool harmony of silvery grays and old gold. Even more characteristic, if less sensitive, is the perhaps slightly later portrait of a man and wife in a parklike landscape, at Amsterdam. The richly dressed citizen slouches joyously at his ease, while his proud wife looks askance in a somewhat shy and cattish complacency. The holiday mood of these privileged persons is caught with swift and infallible sympathy. Material and physical well-being loomed large in Frans Hals' cosmos, and no painter has celebrated it with greater conviction and success. So captivating is this picture that it seems ungracious to note minor technical shortcomings—as that the massive figures are rather on than in the landscape, while the landscape itself is flimsily felt and yields little sense of space.

The high-water mark of this early manner is reached in the justly famous Portrait of an Officer, 1624, in the Wallace Collection, London (Fig. 239). The doublet of various reds, with yellow and white embroidery, gives a superb decorative effect. The face and figure exhale a fine defiance, as of a character that knows how to deal with foes of all sorts. The details of slashed and embroidered stuffs and lace are dashed off with the most brilliant and truthful audacity. The arrangement as pattern is impeccably right. It is one of the rather few unforgettable pictures. Something of its self-confident vitality passes to the spectator and permanently fortifies him. It is hard to realize that we after all have to do with the old, linear procedure with secondary modeling in light and dark, so simple and immediate is the effect of construction. It will seem unhandsome to observe that the technical skill is imperfect. The placing of the masses through values has had to be helped out by introducing a non-existent irradiation about the brim of the big hat and behind the wavy hair. This cuts them out artificially from the background. It is a crude expedient which Frans Hals will soon eschew in favor of placing his forms through subtle modulations of closely related tones. It is not a deeply interpretive or profound portrait—there was nothing profound in this admirable swashbuckler to be interpreted—but it is one of the finest objective portraits in the world.

While in his professional portraiture Frans Hals was pursuing a conservative course, in genre painting he was working out an unprecedented and entirely personal style. Such painting of his boon companions and his children and their young friends was made to please himself; there was no patron whose taste must be considered. Ultimately such genre painting, for its brilliancy and vividness, became popular and salable. Indeed, today Frans Hals' fame rests largely on such pictures as the Merry Toper, the Gipsy Girl and the various versions of Malle Bobbe, so-called Witch of Haarlem, pictures which fairly reek with laughter and physical well-being.

To convey the zest of such characters something other than the old method of painting was required. Dealing with very transient expressions the painting must be equally swift. The old system had implied two separate processes, a carefully drawn contour, which was subsequently modeled up. This would do for a portrait which could be studied and restudied, and aimed at some aspect of permanence, but the outburst of laughter, or the joyous exuberance of tipsiness, had to be caught with the tip of the brush. Such subjects freeze when recorded in careful outline. So the new painting was to be what we call today direct painting, a single not a double process, areas of paint simulating the main constructional planes, and reflecting light as the actual planes do, rendering a similar optical effect.

Here it should be noted that the painter normally presents not an optical, but a mental, image. He paints what the mind has learned and, after repeated observations, has found significant. Such painting, because it implies careful analysis of many appearances, we call analytical painting. Ultimately it depends largely on selective memory. The portraiture of Holbein and Ingres is emphatically of this kind. There is little in such portraiture that the artist or anybody else could actually see at any given moment. Any truly optical image of the sitter would be of a completely different sort—more vivacious, more vividly present as a visual experience. But the mental image has something of permanence, dignity and importance which the optical image lacks. And these qualities great painters, with singularly few exceptions, have preferred to an accurate rendering of the actual look of things. The more the mental image implies previous analysis and criticism, the greater ordinarily the sacrifice of painterlike quality in favor of a kind of drawing. Again Holbein and Ingres excellently illustrate this case. Accordingly, the painter who wishes to employ the full resources of his craft will either try to cope with the difficulties of the optical image—as Hals and Velasquez were ultimately to do—or will find some compromise between the two endeavors. Such compromise may, with Raphael and Poussin, favor the mental image, or, with such Venetians as Veronese and Tiepolo, favor the optical image. Titian and Rubens may be said to mediate on nearly equal terms between knowledge and appearances.

Now the painters of the mental image always have the public with them, because their vision is that of the average person. It is only a very highly trained eye that distinguishes what it actually sees at any moment from what memory of former observation contributes. In short, real seeing involves difficult inhibitions of associative processes, is not a gift, and has to be learned. Most people do not need or care to learn. They use their eyesight merely as a means of identification, and stop seeing as soon as the identification is made. Thus the painter who tries to keep as near the actual look of things as the technical limitations of his art permit, is generally misunderstood, disliked, or neglected—in any case succeeds only on condition of re-educating the seeing of his public.

Frans Hals was fortunate in moving very slowly towards his new vision, and in applying new methods to subjects so full of human interest that any legible method was sure to be accepted, if only because the method seemed unimportant. What he ultimately arrived at was twofold: a procedure in which a carefully modulated and modeling color edge replaced the traditional outline, and an apparently coarse but really most skillful mosaic of color areas which were so many optical equivalents in paint for the colored, light-absorbing or light-reflecting planes which the eye and mind read into external objects. Unlike the painted mental image, which has equal vividness and meaning within the range of visibility, the painted optical image will disintegrate on too near view into casual patches of color. At the proper distance, these patches will snap together and give a far stronger optical effect of presence than the painted mental image ever gives. Such painting, with equivalents of the elementary data of vision, is called synthetic. This means, on the creative side, that the painter selects and puts together the simplest data that will create the sense of mass and space; on the receptive side, that the beholder must make the expected synthesis from such data. To do this the beholder must very definitely co-operate with the painter, accepting and repeating his habit of vision. To do this requires effort and a certain humility, and this is expressed by the phrase that in order really to learn the look of things, we must recover the innocence of the eye.

One must not think of Frans Hals as approaching the problem of the look of things in any scientific or even systematic way. He was naturally the most eye-minded of painters, and with experience his vision constantly grew finer and truer. Naturally his inherited practice grew with his vision, became more subtle, swift and truth-telling. The whole progress rested in instinctive tact and trial and error. So much is the artist bound by the habitual vision of his time, that it took Frans Hals some twenty years to attain that innocence of the eye which an art student of today may reach in as many months. The actual working out of the new synthetic technique was favored and accelerated through his turning for recreation from professional portraiture to genre painting. Here there were no set standards or expectations; here were passing expressions for which the old technique was evidently ill adapted; here, thus, he was free to experiment freely and unrebuked.

The earliest of these experiments, surely before 1620, is to me perhaps his most repellent picture, but withal a most instructive document—the Merry Company, at New York (Fig. 240). Three tipsy men and a wench are singing raucously over a well-stocked tavern table. They are all at the silly stage of drunkenness—and whether in a picture or in real life this is never a pretty spectacle for a sober onlooker. The figures are huddled together in no space that can be felt, and there is no arrangement in pattern to offset the overemphasis of leering expressions. The impudent face of the wench beating time to the din should be the focus of the composition; it seems merely extruded and unrelated to the rest. What, apart from its vitality, is important in the picture is the construction of the figures and faces. Everything is carried off with broad brush strokes which create the form in terms of colored light. There is no longer any question of line or contour. Slashes of tone and color do the work. The color itself is strident, unharmonized, disagreeable, especially the ruddy shadows in flesh which seem to imply a crude adaptation of Rubens' technique. One should turn to the professional portraiture of about the same time, for example, to the Nurse and Child (Fig. 238), to feel the fairly revolutionary innovation of a technical sort involved in making the Merry Company. Its vitality and raciness of characterization, its more positive assertion of form, are new assets which second thought and better taste may turn to good account.

We find taste disciplining this new virtuosity in the picture of Junker Ramp and his Girl (Fig. 241), in the same museum, and only four or five years later. Here again the theme is the hilarity of tipsiness, but it now is qualified and made acceptable by the possessive pride of the man, the devotion of the woman; by a beautiful weaving of the diagonals and great curves into a compact and stable pattern, by the harmonizing of the sharp colors, by making the figures imply the necessary space, and by giving an outlet beyond the curtain to a mysteriously illuminated wall and ceiling rafters. The construction of the faces and hands is of the finest. Only the essential planes are recorded. Between this picture and the Merry Company there has been much elimination and self-criticism.

It is impossible to call the roll of the laughing, singing, drinking, playing figures which soon constituted and still constitute Frans Hals' popularity—the Joyous Drinker, Amsterdam; the Flute Player, Toledo; the Gipsy, Paris; the Fool playing a Lute, Baron Rothschild, Paris; the portraits of the genial Witch of Haarlem, Malle Bobbe, Berlin and New York; perhaps the most masterly of all, the Sand Runner, Antwerp (Fig. 236)—these are so many masterpieces of brisk and expressive execution, of sympathetic interpretation of the humors of simple folk. Then there is that charming series of little sketches of the heads of boys and girls, pretty certainly his sons and daughters by the wayward Lysbeth Reyniers. The charm and gusto of childhood has never been more fully felt nor more skillfully painted. There is much inequality in this genre painting, frequent overemphasis, occasional ugly display of mere dexterity, but the best of this class are so captivating that one has to shake himself in order to realize that these pictures only enlist the virtuoso in Frans Hals and not the intermittent great artist. His triumphs were attained by applying to his more serious professional work the methods worked out in what must have been his playtime.

The new synthetic manner was first tried on an impressive scale in the Doelen made for the Harquebus Company of St. Adriaen's (Fig. 242). The picture was installed in 1627, but there are reasons for thinking it may have been painted three or four years earlier. In comparison with the Doelen of St. George's, of 1616, the composition is more dense, animated and elaborate. The group is no longer in two ranks, but is four figures deep, with a corresponding improvement in spatiality. The composition is built out of diagonals which form lively zigzags and are all buttressed by the standing figure at the left. The large, plumed hats which, as offering difficulties, were omitted in the earlier Doelen, are now effectively introduced as fine ovals contrasting with the general angularity of the composition. The color is fresh and brilliant as compared with the general somber tonality of the first St. George's, but the color effect is gay and attractive rather than harmonious. Everything is now touched in crisply with hardly a hint of anything like outline. The edges of the figures are no longer hard, isolating boundaries, but mobile contours that advance or recede with the form. The flesh tints are, on the whole, silvery, with no trace of the conventional ruddiness of ten years ago. The stuffs, cartwheel or falling ruffs, gay-colored scarves, etc., are painted with the greatest lightness and zest. In every way this is a more richly and delicately painted picture than the first St. George's, but perhaps not really a better picture. The new animation and complication of arrangement produces an effect of restlessness. There is a sense of permanence and importance in the far less-skillfully painted Doelen of 1616 which the more brilliantly conceived first St. Adriaen's lacks.

The second Doelen of St. George's, 1627, is more massively felt, composed in much the same diagonal, baroque fashion, but more simply; the mere handling is less overtly brilliant, but supremely right and telling. The general look of the group, despite great differences in technique, is much like that of St. George's of 1616. There is a similar sense of important common purpose, of permanence. Between the first St. Adriaen's, probably 1624–1625, and the second St. George's, 1627, Frans Hals seems to have mastered a new virtuosity which had threatened to master him. So colorful and characterful a group as the second St. George's can only be improved by infinitesimals. But it is precisely with infinitesimals that taste produces its most admirable results. The case may be convincingly illustrated by a comparison of the second St. George's, 1627, with the second

St. Adriaen's, 1633 (Fig. 243), which marks the peak of Frans Hals'
gay manner.

A larger scale and a longer oblong have permitted a looser and
easier disposition of the group. The open-air space overhead is skillfully punctuated by picturesque forms of banners, pikes and halberds.
Such features give to this picture uniquely in its class a sense of imminent martial decision. The arrangement of these features, generally
slanting but with the folded company colors upright, is that of the
figure group. It is balanced in converging curves from the right and
vertical repeats at the left about the central officer who, in greenish
yellow and blue costume, looks over his shoulder. And there is a
secondary pattern consisting in the odd balance between the dense
concentric group about the commander and the loose group at the
right. This group balances the actually heavier group at the left by
reason of greater energy of pose and the reinforcing patch of light
where the sky shows between trees. The faces are painted with a
sober brilliancy, without display of any sort, the expressions are gentler
and more thoughtful. The man now interests the painter more than
the military officer. Display of brush strokes is pretty well confined
to the touching in of scarves of flower-bed variety of hue and texture
—in short, virtuosity now serves its legitimate purpose of coping with
difficulties of representation. However often quoted, Fromentin's
superb paragraph on the great masterpiece seems still indispensable.
He writes:

"An art of being precise without explaining too much, of making
a thing understood by hints, omitting nothing, but letting the unimportant be merely divined; a touch swift, ready and exact; the just
word and nothing but the just word discovered instantly and never
hackneyed by emphasis; no turbulence and no superfluity; as much
taste as in Van Dyck, as much manual dexterity as in Velasquez, with
the hundredfold greater difficulty of a far richer palette, for instead
of being reduced to three tones it is a repertory of all the known
tones whatever—such are, in the brilliancy of his experience and zest,
the almost unique qualities of this magnificent painter. . . . No one
has ever painted better; no one ever will paint better."

Frans Hals was still to paint two Doelen. Captain Reael's
Company, Amsterdam, was started in 1633, and had it been finished
by Hals himself, it might have rivaled, or even excelled, St. Adriaen's
of 1633. The arrangement is very similar, with the captain the center

of a group at the left and the minor officers more casually disposed at the right. But the great scale permitted the martial figures to be shown at full length, and their relation to the upright measurement, about six and a half feet, is more restful. The quarrel and ultimate breach with the patrons impaired a consummately fine picture, but had the incidental advantage to us of telling, at least inferentially, how Hals made these great compositions. There must have been a composition sketch determining the poses. All heads were painted from life on a small scale. With this material, the picture was laid in in the studio. After which the last touches were made as the sitters presented themselves. We may fairly assume that the preparation was more careful and elaborate than the finished work. The final swift brush strokes were certainly not improvised, but made from life.

The difficulty in the case of Captain Reael's Company was that Hals insisted on painting at Haarlem the great canvas destined for Amsterdam. This meant that the officers must come according to a schedule to Haarlem. When this turned out to be impracticable, Hals honorably threw up the job. But he finished in his own way the group at the left. It is the most monumental composition from his hand, and the columnar figures at the wings are as strong and sumptuous as anything he ever painted. In 1637 Hendrick Pot, a good officer and minor painter, whose modest face you may see at the extreme right of St. Adriaen's of 1633, finished the right side of the Amsterdam Doelen so well that only a very good eye could tell the difference between his work and that of Frans Hals.

For his first corporate patron, St. George's, Hals made a third Doelen, in 1639. At first sight it is a rather straggling affair, but it really has a more military spirit than all the others. One feels the company is about to fall in. Since this, in more ambiguous fashion, is the motive of Rembrandt's so-called Night Watch, painted a couple of years later, it is possible, and even probable, that he had studied this picture with profit. This third St. George's is perhaps the most tenderly painted of all the Doelen, for the reason that it alone takes account of outdoor appearances and atmospheric envelopment. The arrangement—a dense symmetrical group about the commander at the left, and a looser group at the right, seems to have become standard with Hals. In this case the scheme has less precision and effectiveness than it has in St. Adriaen's of 1633, and the great Doelen at Amsterdam.

The new synthetic method produced masterpiece after masterpiece of brilliant professional portraiture.  Here nothing is finer than
the three-quarter length of a rather dull and bemused, but kindly,
middle-aged woman, at New York, which seems to be a companion
piece to the equally vivid portrait of a man in the Frick Collection.
The similar type of triangular composition and the introduction of
the base of a great column as accessory—a borrowing, perhaps, from
Van Dyck's stately settings—make it probable that the portraits are a
pair, representing a man and wife.  But I cannot follow Dr. Valentiner in finding here portraits of the painter and his wife.  The age
of the persons represented makes such a theory untenable.  The pictures are of 1635, when Frans Hals was nearly fifty.  A contemporary
print gives the age of the woman as forty-eight.  A man who had led
Frans Hals' convivial life would hardly be so well preserved at fifty.
Indeed, it is hard to imagine that the sitter for the Frick portrait had
reached any such age.  Then, the frail and fertile Lysbeth was probably considerably younger than her gifted husband.  Her mere record
of childbearing suggests it.  But all this is of minor interest.  What
is important is the vigor and solid existence of these two portraits,
the mere hints by which the forms are accurately and vividly established, the rich sense of color where positive color is almost lacking,
the broad, transparent play of light and shadow through the spaces,
the just placing of the figures in distance and atmospheric envelopment, the perfect compositional relations of the figures to the rectangular setting, finally the complete and telling expression of character.  To adapt Fromentin's phrase—it might be possible to find
more interesting persons to portray, but it would be impossible to
portray anyone better.

Perhaps the show piece of the single portraiture of this period
is the Willem van Heythuysen, Liechtenstein Collection, Vienna, the
only life-size, single, full-length portrait that Frans Hals ever painted
(Fig. 244).  It is a picture that would hold its own in any company.
Heythuysen was actually a charitably disposed burgher who had the
innocent vanity, as a slightly later seated portrait, at Brussels, shows,
of playing the soldier and the sport.  Hals humored this mood to the
limit, and produced a portrait which in sheer swank yields to none.
The generous contributor to Haarlem charities looks ready to take
or give a life on the biting of a thumb.  All this is legitimate dramatization of an accomplished sort, and it goes far to make the picture.

The rest is mostly the magical swiftness and certainty of the handling. It is a masterpiece which justifies Fromentin's perhaps too sweeping characterization of Frans Hals' genius as a whole: "Hals was only a practician, I tell you that straight off, but as a practician he is one of the most able and expert that has existed anywhere—even in Flanders, in spite of Rubens and Van Dyck; even in Spain, in spite of Velasquez." Later we may find reason to shade and extend this definition of Hals as merely a virtuoso. Meanwhile it applies accurately to pretty much all of the work we have been studying up to now, and his early fifties.

It was the alert, colorful style which we have been considering that guided the school of Haarlem and much of Dutch painting outside. For many years Hals had no local rivalry and enjoyed an unstinted patronage. In the 1630's our incomplete lists record seventy individual portraits and three great Doelen; in the 1640's we have forty separate pictures registered and a corporation group. With any reasonable management of his affairs, he should have enjoyed affluence. But occasional notices show the family gradually going down hill. Early in 1639 an imbecile son, Pieter, was sent to the country at the city's expense. Two years later, on the mother's request, a wayward eldest daughter was put in the workhouse; in 1642 he refused to pay his guild dues; in 1654 he assigned his furniture and some pictures for two hundred gulden due a baker for bread and cash loans. And so it went on till he entered the poorhouse upon the foundations of which has risen in our times, in his honor, the Frans Hals Museum.

But these years of narrowing circumstances saw an extraordinary broadening of his style, the creation of a third or "black" manner, in which he achieved perhaps not his most brilliant and alluring, but his greatest works. Here the, I hope, skeptical reader may protest: why do you critics almost always fit out an artist with just three manners? On what is this rule of three based? It is based simply on the difference in outlook between young manhood, maturity, and old age. We all have three manners of living, or ought to have. If an artist has less than three manners it is either because there is no principle of growth in him or he dies young. An unusually long-lived or versatile artist—Titian, Rembrandt—may develop more than three manners. To subdivide such manners is almost always possible, and generally unenlightening.

The Doelen groups of 1625–1637 are about the last pictures in which Frans Hals revels in a brilliant polychromy, and these pictures already show a tendency to reduce sheer color in the interest of harmonious tonality. From about 1637, when he must have been past fifty, the "black manner" gradually dominates his painting. That manner may be more accurately described as an enriched monochrome. While the basis is black and white, the grays carry hints of color—warmed by a tinge of yellow or red, cooled by a hint of blue. There is really as great variety and richness of color as there was in St. Adriaen's of 1633 and the famous genre pieces, but it is a color of another sort, implied, not asserted, a question of tones and tints achieving effect without strong contrasts. Velasquez, in distant Spain, was working in a similar direction in the same years, and so was young Rembrandt in nearby Amsterdam. Eighty years earlier Titian had passed from a splendid polychromy to a somberly rich monochrome, and seventy years earlier still Leonardo da Vinci had remarked on the beauty of forms seen in twilight.

Such parallels should warn us off from too simple explanation of Hals' "black manner"—as that it corresponded to his own sadness in poverty and old age, or was due to the fact that he could now afford only the cheapest pigments, or to the new fashion of dressing in black. Such considerations may have been contributory to the change, but the causing cause must have been the need of a more serious expression, the desire to subordinate overt and objective methods to subjective and spiritual values. On the practical side, this meant the selection of appearances that let such values assume maximum effectiveness.

While the range of color is reduced without loss of real colorfulness, the method of construction remains unchanged. We find still the amazingly swift and accurate brush strokes that denote form, the same avoidance of linear features and of harsh contrasts of light and dark. But all this is best studied in the pictures themselves.

It is customary to date the new manner from the group of the Five Regents of St. Elizabeth's Hospital, 1641, Haarlem, but this picture, as Karl Voll long ago pointed out, is really transitional. The sharp detachment of the group from the background, the emphasis on such details as the ruffs and wristlets, is in the old manner. What is new is the endeavor to celebrate the sagacious kindliness of these prosperous men who hold their wealth in stewardship for the ailing poor. In this regard these portraits seem to show a new insight in

Frans Hals, and to mark a spiritual progress. But the individual expressions are perhaps overemphasized so that there is some lack of
ease, some failure to convey the tranquilizing effect of a common
beneficent purpose. This material and spiritual unity Frans Hals will
attain in somewhat later portraits which look to the consummation
of the artist's deeper vein in the Regent groups of 1666.

Karl Voll found the fullest anticipation of Frans Hals' last manner in the half-length of a Fisher Lad—sometimes called the Sand
Runner—at Antwerp (Fig. 236). It is an amazing achievement of
stability through methods the most swift and nervous. The lad seems
of a piece with the merely glimpsed sea, sand, sky and dunes—to be
their very spirit, and to exult in the fact. Superficially one of the
brilliant Halses, it is really profoundly conceived. Even if it be as
early as 1635, which I doubt, it has, in its telling, broken surfaces, as
in its unity and concentration of meaning, all the characteristics of his
perfected style. To illustrate his technical greatness in his last manner, one need hardly go beyond New York; its spiritual triumphs are,
of course, the Regent groups at Haarlem. Just as a technical exhibit
one cannot go wrong in choosing the bust portrait of Balthazar Coymans, in the National Gallery, Washington (Fig. 245). The gamut
of tones, from deepest blacks to blued or ruddied pale grays, is handled with the most elegant mastery. Nothing is overasserted, nothing
scamped. Merely as a figure enveloped in atmosphere it is in no way
inferior in refinement to a Rembrandt or a Velasquez of the moment.
And it tells everything needful about the wealthy, somewhat melancholy and shy young patrician who has accepted and deeply felt his
responsibilities as a magistrate. Coymans was only twenty-seven in
1645, when the picture was painted, but he has evidently fully accepted the moral responsibilities of wealth and position—is, in the
best sense, an old head on young shoulders.

From these later years there is no more exquisitely painted portrait than the three-quarter length of a middle-aged man, at New
York (Fig. 246). The realization of a quiet, firm and kindly human
dignity is complete and inescapable. The mere painting is a feast
for the trained eye—the working out of form and texture with slightest indications and without sharp contrasts, the absence of formulas,
the directness with which every touch ministers to expression, the
subdued richness of the subtly varied monochrome, such details as
the sufficient suggestion of the closed right hand—all this is Frans

Hals at his magical best, whether in construction or interpretation, about 1654.

It is instructive to compare this tranquil masterpiece with a superficially similar portrait of about the same date, in the Frick Collection. Traditionally, and probably without good reason, the sitter is identified with the famous Admiral van Tromp. At any rate, it is a likeness of an aggressive and even truculent person, and this has caused appropriate modifications of arrangement and technique. The somewhat restless, not quite harmonious predominance of the whites, the crisp and almost metallic edges, the more incisive constructing strokes in the face—all these differences from the more urbane handling of the portrait in the Metropolitan Museum tell eloquently of the harder and coarser fiber of the sitter.

A few years later we have the little bust portrait of Frans Hals himself—several versions, the best in the collection of Dr. G. H. A. Clowes, Indianapolis. It is a rather pitiful effigy of a disheveled and discouraged man, maintaining with difficulty any presentable physical and social form. Frans Hals, as in the lassitude of his nearly seventy-five years, he looked to himself!

Circumstances were narrowing painfully upon him. In 1662 the painters' guild gave up a nearly twenty-year struggle to collect his dues, and, exempting him from further payments, made him a kind of shabby honorary member. He had certainly deserved no less. The next year he was put on the poor rates at one hundred and fifty gulden annually, and still a year later this alms was raised to two hundred gulden. Frans Hals was to die a pauper, but a pauper surely of an unprecedented sort.

We may take leave of him as a painter of individual portraits with the tiny sketch of the exiled French philosopher, Descartes, Copenhagen (Fig. 247), the preparatory study for the famous portrait in the Louvre. In his early fifties, the great scientist, psychologist, and metaphysician was ravaged and wasted by too great stress of thought. The lifelong contemplation of man as a knowing and feeling creature had brought to premature old age no comfort or hopefulness. Possibly he realized that he had unsettled coming generations to no good end. He had only a year or so to live, and he looks as if it were enough. Between the tragic portrait and that of Frans Hals himself there is a curious and paradoxical kinship, as if there were a similar penalty for living too immoderately on whatever plane. All this transpires with a more poignant eloquence from the little casual sketch than from the finished picture of the first really modern philosopher.

In these last years of weariness and poverty Frans Hals painted what, everything considered, are his greatest masterpieces—the Male Regents of the Old Men's Home, and the Female Regents of the same almshouse, 1664, Haarlem. Frans Hals was nearing eighty. His eyes are feeble, his hand no longer obeys his resolute mind. The brush which used to dash now fumbles. Still it does its work, and the expression of a beneficent thoughtfulness, of a collective prudence and efficacy in a good work, is complete. Between these two pathetically great pictures there is little to choose, yet I love better that of the Female Regents (Fig. 248). Formally, it has greater beauties in the effective balancing of the table top with the merely suggested rectangles of the paneling. Spiritually, the sense of fine purpose enlivening the tired and wasted faces of these aged gentlewomen is irresistibly moving. The mere arrangement of gnarled hands, silvery ruffs, discarnate faces, is thrillingly just. Nothing in the big canvas could without detriment be moved a fraction of an inch. Unless it be Rembrandt's Syndics of the Cloth Guild, no finer group picture has ever been painted.

Fromentin, while analyzing unsparingly the technical weaknesses of these two great Regent groups, adds that the "painter's feelings are golden." And this is the sufficient recantation of his earlier too sweeping verdict that Hals is merely a virtuoso. In the sad last years it is plain that Frans Hals rose above his amazing virtuosity and steadily grew in understanding and sympathy, achieving his greatest art when old age had left of his virtuosity hardly a trace.

On August 29, 1664, being about eighty-two years old, Frans Hals died, and, though a pauper, was honorably buried in the choir of St. Bavon's. Eleven years later his widow received a tiny stipend of fourteen sous a week from the city of Haarlem.

As a final estimate it may be said that Frans Hals was possibly the most brilliant executant of portraits the world has seen, and at his rare best one of the finest interpreters of character. In these two regards his only serious rival is Velasquez, who, as his production was more evenly at its high mark, may justly be regarded as the greater painter. The historical value of Frans Hals' portraiture is immense. In his work the stalwart, courageous, patient and sagacious men who made Holland a free nation come alive, as do their sturdy, competent, nerveless, housekeeping wives. In the technical sense he is a painter's painter, and no layman can fully appreciate his excellence; on the human side he is every man's painter, sharing the tastes of every full-blooded man and celebrating them with unabashed gusto. So great an art as his is seldom so accessible. His magic is entirely aboveboard, and though for more than two centuries he was virtually forgotten, it is hard to imagine any future turn of taste that would impair his popularity.

The straightforward brilliancy of his second, or colorful, period was imitable and widely imitated. It set the pace for the school of Haarlem and was an influence throughout Holland. In spreading this influence his younger brother, Dirck (1591–1656), was an important factor. He multiplied little conversation pieces, the dashing execution and good humor of which commended the work widely to Dutch and foreign amateurs. He was an artist of no marked originality, repeating motives and compositional features from picture to picture. His pictures, unlike those of his far abler brother, were scattered widely, advertising throughout the Low Countries the colorful and brilliant manner of Haarlem.

With extraordinary deftness and a fine sense for interior lighting, Anthony Palamedez (1601?–1673) turned out conversation pieces in the manner of Dirck Hals, but his work tended to settle into formulas and he lacked the congeniality of his exemplar.

Frans Hals' best pupil was Judith Leyster (1600–1660). At the very mature age, for a Dutch bride, of thirty-three, she married a painter ten years her junior, Jan Miense Molenaer. It was an ill-assorted marriage, and at times the family brawls were carried to the courts. Jan Miense even capitalized Judith's prowess in a series of little pictures. Judith Leyster at her best commanded, with possibly greater delicacy, all the audacity of her master. Like him, she laughs habitually and consumedly, but her laugh is lighter. She is not yet appreciated at her full worth, because her works are so rare that art lovers seldom see them. I imagine some of the sketchier and blonder Frans Halses will some day be transferred to her scanty list. Among the best of her works are the Smiling Man (Fig. 249) and a Family Group, at Amsterdam.

Jan Miense Molenaer belonged to a family of artists and increased it through his own children. The clan produced little genre scenes of family and pothouse life on the humbler level. Everything is handled with technical delicacy and invested with a quiet, sympathetic humor. In an English private collection is a picture which seems to celebrate a rare moment of precarious good understanding between Jan Miense and his quarrelsome Judith (Fig. 250). The art of Jan Miense and his kin is underestimated for the opposite reason to that which has limited the fame of Judith Leyster—there are too many Molenaers and they may be bought so cheaply that their modest charm and veracity are simply overlooked. I am sure that if nine-tenths of the Molenaers were plowed under, the remaining tenth would fetch sensational prices in the auction room. The fate of pictures is often as odd as that of books.

While something must be laid to similar subject matter and parallel development, the dashing style of Frans Hals inspired such sterling portraitists and makers of corporation pictures as Thomas de Keyser, Dirck van Santvoort and Bartholomew van der Helst at Amsterdam, as it did the kindred art of Jan van Ravensteyn at The Hague. Further afield such masters as Adriaen Brouwer, Jan Steen and Adriaen van Ostade profited directly or indirectly by the example of Frans Hals' second manner. Indeed, the school of Haarlem, which had run its course almost within Frans Hals' lifetime, offers the most consistently even accomplishment, and perhaps the ablest exemplification of Dutch taste at its best, of all the regional schools of Holland, and I believe it still has lessons for any painter of today who is lucky enough to be born an extrovert.

# CHAPTER XVI

# REMBRANDT AND THE SCHOOL OF LEYDEN

Fig. 251. Rembrandt. Self-Portrait.—*Frick Collection, New York.*

Fig. 252. Rembrandt. The Angel Halts Balaam. Fig. 253. Rembrandt. Simeon in the
—Musée Cognacq-Jay, Paris. Temple.—The Hague.

467

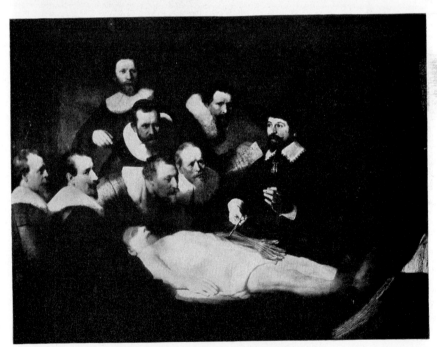

Fig. 254. (Upper left) REMBRANDT. Self-Portrait, 1629.—The Hague.
Fig. 255. (Upper right) REMBRANDT. Portrait of His Sister.—Coll. Mr.
Robert Treat Paine, Boston.
Fig. 256. (Lower) REMBRANDT. Dr. Tulp's Anatomy Lesson.—The Hague.

468

FIG. 258. REMBRANDT. Lady with a Fan.—Buckingham Palace.

FIG. 257. REMBRANDT. Rembrandt and Saskia.—
Dresden.

FIG. 259. (Upper) REMBRANDT. Danaë.—Leningrad.
FIG. 260. (Lower) REMBRANDT. Saskia Ill (drawing).—Coll. Prof. Paul
J. Sachs, Cambridge, Mass.

FIG. 261. REMBRANDT. The Night Watch.—Amsterdam.

FIG. 262.  REMBRANDT.  Supper at Emmaus.—*Paris.*

FIG. 263.  REMBRANDT.  Hendrickje.—*Paris.*

FIG. 264. (Upper) REMBRANDT. The Polish Rider.—*Frick Coll., New York.*
FIG. 265. (Lower) REMBRANDT. Landscape with Ruins.—*Cassel.*

FIG. 266.  REMBRANDT.  The Syndics of the Cloth Guild.—Amsterdam.

474

CONSIDERED from the point of view of technique, Rembrandt is merely the adapter and perfecter of that so-called "dark manner" of painting which Caravaggio and his disciples had spread widely through Western Europe. Considered more intimately, Rembrandt is the exponent of a romantic sympathy and glamour all his own—of a personal poetry which entirely transcends the Dutch School. Thus Rembrandt is the first great painter on record who habitually reacts against his environment, preferring to live in proud isolation, the first rebel genius in painting, the first painter of the modern sort.

He reached this position of dissent gradually, after fifteen years of conformity. It is the less personal work of his beginnings that, through the school of Leyden, shaped Dutch genre painting. The sometimes noble, sometimes merely fantastic, glamour of his mature style, while occasionally an inspiration ever since, has remained, on the whole, inimitable. It is personal to him, and out of the evolutionary line. It is, one may say, the promise of a substitute in individual experience for the old collective poetry and mythology which the Protestant Reformation had ruthlessly swept away.

Rembrandt's career was troubled from without and within. His material adversities he shared with many contemporary artists; his moral maladjustment was of his own making. He rose above it through many painful steps. His seems a dual personality that tardily attained to unity. In one aspect he is merely the most faithful of Dutch portraitists and most literal of Dutch narrative painters. In the other aspect he is a seeker for strangeness and mystery—an incorrigibly romantic temperament equally capable of the romantic sublimities and puerilities. He can descend to cheap masquerade; he can rise to heights of imaginative vision.

This duality runs through the nearly forty years of his activity. Side by side with his most visionary creations, he paints the most truthfully objective portraits. He can be very great in either mood—great in the Lady with the Fan; in the Saskia, at Cassel; in the Jan Six; even greater and more himself in the Good Samaritan and the Supper at Emmaus. He fails, relatively, when he cannot harmonize the two aims, as in the Anatomy Lesson, which, with great reality, has no glamour, or the Night Watch, which, with extraordinary glamour, lacks reality. He is greatest when he invests palpable reality with glamour, as in the Portrait of Himself, in the Frick Collection, and the immortal group of the Syndics of the Cloth Guild.

Rembrandt Harmensz van Ryn was born at Leyden, July 15, the year probably 1606, though possibly 1607. His father was a miller, fairly prosperous and ambitious for the family, for he sent the boy to the Latin school in preparation for the law. This plan yielded to young Rembrandt's evident vocation for painting. He studied three years with Jakob van Swanenburch, an Italianate painter of modest but agreeable talent in idyllic landscape, an intelligent imitator of such Italianized Northerners at Rome as Adam Elsheimer and Paul Bril, and what was perhaps more important for Rembrandt's training, an accomplished etcher. Later young Rembrandt worked six months with a more vigorous, but still Italianate master, the Caravaggian Pieter Lastman, at Amsterdam. By 1626, when Rembrandt was about twenty, we begin to get little signed pictures of a strenuously ugly sort which show the youthful master struggling seriously with the problem of representation. This endeavor was successfully completed in about six years, in 1632. It is the period of Rembrandt's technical self-education.

He wishes to construct in the new and fashionable "dark manner" which had pushed its way from Caravaggio, lately dead, through his emulator, Gerard Honthorst, at Utrecht, into Southern Holland. The "dark manner" required a waiver of the old decorative color schemes in favor of solid construction in light and dark, dark predominating, and it also implied an assertion of the interest of common folk and their ways as against the aristocratic and somewhat conventional dignity of the Renaissance style. Young Rembrandt wants in form, maximum emphasis of construction; in expression, maximum emphasis of emotion, and with these ideals for three or four years he painted the most repellent early pictures that were ever perpetrated by a great painter. A look at them is enough and often too much—Tobias and his wife, 1626, Amsterdam Art Market; Balaam and the Angel, 1626 (Fig. 252), Musée Cognacq-Jay; Jesus expelling the Money Changers, 1626, Moscow; the Gold Weigher, 1627, Berlin—except for unchallengeable signatures it would be very difficult to see in such

forced and labored work the beginnings of the creator of the Night
Watch, the Supper at Emmaus and the Syndics of the Cloth Guild.

There is a hesitation between line and edge—both are hard, wiry
and ugly, perhaps because not hard enough.   There is everywhere
concern with sensational effects of lighting, as the candlelight in the
Gold Weigher, but these effects are not realized either as natural
appearances or as factors in imaginative design.   There is a technical
vacillation.   Young Rembrandt likes the broad, untroubled, rather
opaque shadows of the tenebrists, but he also wants them transparent,
and he loads the shadow to cause coruscations which, while well suggesting textures, complicate and disturb the simplicity of the method.

Soon the little narratives improve, lose something of sensationalism in handling and expression, attain a fair harmony of tone.   Such
a picture as the little Andromeda, Bredius Collection, The Hague, so
homely, yet so picturesquely conceived, is already masterly.   The tiny
Bathsheba, at Rennes; the theatrically effective Supper at Emmaus,
Jacquemart-André, Paris; the romantically staged Simeon in the Temple, 1631, Hague (Fig. 253), with its intent, spotlighted group, its
vague Orientalism, and its high spaces where mysteriously light and
dark interpenetrate—all these show a great talent of a dramatic sort
rapidly discarding cruder melodramatic defects, steadily refining on its
methods of presentation, plainly coming to its own.

But the mark of the young lion's claw appears more clearly in
the numerous small portraits of these juvenile years.   We have about
a hundred of them, mostly of himself or his father, mother and sister.
Possibly the earliest, and surely the most instructive of these, is the
familiar little self-portrait at Cassel.   It shows a rather coarse and
sensual mask, withal in the unconsciously open lips and the deep eyes
nearly effaced by shadow there is a hint of the discontent and volatility of the visionary.   The method, with fairly even distribution of
sharply contrasting light and dark, is pretty much that of Caravaggio.
But I think the touseled, curling hair, so well suggested in mass with a
few individual strokes, could hardly have been painted that way without first seeing something by Tintoretto.   One gets the sense of a
formidable and sullen character still living in some confusion of the
aims of the flesh and the spirit.   It was indeed a confusion that Rembrandt outgrew very slowly.   By the self-portrait of 1629 (Fig. 254),
at The Hague, Rembrandt looks as if he had found himself.   He faces
the world with confidence, is already fully conscious of his own mas-

tery. The handling is more urbane; the uncalled-for steel gorget is a bit of masquerade which Rembrandt will use and often abuse in portraits of himself and of others.

Rembrandt's progress towards such mastery was rapid, but also broken. There is much inequality in these little heads dashed off so passionately. Many have nothing valuable about them except the monogram R. H. L., which tells that Rembrandt, the son of Harmen of Leyden, painted them. And there, too, the habit of signing these slighter studies evinces a vanity from which most painters as great as Rembrandt have been free. An excellent landmark of his progress in these student days is the portrait of 1629, of himself in a plumed hat, in the Isabella Stewart Gardner Museum, Boston. To the old energy it adds urbanity and distinction. It still lacks the richness of tonality which he will soon command, but it already shows the great master.

By 1632, in his late twenties, Rembrandt had carried realistic portraiture as far as his early technique permitted. Here the capital document is the oval bust of his sister, in the collection of Mr. Robert Treat Paine, Boston (Fig. 255). It has pretty nearly everything that goes to make a great portrait: strong rendering of form with very delicate means, a true and sympathetic grasp of fine and sturdy character, admirable composition in pattern and in atmospheric depth. The hackneyed expression, a speaking likeness, flies to the pen, for this competent and noble Dutch girl seems about to say some sensible and friendly thing. To realize the vast superiority of this portrait over the seven or eight others of the same young woman is to learn a lesson in taste. Except for a certain warmth and charm of tonality, it lacks nothing of the perfected Rembrandt.

We may regard 1632 as the year of Rembrandt's graduation from student estate. A year earlier he had left Leyden to seek broader fortunes in the commercial capital, Amsterdam.

Besides his painting, he had made many etchings. As a class these early scratchy plates are not impressive, but such etched portraits as those of his mother, dated 1628 and 1631, announce his approaching mastery. To mark his graduation a diploma piece was necessary, and this he furnished in Dr. Tulp's Anatomy Lesson, The Hague, 1632 (Fig. 256).

It is probably the most overpraised picture in the world, for while it abounds in accurate observation and tenacious handling, it lacks unity and dignity. In color it is rather neutral and raw. The over-insistence on the plastic effect of the heads impairs any pattern there is, and makes the surface disagreeably lumpy. The group is even ambiguously placed—how far is it supposed to be from the picture plane? The arrangement of the heads with too many parallel postures is monotonous, and the relief attempted by making three men peer out of the picture is unmotivated and artificial. Dr. Tulp himself is singularly insignificant. The cadaver is slack and without the fine rigidity of death. One must imagine it painted from a living model. One need only compare this group with Frans Hals' first Doelen of St. George's, sixteen years earlier, to realize its inferiority in the essential matter of fine composition.

Of course, an overestimate lasting for centuries must have its reasons. The solid merit of the picture—a stupendous creation, after all, for a painter only about twenty-five years old—lies in the professional thoughtfulness and concentration of the heads. Taken individually, they are superbly characterful; they are merely not organized into a picture. Rembrandt has not yet reached the taste and judgment for such a task. However, any prosperous Amsterdamer who saw this picture would rightly want Rembrandt to paint his family portraits. And this is what actually happened. For nine years, until 1641, and the Night Watch, Rembrandt prospered mightily as a professional portrait painter, perfected his "dark manner," by making the darkness even more penetrable, by giving to harmonized tone the richness and value of color.

This phase of his progress may be most readily grasped from a picture too familiar to need reproduction, the Little Scholar near a Winding Stair, 1632, Paris. Though much of the surface is very dark, there are no dead areas. The construction is clear, even where it is nearly lost. Everything is most tenderly painted, with no loss of strength, emphasis or character. Finally, the small figure of the thinker oddly dominates a large scene which in one aspect is merely his study; in another, seems a sort of emanation of his contemplative mood. Painted wholly in browns, there is no feeling of monochrome. One accepts it as so much rich and varied color.

His gain in refinement as a portraitist may be measured by the two double portraits—the Shipmaster and his Wife, 1633, Windsor, and the Mennonite Preacher Cornelis Claesz Ansloo and his Wife, 1641, Berlin. Both pairs are cleverly caught in momentary, almost obvious, relations, but relations that are significant. The shipmaster's wife will disappear the moment the letter is delivered. Her hand has not left the door handle—no more interruption of ship design than is absolutely necessary. The preacher's wife listens with attention and respect to what seems to be a well-started sermon. It is her wifely part, and she has willingly accepted it. Both interiors are admirably suggested, the later picture with subtler and richer modulation of lights and darks, and with a more vibrant sense of spatiality.

On June 10, 1634, Rembrandt married a comely and amiable girl, and incidentally an heiress, Saskia van Uylenborch. Their happiness is almost too emphatically advertised in the famous picture, at Dresden, with Rembrandt raising a wineglass, while he fondles Saskia on his knee, 1635, Dresden (Fig. 257). It is an exultant masterpiece, and magically painted.

It is customary to date a dramatic and sensational phase of Rembrandt's art from his marriage, as an expression of sexual exaltation, and that is possible. In any case, alongside objective portraiture we find a new interest in sensational themes. It is the time of the Rape of Proserpina and Samson threatening his Father-in-Law, Berlin; the Blinding of Samson, Frankfurt; the Danaë, Leningrad; big pictures, often tumultuously overemphatic. Etchings of like character are Christ expelling the Money Changers, the Stoning of St. Stephen, the Death of the Virgin, the Angel departing from the Family of Tobias, the Raising of Lazarus, the Descent from the Cross, the two Lion Hunts.

Now it is a pleasing hypothesis that Rembrandt found in Saskia's arms the inspiration for the expression of an energy chiefly physical; but, after all, he had liked these subjects in his late 'teens, and it is more reasonable, if also more prosaic, to imagine that he returned to such themes when his own patronage and Saskia's dowry seemed to justify his painting to please himself.

In the professional portraiture of this second period there is naturally some inequality. The habit of imposing fantastic and inappropriate accessories—armor, sham Oriental headgear—is almost disagreeable at times. It corresponds to the cheaper side of his fantasy. But it also reveals the great technician who loves to multiply difficulties. And, in general, the portraiture of his early maturity is admirable for its unflinching rectitude. Unforgettable portraits abound —the oval of himself bareheaded, 1633, Paris; the infinitely just and delicate half-length of Saskia in profile, Cassel; or the smaller and less sumptuous profile, in the Musée Jacquemart-André, Paris; or the tranquil and unassuming perfection of the Herman Doomer, "The Gilder," New York; or the aristocratic quietude of the half-length of the Lady with a Fan, 1641, Buckingham Palace (Fig. 258). These portraits of his early prime, once seen, are never forgotten. Later he was to paint more profound portraits with a deeper investiture of sympathy and mystery, but merely as a painter he was hardly to surpass these best portraits of his young manhood. Only the best Frans Halses and Velasquezes of the same years may be safely compared with these rather early portraits by Rembrandt. The Halses will seem a little overasserted and brittle; the Velasquezes, while equally discreet as painting, may seem less humanly significant.

Again the hint of multiple personality in Rembrandt seems justified by the considerable inequality even of his portraiture—its tendency to overindulge in puerile masquerade, and even more by the fact that contemporaneously with his superb objective portraiture he paints pictures outrageously sensational or cheaply melodramatic, and at the same time begins to paint Bible themes with a unique seriousness and penetration, with new interpretations wholly his own. The greatest work of this sort falls in his last period, but the tendency was firmly established in these six or seven years of probably extravagant happiness, and certainly of extravagant living.

Rembrandt agreed with the inventor of the "dark manner" that the Bible folk had no classical dignity, but were poor folk like those of Rome and Amsterdam. In this they both took sharp issue with the tradition of Hellenizing decorum transmitted by the Italian masters. Rembrandt's reaction was all the more remarkable that, unlike Caravaggio, who scorned the noble conventions, he himself appreciated these qualities, studied Italian pictures constantly, even collected them. As a good Protestant and believer in the literal truth of the Scriptures, Rembrandt went beyond Caravaggio's generalizing formula —that the people of the Bible were humble folk—and specifically insisted that they were Jews, such Jews as swarmed in the poor quarters of Amsterdam. It was all of ten years before he realized in his art the full value of his own point of view. The Passion series, Munich, which he made in the 1630's for Frederik Hendrik of Orange, uses the new ideals only superficially, and betrays much of the sensationalism of what we must call Rembrandt's tumultuous years. Even the technique is backward-looking, as if Rembrandt had to learn all over again in Biblical subjects the lesson he had already mastered in portraiture.

Perhaps the most accomplished masterpiece of painting in the second period is the so-called Danaë, 1636, Leningrad (Fig. 259). In the delicate liveliness with which the nude woman is represented Rembrandt successfully rivals all the great chiaroscurists—Correggio, whose painting he knew well; Velasquez, who had not yet painted his Venus. Amid accessories of furniture heavy and tasteless in itself, but, as illuminated, part of a fairyland, the nude and ardent girl is ready to greet the lover whose face just appears beyond the curtain. The reflections from the warm ivory of her body and from the white bedclothes seem to irradiate the fantastic scene, glinting here and there on carved wood, edges of velvet curtains and on an inherently absurd, but pictorially valuable, cupid hovering over her head. Of all the rather early Rembrandts this is probably the one that a painter would most value. Quite simply conceived as a legitimate glorification of physical passion, it is a veritable treasury of fine painting. It brings into a singular harmony the rectitude, sensationalism and exoticism of Rembrandt's prosperous years.

Meanwhile he was living in reckless extravagance. The fine house on the Bree Street was becoming a museum. Rare pictures and objects of art, with the incorrigible optimism of the collector, he regarded as safe investments of Saskia's little fortune and of the money that came in so easily from portrait painting and teaching. Along with what may seem merely pardonable bad judgment seems to have gone some relaxation of character. He had dozens of pupils and sold their work profitably, doubtless as his own. This fact may account for the over three hundred inferior pictures in the standard lists of about seven hundred Rembrandts. I am mentioning in this chapter only pictures which I feel sure are wholly by the master himself.

A word on Rembrandt's way of working. Like Frans Hals, he constantly made little oil sketches of heads—many for practice, apparently, for very few correspond to finished portraits. More summary studies of figures, figure compositions and landscapes, were dashed off constantly with the coarsest of tools—big brushes, the reed pen, a softwood stick, his fingers. A heavy line serves both as contour and modeling shadow, being an abstraction for both. These drawings have the most extraordinary form-giving and space-making power.

Often emotional are ignored in favor of material values, but there are also drawings rich in emotional overtones, such as the study of Saskia ill in bed (Fig. 260), or his widowed self trying to feed baby Titus from a spoon. The method, by which a single process—a modulated coarse line—conveys at once the pattern in plane and the existence in depth and mass of a design, is akin to that of the great Chinese and Japanese ink painters. In Hokusai you will find it in perfection. So it is no wonder that Far-Eastern amateurs, who are generally averse to what they regard as the literalism of Occidental draughtsmanship, accept and admire the drawings and etchings of Rembrandt.

All the extravagance and romantic excess of Rembrandt in his early thirties is embodied in his most famous, if far from his best, picture, the so-called Night Watch, 1642, Amsterdam (Fig. 261). It was to be a Doelen, a portrait of Captain Banning Cocq, with some fifteen officers of his military company. The formula for this sort of group was solidly established. All the patriot warriors were to be represented in most recognizable fashion and each was to receive a prominence in the group roughly corresponding to his contribution and his rank. What each officer wore was almost as important as the look of his manly face. Within this formula, Frans Hals, at neighboring Haarlem, had painted admirably free and spirited Doelen. Rembrandt rejected the sound principle that the task was one of straightforward portraiture, substituting therefor a mystery and glamour entirely unreasonable in the circumstances. In so doing he not merely offered an unconscious affront to the taste and thrift of his patrons, but also repudiated what was dearest to the national taste. What matter, if through such apparently willful self-expression he created a great masterpiece? I hear an individualist art lover protest. But did Rembrandt create a great masterpiece, or something which, made with that intention, fell short of its goal? In the case of a much, I feel, overadmired picture, this fundamental query must be approached cautiously.

It is easy to see why Captain Cocq's officers felt they had not had a money's-worth. Out of the staff of some fifteen, only four or five were easily recognizable. The pictorial focus was not the captain, but the adjutant, in silvery yellow. There were queer features, like the female dwarf in white gliding with a cock in her hand amid the legs of the soldiery. The place and the time of day of the assembly were entirely ambiguous. Finally, a well-trained company was represented as in pointless confusion.  No wonder that the officers quarreled over the price, and made the best of the matter by having at least their names plainly inscribed on a tablet.  Their attitude is easily understandable—and I do not see how any sensible person can gainsay its correctness.  Their entirely reasonable expectations had been flouted.

What is much more interesting and less easy to divine is Rembrandt's attitude in the matter.  Probably the great scale of the picture, over twelve by twenty feet, allured him to try to extend the colorful "dark manner" which he had worked out successfully on the small scale of narrative and portrait.  This decision was to make the great canvas not a portrait of a military company, but a battlefield of light and dark, the officers and the military apparatus serving merely as absorbers or reflectors of light.  This was to make phantasmal an entirely familiar scene.  To justify the procedure he chose the moment of apparent disorder before a military group snaps into formation.  This may have made matters right with himself, but not with his patrons.  Indeed, the relative success with which Rembrandt carried off an essentially unreasonable endeavor—for the picture has a fascinating glamour—should not blind us to the fact that his method was and is applicable only on a rather small scale.  A big narrative or historical picture wants more clarity, more conventionality, and the successful painters of such pictures—the Tintorettos, Veroneses, Halses, Rubenses and Velasquezes—have remained modestly within the convention.  And here it is significant that, save for the Night Watch, the handful of big historical canvases by Rembrandt are so negligible that critics rarely even mention them.  They all fail for the same reason, that a luministic method suitable for small and intimate pictures becomes empty and meaningless when applied to big pictures of public import.  One may add that on this great scale the eye reasonably demands more richness and variety of color than Rembrandt's method permits.

So, although the Night Watch, simply for isolated passages of magically light and imaginative painting, is a fascinating field for observation, it is as a whole a masterpiece gone wrong, and the somewhat cruel verdict of Fromentin is sound.  Writing of Rembrandt's technique, he insists Rembrandt is at his best when his technique "is fortunately subjected to obligations to be perfectly natural, or else when it is inspired by the interest of an imaginary subject.  Outside of these conditions, and such is the case with the Night Watch, you have only a mixed Rembrandt, that is to say, the ambiguities of his mind and the false appearances of his mere dexterity."

This is a harsh judgment, but I believe any close observer of the Night Watch must admit its fairness. A champion could only protest that he loves ambiguity and confusion, when it is Rembrandt's. Such an attitude is, of course, impregnable, and it would be foolish to attack it, and, after all, the lover of confusion may some day grow up.

It is customary to date the tragic fall of Rembrandt's fortunes from the controversy over the Night Watch, and its general unpopularity. In this view there is probably some dramatic exaggeration. We probably make everything more sudden than it actually was. But the general truth stands that after the Night Watch the paid portraits shrink to few. Rembrandt paints his friends, the somber Jews who attract his curiosity and sympathy, Bible scenes of profoundest insight made, probably not for pay, but for his own eye. And merely as a matter of chronology, when Saskia died in June, 1642, within a few weeks of the finishing of the Night Watch, Rembrandt's personal happiness collapsed with his professional fortunes. Rembrandt was left in the big, cluttered house with an ailing son, Titus, nine months old, survivor of four children who, coming within as many years, had naturally died in early infancy.

The critics usually write of a period in Rembrandt's art limited by Saskia's death in 1642 and his bankruptcy in 1656. Since this stretch of years saw the synthesis of his fantastic and realistic endeavor, the making of his finest prints and practically the end of this activity, the division seems justified. But it should be noted that there is no marked difference in ideals between such a third period and the work of his latest years, rather a difference in opportunity and accomplishment. He entered this period a strong and proud man of thirty-five or so, he ended it at forty-nine enfeebled and prematurely aged.

In these days of narrowing fortunes, he made himself a new and humble happiness. The faithful nurse and housekeeper, Hendrickje Stoeffels, a young woman of utmost gentleness and kindness, as his numerous portraits of her show, became his mistress and, since the relation was unconcealed, in all but name his wife. In these days he must constantly have read the Bible, perhaps not so much for religious consolation as for its amazing repertory of poignant human relations—

stories of his fellow sufferers of old time.   Within these years fall
the greatest religious pictures—the Good Samaritan and the Supper
at Emmaus (Fig. 262), Paris; the Vision of Daniel, Berlin.   While
the method has not changed materially, the penetrable gloom with
which Rembrandt loved to veil and relieve his figures has assumed a
new and spiritual value.   It seems to partake of and enhance the dominant emotion, is now not merely a means of construction, but a
factor in expression.   Thus the compassion of the Good Samaritan,
the graciousness of the Christ, the wonder and awe of young Daniel,
pervade every part of the picture surface, one might say vibrate in
every thread of the canvas.

There are many portraits of Hendrickje, none more perfect than
that in the Louvre, so instinct with benign humility and modest
steadfastness (Fig. 263).   She wears unconsciously and without pride
rich jewels, probably bought with Saskia's money.   The few professional portraits of these years are of finest quality.   That of his friend
and patron, Jan Six, Amsterdam, 1654, is inferior to no portrait in
the world, whether in swift and massive construction, rich decorative
effect or in sympathetic visualization of character (Frontispiece).   For
so entirely perfect a painting all verbal praise is an impertinence.   The
only real homage is to forget yourself while looking at it.   Velasquez
or Hals never painted anything more deftly and rightly, thinking
merely of the material representation, while the portrait has an emphasis on character and worth that even these great rivals hardly commanded.   We may note in leaving this great masterpiece the discretion of the technical means—none of the usual loading of pigment to
secure luminosity—each smooth stroke carries with it the requisite
light.

These drab and lean years saw most of his finer imaginative creations.   We have the very embodiment of youthful hopefulness and
adventure in the Polish Rider, Frick Collection, New York (Fig. 264).
How confidently the stripling faces certain peril and possible death.
Horse and rider are of a piece—both thoroughbreds.   Even the mount-
ing, broken landscape conveys a sense of lurking danger.   In this time
fall most of his landscapes.   He conceives nature as ominous and unfriendly—a place of imminent storms, threatening alike trees and the
constructions of man.   In these landscapes there is more emphasis
of tragic mood than truthfulness.   Indeed the method, with its extreme contrasts of light and dark and its reduction of color to tone,

is essentially dramatic, not descriptive. In two of the bigger pictures, the Landscape with Ruins, at Cassel (Fig. 265), and The Mill, Widener Collection, Philadelphia—a masterpiece which some critics deny to him—Rembrandt has caught the diffused peacefulness of eventide. It seems to me Rembrandt was fundamentally a city man, probably rarely gave much direct observation to nature, and merely wreaked his romantic excess in studio improvisations which were less landscapes than release for his own tumultuous moods. His fine observational work in landscape is not in his paintings but in his etchings. His best nudes are occasional recreations of these middle years. The Danaë, merely as painting the loveliest, we have already considered. I pass with mere mention the charmingly felt and magnificently executed Bathing Woman, at London, and the great Bathsheba, at Paris, whose unchoice forms, as Renoir was later to say, "take the light" beautifully. Such were some of the sufficient solaces for dwindling health and fortune.

Etching, which in the prosperous years may have been chiefly a recreation, soon begins to be a main source of breadwinning. The early 1650's saw the creation of such masterpieces as Christ Preaching, Christ healing the Sick, Christ before the People, Dr. Faustus. The old romantic emotionalism reappears in chastened and disciplined form in the Three Crosses, in the Sacrifice of Isaac, in that most pathetic of evocations, Blind Tobit. The price of any one of these prints today would have kept the little family comfortable for many a year. As things went, the family situation steadily grew more distressful. Rembrandt's collector's lust was insatiable. Saskia's dowry and what little money he earned himself slipped through his loose fingers.

Finally Saskia's relations intervened legally, and salvaged a little to form a trust for young Titus. In 1656 the big house on the Bree Street was inventoried for a bankrupt sale. Two rooms contained more than fifty paintings, many by esteemed Italian masters, not to mention arms and armor, Persian miniatures, rich stuffs, and hundreds of prints. Rembrandt, in May of 1656, tried to forestall his creditors by conveying his property to Titus. The auction sale, from which Rembrandt had fondly hoped to recoup himself, went off disastrously. Only after nine years and much litigation, Titus recovered the small sum due him.

The big house sold over their heads, the little family moved to the Inn of the Crown.  Rembrandt probably made a little from his etchings, but when, in 1660, Hendrickje and Titus set up a print shop, their articles of partnership declared Rembrandt incapable of earning anything.

But not incapable of painting great pictures!  The self-portrait in the Frick Collection, New York (Fig. 251), was painted in the year of Rembrandt's bankruptcy.  We have a man sad and worn, but confidently maintaining his dignity as a great personage.  Rembrandt ruined is still Rembrandt.  There is something about the portrait that inspires, with sympathy, a certain awe.  We behold a king, to be sure in shabby regalia, but still a king.  The picture has a sort of monumentality which is the new note in many of the later portraits. It is strongly present in the Jan Six of 1654, and equally marked in an Old Woman cutting her Nails, New York, as in the supremely elegant Lady with an Ostrich Feather, Widener Collection, Philadelphia, one of the latest portraits from his hand.  This monumental quality must have been superb in the Anatomy Lesson of Dr. Joan Deijman, of which the central portion is preserved at Amsterdam. The sharply foreshortened corpse has the grandest accent, as have the firm and skillful hands of the demonstrator.  The fire that early destroyed most of this great picture of 1656, has, after all, left us sufficient evidence of its mastery, and a composition sketch shows that the theme was conceived monumentally.  A comparison of the fragment with the Anatomy Lesson of 1632 will tell how far Rembrandt had traveled in twenty-four years.

The greatest picture of these narrowing years is, of course, the Syndics of the Cloth Guild, Amsterdam (Fig. 266), painted in 1662. It is surely the greatest portrait group existent.  Out of a mere committee meeting of five business men, Rembrandt has wrought a universal symbol for rectitude and prudence.  There is an amazing range of clearly denoted character—irony, simple good nature, bluff straightforwardness, suspecting shrewdness, dull tenacity, here find embodiment.  And these various temperaments are concentrated on the single purpose of safeguarding the interests of an important trade, which is virtually a public service.  It is the sense of togetherness, of mutual friendly understanding, that is the spiritual content of the Syndics.  Two years later, at Haarlem, aged and decrepit Frans Hals was to express the same feeling as faithfully, and even more poignantly, in the Female Regents of St. Elizabeth's Hospital (Fig. 248).

But he was no longer able, indeed never had been able, to embody such a vision with a beauty of workmanship approaching Rembrandt's.

In some mysterious way the dull red of the Oriental rug which serves as tablecloth seems to pervade the entire brown surface. The impeccable arabesque of the group is admirably set off by the rectangular elements in the table, the chair, and the wainscoting. The figures live in their own atmosphere. As you gaze at this arrangement of cool and flushed browns, you look into a world which is most precisely the everyday world of great affairs, but also into that world transfigured into something more urbane and noble than any eye but Rembrandt's has ever seen in a committee room.

The Syndics was really Rembrandt's swan song, and a superbly sonorous song it was. A year earlier, 1661, his last etching is dated. His tired eyes are no longer fit for such close work. How it stood with him towards the end one may divine in the self-portrait at Kenwood House, London. Nothing is left of the princeliness of the Frick portrait. A wearied and almost broken old man, huddled down for warmth, looks out almost unseeingly beyond the hand that holds the palette and brushes. Fine white hair is untended. With the wisdom of resignation, Rembrandt has accepted the position of a poor and shabby man. The face is not sad; the artist has the solace of his art. It is a face that compels sympathy to the point of tears, without really making any claim on pity. Oddly, this mild and gentle apparition has a strange, and, with its complete reality, a spectral monumentality. With the Syndics it shows how great Rembrandt could be when actual appearances and imaginative vision jointly challenged his genius.

In the old age of every strong man there must be black moments when he realizes the sheer hideousness of the gradual degradation of his body. In such a moment, surely, Rembrandt painted the self-portrait at Cologne, in which he leers at us and himself in impotent defiance. And this grimacing specter is the portrait of a man well short of sixty years old. Here is matter for depths of pity, but the picture is not self-pitying. It merely reckons unappalled with the appalling facts, and the sordid effigy of human wreckage is strangely glorified by a golden light, as that of sunset might transfigure a hulk rotting sordidly on the beach.

The loving drudge, Hendrickje, died in 1661. The ailing son,

Titus, followed her to the grave in 1668. There was still a year of loneliness left for Rembrandt. He was buried in the Westerkerke, October 8, 1669, in his early sixties.

Through unrestrained curiosity, passion, vanity, prosperity and adversity, Rembrandt finally attained to personal wisdom which, without loss of emotion, exteriorized itself in his paintings as taste—for taste is just the wisdom of art. The whole development is admirably summarized by Fromentin, who, considering Rembrandt's technique and the Syndics, writes a paragraph which is applicable to all the masterpieces of Rembrandt's latest years. The Syndics "is at once very real and very imagined, at once copied and conceived, discreetly conducted and magnificently painted. All Rembrandt's efforts have succeeded; not one of his researches has been in vain. In sum, what was he trying to do? He meant to treat a vivid natural appearance as he generally treated his own fictions, to mix the ideal with the real. Thus he brings together all the threads of his splendid career. The two men who have long divided the powers of his soul clasp hands at this moment of perfect success. He closes his career with an act of self-understanding and a masterpiece. Was he made to know peace of mind? At least, when he signed the Syndics, he could believe the day of peace had come."

When Rembrandt died Amsterdam probably knew it had lost a very eccentric and interesting character, but, I fancy, had no sense that a great painter had departed. Dozens of young painters, many Rembrandt's pupils, knew better than this. They valiantly tried to imitate what was almost inimitable, his pictorial style, and more ill-advisedly still, what was entirely inimitable—his personal emotion. Thus a Govaert Flinck echoes raucously his friend's sensationalism; a Gerbrant van Eckhout repeats on a feeble basis, but also with sensitiveness, his master's fantastic and romantic vein; a Nicholas Maes imitates charmingly Rembrandt's domestic vein, and makes very characterful portraits; an Aert van Gelder reproduces superficially and reduces to a mere treacle the free brushwork of Rembrandt's latest years; a Gerard Dou through a long life pursues the niggling methods of Rembrandt's student days, and imposes it upon the entire school of Leyden.

The immediate fruitful influence of Rembrandt was less on his pupils than on intelligent young painters who saw his work occasionally and caught something of its principles. On the technical side, as against the persuasive polychromy and overtly brilliant handling of the school of Haarlem, Rembrandt's example established the "dark manner" and discretion in handling as standard for the Dutch School. He also confirmed the national faith that portraiture was the essence of their art. And to painters of creative bent he taught that, at least for a Dutch painter, the way to see things in an imaginative and eternal aspect is through first seeing them very precisely as they look. Young Vermeer of Delft will read this lesson profoundly.

CHAPTER XVII

DUTCH GENRE PAINTING OF THE
SEVENTEENTH CENTURY; GENERAL
CONSIDERATIONS AND THE SCHOOL
OF HAARLEM

FIG. 267. BROUWER. Peasants Fighting.—Munich.

494

Fig. 268.  (Upper) Honthorst.  Nativity.—*Florence.*
Fig. 269.  (Lower) Ter Brugghen.  The Calling of Matthew.—*Utrecht.*

495

Fig. 270. (Upper) Brouwer. Drunken Peasants.—Amsterdam.
Fig. 271. (Lower) Brouwer. Singing in the Kitchen.—Madrid.

FIG. 272. A. VAN OSTADE. The Village Schoolmaster. FIG. 273. A. VAN OSTADE. The Strolling Fiddler.—*The* —*Paris.* *Hague.*

497

FIG. 274. (Upper) A. VAN OSTADE. Smoker and Drinker.—*Princeton.*
FIG. 275. (Lower) A. VAN OSTADE. The Alchemist.—*London.*

498

FIG. 277. JAN STEEN. The Flemish Feast.—Paris.

FIG. 276. JAN STEEN. The Menagerie.—The Hague.

499

FIG. 279. JAN STEEN. Doctor and Patient. "Love Sickness."—Amsterdam.

FIG. 278. JAN STEEN. Bad Company.—Paris.

Fig. 280. (Upper) TENIERS. The Smokers.—Dresden.
Fig. 281. (Lower) TENIERS. Temptation of St. Anthony.—Madrid.

Fig. 282. (Upper) TENIERS. Teniers and His Wife, at the Three Towers.
—London.
Fig. 283. (Lower) TENIERS. The Guardroom.—Dresden.

502

Why the universal Dutch taste for portraiture included genre painting has already been discussed. This taste changed both the character of patronage and that of genre painting itself. The picture must be of a sort to attract the average prosperous person, not too big to fit into a modest house, must generally offer possibilities of profitable resale. In short, the economic conditions confronting the painter in Amsterdam in Rembrandt's time were very much those which the painter still faces in New York, London, or Paris. Now the Dutch being the sound materialists they were, what tended to make a picture salable was fidelity to natural appearances as grasped by the average eye, and overtly fine and careful workmanship. A Rembrandt who only exceptionally met either condition of popularity, inevitably died in poverty.

Fidelity to appearances being required, the problem was to create a style within the limitation. Here there really were no precedents. The big tavern and bordel pictures of Aertsen and Hemessen had been composed after an Italian and exotic style. The popular narratives and spectacles of Pieter Bruegel the Elder had developed loose laws of their own, which were inapplicable to the intimate and familiar subjects now in vogue. A Dutch style had to be built from the ground up. This was characteristically achieved within the limitations of what the Dutch genre painter habitually saw.

Painting mostly interiors, he saw the human figure, single or in groups, with its curvilinear construction oddly and happily contrasting with the rectangular forms in which a Dutch room abounded. The obvious course for an artist of taste was simply to play up this contrast, making such selections, eliminations and rearrangements as might serve the purposes of the composition. Practically this meant skillful playing with the given architectural counters—quadrilaterals of every conceivable form, as the fundamental rectangles were distorted in perspective—an equal variety of cubical or rhomboidal forms in furniture, window-casings, doorways, and the room itself. While the arrangement of such geometrical forms was primarily in pattern, the same elements were considered as factors in composition in depth. We have room opening upon room, glimpses of indoors from out-of-doors, and vice versa. All this stylistic play had to be conducted with a lighting and coloring which, though generally subtly conventional, must seem absolutely natural.

Within these strict limitations, for about forty years, between 1630 and 1670, the little Dutch masters produced thousands of small paintings whose apparently simple, but really very complicated perfection is the despair of modern artists. One may see the formula already settling the composition of the best corporation groups of Frans Hals and Rembrandt, accepted uncritically by such a pioneer as Dirck Hals, worked out admirably in simple arrangements by a Metsu and Terborch, worked out with the most elaborate felicity by Vermeer of Delft. Of course, such expression of taste in composition is usually and normally unconscious. But we may be sure when a Pieter de Hooch develops his cubical or rhomboidal elements in depth, or a Vermeer builds up so successfully sophisticated a fretwork as we find in the Music Lesson, Windsor, and the Love Letter, Amsterdam, both artists knew perfectly well what they were about.

The actual handling of Dutch pictures needs only a word. Except for the use of brown preparations instead of white—doubtful gift from Italy and exaction of the new "dark manner"—the method remains that of the great Gothic pioneers of oil painting. Just technically, for example, the difference between the painting of Hubert van Eyck and that of Metsu, Vermeer or Terborch is really very slight. The surface is brought to the finest translucent polish. Upon this are sparingly set a few loaded touches of pigment, which have great value as suggesting texture, and as coruscating points in illumination. The late Sir Charles Holmes, who from a painter's point of view had studied these technical matters with care, believed that from the Van Eycks down Dutch pictures were mechanically honed to a finish with an agate or similar burnisher, and the few loaded passages then added to relieve the monotony of the shine and give liveliness of effect. In this connection it is interesting to note how quickly the bolder, rougher and optically more effective handling of Frans Hals and his followers was abandoned even at Haarlem. In part it merely yielded to the new "dark manner," in greater part to the general conviction of the Dutch patron that a picture which was less lustrous than his own well-kept boots was but a slovenly affair. Thus the Dutch merchant-painter—for such he really was—prepared his alluring wares and, on the whole, he flourished. Many inventories of Dutch painters published by Dr. Bredius show big houses well filled with collections of pictures, many of these Italian.

The more scholarly critics generally group the little masters of Holland by local schools. Except in the few cases, as in those of Haarlem and Leyden, which had a fairly coherent character, such a grouping seems unenlightening. Accordingly, I am following it for the two schools just mentioned and otherwise dividing by subjects, trying to follow a chronological course within each branch. This method avoids such absurdities as classifying De Hooch with the school of Delft because he happened to begin there, or with that of Amsterdam because he long practiced there. For similar reasons it does not seem sensible to insist on a school of The Hague, Rotterdam, Dordrecht, etc., just because there were painters, of most various sort, in these cities.

Since the school of Utrecht was early in the field, rather influential and somewhat exotic, we may get it out of the way briefly. Utrecht was and is exceptional in Holland in being Catholic territory. Both in religion and in art she was in close touch with Italy. Utrecht's continuity with the classical tradition of the Renaissance was maintained by a not very significant painter, Cornelis van Poelenberg (1586–1667). He worked with the Italianate Abraham van Blomaert, later passed three years at Rome where he assiduously studied Elsheimer, Raphael and the antique. The result of these studies was tiny landscapes enlivened by groups of nude nymphs or goddesses. These harmlessly idyllic pictures won immediate popularity in many lands. He worked as far as England. His pictures abound in museums, from Madrid to Leningrad. At bottom their smoothly finished Arcadian designs are of slightest importance. Symptomatically they are instructive as showing the homesickness for antique beauty that persisted in the Roman Catholic outposts of empire.

Gerard van Honthorst is a far more substantial figure. He was born in 1590, was studying with the Italianate painter, Blomaert, in

1610, soon thereafter went to Italy, where he stayed for ten years. Caravaggio had just died, but Honthorst carefully studied his pictures, and those of his numerous imitators. Honthorst, adopting the heavy shadows of the tenebrists and their simple constructions, carried the "dark manner" forward in experiments of his own. From his successful handling of night scenes with sensational artificial light he received the nickname, "Gerard of the Nights," *Gerardo delle Notti.* Here a Nativity, at Florence (Fig. 268), is sufficiently characteristic. His pictures sold readily in Italy and he returned to Utrecht a celebrity. There he continued to paint, on the large scale of the Italian picture, genre subjects and excellent portraits. His pictures had the attraction of novelty and were widely influential. Without the example of Honthorst one can hardly imagine young Rembrandt adopting the "dark manner," and this choice of Rembrandt fixed the character of the greater part of Dutch genre painting.

Honthorst was one of the earlier cosmopolitan painters, worked far afield, serving no less than five sovereigns—those of Tuscany, Poland, Denmark, Holland and England—everywhere won praise and money. He died at Utrecht in 1656. His evolutionary importance is great. He had set a fashion which Rembrandt and his best emulators promoted to a style.

Far the ablest of the Utrecht Caravaggians was Hendrick Ter Brugghen. He was born at Deventer, in 1588, studied with the Italianate, Abraham Blomaert, went to Italy at sixteen, 1604, and stayed there ten years. In Italy he knew Rubens, who later was to praise his talent. Caravaggio, whom Ter Brugghen must have frequented, is the chief influence on his art. But the young Dutchman was to give the Italian tenebrism a very personal application. Beyond serving plastic effect, it yields a sense of diffused light. The Ter Brugghens, as the English critic, H. Collins Baker, has justly observed, anticipate modern *plein air* painting.

For the rest his mood was lusty, often sensational, tinged with a rather obvious romanticism. Like his exemplar, Caravaggio, and his fellow townsman, Gerard Honthorst, he prefers in all subjects contemporary and plebeian types, and always emphasizes, often over-emphasizes, character. Such a picture as Sleeping Mars, at Utrecht, well represents his merits. A wearied soldier in fine armor dozes, resting his elbow on a drum. His hand lightly holds his sword hilt. What makes the picture is the honest and emphatic presentation of a rather characterless face in relaxation, and a fairly Rembrandtesque beauty of illumination. The light, very broadly disposed, is most subtly modulated. The head and bust of a buxom girl in the same museum show Ter Brugghen's skill in modeling with large areas of transparent shadow, his avoidance of smaller definition in favor of the larger truth of rounded mass. Such a head as this, dated 1629, might well have given lessons to Vermeer. The Calling of Matthew (Fig. 269), also at Utrecht, is a densely composed character study in oblong form, quite in Caravaggio's vein. But the insistence on relations of surprise and the artful balance of large passages of light and shadow bespeak a more complicated dramaturgy which was Ter Brugghen's own. On his return from Italy, in 1616, he joined the Guild of St. Luke at Utrecht, and passed the rest of his short life there, dying in 1629, only forty-one years old.

We must imagine the "dark manner" as generally pervasive, and as influencing even those painters who continued the brilliant polychromy of Frans Hals' mature style.

The earliest and best Dutch painters of scenes from lowly and bourgeois life, were in one way or another associated with the school of Haarlem. Adriaen Brouwer, Adriaen Ostade and Jan Steen are the outstanding names in this class. Between them they cover, save for its patrician phase, the whole range of Dutch genre painting.

Brouwer lived the life of the stews and pothouses, and in them paradoxically finds the raw material for a very delicate art. What contemporary or later gossip tells about his short and disordered life suggests an odd blend of a roisterer and a cynic philosopher. He hated the social hypocrisies, perhaps also the social decencies, and made a point of showing them up. He was born at Oudenarde in Flanders about 1605, was early at Amsterdam, in 1626, became a fellow member with Frans Hals in the Haarlem chamber of rhetoric called "Love above All." Earlier he must have been Hals' pupil, surely a close student of such pictures as the Merry Company (Fig. 240). He was precocious—at twenty-one hailed as a master, if by a poor poet.

For the five years between his initiation into "Love above All" and his registration in 1631 as a master in the painters' guild at Antwerp, we have only vague tradition—perhaps he was seized and robbed by pirates, perhaps he served on land against the Spaniards (Dr. Bode's surmise); nothing is certain. Within a year of his settling at Antwerp we find him deep in debt, his entire property hypothecated to a friend to save it from hostile creditors. Still another year, and we find him a political prisoner in the Spanish castle. A contemporary writer says he was imprisoned for approaching the castle "dressed as a Hollander." However unlikely this seems, it indicates that Brouwer was suspected of Dutch and Protestant sympathies. It was not a harsh imprisonment, for Brouwer's expense account, met by a friend, for about six months was five hundred gulden, with a modern purchasing power of some twenty-five hundred dollars. In that highly organized Alsatia which great prisons then were—where a prisoner could freely enjoy any pleasures for which he could pay, the bankrupt painter was living at the modern rate of about five thousand dollars a year.

Legend has it that Brouwer rejoiced in a sordid shabbiness of person and clothing, but he must, after all, have been reasonably housebroken, or Rubens' staid engraver, Paulus Pontius, would hardly have taken him in as a boarder. Within a year, Pontius had to commute Brouwer's board bills, for pictures, in the presence of a magistrate. Van Dyck's etched portrait of Brouwer, made probably in 1634, suggests a man of sensitiveness and dignity, even if he is described in the caption as *pictor gryllorum,* "painter of oddities."

Brouwer had, with the defects, also the qualities of his Bohemianism—a ready wit, friendliness and generosity, a scorn of pretense and hypocrisy. He sold his little pictures at very high prices, and is said to have destroyed a picture before a haggling patron rather than abate the price. He had reason for such pride, for Rubens bought no less than seventeen of his pictures, Rembrandt, eight and a book of sketches. There could be no higher compliment to any draughtsman than to have his sketches desired by Rembrandt. Brouwer's brief, stormy and brilliant career was cut off abruptly towards the end of 1638, probably by the plague. He had just entered his thirty-third year. He lived on in local legend as a wag and boon companion.

Brouwer's early painting at Haarlem has been identified by painstaking connoisseurship. Its feeling is drastic, even brutal, rather painty, with the edgy sort of construction practiced by Old Bruegel and his imitators. It is like Old Bruegel also in a tendency to caricature—squat proportions, incredibly bestial faces. In these early pictures, he tends to employ the greatest variety of local color that the subject permits.

This early, really juvenile, manner may be sufficiently represented by Drunken Peasants, Amsterdam (Fig. 270). He is unsparing in his emphasis of the ugliness of raucous intoxication. These figures are dehumanized, have ceased to be a company, are so many maudlin individuals. But the pictorial arrangement is as refined as the feeling is coarse. The scene is one Brouwer always loved—a basement taproom with the light filtering in from above. The shadow at its deepest is aerial and transparent, never vague or dead. The compact group is admirably composed both in pattern and depth. The play of light and dark on faces and headdresses is most picturesque and expressive of form. The incidental still life is touched in with tenderness and strength, and unobtrusively enhances the character of the scene. The figure construction is large and simple. Paradoxically, the effect is at once lively and stable. We have drunkenness seen very specifically, but yet in a sort of eternal aspect. Within a few years Brouwer was to paint with greater finesse—indeed, this picture shows nothing of his later glorification of tavern life—but it does already give promise of a great master.

Within an activity of only about a dozen years Brouwer's art passes through the phases that usually imply a long career. With all the irregularities of his life, he must have studied incessantly, or perhaps he belonged to that happy race of artists who, as it were, without taking thought, ever experiment as they work. What we may call his second manner, between his leaving Haarlem and settling at Antwerp, was marked by a greater concentration in composition, a finer economy in the use of colors and pigment, a swifter and lighter handling of the brush. Since he did not date his pictures, it is fair to admit that these "periods" are inferences from the style of the pictures.

Instead of the various colors of the Haarlem days we now find a single focal accent—the faded blue of a peasant's blouse, more rarely a faded rose. The rest of the picture is swept in with warm and translucent grays and browns, the whole effect more atmospheric. The solid and energetic construction of the figures is now effected through infinitesimals of light and dark—no longer heavy edges. Any of the seven or eight pictures of tavern fights (Fig. 267) or singsongs— Munich is rich in them—will sufficiently illustrate this new aspect of his genius.

What is admirable in these pictures is the clarity and force with which the main theme is asserted—in the fights one listens for the crack of broken skulls. Admirable as well is the sense of place. These reeking basement rooms, with the hint up cellar stairs of better air outside, convey with an unsparing sense of the foulness of the scene also a sense of strange beauty, as if all the varieties of transparent dark and half-light had found a harmonious rallying ground. One is tempted to apply to Brouwer the term too often misapplied to Rembrandt—namely, mystery. But the facile temptation should be resisted. There is no mystery in Brouwer; everything is plainly stated and accounted for. The dusk rather enhances than veils or attenuates the drastic vigor of the action.

What Brouwer seeks and achieves is a sort of transfiguration. The planless exuberance of revelry or drunkenness assumes a sort of daemonic character—has some kinship with the divine intoxication of the Greeks or of Dr. François Rabelais. Treated from the point of view of human relations, drunkenness is simply revolting, and no subject for art. Isolated and unrelatedly, as Brouwer treats it, intoxication has its fascination and even its splendor. Brouwer's superiority is that he could both be one of his drunken protagonists and abstract himself until they became pure objects of observation and contemplation. As he sat in the pothouse his mood must have readily shifted from participation in its rowdiness to complete detachment. It was, of course, in such detachment that he made those wonderful drawings which Rembrandt coveted, and, of course, only a completely sober man, in full command of his faculties, could have exercised the dark magic that inspires Brouwer's impeccable workmanship.

In the last two or three years of his life the handling grows still lighter, the pigment still thinner and more translucent; color yields further to tone. We have occasionally pictures nearly on the scale of life, character studies, caricatures, if you like, somewhat reminiscent of Frans Hals. Such are the Bitter Draught, Frankfurt, and the Smoker, Paris. Singing Peasants and Soldiers playing Dice, Munich, are representative of this last phase, in which the old rowdiness is giving way to simple jollity. One of the best pictures of this time and type is Singing in the Kitchen, Madrid (Fig. 271). In the Quack Doctor Operating, Frankfurt, Brouwer treats with racy satire and sympathy a subject to which Bosch and Bruegel had given a more sinister interpretation. It is plain that Brouwer was incapable either of condescension or of scorn. There is nothing of the moralist in his work, and, withal, nothing to offend the moralist of any broad-mindedness. He loves the play activities of the human animal, and since the human animal of his day indulged play activities hardly at all except under the influence of liquor, Brouwer simply accepts the fact and turns it to his artistic purpose. There were better moments when he deeply felt the purifying loveliness of nature, but his few landscapes are so important that I shall treat them, not here, but in the chapter on landscape in the Low Countries.

Once more we find in Adriaen Brouwer an apparent lack of connection between character and genius. The artist in him was ex-quisitely disciplined; the man always at loose ends. Again it seems as if the creative part of the man were a sort of second personality—a better self. Until psychology solves these paradoxes—and I much doubt if it ever will—we must be content to receive great art from whatever hands make and offer it, even if these hands are not clean.

For his vividness, delicacy, and taste in composition, Brouwer seems head and shoulders above the scores of excellent little Dutch masters who dealt with his themes. His influence upon such masters as Adriaen van Ostade, Jan Steen, and even David Teniers, was con-siderable, and he inspired a group of closer imitators who are too un-important to be considered in a general survey. Whether as a crafts-man, or conceptually, Brouwer is possibly the greatest painter of the lowness of low life that the world has seen.

A more decorous follower of the brilliant painting of Frans Hals and Dirck Hals was Adriaen van Ostade. Born at Haarlem in 1610, admitted as a master painter in 1634, he was married in 1638, and a second time, to an heiress at Amsterdam, in 1657. No less than three times the guild chose him as headman. He died at a good old age in 1685 and was honorably buried in the Church of St. Bavon. Al-though Ostade learned from two most exuberant geniuses, Hals and

Brouwer, he became the most discreet of executants. In his extraordinarily thoughtful and skillful handling everything is for character and truthfulness and nothing for show. His is an art that charmingly combines ready sympathy of observation with reflection.

His subject is the peasant or workman in moments of ease or recreation—dancing, singing, drinking, fighting, merely loafing in his dooryard. Children are often present in his pictures; he loves to represent the laborious quiet of schoolrooms. His art, even when the pothouse is the scene, is not so shut in as Brouwer's. One generally feels the country near, and often glimpses it. His economy in composition is inferior to Brouwer's, but always adequate to his theme. He has not the same perfect tact in the choice of still life and accessories, prefers larger groups. The relations and composition of his figures he studies most carefully, in numerous sprightly drawings, and in a delightful series of etchings. His art developed under the influence of Rembrandt's, whose permeable dusk he emulated in his interiors. This dusk reduces the really considerable variety of colors in Ostade to hues, so that his pictures, really more positively colorful, yield less sense of color than those of Brouwer, which are built around a single accent of frank color.

Unlike Brouwer, Ostade has no part in the life he studies. He is a gentleman with a hobby for the observation of peasant life. His attitude is kindly and understanding, just a little condescending. Accordingly his peasants have not the raciness and complete authenticity of Brouwer's. Ostade sees the peasant in terms of a grotesqueness which is not inherent, but relative to a middle-class point of view. Where Brouwer paints individuals, Ostade frequently resorts to types, and practices, in his squat, gnomelike proportions, a gentle and effective caricature. I must drop the parallel, for it unduly minimizes Ostade's very sensitive and accomplished art. We must simply take him for himself.

When Ostade was still in pupil estate, in the late 1620's, Brouwer was at his brilliant beginnings at Haarlem. His influence is unmistakably dominant in the early Ostades. The peasant fights, at Munich and Dresden, the carouses, at Munich and Darmstadt, are conceived entirely in Brouwer's drastic vein, but are conducted without his conciseness and fine compositional economy. Ostade was evidently self-critical enough to realize his limitations, and soon abandoned subjects alien to his gentle disposition.

From his early thirties we have his characteristic pictures, such as Interior of a Peasant Hut, 1642, and the Village Schoolmaster, both at Paris. The Peasant Hut has pretty much everything one would want in an Ostade—farm gear quietly visible in the dusk, handsome modulation of the light about a focus, suggestion of work and of the care of children—all cunningly wrought into a cozy fairyland. The Village Schoolmaster (Fig. 272)—a subject Ostade loved and many times repeated—has a similar charm of interior lighting and a precious humoristic touch in the uncomfortable slouchiness of the pedagogue's little victims.

Ostade's interest in character and in the state of mind of groups is as great as his interest in action is slight. So the quintessential Ostades are perhaps the numerous tiny figures, usually seated halflengths, which show the Hollander pleasantly off duty. The Reader, Paris; the Old Woman looking from a Window, Leningrad; the Herring-Eater, Cassel are among the best. Probably the masterpiece in this vein is the Smoker, 1655, Antwerp. In the swiftness and lightness of the handling we are still near the procedures of Frans Hals and Judith Leyster. That blissful nirvana which the convinced smoker occasionally attains is capitally suggested. The quadrangles of the window opening, the merely indicated casement, the reserved panel of the wall, and the diagonally presented table top are given a maximum compositional value. We have to do with an exquisite example of that standard Dutch style which we have already considered.

In his late forties Ostade came under the influence of Rubens' blond and transparent painting, and, I believe, may have studied the technically similar work of David Teniers. Ostade brightens his palette a little, gives a larger place to light in his pictures, enriches his neutrals with opalescences of many tints, handles the pigment even more thinly and lightly. He tends to set his groups out-of-doors: the amazingly fresh and genial Strolling Fiddler (Fig. 273), The Hague; the Inn on a Country Road, Amsterdam; a Skating Scene, at Paris. To this period belong the admirable family group, After Dinner, in Buckingham Palace, London; the Backgammon Players, in the same collection; the Engaged Table (Stammtisch), with its comfortably arranged group of cronies, Dresden; and two very interesting pictures of himself painting in his studio, at Amsterdam and Dresden. In both he is working on a landscape, and the light pouring in from a window is thrown down, softened and diffused by a velarium. Thus his effective illumination is rather arranged and observed than invented.

The beginning of his colorful and diaphanous manner may be studied in Smoker and Drinker (Fig. 274), at Princeton. It is here first published. For a restrained and discreet richness of color in the minor key few Dutch genre pictures surpass it.

To such a temperament as Ostade's the alchemist fussing about his murky laboratory offered an attractive theme. He painted it a number of times, an excellent example at London (Fig. 275). Ostade brings to the subject a gentle satire, a loving observation of incidental still life, and effects of illumination.

Occasionally he paints people of his own class, and carries off the unfamiliar theme with quiet distinction—the Marriage Contract, The Hague; the so-called Portrait Group of his Family, Paris; the latter most graciously composed, animated in the characterization, with an interior spacious, atmospheric, and refined in design. The whole thing is instinct with ease, affection and unpretentious dignity.

The ideal behind Adriaen van Ostade's art is that of a humorous poetizing of the peasant at ease—an exaltation of the peasant's canniness and ready friendliness. It is enough to make him one of the most companionable of painters, as he was one of the most delicately conscientious of technicians. Adriaen van Ostade died in April, 1685, having apparently been inactive for the last ten years or so of his life. He left to his only daughter, Maria, a handsome inheritance and no less than two hundred of his unsold pictures. There seems to have been no element of struggle in his life, and his art is rather fastidious than strenuous. Within its limitations it is quite perfect.

Jan Steen, though born and trained at Leyden, must be regarded as an honorary member of the school of Haarlem, for he early came under its influence, adopted its technical methods and at Haarlem painted his best pictures. He is a kind of link between the older and younger genre painters, less objective than, say, Ostade and Terborch, less sentimental than the Mierises. He possibly gives himself too unreservedly to his subject matter, somewhat neglecting pictorial, in behalf of human, expression. His themes are not merely stated, but are usually invested with his own humorous, moralizing or satirical comment. He can at times play the showman egregiously, tweaking the beholder's elbow lest he miss something. Behind his pictures one feels the genial, sensitive and quizzical man.

No Dutch painter has studied the relations of children with grownups with more insight and charm. He conveys infectiously the animation of games and work and family festivals with eager participants, and he catches equally well some exquisite and unexpected aspect of a solitary figure—as that glimpse of his fair wife about to put on a stocking. Almost alone of Dutch painters he is fully aware of the comedy played between doctors who are half quacks and pretty women who are imaginary invalids. His was a widely roving eye and sympathy.

Such mobility of temperament is hardly Dutch, as it was hardly Dutch to remain a good Catholic. The Dutch, who, after all, adored him, had their revenge in loading his legend with all the peccadillos and some of the sins. Here legend has probably made too much of the fact that he was generally in straits and normally convivial. No wastrel can have painted in less than thirty years of activity the upwards of five hundred carefully finished pictures that bear Jan Steen's name.

He was born at Leyden in 1626, studied with an otherwise unknown painter named Knupfer, at twenty was transiently enrolled as a student of letters in the university, soon went for a short stay at Haarlem, where he inevitably came under the influence of the Halses and Molenaers, and at twenty-two, 1648, was admitted as a master in the painters' guild of Leyden. The next year he was working at The Hague, where he married the fair Margaret van Goyen, daughter of the famous marine and landscape painter. Her gracious form appears in many of Jan Steen's pictures.

Before this time he had painted a few coarsely drastic pothouse pictures, probably under the influence of Frans Hals in this vein. The father-in-law was a disturbing acquisition—an excellent and successful painter, he frittered away his gains in speculating in town lots and tulip bulbs. Evidently painting ill maintained Jan Steen's rapidly growing family, for in July of 1654 we find him renting a brewery at Delft for five years. Two years later the father-in-law died, leaving nothing but debts. Still a year later his own father, on whose security the lease had been drawn, came to the rescue of the brewery business from Leyden, saving it from bankruptcy. Jan was probably an absentee manager at The Hague.

From about 1660 to 1671 Jan Steen painted at Haarlem. This is the moment of his prime and of his best pictures. In 1669 his wife, Margaret, died and a year later the apothecary seized all the pictures in Jan Steen's house and auctioned them publicly to cover a bill of ten gulden. After this chagrin Jan Steen moved back to his native Leyden, where, in 1672, he was licensed as a tavern keeper. The next year he married the widow, Maria van Egmont. His remaining six years seem to have passed in relative tranquillity. Some money probably came with the widow, and he himself had excellent personal qualifications as a host. He died in 1679, only fifty-three years old.

The instability of Jan Steen's character is naturally reflected in his art, which is of a very uneven quality. In general, his elaborate compositions with many persons are, though carefully studied in details, crowded and confused as wholes. His best pictures are those in which the comedy is played by two or three figures. All this suggests that he improvised rather than thought out many of his works.

The earliest pictures by Jan Steen represent bad company without attenuation. The joyous aspect of intoxication is the theme of the Revelers, at Berlin; its beastly aspect, that of Resting Up, at Amsterdam. Neither is precisely a good picture, though the latter has beauties of illumination, but both illustrated the theme with a drastic and truth-telling emphasis which we shall not find again till Hogarth's time.

The Menagerie, 1660, The Hague (Fig. 276), was painted either at the end of his stay at The Hague or soon after his move to Haarlem. It shows him quite at his best. The exquisite figure of the seated little girl, who offers a bowl of milk to a lamb, dominates the large space. The German critic, Lemcke, has justly remarked the Mozartian graciousness of her innocent charm. A bald-headed workman coming in from the right with a basket of eggs, and a dwarf at the left and higher up the steps, beam upon their little queen with a courtierlike pride and affection. The platforms above and below the presiding figure are animated by domestic fowl of every decorative sort, all studied in their character from life. There is a peacock on a blasted tree to the right, and above the archway through which one glimpses between trees a moated castle, a white dove soars. The castle looks like the Steen, at The Hague. If so, this picture was at least started in that city. Everything is considered in composition—the dark and light areas, the contrast of the obliquely presented rectangle of the pool with the formality of the arched portal. And yet the picture has the unexpectedness of a vision; one is afraid to look at it too intently lest it vanish or become something other.

A similar triumph in the visionary vein is the Bedroom, at Buckingham Palace, London. It is dated 1663. One looks through an arched doorway whose dark mass serves as a frame, beyond a lute and an open music book on the threshold, to a room shimmering with straw-yellow and pale-blue stuffs, where on a bed a pretty young woman, his wife, dressed in a yellow, furred coat and a blue skirt, sits with crossed bare legs, reaching down a fine hand to draw on a stocking. Again there is a sense of surprise and revelation, as if one had had the good luck to walk past this door and happen on this gracious apparition.

Jan Steen is rarely at the level of these two pictures. Indeed, he is best known for his pictures of large groups, family festivals, busy inn courts—so many documents of Old Holland at play. One of the earliest is Prince's Day, Amsterdam. The birthday, November 14, of the future deliverer of Holland, William of Orange, was celebrated by the common folk, who rightly saw in him their champion against the wealthy patricians. What we have in this picture is rather a patriotic rally at an inn than a family affair.

In this animated composition of some twenty figures the eye finds little leading in necessary exploration, and few points of rest. One may say that three pictures are arbitrarily juxtaposed—the group at the right behind the bald-headed man who, burlesquing a knightly act, kneels with a wooden sword before an amused young woman and an offish little group; the fine young pair at the left center; the card-players at the left. There is some suggestion of Old Bruegel, whose pictures Jan Steen must have known, and the comparison suggests the superiority of Bruegel's linear and flat painting, for this sort of subject, over Steen's atmospheric tonalities. Again, the big caldrons and platters in the foreground seem put in to fill an unexpected void, without plan. The defects of this picture, which, after all, abounds in accurate and genial observations, are found in all of his more elaborate compositions.

His best groups are less populous and on a smaller scale. Entirely winning is that of his own family, at The Hague, date 1663. Except for two old people engrossed with a little girl, the rest, to the setter dog, are listening with pleasure and perhaps a shade of ridicule to the earnest piping of the eldest son. The light falls in handsomely, picking out faces, headdresses, tablecloth, massive copper kitchen utensils on the floor, and a hanging wicker bird cage which relieves effectually the general gloom of the upper part. Of very similar attractiveness is St. Nicholas' Day, Amsterdam, where the chief motive is a roguish little girl refusing to show her presents to her mother. The various attitudes and dispositions of the celebrators are admirably caught, and the whole picture yields the intended sense of decently convivial merrymaking.

As typical of this kind of picture I reproduce the Flemish Feast, Paris (Fig. 277). It shows at about their best Steen's animation and ability in catching transient expressions and postures—is perhaps just a little over-rich and overcrowded.

Of the pictures of this class a puristic criticism would be inclined to observe that they are merely illustrations, overstress the human interest, offer too many competing attractions. This matter I do not wish to argue, beyond remarking that if these be mere illustrations and narratives, at least few story-telling pictures have an equal truthfulness, vivacity and charm.

In general, Jan Steen is more regardful of pictorial unity in subjects with few figures, such as the Fighting Card-Players, Munich, where the quarrel releases a little avalanche of plunging figures and falling furniture; the Card-Players, Buckingham Palace, London, one of Steen's sparsest and neatest compositions, in which everything is as clear as in a Bruegel.

Bad Company, Paris (Fig. 278), takes up with finer artistry the moralistic motives of his early pictures. The disheveled debauchee slumbers heavily, with his head on the lap of his richly dressed light-o'-love, who guards him carefully while another frail fair one daintily hands over his watch to the rapacious proprietress of the house of pleasure. Dim in the left background a violinist in the poor gull's pay soothes and continues his sleepiness. The figure group, whether in characterization or composition, is one of Jan Steen's best. It expresses moral disorder in an orderly way, quite as the richly-frocked courtesans simulate gentility. Jan Steen, however, has been so concerned with his moral lesson, which he makes very explicit, that he has treated the interior, which must have had its own character and interest, most perfunctorily.

My favorite Jan Steens are the doctor and patient pictures, of which in his last years he made some half-a-dozen. The most accessible are at Amsterdam, The Hague and Munich. Nobody at the time, except Molière, grasped that curious blend of diplomacy, charlatanism and shrewd common sense that medical practice had to be in the seventeenth century, and nobody has equaled Jan Steen in showing in the bedside manner the doctor's consciousness of the comedy he has to play. Perhaps the finest of the doctor series is Love Sickness—a sentimental title which may be wrong—at Amsterdam (Fig. 279). The invalid, sweetly relaxed in her chair, charmingly attired for the visit, fully aware of her feminine attractiveness, the courtierlike physician considering whether a compliment will go farther than a pill, the excellently placed and patterned accessories, such as the lute hanging silently beside the curtained bed—all this is the last word both in fine picture-making and in covert social satire. Hardly inferior is the Doctor's Visit, The Hague. Indeed, this picture, in the touching confidence of the pretty patient which enhances both the solicitude and the inner worry of the doctor, has a more amusingly involved psychology. But the accessories are less harmoniously disposed, while the sympathetic spaniel in the foreground is sentimentally intrusive.

The companionableness of Jan Steen's art is so obvious that any critical summary, beyond the analysis of his pictures, already given, seems superfluous. It is also unnecessary and ungracious to emphasize his artistic inferiority to such Dutch little masters as Brouwer, Ostade, Vermeer and Terborch. These differences in quality must be experienced through the eyes, and not through the ears, and everybody must experience them for himself.

Jan Steen died in 1679, at fifty-three, probably reluctant to leave the life which, while it had used him hardly—perhaps because he misused it—had never failed to interest and amuse him.

Though only remotely associated with the school of Haarlem, David Teniers II stylistically belongs with the bright painters, and may suitably be considered at this point. He was born at Antwerp, in 1610, admitted to the mastery in 1633, married a rich heiress, and received every honor up to a title of nobility. His father, David Teniers the Elder, was a painter who had studied at Rome with Elsheimer. The young David saw his father paint little mythologies and idyls, tavern scenes, pictures of sorcerers and alchemists. That great vagrant genius, Adriaen Brouwer, was at Antwerp in the early 1630's, and his was a leading influence on young David Teniers until his fortieth year. In the general manner of Brouwer he painted no less than a hundred tavern scenes. Technically, there is a predominance of Brouwer's diaphanous browns about a single color note. Psychologically, the attitude is quite different. For Brouwer the pothouse was a place of joyous or frantic disorder; for Teniers it was a place of decent conviviality. And, while he repeats Brouwer's cellar installation, with large still-life features in foreground, Teniers does not shut the space in in Brouwer's sinister fashion. Teniers likes to give glimpses into adjoining rooms, ordinarily introduces, with less action, more figures. Of the many pictures of this sort the Smokers, Dresden (Fig. 280), is one of the most handsomely lighted, constructed and composed. The view of people about a fireplace in a back room is charmingly introduced and most skillfully subordinated. Of similar tact in placing many figures at varying distances is the Smoker, Munich. A personal interest attaches to the Self-portrait in an Inn, Dresden. The handsome young painter looks out between the big wineglass which he holds in one hand while he keeps a magnificent five gallon jug at uneasy balance on the floor with the other. The still life, a cask, the big jug, a rude bench with pots on and under it, is delightfully painted, and there is the usual reassuring glimpse of a group, in the back room, quietly occupied about a table and before a fireplace. These pictures all fall about his thirtieth year and show a fine accomplishment.

Soon Teniers got a great reputation for incredibly speedy workmanship. It is recorded that he could finish one of these carefully painted pictures in the late afternoon hours. They were called, whether mockingly or admiringly we do not know, his "after dinners."

While chiefly engaged with his tavern themes, Teniers sought a wider interest in certain pictures of alchemists busy in their laboratories, or desert saints afflicted by diabolical temptations. His father had treated such subjects, and Jerome Bosch had with rare mastery interpreted the theme of temptation as hallucination. The alchemist pictures, good examples at The Hague and Dresden, are among the most complicated Teniers ever attempted. He rejoices in the jumble of scientific apparatus and multiplies secondary incidents. In his handling of the subject there is no satire. He takes the alchemist at face value, as a scientist, which suggests that he himself was credulous, for, with the beginnings of real science alchemy was already losing prestige. Perhaps the best of these pictures is at Dresden. The grave figure of the alchemist seated while he blows the little fire under a retort admirably dominates the scores of accessories and the secondary group in the background. Teniers' capacity to harmonize concentration with dispersion is somewhat mysterious, and would repay an analytical study, which I cannot make here.

The Temptations, examples at Dresden, Madrid and in the New York Historical Society, are more amusing than impressive. Teniers never rises to the grotesque and horrific possibilities of the theme. He is a true Netherlander in feeling that no woman is sexually alluring unless she be expensively dressed, and in the latest mode. Thus the temptresses who are led up to St. Anthony by an ingratiating horned witch look like the modest Dutch gentlewomen whom Metsu painted so admiringly. St. Anthony himself seems rather mildly shocked at the impropriety of a woman invading his wilderness than deeply moved by the woman's attractiveness. The property demons and monsters who sit or fly about are made up from stuffed fish or monkeys, and again are mildly amusing, and produce no terror. All this may be verified in the Madrid picture (Fig. 281), which is one of the best of its class. It has much romantic charm and no seriousness whatever.

In 1637 David married, with customary prudence, Anna, the orphan daughter of the popular and prosperous painter, Jan, "Velvet," Bruegel. The seventeen-year-old bride brought a rich dowry. The Tenierses took a good old farmhouse in the suburb of Perck. David Teniers built three superfluous towers, apparently for the sole reason that he might hail from the "Three Towers" as a country gentleman's address. Children to the number of six came along rapidly. Meadow landscape, picturesque peasant huts, groves, canals, peasant jollifications, met his eye when he took his morning constitutional or strolled out after the completion of the almost daily "after dinner" picture. Out of the freshness of these new impressions grew his most charming works—the kermesses, peasant games out-of-doors—occasionally he and Anna taking the air within sight of the Three Towers (Fig. 282), London, or seated on the terrace, as the versatile artist plays the obbligato to a song, on a big 'cello, with the belfry of the parish church, and a pet monkey on a parapet against the sky, and a well-stocked wine-cooler prominent in the foreground. The picture is at Berlin, and from the age of the singing boy may be dated about 1645 or a little later.

Rubens had been a witness at Teniers' wedding, and from that year or perhaps a little earlier his influence is marked. The brown sauce of Brouwer pretty well disappears from Teniers' palette, his pictures are still tonal rather than colorful, but the tone is subtly achieved through a harmony of many hues and tints. Rubens, in his diaphanous last manner, had abandoned his old frank color in favor of a magic which is able to give his warm neutrals a suggestion of every sort of color. His opalescences were inimitable, but Teniers intelligently grasped the principle behind them and applied it in his own cautious fashion.

The famous kermesses represent this new open-air phase most strikingly. It is a problem of giving to fifty or so tiny figures sufficient individual character without losing the animation of the dance, of studying the effect of light on crumbling plastered walls and on thatched roofs, of representing the looming of crisp masses of foliage against the sky, and the fading hues of distant foliage. All this the country gentleman, David Teniers, manages, arranges and carries off with the skill and animation of a peasant dance manager. There is little to choose among the score or so rather big pictures of this sort— all are masterly, all lack the daemonic energy that Old Bruegel, the Dionysiac rapture that Rubens gave to such themes. Teniers feels nothing beyond the collective jolliness. It is enough, however, to inspire many delightful pictures. I happen to like especially the big Kermesse, at Vienna, for its clarity, animation, well-unified variety and an especially fascinating distribution of the larger lights and darks.

Possibly even better are the landscapes in which the figure interest is slighter. Here the picture of himself and his wife before his country house is notable, London (Fig. 282). Men are hauling a net in a canal before the point from which two of the three towers rise proudly before the evening sky. Teniers, booted, hatted and cloaked like an officer, stands indifferently while an aged and obsequious fisherman is about to offer a fine fish to Madame, attired like a princess. A superfluous maid and page emphasize the gentility of the pair. This group is merely tucked in a corner, the picture being essentially a landscape, but the corner tells a lot about the painter who would be a gentleman.

Pictures of this general sort, in which cottages, trees, meadows and sky share the interest with foreground groups of bowlers, drinkers or talkers, Teniers painted all his life, and the best are perhaps the tiny pictures which he made probably more for his own pleasure than for sale, in his old age. I think they have been somewhat overpraised. They depend rather upon clever formulas for scenic values than upon repeated or loving observation. Perhaps it is unfair to press damaging comparison with such contemporaries as Goyen, Brouwer, Rubens, Hobbema, Cuyp—to mention only artists who, like Teniers, treated landscape only in its friendlier aspects. Yet such comparisons reveal the tinge of artificiality and the lack of depth of interpretation in these engaging ruralisms of David Teniers.

In 1644 he was chosen dean of St. Luke's Guild. As if to mark the honor, he extended his repertory. The soldiers of the Spanish garrison attracted him. He painted guardrooms where the warriors are killing time. In one of these pictures, at Amsterdam, the guard plays cards, armor and accouterments lie about picturesquely in the corners. A similar picture, at Dresden, serves a double purpose, for it is a guardroom of the day, but the angel is delivering St. Peter in a cell at the left and behind (Fig. 283).

The abundant still life in these pictures Teniers handles most cleverly, also arranging it with taste. The little action involved is well indicated. One feels an ease the more complete because it may at any time be broken by an emergency call. Whoever has done guard duty will admit the naturalness of Teniers' interpretation of that life.

In the 1640's begin a capital series of kitchens. The subject, with its variety of still life and picturesque possibilities of illumination, had attracted many good Dutch painters. Teniers gave it its most sumptuous expression in the famous Kitchen, The Hague, 1644. The well-dressed housewife—it can hardly be the cook—sits and peels an apple, a little page holds a basin ready. She is surrounded by what is virtually a market; a great dinner must be in hand. The mounted skin of a swan on a table is ready for its ornamental function. Under the table is a big hare; a leg of mutton, with pheasants and ducks, on the floor; at the right, beside a copper wine cooler, big turbot and smaller fish lie on the floor. Above the housewife's head a plucked turkey hangs by the feet on the wall, forming a sort of trophy and a superbly decorative spot. In the left background are three figures, one of whom superintends the sizzling of no less than twenty roasts of various kinds and sizes on three spits. All this sounds like illustrative features carelessly heaped up. On the contrary, all the odd forms, colors and textures have their compositional value. Nothing could be shifted, taken away or added without some impairment of pictorial unity. Perhaps the picture should be regarded chiefly as a stunt—if so, a stunt magnificently carried off.

The coming of the new regent, Archduke Leopold Wilhelm, in 1647, was a turning point in Teniers' career. He was promptly appointed chamberlain and court painter. These honors were to have odd sequels. Teniers was to build up an art business as the regent's adviser, was even to paint the regent's gallery with the pictures about. In order to be near his patron, he was to move in 1651 from Antwerp to Brussels, and indulge great extravagance in living, to incur severe criticism from his fellow painters. In particular, having achieved the position of country gentleman, he aspired to a title of nobility; for seven years, from 1649, he bothered the genealogists to find him a qualifying ancestor, and the College of Heralds and even the king to admit his claim.

Meanwhile his patronage grew more distinguished. Besides the regent, Philip IV, William of Orange, and Queen Christina of Sweden, bought his pictures in quantity. He could take his choice on holidays of three golden chains, the gifts of monarchs. He designed for tapestry, conducted picture auctions, began to build a fine town house—in every sense was out for money and spent it rather faster than it came in.

Teniers' late forties and early fifties were a time of embarrassment and distress. In 1655 his wife died, and, though in less than a year and a half he replaced her with another heiress, very soon he was in litigation with his sons about their mother's will. The Guild of St. Luke took legal action against his auctions. His extravagance imperiled the tenure of his beloved Three Towers. Worst of all, the Spanish College of Heralds, which ultimately granted his request, reported that he could become a noble only on condition of ceasing to keep shop and painting for pay.

Meanwhile he worried along. Leopold Wilhelm died, in 1557, but his successor, Don Juan of Austria, continued Teniers' court offices and perquisites. Teniers carried on with his old repertory of subjects, in 1657 made cartoons for tapestry, later made a thrifty use of the little oil copies which he had made of Leopold Wilhelm's pictures by having them etched and published in a big folio, in 1660, under the sounding title *Amphitheatrum Picturarum*. It was the first published and illustrated catalogue of a great collection, and it achieved a successful sale through several editions. It still gives valuable information concerning masterpieces which have been lost or changed in form.

In his fifties Teniers gave his first sign of public spirit. At a time when the painter was a specialist and had little need of assistants, the old wholesome practice of apprenticeship was so breaking down that it was hard for a young painter to get the necessary training. Teniers thought to remedy this by founding an academy at Antwerp. To do so involved several years of negotiation with the old Guild of St. Luke, whose good will was indispensable. The academy was opened in 1665. Teniers wisely effaced himself, leaving the instruction with the deans of the guild. The academy was conducted in a liberal and sensible spirit, and flourished for a century or so.

David Teniers still had twenty-five years to live, but he had little new to say, merely varying his old repertory with always skillful repetitions. He had evidently studied with care the solemn antics of the pet monkey who appears in a family picture, and in his later years he made a number of pictures in which monkeys are shown enacting the parts played by men in the early pothouse scenes. To suppose a serious satirical intention in this work would be, I feel, gravely to misunderstand Teniers. I think he merely capitalized an obvious and rather negligible drollery. Technically, some of these pictures, like the Monkey Kitchen, Leningrad, are among his best, irrespective of the monkeys, and simply as beautifully arranged and lighted interiors.

In 1690 David Teniers died at Brussels, nearly eighty years old. His body was taken to Perck and buried in the little parish church within sight of the Three Towers. For a couple of centuries his name was to be synonomous with Dutch genre painting at its best. Old-fashioned tourists still probably exclaim "A Teniers!" when in passing they catch a glimpse of a dusky room occupied by peasants.

While his character seems to have been vain and self-seeking, nothing of that appears in his art. His pictures of all sorts run into the thousands, and among them it would be hard to find one that is either neglected or pretentious. As an artist his self-knowledge seems perfect, and he never rebelled at his limitations. The revived interest in such far greater painters as Brouwer, Ostade, Terborch and Vermeer has caused an unwarranted reaction against Teniers' previously exaggerated fame. There is much to be said for an artist who is so consistently amusing and skillful. He had the positive merit of retaining his interest in the rich and wholesome theme of peasant life for a quarter of a century after it had gone out of fashion. The would-be country gentleman and small nobleman viewed his peasant neighbors without caricature or condescension, painting them precisely as he saw and understood them. Again, the courtier never yielded a whit to that invasion of false French elegance which was rapidly undermining the sturdy native tradition of the Low Countries. In short, few minor painters of his time, or of any time, give more reasonable grounds for praise than David Teniers. A necessary qualifying consideration is that his brush was far more witty than his mind.

CHAPTER XVIII

DUTCH GENRE PAINTING; SCHOOLS
OF LEYDEN, DELFT, ETC.

Fig. 284. Vermeer of Delft. The Milkmaid.—Amsterdam.

Fig. 286.  Metsu.  The Vegetable Market, Amsterdam.—
Paris.

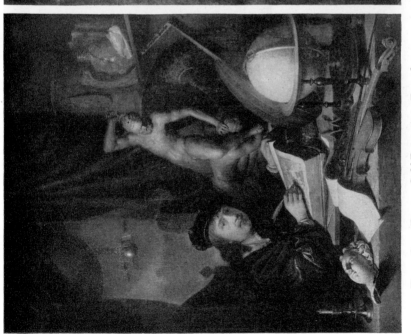

Fig. 285.  Dou.  Self-Portrait.—Dresden.

529

Fig. 288. Frans van Mieris. The Painter in His Studio.—Dresden.

Fig. 287. Metsu. The Intrusion.—Lord Northbrook's Collection, London.

Fig. 289.   (Upper) Carel Fabritius.   St. Peter Escaping from Prison.
—Providence, R. I.
Fig. 290.   (Lower) Leonard Bramer.   Presentation in the Temple.
—Philadelphia.

FIG. 291. VERMEER OF DELFT. The Pearl Necklace.—
Berlin.

FIG. 292. VERMEER OF DELFT. Woman at a Casement.
—New York.

Fig. 293. Vermeer of Delft. The Music Master and Fig. 294. Vermeer of Delft. The Studio.—Coll.
His Pupil.—Windsor. Count Czernin, Vienna.

FIG. 295. (Upper) PIETER DE HOOCH. Mother by a Cradle.—Berlin.
FIG. 296. (Lower) TERBORCH. Signing the Treaty of Münster.—London.

534

Fig. 298. Terborch. Lady Washing Her Hands.—
Dresden.

Fig. 297. Terborch. The Piece of Money.—Paris.

FIG. 299. (Lower) VERMEER OF DELFT. The Supper at Emmaus.
—Rotterdam.
FIG. 300. (Upper) WILLEM KALF. Breakfast.—Detroit.

THE SCHOOL of Leyden grew inauspiciously out of the strenuous and ugly practice of young Rembrandt as continued by his pupil, Gerard Dou (1613–1675). Such minute modeling with sensational light effects was proper enough to a young talent finding itself, and Rembrandt soon abandoned the method. But Rembrandt's move to Amsterdam about 1630 left his seventeen-year-old pupil with a permanent technical investment which he never changed in any way.

Possibly because Leyden was a university city and a center of book publishing, her painters seldom dealt with the peasant or the life of the pothouse. Here they followed the example of the pioneer, Gerard Dou, whose interest was in the solid middle classes.

Perhaps his best, or rather his least bad, pictures are the numerous tiny character studies of single figures, busts or half-lengths. In this manner he painted Rembrandt's mother and father, his own portrait, pictures of hermits, philosophers, etc. Characteristic is the self-portrait, at Dresden (Fig. 285), where the artist is fairly lost amid accessories painted with meticulous literalism, and having no air of belonging together.

Dou prospered, in 1648 was prominent in founding a painters' guild at Leyden, had many pupils, some of whom, like Gabriel Metsu and Frans Mieris, attained prominence.

Dou's larger genre pictures were and are popular. Indeed, there is something solacing to a tourist herded through a great gallery in an art that dots all the i's, crosses all the t's, and requires no effort of the beholder's imagination. Some of the larger pictures, such as the Young Mother, The Hague, and the Dropsical Woman, Paris, have a minor attractiveness because of Dou's evident love of his material and his pride in his workmanship. I think the latter is his dominant motive. It is possible to paint very doggedly with an object before you at which you hardly look, and while Dou did observe single objects very minutely, I fear he never saw his scene as a whole, but built it up while he looked proudly at the point of his little brush doing what seemed to him wonders on the panel. There is no contemplation behind his pictures, and that is perhaps why they are liked.

Dou transmitted his small and sleek manner to his pupils, but the best of them outgrew it. If one had to pick just one Dutch genre painter, one might do well to choose Gabriel Metsu. While his taste and imagination are not of the first rank, he is rarely below a high level of professionalism; his perceptive good humor is unflagging; his curiosity and interest extend to every aspect of domestic life, from the market place and kitchen to the drawing room and music room. Through his pictures one may share the life of a prosperous Dutch household, a tranquilizing vision when the household itself seems to be passing into obsolescence, and the kitchen yields everywhere to the cafeteria. The reasonableness and pleasantness of domestic life is Metsu's theme, and he illustrates it with the greatest variety and geniality.

He was born at Leyden, about 1630, received his first training from Gerard Dou, whose sleek and minute manner he soon transformed into a finer one of his own. Of the good work of able contemporaries he took intelligent account. The example of Hals, Steen, Rembrandt and Maes served to educate him in finer tonalities, in discreet brilliancy of handling, in bringing color into the "dark manner" in which he began. In 1648 he is inscribed among the founders of the painters' guild. In 1655 he moved to the richer patronage of Amsterdam, where two years later he married. He died under the hands of an unlucky or unskillful surgeon in 1667, not yet forty.

In his young manhood he painted a number of Biblical subjects somewhat in the disorderly manner of the former Leydener, Jan Steen, in this branch, and perhaps encouraged by Rembrandt's early success with such themes. But Metsu lacked the imagination which alone gives such subjects significance, as may be proved from the very Steen-like Prodigal Son among the Harlots, at Leningrad. Quite early are pictures of Blacksmith Shops, at Amsterdam and London. Oddly, these pictures of honest toil are unique in Dutch art. They imply a careful study of Rembrandt's admirable interiors, and Metsu has caught much of Rembrandt's magic in making the prevailing dusk a means of revelation and expression. At thirty, in Amsterdam, he strikes his gait, and becomes the celebrator of the comfortable and dignified domesticity of the prosperous families. Here I may only hint at his very various production.

Entirely typical are the two Market Scenes, at Dresden, especially animated the one in which a fine old lady in a nunlike costume bargains for a chicken while a disheveled and disinterested old gentleman seated on a cask smokes seriously, and a spaniel registers interest in the transaction. Finer and more broadly conceived is the more populous Vegetable Market, Amsterdam, with its shadowing tree and picturesque background of old gabled houses beyond a canal—a pleasant episode in the ritual of housekeeping fully understood and expressed. Perhaps the best of these pictures on the subject of marketing is the one at Paris (Fig. 286). The sheer animation, the sheer pleasantness of it are captivating, and its pleasantness depends as much on fine selection and arrangement and sensitive study of the lighting as it does on sympathetic understanding. More concentrated and more tenderly painted is the Young Girl peeling Apples, Paris. The act is accomplished with automatic grace, while the fair worker smiles inwardly over such culinary resources as a basket of big apples and a sizable unskinned carcass of a large hare on the ledge before her.

The richest of Metsu's pictures in compositional pattern is the Music Lesson, London. It is uncommonly bright in color, the seriousness of giving and receiving instruction is well realized, while the contrast of the arabesque contours of the figures with the ingeniously interlocking rectangles of the spinet, picture and pavement is an admirable example of what we have called the standard Dutch style. Aside from this, all the forms are massively asserted, but pictorially, without crowding and without mere bulginess.

Unlike Steen and Terborch, Metsu approaches the social scene descriptively, approvingly, and without a suspicion of satire. Thus the Morning Visit, Paris, where an assiduous officer courteously looks down on a richly dressed young girl seated and holding a glass of wine, is a pure Terborch subject, but there is no hint of solicitation that goes beyond civility. The most elaborate Metsu of this aristocratic kind is the Visit to the Nursery, New York. The reds and golds against the general brown are sumptuous—sharp, yet harmonious. The various moods of the proud parents, of the attentive or merely curious servants, of the demonstrative fine lady making the visit, are sensitively recorded without undue emphasis. The relations of the figure group to the large architectural rectangles, details tactfully suppressed, are entirely just and exquisite. Such a passage as the lights and darks and swaying contours of the maid against the bright rectangle of the door at the left might serve as a lesson in beautiful design. Such a picture suggests that if Metsu had lived on into his sixties he might have challenged the laurels of Vermeer. Of such aristocratic Metsus none is more engaging than the Intrusion, in Lord Northbrook's collection, London (Fig. 287). However eager, the intruding gallant is harmless enough and, except for the faithful terrier, he has the sympathy of all concerned. The odd V-shaped composition and the bold plotting of the white areas are very original and effective.

Undoubtedly the most popular Metsu is the Sick Child, Steengracht Collection, The Hague. In its overt and irresistible pathos it recalls the best works of Maes, but it is finer, more thoughtfully composed, less insistent. How incapable Metsu is of indulging satire, or even of poking fun at his creations, is shown in his single doctor picture, the Sick Lady, Leningrad, which may be profitably compared with the superficially very similar masterpieces of Jan Steen. Unlike Steen, who finds satirical comedy in the situation, Metsu accepts and respects everybody concerned. The exhausted patient does nothing to attract the doctor, he, doing his level best with a urine glass, pays no attention to her, the old servant awaits the diagnosis with natural concern. The composition is one of the densest and finest from Metsu's hand, the severe geometry being tastefully varied and attenuated, and the whole effect singularly lucid, massive and dignified.

It should be clear that while the bonhomie of Metsu may seem his leading characteristic, it is by no means the whole of him. It is expressed through a masterly handling of his materials, and reinforced by penetrating observation and fine selection. With such capacities there can be, despite the radical doctrinaires of today, a very fine artistry which includes no criticism of life.

The sleek style of Gerard Dou persists, but with a better color sense, in the work of another of his pupils, Frans van Mieris. Mieris is interested only in rich people, their easy way of living, their more or less shoddy aristocracy, their social pleasures, their dissipations. Upon the representation of stuffs, silks, satins, fur borders he spends himself, with the result of a literalism that is happily exceptional in Dutch artists of his talent. He really concerns himself with surfaces, and prosperous Holland was busily building up a French surface in costume, manners and morals. This surface Frans van Mieris painted excellently—painted it as well as it deserved to be painted. But it is an art of low vitality and of no raciness at all. His numerous richly clad, portly women playing the lute or receiving attention, I leave the reader to find for himself. The public museums everywhere abound in them, for Frans van Mieris was popular and prolific.

He was born at Leyden in 1631, admitted to the guild in 1658, and died full of honors in 1681. We perhaps see him at his best in the picture of his own Studio, at Dresden (Fig. 288). There is much that is admirable in the painting, but the composition is relaxed. The interest has passed from making a clear and emphatic composition in the Dutch style to producing a general sense of opulence and aristocracy. After all, Frans van Mieris was a fine type of fashionable painter. As much can be said for such contemporaries as Jakob van Ochtervelt, Eglon van der Neer and the Heidelberger, Caspar Netscher.

The full depth of the decadence is not reached till the next generation and the last decades of the century, when we find in Frans van Mieris' son, Willem, and in Adriaen van der Werff nothing left but a disagreeably oily and slippery technique applied indiscriminately to the clothed and unclothed female who, with a fine impartiality, in either condition is made equally insignificant. A similar decadence draws in the excellent painter of interiors, Pieter de Hooch; such accomplished pupils of Rembrandt as Ferdinand Bol and Nicolas Maes show the same deterioration in their later portraiture. It loses strength and character, affects a borrowed Van Dyckish elegance, achieves a studied superficiality.

Delft, perhaps most exquisitely neat and attractive of all Dutch cities, developed a great master in Jan Vermeer, and in Pieter de Hooch a considerable talent, but never built up a consistent school. Since most of her painters followed the "dark manner" of Rembrandt, they may be appropriately considered at this place. In Michiel Jansz Mierevelt, 1567–1641, Delft had an excellent portraitist who worked rather in the old Cosmopolitan Style. In Holland and England he painted many celebrities with fidelity and a quiet distinction. Through him we see today such heroes of the liberation as William the Silent and John of Barnevelt, both portraits at Amsterdam. But Mierevelt, who was much away from Delft, had little to teach an aspiring young painter who was growing up in the 1640's. Such painters as Carel Fabritius, 1624?–1654, and Leonard Bramer, 1596–1667, instinctively turned to the new marvel of Rembrandt at the moment of the Night Watch. Both Fabritius and Bramer may have had some part in the training of Vermeer, though we have no sure evidence that such is the case. Fabritius painted a few very sensitive portraits in the style of Rembrandt towards 1645. Notable among them is the bust of an eager and also somewhat melancholy young man, at Rotterdam, which may well be a self-portrait, and a more confident self-portrait, at Munich. At Rotterdam is an exquisite painting of a Finch on its House, signed and dated 1654. Out of so slight a motive Carel Fabritius made an unforgettable masterpiece, simply by recording the play of light on the wall, the textures and tints of the plumage of the tiny bird, its gay and confident bearing. In a recently identified picture, at Providence, R. I., Fabritius reveals an unexpected dramatic gift (Fig. 289). While the guards sleep, St. Peter moves cautiously away. The figures are fairly splashed with a spectral light. Such a work implies a careful study of the Caravaggians, probably of Ter Brugghen. From pictures of this painterlike fastidiousness and originality young Jan Vermeer might have learned much. Any long contact between Carel Fabritius and Vermeer is improbable, for Fabritius was killed in a powder explosion in 1654, when Vermeer was only twenty-two years old. The more or less accepted list of Fabritius' paintings rests less on signatures or documents than on stylistic attributions, and is far from certain. We gain a sense of an exquisite gift, without being sure of its concrete expressions.

Leonard Bramer (1596–1667) is at least a substantial figure. He was trained in Italy, came under the influence of Elsheimer's idylism, was repeatedly headman of the painters' guild of Delft up to 1665, at a time when Vermeer was probably pursuing his studies. Bramer was a man of considerable culture, and if we need suppose an intermediary to explain Vermeer's transient Italianism, Bramer well serves the purpose. As for Bramer's pictures, they show, with the exception of a few early Caravaggian pieces, no Italian influence, but are derived from the fantastic and theatrical vein of Rembrandt in the early 1640's. They employ his coruscating light and borrow something of his magic. There is nothing of this ambiguous appeal in Vermeer at any time.

Bramer was born at Delft in 1596. From his eighteenth year he studied for several years in France and Italy. At Rome Caravaggio's tenebrism was a novelty, and Bramer yielded temporarily to its spell. He returned to Delft in 1625 and four years later joined the guild. Thus he was a finished painter before Rembrandt had developed his personal style. However, Bramer carefully studied Rembrandt's paintings of the late 1630's and 1640's and from them drew his developed style. This he did with more ability and originality than most of Rembrandt's direct pupils. There is glamour and romance, perhaps too insistently, in such Rembrandtesque Bramers as Solomon and the Queen of Sheba, Dresden; Simeon in the Temple, Brunswick; the Presentation in the Temple, Philadelphia (Fig. 290); the Descent from the Cross, Rotterdam. From the evolutionary point of view, Bramer shares with Carel Fabritius the credit of introducing Rembrandt's style in Delft.

Recovered from complete oblivion by the research of the past eighty years, the forty pictures or so which can be confidently ascribed to Vermeer of Delft are now regarded as the consummation of fine painting in Holland, and it is not likely that the future will challenge the verdict. Technically considered, Vermeer is simply the most able and exquisite practitioner of the bright style that Holland produced. There never was an observation more exquisite than his of the degrees of absorbed or reflected light, a more scrupulous care in decorative and modeling edges, a more careful regard for substance and texture, a more simple and gracious method of construction. He was also the greatest exponent of the Dutch formula of composition. No one gave greater value to the arabesque of the figure locked into a pattern of architectural quadrilaterals. He had refinements of color all his own—ineffable harmonies of pale blue and straw yellow. More briefly, as Mr. E. V. Lucas has felicitously written, as a creator of light, Vermeer exercises a "white magic" uniquely his own.

So far I may go with his eulogists, Mr. Lucas and Mr. Philip L. Hale. But these material perfections, though much of Vermeer, are by no means the whole of him. After early experiments in bordel scenes, religious subjects and mythology, he settled practically to one theme—women serving or reigning in an exquisitely kept home. His finest pictures show only one woman—the Milkmaid, the Pearl Necklace, the Girl making Lace, the Woman reading a Letter, the Portrait of a Girl, at The Hague, the Woman with a Water Jug—these are admittedly the finest Vermeers. When he adds a second figure, the picture loses; when he adds a third, the picture ceases to be a fine Vermeer. In short, people as related to each other, the very staple of Dutch genre painting, did not deeply engage his interest. He was engrossed with another relation—that of a woman to her home. That he made fairly sacramental, and such was the root of his peculiar poetry.

Mr. Van Zype has called Vermeer's attitude chivalric, and, without wholly accepting the term, one need not quarrel with it. Nor does it seem sentimental to emphasize the fact that this cultus of the home, this delicately worshipful feminism, seems to center around his fair and doubtless efficient wife, Catherine Bolenes, whom he married at twenty-one, who was still in her modest beauty when he died at forty-three.

Jan Vermeer was born at Delft on Allhallows of 1632, the year young Rembrandt signed the Anatomy Lesson. In April of 1653 Vermeer married, and at the end of the year was admitted as a master by the painters' guild. He was the headman in 1662, 1670 and 1671. He died in December of 1675, leaving a widow and eight children and considerable debts to his baker. Biographically, we know little more about him than that.

Only one of his early pictures, the Procuress, 1656, Dresden, is dated. So any chronology is dependent on inferences from style, and must be regarded as uncertain. The Sleeping Servant, New York, is more Rembrandtesque and looks earlier than any other Vermeer. It is sensitively executed in browns, in a manner suggestive of Rembrandt, and even more of Nicolas Maes, then a young pupil of Rembrandt. None of the luminous blue-grays so characteristic of Vermeer's developed style are present. The composition is loose, and without the later complicated refinements.

Two rather large pictures, Christ with Mary and Martha, at Edinburgh, and Diana and her Nymphs, The Hague, offer a curious problem. Both are distinctly Italianate. Already the luminous blue-gray tonality is delightfully used. Christ with Mary and Martha is perhaps Vermeer's greatest invention, if not his finest picture. Most painters of this theme have taken sides with the idealist, Mary, against her practical sister. Vermeer faithfully follows the New Testament in giving Mary a superiority in spiritual and physical loveliness, but he makes Martha, insisting on the dignity of her household task, equally noble and impressive. Since the dignity of the household task was to be Vermeer's best theme, this impartiality is significant. Apart from these literary and moral considerations, the picture is very strongly constructed and composed. The foreshortenings, swaying inward and outward of the powerfully realized bodies, yields an uncommon sense of space and actuality. The linear pattern seems of little consequence, and this again is curious in an artist who soon was to make the most fastidious use of linear pattern.

Still of a different sort is Diana and her Nymphs, The Hague. The composition is of baroque type, moving from left to right in asymmetrical balance. The blue-gray tonality, now with contrasts of yellow, is about that of Mary and Martha. The look again is Italianate, but with a difference, for an Italian would as a matter of course have represented Diana and her nymphs nude. Vermeer instead gives the general sense of a group of wholesome Dutch girls modestly dressed, but barefooted, and about to go on a wading party. But this charmingly rustic first impression is deceptive. These are plump and attractive Dutch girls, to be sure, but they wear nothing that their admirers would recognize as contemporary costume. These robes are a sort of compromise with the ideal of classical drapery. In this, as in Mary and Martha, certain solutions of the pictorial problem which at first sight seem obvious really rest upon a very discriminating act of taste. At all times we may be sure Vermeer painted only after prolonged contemplation on his theme.

These two pictures may reasonably be dated in 1654 or 1655. They show Vermeer very seriously occupied in assimilating the Italian Renaissance style as interpreted by the best eclectic or baroque masters. One is tempted to ask how far he might have gone, had he continued the vein. Evidently he could have held his own with the best baroque painters of Venice and Naples.

As I write, a recently discovered Vermeer has been bought by the Boymans Museum, Rotterdam, which confirms the opinion and casts a new light on his early Italianate manner. It is a Supper at Emmaus (Fig. 299), figures nearly life size, and it already shows in its incipience the favorite balance of pale blues and yellows. The painting is searching, with the fullest concern for all textures, so much so that at first glance one might think the picture Spanish. The group is admirably arranged; the sharply defined bright oblong of the tablecloth and the hint of the window at the left contrast effectively with the otherwise massively rounding forms. The placing of the four figures at four distances is superbly achieved; all the masses are securely established, yet kept well behind the picture plane and carrying with them more sense of space than is usual in Vermeer's later pictures.

On the expression of the faces Vermeer has spent himself. The Christ revealing himself as he breaks the loaf is infinitely pathetic and benign. One feels deeply the nearness of the ordeal of Calvary. The rapt attention of the two pilgrims and the woman attendant is expressed with poignancy, and thoughtfully varied according to the character involved. Very masterly is the expression of the pilgrim with his back turned and his features hidden. A most exquisite compositional passage is the arrangement of the three visible hands in a sort of reversed crescent.

My friend and colleague, Professor Erwin Panofsky, has suggested to me that the distribution of light and the method of construction of this picture imply study of the Utrecht Caravaggians and specifically of the work of Hendrick Ter Brugghen. I fully agree with him. What seems to be the case is that young Vermeer was singularly impressionable to the finer Italian and Italianate feeling of the moment, and, had circumstances favored, would have developed as one of the finest painters of religious and mythological subjects of his times. But no such career was possible for a young painter who had to support a family by his art in the Protestant city of Delft. The frustration of Vermeer's dearest ambition may after all have been a gain for us, as we shall see.

The question how Vermeer came to study the Italians, what pictures he may have seen, is interesting but really not very important. It is probable that Leonard Bramer brought back Italian pictures or engravings that would deeply move such a sensitive and searching spirit as was Vermeer's. In any case, good reproductive engravings of earlier and recent Italian paintings abounded, and one need not necessarily look beyond such material to explain Vermeer's Italianate beginnings. Nor was this effort wasted, even if it was not followed up. The study which Vermeer devoted to the making of Mary and Martha, Diana and her Nymphs and the Supper at Emmaus amounted to a liberal education in composition, and in taste generally, and this education he was soon to put to use along sound Dutch lines.

It was probably chiefly because there was no livelihood at Delft in such work that he tried a new experiment, in the Procuress, Dresden, dated 1656. This brilliantly colored character study in half-lengths and in a curiously divided square suggests compositionally

Caravaggio and his school, and even more strikingly, though the mood is wholly different, the comicalities of the Italianate Hollander, Van Laer, nicknamed "Il Bamboccio." It is beautifully painted, the sharp colors as well balanced and harmonized as those in Frans Hals' work of twenty years earlier. Except for the young courtesan, whose face is as pure as that of Mary of Bethany, the characterization is definite and masterly. The sensual young sport and the scheming old bawd are fully alive. But there is little sense of relation between the figures, and the social joys of the bordel are not even suggested. I believe we have to do with a magnificent potboiler which happily failed to attract patronage.

Probably while he was engaged in these experiments he painted the first picture which the average art lover of today would recognize as his, the Milkmaid (Fig. 284), Amsterdam. It shows the cool splendor of his blue-gray luminosity, the ample figure is large and noble in its construction, the ordinary act of pouring out milk thoughtfully is invested with an almost sacramental solemnity. The woman's attitude seems immediately seen, even surprised, but worked out with severest reflection. Such a feeling was hardly to recur in the art of painting until two centuries later Jean François Millet painted at Barbizon, and he never sought or captured Vermeer's "white magic," which first asserts its spell in this admirable picture. Perhaps because a kitchen does not offer, in furniture, pictures, etc., the elements of Vermeer's later compositional complexities, the pattern of this picture may seem uninteresting, as compared with that of the later works. I feel the picture is rather the better for a simplicity which is of the essence, and it does not seem to me that Vermeer ever really surpassed the Milkmaid.

The pictures which we shall next consider were probably all painted between 1656 and 1666, Vermeer's twenty-fourth to thirty-fourth year. In them he capitalized the heavy but benign burden of an expensive home and a rapidly growing family. These little pictures are generally built around the figure of a woman working or at leisure in a room of a fastidiously appointed and beautifully kept house. The light usually falls gently in from a casement at the left, stealing over cool, gray walls, caressing pewter or latten jugs, drawing out the deep hues from an Oriental rug which serves as a tablecloth, glinting on the carving of massive chairs or picture frames, hinting at the geographical pattern in a hanging map, finally, and most important, bringing out the rounded forms of the woman with an authority as convincing as it is gentle. This handling of the light, without strong contrasts, as a factor in construction is the distinguishing technical merit of Vermeer's painting, and it allies him with the greatest figure painters of all times.

Of these pictures with one woman as focus, the Pearl Necklace (Fig. 291), Berlin, if I may trust long memory, is the most exquisitely painted—in the perfection of its enamel and its iridescences of pale yellow and blue. The posture, the hands raising the bight of the necklace, is, while apparently casual, really very studied, as expressing a modest pride in possession. Everything seems to emanate from the pearls and the pearl-like delicacy of the face of their wearer. All the painting is of the most exquisite sort. Mr. Lucas rightly asserts that any square inch of the plastered wall would be a precious possession.

More meditatively conceived, and possibly more rich in variety of surface, if less precious as color, are two pictures, Dresden and Amsterdam, on the theme of a woman standing quietly as she reads a letter. Possibly a shade the finer is the picture at Amsterdam, for the largeness of the construction of the figure and the close, fretlike pattern of the map and the rectangles made by it and the chair backs. It also has an attractive homeliness which the more aristocratic version at Dresden lacks.

Personally I love best among these interiors with a housewife the superb little Vermeer at New York, which is variously called a Woman at a Casement, or with a Jug (Fig. 292). The woman is merely letting in the morning air as she tidies up, but she tidies up with a gesture as grand as that of a sibyl by Michelangelo. The grandeur is of the essence, and not stylistically imputed. Vermeer had seen and remembered precisely such an attitude as the daily ritual which made his home a delight was being accomplished. He records it with gratitude and affection, enhances it by every compositional device which might express its dignity and convey the character of the place. All his perfections in balance and manipulation of light-creating and form-giving color are so quietly present in this picture that it is easy to overlook them. Once understood, this picture will be one of its lover's most permanent memories.

For concentrated elegance in feeling and tone, the little Girl making Lace, Paris, has no rival. And again it is not any elegance arbitrarily imposed upon the efficient girl at her feminine task—the elegance is in the act itself, in the busy, skillful hands going carefully about a routine act. Vermeer does not in the ordinary sense idealize, and never sentimentalizes these household offices, rather he discovers and reveals them in a beauty which is generally obscured by use and wont.

In his few formal portraits, such as those at Budapest and Brussels, Vermeer follows discreetly the example of Rembrandt in his first objective manner, and sensibly waives the studied, decorative effect of his genre pictures. Such work did not deeply engage his imagination, and in this phase he is merely one of a dozen superior Dutch portraitists of the moment. Exception must be made for the Head of a Girl, at The Hague. With its extraordinary reality, it is rather a character study than a portrait in the formal sense. Simply as construction of form in tints which have the value of light it seems to me one of a dozen finest pictures in the world. And here it may be noted that the forms of a fine painter are never bulges, are never thrust out towards the eye, have no relation to the forms of sculpture. They merely exist in a pictorial world which the eye is invited to enter and explore. It explores and ascertains the presence of the forms and their validity. Such is the way of Rembrandt, Hals, Velasquez, and technically Vermeer is of their great company. Aside from the technical perfection of this Head of a Girl, is its richness of characterization—its suggestion of physical and moral vitality, of human worth and amiability. The study of this little picture, which holds Vermeer's genius in epitome, should show that human imponderables of admiration and sympathy are quite as important in it as its accuracy of observation and its perfection in technical resourcefulness.

A few very fine compositions with two figures probably fall within this marvelous decade. The Music Master and his Pupil, at Windsor (Fig. 293), is the most remarkable. The two figures, the girl at the spinet seen from behind, are placed deep in the picture and subordinated, as repeats of such round forms as the 'cello on the floor and the stoneware vase on the table. While the figures are very necessary, and the relation of master to pupil well realized, the picture has really become portraiture of a room. The general, severe pattern of varied quadrilaterals is varied by the heavy Oriental rug which falls heavily and irregularly from the table and spreads out over the floor. Absolutely indispensable is the little gray jug on the table which brings to a sort of focus the few round elements in a composition generally

rectangular. Think the jug away, or cover it with a finger in a reproduction, and the whole picture grows dull. Except for the Love
Letter, Amsterdam, where the compositional complications are perhaps too overt and sophisticated, this is the most complicated of all
the Vermeers, and without loss of naturalness of effect.

What are the late Vermeers is a matter of inference. The Geographer, Frankfurt, is dated 1669, and seems to carry with it, for the
costume of the man, such courtly conversation pieces as those at
Berlin, Brunswick, and the Frick Collection, New York. These pictures of a young woman receiving company are all remarkable for the
deferential and chivalric attitude of the young men. This is as different from the simple sociability of Dirck Hals, Jan Steen and Metsu
as it is from the unabashed male possessiveness of Terborch. Beyond
this there is little notable, for a Vermeer, in this ingeniously composed and fastidiously painted group of pictures.

In it he makes moderate concessions to the new French influence, yielding to it entirely, or to some worse influence, in the big
and silly Allegory of the New Testament, New York. A portly and
indifferent lady in blue impersonates the theme somewhat self-con-
sciously. Like all Vermeers it is delightfully painted, but it is stupidly
felt, or rather, it is not felt at all. The inferiority of this and the
Geographer pictures drove the fine critic, the late John van Dyke, to
suppose a namesake trained in the Utrecht school to explain such
works. It seems to me foolish dictation of a patron and Vermeer's
difficulty in keeping bread in the mouths of his eight young children
may sufficiently explain such lapses from his habitual taste.

His single outdoor picture, the View of Delft, The Hague, is
usually dated pretty early. Since it shows every resource of his later
style, I am inclined to date it well along in the 1660's. The general
effect is due to the contrast of the dull red of the tiled roofs with a
prevailing gray which here and there flowers into deep blue. The
sense of texture in the brick houses and heavy barges is given by a
system of heavy dots which yield a positive coruscation. The neutral
tint of the bit of nearby strand is a terra-cotta inclining to salmon-
pink. Throughout, the painting is of the most precious sort, though
the effect is merely unpretentiously natural and right. There could
be no more delicate homage from a painter to a beloved, native town.

Among what seem to be late Vermeers, Lady and Servant, Frick
Collection, New York, is very handsomely painted, but the slight

motive hardly justifies the large scale. The picture balances uncertainly between portraiture and genre painting, and is not convincing on either score. For intricacies of composition, the Letter, Amsterdam, is one of the most interesting Vermeers. It is built in sharp opposition of tall rectangles, oblongs, and the diamond pattern of the pavement. One looks through a vestibule, through an open door to where a richly dressed woman, seated and holding the keyboard of a lute, looks sharply over her shoulder at a deferential maid who has just delivered the letter still unopened in the lady's free hand. A little drama is implied, and perhaps the staginess of the presentation is appropriate. There is a strange apparitional effect, as of an event happening in another light, and almost in another world than that of the beholder. While I do not much like the picture, I admire greatly its ingeniousness.

The spiritual being in Vermeer is, it seems to me, easily read. He was an inerrant eye, a fastidious and self-conscious artist, a devout admirer of women, whether in the aspect of graciousness or serviceability, a lover of his home. It seems as if he felt such a broadly moral estimate must suffice us, for the single portrait of himself turns its back to us. The famous and rather large picture, the Atelier (Fig. 294), Czernin Gallery, Vienna, consummately well painted, repeats in unobtrusive form those refinements of composition which we have just discussed in the case of the Letter. The painter at the easel, in his fantastic striped jerkin and rumpled silk stockings, is in our world. The heavy, brocaded curtain, the table, the rafters, the big map, cut off another space, another world through which is passing the strangest of apparitions—a woman rather Javanese in aspect, her eyes closed, her hair fantastically decked out with big leaves, her left hand holding firmly a big folio volume, her right hand delicately balancing horizontally a long, straight trumpet. What does it all mean? Perhaps we were never meant to know, possibly Vermeer himself did not know. It is easy to see that the bulging and broken contour of the woman's drapery—it is that, and not a frock—was just what was needed between the corner of the table and that of the map, that the foreshortened quadrilateral of the big book carries the diaper of the pavement into the upper part of the picture, that the fantastic headdress relieves the oval of the head from what might otherwise have been an insipid presentation. In short, there are sound stylistic reasons for whatever may seem bizarre and enigmatic in the picture.

I am inclined to guess that there is also a meaning in the ordinary sense. Perhaps Vermeer saw one of his daughters masquerading at Christmas time as an angel of the Nativity, and there found the focus of a picture which should have a strange and ambiguous beauty. It is the paradoxical blend of worldliness and other-worldliness that constitutes much of the fascination of this unique Vermeer, and with it we may well take leave of him.

Many genre painters of Holland exceeded him in energy and in scope. None, not even Rembrandt, commanded an expression at once so lyrical and so completely truthful. His theme, the sacredness of the woman who makes a happy and well-ordered home, seemed to him to admit of few variations and to need neither emphasis nor ornamentation. To that extent his art may seem to be objective and in a measure austere. But the austerity is warm with implicit feeling and expressed in a style that is always sumptuous, if restrainedly so. His pictures recall certain very precious lyrical poems which similarly glorify routine service—as George Herbert's lines:

> "Who sweeps a room but in Thy Name
> Makes that and th' action fine."

That delicate balance of interest between persons and things which was the problem of the Dutch genre painter, Vermeer, with most of his fellows, established on the side of persons. His fellow townsman, Pieter de Hooch, when at his best, chose for things. There is a point where their art overlaps. Both loved interiors, both searched the lighting most carefully, both made exquisite compositional use of the numerous quadrilaterals which these interiors presented. But by De Hooch, in his early and best work, the figure is little studied for its own sake. It became rather a valuably contrasting element in still life—a curved thing quietly varying what might otherwise be monotonous in the generally rectangular pattern. And De Hooch approaches the problem of painting interiors almost without preconceptions. He takes his color and lighting about as he finds them, without Vermeer's dislike of swarthy shadows and preference for blue-yellow tonalities. A Vermeer, while it seems equally real, is actually more stylized. The influence of Rembrandt, which was transient in Vermeer's art, is lasting in De Hooch's.

Even for a Dutch painter, De Hooch's origins were humble. He was born in 1629, the son of a butcher of Rotterdam. After his baptismal record, the next is of 1653, when, at twenty-four, he is mentioned as a "painter and footman" in the service of Justus de la Grange. That rich merchant-adventurer was evidently a kind master, for he owned no less than ten pictures by his footman, who, in occasional visits to Leyden and The Hague with his master, had the privilege of seeing good pictures by Metsu, Steen, and perhaps Maes.

In 1654 De Hooch seems to have been free of service, for he married a Delft girl, moved thither, and in September of 1655 became a member of the guild. Within the following ten years—his thirty-sixth to forty-sixth—his finest pictures were painted, probably somewhat in emulation of Vermeer's. De Hooch prospered, and in 1664 moved to the commercial center, Amsterdam, where he practiced very ably, but with much loss of quality in his art, the new Frenchified style. He died sometime after 1677, in his late fifties. Since his early situation as a house servant probably precluded anything like regular instruction in painting, it is of minor interest that his first master was probably the Italianate, Nicolas Berghem, landscapist and cattle painter. Since Berghem sought and caught very accurately the general blond tonality that prevails out of doors, De Hooch could have learned from him only the need of harmony in tone. He probably learned mostly from his observation of interiors as he served, and if we must suppose an artistic influence, it is that of Rembrandt, whether direct or mediated through such intelligent imitators as Vermeer, in the earliest phase, or Metsu. The leading motive in the best De Hoochs is a houseman's proper pride in a fine house, a very intimate feeling, which, entirely without depreciation, is to be distinguished from that householder's pride which Vermeer so eminently represented.

De Hooch's favorite problem was that of suites of rooms receding in refinements of aerial perspective and intricacies of linear pattern. A very distinguished solution of such problems is the little Interior, at London, with a standing woman and child. The way in which the doorways cut the figures and each other is exquisitely chosen, even the variation in the set of the floor tiles is important, and the chair is essential to the arrangement. In such a picture the mere space develops a kind of poetry, and in addition there is the charm of textures very delicately observed and indicated, and a quietly vivid play of light. Of similarly delightful quality is the Dining Room, at Berlin, with its gracious standing figures of a woman and a little girl, and its contrasting outlets into a velvety dark closet, left, and an opaline inner room, right, through the casement of which you look out of doors.

There are many intimate De Hoochs of this quality, and save the Vermeers, no Dutch interiors of a realistic sort can bear comparison with them. Characteristic is the Mother by a Cradle, at Berlin (Fig. 295). It is impeccable in compositional pattern of a very rich sort, in spatial relations and in sensitively studied and most various illumination. And this elaboration is modestly subordinated to intimacy of effect. Sometimes he moved out of the house to the door-yard, and painted the house from the outside. He is equally felicitous in such themes, though they have to be worked out with simpler compositional forms. London again gives us a capital example in the Courtyard of a Dutch House, in which the natural foreshortenings of the walls serve as very interesting compositional features. Of somewhat similar attractiveness, though later in date and simpler in arrangement, is the Country House, Amsterdam. Indeed, for a De Hooch, it is a little dry and obvious in composition, depending for its effect upon light falling pleasantly upon tiles and bricks, and the masterliness with which the form of the woman in middle distance is asserted in pure color, in Vermeer's fashion. The group around the table in the foreground is not quite assimilated, being too large in scale, hence dwarfing the house. Such negligences are not uncommon in De Hooch's latest years.

In his last fifteen years De Hooch surrendered to the new French elegance, and though he still painted pictures of a brilliant and fastidious workmanship, such as the fine conversation piece in the collection of Mr. Robert Lehman, New York, on the whole his work went off badly. Even technically, he no longer observes closely, but repeats his old formulas. The pictures tend to be bigger and emptier. The bad De Hoochs the reader must find for himself. I may merely help him to a peculiarly bad one, at Amsterdam, where, if the main feature, an inquisitive puppy, does not immobilize your gaze, you look out through a door to a passing little girl with a fishing rod, across a canal to sunlit houses. The eye returns to the starting point, and, again dodging the inquisitive puppy, finds a seated lady, her attention divided between a puppy on one knee and a letter on the other. A male attendant offers her what may be either another letter or a cracker. She ignores the offer. This rambling inventory is hardly more incoherent than the picture itself.

De Hooch's decline suggests that, with all his skill, his reserves of taste and character were too small to cope with the demoralizing influence of Amsterdam. I feel, but cannot substantiate the surmise, that during the nine good years at Delft, Vermeer may have been a steadying and encouraging influence, perhaps as much through personal advice as through the example of his art. In any case, the really precious residuum of De Hooch's pictures were all painted almost within hailing distance of Vermeer's house.

Chiefly because he practiced the "dark manner," Gerard Terborch is considered in this chapter. He has the distinction of being the only Dutch genre painter with the experience and outlook of a man of the world. His art has a corresponding narrowness and refinement. He has a gentleman's dread of overstatement, and his pictures, mostly executed in grays and blacks with a single flash of positive color, are marvels of an entirely reticent emphasis. Beyond his own world he has no curiosity and makes no explorations. It is the world of his boon companions, officers off duty and variously on pleasure bent. One sees the officer bargaining for a girl's favors, Paris; at his ease in a well-conducted brothel, Amsterdam and Berlin; interrupted in his dalliance by the unwelcome appearance of an orderly, The Hague. The theme of the officer in search of his woman is carried back to the guardroom in two pictures at The Hague, the Officer writing and the Officer reading a Letter. This life he presumably knew at first hand and it may have been especially vivid to him, for a brother had died gallantly when the Dutch fleet vaingloriously invaded the Thames.

These pictures imply a very simple pattern for living. It is man's function to pursue and possess, woman's function to accept the situation sensibly and gracefully—to attract pursuit and reward possession. Terborch never shows any misgivings over his faith in the conquering male. He exploits the theme absolutely without criticism and with that imperturbable veracity which, two hundred and more years later, Guy de Maupassant was to exemplify in fiction.

Occasionally in his later years Terborch paints women of good social class, taking music lessons, receiving visits, at their toilette. But it is still a man's world. His women are pliant, feline creatures whose charm is for man's benefit and at man's disposal. In the few conversation pieces of this sort, the early attitude has only changed to the extent that the man of the world or officer off duty is provisionally on his good behavior, remaining, after all, the same dominating and predatory male.

Gerard Terborch was born in 1617, at Zwolle, central port of the Zuyder Zee. His father, an unsuccessful painter, but a widely traveled and acquainted man, had settled down to making his living as tax collector. Three marriages were blessed by no less than twelve children, half of whom developed as amateur painters, musicians, or both. The father, a man of considerable education and of ready sympathies, was proud of his talented brood, and did what he could to further their interests. There are drawings by Gerard as early as his eighth year, and really spirited sketches of skaters which he did at fourteen. At eighteen, Terborch was at Amsterdam, having earlier been a pupil of Pieter Molyn at Haarlem. It speaks for his independence that, seeing in the impressionable years the most brilliant painting in the world, the mere boy maintained the sobriety of his own handling and outlook. Before he was twenty he had visited England. Probably he painted there some of those characterful little oval half-lengths and full-length portraits which we are unable to date. Indeed, it seems that before his fifties his activity was chiefly in small portraiture. Probably he found the competition at Amsterdam too pressing, for in 1646, at twenty-nine, he went to Münster, in Westphalia, to profit by the peace conference—much as ambitious young portrait painters naturally went to Versailles in 1920.

The permanent result from this adventure was the extraordinary little group, the Delegates swearing to the Peace Treaty (Fig. 296), London. The picture is of 1648. The group is composed with clarity and dignity, the tiny heads have much character, the decorative character and impressiveness of the scene are well felt. Usually we feel sure Terborch practiced a gentleman's phlegmatism, but even he must have had a catch in the throat over the ceremony that ended the

Thirty Years' War and gave legal sanction to the independence of Holland. He seems to have painted this grand little historical piece on his own account, and not on a commission. It is not only intrinsically his most important picture, but also one of the most instructive for its sure and early date.

From Münster, having, according to credible tradition, won the good will of the Spanish envoy, Penaranda, Terborch went on to Madrid, where he painted a portrait of Philip IV and received the gift of a golden chain. Terborch's sojourn in Madrid raises the alluring possibility of relations with the art of Velasquez, which, in its objectivity, reticence and rectitude has much in common with his own. It seems to me that this possibility of direct influence from Velasquez has been too summarily dismissed. Velasquez himself left Madrid for Italy shortly after Terborch's arrival, but the works of his glorious prime were readily accessible. The somewhat heavy courtliness of their accent was thoroughly congenial to Terborch, and might have taught him much. In particular, the example of a workmanship which, without calling attention to itself, gave great emphasis to the painted forms, might have been valuable to a young painter who had been influenced by the overt and almost overadvertised dexterity of Frans Hals and his followers at Haarlem.

I feel quite a definite influence from Velasquez in the stance and compositional arrangement of the little full-length portraits of Terborch's maturity—the portly effigy of himself, at The Hague; two male portraits, Berlin; a Husband and Wife, London; and the very sensitive portraits of Jan van Doren and his Wife, in the collection of Mr. Robert Lehman, New York. Something entirely undefinable in the refinement of the lighting may be coincidence, but the setting of the figures on a floor rising steeply in perspective to the actual horizon, is rare in Holland and, I believe, invariable in Velasquez. The stance gains a piquancy from admitting the optical facts. Generally, in full-length portraiture the horizon is arbitrarily lowered in the interest of making a more stable base for the figure.

On St. Valentine's Day of 1654, being thirty-seven years old and ready to settle down, Terborch married the prosperous widow, Gertrude Matthyssen, who lived at Deventer, twenty miles up the Issel from Zwolle. He moved to his wife's property, became a magistrate, doubtless continued to frequent the company of officers off duty, and otherwise varied the possible tedium of public service and a childless

marriage by painting a few very fine pictures. He died near the end
of 1681, at sixty-four.

It is not the range but the intensity of Terborch's art that counts,
and for our purposes a few pictures will sufficiently tell of him. In
all, the interest centers on the figures, and the setting is carried only
to the point of suggesting the general character. Depth and sense of
space are of minor concern to him. So is atmospheric envelopment,
though it is always sensitively considered. The compositional patterns
again are generally of the simplest kind, deriving from the figure in
focus or the relations of the group. It is a rich and dusky world, that
of Terborch. The women wear sheeny satins, or velvet bordered with
ermine; the men are got up in all masculine bravery; generally a velvet
table cover of crimson hue echoes the richness of the costumes. This
art, which rests on the discreet use of really very simple elements, has
a singularly aristocratic flavor. It seems as if Terborch imposed himself almost as much by his eliminations as by his positive assertion—
just as a gentle person is almost as well known by what he never
deigns to do as by what he actually does.

A most characteristic Terborch is the picture miscalled Paternal
Admonition, versions at Amsterdam and Berlin. The traditional
title fooled as shrewd a critic as Goethe, but a little scrutiny of the
picture will show that there is nothing fatherly about the plea of the
confidently seated young blade to the fine young woman with her
back turned to us. Nor is the shrewd old woman drinking a glass of
wine a chaperon. She is rather a referee in a business matter with
amorous implications. The building of the group against the standing figure in a sort of sidewise pyramid is simple, odd and very
effective.

The same motive is presented overtly in the Piece of Money,
Paris (Fig. 297). This time the officer is too much in a hurry to
establish his winter relations to remove his corselet and change to
civilian costume. He makes no pretense of courtliness, but shows a
handful of gold pieces to the pretty girl who, without putting down
her wineglass and pitcher, studies the offering very thoughtfully. She
shows no more hesitation in considering the offer than he shows in
making it. On both sides is a world where the buying of a woman's
favors is entirely in the day's work. The contrast of types—the predatory male and his predestined prey—is effected without apparent emphasis. The picture is at once most concrete and a universal symbol.

Of the numerous pictures of women of his own class, those with one or two figures are the best. They have a quiet and irresistible elegance of mere execution. A couple of centuries later Fortuny and Alfred Stevens were to reveal a similar gift. The various Music Lessons and Concerts by Terborch all seem to me well below his best accomplishment. Perhaps the theme did not really interest him, and he tried not too successfully to give it animation. Such waiver of cool and impartial observation would be very impairing to such an art as his.

We perhaps see him at his painterlike best in such pictures as Lady in her Room, Dresden. It is just a view of the back of a lady clad in white satin, with the merest suggestion of a well-appointed room, but the costume tells a lot about a soft type of woman, living a life of privileged ease. More intentionally picturesque is the Concert, Berlin. A woman seen from behind bows the 'cello, while another woman, seated behind a harpsichord, plays the accompaniment. It is a picture which, in its bright and harmonious coloring and its odd pattern, competes with Vermeer, but with only partial success, for the placing of the distant figure is ambiguous. It could be a bust on the harpsichord. Again the elaborate pattern yields little sense of space. The mere painting of the back of the 'cellist is at once brilliant, restrained and sumptuous. While, on the whole, Terborch shows less gusto in painting honest women than in depicting the other sort, surely one of his best pictures is the Woman washing her Hands, at Dresden (Fig. 298). It is in the best tradition of Dutch genre painting. It dignifies an ordinary act without sentimentalizing it, it expresses truly and charmingly the artist's difference in attitude towards the pretty hands of the lady herself and those of the servant. The realization of a rich interior, though on a lower key, is as complete as Vermeer's, the touching off of details, such as the jug and the carved picture frames, is of a magical and entirely unpretentious dexterity, which celebrates not itself, but the object under observation. It is one of the most elaborately composed Terborchs, without any sacrifice of the simplicity of central motive, which is merely the desirability of a comely and well-groomed woman.

In summing up Terborch's accomplishment I recall the wise saying of George Moore about a kindred genius, Manet. In substance it runs: there is nothing but fine painting in him, and it is foolish to look for anything else. This is the general truth about Terborch.

But just as Manet through his fine painting after all expressed the\
attitude of a man of the world, so did Terborch two centuries earlier.
It is an attitude that lacks breadth, generosity and idealism, but it has
the advantage of coherence and of corresponding exactly to the theory
and practice of a large part of the human race. To express it dis-
passionately in any art is to help one both to see and to think. In the
art of painting Terborch expressed it with the completest clarity and
understanding. Irrespective of the value of the attitude itself, this is
enough to insure his minor immortality.

And there is another reason for respect towards Terborch. Living in social circles dominated by the new French elegance, as an
artist he never yielded to it. Where most of his contemporaries compromised, he retained to the end his Dutch probity. In so cosmopolitan a person this evinces sturdy self-knowledge and fine self-
criticism. Among the little masters of Holland, he seems one of the
best intelligences.

Chiefly because the still-life painters worked on indoor subjects,
and this small group is hardly worth a separate chapter, I treat them
here with the painters of genre. They remind us how completely the
Netherlands repudiated Leonardo da Vinci's dictum that the painter
should be universal. The still-life painters merely bring to an extreme that specialization which was the general tendency, and which
such a master as Rembrandt ignored to his financial disadvantage.

Before Dutch and Flemish still life emerged as a separate branch
in the 1630's, it had had a distinguished ancestry. From the Van
Eycks to Frans Hals the Netherlandish painters of whatever school
had painted it incidentally, with exquisite care. Its promotion to a
specialty simply accompanied the growing love of possessions in the
thrifty Low Countries. This still-life painting can be minutely classified by subject—as dead game, fish, flowers, fruit, kitchenware, tableware—but the two last classes are the most important. In such modest
arrangements of kitchen utensils and foodstuffs as Pieter Claesz and
Willem Claesz Heda loved, we experience that intimacy which is the
most endearing trait of Dutch painting, while in the elaborately composed breakfasts of De Heem and Kalf, with their magnificent porce-

lains, glass, metalware, rugs, etc., we have subjects that challenged the technical skill and brilliancy of the Dutch painter. In either the homely or pretentious sort of still life, the artist had the advantage over the genre painter, who must take his world about as he found it, of being able to make his little world to suit himself.

While the two sorts of still life were practiced side by side, the earlier painters favored the kitchen and the later painters, the dining room. The pioneer was Willem Claesz Heda. Born at Haarlem about 1594, he was headman of the guild in 1631 and died about 1670. His best pictures are of small dimensions. The elements are the copper and clay pots found in every kitchen, a loaf of bread, a cut ham, perhaps a wineglass for the sake of contrast. His arrangements are open and simple; he paints in grays and russets, with a fine regard for tone and texture, on the whole avoiding brilliant color. Luster and sparkle do not attract him. He likes rather the dull and mellowed patination of objects of common use. In these preferences he anticipates Chardin by a century, and while it would be foolish to equate his innocent charm with the magic of Chardin, the art of the two is of similar character.

Among museum directors and art dealers the favorite Dutch still-life painter is Jan Davidsz de Heem, and, indeed, his sumptuous breakfasts are brilliantly enough painted to deserve their popularity. But he seems to me fundamentally a virtuoso, more enamored of his own skill than of the objects he paints, and much inferior to such artists as Willem Kalf and Van Aelst. In contrast with such slightly older contemporaries as Claesz and Heda, De Heem multiplies colorful objects and paints them colorfully. There is little intimacy in his pictures. He tends to build up his compositions conically about some splendid metal ewer as axis. He loves glittering objects which abound in reflected lights.

De Heem was born at Utrecht in 1606, and possibly never fully outgrew the sleek and oily style of that city. At twenty he was at Leyden and married. He seems to have moved thence too soon to undergo the influence of Rembrandt and Dou, for in 1636 we find him free of the guild at Antwerp. There he made most of his career, moving back to his native Utrecht for three years, from 1669 to 1672, and returning to Antwerp to die about the end of 1683, the exact date is uncertain, at the good old age of seventy-seven. The German art historian, Sandrart, writes that De Heem preferred Antwerp because its markets supplied the biggest and finest plums and peaches during much of the year.

Far the ablest of the colorful painters of breakfasts was Willem Kalf, who was born in Amsterdam in 1622, and died there in 1693. He showed admirable taste in choosing and arranging splendid objects. He thinks most sensitively in terms of color. Frequently he sets his vessels on a crumpled Persian rug, the velvety texture of which offsets the generally polished surfaces of the tableware, while offering as well color notes which are echoed by the bloom of ripe fruits. His arrangements are not merely sumptuous, but aristocratic. Among the many superb Kalfs, the breakfast, at Berlin, with its bowl of whole and half-peeled fruits, its mounted nautilus shell, crystal pokal, and Persian rug, is one of the finer. Simpler and even finer in arrangement is an example at Detroit (Fig. 300). With all this richness there is no sense of ostentation. Kalf plays with forms and colors because he loves them, and not to show off his own dexterity. Apart from his still lifes, Kalf was a genre painter of much charm.

One could go on indefinitely with this minor theme, but the reasonable restrictions of a survey forbid. I cannot, however, leave the subject without a word on Abraham Hendriksz van Beyeren (1620–1677), who made a specialty of fishmongers' stalls, at The Hague. There is next to no artistic arrangement in his generally big still lifes. He takes his stalls as they come, overloaded with shiny, but also opaline, fish. But he commands a true and fine color and a magically swift and light touch, is in his specialty a superb technician. To see his equal as a pictorial fishmonger we had to wait nearly three centuries for William M. Chase. The value of Van Beyeren is simply his gusto, and it is enough. He painted as well excellent marines, in the general low tonality of his more famous fellow townsman, Jan van Goyen.

In leaving the subject of still-life painting in the Low Countries, it is the part of honesty to admit that the choice, out of scores of admirable practitioners, of a mere handful as especially admirable, may be arbitrary and more or less fortuitous. I am constantly amazed by the quality of still lifes by Dutch painters of whom I have not even heard. Possibly the fame of the half-dozen famous Dutch still-life painters may be due to distinguished patronage, to shrewd salesmanship on the part of dealers or of the painter himself, which early distributed the work of such privileged artists among famous collections where they have been constantly seen and admired. My guess is that there may be many more excellent still lifes by entirely unregarded painters in the storerooms of the museums which proudly display in their galleries their Hedas, Claeszes, De Heems, Kalfs and Beyerens.

And in a lesser degree the same elements of early luck may have fixed the standing of Dutch genre painters generally. It is a little staggering to realize that David Teniers II, at best a second-rate painter, has, from his own day to almost yesterday, passed for the greatest Dutch genre painter. Why? Simply because kings were his good customers, and the royal collections became the great public museums of Europe. Thus in any famous European museum you can see a dozen Tenierses for every Brouwer, Terborch, Metsu or Vermeer, and the numbers count.

It would be ungrateful to leave this theme without hailing the scores, probably hundreds, of Dutch genre painters of fine and sincere talent who, for one reason or another, have never attracted the attention of critics, dealers or museum officials. You may pick up their pictures for a couple of hundred dollars or so from the small antiquaries of any great city. You could fill the walls of a house with them for the price of a second-rate Post-Impressionist painting, and it would be a charming house to live in. Whoever hears of Abraham Begyn, admirable flower painter and proficient in many branches; of the Molenaers; of Martin Sorgh, painter of intimate interiors? These names must stand for scores. I sometimes feel that in many cases it is merely a sort of chance or luck that painters no better than these forgotten little masters have gained and kept prestige. However that be, no estimate of Dutch genre painting is complete which ignores the extraordinary high average of excellence of painters whom even the instructed art lover never so much as hears of.

## CHAPTER XIX

## OPEN-AIR PAINTING IN THE LOW COUNTRIES

Fig. 301.  Ruysdael.  A Waterfall.—London.

FIG. 302. (Upper) JAN BRUEGEL. The Windmills.—*Madrid*.
FIG. 303. (Lower) SEGERS. View of Rhenen.—*Berlin*.

Fig. 304. (Upper) SEGERS. Mountain Gorge.—London.
Fig. 305. (Lower) REMBRANDT. The Mill.—Widener Coll., Elkins Park, Pa.

Fig. 306. (Upper) Van Goyen. Landscape with Two Oaks.—Amsterdam.
Fig. 307. (Lower) Van Goyen. The River Mouth.—Bredius Museum,
The Hague.

Fig. 308. (Upper) Van Goyen. View of Rhenen.—Corcoran Gallery,
Washington.
Fig. 309. (Lower) Brouwer. Moonlight on the Dunes.—Berlin.

FIG. 310. (Upper) JAKOB VAN RUYSDAEL. River Scene.—Detroit.
FIG. 311. (Lower) JAKOB VAN RUYSDAEL. The Hunt.—Dresden.

571

FIG. 312. (Upper) JAKOB VAN RUYSDAEL. The Jewish Cemetery.—*Detroit*.
FIG. 313. (Lower) HOBBEMA. The Water Wheel.—*Amsterdam*.

572

FIG. 314. (Upper) HOBBEMA. The Avenue, Middleharnis.—*London.*
FIG. 315. (Lower) PAUL POTTER. Cow and Her Reflection.—*Paris.*

573

Fig. 316. (Upper) Cuyp. River Barges.—*Liechtenstein Collection, Vienna.*
Fig. 317. (Lower) Cuyp. Landscape with Cattle.—*London.*

Fig. 318. (Upper) Wouverman.  Cavalry Camp.—*Frick Collection, New York.*

Fig. 319. (Lower left) J. Berckheyde.  The Bourse.—*Amsterdam.*

Fig. 320. (Lower right) G. Berckheyde.  The Great Church, Haarlem.—*Detroit.*

575

FIG. 321. VERMEER. View of Delft.—The Hague.

THE PIONEER of realistic, Dutch landscape painting was the Flamand, Pieter Bruegel the Elder (1525–1569). Though he freely introduced Alpine features into his wide panoramas, these composite landscapes retained, after all, much of the character of the river plains of the Low Countries, and occasionally, as in the Harvest Scene, at New York (Fig. 185), and The Blind leading the Blind (Fig. 181), he painted the scenery about Brussels with ability and feeling. On the whole he preferred neutral tones to sharp local color, and this preference was to be formative for most landscape painting in Holland and Flanders for more than a century.

In a copyistic way his son, Pieter Bruegel II (1564–c. 1637), kept the paternal style alive and popular for an additional sixty years or so. By him we have, usually after his father's pictures, winter scenes with skating ponds and bare-branched trees. A more original emulator of Old Bruegel's tonal and panoramic landscape was Lucas van Valkenburgh (1540–1625). He was born at Mechlin, worked as far afield as Frankfurt-am-Main, but made most of his career at Brussels.

The tonal and panoramic vein was pursued also by Joos van Momper (1565–1635). He went to Italy, but brought little back except landscape sketches of cliff scenery, with which he embellished the foregrounds of his landscapes. His was an improvising and romantic spirit. Much of his work was of a minor decorative order, for the panels of doors, the inside of the covers of keyboard instruments, over-mantels and the like. He settled down to a formula—a rather cottony brown crag in the foreground at one side, a green middle distance and an artificially blue distance. He worked mostly at Antwerp and may be regarded as a link between the old tonal manner and the more colorful manner which was soon to prevail in Catholic Flanders.

Jan, nicknamed "Velvet," Bruegel (1568–1625), the youngest son of Bruegel the Elder, is again a connecting link between the two styles. In such a landscape as the Windmills, Madrid (Fig. 302), Jan, with some loss of strength, is fairly faithful to the tradition of the great father he lost when only a year old. In registering distances in atmosphere he is more skillful and modern. But Jan made the consecrated Italian trip when he was about thirty, and there he spent four years, 1593–1597. It was the moment when the landscapes of the expatriate Flemings, Mathys and Paul Bril, were in favor, and Jan must have considered their work admiringly. Their feathery trees, made on a formula of touches in yellow and bluish green, pass into his own later landscapes; so do their indigo-blue distances. The whole effect of these later Jans is highly artificial and tapestrylike. They were very popular, and are today esthetically insignificant. Jan became a friend and aid of Rubens, who occasionally painted figures into his senior's landscapes, Adam and Eve in Paradise, The Hague. Jan painted flower garlands around Madonnas of Rubens, was associated in one way or another as a collaborator with many of the best painters of Antwerp. He died rich, and Rubens composed a far too flattering Latin epitaph.

Except for Old Bruegel, the painters we have been considering are of importance only because they created a demand for landscape, which meant opportunity for their greater successors. The landscape painting of Rubens, which lies outside the local development, has been treated in the chapter on the Flemish school of the seventeenth century (Fig. 225).

In general, after the separation of Holland from Flanders the Flemish landscape painters, following the lead of Jan Bruegel and Rubens, worked in a rather decorative and colorful fashion, witness the landscapes of David Teniers II. The Dutch landscapists, on the contrary, continued the tonal manner of Old Bruegel, seeking, however, greater intimacy, more limited views, a more subtle tonality, and in most cases a more strenuous construction. As the Dutch landscapists considered profoundly the permanent characteristics of the scenery of their hard-won fatherland, they developed a convention. They observed the long, level stretches of meadows strongly marked by shadows from towering cumulus clouds, the interesting patterns of roads and canals; the bloom of brown and russet towns beyond their gray harbor; the impressive rise of really low dunes and hills from the general level; the torsion and density of great wind-resisting trees; the tense flicks of cold light on the crest of wavelets; the velvety reflections in quiet waters. To express all this emphatically they perfected a convention. Avoiding strong local color, they painted mostly in brown and gray. The browns might tend towards russets or yellow; the grays towards blue or, sparingly, towards green. Such was the convention that ruled serious landscape painting in the North until John Constable protested against the brown tree.

Admitting the heavy sacrifice of color required by the formula, it perhaps, after all, expressed what the Dutch painter felt about landscape better than the more colorful methods of Rubens and Claude. The Dutch painter took his landscape wistfully, if not tragically, and the brown-silver convention gave him the rhetoric suitable for his personal poetry. When you find a Dutchman or a Flamand painting joyously and in full color—a Rubens, Vermeer, Jan Both, Berghem, Cuyp—you find either an individualist or an eclectic indoctrinated from Italy. The brown-silver formula seems to originate in the painting of interiors—moderately in Old Bruegel, fully developed in the admirable church interiors of Hendrik van Steenwyck the Elder (1550–1603) and in those of Pieter Neefs the Elder (1577–c. 1657). Indeed, the simplest accounting for the convention is that the Dutch painter carried into the country the colors he had observed and the tonal preferences he had formed in his own mellow painting room, or in the narrow streets and shadowy arcades of his own city.

The first painter to put the formula to high artistic use was a short-lived and ill-fated man, Hercules Segers. His was an experimental spirit, for he invented a method of printing in chiaroscuro from the etched copperplate. One represents the unexampled theme of a town seen from deep in a room through a window. The rest of the sixty are mostly craggy landscapes. It was the study of these immensely rare chiaroscuros that enabled recent criticism to rescue the few painted landscapes of Segers from false attribution or from anonymity. The list hardly runs to ten.

Hercules Pietersz Segers was born in 1590, probably in Haarlem, and was trained in Amsterdam by the panoramic, old-fashioned landscapist, Gillis van Coninxloo. He was free of the Haarlem guild in 1612. Remaining notices are largely of wanderings to Utrecht and The Hague, and of debts. He married early a considerably older woman, who amiably received his natural daughter into the household. His last years were spent at Amsterdam, where he died in 1640, about two years before Rembrandt signed the Night Watch. Rembrandt cared enough about Segers' copperplates to buy a number, revamp them and sell the prints from them thriftily as his own. From these scanty notices one may infer an unstable, highly experimental and gloomy character—an estimate borne out by the feeling of Segers' etched and painted landscapes.

His only signed painting is the View of Rhenen, at Berlin (Fig. 303), and though it is probably a rather late work, we may well begin with it. Unlike the old, panoramic landscapes with the skyline set unnaturally high, Segers accepts the low horizon he saw, and builds up a vast height of veiled sky, which, though unmodulated, is impressive. The city is set back from a very dark foreground by successive strips of light and dark—an expedient which we shall see more artificially developed by Van Goyen. The church tower and the windmill, though they are tiny and barely rise above the horizon, have a sense of height and even of monumentality. The generally pleasant alternation of dark and light is varied by a glimpse of a river with reflections at the extreme right. Such features as tufts of trees are very thoughtfully placed, to give the greatest sense of distance. In general, the look is that of Van Goyen and his followers, but the general brown and gray tone has implications of pearly color. I think Rembrandt may have had this landscape in mind when in 1640 he etched his marvelous View of Amsterdam. The tranquil richness and amenity of Dutch landscape is fully expressed. It may represent a passing, life-accepting mood in an artist whose temper is habitually melancholic.

This melancholy is gently asserted in the larger Landscape with Cattle, collection of Sir Edward Speyer, London. The whole left side of the composition, a river under a hill, is kept very dark except for the bright spots formed by the grazing cattle in the stream. The expanse of water seen on both sides of a dark, wooded point is darkly lustrous. All this gives prominence and luminosity to the hilltop which rises bright before a dark slope cut by two dark towers. A windmill against the sky on the slope which falls to the right to end in the dark, wooded point is an animating feature. It seems to greet the breeze suggested by the thin, mixed clouds which marble a faintly blue sky. Few Dutch landscapes evince so deeply elegiac a mood.

Deeply tragic is the most accessible and famous of Segers' landscapes, which wandered to Florence as a Rembrandt. The balance is now at the right in a retreat of shattered crags. The foreground, a knoll, varied by dead or wind-beaten trees, is kept light. Beyond a dark middle distance, there is a hint of a distant river and of a hill above which a dark storm mist invades from the right a veiled but bright sky. The russets with which the crags are painted give much sense of color. Without insistence, the mood is that of impending storm.

The tragic mood of Segers receives its fullest expression in the Landscape at London (Fig. 304). One looks over a very narrow, dark foreground of boulders to a sharply lighted deep foreground from which a torrent bursts through a rocky gap bridged by a spiky log. Beyond, the river valley is very dark up to the meeting of the converging mountain edges with boiling clouds. The effect is ominous and fateful, as of a nature hostile to man and his works. The painting is here and there more heavily loaded than is usual in a Segers. From such a landscape as this Rembrandt might have learned much.

This brief survey will show that Segers, within his tonal convention, is really very various in his method of composing his landscapes. In comparison the contemporary tonal landscapes of Van Goyen are somewhat monotonously systematic. That Segers was a leading influence in the landscape painting of Rembrandt cannot reasonably be doubted. Rembrandt's beginnings in the branch, about 1638, coincide with Segers' too brief prime. Unquestionably one of the greatest Dutch landscapists, Segers was promptly forgotten, though his influence must have survived in Van Goyen and his fellow tonalists. One studies Segers with a mixture of regret and admiration, withal, of expectation, for there must be many of his landscapes lying about unconsidered which will eventually be identified as his. Future art lovers will know him more fully.

The fifteen or sixteen landscapes by Rembrandt have already been briefly characterized, and perhaps I should do well to let it go at that. But as I see this work in its setting of Dutch landscape painting, I feel there is a little more to say. As I review these pictures, I am amazed by their general romantic falsity and extravagance, by their unduly sensational contrasts of light and dark, by a treacly and unpleasant use of the prevailing brown sauce, by dark areas that are nearly empty and almost muddy, by energetic passages that seem energetic on general principles and not for specific effect, by a tasteless accumulation of untelling details. It should be recalled that most of these landscapes date from Rembrandt's tumultuous years from 1636 or so to 1646, and naturally share the overemphasis that marks too many of the other pictures of this period.

There are, of course, exceptions. The Landscape with the Baptism of the Eunuch, 1636, in a dealer's hands, at London, has many of the qualities of a fine Segers in its fine rock forms and impressive distribution of light and dark. The Evening Landscape with a Horseman, at Oslo, has a fascinating tranquillity and great probity in suggesting the barrier of trees against the sky. The River Landscape with a Ruin on a Hill, Cassel (Fig. 265), though badly cut up and overcrowded, has, after all, great fullness of romantic effect. Such pictures, for me, show a good but hardly a great landscape painter. The best landscapes by Segers and the best by Rembrandt's own pupil, Philip de Koninck, seem to me more handsomely organized, more sensitive in their tonality and distribution of light and shadow, and distinctly more faithful to effects of natural beauty. Rembrandt's standing as a great landscape painter, for me, hangs on a single picture, the Mill (Fig. 305), in the Widener Collection. While it is probable that he painted this tranquil vision of eventide, it is also uncertain. It was his habit to sign, and the absence of a signature on a picture of this importance is anomalous. A number of good critics think it a Segers. If so, it is his masterpiece. But perhaps such problems should not be raised in a book of this kind.

The general second-rateness of Rembrandt's painted landscapes is in baffling contrast to the perfection of many of his landscape etchings. They are much better in composition, in subtle modulation of light and dark, in finesse generally. Usually, but not always, the scene is more limited and intimate. From Rembrandt's time on they have been the inspiration and the despair of generations of landscape etchers. The etcher who would fathom every resource of the needle and acid bath must study the Omval; he who hopes to evoke air, light and distance by the open line must constantly peruse the Goldweigher's Field, with its strong and lovely calligraphy, and who would get the greatest effect of space and substance by linear accents must pin the View of Amsterdam on his walls.

Now the paradox between the greatness of the etched landscapes and the relative inferiority of those that Rembrandt painted may admit of a very simple explanation. Surely drawings for the landscape etchings were mostly made before the subject itself, and that challenged the honest realist which was one half of Rembrandt's genius. He was incapable of betraying nature when in her presence. But the painted landscapes were improvised and dreamt out in the studio rather irresponsibly under the direction of the other half of his genius, the undisciplined and extravagant romanticist. Such a view seems to explain the discrepancy.

It was Jan van Goyen of Leyden who perfected the tonal method of landscape painting. He was born in 1596 and early showed his volatile and restless temperament by seeking and quitting in quick succession no less than five masters. He married in his native Leyden at twenty-two, left it some thirteen years later, and in 1634, at forty, came to an uneasy anchorage at The Hague. There his pictures won popularity, and but for an incorrigible habit of speculating in many fields—pictures, real estate and tulip bulbs—he should have prospered. But our notices concerning him are chiefly of bankruptcies and forced sales. He would pay at a pinch sixty gulden for a rare bulb, while a picture by him fetched considerably less. Naturally, if the bulb market blew up, as it did, his end was inevitable.

All the same, in picture-making he maintained at a high level a constant and systematic activity. He sketched constantly from nature with the black pencil and thus assembled an extraordinary repertory of Dutch scenery and outdoor life which was easily convertible into painting. There are early landscapes which show much of the crispness and dryness of his ablest master, Esaias van der Velde.

While his characteristic subjects are river and harbor scenes, there are also pure landscapes of an effective character, such as the one, dated 1641, at Amsterdam (Fig. 306). Goyen, essentially a refined talent, here appears in an exceptionally robust vein. It already shows his characteristic dark foreground and his distance-making formula of alternating streaks of light and dark.

This somewhat arbitrary formula he applied with such refinement that one is conscious of it only on analysis. As he grew older, he holds ever more firmly to unity of tone, experimenting therewith in several directions—cold grays, green grays, brownish yellows. At times, particularly in the yellow Goyens, the convention obtrudes itself, but generally with his unfailing tact he makes it seem acceptable and natural. In his later years he preferred to paint big panoramic pictures—marines, towns seen over an expanse of meadows, or beyond tranquil or wind-swept, choppy harbors. In this last-named class of work he is one of the most vigorously truthful of Dutch painters. An admirable picture of this sort is in the Bredius Museum at The Hague, with its jumping chop over the shallows, its sense of weight in the fishing boats, its billowy, forward-coming clouds (Fig. 307). It is also exceptional for attaining spaciousness without much insistence on his usual conventions of alternating light and dark streaks.

Holland, with its abundant canals in humid polders, is the cloud-making country par excellence. Nobody in Holland studied clouds more carefully—their density, their distance. Goyen's clouds are always a canopy and never a mere backdrop. In his careful and sensitive observance of tone Goyen has remained an example for landscapists of that predilection up to Jongkind and Whistler. He is one of the few Dutch landscapists who has always been popular.

Before attempting a summary of his amiable art, I choose to represent his panoramic phase, one of his many views of the city of Rhenen (Fig. 308), so that we may compare it with Segers' smaller but much more profound version of the same subject (Fig. 303). Goyen's great picture, in the Corcoran Gallery, Washington, does not suffer too much in the comparison. It is more crisply executed and more consciously dramatic, and less subtle. It must stand for many distant views of towns, all scenically effective, but none in my feeling superior to this exceptionally somber example.

Of Goyen's work in general the cavil much later applied to Turner's—that they look like big water colors—may seem to be justified. That is, they lack something of the richness of handling which we have come to expect in oil painting. Again, it is possible to regret that he failed to capture Segers' manner of suggesting considerable variety of color within a unified tonal scheme. But, on the whole, I feel it is unwise to urge such might-have-beens. We do well to take great artists as they come, and in his own fashion Goyen was a great artist. His pretty daughter Margaret married Jan Steen and in many of Steen's pictures we may see what his genial and able but eminently unreliable father-in-law looked like.

Salomon van Ruysdael gave to the tonal formula a more robust and masculine character. While he uses the expedients of Van

Goyen, he uses them less systematically and with constant reference to nature. On the whole, he prefers more intimate subjects—river vistas with boats, houses and great trees prominent. He gives the substance and structure of such things with a pervading luminosity, and with a quiet personal poetry which would have won him greater fame, had he not, while anticipating the Wordsworthian quietism, also anticipated something of the Wordsworthian monotony. At his best he is quite perfect, and among all Dutch tonal pictures it would be hard to find one of a lovelier richness than the Canal Scene, at Berlin, dated 1642. Without any loss of strength it has a velvety attractiveness, and the relations of the forms of the clouds to those on the land are as precise and felicitous as those which were soon to be worked out by his thirteen-year-old nephew, Jakob. Indeed, it is chiefly as a link between Jan van Goyen and Jakob van Ruysdael that Salomon van Ruysdael is remembered. On his own account he deserves something more than that.

His life was a tranquil and stable one, with the quality of his pictures. Outside of his native Haarlem there is no record of him. Since he was headman of the guild in 1623 his birth must fall rather before than after 1600. He was honored and prosperous until his death in 1670.

The few landscapes of Adriaen Brouwer belong only partially to the tonal school. They are freer, less conventional, more intimate— in every way surprising in the painter of pothouse brawls. But the capacity for strong emotion usually works quite variously. One may imagine Brouwer dizzy with the reek and clamor of the tavern, heavy with liquor, finding welcome solace, release, and a sort of purification in the cool moonlight outside. Such is the mood of that most imaginative little picture, the Dunes by Moonlight, Berlin (Fig. 309). There are no precedents for it, unless it be, vaguely, Rubens, while it looks forward to Millet. Brouwer rarely again reached this height, but he painted a few other landscapes of a similar lyrical feeling—all improvisations and free from current formulas, all deeply impregnated with the character of a particular place and moment.

The greatest of all Dutch landscape painters, and one of the greatest of all time, Jakob van Ruysdael, transcends the tranquil character of the school. He is more intellectual, more tragic, in his last phase more consciously romantic. He was born at Haarlem in 1628 or 1629, and after preliminary studies as a physician, turned to landscape painting, probably under the instruction of the local tonalist, Cornelius Vroom. Though he adopts, or rather adapts, the tonal formulas, he does so with considerable differences of his own. Where the tonalists sought breadth and transformed portraiture of place in decorative and lyrical directions, Ruysdael at his beginnings seeks minute and specific truthfulness and objective portraiture of place. The style is descriptive.

An early River Scene, at Detroit (Fig. 310), clearly shows the style. The method is small and analytical, but also drastic and expressive. The innumerable touches are carefully calculated to give the effect of bristling growth in foliage and shrubbery, the torsion and substance of trees, the complicated etching of currents upon the water, and already there is a new unity of relation between the lights and darks of earth and those of the clouds forming a semidome overhead. Withal, though local color is subordinated, it is more fully indicated than it ever is by the painters of the brown-gray manner. The velvety play of reflections in the water suggests a possible influence from his uncle, Salomon van Ruysdael. There are many of these minutely studied descriptive pieces of the early 1660's, and they differ so greatly from Ruysdael's mature work that certain critics have doubted they were his. Since most of them bear his genuine monogram and all reveal a sort of intense research, the fruits of which are garnered in the developed work, such skepticism seems unjustified.

As he matured, his style grew in breadth and energy. The pictures assert a more personal mood—show something of the tragic tension of Segers and Rembrandt. The skies are finer and more actively in motion. It seems that Ruysdael moved to Amsterdam when about twenty-five, assuming citizenship some five years later. About this time, or somewhat earlier, we may date the vast and noble View of Haarlem, Berlin. One sees it under a towering, troubled sky, across dyers' vats in the foreground and miles of meadows and rivers. The grasp of facts is firm, but the facts are more thoughtfully selected, while the mood has changed from curiosity to an elegiac melancholy.

At Amsterdam Ruysdael worked out under difficulties the style in which he is incomparable. It is the expression of a soul that is burdened, but neither dismayed nor disillusioned. Long hampered by the need of supporting his father, Ruysdael never married, never knew guild or civic honors, never enjoyed even a moderate prosperity. A member of that mystic and ascetic community, the Mennonites, his religion was presumably of an intense and somber order. All this transpires from the great pictures of what we may call the dynamic style. Two centuries before Cézanne repeated the discovery, Ruysdael grasped the truth that nature is not static, but dynamic—built and destroyed in conflict of eternally warring forces. Great trees push up and down painfully and rise distorted by the perpetual protest of the winds against their growth. The earth is torn and shaped by destroying torrents; even the rocks hold their form more or less at the mercy of wind and water. Ruysdael's intuition of a perpetual Armageddon in nature gained esthetic validity through his perception that the strife becomes visible in mighty rhythms. So the observer of a great battle might find a terrible beauty in the geometrical orderliness with which the work of destruction was executed. The pictures of this style are no longer portraits of places, but deliberately composed in the studio to express these ideas.

These landscapes are not Dutch, but exotic. We enter a broken country where there are great spiraling oaks, crags, heavy waterfalls. We may be sure that Ruysdael sketched on the Lower Rhine, towards Cleve—the nearest point where such scenery existed—and virtually memorized its elements, as Pieter Bruegel a century earlier was said to have swallowed the Alps.

All the qualities of a dynamic Ruysdael are found in the Hunt, at Dresden (Fig. 311)—the chill of dank fenlands, the persistent strength of wind-ravaged oaks, the fine accord of cloud and land forms, the bleakly accurate play of light across swampy pools and the broken terrain—everything characteristic is here. It is a lucid, melancholy, noble and thoughtful art, without charm of any sort, and to appreciate it one must bring to it a certain responsive nobility and austerity of his own.

The theme of strife in nature found its most compact symbol in the numerous cataracts of Ruysdael. Here the master spent himself in realizing the gnawing force of the tumbling water, and in echoing it in twisting tree trunks with branches warped or shattered by the winds. Clouds beaten into shape and driven about by the winds carry the motive into the sky. A Waterfall (Fig. 301), at London, expresses the mood of the class. It has, as is frequently the case, just a hint of habitation, as if to remind us how provisional and hazardous man's tenure is amid these inconscient energies of nature. We have reasonably supposed that Ruysdael had explored the little watercourses that join the Rhine below Düsseldorf, but it is unlikely that he had ever seen a powerful waterfall with his outer eye. Hence it has been suggested that he got the necessary data from a younger contemporary, Allart van Everdingen, who had etched and painted cataracts in Norway. A waterfall of his, at Dresden, shows Everdingen's competence, and as well the very small element of subjective interpretation in his art. At most, I feel, Everdingen may have suggested the interest of the theme to Ruysdael. As for data, an artist of Ruysdael's constructive imagination could easily have made his big waterfalls from sketches made along the brooks near Cleve or from simple observation of the water rushing over the tail of any Dutch sluice.

Earlier painters like Old Bruegel had painted snow scenes skillfully, but they treated snow as a friendly element, helping the hunter or gracing the nativity of Jesus. In the few snow scenes of Ruysdael, of which perhaps the best is at Amsterdam, he emphasizes instead the squalor and misery that snow means in a damp climate. Indeed, in this picture a moroseness of mood is emphasized almost melodramatically. Such exaggeration tells much about Ruysdael's attitude towards nature. One can hardly think of him as loving it, rather as profoundly impressed by the extent and variety of its powers. One feels a manly and necessarily tragic acceptance of the fact that nature is entirely indifferent to man's feelings or needs, and since nature is very powerful, her impartially wreaked forces are always contingently hostile to puny man. This seems to be the attitude that underlies most of the mature Ruysdaels. In his later years we shall see submission to the destructive forces of nature bringing about a kind of reconciliation and peace.

In the fertile middle period between 1660 and 1670 Ruysdael now and then returned with greater breadth and insight to portraiture of place. Here nothing is more grand than the justly famous Windmill, Amsterdam. In it entirely familiar elements attain a splendor both gracious and austere from noble distribution of light and dark, from simple veracity in the statement of vertical and horizontal relations, from a vast and moving system of irradiated cloud forms. And this larger and simpler organization is reinforced by every minor refinement. Hardly elsewhere in European art will you find such strong and delicate indications as those of the foreground reeds. For their like you must go to the great ink painters of China and Japan. And rarely elsewhere will you find familiar aspects of the world assuming sublimity without distortion or indeed obvious emphasis of any sort. The grand quietism of such a masterpiece is appropriate to the religious quietism of its Mennonite painter.

Other fine descriptive Ruysdaels are Wheat Fields, New York, and the Landscape, at Florence. The Wheat Fields is exceptional for the absence of the usual abrupt contrasts, for its construction in very large areas and gentle curvatures, which grow moderately tense only in the magnificent rising clouds. The Landscape, in the Uffizi, is especially instructive in the way in which the spiraling growth of the bent and blasted oak in the foreground is taken up and extended in the winding road, in the edges of the light and dark areas, and brought to crispness in the treetop, now dark, now light, against the sky. In order to emphasize this terrestrial rhythm, the sky, which is rare in a Ruysdael, is almost unmodulated. The curves below die in the edges of very distant and faintly defined clouds. The picture is composed on the principle of a musical theme with variations. It has the simplicity, clarity and effectiveness of the slighter compositions of Bach, with something of his unpretentious probity and fairly mathematical objectivity.

Many times Ruysdael studied the troubled surface of the North Sea, driving its murky waves shoreward over the shallows. There is no charm in such a spectacle, but there may be a tonic fascination. So Ruysdael made the theme his own in many a fine picture. Almost at random I recall the Beach, at The Hague, to represent the class. Where the professional marine painters, such as Backhuysen and Peeters, liked to make laboring and imperiled ships prominent, relating the scene to man's toil and interest, Ruysdael subordinates such features. For him the sea goes grimly about its own business, in which man is wholly unconsidered.

By 1670 Ruysdael was only forty, but he had suffered much from poverty and neglect. Apparently his health was impaired, for there is no longer any indication of study out of doors. These narrow days produced what the critics were to call the great romantic Ruysdaels. In his studio he now dreamed out great canvases of a more tranquil nobility than the earlier ones. The old subjects are repeated, but there is less sense of tragic strife. Above the cataracts now rises some hilltop warm in the evening light, a point where earth and sky meet in peace. Ruysdael has so far accepted the indifference of nature to man, and man's unimportance in the ongoing of nature, that he seems to find consolation in the fact. Indeed, his humility recalls the maxims of the great Chinese landscape painters, little as his practice resembles theirs. For both there was peace in accepting the world. There is not actually more color in these latest pictures, but there is more sense of color, more urbanity in the use of light and tone. These are emphatically mental pictures, made for consolation and chastened delight; as such they have no equals in Western art, save the great landscapes which Poussin had finished only a few years earlier at Rome.

Of these romantic Ruysdaels the most famous and perhaps the greatest is the Jewish Cemetery, at Dresden, an even more overtly dramatic version at Detroit (Fig. 312). The theme is nature endlessly consuming and renewing itself and incidentally annihilating the most enduring works of man. Not merely man's constructions, but even his best-planned memorials yield to the gradual attrition of storm, frost, eroding water, as to the more constant and slower process of decay. Such is the meaning of the picture as Goethe read it for us nearly a century and a half ago. It is full of symbolism behind its superbly decorative and emotionally appealing features. There is promise of the eternity of the torrent in the glimpse of boiling, wet clouds above the falling tombstones; behind the blasted oak a new tree burgeons in as yet intact beauty; death and renewal for nature— for us, what? As a good Mennonite, Ruysdael had the answer, but he holds it as a humble affirmation of faith, and paints instead nature's impersonal recurrences.

This picture is his testament. There are others equally noble and less tragic. It is unnecessary to enumerate them, for they merely repeat the theme with solemn variations. Meanwhile his own strength was failing. In 1681 he returned to Haarlem to enter the Mennonite hospital. The next year, being just past fifty, he died. No great Dutch painter had been so sorely neglected, and none save Rembrandt has left a greater fame. Ever since, such painters as have wished to pass beyond the decorative effect of landscape to its meaning have necessarily consulted Ruysdael. You may trace him in the sturdier aspect of Constable, and throughout the work of Théodore Rousseau. It was perhaps the tragedy of a somewhat like-minded painter, Paul Cézanne, that he could not or would not consult Ruysdael. Jakob van Ruysdael will never be popular, and he will never be forgotten.

Meindert Hobbema, an attractive landscapist in his own right, is, after all, chiefly important as a foil for Ruysdael. Born at Amsterdam, in 1638, he had the good sense or good luck to marry at thirty a maidservant of the burgomaster. The marriage, at which Ruysdael was a witness, meant political influence which soon brought Hobbema a small position in the wine customs, thus freeing him from dependence on his painting. He had already learned what could be easily learned from Ruysdael—the pattern of his fine skies, his general russet, olive and gray tonalities, his agreeable compositional arrangements. Beyond this, Hobbema added his own joy in the sparkling and shadowy groves about Amsterdam, in the pleasantness of old farmhouses, barns and mills. To express these likings he adopted an appropriate technique—swift flicks of the brush to suggest the crisp reflections from dense masses of foliage. His characteristic compositions are much like the early, rural Ruysdaels, but looser, less simple, with less strenuous study and more emphasis on habitation.

A thoroughly sound and cheerful Hobbema of this sort is the Water Wheel (Fig. 313), at Amsterdam. It is charmingly neat and intimate, and not much else. It would hang untaxingly and agreeably on any wall. It is entirely typical of some fifty similar subjects, for Hobbema never hesitated to repeat a good thing. When a great subject presented itself ready-made, he was equal to the opportunity. Such was the case with the Avenue, Middleharnis (Fig. 314), at London. Here, as the late Sir Charles J. Holmes has written:

"Hobbema's geometry enables him to make noble use of these large elements, to order his horizontals and uprights so that we may feel every yard of the plain receding to the village on the horizon with its quaint church spire, and then may follow the line of the poplars upward to that silvery sky with its nobly marshaled clouds."

It seems to be the only work that he painted after 1670, his thirty-third year, and it represents a rare moment of elation and expansion in a usually contentedly prosaic soul. For his last twenty years he lived on his pay, which was not enough to keep him from a pauper's funeral when he died in 1691.

The genial and accessible character of his work has made it episodically an influence over like-minded painters ever since, while its rarity has continuously given his landscapes an exaggerated vogue with museum officials and private collectors.

The last of the tonalists who need occupy us is the marine painter, Willem van der Velde II. Within his specialty of tall ships riding or drifting in a calm sea he is extraordinarily skillful. He finds unexpected beauty in the turbid North Sea. Under his brush its tranquil surfaces, damasked by currents, become gray-pearl, blue-pearl, brown-pearl, and these tints are carried in attenuated values up through the picture in broad, creamy sails and bossy clouds. He fully understood the essentials of the theme—the lightness of hollow ships afloat, the heavy sag of lifeless sails. Indeed, except for a panoramic emptiness and monotony in his large canvases, he is within his chosen limits quite perfect. He painted sea fights, with the big ships of the line doggedly exchanging broadsides, and more rarely he painted fishing craft in heavy seas.

He was born in Amsterdam, in 1633, and schooled by his father. In 1677 his manifest abilities as a naval painter drew him to England, where Samuel Pepys' new navy was already beginning to rule the waves. There Van der Velde lived out his life as official glorifier of the British navy, dying in 1701, at Greenwich, within sight of the great square-riggers which he loved so much. The very even quality of his work is well represented by Shipping in a Calm, at London.

Except for Van der Velde the professional marine painters of the Low Countries, such as Bonaventura Peeters (1642–1652) and Ludolf Backhuysen (1631–1708), of Amsterdam, are not impressive figures. The finest Dutch marines are those of Van Goyen and Ruysdael. Indeed, from Old Bruegel to Courbet and Winslow Homer, the principle seems to hold that the best marine painter is a good landscape painter.

Alongside the tonalists there flourished many painters who declined to make the sacrifice of local color to tone. To discuss them thoroughly would involve a digression impossible in a book of this kind. Moreover, most of them were Italianate, worked in a more or less exotic manner, and constitute at best an expatriate branch of the Dutch School. So I pass with bare mention such variously able painters as Nicolas Berghem, Jan Both and Karel Du Jardin. These were all excellent technicians, richer colorists and closer observers of natural appearances than the genuinely Dutch landscapists. As a class, however, the Italianates seem insignificant, perhaps because of their relative objectivity and their failure to reflect over their themes up to the point of attaining vital conventions. Adriaen van der Velde (1635?–1672), excellent painter and etcher, tempts to delay. In the 1660's he painted many landscapes and marines in full local color. He loved to introduce cattle into his pictures, and took the pains to make preliminary studies of them in clay. He was an accomplished technician, and, unlike most Dutch landscapists, painted the figure with ability. His are the figures in many landscapes of Hobbema, Ruysdael and half a dozen others. So good an all-around man, even if he be of the second order, cannot be ignored. Such a picture as the River Landscape, at Berlin, anticipates much of the charm of Cuyp.

Paul Potter is the most famous of the colorful landscapists of Holland. Born at Enkhuysen, in 1625, a pupil of his father and of Jakob de Wet, at Haarlem, he lived most of his short life at Amsterdam, dying in 1654, only twenty-four years old. These were years of strenuous research almost unguided by taste. A colorist he was only in the sense that he accepted local color uncompromisingly. His microscopic vision prevented him from using color harmoniously. But his minute fidelity promptly brought him popularity and profitable employment in portraying the massive horses and cattle of prosperous Amsterdam merchants. His chief exhibit is the famous Bull, at The Hague. It is a very big animal painted in a very small way. For its exaggerated, minute realism it has found a place on all the foolish Victorian lists of The World's Ten Most Famous Pictures. One gets about the same pleasure from it that he gets from looking at a well-conditioned bull, and there is really nothing more to say about it than, that for a painter barely twenty, it is a truly amazing diploma piece. There are many Potters in this small and cramped style, and a few more agreeable ones, such as the Cow and her Reflection (Fig. 315), at Paris. Painted in his last year, it shows that Paul Potter, without losing his zeal for the smaller facts, is beginning to study the larger facts of composition and atmospheric illumination. Its quiet sunniness and modest rural feeling suggest that Paul Potter was capable of a growth which fate did not vouchsafe him. But, since fine color is a gift and not a conscious achievement, I cannot imagine that Paul Potter could ever have become a great landscape painter, could seriously have challenged the laurels of such born colorists as Adriaen van der Velde and Aalbert Cuyp.

In the work of Aalbert Cuyp the colorful landscape painting of the Low Countries comes to a worthy end. He was descended from two generations of painters, and developed various gifts by inheritance. Beside his famous cattle pieces he painted pure landscapes, cavalcades, river and boating scenes, marines, genre pieces, portraits— and all excellently. This uniformity of merit, with the fact that few of the finest Cuyps have never reached the public galleries, has caused him to be taken for granted, as a good animal painter, and estimated below his worth. Actually, he is not merely a versatile talent and a clever technician, but as well a very original artist. His life was as uniform as his art was various. He was born at Dordrecht, in 1620, schooled by his father, married prosperously at the ripe age of thirty-seven, thenceforward alternated the occupations of magistrate, country gentleman and painter to his death in 1691.

In his early years Cuyp was influenced by Van Goyen. A River Scene, Berlin, shows Goyen's even, golden tonalities, but the forms are bolder, the arrangement and accessories less conventional, and the sky more varied and transparent. Already we find Cuyp's preference for centering the interest in the foreground and letting picturesque forms cut the low skyline or a hazy distance. What is virtually an amber monochrome has charming suggestions of color. An even richer Cuyp of this early sort is River Barges (Fig. 316), in the collection of Prince Liechtenstein, Vienna. The monumental scale of the sailing barges and their sense of flotation is given with admirable directness. The painting of the water full of reflections and of the clouds responding to a change of wind is amazingly varied and expressive. At times the color is applied with the thinness of a watercolor wash; again it is loaded heavily, and these loadings become coruscations. It is a subject that has been painted a thousand times, but I doubt if it has ever been painted better.

In the Landscape with Cattle (Fig. 317), at London, we find Cuyp's personal formulas completely and most skillfully developed. The foreground, instead of being a mere shadowy vestibule, almost constitutes the picture. The eye practically skips the middle distance and passes immediately to the vaporous distance. In the long levels of Holland there is no middle distance unless you find a high position. The foreground features of this picture, whether the tangle of brush and weeds or the forms of the cattle and their tenders, are broadly and strongly asserted in their ruggedness and lustrousness.

The shaggy hides of the cattle seem to soak up the dispersed radiance of a golden eventide. The composition is based on what today we call a close-up of the foreground group. Here and there it cuts the sky in the vaporous distance. That gives the group importance and sets the sky back. The effect of a golden late afternoon is one that Cuyp loved and often repeated with choice variations. The touching in of the luminous edges of the clouds in this picture is light and nervous and paradoxically precise and delicate. Here is a fine, typical Cuyp which justifies Fromentin's enlightening paradoxes concerning his style: "A fine and true Cuyp is a painting at once subtle and coarse, tender and robust, aerial and massive." Which means that Cuyp frankly accepted the dissonances of nature itself, declining to level them into a conventional harmony for the sake of the picture.

Cuyp's simple and reasonable formulas were readily adaptable to various subjects and scales. As foreground features, instead of the usual cattle, you will find bands of horsemen, strollers taking the air, even skaters. But the general distribution is always about the same, and it never seems monotonous, for it is nature's scheme as she reveals herself in Holland. There is an attractive picture of himself, well cloaked and seated on a camp stool, sketching a broad plain. An admiring groom holds the two fine horses while he looks over his master's shoulder. Cuyp was probably the only Dutch landscape painter who could afford to keep a groom and two saddle horses waiting as he jotted off a note in his sketchbook. Evidently he put his affluence at the service of his art.

To the end Cuyp maintained his wholesome love of the look of ordinary things. He was a country gentleman with a sense of the soil. Naturally this candor and veracity has endeared him for generations to the picture-collecting country gentry of England. In their hands his best pictures still remain. His influence survived, again chiefly in England, among painters who shared his robust taste, such as Loutherbourg and Old Crome. As long as men continue to love the rural scene, Cuyp is sure to be remembered and admired.

For the sake of completeness a line or two on Philip Wouverman, prolific and able painter of scenes in which horses appear—hunts, battles, pleasure rides, stable yards and interiors. Wouverman was born at Haarlem, in 1619, probably studied with Frans Hals, was free of the guild in 1640, traveled in France and possibly in Italy, and died at Haarlem in 1668, leaving behind him something like a thousand pictures for a working career of less than thirty years. He profited greatly from this quantity production, and his pictures have always been favorites with museum officials and collectors. Personally they leave me cold. I see their neatness, accuracy and animation, but it does not much interest me. His pictures seem to me to lack fine color and distinguished arrangement, to be rather good illustrations than fine pictures. I fancy the trouble may have been that his interest was exhausted with horses and riders and did not reach to buildings and landscapes. But in these matters the reader must judge for himself from the reproduction of a very good Wouverman, the Cavalry Camp, in the Frick Collection, New York (Fig. 318).

The Dutch towns, for their picturesqueness, well deserved portraiture. The painting of street scenes and architectural interiors became a recognized specialty. Such painters of church interiors as that of the younger Steenwycks and Neeffs and Emanuel de Witt need nothing more than bare mention. The work of Job Adriaensz Berckheyde has such documentary value, in preserving the look of changed or perished buildings, that we cannot ignore it. Berckheyde was born at Haarlem, in 1630, studied with Frans Hals and Jakob de Wet, and entered the guild in 1654. He traveled as far afield as Cologne and Heidelberg, and painted some of their famous buildings, specializing in church interiors. He died in 1693. He paints with great accuracy in a blond key based on warm gray, which gives more sense of out-of-door light than most Dutch pictures. Until one has seen a number of Berckheydes one is likely to overvalue this exceptional luminosity. From the study of a series of his pictures it becomes apparent that they really are of the class of architects' renderings. There is a formula for everything, and beyond noting the essential forms of buildings, there is very little observation. I feel the situation will be plain enough even in the tiny cut of the Bourse (Fig. 319), Amsterdam.

His younger brother Gerrit (1638–1698) had about the same training and followed a similar course. He preferred the outer to the inner aspect of buildings, painted a handful of good genre pictures, such as the Studio, Leningrad. He was popular with eighteenth-century collectors and thus has gained a prominence in museums beyond his importance. The Great Church, Haarlem, at Detroit (Fig. 320), is a typical work. The two brothers have chiefly documentary value today.

Of all the Dutch pictures in that richest of small museums, the Mauritshuis, at The Hague, the most startlingly original is Jan Vermeer's View of Delft (Fig. 321). It is an amazing thing to have been painted about 1660; indeed, it would have seemed a triumph in the Impressionistic 1890's. Vermeer accepts all the facts; there are no conventions. One enters the picture, not over the usual stereotyped dark foreground, but over a strip of salmon-colored sand, as pale in value as the adjoining blue-gray water. Beyond, there are cool reflections, while on its level site the city hangs lightly between lagoon and sky, its red roof tiles throwing off reflections here and there from the veiled sunlight. Everything is most sensitively studied, and has the quiet and penetrating beauty of all devout and meditative observation. It is this quality of permanency which makes the View of Delft superior to many apparently similar pictures of the last century, in which the mere registration of light, and sense of time of day, may seem to be captured with equal skill.

It is difficult and perhaps superfluous to bring our studies of Dutch portraiture of place to a single, critical generalization. At least the great variety of expression within an ideal of true portraiture may tell us this—that however realistic and objective the approach to nature, in a good artist nothing like literal representation ever results. From the outset, preference and selection produce transformations. The quality and type of attention force reorganizations of the actual appearance which are as personal as they are unconscious. Thus the forms of the painter's apprehension impose themselves on the picture as conventions which are expressions of himself as man and as artist. The thing seen is thus subtly and slightly, but also essentially reshaped in terms of a world which is uniquely his. What is nominally Holland becomes in a far truer sense several kindred countries —so many kingdoms of Segers, Goyen, Vermeer, Rembrandt, Ruysdael, Cuyp, so many domains of choice human spirits open to us if our own spirit be fine enough. And this inevitableness of creative transformation, even under the most realistic maxims and intentions, is perhaps the most valuable single lesson that the Northern schools of painting may give to the lover of art.

CHAPTER XX

SPANISH PAINTING IN THE SEVEN-
TEENTH CENTURY; RIBERA, ZUR-
BARÁN, VELASQUEZ

FIG. 322. VELASQUEZ. Las Meninas.—Madrid.

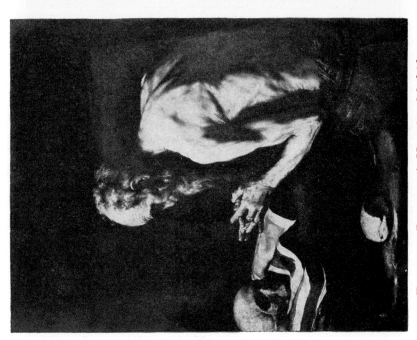

FIG. 323. RIBERA. A Hermit.—Madrid.

FIG. 324. RIBERA. Adoration of the Shepherds.—
*Paris.*

601

Fig. 325. (Upper) Zurbarán. Bonaventura Refers Thomas
Aquinas to the Crucifix.—*Berlin.*
Fig. 326. (Lower) Zurbarán. St. Hugo Enters the Refectory.—
*Seville.*

Fig. 328. Velasquez. The Poet Gongora.—Boston.

Fig. 327. Zurbarán. St. Mathilda.—Strasbourg.

FIG. 329. (Upper) VELASQUEZ. The Supper at Emmaus.—New York.
FIG. 330. (Lower) VELASQUEZ. The Maid.—Chicago.

FIG. 331. VELASQUEZ. Philip IV.—New York.

605

FIG. 332. (Upper) VELASQUEZ. Los Borachos.—Madrid.
FIG. 333. (Lower) VELASQUEZ. Joseph's Bloody Coat.—Escorial.

Fig. 334. Velasquez. The Sculptor Montanes.— Madrid.

Fig. 335. Velasquez. Head of a Little Girl.—Hispanic Society, New York.

607

Fig. 336. Velasquez. Prince Balthasar Carlos.— Fig. 337. Velasquez. Pope Innocent X.—Doria
Madrid.                                                   Palace, Rome.

FIG. 338. VELASQUEZ. The Surrender at Breda (Las Lanzas).—Madrid.

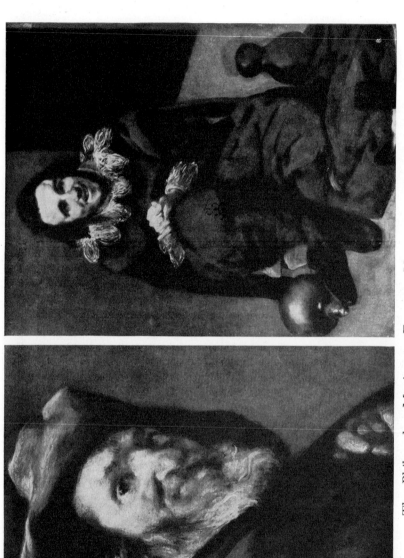

Fig. 339.   Velasquez.   The Philosopher Menippus   Fig. 340.   Velasquez.   The Idiot of Coria.—Madrid.
(detail).—Madrid.

Fig. 341. Velasquez. The Infanta Marguerite.—Madrid.

611

FIG. 342. VELASQUEZ. The Tapestry Weavers (Las Hilanderas).—Madrid.

D URING the second half of the sixteenth century the most progressive Spanish painters ostensibly were trying to master the secret of Renaissance grace and grandeur. What they were really doing, from the evolutionary point of view, was learning a new technique with which things seen could be represented with greater truthfulness. We have noted in their grandiose compositions the constant intrusion of incompatible, realistic features. This is the Spanish spirit seeking under difficulties to express itself. We have seen in Herrera the Elder (Fig. 200) an austere and drastic realism actually attained in the early years of the new century. All this is the necessary preparation for the Impressionistic realism of Velasquez, which is as unthinkable without its antecedents in the mixed art of a Roelas, Ribalta, Pacheco and Vargas, as Rubens' assimilation of the Venetian style is unthinkable without its antecedents in the mixed art of an Orley, Vos, Frans Floris and Van Veen. But before considering the culmination of Spanish realism in Velasquez we must at least glance at the work of two of his older contemporaries, Ribera and Zurbarán, both considerable artists in their own right, who may be regarded as a link between him and the Italianates.

Since the career of Jusepe de Ribera was made in Italy, and his direct influence probably slight in Spain, we must dispatch him with a brevity which may seem unmerited. He was born at Játiva, near Valencia, probably a little earlier than 1590. He came of a distinguished family. His father was adjutant at the important outpost, Castelnuovo, Naples. Ribera studied with the good Valencian painter, Ribalta (Fig. 203), who was somewhat influenced by Caravaggio's tenebrism. Probably at Ribalta's suggestion, Ribera went to Italy. He was for some time in the north, at Parma, Padua and probably Venice. Any influence from Correggio and the Venetians he soon shook off—Caravaggio's proletarian tenebrism influenced him permanently, though he developed a technique of his own. In 1616 he married at Naples the daughter of an Italian painter, attracted the notice and gained the patronage of the new Spanish viceroy, the Duke of Osuna, and throve mightily.

Like Caravaggio, Ribera chose his models from humble folk. He liked the character of old men, which had through the years corrugated their bodies and heavily lined their faces. From such models he multiplied character studies, mostly busts or half-lengths—laughing and sad philosophers, apostles. These Riberas have, for me, an unpleasantly aggressive quality. With every regard for construction and character, there is little concern with composition, color and the refinements of picture making generally. A superior example of these character studies is the nearly nude A Hermit, at Madrid (Fig. 323). Superficially, in its deep shadows and broad areas of light, the work resembles Caravaggio, but only superficially. Where Caravaggio effaces the brushwork, Ribera asserts it. The surface is heavily loaded and streaked, and this produces a positive coruscation quite unlike the smooth painting of Caravaggio. The method is very similar to that of Herrera, and it is possible that Ribera had profited by the study of Herrera's pictures before going to Italy. Ribera's color in these early pictures is hot and unpleasant and lacks harmonious relations with the sparse accessories and simple backgrounds. We have to do rather with powerful studies than with good pictures.

When Ribera paints subject-pictures, he chooses the most sensational themes. St. Jerome hearing the Last Trump, Naples, the Martyrdom of St. Bartholomew, Madrid, the Martyrdom of St. Andrew, Budapest, are still character studies with dramatic effect. Composition is obvious and unstudied. There is plenty of light, but no air. The construction is massive and powerful, but also disagreeably lumpy. The form is thrust out at you, as the expression was insisted on in the character studies. With all these defects the Martyrdom of St. Bartholomew is a very powerful and sincerely felt picture, the expression of an extraordinary talent, while the Martyrdom of St. Andrew is finely dramatic and, for Ribera, of unusual decorative beauty. It is the masterpiece of its time and class.

It was work like this that won Ribera in 1626 the honor of election to the Academy of St. Luke, in Rome. The scholar and critic, Jusepe Martinez, tried to get him to return to Spain, and he retorted that "Spain was a tender mother to foreigners, but a cruel stepmother to her own people."

When Ribera was in his late forties, 1635, his style changed for the better. The color becomes cooler and more harmonious, the construction less aggressive, the composition more carefully considered. Ribera's best biographer, Dr. A. L. Mayer, dates this change from the Immaculate Conception, of 1635, at the Augustinian convent in Salamanca. It is not a good picture, the Virgin Mary being singularly dwarfed by the wide margins crowded with tumbling cherubs, and the baroque swirl of Her robe is overcomplicated, but at least we have a reasonable distribution of light and shade and an approach to pictorial unity. It will be interesting to compare this Assumption with the later more successfully operatic and sentimental versions by Murillo and his contemporaries.

Perhaps the greatest picture of this mature sort is the Lamentation for Christ, at S. Martino, Naples. It is very large in feeling, poignant without sentimentality, and the faces are near enough the model to keep the effect idiomatic and Neapolitan, without waiver of nobility. The portraits and character studies of this period are more restrained and more effective than their predecessors of some twenty years earlier. The magnificent bust-portrait of a Musician, once Ex-Strogonoff Collection, now at Toledo, would live comfortably in any company. The St. Mary of Egypt, at Montpellier, has utmost intensity of ascetic character, and the relation of the gaunt figure to the craggy background is very handsome. Ribera's touch and taste are still uncertain. The very famous St. Agnes, at Dresden, is painfully sentimentalized. There is much pleasure-giving quality in the sturdy and lucid prose of one of his latest pictures, the Adoration of the Shepherds, at Paris (Fig. 324). In it we have an art of plain statement, without overtones of any sort, and it shows the normal mellowing of his harsh talent in old age.

To the end Ribera interpreted his task rather narrowly, as emphatic construction of form and assertion of facial expression. He seems to lack vision of the picture as a whole. Velasquez visited him in 1649 and doubtless was polite and complimentary to his famous senior. One would like to know what Velasquez really thought about Ribera's work. Ribera died in 1652 full of honors, leaving his stamp upon his Neapolitan contemporaries. About his memory grew up a legend of arrogance and violence. Here, though one cannot imagine him a well-balanced temperament, there is probably a certain exaggeration. It is the view that one would expect Naples to take of a very successful foreigner who was always called the "little Spaniard," *Lo Spagnoletto*.

The austere aspect of religious realism in Spain is best represented by Francisco de Zurbarán. The ascetic religious orders naturally made him their painter, and his best work is associated with monastic legends. His style is, paradoxically, tight, linear, and yet wholly painterlike. He uses freely the broad, dark shadow of the Caravaggians, but keeps it harmonious with his positive color. He modulates his smooth surfaces so that they express every sort of texture. His art is both emphatic and reticent, entirely other-worldly even when it seems most specific. He is in his own fashion one of the most uncompromisingly Catholic and serious painters the world has seen, and of all Spanish painters of the seventeenth century, perhaps the most Spanish.

Francisco de Zurbarán was born in 1598 of a peasant family in the village of Fuente de Cantos in Northern Andalusia. He early went to Seville, where first he studied under a follower of Morales, later with Juan de Roelas, and an obscure designer for embroidery, Pedro Diaz de Villanueva. I sometimes think the discreet luster of closely laid silk threads may have furnished suggestions for Zurbarán's very subtle handling of his paint. He soon became the favorite painter of the older and more ascetic monastic orders—Augustinians, Dominicans, Carthusians, Franciscans. It should be recalled that the reforms instituted by the Council of Trent had had a twofold effect upon the forms of Catholic piety. In the monastic orders, which were largely enlisted in the cruelties of the Holy Inquisition, the Counter Reformation wrought a new emphasis on faith and a return to severe discipline. Of this regenerated and hardened monasticism Zurbarán is the visual chronicler, unique for his power and veracity. But among the laity, particularly among women, the Counter Reformation, ably seconded by the Jesuit Order, fostered a new and highly emotionalized pietism, not to say sentimentalism. The Mother of God, whether in the Nativity or in Her Assumption amid clouds, must be a very pretty and appealing girl, monastic saints cuddle the Christchild, or passionately clasp the feet of the Crucified Christ. The attack upon the sensibilities is unsparing. Of course, Murillo is the painter who most fully visualizes this sentimental pietism. Zurbarán now and then makes concessions to it, and when he does so, in his Madonnas, Holy Families, youthful Marys in prayer or knitting, he is often sentimental to silliness.

Since there is really little development in Zurbarán's style we may omit relatively unimportant early works and pass to such a masterpiece of his early maturity as St. Bonaventura referring St. Thomas Aquinas to the Crucifix, Berlin (Fig. 325). It was painted in 1629, as one of a series for a Franciscan convent. Like all such series it was dispersed when the religious orders were suppressed and the single pictures scattered in many galleries. The legend behind this picture is that the great Dominican master of theology, Thomas Aquinas, visiting the cell of the Franciscan theologian, Bonaventura, at Paris, asked him the source of his divine wisdom. Bonaventura, turning his back on the shelves loaded with the books of the great Church fathers, draws a curtain and points to a Crucifix. Thomas Aquinas raises his hands in amazement. Behind him a group of four Franciscans observe the scene with edification and delight.

This is one of the most dramatic pictures of a time and race that valued the dramatic. But the drama is reserved and noble. Without knowledge of the legend one would feel some kind of a moral emergency. That impression merely deepens when we realize that a too rationalizing spirit is being recalled to the true source of all valid knowledge. Technically there are few finer Zurbaráns than this. It is hard, or in painter's phrase "tight," but its tightness is very expressive and precious. Much of the effect depends on the subtle modulation of the apparently hard and uniform edges. Here perhaps lies Zurbarán's technical superiority over Ribera. Compositionally the spotting of dark and light areas—the chair, Bonaventura's books on the table and shelves, the curtains, the crucifix, Thomas Aquinas' hand and white sleeve, the opening of the doorway—is brilliant and even exciting, introducing an element of animation into a generally very static design. Again, the apparently flatly painted, broad areas are very carefully varied to suggest the texture of woolen stuff or silk, flesh, wood, vellum—all this with minimal indications of greatest refinement, such as we expect rather in a Dutch genre painter than in a Spanish painter of religious legends. It is this paradox of a very painterlike exquisiteness in work that offhand seems entirely unpainterlike that constitutes much of the esthetic appeal of a fine Zurbarán.

The most grandiose, the most Renaissance in feeling, of Zurbarán's compositions is the Apotheosis of St. Thomas Aquinas, 1631, Seville. Below, in a cloister, eight monks or regular clergy look upwards to a vision where St. Thomas with his pen and book stands on a cloud that supports the seated Four Latin Doctors. The arrangement of the five figures is a foreshortened semicircle, which is repeated high up and further away by four holy figures in the upper heaven. In its general lines the composition goes back to some symmetrical composition of the Renaissance, like that of Raphael's Dispute concerning the Sacrament. El Greco's Entombment of Count Orgaz, at Toledo, might have been the intermediary, though Raphael's compositions were entirely accessible in engravings. The effect of the Apotheosis of St. Thomas rests largely upon the success with which realistic figures are fitted into a composition which would naturally call for stylization of the figures. Few pictures express so much spirituality through earthy elements. Zurbarán locates his vision in a loggia through the arches of which you look out to a Spanish cathedral square. Even the clouds which support his glorified saints seem as capable of meeting the weight as the roof of a limestone cavern. There is none of the conventional poetry which usually characterizes such subjects and compositions; instead, just a manly and sonorous devotional prose.

The pictures painted in 1636 for a Carthusian monastery are fine Zurbaráns, being free from Renaissance influence. The most striking of the series is St. Hugo entering the Refectorium (Fig. 326), Seville. Seven stern Carthusians are seated about a table at the moment of saying grace. From the right the aged and decrepit cofounder of the order, St. Hugo, totters in unobserved except by the waiter. The general sternness and stiffness of the composition is enlivened by the big picture on the wall and by the glimpse through a door at the right. The effect depends less on stylistic features than on energy of characterization and those refinements of workmanship which we have already described.

In 1637 Zurbarán was called to Madrid to paint the labors of Hercules for the royal palace of Buen Retiro. The work, in which assistants doubtless participated, reveals his limitations. He used vulgar models, exaggerated all muscular efforts, and in general did about as badly with the theme as any Italianate Flamand of the generation before him. For that matter, has any Spaniard ever painted a classical subject with any conviction—not to say, with any poetry? The sense of a lovelier and grander youth of the world seems simply lacking in the national temperament.

Dr. Kehrer writes that Zurbarán's chief endeavor was to paint the single figure in the most monumental way. This being the case, he is perhaps better represented by his best single figures than by his compositions. Eminent among many ideal portraits is that of the German mystic, Suso, Seville. It is remarkable for the gentleness with which religious ecstasy is expressed, and this tenderness is echoed in an idyllic landscape. Among the few pure portraits none is finer than that of a Reading Carthusian, Hispanic Society, New York. As usual, Zurbarán emphasizes, perhaps a little overemphasizes, awareness of a spectator. But the painting is of the most soberly sumptuous kind, the modulations of the shadows of the greatest refinement, and everything telling for melancholy yet steadfast character.

Probably the most famous and popular Zurbaráns are his full-length, ideal portraits of the best-loved female saints. He represents them as great ladies of his own Spain. Thus their rich costumes give him opportunities as a colorist such as his monastic subjects fail to afford. To choose among them is difficult. The most maidenly and decorative is the St. Elizabeth, in the Van Horne Collection, Montreal. I like a shade better, for its Spanish pride, the St. Mathilda (Fig. 327), at Strasbourg. In order to give the personage and the rich costume full value all the pictures of this sort are painted without accessories and with the simplest background. It should be noted that the effect is as massive as it is rich.

Possibly the exquisite technician in Zurbarán is even more apparent in a few still lifes which recent research has restored to him. In representing the rows of metal and pottery vessels arranged in a long oblong, Zurbarán commands the spectral emphasis of our modern surrealists, while, unlike them, he suggests the varying textures reticently but completely. The work shows the pure painter liberated from religious pressure.

About Zurbarán's latest years there is little to note except an intensification of his religious sentiment and an expression thereof which occasionally departs from his usual plain statement and enlists mystery. Such is the case with the St. Francis, London, where even with the face and eyes almost hidden in shadow there is the fullest sense of passionate prayer. Just as painting, the handling of the edges of the figure is consummately strong and delicate.

In 1658 Zurbarán was called to Madrid again and about that time received tardy recognition as a painter of the king. Very curiously he was a sponsor for Velasquez's petition for membership in the distinguished Order of Santiago, testifying that Velasquez came of gentle ancestry. In the later years there are hints of an unhappy influence from the youthful wonder, Murillo, in certain highly sentimentalized Madonnas, at which, after all, one does not have to look. Almost his latest and most remarkable memorial of himself is the strange picture in a private collection at Madrid which represents the aged and haggard artist looking up to the Crucified Christ. It is a very painful picture, in a sense a bad picture, but it is also a most impressive picture for its expression of deeply religious compassion. Shortly after he painted it, in 1664, at sixty-six, Zurbarán died. Upon his own Spain he left a lasting impression. In our grandfathers' time Gustave Courbet regarded him as a marvel. When at the end of the eighteenth century the Spanish religious orders were proscribed, the museums of the world were glad to buy his dispersed pictures, with the result that he is perhaps of all masters of Spanish painting the most accessible to art lovers generally. His incisive art is one of plain and complete statement and no painter less needs critical commentary. It is easy to see his limitations. To regard them as defects would be foolish, for of these very limitations he made positive qualities in his really quite various illustration of the theme of ascetic piety.

In the early years of the seventeenth century the realistic endeavor which for two centuries had been latent in Spanish painting found a robust expression in the work of Ribera and Francisco Herrera the Elder. Both consulted actual appearances most strenuously, but both inclined to reduce the infinite variety of appearances to a kind of monotony through their preference for certain formulas of handling. It remained for Diego Velasquez to fulfill and perfect the realistic endeavor by a consummately fine observation, by an amazing ingenuity in organizing his tints and hues so that they became equivalents of what he saw and felt in nature, by a technique as various and subtle as that by which nature reveals herself to a sensitive eye. To reach this perfection required nearly twenty years of constant study and experimentation. It was a course possible only for a painter under favorable circumstances, and I believe Velasquez's lifelong service as a court painter, which has often been deplored as a servitude, really provided the conditions which were essential to the flowering of his art. He was to suffer distractions and interruptions from his duties as a chamberlain, but his livelihood never was in question. In Philip IV he had a patron who let him paint in his own way. I doubt if Velasquez's art could have developed under any private patronage that Spain then afforded.

Diego Velasquez was born in Seville, in 1599, his father being of Portuguese and gentle extraction, his mother of patrician Sevillian stock. At thirteen Velasquez was taken from the Latin school and placed with Francisco de Herrera. Within a year Herrera's notoriously brutal manners had become unbearable, and the fourteen-year-old boy was articled for five years on very onerous terms to the cultured and friendly painter, Francisco Pacheco. No very definite influence of Herrera appears in Velasquez's early works. Indeed the fury of Herrera's workmanship, his combing and streaking heavy loadings of pigment about, must have been distasteful to a pupil who from the first sought refinement and reticence. Yet I am sure that on broader lines the pupilage with Herrera was fruitful. He was the only painter then working in Spain who knew that pigments may and should be convertible into colored light, that modeling is merely the registration of the significant degrees of light reflected to the eye from the form under observation. The task of Velasquez was merely to pursue this principle to its ultimate and exquisite consequences.

In the task Francisco Pacheco could help young Velasquez very little. He was, on the whole, a well-meaning and kindly pedant, with the saving grace of a lively curiosity as to the art of the present. He adored the Renaissance style and tried to follow it. Eventually he wrote a treatise on the art of painting, *Arte de la Pintura*, in which, with much good advice to young painters, he embodied the gist of the more important artist lives of Vasari, adding on his own account such information as he could gather concerning contemporary Spanish painters. Pacheco had the acquaintance and good will of the art-loving intelligentsia of Seville. To be his apprentice was after all an admirable training for a youth who was to become a court painter. The dignified and serious pupil readily won the master's favor and, just short of nineteen, Diego Velasquez married Pacheco's daughter

Juana. It is the last that we hear of her, but in the marital relations of artists no news may be presumed to be good news.

For some five years, with Pacheco's influence behind him, Velasquez seems to have practiced independently at Seville, painting, so far as surviving pictures indicate, rather tavern pieces (*bodegons*), and religious pictures, than portraits. In 1621 Philip IV came to the throne, called Count Olivares, a notable patron of poets and painters, from Seville to be prime minister. Scenting opportunity, Velasquez and Pacheco hastened to Madrid, without success. Two years later, in 1623, Velasquez repeated the visit, and through the kindness of Olivares got a sitting from the king. The resulting equestrian portrait was early destroyed, but it must have been satisfactory, for Velasquez was appointed court painter and, at twenty-four, assured of an adequate and permanent livelihood.

Of the score or so of pictures that have come down to us from Velasquez's six Sevillian years, none show any trace of the prevailing Italianism. All are soundly Spanish. It appears then that Pacheco had the good sense to let his talented young apprentice and son-in-law alone. In his later writings he deprecates in principle the painting of bodegons as an inferior branch of art, but approves them when they are as well painted as those of his son-in-law. They show the future great painter more plainly than the few religious pieces and portraits of this early period, but before considering the bodegons, a word on the other pictures. In such religious pictures as the Assumption and St. John on Patmos, Frere Collection, London; the Epiphany, Madrid; the Investiture of St. Ildefonso, Archbishop's Palace, Seville, nothing is very remarkable except the tenacity of the modeling in harsh contrasts of light and dark, and the Spanish types. We have the work of a very strenuous young painter coping with the difficulties of construction and character, acquiring his fundamentals. He hardly knows what to do with these hard-won elements, compiles them rather casually into pictures which in their metallic protuberances give an unpleasant sense of effort. But there is progress towards unity. The Supper at Emmaus, New York (Fig. 329), is really a transfigured bodegon, has dignity, a cool harmony of silvery color, while the swing of the figures of the disciples, and the outstretched, foreshortened arm of the nearer one, give a fine sense of space, which is enhanced by the transparent grays of the prevailing tone. The modeling of the face and the shoulder of Jesus is strong and sensitive.

The very detailed account of such features as the drapery and the tablecloth is singularly large in feeling. On the religious side, Jesus is merely serious and affable, the disciples merely astounded. The reading is adequate, not penetrating. It is, to repeat, a sort of glorified bodegon, as if, to the amazement of the honest frequenters of the tavern, a devout and dignified wayfarer were to say an unexpected grace.

The Investiture of St. Ildefonso has evoked little admiration, yet I like the asceticism of the saint who maintains before a miracle in his favor a hidalgo's imperturbability. I like, too, the practical sense shown in bringing the baroque cloudland peopled by Sevillian girls down to a level which makes the Virgin really bestow the vestment on the saint. A sort of housewifely carefulness with which she performs her office is most happily expressed, and is altogether entrancing. When one recalls the scores of operatically conceived St. Ildefonsos, the rigorous prose of Velasquez's reading of the theme will seem, not merely very Spanish, but very distinguished.

Of the three or four portraits from the Sevillian years, far the finest is that of the poet Gongora, at Boston (Fig. 328). It is modeled up in neutral tints with great energy, and though elaborately, with a fine sense of the larger forms of the hatchet-faced head. It has heavy passages—the unmodulated shadow of the farther side of the face, the unsatisfactory placing of the shadowed eye, the hard further contour which interrupts the rounding in space. With all these signs of inexperience, it conveys the somewhat vain and aggressive character of the self-conscious stylist and fashionable poet; is for a painter of twenty-three an extraordinarily competent and promising performance.

But it is in the bodegons that the future master most plainly declares himself. Of these tavern or kitchen pictures there are, according to the authority you consult, a dozen, more or less. With a single exception, the Water Carrier, these are all half-length character studies in oblongs, after the fashion set by Caravaggio and his followers. The Caravaggian tavern pieces, however, are in feeling a world apart from those of Velasquez. Where the Caravaggians rested their appeal on sensational human relations—generally on something strange, sinister, overtly picturesque in the action represented—on exceptional and exciting human relations, Velasquez dispenses with action altogether, or merely emphasizes the dignity of habitual and routine relations.

The few bodegons in which he seeks animation or drama—the Musi-cians, Berlin; the Old Fruit Woman, Oslo—are the poor bodegons. While the Caravaggians stood on the dramatic appeal of some odd event happening in the place, Velasquez stands on the worth and interest of the place itself, and of those persons who normally frequent it. One may say that to the end his art was merely a vindication, as against all sensationalism, of the thrilling interest of what anybody could see any time—if his eye were good enough.

What may be Velasquez's earliest bodegon is also one of the finest—the Maid, in the collection of Mr. Otto Beit, London. A good replica is at Chicago (Fig. 330). The sturdy figure of the girl, foreshortened as she leans over the table, dominates the long oblong. The curves of her face and white headdress are repeated along the bottom of the canvas by a fine assortment of kitchen bowls and pots, mostly in glazed pottery; one piece, copper. There is a suggestion of a tidy little world, of permanence and dignity. The posture of the girl preparing for her work is very grand. Velasquez has anticipated Millet in asserting the monumental character of the commonest useful actions. The modeling, through light, is at once very emphatic and tender. As in all his early works, the figure is pushed forward to the picture plane, but shows no tendency to transgress its bounds. There are empty or ambiguous areas at the upper corners, but they hardly impair the concentrated effect. The full lights on the head and sleeve of the figure, and on the kitchen gear, are most subtly modulated—no repetition, no wide intervals. For the work of an eighteen-year-old youth, this picture is amazingly complete and skillful.

The grandest of the bodegons seems to me not the famous Water Carrier, *El Aguador*, at Apsley House, London—superb as that great picture is—but rather Two Young Men Eating, Budapest. Though the figures and still life crowd the oblong frame, there is a sense of ample space. That is achieved by various means, the swing in and out of the figures, the foreshortening of the table, the carefully observed distances between the four rows of kitchen utensils on the table, but even more by the translucency of the all-enveloping atmosphere. The composition is very interesting. The roughly crumpled napkin is the central accent. Its mobile lights are physically exciting. All other lights are kept smooth and globular and tranquilizing. The heavier off-center weight and mass of the two men is oddly but effectively balanced by the greater number of lighter forms on the table to the left, and by the prominence given to the table top. The whole arrangement shows a sensitive regard for linear composition, which will soon yield to other interests. Again, in the grandeur discovered rather than imputed in these habitual postures and everyday acts, lies much of the greatness of the picture.

We may recall in passing that the mood is Spanish. In Spain a workman is still hailed as *caballero*, knight. Other painters of bodegons shared this mood. None expressed it with the integrity and finesse of young Velasquez.

It might reasonably be argued that Velasquez's first six years as a court painter mark a retrogression in his art. Certainly nothing made in this period is as pictorially accomplished as the best of the bodegons. These were years of re-education chiefly in the elements of construction. In the rich galleries assembled by Philip II at the Escorial and Madrid, Velasquez had before him masterpieces of Titian and El Greco. At the moment, they helped him little, if at all. Both predecessors indulged conventions of picture-making which were alien to his spirit. As for himself, he wished to approach natural appearances as much as possible without preconceptions, wanted the picture to grow out of the observation itself. It was an unprecedented quest in which he had to find his own way. Luckily, handsomely supported by salaries as a court painter and minor chamberlain, he could take his time without worry. And he was positively encouraged by frequent visits from the young king to the basement studio in the old palace.

The new manner is admirably illustrated in the standing portraits of Philip IV (Fig. 331) and of Olivares, at New York, both made in 1624. As pictures, both portraits, with all their impressiveness as readings of character, have an unpleasant stiffness and coldness. The forms seem rather casually set in the frame and tend to break through the picture plane. The merely silhouetted legs give an inadequate sense of support. There are dead areas in the expanse of black costume, and the accessories, just a table or a chest, are of little compositional value.

But these apparent defects are the result of calculation, and not of negligence. In observing the forms, Velasquez resolutely focuses on the faces and hands, which he models up with the utmost care. When the eye focuses on such points, the mass and projection of the whole figure is only vaguely seen and apprehended. He will paint the body and legs only as he sees them when he is looking intently at the face. It is easy to say that by waiving this principle of focus and optical center of interest, and painting the figure not as he saw it, but as he knew it to be, Velasquez could have made more attractive pictures of the king and Olivares, but he could have done so only on condition of abandoning that long quest which was to lead to his most personal and beautiful discoveries.

As modeling in light and dark, in careful gradations of tone, these portraits mark an advance over the Gongora and the heads in the bodegons. The modeling shadow is lighter and more transparent; nothing is lost in it. The edges no longer check the rounding away of the form. But the construction of the entire picture in modulations of tone is as yet beyond his powers. He comes to passages where the forms will not detach themselves from the background, and has to help himself out by arbitrarily whitening the background alongside the refractory edge. The contours of the Olivares show five or six such cobbled-up transitions. It is an expedient which Velasquez will employ for many years before he is able to make the tone tell everything about form and envelopment. The king and Olivares showed great generosity and open-mindedness in encouraging a new style which outraged the decorative and linear conventions of official portraiture in Spain, while lacking the charm of the popular Venetian manner.

It is a moment of acute self-consciousness for Velasquez, which results in such disagreeably assertive portraits as the so-called Geographer, probably rather a court fool, at Rouen, and finds its ablest and most emphatic expression in the famous and, to me, almost equally disagreeable masterpiece, the Drinkers, *Los Borachos*, Madrid.

Shortly after the painting of Los Borachos the great Peter Paul Rubens came to Madrid and worked in a studio in the old Alcazar near that of Velasquez. The younger and older painter, both men of the world, maintained friendly relations, though there was probably little that either approved in the other's work. I fancy Los Borachos would have shocked Rubens for its chaotic emphasis. He himself, during his nine months' stay, was mostly copying the king's Titians. From Rubens, whose decorative formality must have been distasteful to Velasquez, could be learned only that a plenitude of form could be expressed with smallest contrasts of blond tints. It was a lesson which Velasquez was already learning through direct observation of nature, and I doubt if the example of Rubens' highly stylized sketches did much to further Velasquez's new endeavor. But the generous and open-minded Rubens cannot have failed to recognize the prodigious talent of Velasquez, and also the fact that it needed some central principle of direction. It is a reasonable guess that Rubens' advice counted for much in Velasquez's decision to visit Italy in 1629 and 1630.

I think Los Borachos may have been Velasquez's challenge to the Italian and Italianate painters about the court. Lacking grandeur, grace, everything to which, while not commanding themselves, they gave lip service, Velasquez must have seemed to them just a journeyman portraitist of an inferior kind. It seems as if Velasquez may have decided to meet these cavilers on their own ground in an elaborate composition with many life-sized figures.

Evidently the gusto and vitality of Los Borachos (Fig. 332) easily put down the anemic work of the Italianates, and the picture has ever since been enthusiastically acclaimed. Such praise it well deserves for its power of construction and characterization, for its superabundant vitality. Yet a sum of superb parts does not necessarily count up to a fine picture, and this is far from being a fine picture. One thinks of a more genial Ribera. Everything to the right is a bodegon motive enhanced and taken into the open air. In a mock ceremony a drinker, nearly nude and burlesquing Bacchus, places a wreath upon the head of a kneeling initiate. In this group of unforgettable heads there is no principle of focus, no point from which the eye must begin its explorations. The total effect of the group is restless, lumpy and crowded. The two figures at the left are entirely alien and unassimilated. The foreshortened torso of the youth at the upper left has a borrowed, Venetian elegance; the seated figure below, silhouetted in an entirely unexplained and illogical half-light, again might have come directly from a Venetian pastoral. The Drinkers makes it clear that, having abandoned the chiaroscuro construction of the bodegons, Velasquez at twenty-nine had arrived at no principle under which he might organize an elaborate composition. It is as if he felt the need of study that he passed most of his thirtieth and thirty-first year in Italy.

Velasquez spent most of his time in Italy in Venice and Rome. Rome had very little to his purpose, for he was far in advance of the new Caravaggians, while the stately or pompous way of the Renaissance masters was not his. Venice, on the contrary, offered much to his purpose. The Venetian compromise between decorative and optical effect was to dominate his art beneficially for nearly twenty years. Just from whom he drew the new principle is not easy to say, and does not greatly matter. From the informal composition and general silvery tone of the pictures which he painted in Italy, or immediately on his return, I am inclined to guess that the colorful monumentality of Titian, Tintoretto and Veronese, attracted him less than the calmer tonality and looser arrangements of such outlying Venetians as Lotto, Savoldo and Moretto. It is of these masters that I am reminded when I see the two big pictures which he painted in Italy, in 1630, Jacob sees Joseph's Bloody Coat, the Escorial, and the Forge of Vulcan, Madrid. In certain expressions and attitudes they also recall the dramatic mood of Strozzi, who, during Velasquez's stay at Venice, was the leading painter.

Both pictures must be regarded as study pieces, and as such they mark a long stride beyond Los Borachos. In Joseph's Coat (Fig. 333), the pictorial focus is sharply established in the two jealous and lying brothers and in the coat which they hold between them. This involves a veiling of the figure of Joseph, at the right, in half-light, with a consequent attenuation of the narrative interest. The glimpse of landscape behind the group of brothers through the open door is felicitously managed and gives a liberating effect. The relation of the group of three to the rectangular aperture which it overlaps is happily felt. Velasquez is beginning to pay attention to pattern. The conscious effort involved in the composition betrays itself in the handsome but unfunctional posture of the nearly nude figure at the left, and in the two uncertainly placed figures in middle distance who are merely stop-gaps.

As a linear composition the Forge of Vulcan is more thoroughly thought out. Velasquez has found a function for the postures of the four brawny seminudes, and a sufficient topical motive in the almost irate astonishment with which Vulcan regards his celestial cousin, Mercury, who breaks the news of Venus's infidelity. The peasant masquerading as Mercury is inherently rather silly, but the classically draped form, with the torso and one arm bare, is at once the necessary counterfoil and echo of the four almost-nude smiths. The picture is well unified by a cool, silvery tonality, the accessories are skillfully subordinated, and the play of light and shadow about the space is handsome.

The next fifteen years or so saw the painting of all the most famous and popular portraits. Velasquez's construction is now both sure and various. He can make his tones say anything he wants, and at all degrees of emphasis and definition. He knows that a face looks one way under a fixed top light and quite another way in the diffused light outdoors and, outdoors again, the difference in appearance between the face of a sitter at rest or riding a galloping horse. He studies most assiduously the relations of tones in the ensemble, attaining unprecedented refinements in their adjustment. This adjustment is still somewhat artificial, in the Venetian manner. In as fully achieved a masterpiece as the Surrender at Breda, one figure receives the light from in front and a neighboring figure is seen dark against light coming from behind. Velasquez, like the great Venetians, as yet uses the light as a resource of stage managership, as an arbitrary means of emphasis or subordination. He is still far from the thoroughgoing luminism of his last years.

In composition again, with a less decorative feeling than the Venetians, he adopts their compromise between presentation in naturally illuminated masses and areas and presentation in agreeable and legible pattern. It is an expedient that is almost inevitable, as R. A. M. Stevenson has shown, when the field of a picture is wider than the natural angle of vision. In such a case, unity can only be obtained by the use of decorative conventions, without which the picture breaks up into several pictures or blurs off into illegibility. All this by way of preparation for the great masterpiece of Velasquez's maturity, the Surrender at Breda.

But before treating it, a word on the portraits. One of his earliest and best portraits of children is Prince Balthasar Carlos and his Dwarf, Boston. The general stately setting is one that Titian would have approved, but Titian would not have given the floor its rise in perspective, thus throwing the dwarf forward and lower. This acceptance of the actual perspective distinguishes most of the full-length portraits. It gives liveliness to the stance of the figures. The details of the little prince's costume are touched in with snap and precision. His head is constructed with infinitesimal gradations of blond tones, contrasting with the heavy shadow employed in constructing the heavy, moody face of the dwarf. This difference of treatment brings out the physical frailty of the ailing and short-lived little prince. His fixed, somewhat distrustful eyes singularly hold the attention. The total feeling is of rectitude, permanence and completeness, as if everything had been said that needs to be said, and not a syllable more. The date is just after the Italian journey, 1631.

Merely mentioning a number of indoor portraits of members of the royal family, which differ from those of the second period chiefly in greater ease of workmanship, we may pass to the portrait of Velasquez's friend, the sculptor Montanes, 1637, Madrid (Fig. 334). At first sight it is merely such a wholesome, full-blooded portrait as the Venetians, for example, Moroni and Francesco Bassano, produced in abundance. On closer inspection its superiority begins to appear. The head is constructed in a larger and simpler fashion, with modulations of fewer values, the definition of everything is adjusted with regard to its distance from the face, and this principle reduces the heroic head on which Montanes is working to a mere indication. A Venetian painter would have represented it completely, to the detriment of pictorial concentration. And while the Venetians, as born colorists, were adepts in the use of black, they rarely, if ever, created a black like that of the sculptor's coat, so lively, so full of implicit color. The sense of a robust, self-confident nature, fit for great executive enterprises, is vividly conveyed. Except in the treatment of the hair and beard there is no apparent dexterity, just the plainest and most inevitable statement of the visual facts. It is as if when painting a fellow artist Velasquez worked with a kind of humility and homage. Montanes was of a character to dispense with pyrotechnics.

Velasquez's unpretentious perfection in these years may be more readily grasped in the small compass of the Head of a Little Girl (Fig. 335), in the Hispanic Society, New York. The processes are entirely effaced. The fine, rounded face seems to bloom out of the background in all its dignity and graciousness as a mass of coral detaches itself from the seaweeds as your boat drifts over shallow waters. Of an art that conceals its art, this is one of the finest examples I know.

Velasquez, on the contrary, employs every audacity of handling in the outdoor portraits of these middle years, and logically, for the large scale of the pictures required a broader treatment, and a method at once more summary and emphatic was needed to make the forms and textures count in that great leveler which Leonardo da Vinci called "the universal light." The great pictures of this sort are all at

Madrid—the standing portraits of Philip IV and Prince Balthasar Carlos with their fowling pieces; the equestrian portraits of Count Olivares, the king, and the prince. The brilliant handling of these pictures is so obvious, their freshness and vitality so captivating, that they are equally popular with the layman and the connoisseur. It seems as if the naturally clean and silvery air had been especially washed for the reception of these great personages. Such details as purple scarves and gold trimmings are quietly splendid, but without the sumptuousness a Venetian painter would have given to such features. Here comparison of Titian's magnificent Equestrian Charles V, in the same museum with Velasquez's equestrian portraits, is most instructive. Titian insists more on his few color features; they have a value of contrast as against the prevailing neutrals. In Velasquez the positive color is merely the high note in a chord, is not different from, but in the general scale of, the prevailing neutrals. Again, because Titian keeps the key low and maintains a merely decorative unity of tone, he is able to detach his horse and rider without resort to such expedients as arbitrary irradiations around the contours. This dodge, which Velasquez had outgrown in his indoor portraits, is freely used in all these outdoor pictures. He has not arrived at the point of making the natural light create the sense of relief. But these illogical accents are in such decorative accord with the generally brilliant handling, that only a detective eye ever notices them.

In the three equestrian portraits, the landscape is treated with panoramic breadth. The eye sweeps easily over the miles between a brown foreground and the snow-covered crest of the Guadarrama mountains. In the Philip and the Olivares a fine poplar, with leaves that seem to twinkle, brings the sense of growth into the composition. In these landscapes there is steady progress in breadth and energy. In the Olivares, painted before 1634, the landscape is somewhat sensationally cut up, and the billowing clouds are theatrical. In the Philip IV, about two years later, all landscape forms are simplified and tranquilized. The level clouds which veil the sky echo the easy diagonal parallel lines of the landscape, the growing poplar is set further away. All this centralizes the energetic elements in the horse and rider. The dignity of the main theme is once for all asserted in its own right, and needs no repetition or extraneous advertising. The false accents of light along the contours used profusely in the Olivares are here frugally employed. Velasquez is learning that subtler registration of tone which gives assurance of form. The prevailing feeling of the picture is less of force, though that was probably intended, than that of a reticent dignity. The king, despite his cuirass and firmly held baton of a field marshal—compare the way in which the king holds his baton, low, level and inconspicuous, with the operatic way in which Olivares brandishes his—the king seems rather a distinguished aristocrat than a resolute military commander.

Interesting details tell us how the Philip IV was composed. A pair of hind legs of the horse, which had been painted out, have faintly reappeared, and strips about six inches wide have been added at the sides. It is evident that the composition was not thought out in advance, but corrected as the painting proceeded, and that even the size of the rectangle was not pre-established. The painter began with the leading motive, which developed its own accessories more or less unpredictably. A Florentine, who before painting fixed his composition irrevocably in a cartoon, would have been shocked at such a procedure. Even a Venetian, who had the habit of working out the composition approximately in a sketch, would have thought Velasquez's habit far too casual. It remained his practice to the end, as is shown by seams and cuts in many of his canvases. It may have been inevitable when the arrangement rested rather on very subtle relations and balances of tone than on anything so concrete as linear pattern and equipoise of mass and motion. With these factors known, the amount of space necessary can be foretold; when the bounds are merely those emanating as tonality and light from a central theme, no such pre-establishment of their extent seems possible.

I suppose the popular favorite among the equestrian portraits will always be the Prince Balthasar Carlos (Fig. 336) on the barrel-bellied pony that almost leaps out of the frame, before a spacious panorama of riverland, mountains and clouds. And for once the popular verdict seems to me sound. The picture carries the whole freshness of a windy morning with it. While the confident boyish face, and the large, fatal eyes of the lad soon to die are the center of attention, the eye readily grasps the snapping scarf, the bristling tail and mane of the pony and the active, docile mass of the beast, who rears as the little hand of his rider just feels the curb. I sometimes think one must have been a horseman fully to appreciate these equestrian portraits of Velasquez. So many painted horses are badly ridden. The diagonal plunge of the pony is magnificently increased by the opposed diagonals of the landscape. The landscape itself, with its sense of vastness, obtained with a few carefully chosen features rendered almost in monochrome, has scant analogies in European painting. One must seek them rather in the early landscape painting of China and Japan.

In none of his pictures has Velasquez paid closer attention to linear pattern, and he does so without abandoning his quest of the subtlest relations of tone. Thus the Balthasar Carlos combines the old equipoised composition of the Renaissance with that new principle of equipoised atmospheric relations which was his own discovery. All the portraits, indeed, virtually all of the pictures of the twenty years between the two Italian journeys, reveal the same compromise. In accepting the Venetian compositional scheme, while rejecting the decorative splendor of Venice, these pictures are not quite consistent. They look forward to a kind of picture which should have the strongest appeal, while dispensing both with the established compositional formulas and with the consecrated color conventions.

The masterpiece of this period by common consent is the Surrender of Breda, better known from its mass of lances against the sky as *Las Lanzas* (Fig. 338). It was finished about 1635, as one of thirteen mural decorations for a hall in the new palace of Buen Retiro, and this explains an arrangement which virtually omits the middle distance. What was to count decoratively at distant view was the picturesque mass of the group as a whole, such contrasting elements as the horse seen from behind, and a wide prospect of smoking, level country glimpsed over the heads of the soldiers or between the uncertainly held pikes of the defeated Hollanders and the rigid palisade of the lances of the victorious Spaniards. And all this was to serve merely as a sort of elaborate margin for the central feature—a magnanimous victor declining to humiliate a beaten foe, rather greeting him as an honored brother in arms.

This great invention really makes the picture. R. A. M. Stevenson has justly remarked that you could imagine these two central figures cut out and the loss in the marginal features would be surprisingly small. But a given space had to be covered, and the extensions of the theme are appropriate. In 1629 Velasquez had made the considerable voyage from Barcelona to Genoa in Spinola's train, and doubtless his chivalric courtesy in this picture corresponds to Velasquez's personal estimate of the man. Such an invention should dispel the legend that Velasquez was a frigid character, a mere technician. No frigid person imagined this meeting of the Marquis of Spinola and Justin of Nassau.

Even the best reproductions misrepresent Las Lanzas, push the figures too far into the foreground, diminish the expanse of the landscape, and the canopying effect of the marbled sky. But even in a mediocre reproduction the dignity and completeness of this greatest of military pictures is apparent. In order to harmonize with the other battle pieces in Buen Retiro, Velasquez had to follow what we have called the Venetian manner of composition, as usual studying the actual illumination more closely than the Venetians ever did. The picture was finished about 1635, ten years after the event commemorated. Spinola must have regarded it with mixed feelings, and with a retrospective consolation, for meanwhile his battalions, victorious in the Netherlands, had been shattered in France before the army of the Great Condé. Having himself tasted the bitterness of defeat, it must have pleased him to be immortalized as softening the defeat of a gallant foe.

As if to show that he could still paint a conventional subject in a conventional way, when Velasquez was commanded, about 1641, to paint a Coronation of the Virgin for the queen's oratory, he produced a picture that at first sight might have been made a century earlier, in, say, Brescia. Even the Madonna is a type. Velasquez repeats the formal symmetry of the Renaissance in the composition, and avoids baroque extravagance where it would have been effective, in the clouds and draperies. As his repudiation of the baroque, this picture is chiefly significant.

In January, 1649, Velasquez sailed for Italy, and made his way as quickly as possible to Venice. This time he came not as a student, but as a master, with a commission to buy pictures and engage decorators for the king's new palace. He bought chiefly the Venetians, notably Tintoretto's sketch for the Paradise. Passing to Rome, he was well received by such leading artists as Bernini, Poussin and Salvator Rosa. Salvator questioned him as to his favorite Italian painters and heard with amazement that Raphael did not please Velasquez at all. Pursuing the inquiry, he got the opinion that Titian was the "banneret of painting." The anecdote is interesting as showing a blind spot in Velasquez's taste, and as showing that, even for the romantic and ruffianly Salvator, Raphael's pre-eminence was axiomatic.

From Pope Innocent X came an unexpected and, since Velasquez was very busy, possibly unwelcome command for a portrait. To get his hand in, Velasquez painted the head of his mulatto assistant, Pareja, and then began the astounding portrait now in the Doria Palace, which Sir Joshua Reynolds was later to call the finest picture in Rome (Fig. 337). Perhaps no other portrait in the world grips so promptly and holds so strongly every sort of beholder. Why? Not for the usual reason of charm. The reds and whites in which it is painted are rather strident than harmonious; the man himself, repellent. There he sits eternally, sensual without geniality, choleric yet sly, and he is God's vicegerent on earth. I suppose it may be this disparity between the gross male and his sacred office that constitutes the irony of the presentation and much of its effect, yet I doubt if such considerations were in Velasquez's consciousness in the few breathless hours in which he made mere paint strokes give the look of the man before him. While the figure is admirably set in the frame in the Venetian fashion, no one would think of it as decorative or composed. The greatness of the work grows out of the sinister interest of the subject matter. Everything is rather discovered afresh than made after any pre-existing pattern. So this great portrait is at once Velasquez's highest triumph in what we may call his conservative vein, and also the prelude to the unprecedented masterpieces of his remaining years.

Velasquez stayed so long in Italy that the king, who valued his company as much as his services, repeatedly called him, and got him back in June of 1651, after an absence of more than two years. During this period Velasquez was too busy to do much painting. We may imagine him resting up and thinking much, and more or less disinterestedly training his eye to finer observation. The king appointed him marshal of the palace, which put him in charge of ceremonies, entertainments, of the higher royal housekeeping generally. It was a position that required tact and took much time. Knighthood promptly followed this honor. The king had remarried, and the entertainments for Maria Anna of Austria taxed the marshal's time and energy. Often he must have looked at two little sketches of the Villa Medici which he had brought back from Rome, and perhaps sighed when he thought how difficult it was to find time to realize what these modest studies foreshadowed.

These little sketches, at Madrid, simply show that charming concord of formal planting and formal architecture which still makes the Villa Medici one of the most delightful garden spots in the world. What composition there is is simply that of the architectural features in the foreground; the rest is bristling ilexes with the light sifting through, tall cypresses melting into the sky, clipped hedges, the tops of which draw down the light. There is no great variety or force of color, but the neutral gray, green and brown fully express the play of the universal light about the forms. In landscape nothing similar had been done, nor was this achievement to be equaled until after a century and three quarters young Corot painted at Rome.

The prophecy of Velasquez's fourth and final manner is found in certain character studies and portraits of court fools and dwarfs painted well before the second Italian journey. In these records of social nobodies Velasquez was perfectly free to experiment. What he was seeking is clearly shown in the full-length portraits of two vagabonds, Madrid, posing as the philosopher, Menippus, and the fabulist, Aesop. These figures, which nearly fill the space and are presented without compositional accessories, are more impressive than the royal portraits of the same date. The contrast in handling is instructive. The constructional planes of the Aesop are strongly and crisply asserted. It is the technique that Manet will later repeat with great mastery. The Menippus (Fig. 339) seems to be merely a varying luminous surface which becomes face, features, body, drapery, by some magical modulation of tone and light. One can hardly speak of workmanship. The brush simply bestows the light that is necessary to create the form. These pictures are usually dated about 1640.

This inscrutable technique reappears in several of those most pathetic portraits of dwarfs, notably in the lolling idiot, El Primo, and in the Idiot of Coria, both of about 1647, and at Madrid. The head and the lace ruff of the Idiot (Fig. 340) are documentary for the new style. There are no linear accents, really no edges, no sense of linear pattern, simply a rounding of variously illuminated forms in space. Velasquez has arrived at a complete synthesis, has found equivalents in pigments for those subtle modulations of lighter or darker tones which the eye reports to the mind and the mind interprets as forms.

On his return from Italy in 1651 Velasquez pursues a twofold course. The royal portraits are still conceived in the Venetian manner, but are brushed with an ever-increasing dexterity which is, after all, devoted to simple truth-telling. Notable among the royal portraits are that of the Infanta Maria Teresa, Vienna, all muted silver about the proud, warm face; the adorable half-length, unhappily defaced by a big inscription, of the Infanta Marguerite, Paris; and, perhaps most brilliant of all the royal portraits, that of the Infanta Marguerite (Fig. 341), now grown into her 'teens, at Madrid. In her absurdly stiff and hoop-skirted costume she becomes a princess of a luminous fairyland, in which the brush strokes that create the curtain and describe the cherry-red ribbon laced through her silvery frock are beyond their connotation a circumambient glory of light and color. It is one of the few official Velasquezes that seem to be joyously executed, as if he had emerged from long effort into a realm of effortless and rapturous creation. It was painted in 1662, a little before the master's death.

The Venus and Cupid, London, was painted five years earlier, in 1657. I would much rather not write about it, for it seems to me a badly over-rated picture, and since it is also a very famous picture, my view of it may be unpopular. Intrinsically, it is just an academy, an alert, slender female nude seen from behind. The method of construction is, for the moment, strangely linear. Naturally so, for the supple line that runs the length from the nape of the neck to the relaxed instep has interested Velasquez. I wish he had left it as an academy with few accessories, for the accessories which make a nude into a Venus are ill-chosen and untelling. The stuffy draperies serve no compositional purpose; the enlarged reflection of the face in the mirror is obtrusive and confusing, the plump, well-conditioned Cupid who holds the mirror is extraneous and silly. In short, the picture should either have been more naturalistic or of a more studied conventionality. Even granting the beautiful painting of the nude, the picture compares badly with the honest naturalism of Courbet and Manet in this vein, as it does with the provocative sensualism of Goya's Maya, or the artificial grandeur of Titian's Venus and Danaë. One should perhaps regard Velasquez's Venus as a very able but unsuccessful attempt to dispute Titian's inalienable laurels. Velasquez, whose intelligence was probably as narrow as it was acute, had not learned that there is no equivalence between a naked woman and a nude Venus.

At about fifty-seven Velasquez painted the two pictures, the Maids of Honor, *Las Meninas*, and the Tapestry Weavers, *Las Hilanderas*, which most fully expressed his lifelong ardor of research. For nearly a century they have been a bourne of pilgrimage for ambitious young painters of impressionist sort, and, despite the present vogue of anti-impressionism, it is hard to foresee a time when these pictures will lose importance.

Before considering them separately and carefully, a word on their composition. In both cases it is entirely unprecedented. The pattern of Las Meninas (Fig. 322) is fixed once for all by the character of the interior—the repeated rectangles of windows, a door, picture frames, the exposed edge of the big canvas on which the artist is working. Within the big, shadowy, yet luminous space which opens before you, the figure group forms at the level of the heads an undulating curve which counters the general rectangularity. The curve comes down and out to the picture plane in the head and body of the fine hound at the right.

Las Hilanderas (Fig. 342) offers a composition of quite a different sort. You look through a larger, dusky world, animated by the magnificent gesture and pose of the woman reeling yarn, through an arch into a world higher up and quivering with light, in which courtly women view a tapestry, their figures just distinguishable from its woven figures. It is a kind of picture within a picture—a fairyland created by the skillful work of the toilers seen in the nearer space.

Strangely enough, within a dozen years or so the finest eye among Dutch painters, Vermeer's, was to make compositions of much this sort, and, of course, without knowledge of these masterpieces of Velasquez. But Vermeer was to conduct his experiment on a small scale. It is doubtful if he could have carried it off on the scale of life. It needed the eye and hand of a Velasquez to heroize what are essentially genre subjects. In viewing Las Meninas I think one is first aware of the vast, dimly lighted space, of which the figures seem a sort of incident. Yet when you consider the group as such, it expresses a singularly tense solicitude for the lovely child in the center. R. A. M. Stevenson has justly remarked a devotion which has almost a religious character, like that of the saints in some Italian Adoration of the Virgin.

Perhaps the appeal of Las Meninas is chiefly technical. But here we should realize that the technique is merely the expression of a noble and gracious way of seeing. For the value of any picture is simply that it enables a sensitive beholder to experience the disciplined rapture of the artist's creative act. Everything depends on the fineness and breadth of the artist's vision. If he sees in a small and mean way, his king, his saint, his Olympian deity will have a small and mean effect. If he sees in a large and generous way, his beggar will have grandeur. Very rightly Delacroix insisted that a ragged Jew by Rembrandt could be as sublime as a Sibyl by Michelangelo.

This largeness of vision develops the appropriate technical means. The size of the picture is very carefully adjusted to the natural angle of vision. The natural spaciousness is maintained at all sacrifice. The play of the light in space is fastidiously registered. And all these factors in simple representation become as well elements in decorative effect. "Velasquez decorates a space by the use of tone more than any painter before him," writes R. A. M. Stevenson. It is an unusual means of decoration. The eye trained to swirling lines and balanced areas of positive color easily misses it. And because most of us see in a small way, it is easy to find Velasquez's airy spaciousness empty and uninteresting. His pictures, then, are an invitation and a challenge to see largely.

As for the magic of his tonalities, we can study his palette as he paints in Las Meninas. It contains only black, white and red. Yet the picture gives the sense of great variety and richness of color. All these technical values were first values of contemplation to Velasquez, and may be values of contemplation to us.

At first sight Las Hilanderas (Fig. 342) has a stranger beauty. Its values are those of action deeply contemplated. On closer study, the picture stands less apart than Las Meninas, falls more in line with established attractions, recalls, say, the athletic romanticism of Tintoretto. The picture was painted in 1657, a year after Las Meninas. It is as if Velasquez, having created a masterpiece along completely unprecedented lines, wished to show that he could create a striking novelty while working under established procedures. Except the inner room, the fantastic picture within the picture, there is little that would have struck Tintoretto and his followers as new or odd. Even the greater subtlety of construction would have been approved by a Fetti or a Strozzi.

The composition may be regarded as a sort of emanation from the superbly posed head, back and arm of the spinner at the right, just as the light from her flesh and her white basque seems to pervade the space in radiating diminuendo. The theme, in a narrative sense, is artistic creation in two aspects—that of the worker and that of the beholder. Velasquez asserts the grandeur of the mere work, and suggests the joy that work makes possible. The picture is more brilliantly handled than Las Meninas, with larger sweeps of the brush and heavier applications of pigment. Again I feel Velasquez had his favorite Venetian, Tintoretto, in mind.

The composition is exceptional in Velasquez in observing central symmetry—a formality well disguised by the variety, energy and absence of symmetry in the balanced elements. There are delightful subtleties in the balance, as the compensation for the lesser definition of the group at the left, in shadow, by its greater complication and richness of accessories. The ladder that catches the light alongside the portal is an indispensable element in composition. Without it the central symmetry would be too apparent. Again, it required utmost tact to give the courtly scene in the inner room its fairy charm without sacrificing its reality. Perhaps the larger motive of the picture is that of the two phases of the work of art, creation and appreciation, the work of creation is the more real and significant. Such a reading at least corresponds to the emphasis which Velasquez has given to the two spaces which constitute this great picture.

Of these two pictures R. A. M. Stevenson writes: "In keeping with its more lively color scheme, the composition lines of the Spinners flow more sinuously and harmoniously than the rigid forms of Las Meninas, and the masses twine and interweave in a more rhythmic and balanced pattern. Las Meninas is graver, nobler and more imposing, also less expected, less formal, and less aided by artificial elegancies of arrangement. Las Hilanderas is more supple and insinuating in its grace of pattern, more enchanting and varied in its treatment of color and detail."

I sometimes feel that this last great picture of Velasquez really marks a willing compromise with those conventions of picture-making against which he had consistently striven. Were these preconceptions and traditions really hindrances to seeing? might they not rather be helps towards seeing in a large way? If so, the part of painter's wisdom would be to use the conventions after his own fashion and not be used by them. Something like this seems to emerge as the teaching of Velasquez's career, that style is really a by-product of an endeavor that does not take it into account. In the case of Velasquez, it is the endeavor to see accurately and to find equivalents in paint for the thing seen. So he attained to innocence of the eye long before the phrase had been coined.

But the innocent eye, after all, only delivers raw materials to a mind that is more or less educated. Should the artist seek also an innocent brain? The question answers itself. We can only see what we are predisposed to see, but we may let our predispositions harden or keep them flexible. Only on that condition can there be progress in our visual experience. Velasquez's visual experience was one of continual progress. His style in his most characteristic work was as nearly as possible a by-product of accurate observation and faithful representation. Yet it would be an error—as fine a critic as R. A. M. Stevenson occasionally falls into it—to regard that Venetian tradition of picture-making which he habitually followed as cramping his style. Next to his exquisitely observant eye, it was probably the best thing he had.

In June of 1660 they married the Infanta Maria Teresa to the young King of France, Louis XIV. The ceremony, which was held on the Isle of Pheasants, in the river dividing France from Spain, had to be planned by the aging marshal of the castle, and apparently overtaxed his resources, for on his return to Madrid he was stricken with a violent intermittent fever, and a little past midsummer he died. He had won generous acclaim from fellow artists, but apparently the laity regarded him simply as one more portrait painter. His pupil, Murillo, was far more widely known and admired until about seventy years ago. In the eighteenth century the magnificent Velasquezes owned by the king of France were hung, not in the public halls, but in the bathrooms. Similarly, a great American art patron of recent times relegated the Cézannes to the servants' quarters. The critical rehabilitation of Velasquez came with impressionism, the ancestor and incomparable model for which he obviously was. Now that impressionism itself is everywhere in retreat, one would expect a corresponding abatement of Velasquez's fame. But nothing of the sort seems to be happening, which is perhaps a sign that his impressionism is, after all, merely one of many capacities that constitute his greatness.

# CHAPTER XXI

# THE SCHOOL OF SEVILLE

Fig. 343.   Murillo.   Vision of St. Anthony of Padua.—*Cathedral, Seville.*

Fig. 344. (Upper) Murillo. Miracle of S. Diego.—*Paris.*
Fig. 345. (Lower) Murillo. John Tells His Dream to Pope Liberius.—Madrid.

FIG. 347. MURILLO. Young Beggar.—Paris.

FIG. 346. MURILLO. Holy Family.—Paris.

646

Fig. 348. (Upper) MURILLO. The Prodigal Son among Harlots.—*Coll. Alfred Beit, Esq., London.*
Fig. 349. (Lower) MURILLO. Moses Striking the Rock.—*Seville.*

Fig. 350. Murillo. Immaculate Conception.
—Seville.

Fig. 351. Murillo. Soult Immaculate Conception.—Paris.

648

FIG. 352. VALDÉS LEAL. Temptation of St. Jerome.—Cathedral, Seville.

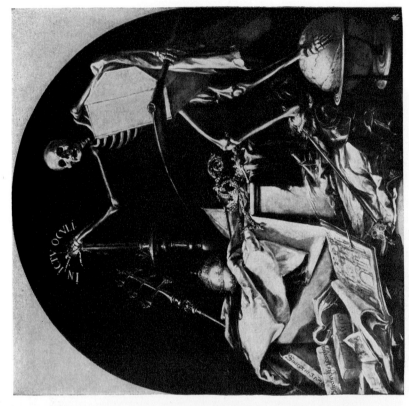

FIG. 354. VALDÉS LEAL. In the Twinkling of an Eye.—Seville.

FIG. 353. VALDÉS LEAL. St. Bonaventura,
Dead, Writing.—Coll. Sir Robert Cook,
Richmond.

Painting at Madrid, like the city itself, was to a considerable degree exotic and artificial. The artists revolved about the court, and, not excluding Velasquez, were conditioned by its requirement of pomp and decorum. It was not so at the pleasure-loving city of Seville. There had been effected the assimilation of the Italian style and its transformation into a native manner. There fell the gracious twilight of Spanish painting in the art of Murillo. While Zurbarán was strenuously studying the ascetic piety of the historic religious orders, Murillo was sharing and expressing the easy-going, sentimental piety of the citizenry. We are told on eminent authority that the mark of all true religion is other-worldliness. This quality Zurbarán had in the highest degree. But there is also a religion which meets the world halfway, consults its predilections, foibles and prejudices. Such a religion thrives not on authority but on persuasion. It was that sort of religion that the Jesuits fostered throughout Catholic Europe and nowhere more successfully than at Seville.

To this work of persuasion the orphan lad, Bartolomé Estában Murillo, early gave himself. He had the originality to perceive that the most persuasive object in God's creation is a pretty girl. Through her charm you could sell religion, much as today the pretty face on the cover sells the magazine. This discovery dictated the character of his art. Where the baroque painters of Italy and elsewhere offered to the believer the less persuasive fine-figure-of-a-woman, Murillo a hundred times offered the modest and appealing and invariably comely maiden of Seville. It seems as if he not only painted her, but painted for her. Nothing tragic in the Christian story was to shock her maidenly sensibilities. Among the nearly three hundred Murillos that have come down to us there are barely a dozen that deal with the cardinal event of Christianity, the passion of Christ. There are scores of big-eyed, girlish Madonnas looking out wistfully at you; scores of Holy Families with the genial old folks rejoicing over the young; in a dozen or so Assumptions the sweet Sevillian maiden rises cloud-borne to heaven, while pearly cherubs flutter about her ascending form. Or we have the Madonna or the Christchild miraculously descending towards the praying hands of an expectant saint. Such pictures are less hymns than the society verse of religion. In thus analyzing a certain superficiality in his outlook, I do not mean to disparage one who was in his own fashion, and when at his best, just short of a great painter.

He was baptized at Seville on New Year's Day of 1618; by eleven was orphaned of both father and mother. While in charge of a kindly uncle, a physician, he was apprenticed to the Italianate painter, Juan de Castillo. Castillo was about the only Sevillian painter whose manner was gentle and elegant. His teaching must have confirmed the tenderness with which Murillo was born, and must have turned the young student from those Sevillians who painted robustly and with monumental ambitions. The apprenticeship was probably short, for in 1639, when Murillo was twenty-one, Castillo moved to Cadiz.

We have virtually no pictures that can be dated before Murillo's twenty-fifth or twenty-sixth year. It is probable that he made his living by painting banners and temporary decorative cloths. It is clear, however, from his rare early works, that he had carefully studied the paintings of Roelas. In 1642, at twenty-four, he found the way to Madrid, where Velasquez befriended him. There he studied the Riberas and the Venetian masters in the royal collections, probably paying special attention to the few Correggios. The result of such studies was perhaps confusing, for he emerged neither a colorist nor a tonalist. He learned to paint flesh with great sensitiveness, but his ensembles are coloristically timid. He reduces the positive colors to tones or tints and harmonizes a rather characterless color scheme by painting in enough warm brown and amber yellow. The scheme is often attractive and generally adequate to its purpose; at times it is merely cheap.

A Holy Family, in the Heinemann Gallery, Munich, is certainly painted before 1642 and the Madrid years and is among the earliest Murillos. He will do such subjects with greater skill, but with no real change of point of view. Everything centers upon the upturned inspired face of the little boy Jesus, who walks towards us guided by His Mother's hand and reaching for the hand of Joseph. Above in the clouds a dimly seen God Father sends down the Dove of the Holy Spirit, while angels and cherubs hover in the clouds. Contrary to the Gospels, immensely old St. Joseph is represented as in his prime, proudly bearing his rod which blossomed as a lily. The multiple inveracities and sentimentalities of this picture need no comment.

On his return to Seville, in 1645, Murillo received his first important commission, the decoration of the smaller cloister of the Convent of St. Francis. He rose handsomely to the opportunity, and was not greatly to surpass the best work of this series. It betrays various influences. Angelic visions of St. Francis, at Madrid and the Palazzo Bianco, Genoa, suggest the study of Ribera and Zurbarán. Again, very like Zurbarán is S. Diego of Alcalá feeding the Poor, Madrid, for its carefully studied old faces and its loose and casual arrangement. The Death of St. Clare, Dresden, is surely composed under Paolo Veronese's influence. It represents the Virgin placing a rich shroud upon the body of the dead saint, while a throng of Franciscans at the left, and of virgin martyrs at the right, intently witness the miracle. The picture reveals Murillo's preference, despite his eminently baroque exuberance, for the stately compositional patterns of the Renaissance. It would be easy to argue that had he let himself go in a fully baroque direction he would have been a better painter. The present picture is one of the few that has the dignity required by the compositional formulas.

His originality emerges in its most pleasing aspect in the Angels in S. Diego's Kitchen (Fig. 344), 1646, Paris. While the saint is levitated by the force of his ecstasy, to the admiration of lay and religious bystanders, angels have come down from heaven to serve in his neglected kitchen. Two strong-winged angels form the axis of the composition, others are at work over the tables and among the pots and pans. The elaborate narrative is restless and disorderly as a composition, there are holes here and there, but the total effect is animated and charming. Throughout his career Murillo will show an inventiveness in pure narrative—in the series devoted to the story of Joseph, the parable of the Prodigal Son, the deeds of Moses—which he lacks in his conventionally prettified devotional pictures.

The year he painted these two pictures, 1646, he married. A son and a daughter entered monastery and convent. Another son disappeared in the New World. It is a reasonable supposition that the numerous Madonnas of this period represent the features of Doña Beatriz and their children. These are, or recently were, much-loved pictures, and in suggesting their limitations we must tread lightly. The real defect of these numerous attractive Madonnas is that they are a compromise between domestic genre and devotional art. The appeal of these Madonnas is simply that they are young and good-looking mothers very devoted to their baby. This is no new appeal. The Florentine painters of the fifteenth century and their Flemish contemporaries constantly emphasized the girlish grace of Mary, but they managed to convey the feeling that something more than ordinary motherhood was involved—they gave at least a hint of the mystery of the Incarnation. In Murillo's Madonnas there is no such suggestion.

In 1656 Murillo agreed to paint a Vision of St. Anthony of Padua (Fig. 343) for the baptistery of the cathedral. The enormous canvas, about eighteen by ten feet, was finished within eight months. It is one of the finest Murillos, the operatic treatment being proper enough to the theme. The nude Christchild stalks down His cloud-way with chubby arms extended towards kneeling St. Anthony, with his arms open to receive the visitant. The Christchild in His saffron aureole, surrounded by a border of hovering cherubs and angels, holds the eye. There is compensation for the baroque instability of the vision in the solidly realized form of the saint, in the effective silhouette of the table and the fine spot of His emblematical lilies in a vase; and there is reassurance as to the reality of the whole in the Zurbaránlike glimpse through a doorway to the palaces beyond a piazza. The whole picture is staged with taste and sensitiveness, so that the eye and mind readily accept it as a thrilling fact. Murillo has rarely commanded so thoroughly the resources that make for esthetic illusion.

Such work precisely met the volatile and pleasure-loving temper of Seville. There was no tax upon the intelligence; it went straight to the ordinary sensibilities. Murillo rapidly added to his already great fame and when in 1660 an academy was founded at Seville, he was the inevitable president. His work in these early years of maturity, his forties, can be treated here only in general terms. It runs from his successfully operatic Assumptions, through his egregiously sentimental juvenile Marys, St. Johns and Jesuses to his soundly realistic Holy Families. Perhaps the best of these is the so-called Virgin of Seville (Fig. 346), painted about 1670, and at Paris. Fundamentally it is a Renaissance composition, with superfluous baroque trimmings. An Andrea del Sarto would not have arranged the dense pyramidal group very differently. But, although he was a mundane spirit, his group would have had esthetic distance, would have seemed a Holy Family, without the testimony of God the Father to the fact. It may evince both the limitations and the tact of Murillo that he felt nobody would be sure his group was a Holy Family unless he cited the Father, the Holy Spirit and the cherubs as witnesses. Thus the baroque upper portion of his picture is in the nature of a gloss or commentary to explain that we are dealing with very holy personages. In an Italian Renaissance picture, even without any more specific religious inspiration, a more thorough stylization would produce the necessary illusion of other-worldliness. All the same it is a fine picture, and one of the best Murillos.

About 1665, in his late forties, Murillo was called to decorate in the Church of Our Lady of the Snow. He chose his themes from the charming legend of the foundation of Her church, Santa Maria Maggiore, at Rome. The pictures, in lunettes, are virtually illustrations, and as such they manifest Murillo's gift for narrative. The Dream of the Roman Patrician, Madrid, is one of the best of the series. As the patrician John and his wife doze, the Madonna appears to bid him erect a church where a miraculous summer snowfall shall mark the foundation. The handling of light and dark in the picture is very sensitively and quietly dramatic. Just in this technical regard it is unique in Spanish painting, and there are few real parallels in Italy. The light is directed to pick out the essentials of the Madonna, the sleeping pair, the white cloths, the precious bit of illuminated wall, but there is no sense of emptiness in the large areas where the light fails. Of similar ingeniousness is the companion piece, John tells his dream to Pope Liberius (Fig. 345), Madrid. Both the one-sided arrangement in the lunette and the play of the light are charming.

From now on such narratives followed, series after series. One of the best is the story of Joseph. Here the finest picture is Isaac blesses Jacob, Leningrad. The little scene at the right is sufficiently emphasized, and the marginal features in architecture and landscape are delightfully painted from the point of view of illumination. Other pictures of the series have idyllic landscapes which are rather superficially felt and without decorative arrangement. The date is about 1670.

Perhaps the most delightful of these narrative series is that painted somewhere about 1680, and devoted to the parable of the

Prodigal Son. The subject permitted contemporary treatment, and Murillo conceived it in terms of what he could see. The most richly painted of the series is the Prodigal Son among Harlots (Fig. 348). There is no moralizing, no sense of revelry in bad company. Here the contrast is striking with Dutch and Flemish versions of the theme. Dissipation is conceived as it was practiced by the privileged classes of Seville, as a gentle pursuit. There is little coping with the pathos and tragedy of the parable. We are in an atmosphere of romance tempered by the habit of good society. The Prodigal Son rides off adventurously from his sorrowing parents in the doorway; he runs ragged and disheveled before the threat of broom and rod wielded by harlots who have ceased to be ladylike; he prays expostulating among his swine in the posture of a tenor holding a high note; so it goes. It is a Sevillian rake's progress very sympathetically told by one who has a fellow feeling for the rake. One imagines in Murillo a very gentle spirit hardly capable of really facing suffering or even indulging moral indignation. Incidentally, the swiftly indicated landscape in the swineherd picture is spacious, romantic in feeling and quite worthy of its Venetian precedents. The pictures of this series are in the rich collection of Alfred Beit, Esq., at London.

In 1674 the ancient aristocratic confraternity of the Caridad, which had fallen upon hard times, was put on its feet again through the generosity of a patrician friend and patron of Murillo. He himself was honored by election as a member. For the new building he painted many subjects, most of which are widely scattered today. The most famous, Moses striking the Rock (Fig. 349), or, as the Sevillians call it, the Thirst, El Sede, remains in place, and is the pride of the city. Relatively, it well deserves its favor, for it is one of the finest populous narratives ever painted in Spain. Absolutely, it is neither better nor worse than the work of any one of a dozen followers of Tintoretto. Indeed, in the poses and arrangement Tintoretto is constantly recalled. Murillo can hardly have seen any important Tintoretto, but his pictures were available in engravings, and his compositional style was represented by Luca Giordano, who had painted much in and about Madrid. The main motive of El Sede is not very clearly asserted, for the people struggling for the water are deeply veiled in an entirely illogical shadow. As a picturesque ensemble and a repertory of charming and idiomatic motives the picture is notable, but it would be absurd to rank it with the great Venetian narratives which superficially it resembles. The companion piece, the Miracle of the Loaves and Fishes, at the Caridad, again combines skillfully enough idyllic features delightful in themselves, but it lacks fine compositional balance. From these pictures, painted in his full maturity, it would seem that Murillo lacked the capacity to organize these big oblong compositions into pictorial wholes. As compared with his minor compositions with few figures, the stories of the Prodigal Son, for instance, the big pictures, with their abundant felicity in details, seem pieced together.

I sometimes think that Murillo was a good genre painter gone wrong, that with more favoring circumstances he might have been a sort of Sevillian Jakob Jordaens. But a look at his famous genre pictures of street Arabs shows that the formula is too simple. These pictures are admirable for animation and character, but they betray an element of showmanship which is alien to sound genre painting. Murillo nudges you to remark on the picturesqueness of his waifs, and the waifs themselves are too often conscious of their own picturesqueness. One need only recall the integrity with which the Flemish and Dutch, or for that matter Velasquez, did this sort of thing, to see that the taint of sentimentality is constant in every phase of his art. It is at its minimum in the picture Street Boys, Eating, Munich, while technically one of the best of this popular class is the Young Beggar (Fig. 347), at Paris.

No less than fifteen times Murillo painted the Immaculate Conception of the Madonna, a subject visually indistinguishable from the Assumption. These are his best-known and perhaps his best-loved pictures. The arrangement is always the same. The Virgin Mary rises heavenwards amid a glory of clouds peopled by exultant cherubs and angels. The pictorial effect depends largely on the contrast of pearly flesh with masses of gray and brown. The Madonna is usually very young, wide-eyed and appealing, gracefully posed for effective display. The whole feeling is operatic; one can easily imagine an obbligato of coloratura melody. We are dealing not with that "eternal womanly" which Goethe in the closing lines of Faust says draws us upwards; we are dealing with the transient and evanescent spell of adolescent girlhood, arbitrarily enlisted in the service of pietistic sentimentalism. These facile Assumptions are in no sense great pictures. Indeed, most of them are quite flimsy merely as construction. But they are evocative of an agreeable confusion between the prettiness of chaste and gentle girlhood and the beauty of holiness. One yields to the spell somewhat against his better judgment, just as against his better musical judgment he yields to the crystalline elaboration of the singing of a choir of nuns.

For me the finest of these Immaculate Conceptions is the earliest, painted somewhere about 1660 for the Franciscans (Fig. 350), Seville. Compared with the later versions it is robust, in the broad use of light and shade, in the matronly aspect of the Madonna, in the powerful swirl of Her robe, in the energy of the few cherubs sturdily about their business of pushing Her up. Happy, too, is the thought to make the Madonna's eyelids droop as if for a last look at the earth she is forever leaving. In the later Assumptions the Madonna's wide-opened, lovely eyes all but ogle you. In comparison, this Assumption has power and self-contained dignity, is worthy of the great Venetian precedents which at first or second hand Murillo surely consulted when painting it.

Of the numerous later Assumptions none is finer than the so-called Soult Conception, at Paris (Fig. 351), painted about 1678, some four years before his death. The Madonna in her ascent has time to assume a gracefully statuesque pose. Her eyes are rolled heavenward, but I feel she is aware of their earthly appeal. Murillo has fairly squandered rosy cherubs, but he has disposed them cleverly, and by dividing dark and light diagonally, he has relieved a rather simple symmetrical pattern. I feel the ungraciousness of subjecting to any unfriendly analysis what is, after all, a sensitively magnificent achievement in showmanship. Given Murillo's defective conception of a solemn theological theme, the picture could hardly have been made better. And, such as it was, Murillo's religion was entirely personal and sincere. He gave to it what he had, and high seriousness was never among his mental or emotional possessions. There is a tradition that he often spent hours before Pedro Campaña's great Descent from the Cross, which at least proves sympathy for work more deeply felt than his own.

Early in 1682, while working on a Marriage of St. Catherine, for Cadiz, Murillo fell from the scaffold, failed to rally from the shock, made his will and died. He was appropriately buried in the chapel containing Pedro Campaña's masterpiece. He left abundant bequests for masses for the repose of his soul.

Though Murillo is commonly regarded as the most brilliant exponent of the so-called Jesuit style, hence as a typical baroque artist, the case, as Dr. A. L. Mayer has pointed out, is not so simple. The robust exuberance of the baroque is very rare in Murillo; its open dynamic patterns, which strain at their boundaries, he seldom employs. Instead he uses the compositional formulas of the Renaissance, but with little sense of their monumental value. His art, in its volatility, animation and susceptibility to adolescent female beauty, looks forward a full generation to the rococo.

Imagine for a moment that Murillo's principles had permitted him to paint the girls of Seville in their gracile nudity. Such pictures would have been tremendously alluring, and akin to the art of François Boucher. Deep into the rococo period in Spain itself Murillo's art retained its popularity and was continued by such imitators as Tobar (1678–1758). Alongside this potential rococo painter worked a good genre painter in the straight tradition of Spanish realism. One gasps when one faces the paradox that the painter of the Dream of the Patrician and of the parable of the Prodigal Son is also the painter of the Immaculate Conceptions. We seem to confront rather a versatile and sensitive talent than an integral genius, and the comparison of Murillo's best work with that of the admittedly great painters is simply cruel. It is also, I feel, unnecessary, for, after all, Murillo was singularly responsive to the easy-going romanticism of Seville, where between dueling, guitar playing and bullfights, you could agreeably fathom the mysteries of your faith in the big brown eyes of any nicely bred and pretty girl.

Vain, melancholy, violent, cantankerous—at Seville, Juan de Valdés Leal seemed the predestined foil for the too gentle and reasonable Murillo. Leal was bound to hate him for what must have seemed an unmerited acclaim. And there was this amount of reason in Valdés Leal's essentially unreasonable resentment, that he himself was unquestionably the richer colorist, the more powerful constructor, the more vivid and original imagination. I rather think there are more important Leals than Murillos, though here I have virtually all critics of Spanish painting against me. In any case, his scorn and loathing of Murillo was temperamental and inevitable. He could only despise Murillo's sweetness and superficiality. The littleness of Leal's resentment is expressed in an anecdote. He took Murillo to see his own charnel-house allegories, in the Caridad. Murillo, doubt-less half joking and perhaps half complimentary, remarked: "Com-rade, while looking at these pictures one must hold his nose." Leal retorted: "Yes, your highness, you eat the flesh and I get only the bones, but you have painted a St. Elizabeth at the sight of which I puke." Unduly strong language for Murillo's picture, now at Madrid, which represents St. Elizabeth delousing the sick, and a foul blow, for Leal's contempt was not for such an exceptional Murillo as the St. Elizabeth, but for that habitual sweetness which had made Murillo's fame. Unquestionably Leal's jealousy of Murillo produced a complex which unfavorably affected his own work. Most of his best pictures were painted in the seven or eight years after Murillo's death, when Valdés Leal was free to give more attention to his own practice.

He was born at Seville, in 1622, of Portuguese paternal stock. For his training we have only inferences. He probably studied with the urbane Italianate Sevillian, Antonio del Castillo, perhaps worked for a time with a kinsman who was an engraver and goldsmith. His early career was made at Cordoba, where he married in 1654, moving two years later to Seville to contest the laurels of Murillo. He was associated with the Academy founded in 1660 under Murillo's presi-dency, made himself a nuisance in its affairs, and ultimately withdrew from it.

Among his early Sevillian pictures, the Temptation of St. Jerome, in the Cathedral (Fig. 352), is notable. Valdés was about thirty-five years old when he painted it. It has a most energetic and dramatic character. The play of light and shade is sensationally effective. The silhouetting of the saint's head and shoulders against the bright aperture of the cave is very handsome. Where these tempted an-chorites are usually represented as immensely old and presumably physically immune from the temptation they seem to be undergoing, Valdés Leal presents a vigorous man in his prime who is really strug-gling against the powerful call of the flesh. It is also a refinement on the habitual motive of one woman overtly exercising her seductive arts, that Valdés Leal offers instead a bevy of attractive Sevillian girls about to sing and play—in short, a true symbol for what is most en-ticing in the world the saint has renounced.

The Assumptions of Valdés Leal differ from those of Murillo in

greater energy, in a more colorful character, in more reasonable spatiality, finally in a self-contained feeling which disregards the spectator.  Unlike Murillo again, Leal is likely to keep some link between
the Virgin's cloudland and earth, in the forms of saints or donors in
the foreground.  The Assumption at London, 1661, is pretty near
Murillo in the girlish form of the glorified Madonna, but here eyes
are heavenwords and not wide open for human admiration.  Unlike
Murillo too are the stark portraits of donors at the base and the sense
of celestial spaces far away.  But while the picture has greater sincerity and energy than any of the Assumptions by Murillo, it also
has less pictorial unity, is less completely thought through in its decorative aspect.

A much finer and probably somewhat earlier Assumption by Leal
is or was in the Carvalho Collection.  The Madonna is a matronly
figure, eyes and outstretched hands directed upwards.  Two strong,
adolescent angels—one thinks of Veronese's angels, or Greco's—push
Her up.  A bewildered apostle below raises his hand to shade his
eyes from the glory.  Other holy persons in a near middle distance
inspect the miraculously empty tomb.  In the sky above there is a
sense of infinitely receding radiancies.  The figure composition is in
sharply opposed diagonals, which give a dynamic effect.  It is the
method of Titian in his maturity, and after him of Tintoretto,
Veronese and Rubens.  The broad and very monumental distribution
of light and dark, with subtle transitional half-tones, again has a very
Venetian suggestion, as has the sonorous color.  The difference in
type between these two Madonnas is significant.  Unlike Murillo,
Valdés Leal does not settle down to types or favorite models.  He
is as unpredictable as nature.  This may be partly due to his mere
restlessness, but it is fair to credit it partly to his probity.  Of course,
the picture has much of the operatic expansiveness proper to the
theme.  At least it is grand opera.  Can one say as much for Murillo's Assumptions?

Perhaps the most remarkable invention of Valdés Leal is the
Dead St. Bonaventura finishing his Life of St. Francis (Fig. 353), in
the collection of Sir Robert Cook, Richmond, England.  The legend
told that the greatest of Franciscan theologians was allowed to work
for three days after his death to finish his life of St. Francis.  The
theme then is a corpse concentrated on writing, and Valdés Leal has
expressed the macabre motive perfectly, has given it a gruesome real-

ity. At first glance it seems as if one had to do only with a rigid posture and a set expression, and then it comes over one with a chill that the writer is dead.

Probably most visitors to the Caridad at Seville glance with a shudder at Leal's two great Vanity pictures, and pass on. But no one who has seen these pictures ever forgets them. We have here an eminently Spanish reading of the century-old theme, the Triumph of Death. It had been very variously visualized. The French and Italians thought of a gay cavalcade coming suddenly upon rotting corpses. A Catalan painter at Palermo and Old Bruegel thought of it as a skeleton horseman mowing men down with his scythe. Hans Holbein, with many Northerners before and after him, depicted Death as a mischievous skeleton coming upon people at their work or play. Valdés Leal, with the concrete realism of a Spaniard, thinks of Death as sundering the high in place from their possessions. To what end pile up honor and wealth only to surrender them to Death? This is the challenge of Leal's pictures and, of course, the challenge is as old as the Ecclesiast. Leal merely finds very specific symbols for the most universal of themes.

In so doing he was following the will and probably the directions of a very interesting friend, Don Miguel Manara Vincentelo de Leca, knight of the order of Calatraba, benefactor and brother-in-chief of the Caridad. After a singularly wicked youth and young manhood, Don Miguel turned to penitence, religion and good works. There is probably no blackness of gloom comparable to that of a pleasure-loving Spaniard who has repudiated his pleasures. Witness certain awful designs of Goya a century or more later; witness Don Miguel's expression of Christian pessimism in his "Discourse concerning Youth." He composed his own epitaph. It runs: "Here lie the bones and ashes of the wickedest man in the world."

Valdés Leal never painted more strongly than in these two pictures. They have the emphasis and lucidity of a hallucination, and a beauty of color which somewhat attenuates their sheer grisliness. In the records of the Caridad one of these pictures is called by the quaint but fit title, "Hieroglyphics of the End of our Days" (Fig. 354). We have a kind of altar, upon and about which are all the appanages of worldly glory—crowns, miters, an archbishop's staff, a chain of the Golden Fleece; below the scholar's books, the sword and armor of a knight, a geographer's globe. Using the globe as a stepping stone a skeleton stalks in and smashes his fleshless hand upon the burning candle on the altar. It disappears as an inscription tells "In the twinkling of an eye"—IN ICTU OCULI. Death seems to glare at the spectator as if to insist that the lesson be read. A surrealist picture of the first order.

Again with unsparing, and possibly unpardonable, realism Valdés Leal shows us the physical sequels of death. In the foreground of a charnel pit lie in their coffins the festering corpses of a bishop and a knight. Details are better left unwritten. Above in a light between clouds the pierced hand of Christ holds a balance, the two pans even and labeled "neither more" and "nor less." In one pan are the symbols of the knight's luxury, in the other those of the bishop's service. The moral seems to be the nihilistic one that the two lives were equally nothing, and it is enforced by a label at the bottom reading *Finis gloriae mundi.*

Pictures like this offer a staggering problem to a critic. He deals mostly with face values, and here the face values are cruelly annulled in behalf of a life-denying maxim. One is tempted to discuss the maxim itself and how far a painter should go in maintaining it. Are worms and beetles necessary to tell us that the body decays? Leal's answer would doubtless be that the body decays that way. What is at stake, after all, is not the validity of the tremendous commonplace that earthly glory passes and death is ever imminent, but rather the ability of the artist in finding and arranging symbols for this theme. And here, like or dislike the pictures, we must acclaim the power and lucidity of Valdés Leal. These are not literary pictures. They are immediately legible; they create their own sinister and dreadful world. On the theory that there is something bracing in facing the worst, these are tonic pictures. Their dreadfulness is entirely truthful. Possibly they are the two most Spanish pictures in all Spain.

It is impossible within the scope of this book to follow Valdés Leal's activity in the nearly twenty years remaining to him after 1671, when these pictures were painted. His narrative pictures, which I know only inadequately, seem to me inferior in insight and arrangement to Murillo's. Technically they are often superior. His pupil, Palomino, later the historian of Spanish art, describes Valdés Leal's method of painting. He constantly withdrew from the picture, studied it and walked up to it for a single stroke. It is the procedure of

a painterlike spirit, and is dissimilar as possible to what must have
been the tranquil and uninterrupted quantity production of Murillo.

Valdés Leal, besides his painting, designed retables and temporary decorations and engraved for illustration. After Murillo's death
in 1682 he was admittedly the first painter of Seville. He visited
Madrid in 1674, but was too old to learn much from the Italian
masterpieces there. In 1689 he was disabled by a paralytic stroke,
and, since his was not a temperament to bear invalidism gracefully,
the next year, mercifully, he died.

Valdés Leal is one of the very few Spanish painters who make
upon me the impression of genius. Even Velasquez seems to me
rather an exquisitely and completely cultivated talent than a genius
in the proper sense of the word. But the inborn genius of Valdés
Leal was not backed by the character necessary to make it fully effective, while probably the religious subjects generally assigned to
him were not of a sort fully to enlist his powers. What he might
have done had he extended to other themes the fairly surrealistic
vividness of his macabre masterpieces, we may only guess. He seems
to have had in him the capacity to be a more versatile and imaginative Zurbarán. Instead, by trying to rival Murillo, he more or less
accepted the limitations of Murillo's outlook and practice. He seems
only rarely to have come into the clear, and to have worked habitually in a certain worry and confusion. For this reason, though he
had the technical capacities of a great painter, we must think of him
as among

"The inheritors of unfulfilled renown."

In retrospect Spanish painting of the seventeenth century yields
no coherent memory picture. One recalls rather a few superior artists
doing what they could under more or less favoring, and withal limiting, circumstances. Except Murillo, who uncritically followed lines
of least resistance, the other great or nearly great painters, Ribera,
Zurbarán, Velasquez, were unsupported and uncorrected by a national Spanish taste. For the persistent Spanish realism was quite
as much an esthetic liability as an esthetic asset. Thus, in comparison with their contemporaries in Italy, France and the Low Countries, the Spanish painters had to fend for themselves, without the
support of a like-minded, coherent patronage. It is only for conven-

ience and by courtesy that we can speak of a Spanish school of painting. What common denominator is there between Velasquez, Zurbarán, Ribera, Murillo, Valdés Leal? All the more honor then to those gifted painters who, in relative isolation, made Spain a bourne of pilgrimage for all lovers of the painter's art.

CHAPTER XXII

FRENCH PAINTING IN THE SEVEN-
TEENTH CENTURY FROM VOUET
TO PHILIPPE DE CHAMPAIGNE

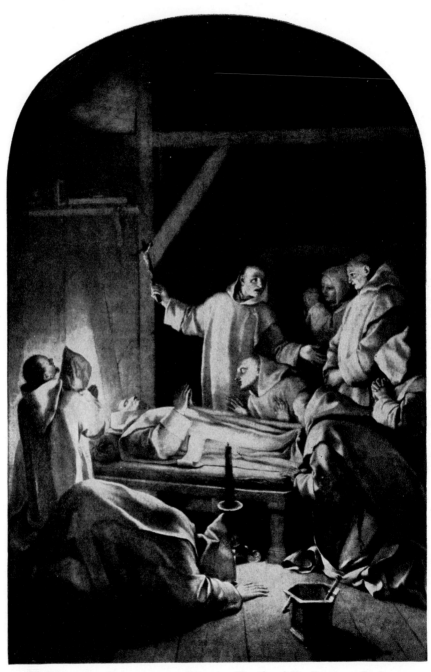

Fig. 355. Eustache le Sueur. Death of St. Bruno.—Paris.

668

Fig. 356. (Upper) SIMON VOUET.  Temptation of St. Francis.—S. Lorenzo
in Lucina, Rome.
Fig. 357. (Lower) SIMON VOUET.  Apollo and the Muses.—Budapest.

FIG. 358. (Upper) JACQUES BLANCHARD. Angelica and Medoro.—New York.

FIG. 359. (Lower) VALENTIN. The Musicians.—Paris.

Fig. 360. (Upper) Georges de la Tour. Nativity.—Rennes.
Fig. 361. (Lower) Georges de la Tour. Peter's Denial.—Nantes.

Fig. 362. Georges de la Tour. Lamentation over St. Sebastian.—Berlin.

Fig. 363. (Upper) Antoine le Nain. The Peasants' Meal.—Paris.
Fig. 364. (Lower) Louis le Nain. Family Group.—Paris.

Fig. 365. Louis le Nain. Venus Visiting Vulcan's Forge.—Rheims.

Fig. 366. (Upper) Mathieu le Nain. The Guard Room.—Paris.
Fig. 367. (Lower) Mathieu le Nain. The Dancing Lesson.—Samson
Gallery, Paris.

Fig. 368. Philippe de Champaigne. Cardinal Richelieu.—Paris.

676

Fig. 369. Philippe de Champaigne. President de Mesme.—*Paris.*

Fig. 370. (Upper) Philippe de Champaigne. Mère Arnauld and Sœur Catherine.—Paris.

Fig. 372. (Lower) Eustache le Sueur. Venus Presents Cupid to Jupiter.—Paris.

FIG. 371. PHILIPPE DE CHAMPAIGNE. The Magistrates of Paris.—*Paris*

679

FIG. 373. EUSTACHE LE SUEUR. St. Bruno Listening to a Preacher.—*Paris.*

IN ORDER to give prominence to such painters as Claude and Poussin, and to the influence of Lebrun, the history of French painting in the seventeenth century has been badly oversimplified. In literature the case has been similar. The student has been taught as if the century began when it was a third gone, with the criticism of Malherbe and the plays of Corneille. Now the confusion that prevailed before the founding of the Academy of Fine Arts in 1648 may not seem worth investigating, and indeed, except for the etcher Jacques Callot and such painters as Georges de la Tour, the three brothers Le Nain and Philippe de Champaigne, there are few artist figures in these years who retain any present importance. However, there is no understanding the classical ideal exemplified by Poussin and imposed by Lebrun and the critics in the second half of the century, unless we first study the diversity of tastes that seemed to require criticism and reform. Hence, if only sketchily, we must describe the artistic situation in France about 1620, when the end of the religious wars and the return to general prosperity again made possible a serious patronage of the fine arts.

The gracile mannerisms of the Fontainebleau School survived feebly in such artists as Sebastian Le Clerc and the painter-engraver, Jacques Bellange; the Michelangelesque mannerisms in Martin Fréminet. There was no principle of life here.

Through François Pourbus the Younger, court painter to Henri IV (Fig. 195), the linear international style fairly held its own in portraiture, and though gradually superseded by richer methods, something of its metallic brilliancy persists in the portraiture of Rigaud, and of minor face painters, at the end of the century. Much of its dogged probity survives in the masterpieces of Philippe de Champaigne.

The etcher, Jacques Callot, with his nervous vitality, his elegance, his sense of character, his gift for caricature, his interest in low life, in the theater and in war, was giving the first visible expression to what we call the French vein—l'esprit Gaulois. Although Callot was the wittiest, and in the technical sense, the most fastidious of draughtsmen, his example was available for all artists who eschewed the official noble style. His influence, however, was stronger in the eighteenth than in the seventeenth century.

Parallel with the influence of Callot was that of Caravaggio's tenebrism and proletarianism. It came to France directly from French imitators of Caravaggio and his Italian followers, and also indirectly through Honthorst and the little Dutch masters who had adopted the "dark manner." There had been a veritable immigration of minor Dutch and Flemish painters to Paris and the chief cities of the provinces. Such painters as Valentin, La Tour and the Le Nain represent this mixed influence.

Rubens' Médicis series in the Luxembourg, finished about 1625, gave a superb example of a florid and colorful classicism to all French artists of painterlike disposition. For most of the century it passed for bad taste to admire Rubens openly—the critics and the Academy had condemned him, but people of unspoiled taste rejoiced in Rubens on the sly, his style was to dominate French painting of the eighteenth century, leaving the Academicians in merely nominal authority.

Italian influence steadily increased. There was a great activity in collecting. Cardinal Mazarin, himself an Italian, shrewdly bought many masterpieces from the gallery of Charles I, as the Commonwealth thriftily peddled them off. These are treasures of the Louvre today. Reproductive engraving had made the compositions of all the greater Italians, down to such contemporaries as Domenichino and Guido Reni, widely available. Any perceptive French painter could study from his portfolio the characteristics of the famous Italian style. But the luckier or cleverer French painters studied at Rome. Having no reason to take sides in the controversy between rightism of the eclectics and the leftism of the tenebrists, they sensibly took what served them from either school. Simon Vouet is the dominant painter of these years at Paris, the best example of compromise between the rival Italian tendencies, and it is significant that his ultimate adjustment was pretty well to the right, with the eclectics. This drift showed what was to come when the new Academy, the salons, the criticism of Malherbe and Dufresnoy, had put an aristocratic but powerful minority behind the doctrine of the grand style. But there was no such dominant minority when, in 1627, Simon Vouet made his triumphal return from Rome to Paris.

Vouet was born at Paris in 1590. By his twentieth year he was working as a portraitist in England. At twenty-one he accompanied the French ambassador to Constantinople. From 1612 to 1627 he was in Italy, a pensioner of the French king, and crowded with commissions and honors. In 1624 he was chosen rector of the Academy of St. Luke—for a foreigner a high honor. In Italy he moved about, sojourning and working at Naples, Genoa and Venice, and everywhere intelligently studying the recent and contemporary painters. Thus the blond clarity of Paolo Veronese's construction left its permanent mark on him, though he failed to grasp the richness and subtlety of Veronese's apparently simple formulas.

Naturally the new sensation of the tenebrists first intrigued him. One must recall that the sharp contrasts of orthodoxy and heresy retrospectively set up by the art historians and critics of Italy and France find little correspondence with the facts of contemporary taste. The same Roman amateurs bought Caravaggio, Manfredi and Saraceni alternately with Guido Reni, Domenichino and Albani, with no feeling of inconsistency. As a Caravaggian, Vouet could easily have rivaled Valentin. The half-length of a swashbuckling officer, at Brunswick, proves it. The motto on a contemporary engraved copy:

> "I, the nursling of Bellona and Mars,
>    Wish for a universal reign of terror,"

suggests a satirical intention, as does the truculent expression of the sitter. He is plainly a *miles gloriosus*, favorite of Roman comedy and of its recent vernacular imitations, familiar enough in real life in those mercenary officers who fought the interminable wars of the century.

A more serious Caravaggian experiment is the Temptation of St. Francis, at S. Lorenzo in Lucina, Rome (Fig. 356). The light drives into the murky cell from a high window at the right, sharply defining the athletic form of the saint, who starts up from his pallet to point a forbidding finger at the temptress. The sturdy, handsome wench leans backwards as she shows a leg and prepares to expose her breast, confident in their seductive power. It is all admirably effective in a way in which realism and melodrama oddly blend. It is a shock to have Dr. Weisbach inform us that sore temptation has contorted the saint's body into the pose of a famous Michelangelesque Venus. The picture is a singular document both of Vouet's incorrigible eclecticism and of his great native talent. To a modern taste, the oddest thing about the picture is that it should have been ordered and accepted by a Christian church.

Vouet was far too shrewd to stay with the tenebrists. He knew their appeal would play out, and that the future was with the conservatives. Accordingly, he found his personal style through study of the Carracci. His religious pictures on his return show forms and colors very similar to those of the Carracci and also stately classical settings derived from Paolo Veronese. Such is the synthesis that lies behind his St. Charles Borromeo and the Pest-Stricken, Brussels, but the loose diagonal figure composition is his own adaptation from the Italian baroque. The superb angel who eagerly prompts the praying saint anticipates later triumphs of the sculptor Bernini.

At thirty-seven Vouet returned to Paris with a staff of fellow Frenchmen, specialists in decoration and sculpture. He expected commissions for mural painting, and the hope was amply justified. Unluckily pretty much everything of this sort has been destroyed and is today represented either by detached fragments or unexpressive engravings. Still in place is a much damaged vaulted ceiling, in the grotto of Wideville, representing Parnassus. The lightly draped deities loll informally and deliciously on a mound from which sprout feathery trees—recalling Rubens and anticipating Corot. The architectural support is painted away by foreshortened figures playing musical instruments. Vouet has gone further with baroque illusionism than is usual with French painters. Everything is casual and slight and entirely gay and delightful. One thinks of the more idiomatic ruralism of Pontormo at Poggio a Caiano. In comparison with what had been done by the Fontainebleau School, this is completely winning and completely French.

Vouet's unflagging activity was sustained by his vanity. At Rome he had declared himself Rubens' superior, and as if to prove it at Paris, he, who freely borrowed from every other source, refused to profit by the obviously available example of Rubens in the Luxembourg. Paris took Vouet at his own estimate. Louis XIII and Cardinal Richelieu almost smothered him with commissions and after their death in 1643 the queen-regent, Anne of Austria, continued their patronage. Vouet designed for tapestry, planned whole interiors, diligently instructed dozens of pupils.

Of his numerous mythologies and allegories, such as Wealth, from the Hôtel Lambert, now in the Louvre, Apollo and the Muses (Fig. 357), at Budapest, or the Europa, in a private collection, at Paris, one must admit that they are invariably superficial but never dull or perfunctory. Vouet loves his own facility, is highly susceptible to his own charm, hence never fails to communicate it. He is always lucid and agreeable, always innocently sensuous. It is no long step from his pictures to the teasing sensuality of Boucher, but it is a step Vouet never takes. His drawing and color are sprightly, never deeply searched, but always good enough for what he had to express. In his facile and joyous professional competence—he was an admirable designer of ornament—in his frank acceptance of the standards of the average sensual man, in his sound instinct for a career, he may claim the distinction of being the first modern French artist and the founder of the school.

He died in 1649, being fifty-nine years old. He had brought French painting to a good professional standard, had salvaged for France what was available from the declining Italian Renaissance, and had cleared the way for the far more considerate art of Poussin. The critic of today who must regard him with qualified admiration cannot think of him without gratitude.

Such younger contemporaries of Vouet as Laurent de la Hire (1606–1656) merely assure us of the continuity of the eclectic tradition. A passing word is due Vouet's occasional associate, Jacques Blanchard (1600–1638). We find him at Rome in 1624, and for two years thereafter at Venice. Such colorful Caravaggians as Fetti and Strozzi there held the field alongside such continuers of Tintoretto's manner as his son, Domenico, and Palma Giovane. Blanchard had the good taste to look rather to Paolo Veronese and Titian for inspiration; indeed, on his return to Paris, about the year of Vouet's reappearance, 1627, Blanchard had the awful luck to be nicknamed "the French Titian." What mural decoration he accomplished in his eleven remaining years has perished, but a few easel pictures remain to tell us that more than Vouet he valued the Venetian color and grandezza. The nudes in the canvas Angelica and Medoro (Fig. 358), New York, are grandly disposed after Titian's example, and strongly, sensitively and colorfully painted. Technically such a picture is a high point in French painting of the moment, and far better than Vouet's best achievement. One realizes with a start that these monumentally constructed and grandly disposed bodies are just those of a pair of Ariosto's idyllic lovers carving each other's names on a tree. Blanchard has captured something of the monumental ardor and decorum of Titian, while remaining his own man. A Holy Family, at Cherbourg, again draws chiefly from Titian, with perhaps a collateral influence from the soundest work of Van Dyck. What Blanchard might have done had he lived on for thirty years is an interesting subject of speculation. A painter with more sap than Poussin, with a richer color sense, with an equal respect for decorum, might easily have offset Poussin's undervaluation of color, might have substituted for a classical tradition based too much on linear draughtsmanship one based on fine painting. In short, a Blanchard come to maturity and authority might have tied pictorial orthodoxy in France rather to the practice of Venice than to Raphael and the antique. Such leadership would have prevented many vain controversies and sterile hatreds. But an elementary history of painting is no place to write an "if" story.

In the second quarter of the seventeenth century few of the younger and more intelligent French painters escaped the spell of Caravaggio's "dark manner"; many yielded to it unreservedly. Since the "dark manner," with its incidental proletarianism, was only an episode, and its more important expression that of a single family, the Le Nain, we must pretty well confine our attention to them. Certain interesting contemporaries must first be very briefly dismissed.

Valentin, born in 1591 in Northern France, early found the way to Rome and made his whole career there, dying at forty-three. He probably knew Caravaggio personally and based his art solidly on that of the pioneer tenebrist. Valentin enlisted generous patronage for his religious pictures, but his most personal achievement was in the half-length character studies which Caravaggio had brought into European mode. He searched more carefully than Caravaggio the human relations involved in scenes from low life, directed upon his characters a less generalizing and more specific sympathy. Thus the Card Sharper, Dresden, which long passed for a Caravaggio, is most energetically dramatized and modulated in its shades of cold rapacity, sinister collusion and gullible innocence. The Musicians, Paris (Fig.

359), again abounds in shades and varieties of feeling in the players and hearers. The dour intentness of the woman playing the lute is admirably caught, as is the resigned boredom of the little lad. The whole is well held together pictorially, though there are dead passages which Caravaggio, after all, inheritor of the grandeur and harmony of the Renaissance, would not have permitted himself.

The most individual and fascinating of the French Caravaggians is Georges de la Tour. Research has only recently dragged him from oblivion. He was born about 1600, at Lunéville, in Lorraine, perhaps studied at Rome, worked at Paris. About him we have almost no biographical information. The dark shadows which Caravaggio used chiefly as a factor in construction, De la Tour used as a means of increasing illumination. In this respect, only technically, of course, he is really nearer to Correggio and early Rembrandt than to Caravaggio. The transitions between the broad masses of light and dark are very tenderly handled. Often an area of almost incandescent scarlet relieves the general effect of warm monochrome. Contrasting with the quite modern technique is a fixed and immobile feeling in his figures. This and the humble character of his personages gives to his pictures an oddly primitive look. One thinks of nativities by the Late-Gothic painters of Germany. His preference is for artificial light, but again it rather envelops and caresses his figures than forces them into plastic prominence.

In the sentiment of Georges de la Tour a curious quietism prevails. You will find it distinguishing the massive and noble Nativity, at Rennes (Fig. 360), and the more elaborate Adoration of the Shepherds, Paris. The light falls from a carefully held candle upon the tightly swathed and deeply sleeping Babe. Otherwise the scene is composed after Caravaggio's fashion, as a character study in half-lengths. In a theme which at the time was treated with baroque eagerness and ecstasy, stillness rules. The five worshiping figures are not merely motionless, but even seem to withdraw a little, for deeper contemplation, and not to disturb the slumber of the Christchild. Their faces glow amid the investing darkness. There is a superb flash of scarlet in the Madonna's robe. A very thoughtful and noble tenderness and reserve set this picture apart from the scores of Holy Nights, from Correggio's down, in which animation is emphasized. There are no real analogies for this masterpiece—

the nearest, perhaps, being the early religious pictures of Velasquez, which relatively are rather stolid than quietistic.

Peter's Denial, Nantes (Fig. 361), is perhaps Georges de la Tour's most original invention. The arrangement, an oblong with half-lengths, and the lighting from a candle, is Caravaggian, but the light and dark are less factors in construction than in the production of a sinister effect. And this effect lies in the picture itself and is not enhanced by stage management. The composition consists of two groups—the two dicing soldiers and three onlookers, and the little maid who, casually turning to Peter, terrifies him by remarking on his Galilean accent. Only two faces are really prominent—the worried face of Peter, the ugly mug of the hard-featured but loose-lipped ruffian which pushes into the candlelight to observe the fall of the dice. Much of the effect of the narrative depends on the contrast between these two faces. The group of five soldiers at the gaming table is strangely and most ingeniously composed. There is a general geometrical sense of globular and cylindrical forms, incandescent at the edges, but this general rotundity is sharply contradicted by the awkward but entirely natural angularity of the silhouettes of the two dicers. The posture of the maid with the candle well expresses the unexpectedness of the challenge to Peter, while her arm and head, dark against the light, carry the eye to Peter's pitiful, weak face. The pious Galilean fisherman has found himself in terrifying company. Fear, even to denial of his Lord, is inevitable under the circumstances. It is consonant with De la Tour's always restrained, allusive and undramatic taste that nobody but the harmless little maid pays any attention whatever to Peter. In short, his treason is both inevitable and unnecessary. It is the profoundest reading of the theme that I know. The decorative effect is heightened by the usual glowing scarlet robe and the bluish glints that the yellow candle-light forces from the helmets.

Loose Company, Paris, is a card-sharper theme such as Caravaggio and his followers had often painted. De la Tour gives it a new turn by letting a courtesan preside. I do not greatly care for the picture. There are too many profiles and the cheating motive is made too overt. It is the only De la Tour I know which lets the stage management appear. All the same, the hard and intelligent efficiency of the courtesan and the self-satisfied dullness of her rich young client are capitally expressed. I sometimes think that the right half of the picture, with these two figures, would better have told the whole story. Quentin Massys would have done it that way, and in an odd, primitive austerity about this picture there is a suggestion, which can hardly be merely casual, of Massys' famous genre pieces.

The Lamentation over St. Sebastian, Berlin (Fig. 362), is perhaps the masterpiece of Georges de la Tour. To realize its distinction one must imagine what such sterling contemporary painters as Ribera or Strozzi would have made of the theme in a dramatic way. And the tenderness of De la Tour's reading of the theme brought the picture, before it was securely identified, a by no means absurd attribution to Vermeer of Delft. Everything is attenuated. With no suggestion of the rigidity of a corpse, the fine, youthful body of the martyr lies as if in easy slumber. A single arrow may be said rather to symbolize than to represent the martyrdom. St. Irene will not approach too near. Her grief is expressed almost formally by her outstretched hands and the concentrated gaze of her fine, unperturbed face. A maid looks mostly to the balancing of her flaming torch, while her left hand touches the wrist of St. Sebastian with the professional coolness of a nurse. The motive of grief is overt only in the maid, who weeps into her handkerchief in upper right. The motive becomes mysterious in the praying hands of a nun high in the center. You see the hands before you see the profile bowed above them in the gloom. A theme inviting to dramatic exaggeration could hardly be more thoroughly purged of the legitimately dramatic. And, oddly, while the picture has become a vision, a visualization of the tenderest aspect of legend, the eye accepts it as a fact.

We are only at the beginning of our knowledge of the art of Georges de la Tour. For nearly three hundred years his pictures were either ignored or wrongly attributed. In the enthusiasm of discovery we are possibly inclined to overestimate him. What seems likely to stand is the praise of being the most fine and various temperament among the French Caravaggians.

In his lifetime, we may infer from the scanty notices, Georges de la Tour was appreciated. Louis XIII was a great patron, as he was of other artists from Lorraine. De la Tour died in 1652, and when only some twenty years later Félibien and Rogier de Piles began to collect material for their critical and biographical works, the official authority of the grand style had put such painting as De la

Tour's completely out of fashion. Hence these early French art historians possibly did not even know of him, and in any case felt they had done their full duty by French painting of low life when they made some brief and condescending mention of the painting of the brothers Le Nain.

The work of these three brothers, Antoine (1588–1648), Louis (1593–1648) and Mathieu (1607–c. 1678), offers a curious problem, for they kept shop together, signed their pictures only with the family name; while of the few dated pictures eleven fall within the years 1640 and 1647, when the brothers were certainly working together. M. Paul Jamot has skillfully classified this work, and, while his results are not beyond doubt, they are consistent and should be provisionally accepted. The opportune discovery of a picture signed Le Nain, 1674, offered a starting point for the work of Mathieu, since the elder brothers were dead. The identification of his work offers few difficulties. Examining the remainder, M. Jamot found it consisted of portrait groups thrown together without regard for composition, and of true genre paintings deeply felt and very thoughtfully composed. The more primitive and less skillful pictures M. Jamot reasonably attributed to the elder brother, Antoine; the fine genre pictures, to Louis. This classification purged the incoherent Le Nain group of its weaker elements and let the figure of a very individual and important artist emerge. We will agree that he is Louis le Nain, though it does not necessarily follow that because he was younger his work must be superior.

The little portrait groups now generally ascribed to Antoine have strong character of individual portraiture and next to no feeling for composition. The color is cold and negative, the drawing rather linear and harsh. In general, the work is of the "dark manner," though it is hard to find any specific influences to which it corresponds. Portrait groups by Antoine, at London and Paris (Fig. 363), have a common defect of mere juxtaposition of the figures and unrelatedness between them. The whole effect has a certain solidity and gravity that wins respect, even if it does not produce much pleasure.

Antoine was born in 1588, at Laon, in Northern France, and according to tradition had a foreign, probably a Flemish master. By 1629 we find him a member of the guild in the Quarter of St.-Germain-des-Près, where the Flemish painters mostly resided. Our earliest date for the partnership of the three brothers is 1633. In 1648 they became charter members of the new Academy, Antoine and Louis in the low category of painters of peasant scenes (*bambochades*); Mathieu in the higher, but still low ranking of a portrait painter. The style of the two elder brothers must have been pretty well fixed by 1615, when Antoine was twenty-seven years old and Louis twenty-two. Thus their work antedates by ten or fifteen years the burgeoning of Dutch and Flemish genre painting, and it is hard to trace any influence from the painters intermediate between Pieter Bruegel and Brouwer. It is a reasonable guess that they drew something from the Caravaggianism that was everywhere in the air, and that they may have been encouraged by the popularity of Callot's etchings of low life. In any case, their appeal must have been to Callot's public.

The almost unique distinction of Louis le Nain is that he found poor folk interesting in their own right, and not just as oddly different from their betters, and so painted poor folk in their inherent human worth and dignity. In this attitude he seems to have anticipated Rembrandt and Rembrandt's disciple, Nicholas Maes, with whose best work that of Louis has close analogies. This attitude of respectful sympathy for the poor has been pretty rare in art. The good genre painter of Flanders and Holland was usually a genial slummer—a student of humors in the English sense—observing poor folk from outside for the racy variety of difference—eccentricity when seen from the prosperous side—between their ways and those of the painter. Of this condescension Louis le Nain never betrays a trace. He admires the patience and prudence of the poor. Nobody else was admiring it at the time except certain young painters at Seville, among them the patrician, Diego Velasquez.

Paris abounds in fine peasant scenes by Louis le Nain; there are striking out-of-doors pictures at Boston and at London. No Le Nain is finer than the Family Group, at Paris (Fig. 364), with two children, two parents and an old woman, listening to a lad who plays the pipe. The way in which the artist completely fills his oblong with his figures suggests an influence from Italy. The Dutch and Flemish genre painters wanted a greater prominence and portrait character for the interior and more elbow room for their groups. From his more compact procedure Louis le Nain gains emphasis and dignity. In the picture we are considering the characterization is very choice. What patient nobility in the seated old woman! what singular, disciplined loveliness in the young mother, what worried prudence in the bearded face of the father and breadwinner! what intentness in the little piper! and all this inherent, nothing overemphasized, but everything legible beyond misunderstanding. Apparently casual, the picture is thoughtfully arranged, but Le Nain has given thought not to exhibiting his own skill but to communicate the personal and collective character of his peasants. In some indefinable way the picture expresses the depth and value of family love.

As for the color, Louis le Nain seems to have been immune to the decorative ideals that were coming in with Vouet. The color is just as much local color as the "dark manner" permits, with little or no attempt to harmonize what nature has put asunder. Indeed, the coldness and dissonance of most of the Le Nains is such that a sensitive eye will generally find more pleasure in a good photograph than in the original.

A few religious pictures, such as the Last Supper, at Paris, show Louis le Nain in a quite Italianate phase, and also in trouble. When, as in these sacred subjects, he must paint classical drapery, he tortures it, and when he must express strong emotion, he exaggerates it. His best mood is that of a complete quietism.

A big mythological picture, the Forge of Vulcan, 1641, at Rheims (Fig. 365), has very interesting analogies with Velasquez's somewhat earlier version of the theme. In both pictures Vulcan and his helpers are sturdy mechanics. Louis le Nain has sought and achieved the more sensational effect in the radiation of the light from the forge through the surrounding gloom and on the faces, limbs and bodies of the workers and visiting Venus. Venus is just a buxom and moderately comely housewife, who happens in without taking the trouble to adjust her *déshabillé*. Vulcan and a swarthy man in the background regard her with measured admiration. The intrinsic seductiveness and piquancy of the familiar subject have meant just nothing to Louis le Nain. He treats it with detachment and without innuendo, as something that might happen at any French armorsmith's. As a composition, in happy distribution of light and dark and in a densely rhythmical character both in pattern and in depth, this is one of the ablest Le Nains, as it is one of the most Italianate. It is possible that he studied in Italy, but I do not think, in the absence of direct evidence, that we need to suppose it.

We may imagine that Louis le Nain depended on a patronage which dwindled with the growing classicism. His art was grim, and no grim art has ever lasted long in France. His art was soon discredited by the critics of the next generation, and has had to wait to our times for its just appreciation.

Mathieu le Nain, born in 1607, was young enough to undergo in his flexible years the various influences that were invading Paris. He settled into his own kind of "dark manner," sought novelties of artificial lighting, in general remained a Caravaggian. But, unlike his brothers, he was a climber, rose to a higher social level, that of officers and gentry, served in the army and won a captaincy and knighthood. Naturally he painted the people and the life he knew.

The key picture for the reconstruction of his work is the Guard Room, signed and dated 1643 (Fig. 366), in a private collection at Paris. The officers of the guard are seated or standing about a round table upon which a wearied comrade has sunk over from his stool in sleep. Most of them hold or smoke long clay pipes. They are caught in free and gallant postures. The light comes from an unexplained source in front and beats upon the table and the wreathing faces. There is a fireplace in the right background and a tub with cooling wine flasks in the right foreground. The portraiture is excellent, the arrangement hardly more than fair, but Mathieu le Nain has truly caught the essential character of the scene—the paradox that men who are on instant call, between times cultivate the ease of a perfect relaxation. A more animated character in his work distinguishes it from that of his really abler brother, Louis.

Mathieu, with his air of good society, can be more charming than either of his brothers, witness the Dancing Master, Samson Gallery, Paris (Fig. 367). Everything is successfully played up—the bonniness of the little girls and their modest self-consciousness, the professional and merely sufficient intentness of the master, the sympathetic gaze of a distant man who, with turned head, is walking out of the picture at the right. The outdoor suggestion is slight, but also pleasant. The rareness of pictures by Mathieu le Nain, as compared with the abundance of those in Louis' manner, may mean not so much that Mathieu lacked appreciators, but rather that he was occupied with other matters and too prosperous to need to be productive. We have an Adoration of the Shepherds, dated as late as 1674, which shows him yielding to the prevailing classical tendency. He had shown little tenacity at any time, and the general interest had shifted from genre painting to so-called historical painting.

Rather for negative than for positive reasons Philippe de Champaigne (1602–1674) may be roughly grouped with the tenebrists. Though his pictures are generally brighter than theirs, he shared their dislike of positive color and their neglect of decorative considerations. Today he seems to us important only as portrait painter; his contemporaries employed him throughout his long career in religious painting and decoration. No contemporary except Vouet enjoyed greater or more constant popularity. A sparse, reasonable and evidently honest quality of his art may account for this. Generally, alongside the artists of richness and charm, France has produced and encouraged artists of austere sort. An Ingres thrives alongside a Delacroix, a Bonnat alongside a Carolus Duran. So there was room in Paris at the turning point of the seventeenth century for artists as different as Philippe de Champaigne and Vouet.

Born in Brussels in 1602, Philippe de Champaigne early found the way to Paris; through Marie de Médicis' favor he aided Duchesne in decorating the Luxembourg; and like the proverbial good assistant, married his master's daughter. Louis XIII and the great Richelieu generously employed him. It is said that Poussin befriended him; if so, without influence on his painting. Nothing we know about Philippe de Champaigne's training accounts for his style—a style fixed very early and never changed. In portraiture it is my guess that he admired the sober and resemblant portraiture of François Pourbus the Elder. In any case, he avoided the minute finish of the younger Pourbus, court painter to Henri IV. In religious pictures his rather dry and simple style derives ultimately from the altarpieces of the Carracci. Their rather formal and sentimental type of composition could be studied in engraved copies and may also have been mediated by such Dutch or Flemish imitators as Carel van Mander or Otho van Veen.

The manner becomes pretty immobile and anemic in such a picture as the Presentation in the Temple, Brussels. In the Assumption, at Grenoble, an earlier picture, there is some mixture of the eclectic and tenebrist technique and a greater animation, which is rather imposed than really felt. Even more unpleasing in its starkness, its surface bulging and giving way with ill-planned projections and unassimilated voids, is the Vow of Louis XIII, painted for the Cathedral of Notre Dame, and now at Caen. The main group, the Madonna and the Dead Christ, has a heavy dignity and emotional sincerity. The king, offering his crown and scepter, is stilted and a bit absurd. There is little sense of a body under his regal robes. The little nude angels prancing above among clouds make no sense at all, whether emotionally or as mere space fillers. Clearly Philippe de Champaigne had no gift for elaborate composition.

But he made one masterly composition in the Last Supper, Paris, originally painted for the Jansenist convent, with which he had close relations of friendship and piety. Doubtless he took uncommon pains with the picture, and he was steadied by the great example of Leonardo da Vinci's Last Supper, of which there were good copies in France. Its general lines he has sensibly followed, with some re-arrangement of the figures to bring two to the near side of the table, thus deepening the grouping. By clearing the table of all properties—Leonardo had shown the table fully set—Philippe de Champaigne emphasizes the sacramental character of the blessing of the bread, giving to the whole picture more the character of a solemn ceremony than that of a dramatic event. The general effect of the group, due to the even lighting and contouring of the figures, is that of a huge cameo, and this simplifying of the relations of light and dark gives to a very consciously made composition a spectral quality and a sense of other-worldliness.

It is as a portraitist that Philippe de Champaigne holds his place in the history of art, and, indeed, in that portraiture which seeks likeness and character, while eschewing extraneous elegance, charm or poetry, he probably has few equals and no superior. Perhaps it will emphasize his greatness to begin with a relative failure, Louis XIII, Conqueror of La Rochelle, Paris, 1628. To celebrate the successful conclusion of the prolonged and bitter siege of the Huguenot citadel,

Louis is represented in half-armor, in the attitude of a commander at ease. The painting is strong, manly, austere, most careful in indicating the textures of leather, steel, silk, lace, yet discreet in avoiding any overstressing of such minor essentials. What would have been a striking and powerful full-length in the general manner of Pourbus is spoiled by the introduction of a plump and insipid Victory, who, dangling inexplicably a foot off the pavement, seeks to impose the victor's laurel wreath with an awkward backhanded gesture of a fleshy hand. Most sensibly, his royal and victorious highness pays no attention to her, and we should be lucky if we could do the same. One need only imagine this motive in the hands of Rubens to realize the entire absence of any expansive or romantic principle in Philippe de Champaigne's temperament. He had what is rarer and perhaps better, a close and respectful observation, a sympathy limited by desire to tell simple truth, a lean and expressive prose that seems to rebuke the poetry of less conscientious masters of the portraitist's art.

One may say that he painted rather the sitter's thought and will than his feeling; indeed, as a class his sitters seem to live on a plane of character where the emotions are of minor importance. This concern with the intelligently directed will made Philippe de Champaigne the idea interpreter of statesmen, as he was of those austere theologians, his friends, the Jansenist fathers of Port Royal. In such full-lengths as the Cardinal Richelieu and the President of Parliament, De Mesme, both at Paris, Philippe de Champaigne may be said to have invented the political portrait. The great cardinal-prime minister (Fig. 368) walks across the space, holding his *beretta* in one hand while with the other he makes a gesture which is a command, or perhaps an explanation which is an equivalent. The fine face, with the mustache and pointed beard of a duelist, dominates the richness of the brocaded curtain which is the background, and that of the crimson silk and white lawn of the cardinal's robes. All this splendor seems simply the man's due, and of no further importance pictorially or otherwise. The nervous, defiant face expresses that indomitable will and inexhaustible craft which systematically broke the power of a turbulent nobility to establish the sway of the king over a strong and united France. Before this great picture one feels the nation-maker.

Superb as is the Richelieu, I am not sure but that the President de Mesme (Fig. 369) is not pictorially a little its superior. If so, it is because of the way in which the bizarre richness and complication of the furred official robes are, while fully expressed, subordinated to the character of the wearer. De Mesme does not seem to have had Richelieu's single-track mind. There are suggestions of irony and sarcasm in the alert and patient face. Here, perhaps, rather than a great statesman, is a great politician, for whom the handling of refractory deputies is as much a game as a career. The more elaborate composition, the absence of neutral passages, again may seem to make this picture technically more masterly than even the Richelieu. All accessories are imbued with a singular fitness and importance. Even the heavily hanging cord and tassel before the sky has an official impressiveness.

For a portraitist to whom decorative considerations were always secondary, the face was naturally the first concern. So the average art lover recalls less vividly such grandiose pictures as the De Mesme and Richelieu than some bust portrait of unforgettable spiritual intensity which has arrested him almost casually. Especially the portraits of Jansenists have the challenging character. One is almost rebuked as light-minded by the Abbé of Saint-Cyran, at Grenoble, by that of Bishop Pierre Camus, at Antwerp. Yet these clerics of inflexible convictions and of unsparing self-discipline look also charitable towards the weaker sort. Plainly Philippe de Champaigne found congenial associates in these Catholic reformers who sought purer forms of worship and a more serviceable Church. Leaders in this reform were the Jansenists of Port Royal until their individualistic theology, in many respects akin to that of the Calvinists, brought on them the condemnation of Rome. Portraits of this Puritan type abound in French galleries and are rare elsewhere. In the United States I recall only a characterful bust of a man, at Princeton, possibly a likeness of Descartes, and a stately medallion portrait of a Jansenist in the New York Historical Society.

The most impressive souvenir of Philippe de Champaigne's relations with Port Royal is the double portrait of his daughter, Catherine, and the Mother Superior, Agnès Arnauld (Fig. 370). It commemorates the miraculous healing from lameness of his daughter, a nun in the convent. The two women are praying together, Sister Catherine very quietly from her invalid's chair, the kneeling abbess ecstatically, as she feels the imminence of the miracle. All this is set down in a hardly needed inscription. Aside from its convincing character, the picture is painted with a massive and impressive economy of means, and is in its own fashion very decorative. But this effect grows out of the essentials, the broad masses of the robes, the picturesque spots of the black headdresses, the contrast between the relaxed seated figure and the tension of the kneeling suppliant. This superb votive picture was painted in the artist's old age, in 1666.

Philippe de Champaigne's portraits were popularized by the admirable engraver, Robert Nanteuil. Thus they promptly gained, and have always retained, a classic standing among people of taste in many lands. Unlike the fame of his contemporaries, which has known wide fluctuations, that of Philippe de Champaigne, portraitist, has never varied. One admires him somewhat coolly, but also without reservations, and that is probably the way he would like to be admired.

Just a word, as we take leave of him, on his groups of civic and guild magistrates and other corporate bodies. In this branch, where he necessarily invites comparison with his great Dutch contemporaries, Philippe de Champaigne does not show their ingenuity in composition. His groups are generally arranged with an obvious and dry symmetry. A good instance is the Magistrates of Paris, in the Louvre (Fig. 371). Such a picture, despite its lack of naturalness and ease, is highly impressive for its gravity and character and for a somber richness of character. It might be argued that its very formality tells much about official deliberations, and that in apparent negligence Philippe de Champaigne may actually have invented the bureaucratic as he had earlier invented the political picture.

Philippe de Champaigne lived on to 1674 and his seventy-third year. Never having experimented with a style early fixed and approved, he shows some signs of falling off in his later work, though still remaining capable of such occasional masterpieces as the votive picture for his daughter's healing. His self-portrait of 1668, Paris, betrays this relaxation. He actually tries to make himself attractive and sentimentally appealing and he poses out of doors before an umbrageous landscape. Done at the instigation of friends, it is one of his few unachieved portraits. He is perhaps troubled by the thought of the elegance of Van Dyck, as in the later religious pictures he is perturbed by the simplicity of Sacchi and by the unapproachable graciousness and dignity of Poussin. But Philippe de Champaigne had earned the right to vacillate. Forty years and more of the utmost rectitude in portraiture had already assured his immortality.

The moderation and reasonableness of Philippe de Champaigne's work, its concentration on draughtsmanship and evasion of conscious arrangements of color, was a strong parallel influence, with that of Poussin, in establishing, as against the gay superficiality of Vouet and the sensationalism of the Caravaggians, the domination of the new classical, or, if you will, pseudo-classical ideals. But these ideals found their formulation through critics and academies, and their expression in the work of Nicolas Poussin, which is matter for a later chapter.

Though Eustache le Sueur was junior to Claude Lorrain and Poussin by some twenty years, his style was less advanced· and his brief career came to its close before these great elder contemporaries had fully come to their own. Le Sueur's activity also falls within the regency for Louis XIV, a period that saw a finer flowering of the French spirit in Corneille, Molière, Pascal, Descartes, Poussin, Claude, the elder Mansart, than the actual reign of the Roi Soleil was to witness. For these reasons we shall disregard precise chronology in studying Le Sueur before some of his elders and betters.

He was born in Paris in 1616, the son of a wood-carver—an excellent parentage for a future master of ornament. He was the pupil of the friendly and versatile Vouet, who generously shared his popularity with his young charge. But Le Sueur's ultimate style was based less on Vouet's eclecticism than on the study of the clear and harmonious designs of Raphael, which were available in prints. Le Sueur's religious pictures, especially his famous series of the Life of St. Bruno, have overshadowed his designs of an ornamental and mythological sort. These begin early in his career, have great charm, and we may well start with them.

Most of the decorative work was done for the Hôtel Lambert, in association with Vouet and others. The mansion was long ago demolished, but many of the panels have passed into the Louvre and French private collections. Entirely typical is Mercury and Venus, at Paris. There is a hint of Raphael's famous stories of Psyche in the Farnesina, but the accent is lighter, more lyrical, more facile.

There is a conscious elegance, a kind of air of good society about the forms which, not amounting to mannerism, faintly recalls the preciosity of the Fontainebleau School. It has been well remarked that in the female nudes of Le Sueur one feels less the woman than the lady.

Of more ambitious composition is the group of the Muses, Clio, Euterpe and Thalia, at Paris. It is again part of the salvage from the Hôtel Lambert. The feeling is wistful, meditative, maidenly, as far from the joyous sensuousness of Vouet as it is from the graver idylism of Poussin. Such features as the exposed breast of Clio and shoulder of Euterpe have the grace of entire unconsciousness. Indeed, at all times the element of showmanship is absent in Eustache le Sueur. He paints for his subject and for himself.

We may represent the panels for the Hôtel Lambert by Venus presenting Cupid to Jupiter (Fig. 372), Paris. It has much of that charm of artlessness which we associate with Domenichino. The execution is not very strong, but direct and simple. The picture is sensitive and unpretentiously elegant.

The charm of Le Sueur's mythologies is so refreshing and positive that any analysis of their making may seem impertinent. Still such is ever the dire task of criticism, and it is not to be evaded in this case. No other artist with any pretensions to greatness has a construction so slack and a color so negative as Le Sueur's. When looking at his nudes, the inevitable association is with artists of the second or third order, with, for example, Angelica Kaufmann or Flaxman. In this branch Le Sueur never for a moment recalls any really great artist—Raphael, Correggio, Poussin. The conclusion would seem to be that this alert and charming painter is not a great artist. To think him so one has to be born French, and I was not born in France.

Near the end of his short life came his most congenial commission, in twenty-nine stories of the Life of St. Bruno, for as many arcades of the cloister of the Chartreuse at Paris. Scattered about the Louvre, we see these paintings as they were never meant to be seen. For their purpose of edifying the Carthusians by constantly reminding them of the life of their founder, it is hard to see how they could be bettered. The theme is solitude as favoring religious perfection through the practice of the contemplative life. The problem was one of narration. Here the slightness of Le Sueur's construction and the defects of his color are of minor importance.  Upon clarity, simplicity and effectiveness of narrative design Le Sueur spent himself without reserve.  What an extraordinary variety of shades of piety there is in the faces and postures of his holy people!  Everything of this sort is completely thought and felt out.

The compositions are highly simplified and concentrated, with fewest accessories and emphasis always on the figures.  But in these simplified arrangements are used the most ingenious perspective devices, which give a sense of appropriate space and reinforce the patterns made by the figure groups.  Such refinements of design may be readily grasped in such a picture as Bruno listening to Raymond Diocres Preaching (Fig. 373).  How surely the sense of a throng and a great space is given with a few figures in a limited area!  The interest balances between the preacher and the rapt face of the youthful Bruno at the moment of conversion.  But mark the faces and figures one by one, their devout intentness, their relative inattention.  All this is conveyed, not in a literary way, but by just disposition of architectural and human forms, and by a broad, sensitive and most expressive distribution of light and dark.  More sensational, but also noble and reserved, is the Death of St. Bruno (Fig. 355).  The scene has great actuality, and also a paradoxical romantic glamour.  No tenebrist ever handled more successfully the problem of artificial illumination.  It is a very devout and tragic picture.

If the whole of the St. Bruno series were at the level of these two pictures, there could be no doubt as to Le Sueur's position as a great painter.  But again the critical spirit asks, What are the analogies?  Such masters of concentrated figure design as Giotto, Zurbarán? or rather such pietistic composers as the German Nazarenes and Flandrin?  I fear his place is with smaller men, even if he be well at their head.

The Life of St. Bruno was finished about 1650, in Le Sueur's thirty-fourth year.  He had some five years more to live, dying in 1655, at thirty-eight.  His later religious pictures show no growth, and it is probable that in his short life he gave qualitatively all he had.  When he passed, Paris was the poorer by an alert, sensitive, devout and eminently French spirit.  His mythologies seem to echo belatedly the fragile grace of the poetry of the Pléiade; his religious pictures seem inspired by the gentle lucidity and austerity of new Port Royal.

# CHAPTER XXIII

## CLAUDE LORRAIN

Fig. 374. Claude. Landscape with a Woman and Angel.—London.

Fig. 375. (Upper) Claude. River Landscape.—Princeton.
Fig. 376. (Lower) Claude. The Forum.—Paris.

Fig. 377. (Upper) CLAUDE. Embarkation of St. Ursula.—*London.*
Fig. 378. (Lower) CLAUDE. Sacrifice to Apollo on Delos.—*Doria, Rome.*

706

FIG. 379. CLAUDE. Landscape with a Piping Shepherd.—*Kansas City.*

FIG. 380.   CLAUDE.   Acis and Galatea.—Dresden.

FIG. 381. (Upper) CLAUDE. River Landscape (pen and wash).—*Author's Collection.*
FIG. 382. (Lower) CLAUDE. The Tiber, Sundown (brush drawing).—*British Museum, London.*

FIG. 383.   CLAUDE.   View of Nemi (pen drawing).—Rome.

Fig. 384.   CLAUDE.   The Fall of the Roman Empire.—Coll. Duke of Westminster, London.

711

Fig. 385. Claude. Aeneas Hunting in Libya.—*Brussels.*

CLAUDE GELLÉE, later called Lorrain, was born at Chamagne, near Toul, in the year 1600. His parents were poor, and he was early left an orphan. At twelve he was apprenticed to a baker, and a little later went to a brother, a wood-carver, who worked at Freiburg-im-Breisgau. There he probably made himself useful both in the kitchen and in the shop.

At fourteen he took the road to Rome with a company of pastry cooks. There he was apprenticed to a landscapist and decorator, Agostino Tassi, whom young Claude served as cook, houseman and studio assistant. Tassi was a versatile and somewhat charlatanistic artist, who had the astuteness to follow a new fashion. Earlier there had been a movement to substitute for formal figure decoration fantastic frescoes of a rustic sort. Even the grave Domenichino had done something of the sort. The Germans, Paul and Matthew Bril, by the beginning of the century were painting such scenic decorations in the Roman palaces and churches. Unluckily, what Tassi painted in Roman palaces and at Viterbo has virtually perished, but contemporary descriptions tell us that amid the frescoed arbors appeared many of Claude's future subjects—especially seaports. Tassi's shop was doubtless a good place in which to acquire executive habits. On Tassi's character the saying of his good patron, Pope Paul V, is instructive. Tassi was satisfactory to deal with, the Pope felt, because he was so plainly a scoundrel, a fact which, in the case of other artists, had to be found out. The Pope died in 1621. His successor did not take so friendly a view of Tassi's defects, and it is probable that, with the waning of Tassi's patronage, young Claude went on his own. With Tassi he had painted two and a half years among the hills of Viterbo; he was later two years with a master whom we know only by his Christian name, Goffredo. Apparently living in other than Rome scenery merely confirmed Claude's love of Rome and the Campagna.

In 1625 Claude returned to Lorraine by the Brenner and served as an assistant at Nancy to a mural painter, Claude Deruet. Of course, in these ten years of his education Claude must have drawn and painted landscapes, but nothing of this early period has been as yet identified. Accordingly, what Claude had learned during his eleven 'prentice years in Italy is pure surmise. One must recall that he was almost illiterate, much of the time a menial, probably no thinker, hence out of the circles where methods and ideals of art were discussed. He learned simply from what he saw in nature and in art. When we try to imagine his attitude in his late 'teens and early twenties, we are merely presenting probabilities or projecting backward the qualities of his work a dozen years later. We may safely assume an innate love of nature, especially in shifting effects of light and air. He was the first to paint such themes for themselves, and apart from any human interest they might enhance. In fifty years of constant production he never took the pains to learn to indicate the human figure with accuracy, generally entrusting the incidental figures in his landscapes to collaborators. It is plain that he loved the mellow ruins about Rome, loved them for their neglect among trees and bushes—for the way in which they caught the Italian sunlight. He loved also the stately way in which the tall, full-bosomed ships rode in Italian harbors—their picturesque geometry of spars and rigging now defined and glorified against sunset skies, now reduced to a ghostly pattern by golden mist. He loved the gentle windings of the slow rivers of the Campagna, their punctuation by fine, arched bridges, their borders of dense shrubbery, their reflections of trees and sky. Such, we may reasonably suppose, were Claude's dearest tastes from boyhood. His particular problem was how to find means of giving visual form to these intimate delights of the eye.

Evidently he could not do anything so novel and difficult without help, and, save for his share in Tassi's apparently quite superficial work, the only help available was the landscape painting that was going on at Rome, and the landscape backgrounds of certain Titians in Roman galleries. We may be sure he studied all this material with the most loving and thoughtful attention. The critics have generally ignored any dependence on Titian, but I feel that such Titians as the Bacchus and Ariadne, the Garden of Venus, Ariadne among the Adrians, may very well have confirmed what observation was doubtless teaching Claude—that the light must not seem to fall upon the picture, but must flood out of it. Most Renaissance pictures had been conceived as agreeable assemblages of plastic objects plainly lighted from in front, as actors on a stage are given prominence by the footlights. With a closer regard for nature, Giorgione, Titian and their contemporaries reversed the process. The picture must seem not to receive, but to emit light. Claude was merely to realize the multiform, exquisite applications of a discovery which the Venetians had only half developed. Of course, he may have worked this out for himself, ultimately did work it out alone, yet I cannot believe he failed to see and study deeply those idyllic Titians which his fellow Frenchman and good acquaintance, Nicolas Poussin, adored.

At Rome enlightened amateurs favored two quite different types of landscape—the luscious and rather romantic landscape practiced by the Brils and Elsheimer, and the more selective and austere landscape invented by Annibale Carracci, only recently dead, and ably continued by his best pupil, Domenichino. Poussin drew chiefly from Annibale and from Domenichino, eschewing what must have seemed to him the meretricious charm of the Brils and Elsheimer. The modest and undoctrinal Claude, I feel sure, admired both sorts of landscape, and profited by that admiration.

The Brils loved especially in landscape its lusciousness, bright coloring and sense of growth. They made no searching study of actual appearances, but they were most ingenious in contriving formulas to express what they liked to see. Thus Paul Bril shingles an area with dabs of yellow, blue and green, and the result is the leafage of a tree. The formula is so close to that of the tapestry weaver that I cannot imagine Paul Bril had failed to study the best verdure tapestries. The pen drawing of both the brothers Bril is so similar to Titian's that one may be sure they had made some study of his methods in landscape. During all Claude's early career Paul Bril was the favorite landscape painter in Rome. He was versatile. His formulas could be adapted to the requirements of a tiny cabinet picture or to those of a big fresco.

To a method very similar to that of the Brils another northerner, the German, Adam Elsheimer, brought a positive poetry. Everything is finer and more eloquent of mood. Elsheimer has aptly been called a reincarnation of Altdorfer, and, indeed, in a naïve romanticism these two charming artists are akin. Elsheimer worked only ten years at Rome, dying in 1610, but his memory was fresh when Claude arrived, and possession of his tiny pictures was disputed by discriminating amateurs, as is still the case.

Now Claude's art was to rest on a repertory of generally available and skillfully selected formulas—a century and a half after his death John Ruskin was to reproach Claude harshly for taking this sensible course. In working out his own formulas one may be sure Claude found the work of the Brils suggestive, and Elsheimer's little masterpieces may well have taught him that a methodical way of working is entirely compatible with intimacy of effect.

The landscape of Annibale Carracci and of Domenichino rested on a more rigorous selection and elimination than the romantic northerners practiced. To keep the clarity of the composition, color is reduced to tone. The effect is not luscious and exciting, but cool and tranquilizing. Everything depends upon a careful balancing of relatively few forms in terms of likeness and contrast, upon clear distinctions of foreground, middle distance and distance, upon large, untroubled areas skillfully plotted to serve the compositional harmony. In contrast with the art of the northerners, which at its best was temperamental, this landscape art of the eclectics is highly intellectual. Their pictures must be architectonic. Now the landscapes of Claude owe their greatness to an entirely similar architectonic. Everything is planned—though the planning may be mostly in the unconscious—nothing is casual, however free and lyrical the total expression may be. So, while we must always feel that Claude found his exquisite balances of form and color, light and luminous mist, in nature itself, one cannot doubt that his discovery was facilitated by the example of his contemporaries, who, doubtless even in his years of mastery, probably seemed his betters. Indeed, in its merely technical aspect, the art of Claude may be regarded as a synthesis of the methods of the northerners and of the eclectics, with a great extension of the scope of both.

We have left Claude working in a church at Nancy as an assistant of an obscure French mural painter. In 1627 Claude returned for good to Italy, via Lyons and Marseilles. His going, according to contemporary hearsay, was hastened through the shock occasioned by the fatal fall of a comrade from a scaffold. We have what seems to be a record of his landing at Civitavecchia, in a pen and wash drawing at Berlin. It is a good, crisp sketch, but has no great distinction and lacks the coloristic quality of his best drawings. If we may venture a generalization from this single instance, at twenty-seven Claude had not attained great skill. The versatile German artist and critic, Sandrart, confirms this view by saying that on Claude's return to Rome he made many small pictures which, because they were not very good, he sold at small prices. All the same, one would like to see them. Something of their quality may be inferred from the tiny landscape at Princeton, which bears the last letters of a genuine signature and the date 1635. It is a fine landscape, unaffectedly charming, possibly even a reminiscence of the pleasant, broken countryside of Lorraine (Fig. 375). From its lack of classical features such an unpretentious little affair might easily strike a Sandrart as not very good. Hence from this delightful little canvas, here first published, one may gain an idea of Claude's breadwinning activities some ten years earlier.

From Sandrart we have a pleasant account of Claude's doings at Rome. They sketched together as far as Tivoli. Sandrart painted in the very mist of the cascade at Tivoli, and induced Claude to paint out of doors—a practice which Claude soon abandoned in favor of the more sensible and comfortable procedure of sketching out of doors and painting in the studio. The talented Flemish sculptor, François Dufresnoy, was often of the company, and Poussin occasionally made the fourth. What is interesting in these reminiscences is that the native wit and good humor of the untutored Claude made him an acceptable companion for three intellectuals of the first order.

Throughout his life Claude sold pictures in pairs—to hang on either side of a door or chimney piece. The earliest such pair consists of a View of the Forum and a Seaport, at Paris. Since the prospect of the Forum was copied by Claude in an etching dated 1636, the oil painting is probably somewhat earlier. The Forum (Campo Vaccino) is one of the few Claudes that is a portrait of an actual scene; the Seaport is fantastically pieced together after his own taste.

The architectural elements in the Forum are represented with reasonable fidelity, but are arranged as wings inviting to look between and down a vista. Since the Forum (Fig. 376) was the left-hand picture of the pair, its left is clearly marked by a retreating perspective of monuments, which begins with the arch of Septimius Severus, cut by the frame, is broken by the Torre della Milizia, arbitrarily introduced, by an arch of the Basilica of Constantine, and closed by the campanile of Sta. Francesca Romana. It rises to precisely the height of the highest part of the Coliseum, which closes the vista. The right wing is kept lighter and more in the foreground. There are two ranges of three columns, with a fine tree interposed to break their rigidity. The warm light comes forward tranquilly from a veiled sky, revealing the architectural masses as creamy areas, in a fashion that young Corot will emulate nearly two centuries later. Much of the picture is in shadow, which Claude has so skillfully handled that there is no loss of definition.

The Seaport is plainly compiled. The retreat of buildings at the right—for it is the right-hand picture—is composed of various contemporary buildings, designed by Claude himself—a rusticated portal softened by a crown of shrubbery, a palace with a giant order, a building which, since it has a campanile, may be a vague formula for a basilical church. Towards the left are the prows of great ships, further away a confusion of moored square-riggers and feluccas with great slanting yards. Again the light comes forward from a veiled sky where float a few small clouds with luminous edges. The surface of the harbor is troubled by the south wind, the light touches the top of the swirls, giving the area a soft, velvety incandescence. Here are the elements which Claude soon will handle with much more finesse and precision. In both pictures the scenic method is complete and only needs to be worked out more subtly.

The foregrounds of both pictures, especially that of the Seaport, are rather cluttered by characterful little figures in the general bizarre feeling of Jacques Callot. They were touched in by the friendly Hollander, Jan Miel. Later such incidental figures will be used more sparingly and with greater pictorial discretion. Here they probably represent a money's worth to an exigent client.

In the same year, or possibly a little later, 1636, falls Claude's finest etching, the Herdsman, *Le Bouvier*. Its delicate luminosity is achieved by a method that, were it not so successful, must be called niggling. The dark masses, always full of half-light, are built up by an infinitude of small flicks of the needle, but the effect is broad and spacious, the feeling a blithe serenity. And Claude's greatest pictures are similarly niggled into perfection with countless small brush strokes —local loadings with solid colors, local glazes with transparent tints. The luminous evanescence of the effect depends on the fact that the brush has fallen as frequently and variously as do rays of light over clouds, water, foliage, buildings. This method has made the Claudes the natural prey of the picture restorer. The slightest overcleaning or impairment of the fragile surface simply ruins a Claude. It remains a wreck, or worse, is refinished by the restorer's heavy hand. So the reader must be advised that when he sees, as he often will, a bleak and colorless Claude, or one reeking with vulgar polychromy, he is seeing a restorer's Claude—either skinned or radically repainted.

By his fortieth year Claude was prospering greatly. The Roman nobility and clergy ordered the pairs of big pictures incessantly. He set up bachelor hall, in the Via Babuino, near Poussin. A brother came down from Lorraine to relieve him of all household and business responsibility. By the early 1650's the household was enlivened by the presence of a little Agnes, a love child of some tardy and probably fugitive amour. His pictures became so costly and popular that they were fraudulently copied and sold as his. To circumvent the forgers he made composition sketches of his pictures, giving it out that he never made replicas himself. Thus was made the famous "Liber Veritatis." He willed it to his daughter Agnes, and it has constituted a higher education in composition for landscapists ever since.

A close study of the Claudes will reveal certain standard expedients. There are little touches which suggest the crispness of foliage, but denote no particular tree; there are picturesque crossed tree trunks that appear many times; the rising of the trunk and its branching are improvised and without much strength or specific character; a certain sort of coarse zigzag stroke means sunlight caught on the tops of little waves. Aside from such details the general composition of his pictures offers only a few patterns. Something tall and massive in the foreground throws the rest of the picture back. It may be stately buildings or great shadowy trees on both sides or on one. Usually there is a central vista seen through wings in the foreground. Sometimes there is a central feature, a tree or a building in middle distance with outlets almost always unequal on either side. He habitually veils and virtually effaces the skyline with golden mist. The eye rests in the middle distance and loses itself beyond.

The vastness of Claude's spaces is first indicated by disposition and stepping back of forms, but the real factor in spatiality is the color which tends to dissolve the forms into an unmeasured but infinite space. Poussin's space is indicated by disposition of forms, but created by relations of tones. In his later works it is often a vast space, but always a measured one.

Now all such schematisms were severely reprehended by John Ruskin, and probably most modern landscape painters would feel Claude's expedients to be unnecessarily formal and artificial. In particular, many modernists would deprecate the sacrifice of substantiality to circumambient colored air. But these dodges—not to mince matters—which Claude to a certain extent shares with the ordinary scene painter, are of the very essence of his art. He loved to paint the hours when, in the constant rivalry between light and things, light triumphs, and things become mere reflectors or transmitters of light, largely lose their substance and entirely their individuality. His formulas merely admit this fact of ordinary observation. His little, apparently timid touches are the only way in which he could give to paint the value of colored air. One must regard things in a Claude sunset as merely hanging in a sort of solution in a vaporous medium. The issue is not of his expedients, which are frankly artificial and undiscoverable in natural appearances—but of the transfiguring power with which he uses them. He prefers to paint moments when nature is rather glorified than revealed by the light; his problem is to enhance this glory on his own account, and he seldom fails to do so. To realize the immense superiority of a Claude sunset, we need only recall the hundreds of merely gaudy sunsets from those of his able contemporary, Salvator Rosa, to those of yesterday. And, oddly, those that are painted with a close regard for the actual data, are false and theatrical in effect. In short, it is through a sensitive conventionality that Claude arrives, not only at a greater brilliancy, but also at a greater naturalness of effect.

Since the loveliness of the good Claudes is of a somewhat monotonous order, and his life offers, save for a few anecdotes indicating his gentleness and amiability, really no events, there is little more to say beyond pointing out a few of his finest paintings, and giving some notion of the preparatory processes before he began to paint. In his forties Claude painted mostly seaports, and as a class these are the least interesting part of his work. He sometimes insists too much on the obvious splendor of sunset, while the made-up character of the composition is often too apparent. The best are magnificent, and certainly one of the best is the Embarkation of St. Ursula, at London (Fig. 377).

Here Claude has avoided the formality of a central vista between flanking wings. The eye reads the picture from left to right. The very elaborate pattern of uneven rectangles in the buildings, steps and quay is gently echoed in the buildings behind the moored ship at the right, and relieved by the picturesque silhouettes of the ships and the blurred diagonal lines of the little waves which catch the level light. The big tree deep at the right, because its soft mass is sufficiently unbroken, balances the buildings. The boat, cut by the frame and the lower left corner, leads the eye back into the picture after the eye has made the circuit from left to right. The sense of ponderous movement in the square-riggers contrasts effectively with the light grip of the shallops on the water. The sky vibrates with golden light, which overflows towards the beholder, resting momentarily on all intermediate forms as it comes. The figures, probably by the Florentine, Filippo Lauri, give a sense of joyous urgency and of stately ceremony befitting the noble architecture and the theme—the embarkation of a princess for her nuptials. That romantic glamour at which Claude aimed in all these seaports at sunset seems here perfectly achieved.

As Claude passed into his forties his skill as a composer grew finer. There is less obtrusion of architectural elements, the figures are more sparsely and appropriately disposed. No picture of this period is more exquisitely balanced than the Sacrifice to Apollo on Delos, Doria Palace, Rome (Fig. 378). The arrangement is at once very formal and very easy. There are two vistas marked by trees silhouetted in near middle distance. The right-hand vista is short, being closed by a stately domed temple; the left-hand vista over a distant zigzagging river, faintly discerned buildings and long arched bridges is illimitable. The very static linear pattern is enlivened and carried deep into the picture by a series of opposed diagonals which begin with the bridge and approach to the temple, and end with a sharp turn of the river as it widens and loses itself in the haze under the horizon. Of the more formal sort this is a perfect Claude—reticent yet rich in cool color, actively balanced without too artificial display of the underlying geometry. This stately masterpiece was painted in 1648.

A similar compositional system which avoids a too obvious symmetry is shown in the Landscape with Figures, London (Fig. 374).

The opposing diagonals are here carried into the sky in a flight of birds.

As Claude passed into old age, accessories of all sorts are more strictly economized and pure landscape interest predominates. Here the Landscape with a Piping Shepherd, at Kansas City (Fig. 379), is one of the finest exhibits. Again the system is one of diagonals in depth, but there are refinements of atmospheric envelopment, edges of utmost delicacy which tell everything of form and distance, and a singularly remote and pellucid sky. It is a quietly musical picture.

Merely from the point of view of the creation of an illusion of colored air in gently irresistible motion, the Acis and Galatea, 1657, at Dresden (Fig. 380), must be regarded as a consummately fine Claude. Everything hovers and swims in a pulsating and humid luminosity which sweeps landwards over the rippling, gently flashing tops of little waves. The classical figures of lovers seem to belong, which is not always the case with Claude, while the fishing boats tell reassuringly that this glorified and transformed world is after all the world we inhabit.

If Claude rarely painted in the open air, he sketched constantly in the face of nature, built himself up an amazing repertory of objects and motives, and even complete compositions, which needed only the transforming touch of his color. All his life he made such drawings, and when the gout seized upon him in old age his greatest affliction must have been less the pain than the inability to stay out in the Campagna in the evening chill. There are hundreds of his drawings in public and private collections—everything is there—ruins, crags, trees, bushes, cattle—everything but people. If he painted by formulas, he had previously observed and recorded with fidelity. For many critics, including myself, there are more first-class drawings by Claude than first-class paintings. The chronology of the drawings, except for the few which can be associated with his paintings, is uncertain. Some surely are earlier than the earliest paintings we know. This is probably the case with a wash drawing on blue paper, in my own collection (Fig. 381). It is a mere blot of transparent brown bistre, but a blot that suggests miles of space and distance.

More often Claude used two washes, blue-black India ink and warm brown bistre. With these two tints he gets extraordinary effects of color, and establishes complete and noble compositions. Because it will reproduce well I choose the famous sheet, at London, the

Tiber, Sundown (Fig. 382). It suggests with a peculiar poetry the vastness and mystery of the Roman Campagna as the darkness is about to engulf it, and I suppose it hardly occupied Claude for half an hour.

Claude's pen drawings are somewhat more conventional, in the tradition that had come down from Titian to the Carracci, Elsheimer and the Brils, but they are also intensely alive. Witness the View of Nemi, in the National Gallery, Rome (Fig. 383). Materially it is a system of preconceived strokes; spiritually it is the rise of cliffs, the rustling of trees, the sweep of wind-blown smoke.

Towards the end of his career Claude painted fewer seaports and more landscapes. In these he tactfully conceals his standard artifices, seeking natural and almost casual effects. He paints larger pictures and now prefers a rather wide oblong. Among the many superb canvases of this time and type none seems finer to me, though I know it only from reproductions, than the Fall of the Roman Empire (Fig. 384), in the collection of the Duke of Westminster, London. The level foreground of pasture, thinly occupied by cattle, sheep and two attendant women, is the near side of the bend of a quiet river, beyond which, between great trees at the left and a ruined triumphal arch at the right, one sees a file of empty and ruined buildings, with the light showing through their arches. Beyond, rises gently the long slope of the Alban Mountains. The sky is cloudless, but vibrant. As Dr. Walter Friedländer has well remarked in his excellent book on Claude, we no longer have a view, but rather a vision, and it is probably this visionary quality which has given the picture a title which, though it may have been deep in Claude's feeling, probably was not in his mind. The figures of animals and people are, I think, Claude's. Deprecating his little skill in this branch, he used to say that he sold his landscapes, but gave his figures free. Of this Sir Joshua Reynolds was later to observe that the figures of Claude are more appropriate for his pictures than those touched in by his abler collaborators. Nowhere is the pensive and elegiac mood of Claude more fully expressed than in this great picture; nowhere are his artifices truer to natural effect. We have here in exquisite balance whatever he most loved—the simple rusticity of the herd and keepers, the glooming of great trees against the sky; the stretch of tranquil water darkened by reflections, brightening by the foam of distant rapids, mirroring the sky; the stately forms of ancient ruins which have become one with the landscape; the high towering of a pellucid sky which is a cover rather than a background—all this you have combining in a chord in which love and a noble melancholy vibrate in complete harmony.

Claude was to live over twenty years after this great picture was signed in 1661, but he was hardly to surpass it. Perhaps he did in his most energetic and vibrant landscape, Aeneas hunting in Libya (Fig. 385), Brussels. Here everything vibrates in unison, and an extraordinary luminosity is achieved through low values with avoidance of sharp contrasts. Of all the Claudes I know it is the most fully and legitimately romantic in effect, and without a tinge of his artificial stage managership. When he signed it in 1672 he was a very tired and ailing old man. It is notable among the many defiances that great artists have made of the descending scythe of Father Time. At eighty-two, in November, 1682, Claude died, leaving his artistic effects to the love child, Agnes.

Ever since, his landscapes, painted, drawn or etched, have been an inspiration to landscape painters of the thoughtful kind. His pictures were early engraved, so that their compositional features could everywhere be studied. Direct imitation of his methods and subjects —from Patel to Turner—has generally led to pyrotechnic vulgarity. What was and is available is his main principle that landscape usually cannot be merely compiled or discovered, but must be created— created, however, by a painter who, like Claude himself, has first been sensitively diligent in observation and discovery.

# CHAPTER XXIV

## POUSSIN

Fig. 386. Poussin. Et in Arcadia Ego.—*Devonshire House, London.*

FIG. 387. (Upper) POUSSIN. Echo and Narcissus.—*Paris.*
FIG. 388. (Lower) POUSSIN. Massacre of the Innocents.—*Chantilly.*

FIG. 389. (Upper) POUSSIN. Triumph of David.—Madrid.
FIG. 390. (Lower) POUSSIN. Sleeping Venus.—Dresden.

728

FIG. 391. (Upper) POUSSIN. Triumph of Flora.—*Paris.*
FIG. 392. (Lower) POUSSIN. Lamentation over the Dead Christ.—*Dublin.*

729

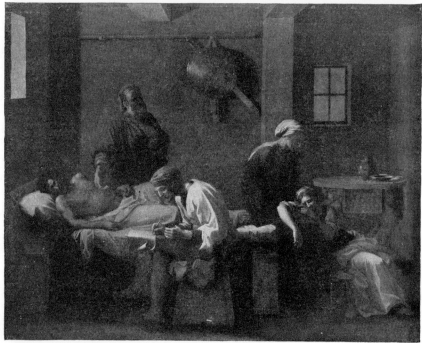

FIG. 393. (Upper) POUSSIN. Et in Arcadia Ego.—Paris.
FIG. 394. (Lower) POUSSIN. Testament of Eudamidas.—Copenhagen.

730

FIG. 395. POUSSIN. Time Rescues Truth from Envy and Discord (oil sketch).—Lille.

731

FIG. 396. (Upper) POUSSIN. Sacrament of Marriage.—Bridgewater
House, London.
FIG. 397. (Lower) POUSSIN. St. John the Evangelist on Patmos.—
Chicago.

732

FIG. 398. (Lower) POUSSIN. Orpheus and Eurydice (drawing).—Chantilly.
FIG. 399. (Upper) POUSSIN. Orpheus and Eurydice.—New York.

FIG. 400. (Upper) POUSSIN. Orpheus and Eurydice.—*Paris*.
FIG. 401. (Lower) POUSSIN. Winter—the Deluge.—*Paris*.

A YOUNG Norman painter, Nicolas Poussin, was working on the decoration of the Luxembourg Palace while Rubens' great pictures of the career of Marie de Médicis were being installed. He left Paris for Rome about a year before this magnificent series was publicly inaugurated. It is strange indeed that there is not the slightest trace in Poussin's art of the greatest contemporary painting he was ever to see. His immunity was all the stranger that he, like Rubens, was completing for his nation a century-long process of assimilation of the Renaissance style, or, more specifically, of the Venetian manner as represented by Titian. Both were profoundly influenced by the antique. The gulf between the art of Poussin and that of Rubens—so unbridgeable that for half a century artistic Paris was militantly divided into Rubensists and Poussinists—was established by sharply differing personal and national points of view. While Rubens was born of gentle stock and lived the life of a nobleman and courtier, Poussin came of small bourgeois stock in the provinces, married the daughter of a cook, and while at the height of a professional fame that was international, lived in modest obscurity at Rome. In his manners and in his art Rubens displayed the florid expansiveness of a Flemish patrician; in his manners and in his art Poussin retained much of the simplicity, shrewdness and eminently calculating spirit of a Norman peasant.

In taste, what Leonardo da Vinci called the artist's judgment, *giudizio*, there is, I think, little to choose between them; both had it in an extraordinary degree. But it worked at different points of creative activity. It seems as if taste guided Rubens' hand instinctively, as he seemed to improvise, while in Poussin taste worked consciously and reflectively through long preparatory processes, before he put brush to canvas. Here, too, national and racial differences may underlie the contrast. Rubens evinces the ready and ardent opportunism of the Flamand; Poussin the rational and calculating prudence of the Frenchman. One cannot imagine that Rubens burnt the lamp of sacrifice; Poussin seems to have tended it assiduously. His

only expression of pride in his work is the famous saying "I have neglected nothing"; Rubens might have written "I have sacrificed nothing." At a remove of three centuries it is possible to admire both
masters whole-heartedly; in Paris in Louis XIV's time it was virtually
impossible, and such liberal secretaries of the Academy as Félibien
and Rogier de Piles who ventured to praise both artists, got away with
it only by asserting, probably well beyond their personal convictions,
Poussin's superiority. Even today I think only a Frenchman can have
the fullest appreciation of Poussin. In painting he stands for all that
was finest and noblest in the emergent culture of Louis XIV's France
—represents it, I feel, with a more disciplined eloquence than Corneille, with an insight more masculine and heroic than Racine's, with
a logic and methodology vying with that of Descartes.

Nicolas Poussin was born at Les Andeleys, in Normandy, in 1594,
of a stock which later he very candidly described as brutal and ignorant. His vocation as a painter early declared itself, and with next
to no education he was studying with an itinerant painter named
Quentin Varin. On his travels from Flanders to Provence Varin had
picked up at second hand something of the Italian manner. He could
have taught young Poussin little but the mechanical part of painting
—a part more important then, when a painter had to prepare his own
colors and even make his own brushes. The relation lasted about a
year, and at eighteen, in 1612, Poussin went to Paris and plunged
into an atmosphere of eager but misunderstood Italianism. Vouet
and Philippe de Champaigne, who had really assimilated the Italian
style, had not yet come to Paris. There was drudgery with a Flemish
portrait painter, François Elle, and with a French decorator, Lalle-
mant. Amid difficulties, Poussin began one of the most extraordinary
efforts of self-education on record. He fell in with a friendly young
nobleman from Poitou, who engaged him to decorate his château.
These paintings have never been traced. With extraordinary considerateness this young patron took Poussin to see a mathematician
named Courtois, who had a collection of Marcantonio's engravings
after Raphael. These were the clarion call to Poussin that the old
ballad of "Chevy Chase" had earlier been to Sir Philip Sidney. He
now knew what he wanted to do—nothing less than to make over in
his own fashion that ideal and noble world which he had divined in
Marcantonio's thin and bloodless copies of the Parnassus, the Judgment of Paris, the Galatea, the Psyche. Poussin was yet to pass long

years of struggle, but at least he had glimpsed his far-away shining goal.

Unhappily we cannot trace Poussin's early progress. We have no pictures that can surely be dated before his thirtieth year. Indeed, it seems likely that he was making a hard living by assisting other painters, and in these years produced little on his own account; likely, too, that his mind worked massively and unhurriedly, and that, like his future great exemplar, Titian, he matured late. At eighteen or nineteen he was traveling about central France in search of a living, with the result of one of those serious illnesses which periodically ravaged his powerful frame. He passed more than a year of convalescence and attained his majority at Les Andeleys, probably none too happy amid his brutal and ignorant kinsmen. For nearly five years we have almost no notices of him, and then we find him making repeated efforts to get to Italy.

In 1620 he got as far as Florence and for some unknown reason, perhaps from poverty, turned back. In 1622 he was halted at Lyons by a legal extortion which took all his traveling funds, except a pitiful remnant which in good sporting fashion he spent on a fine dinner for himself and his friend. Back in Paris better luck dawned. He was employed with Philippe de Champaigne, by Duchesne, in the minor decoration of the Luxembourg. Rubens' florid masterpieces were coming in, but, as we have seen, they made absolutely no impression upon Poussin. The turning point in his fortunes was his acquaintance with the visiting Italian celebrity, the Cavaliere Gian-Battista Marino. It came about in a curious fashion. The Jesuits held a competition for six pictures representing the history of their order. Contrary to his habit of deliberate execution, Poussin knocked off six water-color designs—unhappily now lost—in as many days. These attracted the admiration of Marino, who with utmost zeal and friendliness helped Poussin continue that effort of self-education which the young nobleman of Poitou and the mathematician Courtois had auspiciously inaugurated.

Marino was a man of vile character, who had made his native Italy too hot for him. But he was an ingenious rhetorician at a time when rhetoric was highly valued, and the artificial elegance of his poem "Adonis," not to mention its unabashed sensualism, made him as much a hero for the flaming youth of Louis XIII's time as James Joyce, for his "Ulysses," was to be for the flaming youth of the reigns of George V and Woodrow Wilson. And like many men of morally vile character, Marino was a genial and friendly person, and probably, with the libertine's nostalgia for his own cleaner days, had a respect for the cleanness of youth. Poussin took no harm from him and got much good. Marino, an accomplished classicist, led Poussin to the great ancient books, opened to the youth's ravished vision the idyllic world of Virgil and Ovid, the heroic world of Plutarch. Where most classicizing painters drew from such stale secondary sources as Ripa's "Iconologia," Poussin drank at the fountainhead. Unless it be Emerson's and Keats', there has been hardly another case of so thorough an indoctrination with the spirit of classical antiquity, without command of the languages.

Marino was a great lion at Paris, and his friendship opened all doors. Poussin had probably already been free to study the antique marbles and casts in the royal collections, and such Italian pictures as were owned at Paris and Fontainebleau. But the great Titians now in the Louvre, from which he had most to learn, were still in England, Italy and Spain.

It has been suggested by French art historians that Marino introduced Poussin to the cultured and highly precious circle of the Marquise de Rambouillet. This seems to me unlikely, for it was never Poussin's habit to seek people out. They had to come to him, from the young Poitevin nobleman and Marino to the artists and gentry who later joined his evening strolls on the Pincio. In 1624, doubtless encouraged by Marino, Poussin at last found the way to Rome, where, with the exception of a brief, unhappy sojourn at Paris, he was to pass the rest of his days. He was thirty years old, and had singularly little to show for over ten years of laborious breadwinning.

The handful of pre-Roman Poussins have been picked out by critical intuition and without substantial evidence, but we may agree with Grautoff that the youthful Bacchus and Erigone, private collection, Paris; the Narcissus gazing into the Fountain, Dresden; and the Echo and Narcissus (Fig. 387), Paris, were either painted at Paris or in his French manner soon after his move to Rome. It is not an impressive group. The tone is that of a gentle idylism, the figures are slackly constructed and stand far from firmly, the placing of the nude forms in the landscape is perfunctory, and the landscape itself hardly more than a decorative screen. Something of the future master, however, reveals itself in the Echo and Narcissus. The looming of the big rock and the trees against the sky is nobly expressed. The gracious body of the mourning nymph is highly expressive and well set in its surroundings of rock and trees; there is a certain monumentality in the little Amor against the sky, and the disposition of the body of dead Narcissus is effective if not correct. Where the two presumably earlier pictures hardly transcend the rather anemic idylism which Le Sueur was soon to represent, and are, for me, less coherent than the superficial mythologies of Vouet, the Echo and Narcissus gives promise of the future master. Probably the two subjects of Narcissus were suggested by Marino, who had duly exploited the theme in that great catch-all, his famous "Adonis."

At Rome, with Marino's influence, the way to patronage seemed clear, but there was still much difficulty ahead. Cardinal Barberini interested himself in Poussin, but was soon sent from Rome to a diplomatic post. Poussin, however, knit a firm friendship with the Cardinal's secretary, the Cavaliere Cassiano del Pozzo, archaeologist, expert, incidentally art dealer—a good man for a struggling young painter to know. Poussin shared lodgings with two classicizing sculptors, the Fleming, Charles Dufresnoy, and the Bolognese, Algardi. Together they studied the antique marbles.

The fixed point in Roman taste on Poussin's arrival was admiration for the somewhat mannered elegance of the late Hellenistic sculpture. Here only the Caravaggians, prominent among them the Frenchman, Valentin, dissented, and I fancy they, too, admired on the sly such robust statues as the Dying Gaul and the Torso of the Belvedere. Everybody but the Caravaggians adopted the proportions of the Vatican marbles and their feeling. This involved a waiver of the massiveness of the Renaissance. Here is the origin of Poussin's figures, whether nude or draped, though he ultimately corrected what threatened to become insipid ingredients by consulting nature and the superb forms of Titian's mythologies. Beyond this consensus of admiration for what we now know to be the inferior antique, all was confusion. Taste in figure design oscillated between the proletarian assertiveness of the tenebrists and the robust eclecticism of the recently deceased Carracci. Their style was being continued in various phases by the facile idylist, Francesco Albano, by the noble and thoughtful Domenichino, by the versatile and sentimental Guido Reni, the hero of the hour. Alongside this imported Bolognese manner, flourished that of the debilitated Renaissance, or unrealized baroque, as you will, in Pietro da Cortona—the most fecund and popular mural painter of the moment.

In the new art of landscape painting there was a similar confusion of counsels. The northerners, Adam Elsheimer and Paul Bril, had introduced an elaborately decorative and intimate, and appropriately colorful, landscape. Agostino Tassi had gained popularity for a superficial and stagey scenic painting. From such sources a Poussin, whose tendency was always to heroize his themes, could draw nothing. The tenebrists left landscape out of their reckoning. Annibale Carracci had left a few landscapes quite spacious in feeling, with carefully selected forms executed mostly in browns and grays. His pupil, Domenichino, was continuing the style in a more colorful manner. Ultimately this work was to have a leading influence on Poussin as a landscape painter.

One must think of Poussin as feeling his way for three or four years amid this welter of new impressions. He even yields momentarily to the tenebrism which he hated, probably induced by the success of his fellow countryman, Valentin. The result was the two battle pieces representing Joshua's Victory over the Amelekites and Amorites, at Leningrad. These are technically very able. Even Rubens had hardly handled masses of struggling men with more energy and clarity. These exceptional pictures, which some critics have doubted, have the interest of showing the dramatic and emotional capacity of Poussin, of proving that the moderation of his mature manner is due not to coldness, but to conscious self-restraint.

The emotional power of Poussin is even more strikingly shown in the Massacre of the Innocents (Fig. 388), at Chantilly. No painter has wrung so completely the horror from the theme. Most painters, notably Raphael, in Marcantonio's engraving, had represented a wholesale massacre with many figures, attenuating the dreadfulness of the scene by the beauty and dignity of the forms. Guido Reni, in a picture now at Bologna which Poussin undoubtedly knew, sought to individualize the horror by virtually limiting his composition to two soldiers slaughtering the infants of two mothers. Poussin carries dramatic concentration to the limit by showing only one woman desperately and vainly struggling with a soldier, with an incidental figure of another woman who walks off tragically carrying the body of her slain child. We have to do with continuous narrative expressing two moments of the fearful event. Preliminary studies show how

Poussin sought the maximum of terror. In an amazing sheet at Lille he takes from his friend Marino's poem on the theme, the soldier holding off the woman by her hair and treading on the babe. In the sketch at Lille the sword has not begun to fall—is horizontal, the foot of the soldier is on the child's body, the other woman seems to be escaping with a live baby in her arms. The screw could be turned a little harder. In the finished picture the sword is cutting down upon the child, the soldier's foot is on the child's tender throat, the escaping woman has dangling before her the body of her dead child. The picture shows only one further change. The mother with the dead child is no longer escaping. Her hand raised high in the drawing to express despair is bent back to clutch at her hair. She walks away very quietly, with a certain acceptance. It is a very terrible picture with its focus of the agonized and distorted face of the mother. It is also a picture of the most imaginative truthfulness, and while for its unsparing painfulness one could almost wish it unpainted, one cannot withhold admiration for the mind that could conceive it.

Stylistic analysis of what is less a picture than an appalling excerpt from life itself may seem trivial. Yet it is worth remarking that in what required utmost exuberance of emotion Poussin had recourse to the most exuberant of styles, the baroque. The curves and diagonals in plane and in depth, the straining against the bounds, are true baroque characteristics. The picture was painted in 1629, when Poussin was thirty-five.

A little earlier Poussin had made for St. Peter's the Martyrdom of St. Erasmus, his first important commission. It, too, is a baroque composition, and, in my opinion, one of the finest. The subject is one of the most disgusting imaginable—the disemboweling of a martyr by gradually reeling out his intestines. But as one sees it in the Vatican Gallery the gruesomeness of the theme is not the first or major effect. It is modified by a large and tranquilizing distribution of light and shade, by a cool harmony of brown and deep amber colors, by the noble postures of the persons engaged in the ignoble business. In this connection one should recall that the nerves of the seventeenth century man were stolid enough to accept judicial torture, by the civil courts or by the Inquisition, as a necessary and meritorious institution. Since our nerves are more tender, at least when we are not blowing people to bits by air bombs, the Martyrdom of St. Erasmus may serve as a signal demonstration of the transforming character of style. It seems to me one of the great Poussins, however anomalous in his activity, and it thoroughly disposes of the criticism which Sir Joshua Reynolds was to make a century and a quarter later, that Poussin was excellent only in small-scale figures and incapable of painting effectively on the scale of life. It is the only picture he ever signed, and he did so "in order that it might not discredit the great painters who worked for St. Peter's."

We begin to get the characteristic Poussins in these years after 1625—the Parnassus, Madrid, overcrowded, a bit rhetorical, somewhat dependent on Raphael's famous fresco; the Death of Germanicus, Barberini Palace, Rome, the first to make the exterior space integral with the whole composition, the first Poussin to catch the masculine gravity of Roman antiquity. While painting these pictures he had been copying the work of the disregarded and sensitive Domenichino, made his acquaintance, defended his Last Communion of St. Jerome against the general charge of plagiarism. The association was soon broken through Domenichino's departure for Naples, new chagrins and a mysterious death. But the sincerity, thoughtfulness and absence of display of Domenichino powerfully reinforced these virtues in Poussin, while, I feel, Domenichino's few landscapes established the broad and grand topography and the austerity of color in Poussin's later landscape painting.

For me, the completest Poussin of these years of re-education is the Triumph of David (Fig. 389), Madrid, one of the few well-preserved and colorful Poussins. Much that most painters would have wanted in the scene is sacrificed to concentration. There is no triumphal procession, no admiring throng—just the lithe young conqueror sitting casually beside the armor and severed head of the giant, seeming unconscious of the winged Victory about to place a laurel wreath on his head, as of the three chubby geniuses who offer wreaths or engrave a commemorative inscription. What is remarkable about a picture which superficially recalls the emptiness of baroque symbolism is its self-contained character and what might be called its seemingly casual monumentality, which is really very studied. All the postures are dictated by function, as in a Venetian design, and not by considerations of animation and grace in a stylistic vacuum. The construction of the nude bodies is at once strong and unassertive; the transforming of the horrid feature of the severed head into a dignified and pathetic accessory, the gentle effect of the really loose and exuberant poses of David and the Victory; the steadying value of the colonnade and of the tablet tilted at precisely the right angle to balance the figures—all this is pure Poussin. It is evidently an art of taste, vigorous self-criticism, unremitting reflection, with a tact which pretty well conceals these preliminary processes. A little earlier Poussin had treated the Triumph of David scenically and profusely—the conqueror, with Goliath's head on a pike, striding behind trumpeters amid an acclaiming populace. The picture is at Dulwich. It abounds in unassimilated dramatic devices, some of which are inherently ingratiating, but it is a stilted affair. Poussin's Triumph of David, at Madrid, may be considered as a sort of repudiation of the procedures of the earlier picture. The comparison of the two tells much about the growth of his artistic intelligence in these first Roman years.

In 1639 it was rumored about Rome that Titian's three Este mythologies and the Giovanni Bellini which he had finished were to pass from the Doria-Pamphili Palace to that of the king of Spain. Poussin is said to have wept at the news. These admirable arrangements of nudes in landscape, products of Titian's glorious maturity, had already evoked his adoration. Now he saw them with that hallucinatory vividness with which we view anything which we know we are soon to see no more. He carefully copied at least two, probably all four, with the result that the full-blown idylism of Titian was to dominate his development for a matter of ten years.

We see the immediate working of this new influence in the full and noble sensuousness of Sleeping Venus with gazing Shepherds (Fig. 390), Dresden, the similar picture, Sleeping Venus and Satyrs, London, and the early Bacchanale, at Paris. In all of these pictures the gleam of the white bodies against a screen of dark boscage is entirely Titianesque, as is the saturated warm coloration of such of these pictures as are well preserved. The sense of space is weak, really weaker than it is in Titian. This problem, which Titian faced only casually and intermittently, was to occupy Poussin's later years. Meanwhile he achieved what was very necessary for his long and strenuous endeavor, domestic happiness. In a serious illness a friendly fellow countryman, Jacques Dughet, cook for a Roman nobleman, took Poussin into his home. During convalescence he fell in love with the young daughter of the house, Anna Maria, and married her in 1630. He adopted her brother, Gaspard, whom he made an excellent landscape painter.

The few really loved Poussins come along in the five years
between his marriage and his unfortunate return to Paris. They have
the gaiety and frank sensuousness proper to a young husband. Perhaps the most gracious of this series are the Inspiration of Anacreon,
Hannover, and the first version of the theme *Et in Arcadia Ego* (Fig.
386), Devonshire House, London. It is all more casual and animated
than the slightly later and far more famous version of the theme at
Paris. Two shepherds and a shepherdess have happened upon a tomb
which bears the inscription "I, too, in Arcady." An old man,
marked as a poet by his wreath, is seen from behind as he contem-
plates the brevity of Arcadian life. The profound and universal pathos
which distinguishes the later version is hardly intimated in this early
rendering of the theme, yet it is one of the lovelier and more satisfying Poussins. The arrangement is highly Titianesque—the tree trunks
looming against the sky opposing the heavy thrust of the three youthful figures which is brought to stable balance by the incoming curve
of the seated poet. Very Titianesque, too, is the contrast between
the face of the girl in full light and that of the shepherd arbitrarily
in shadow. It is the magic of Poussin to keep a casual grace in a fully
calculated composition. The painting of the nude is Poussin at his
best, at once monumental and very much alive. The greenish white
of the woman's robe is taken up in the blue-green and green-white
of the sky. There are far grander Poussins than this, but perhaps
none more fully and graciously appealing.

The most elaborated of Poussin's mythologies of this time is the
Triumph of Flora (Fig. 391), Paris. We see it today sadly dulled by
overcleaning, but enough remains to make it still one of the most
enchanting of his pictures. The car of Flora, drawn by Cupids har-
nessed with garlands, moves from the right before a background of
distant blue hills towards a grove which looms at the left against the
yellowed sky. Everywhere flowers. Nymphs stoop to pluck them,
or offer them to the goddess. Flying Cupids are ready to place
wreaths on her head. The processional motive is steadied by a nymph
at the extreme right, statuesque as a caryatid, holding a basket of
flowers on her head. A lolling couple before the car gently check
its motion, which is repeated by a dancing nymph behind them who
carries the motive to the extreme left. There is much of Titian in
the general arrangement of this picture, something also of Annibale
Carracci, but a certain gravity and measure in its blitheness are pure

Poussin. The feeling of the landscape is chiefly decorative, in Titian's fashion, but there is already a hint of that spaciousness which Poussin was ultimately to develop. The minor adjustments are of the happiest—the heads that here and there cut the skyline, the contrast value of the armored warrior amid the lightly draped or nude forms, the lovely curvilinear geometry of the stooping nymph and the two geniuses before the wheels. There are Poussins of fuller vitality than this, but very few that so abound in compositional refinements.

It will be noted that I am passing the many religious pictures of this time in silence. As a class they seem to me the more negligible Poussins. Especially in New-Testament subjects he equally lacks the active monumentality of the Renaissance and the feelingful exuberance of his baroque contemporaries. About most of his Madonnas and Holy Families there is, for me, something static and even stilted. Possibly in these compositions with few figures his careful practice of modeling the figures and arranging them in a box especially illuminated worked unfavorably. There are, of course, exceptions. The Lamentation over the Dead Christ (Fig. 392), at Dublin, painted in the late 1640's, is a great tragic masterpiece. The Baptisms and other New-Testament subjects in the two series of the Seven Sacraments are among the finer Poussins. But, in general, the Old Testament, with its blend of the austere and idyllic, better served Poussin's purpose than the New. Some of the Old-Testament subjects we shall later study.

Unquestionably Poussin's most famous picture is the second and final version of the theme *Et in Arcadia Ego* (Fig. 393), Paris. What distinguishes it from the earlier version (Fig. 386), in England, where curiosity and surprise dominated, is the complete awareness of the group of the universal meaning of the situation. They not merely are aware of the darkness of the tomb that awaits them, but they seem to point out to the spectator the short tenure of youth and happiness, the certainty of death. And the figures are such as might gain this pensive awareness—no longer young, eager and thoughtless, but grown older and completely reflective. There is no longer that gracious exposure of the limbs of the eager girl in the English version, the enchanting toss of her lovely head—instead a young woman, draped and posed with the gravity of a Roman matron, touches the shoulder of the young shepherd who points out the inscription, as if to console and reassure him. The group is densely and monumentally balanced; the landscape features are fewer and more simplified; the whole thing could be rendered in marble high-relief without great loss of emotional effect. Few pictures show so complete a harmony between the formal and what one may call the literary content. And in this case the word literary merely implies a profound elegiac poetry, for the meaning of the picture would be clear even without the reinforcing inscription "I, too, in Arcady."

Since we are dealing with the highest type of visualized poetry, we may well recall the description of this picture by the poet-critic, Théophile Gautier, in his "Guide to the Louvre":

"The picture of the Shepherds of Arcady expresses with a naïve melancholy the brevity of life and awakens among the young shepherds and the girl who look at the tomb they have found the forgotten idea of death; their brows become pensive under their garlands of flowers, and leaning on their staffs they lean towards the tombstone on which they decipher the inscription: ET IN ARCADIA EGO. No epitaph of the Greek Anthology, summarized in a distych by Meleager, was ever more tenderly sweet."

Late in 1640 came to Poussin a great honor which ended in a great chagrin. He was called to Paris to decorate a gallery in the Louvre with the Labours of Hercules. Everything started well. They assigned him a pleasant house on the Champs Elysées with a garden and a cask of old wine in the cellar. But as the decoration of the Louvre proceeded he was subjected to every sort of interruption, and finally opposition. While occupied in his great task, trivial commissions were imposed upon him. The atmosphere of intrigue among artists at Paris disgusted him. Shortly after beginning the decorations in the Louvre he writes to Cassiano del Pozzo: "If I stay longer in this country I shall become a veritable swindler like the men here. I find no one to second me; studies of ancient life are unknown in Paris, and he who is inclined to do well should keep away from this place." Soon the jealous Vouet and his associates openly decried Poussin's scheme of decoration as too simple and wholly inadequate. He who had reluctantly come to Paris as art director for the king was put in the humiliating position of a defendant. He returned to Rome late in 1642, having virtually wasted about two of his best working years, for the Labours of Hercules soon gave place to other decorations as the Louvre was rebuilt, and we know this series today only in inexpressive engravings.

His farewell to France was appropriately made in a ceiling medallion for Cardinal Richelieu, Time rescues Truth from Discord and Envy. The arrangement is illusionistic and baroque, but the symbolism is specific and the feeling tense rather than merely exuberant. An oil study at Lille shows that the ceiling was originally planned as an oblong, and shows as well that impetuosity which characterizes all Poussin's preliminary sketches. We must think of him as consciously sacrificing something of raw emotion to dignity and permanence of effect. The figures of Truth's foes, Discord and Envy, are far more drastically conceived in the sketch (Fig. 395) than in the finished composition. Richelieu, creator of French nationality, was about to die, leaving behind him a lifetime of contention and misrepresentation; Poussin was about to quit Paris for good under a cloud of small criticism and disloyalty. For both last events this picture is a fitting memorial. Both the great cardinal-prime minister and the greatly misunderstood painter could safely leave their case against Envy and Discord in the hands of Time and Truth.

In the disordered days between the premierships of Richelieu and Mazarin it was too-late felt that the crown had lost prestige in losing Poussin's services, and efforts were made to recall him. These he quietly resisted. He writes to Chantelou with stoic wisdom: "I find I must accept the good and bear the evil. Misery and misfortune are so common to mankind that I marvel how intelligent men resent it and do not rather laugh than sigh over it. Nothing belongs to us; everything is lent us." So philosophical an attitude bears out Dr. Grautoff's theory that Poussin, after all, may have gained morally from the materially disastrous years in Paris. Directly or indirectly some inkling of the new French time-spirit seems to have been his—of the heroic magnanimity of Corneille, of the uncompromising rationalism of Descartes, of the austere morality and theological probity of the champion of Port Royal, Pascal. The pictures of the late 1640's suggest as much. We no longer find joyous idyls and mythologies. Rather grave subjects from antiquity, symbolism of the mysteries of the redemptive process in the series of the Seven Sacraments. Typical of the paintings of this time is the Lamentation (Fig. 392), which has been already considered. Very similar in general aspect is the Testament of Eudamidas (Fig. 394), Copenhagen. The fable from Lucian tells that the very poor citizen of Corinth, being about to die, drew up his will. When it was opened they read that he had left his friends his mother and daughter to support. Poussin has picked out of the general darkness the following scene—a dying man on a couch, a doctor testing the flickering heartbeat, a seated scribe assiduously writing, an old woman, the wife, turned away from the scene, a young woman, the daughter, wearied so that she has slipped into sleep at the foot of the bed. Beyond this only a bare and gloomy room, with the dying warrior's shield and sword hanging on the wall. The whole effect is singularly grim and imposing. No wonder it was Napoleon's favorite picture. He told his minister of fine arts, Denon:

"I knew the Death of Eudamidas in an engraving that I had with me in Egypt. When one has seen that austere composition and the Death of Germanicus, it is not possible to forget them. Denon, our school is weak. We should return to the manner and thought of Poussin."

This great picture and the Lamentation show an emphasis of chiaroscuro which is novel in Poussin. He unquestionably had taken tribute of the enemy Caravaggio and probably of his own fellow countryman, Valentin. But the play of light and dark which in the Caravaggians was chiefly a means of construction is in Poussin a powerful means of expression. It directs the beholder's eye as the artist wishes to a few points carefully selected for emphasis. The light is a command. Raphael, whom Poussin was at this time restudying, had in a simpler way done something quite similar in the fresco of the Liberation of St. Peter, in the Vatican. Despite the great difference, in mere handling, the method is that which Rembrandt was using in far-away Amsterdam, and here we may remark the singular technical and even expressional affinity between the wash drawings of the two masters.

Before going to Paris Poussin had painted for his friend, Cassiano del Pozzo, a series of the Seven Sacraments, now in Belvoir Castle, England. From 1644 to 1648 he made a second series for his patron and confidant, Chantelou. In the second set, now at Bridgewater House, London, Extreme Unction repeats the drastic chiaroscuro method already described. The comparison of the two series subject by subject would be a most useful exercise in discrimination. Here I can only note that in the second series the figures are more sharply defined by light and dark, more isolated, the accessories reduced and simplified, the effect more grave, static and antique. That unity which had formerly been attained largely on a decorative basis by harmony of color and larger rhythmical lines is now secured by careful correlation of posture and perfect accord of feeling. One senses behind the pictures of these years the modeled figurines carefully adjusted in the box lit by candlelight. The intensified dramatic effect of these pictures recalls Poussin's saying that he wished to compose his paintings "according to the rules of the theater," which at that time meant the Aristotelian "three unities" of time, place and action.

The change in Poussin's style may well be illustrated by comparing the earlier with the later picture devoted to the Sacrament of Marriage (Fig. 396). In both cases, because the marriage of Mary and Joseph is the subject, the setting is Roman. Two columns, which in the earlier version rose at the margins without compositional value, are brought forward a little and are useful in setting the group at a greater distance. A small detail, but a significant one, the columns are no longer fluted, and so unrelated to the figures, but smooth. Three openings on the streets of a city vary the background. Hanging garlands in half-light similarly relieve the dark space under the ceiling. The silhouetting of all figures is sharper and now more often in light against dark. The cast shadow and the marble squares of the pavement are more clearly defined. The feeling is no longer ceremonious and solemn, but meditatively joyous. The priest, no longer wearing his tiara and frontal, now sits in profile, bareheaded, in fatherly ease, blessing the young pair rather as a friend than as a mere officiant. The group of twenty-five, though arranged as densely as before, is charmingly subdivided by more varying values of the drapery, by the relations of figures to the columns and doorways. The earlier version seems a little monotonous and starved of light; the later lets the light play from many sources in the most unexpected and fascinating ways. Without sacrificing the necessary sense of a solemn rite, the whole picture has taken on a festive and idyllic character—a visual beauty of holiness. The picture was finished in 1648. It reflects the enhanced thoughtfulness of Poussin in these years.

The renewal of Poussin's style which we have remarked suggests that as he was approaching fifty he sought through study a more conscious control of his genius. We know from his friend, Félibien, that Poussin pondered Leonbattista Alberti's "Essay on Painting," and Dürer's writings on human proportion and perspective. Just before the journey to Paris a new influence of this intellectualizing sort came to him in the "Treatise on Painting" by Leonardo da Vinci.

His friend, Charles Fréart de Chambray, made a French translation which was published in 1651. Poussin furnished illustrations for the verbal maxims. This means that he had read the book most carefully. Characteristically, he thought it too fragmentary to merit publication. In general, Leonardo, who had written that there is no good practice without a good theory, merely reinforced the native intellectualism of his reader, but there were many fine observations on landscape, on the effect of distance on vision, on aerial perspective and the like, which were calculated to arouse in an artist of Poussin's type an analytical and fairly scientific interest in the problem of painting landscape.

From his fifty-second or fifty-third year on, this was Poussin's main concern, and it involved a considerable sacrifice of hard-won gains as a figure painter. It meant also a considerable shift in philosophical point of view. Earlier he had given to human events of many sorts a kind of importance and permanence by keeping the scale of the figures relatively large, staging the action near the picture plane, and minimizing the spaciousness and interest of the place in which the action is performed. In this, in his own words, he is obeying "the rules of the theater" with its shallow and limited stage and the prominence it gives the actor. Now the figures dwindle, the action becomes less important, taking place as it does in the vastness of nature. Nature now becomes the permanent and important feature. Man transiently seizes his brief moment of joy, sorrow, glory, peace, and passes, while nature remains. It is the personal pathos of *Et in Arcadia Ego* given now a universal extension; it echoes his own saying, already quoted, "We own nothing; everything is lent to us." Some two centuries later Victor Hugo was to repeat the sentiment in the famous saying, "We are all condemned to death, with an indefinite reprieve." Of course, all this, from Homer and the Ecclesiast down, has been the essence of the finest elegiac poetry. Poussin's greatness is shown in the fact that he faced a situation, often taken rebelliously and tragically, with entire tranquillity, and even with a measured happiness.

It is probable that Poussin's interest in landscape was encouraged by the success of his fellow countryman and neighbor, Claude Lorrain. Their Italian womenfolk of humble estate must often have compared notes on their great men. But Poussin can have drawn almost nothing directly from Claude, whose enthusiasm was for the evanescent loveliness of nature, while Poussin's was in its strength and permanence. The mere fact that Claude habitually veils parts of his landscapes, notably the horizon, in golden vapors, while Poussin never does, tells the difference. Poussin keeps everything clear, in a cool, equable light, articulates his landscape forms with the considerateness he had used in assembling his little figures in their box, and the painted figures in their group. Now the box serves no useful purpose; the landscape must literally be made out of his head. Thus while a Claude, despite its conventions, always seems to rest on observation of the whole of a landscape effect, a Poussin rests on memories of the essential parts of landscape which are combined into a whole as his taste dictates.

One of the earliest and most delightful landscapes in the new style is the Landscape with St. Matthew and an Angel, Berlin. Among fragments of Roman buildings on a river strand St. Matthew sits and writes, eagerly looking up to the angel who is dictating the Divine words. The figures are small. One looks above and beyond them over a river which bends twice in an S between shrubs and coppices to a little hill on which is the ruin of a castle, beyond which gentle mountain forms recede in two ranges to meet the pale yellow horizon of a sharp blue sky. The tranquil river is velvety with reflections. The geometrical forms of the ruins in the foreground, with their faces sharply defined by the light, afford a handsome contrast to the generally suave masses of the landscape. These ruins are not merely favorite objects which Poussin sketched in his walks about Rome, but symbols of the transiency of man's tenure, even his proudest tenure of the earth. The companion piece, St. John on Patmos, Chicago (Fig. 397), offers a landscape less tranquil, highly accidented and exciting, a fit setting for St. John's more tense inspiration.

There is no more imaginative Poussin than the Orion, at New York. The gigantic blind huntsman, once Diana's lover, feels his way down a path through bristling trees towards the sea, from which rise a rocky promontory and islands. A man, standing on his mighty shoulders, carefully directs the giant's march. Mortals look on in amazement and sympathy. On a cloud which trails down across nearby trees at the left, Diana stands at ease, meditating the transformation of her lover into a constellation. Of course, all this is literary and has to be read into the picture. What may, after all, be read out of the picture, without commentary of any sort, is the contrast between the helplessness of the giant man, his transiency as compared with the permanence of inanimate nature. The pathos is enhanced when, consulting the fable, we realize this is a stricken god denied his joy, doomed to a cold and inconscient immortality as a starry symbol.

Most heroic, in Goethe's sense, of the great landscapes of the middle years, are the Polyphemus, and Hercules and Cacus, at Leningrad. Grandiose mountains tower into the sky. On these peaks or declivities are Titans at ease or in action. In the pleasantly broken country near by are nymphs inattentive to what happens on high. Great trees occupy much of the middle distance. In the heavens the illuminated edges are crinkled nervously. The theme seems to be the entire indifference both of nature and of average mankind to the sentimental pangs of a Polyphemus or the mighty deeds of a Hercules. In such pictures as these every touch, every choice of a lighter or darker hue, represents a definite thought. Everything comes from the depths of the mind, where, to be sure, many observations are stored; nothing rests on immediate observation.

Now this minimizing of the importance of man in the natural order is the very oldest wisdom. The Old Testament abounds in it. It is the very essence of Hindu religion, whether Brahmanistic or Buddhist. Rich Mr. Kuo of Old China, who insisted he had stolen all he had, because everything belonged to nature, was merely expressing some two thousand years earlier Poussin's grim maxim: "We own nothing; everything is lent to us." Yes, this insignificance and impermanence of man has always impressed the great thinkers. The truth of this view is so disagreeable to men that they either deny it rebelliously or pretend it is not a truth. The intellectual lucidity and fortitude of Poussin is shown in his facing this grim fact with acceptance and serenity. It may have been an aspect of his Christian humility. In any case, it sets him apart from those self-asserting masters of the Renaissance whom he often superficially resembles. What Poussin in his ultimately achieved wisdom asserts is something he feels to be much greater than himself—a relatively immortal and self-renewing nature.

This self-abnegating philosophy throve in the face of material success and growing fame. He was fairly pestered with commissions. Very early he had fixed what he felt to be a fair price for his pictures, and he never raised it. As a matter of self-respect he returned whatever a generous patron might give in addition. He never changed his modest manner of life, never sought out the notabilities he knew, but on his evening strolls on the Pincio he made himself accessible to whomsoever might wish his counsel. His health and strength began to wane as he passed sixty. He continued to perfect his work.

The extent of his self-criticism we may measure by comparing the two versions of one of his latest pictures, Orpheus and Eurydice. A bistre drawing (Fig. 398) at Chantilly shows the first conception, which he faithfully followed in the painting (Fig. 399) at New York. In the landscape he seeks an agitation corresponding to the shocking character of the theme. Everywhere trees and bushes bristle; the smoke from a burning castle writhes as it rises; even the clouds form hard zigzags. The disposition of the figures is highly theatrical. A young man has arrested Orpheus' playing and points with an oratorical gesture to the place where Eurydice looks with terror at the adder whose fangs are in her heel. Her arms and those of two girls are raised in despair. Orpheus, with turned head, is frozen with terror. Two reclining nymphs in the foreground turn their fine profiles rather languidly towards Eurydice. In middle distance another nymph shades her eyes to make sure of what is going on. The whole group is very deliberately, even artificially, arranged to direct the beholder's gaze at Eurydice. There are extraneous elegancies—the exposed legs of Eurydice, the sculpturesque torsos of the three nymphs, Orpheus' too fashionable Phrygian cap. It will be seen that Poussin, exceptionally, has indulged the pathetic fallacy—the false assumption that nature responds sympathetically to our moods.

Perhaps a year or two later, in 1659, he took the sketch out of a portfolio, frowned at it, decided that the picture was all wrong and must be painted again and right. The result was the masterpiece (Fig. 400) in the Louvre. The landscape has become completely tranquilized, largely by means of elimination and simplification. Bristling trees and shrubs in the middle distance have given place to a quiet lake. The trees at right and left are gently indicated—none of the nervous, staccato touches of the earlier version. Tree trunks curve gracefully, where before they were rigidly upright. The distant smoke and the clouds now float softly, without the former spiraling or zigzagging edges. Poussin now wishes to depict a nature to which legitimate defensive reaction of an adder and the untimely

death of a fair girl are equally indifferent. And the figures are rear-
ranged in a casual sense—no more theatrical devices. Man is generally as unaware as nature herself of the disasters that brute chance
allots him. The figures formerly dispersed are now grouped about
Orpheus, listening as he plays his lyre. Nobody is aware of Eurydice's fate except herself and a seated fisherman, who turns his head
to see what is going on. The adder, his work done, is gliding away.
The group is contained within the background formed by the gray-
blue lake. Insensate tragedy has intruded upon an idyl. Such changes
bespeak a deeper understanding of the problem of evil and sorrow
in the world. It befalls us when we least expect it; we do not perceive it until it is too late. Nature wills nothing towards us, shares
nothing of our deepest feelings; is neither benevolent nor hostile.
Our part in the universe is very small, and it is a counsel of wisdom
to accept the fact with resignation and humility.

Such seems to be Poussin's ultimate vision of man's place in
the world. It opposes a gentle Christian pessimism—akin to the
teaching of Port Royal—against both the pride of life of the Renaissance and the new optimistic rationalism of Cartesian France. The
validity of Poussin's attitude it is not my task to discuss. Indeed,
these deeper spiritual experiences are profoundly intuitional; they
must be experienced, and discussion does not conduce to such experience. Agreeing or disagreeing with Poussin's ultimate elegiac
quietism, the reader must at least admire the lucidity, tenacity and
magnanimity with which the position is held.

From about 1658, his sixty-third year, Poussin was afflicted with
a palsy. Under these conditions he painted some of his best pictures. For lack of space I can only direct the reader's attention to
the famous series, the Four Seasons, Paris, finished before 1664. The
themes are drawn from the Bible. Spring, the Creation of Eve, is
the only luscious landscape Poussin ever painted. In its handling of
greens and browns it is of a tapestrylike richness. Winter (Fig. 401),
representing almost in monochrome the deluge, is the most vast, dramatic and tragic of Poussin's creations. It has been admired for
upwards of two centuries and a half, and needs no praise of mine.
The quiet, impersonal inexorableness of the flood, the hopelessness
of the attempts to win safety, are fully expressed on the most concise
terms.

Poussin's last picture, Apollo and Daphne, Paris, is a complete synthesis of his art. He ended, as he had begun, as an idylist. The landscape is pleasantly featureless—no heroic elements. The festoon of lightly draped nymphs and deities seems a sort of emanation from or incident of the setting. There is no suggestion of story or action. The figures, for a late Poussin, are relatively large in scale. It is as if he now sought an equivalence of interest between nature and man, restoring to man something of that importance which he had formerly taken away. In mood there is a lovely casualness; in composition an extraordinarily intricate yet entirely natural interweaving of curves. One may think of everything as related to a foreshortened oval of which the group is the arc facing the beholder. All elements count powerfully both in pattern and in depth. Here it stands apart from the composition on a single plane of the Flora and the earlier mythologies generally. Just as a problem, though far less rich and able, Cézanne's Bathers is technically akin to the Apollo and Daphne. What is really instructive is the fact that into every problem of the great technician Poussin passed insensibly the gracious austerity of his taste, the mellow richness of his wisdom. It is this involuntary contribution from the artist's personality that really constitutes the greatness of the work of art. The end, Poussin wrote, is delectation— meaning a high and enduring happiness; the means, he might have added, is magnanimity. It is the absence of magnanimity, of any inner store of wisdom, that makes Cézanne, Poussin's most loyal devotee, less a great artist than a confessedly valiant experimenter.

About the time the Apollo and Daphne was painted Poussin's wife, Anna Maria, died. It had been a childless marriage, and her death left him pitifully alone. His own strength was dwindling, and at the end of a painful illness, late in November, 1665, his release came. He was seventy-one years old. He was unquestionably the most famous painter in Rome, and they disregarded the very frugal limit his will assigned for his funeral expenses, in order to give him public last rites and dignified burial in S. Lorenzo in Lucina.

When Poussin died every well-informed and civilized person in Western Europe felt that she had lost her greatest painter. In France his work became a sort of holy writ of good taste, and the early sessions of the new Académie Royale were largely given to the analysis of his pictures in the interest of the learner. To be a Poussinist constituted a sort of orthodoxy. In the eighteenth century the so-called age of reason paradoxically developed a new cult of pure emotional-

ism, harbinger of the romanticism of the early nineteenth century.
Poussin's authority dwindled.  Sir Joshua Reynolds was, on the whole,
amiably condescending in the matter.  William Hazlitt, champion of
spontaneity, found Poussin, like the parson's egg, good in spots, but
declared his faces to be monotonous.  The great confusion of our
own century has been largely a knockdown fight between smooth
necks and rough necks.  The latter invariably have insisted that
Poussin is anemic and wholly backward-looking.  In the sense that he
never clenches the fist or prognathously squares the jaw, the rough
necks are perfectly right.  But there may be, after all, other expressions of inward strength.  As generally sensible a critic as Dr. Hendrik
Willem van Loon thinks Poussin a man without a country, who
might just as well have been Italian, in the way he looked at the
world and painted—Poussin, perhaps the most French figure of the
Grand Siècle.  So it goes!

On the other hand, painters of markedly thoughtful sort, of
whatever school, have always felt Poussin's greatness.  Delacroix
constantly extols him in his Journal, wrote one of the best essays on
him; the dogged experimenter Cézanne indulged the vain hope,
which was a homage, of painting Poussins after nature.

There is no use of arguing this difference of opinion, but one
may clarify the issue by defining the values involved.  In simplest
terms the fight is between imagination and observation, between the
mental and the optical image, between the inner and the outer eye.
Was Courbet right when he snorted: "Show me an angel and I'll
paint you one"?  Or was Fra Angelico right when he painted an
angel as he imagined one?  Or were both right, though in different
ways?  It all depends on the value you give to mental processes.  As
it happened, Velasquez, greatest master of the outer eye, was a contemporary of Poussin, and so was Rembrandt, equally master of the
outer and inner eye.  Shall we compare them and decide which most
to admire?  I can imagine no more foolish process, for nothing in
their work is really comparable.  Inevitably we shall prefer one of
the three as corresponding more closely to our own temperament,
but there is no balance in which we may objectively weigh the weight
of these artists, and the part of wisdom may be to admire them all
gratefully.

For Poussin it may be said that in choosing the mental image
and in seeking to re-create an older grandeur and happier world he is

in the apostolic succession that, beginning with the fabled painters of Greece, passes through Giotto and Raphael and Titian, and, as an ideal, at least, is still alive today. No painter who, following Leonardo da Vinci's counsel, wishes to work rather from his judgment than from his temperament, can afford to ignore Poussin. From him more is to be learned, as to the right disposition of the reflective artist's soul, than is to be learned from the possibly greater masters, and certainly more resourceful technicians, Velasquez and Rembrandt.

CHAPTER XXV

CHARLES LEBRUN AND THE ACAD-
EMY POUSSINISTS AND RUBENSISTS

FIG. 402. RIGAUD. Louis XIV.—Paris.

Fig. 403. (Upper left) Charles Lebrun. St. Louis Praying for the Pest-
Stricken.—Grenoble.

Fig. 404. (Lower) Charles Lebrun. Atalanta's Hunt.—Paris.

Fig. 405. (Upper right) Mignard. His Daughter as the Genius of Fame.
—Paris.

Fig. 406. Mignard. Assumption.—Dome of the Val de Grâce, Paris.

Fig. 407. Charles de la Fosse. The Car of Apollo (sketch). —Rouen.

Fig. 408. (Upper) Sébastien Bourdon. Julius Caesar at the Tomb of Alexander.—*Paris*.
Fig. 409. (Lower) Sébastien Bourdon. A Gypsy Camp.—*Paris*.

Fig. 410. JOUVENET. Descent from the Cross.— Fig. 411. JOUVENET. The Choir of Notre Dame.—Paris.
Paris.

764

Fig. 412. Largillière. His Family.—*Paris.*

FIG. 413.   RIGAUD.   An Officer.—Aix.

WHEN Poussin returned discouraged to Rome in 1642 he took with him a very serious and energetic young painter named Charles Lebrun. The next year a very intelligent and self-willed little boy of five inherited the crown as Louis XIV. The two were later to create what for over two centuries was to be the official taste of France in the arts. Lebrun was born in 1619 at Paris, his father a mediocre sculptor. When he was a mere lad some of his drawings fell under the eye of Chancellor Figuier, who, recognizing their excellence and promise, took Lebrun into his household and gave and brought him patronage. For a time Lebrun studied with the indispensable Vouet, but in the controversy over the decorations of the Louvre, in 1640, he must have taken Poussin's side. Indeed, his future campaign for the grand style in France was chiefly to be waged in Poussin's name.

Before going to Rome Lebrun had had important commissions at Paris, and in Rome he enjoyed a ready patronage. He spent four years there, professing allegiance to Raphael, but rather drawing from Raphael's heavy-handed disciple, Giulio Romano. Unluckily, Lebrun never saw, or at least never seriously remarked, Giulio Romano's decorations in the palaces at Mantua, in which the often tasteless titan developed an extraordinary taste in decorative ensembles combining painting and sculpture in relief. For such studies Lebrun found a reasonable equivalent in the at once calculated and exuberant frescoes of the Loves of the Gods, by Annibale Carracci, in the Farnese Palace. Upon this famous decoration his own more elaborate and thoroughgoing scheme, best represented at Versailles, was to be based. It is significant that Lebrun never took the pains to visit Venice. Moreover, the great Titians had been taken from Rome before his arrival. Thus, unlike his mentor Poussin, Lebrun never exposed himself to any really painterlike influence, with the natural result that his own pictorial style was as unpainterlike as possible. A poor colorist, he was to make it official doctrine that in comparison with drawing, color is of secondary importance for a painter.

Returning to Paris in 1646, the chancellor renewed his favors, and great commissions for religious pictures and for mythological cartoons—such as the Story of Meleager—overwhelmed the newcomer. This success, within two years, in 1648, emboldened Lebrun to take the extraordinary step, for an artist not yet thirty, of proposing the foundation of an Academy, following the brilliant precedent of the Academy devoted to literature, which had been established fourteen years earlier. The plan won the favor of the new prime minister, Mazarin. The members were granted substantial pensions, and the sole privilege of being named as painters of the king. So the Académie Royale de Peinture et de Sculpture opened with thirty-two members. Among them, besides Lebrun, were Sebastien Bourdon, Eustache le Sueur, Philippe de Champaigne and the three brothers Le Nain. Vouet, already stricken and about to die, was omitted. The real glories of contemporary French painting, Claude and Poussin, were at Rome, and ineligible. Only active members were wanted.

The aims of the Academy were to raise what had been only a trade to the dignity of a profession, to formulate and promulgate correct principles of artistic taste, to maintain a standard of instruction under which these principles might be applied and maintained.

The Maîtrise, the old guild, its vested interests of teaching and licensing artists being sadly diminished, employed every legal and political device to oppose the Academy. The quarrel lasted, the Academy generally winning, until in 1777 the Maîtrise was suppressed. On the whole, the Academy had the right of the matter. The Maîtrise had gone stale; its standards of licensing were low, its teaching casual and without standards of any sort.

Lebrun's most ambitious project was that of establishing a correct body of doctrine. In this he counted on the co-operation of his colleagues. They were to meet periodically, hear a lecture treating some masterpiece specifically, and arrive at conclusions as to its merits and demerits, from which guiding principles might be drawn. The method turned out to be unsatisfactory. The lectures tended to deal in generalities; the Academicians rarely arrived at formulated opinions. Colbert, who often presided himself, complained at the inconclusiveness of the sessions, and insisted that everything be reduced to precepts by which the students of the Academy might profit. The doctrine actually had to be worked out by Lebrun and his literary advisers. Indeed, it was only necessary to adapt to the

fine arts the critical principles which had been proclaimed for literature by such critics as Boileau. Let me summarize the doctrine with
comments.

1. The cardinal maxim was that the ancients offered an incomparable example of perfection which the artist must imitate.

The real sense of this was merely that the ancients left very
fine works of art which the student might profitably study. Unhappily, most of the antique masterpieces available in Lebrun's time were
second- or third-rate sculptures of the classical decadence, or, worse,
lifeless plaster casts thereof. Moreover, if the ancients were unsur-
passable, all moderns must accept defeatism. Finally, while drawing
from the antique was and is useful, too much of it too early will probably disable the beginner for direct and accurate observation of
nature.

2. While nature may be consulted, this should be done with
greatest caution. The finest natural aspects, *belle nature*, should
alone be chosen. Even these aspects should be corrected and improved in the light of the antique.

There is only this much sense in this maxim, that some aspects
of nature are more available than others as subject matter for the
artist. But there is no standard list of such aspects. The artist must
choose according to his personal taste. Any other course involves a
disastrous limitation of research and experimentation. As for cor-
recting nature by the antique, it is possible only in figure design, and
there it discourages direct observation.

3. Only noble subjects should be treated, and preferably from
the great poets, ancient or modern, or from the great historians.

This maxim seems to have, and partly had, the warrant of Poussin's theory and practice. But it was very foolish to assume that
what was right for Poussin was right for every painter. The requirement of nobility in the subject matter was simply infantile psychology. For nobility is in the artist's attitude of soul and not in objects. No one can tell in advance what objects can or cannot be ennobled by the artist's admiring observation and reverent execution.
It was and is sensible for an artist of an intellectual sort to seek his
subject matter in poetry, legend or history, but many artists should
do quite otherwise. The practical result of such a maxim was to en-
courage paintings which were simply overgrown illustrations, not vis-

ually self-explanatory, and needing a verbal interpretation—paintings to be seen not with the eyes, but with the ears.

4. The highest merit of painting was correct drawing, meaning linear drawing. Color is a secondary grace, which should never be exaggerated.

This is the most pernicious article of the Academic faith. It limits drawing, which is merely construction, to linear drawing. It advocates the least painterlike method of construction, condemning implicitly the methods of such great painters as Frans Hals, Rembrandt, Velasquez, Titian, Tintoretto; it tended to deprive painting of its richest and most appropriate resources. Now and then a painter may successfully express himself in colored outlines. If every painter did so, there would soon be no painting worthy of the name. This dogma of the inferiority of color has narrowed the teaching of painting almost to our own times.

It should be said for Lebrun's integrity that he not merely preached but also practiced this doctrine. It was calculated to produce an art just like his—superficially classical, theatrical rather than natural, pompous rather than noble, neutral or discordant in color. Indeed, the real greatness of Lebrun rests on the vast decorative ensembles which he planned, and in no wise on his paintings.

Poussin's theory and practice were often cited in justification of this Academic program. Without warrant. His casual sayings advocate imitation of the antique and choosing a noble subject, but he wisely refrains from defining either the manner of imitation or from listing the noble subjects. As to imitation of nature, Poussin was too good a thinker to divide natural appearances into beautiful and ugly. He merely recommended imitating nature, not literally and thoughtlessly, but patiently and reflectively. To this kind of prolonged and interpretive observation he gave the technical term "prospect." And, of course, the devout admirer of Titian never said or wrote that color was a minor concern for the painter. On the contrary, he had written that color is as necessary to painting as verse is to poetry:

"Colors in painting are like verses in poetry: they are the charms that each of the two arts employed to persuade."

The Academic or pseudo-classic doctrine rapidly gained authority and, despite many revolutions in taste, has never wholly lost it. In replacing with a solid program the anarchy and eclecticism that had prevailed, it did immediate good. In organizing the teaching of art, it assured a minimum professional competence of the artist. It has thus safeguarded the art of France from those disastrous ups and downs which art in other lands has suffered. Its dogmatism was, on the whole, merely an exaggeration of principles sound, if taken genially. The antique still is most useful to the young artist; it is still desirable that artistic expression be noble; it is still essential that imitation of nature be intelligently selective. In short, the first three of the four maxms are still valid if they are interpreted, not in an exclusive, but in a liberal sense. And though narrow and defective in details, the program was right in spirit. It wanted the artist to be a disciplined human spirit, to achieve a certain culture through allying himself to some great tradition, to seek rather to be a man of trained taste than a barbarian or Bohemian with merely a keen eye and a ready hand. Most dogmatisms are warped and narrow; most also gain a tinge of nobility from the fervor and conviction with which they are believed. The dogmatism of Lebrun and the Academy was no exception in either respect to the rule.

Lebrun's reform, for such it was, was furthered by the king's coming of age and by the appointment of Colbert as minister of finance. In 1668 the Academy was reorganized and completed by the addition of architecture, and the continuance of its classical tradition had already been assured in 1666 by the foundation of the École de Rome, again Lebrun's suggestion. Such students of the Academy at Paris as had successfully passed strict competitive tests were accredited to the school for five years, generously maintained, and subjected only to mild discipline and reasonable duties. Today it is the fashion to decry the value of such training, and with some reason. We should not forget, however, what Rome meant in Lebrun's time. It was not then a museum and a manufactory of mediocre or bad art. It was still one of the great centers of living art. The grand baroque churches and palaces were still being built and decorated; the admirable piazzas and fountains were being planned and executed. The feeling of decadence which, with the wisdom of hindsight, we feel today, was absent. To go to Rome was not merely to study the statues and ruins, the frescoes of the Vatican; it was to play a part in the city where creative art was most variously alive. No Frenchman about 1666 could possibly have felt that there was more of the painter's art to be learned at Haarlem, Amsterdam or Madrid. Even Venice, which offered far more to the painter, offered rather little to the sculptor and architect. From such men as Colbert, Lebrun and Louis XIV, who magnanimously undertook the heroic task of creating and shaping a national culture, I do not see how anyone can withhold admiration; nor do I see how any historically minded person can deny that, according to their lights, they built well and permanently. Indeed, the success of their heroic endeavor is proved by the fact that the artist must still reckon with it today. The upshot of the matter seems to be that in the field of taste, as in that of action, a narrow and defective program is much better than no program at all.

Honors and responsibilities continued to seek Lebrun. In 1662 he was made chief painter of the king and keeper of the king's collections. In 1667 he was made chief of the Council of Buildings, looking towards the great enterprise of completing the palace of Versailles. In 1667 he was put in charge of the Gobelins. This state factory, started to take over tapestry weaving from private hands, was developed by Lebrun in many directions. Practically everything for the decoration of Versailles was designed and made at the Gobelins—the paintings, carved wood, furniture, even the hardware. Lebrun chose to live at the Gobelins as leader of fifty artists. It was such a creative community as the world has rarely seen. The members were well paid, exempt from military service and from certain taxes. For their spiritual advantage, a French and a Flemish chaplain officiated regularly. The Gobelins undertook anything—up to designing a coach, as a gift from the king to the Great Mogul.

For the tapestry weavers Lebrun furnished designs for nine series, using in part his older subjects—as the story of Atalanta and Meleager, and the Deeds of Alexander the Great, and furnishing new cartoons for the Elements, the Seasons, the History of the King. Lebrun's orderly and energetic composition and his fine sense for ornament made him almost an ideal designer for the tapestry weavers, and they, with their craftsman's sense of color, made Lebrun's tapestries far more attractive than his paintings. To them we come tardily, and since stylistically they are of a piece, disregarding chronology.

The resolute and intelligent, but also insensitive, manner of Lebrun is, on the whole, favorably shown in such a picture as St. Louis praying for the Pest-Stricken (Fig. 403), at Grenoble. The feeling is Raphaelesque, but with a theatrical emphasis which Raphael rarely indulged. Everybody is just a little posing. As for color, there really are just unassimilated and unharmonized local hues. The balance of the subgroup of three in the foreground is ingenious and handsome. Such a work implies a robust, sincere and intelligent talent.

Such a mythology as the Hunt of Meleager and Atalanta (Fig. 404), at Paris, would hold its own in the company of much better pictures for its energy and picturesqueness, for the charm of the details. Its inferiority would betray itself in a compiled and assembled look as compared, say, with the hunts and battle pieces of Rubens.

In a book of this character Lebrun's real contribution as a maker of decorative ensembles can only be hinted at. His sheer activity in such a decoration as Versailles was unbelievable. To make such interiors as the halls of Peace and War he must have been at his drawing board many hours a day, and in superintendence at the Gobelins and in the palace he did the work of two or three architects. Earlier he had designed the decoration and furniture for the Salon d'Apollon in the Louvre. Although the great ceiling panel has been replaced by Delacroix's superb Apollo and the Python, and incongruous portraits have been set in ovals of the wall, it remains an excellent example of Lebrun's sumptuous and highly orderly method of decoration. The method in its glory must be studied at Versailles. I confess I lack the taste for it. I prefer the more genial effrontery of Giulio Romano and the Carracci—to mention only decoration of a kindred order.

Versailles is, in contrast, completely calculated. Everything is forethought; nothing happy thought. And the design includes the most various ingredients—mural painting, moldings, sculptured medallions, parquetry, furniture; everything related with an unflinching logic and a fully rationalized taste. It is pompous, intended so to be, but one cannot say it is pretentious. The whole thing has a sort of inevitableness which fully reflects the character of Louis XIV and his first painter. Versailles is one of the fullest and finest expressions of the French spirit, and probably only a Frenchman can give full appreciation to these vast decorated spaces. An Englishman and an American wants to keep just a little place for the unexpected, and one may say there is nothing unexpected in Versailles.

Orthodoxies are ever maintained with difficulty, and that of Charles Lebrun and the Academy was no exception. The people who seriously believed the Academic doctrine were rather few—a group of artists probably never amounting to more than a few score. Thousands more, in a general way, accepted the doctrine, but never let it bother them in any practical way. The amateurs and the young artists very much went their own way, while they took pains never to oppose the Academy openly. Thus we read in a guide to Paris of 1684 that the paintings of Rubens, which the Academy disapproved, were constantly visited by young painters for their instruction. The writer, Germain Brice, warmly praises the Rubenses. Of course, the sight-seer in seventeenth-century Paris had as little to do with Academies and doctrines as he has today. As for the collectors, they, too, probably read Dufresnoy's "De Arte Graphica" approvingly, but they bought what they liked, and found no incongruity in hanging Poussin, Holbein and Teniers on the same wall. Poussin himself had collected, besides his classical marbles and portfolios of prints after Raphael, Titian and the Carracci, no less than three hundred and fifty woodcuts and copperplate engravings by Albrecht Dürer.

Soon the Academic doctrine began to suffer, less from outsiders than from its friends. Especially two critics closely associated with the Academy, Charles Félibien and Rogier de Piles, were in the position of extravagantly and quite honestly lauding Lebrun's art while freely contesting his theories. They wrote copiously and had a public. When Félibien wrote of a Venus of Lebrun that "it wasn't Venus enough," he really struck at the principle of decorum. It seems to have been young Rogier de Piles who, in 1671, shocked the assembled Academicians by saying "it was more important for a painter to know color relations than to draw correctly." This, of course, was rankest heresy, and behind the minutes of the meeting one can almost see the flushed and indignant clerk. De Piles, like Félibien, never contested the Academic doctrine, indeed, both accepted it, but they let it in no way limit their taste. For example, De Piles writes disapprovingly of Rembrandt, but he bought one of Rembrandt's paintings, and regarded it as one of his more precious possessions. Both Félibien and De Piles openly admired the colorful masters, Titian and Rubens. They unconsciously built up a liberal party of Rubensists against the Poussinists of the Academy.

Even inside the Academy, opinion was not quite sound. Philippe de Champaigne had to be gently rebuked by Lebrun for suggesting that Poussin had too much pillaged the ancients. Lebrun was subjected to the chagrin of having his famous "Treatise on the Passions" declared a plagiarism before the Academy.

Then the later years of Lebrun were troubled by the personal rivalry of the scheming Meridional painter, Pierre Mignard. Mignard was born in Troyes (Aube), in 1612. After studies with Vouet, he went to Rome in 1636 and there spent twenty-two years. There he became possibly the first society portrait painter in the history of art, an adept in securing commissions by intrigue and retaining them by flattery. He returned to Paris about 1658, at the moment when the fight between the Academy and the Maîtrise was on. He conceived the idea of reorganizing the Maîtrise as the Academy of St. Luke, with himself as rector. This plan found no favor with the king and Colbert. Having mortally offended the Academy, Mignard must climb alone. This he did with amazing success. His personality must have been persuasive, for his art was feeble and saccharine. It is simply amazing to find such personalities as La Bruyère, Molière and Mme. de Sévigné taking Mignard as a great master. Even in the great confusion of the 1870's I doubt if any painter made so great a reputation with so slender a talent. He multiplied sentimental Madonnas, and won the nickname of the French Raphael.

He was hardly a fair portraitist, lacking all sincerity and intensity of observation, but his florid and colorful style set off a fine figure of a woman in a fashion that pleased her and her friends. Such portraits as that of Mazarin's niece, Maria Mancini, or of his own daughter, proudly labeled as Marquise de Fouquières, and as Muse of History displaying the portrait of Mignard (Fig. 405) looking about twenty years younger than he really was—such pictures give the man's measure. His portraits of men are somewhat better, but rarely of any distinction. As a professional portraitist he had fallen on a lucky time. Philippe de Champaigne died in 1674, having been rather inactive for ten years earlier. After him there was literally no competent professional portrait painter in Paris for a matter of fifteen years and the emergence of Rigaud and Largillière. Mignard profited to the full by the situation and won a social support which resulted in great decorative commissions which made him independent of the Academy.

How the queen-mother should have entrusted him with the frescoing of the dome of the Val de Grâce (Fig. 406) is mysterious, even when one considers how such commissions usually are awarded. On the saucer-shaped ceiling, in 1665, Mignard painted what had been painted a thousand times—an Assumption of the Virgin, in concentric tiers of clouds on which the figures of the blest sat or reclined, or from which they popped out. The task of making a paradise overhead in the badly lighted concavity of a dome is desperately difficult. Hardly anybody except Correggio, at Parma, has carried it through creditably. As for Mignard's attempt, it was feeble in the extreme— a blend of insipidities and would-be audacities. A general pearly and rosy tonality commended it to a Paris which the Academy had put on short rations of color. Molière, being doubtless prompted by Mignard himself, wrote in verse a very prosaic eulogy of "The Glory of Val-de-Grâce." He emphasized pointedly, for the Academicians were oil painters, the difficulties and advantages of fresco over painting in oil. In conclusion Molière bids Colbert employ Mignard before it is too late:

> "Attache à des travaux dont l'éclat te renomme
> Les restes précieux des jours de ce grand homme."

Molière was both champion and prophet. The precious remainder of Mignard's days were devoted to a vast mythological series at the palace of Saint Cloud, 1677, to various minor decorations at Paris, and in 1685 he pushed his way into Versailles. He and his art served as a rallying point for those who disfavored Lebrun and the Academy. He made himself and his art agreeable, held no principles and imposed none on others. His pictures were pretty and entirely untaxing. The worse he painted the more he was admired and loaded with commissions. As his prestige grew, that of Lebrun shrank. He accepted the situation with dignity. When the king asked him why he had not visited a decoration Mignard had made, Lebrun answered, if he visited it, he must give his opinion. "If favorable, it would be laid to subservience; if unfavorable, to jealousy." Accordingly he had not gone, and was not going, to see this work. The death of Colbert in 1684 removed Lebrun's stanchest supporter in the ministry. Louvois, the new incumbent, favored Mignard.

In 1690, when Lebrun died, Mignard seemed his only possible successor, and he was appointed to all of Lebrun's dignities and responsibilities. He was nearly eighty, wanted distinction rather than work, and the operations at the Gobelins and Versailles suffered under his mismanagement and neglect. Mignard's appointment had a high symbolic value. It meant that the king and the cabinet had wearied in the task of shaping a French culture, and now were content to let it shape itself. The Academic doctrine was never disowned, it merely retired into a respected but unconsulted background with the stricter articles of the religious creeds. Nearly everybody continued to give lip service to the doctrine of the grand style, but everybody bought or painted as he pleased. And the new painting, which soon was to conquer the world with its sensuous charm, disregarded all the technical precepts of the Academy, and drew unashamedly from that treasure of fine color and vital design which Rubens had left in Luxembourg.

But it would be an error to suppose that the Academic doctrine died with Mignard's rectorship. A well-knit dogma dies very hard, and when it seems to die it may be only latent, awaiting a revival. Thus, less than a century after Lebrun's death, the pseudo-classic program was being imposed with a far greater severity by Jacques Louis David, while in elementary art instruction the program of the Academy was still in my own youth making many thousands of beginners unhappy observers and copiers of dusty casts from the antique. In insisting on mental values in art, the Academy was profoundly in accord with the new French spirit, and even in aberration or decadence the French artist has rarely fallen below a reasonable professional standard. And while the nobility required by the Academic doctrine has at times been caricatured as mere exuberance or sheer pompousness, it has been a constant advantage to French art to have, however vaguely, ideals of grandeur and nobility officially advocated and generally approved. The fact that such ideals are often misunderstood and misrepresented both by artists and by official patronage has nothing to do with the value of the ideals as such. In leaving the Academic doctrine I believe the reader will feel with me that a formulation so eminently French in its qualities and defects cannot wholly die so long as there is a France. For that matter, there will never be a time anywhere when it will be superfluous to remind the artist that he does well to seek nobility of expression, to consult nature selectively, to refresh himself from the inexhaustible resources of older art.

It remains to treat briefly a few of the minor artists in or on the fringe of the Academic movement. The oldest was a Protestant from Montpellier, Sébastien Bourdon, a painter whose extraordinary versatility led him at times to counterfeit the most various old masters and contemporaries. He was born in 1616, and studied in Rome from his eighteenth to his twenty-first year. He yielded to the most miscellaneous tendencies, practiced his art as a forger. Returning to Paris about 1637, he painted mythologies and histories in the style of the popular Vouet, genre pictures in the manner of the Genoese, Castiglione, now and then indulging in close mimicry of Poussin. He was called to Sweden to paint an equestrian portrait of Queen Christina. He was a founder of the Academy in 1648, and its first rector, also diligent as a lecturer at its sessions. Plainly a baffling creature—equally capable of preaching the grand style and forging such vulgarians as Van Laer. The work of such a man naturally shows no consistency: it does show a high level of excellence in its various phases. Bourdon's baroque manner under Vouet's influence is charmingly represented by Solomon sacrificing to Idols, Paris. The king is shown kneeling among the persuasive pagan beauties who have insensibly led him to idolatry. The motive of fascination is clearly presented; the figure arrangement is rhythmical; the composition is eked out in good baroque fashion by the column, the casual curtain and the trees. A superficial picture, but agreeably so, and conducted with an alert taste.

Somewhat nearer Poussin, but more animated and baroque in feeling, is Julius Caesar at the Tomb of Alexander the Great (Fig. 408), Paris. It is immensely inventive and picturesque, theatrical where Poussin would have been grand.

One can hardly think of the same man painting Halt of Gypsies (Fig. 409), Paris. A pair of gentlemen are visiting a gypsy camp. The faces are characterized with energy and truthfulness, the play of light over cut stone, tree trunks, armor, stuffs, is very sensitively studied. Except for an odd and indefinable elegance, this could be a

Dutch picture. Everything is straightforward, specific, functional. Plainly the theme has deeply enlisted the sympathy of the wayward artist, and moved him to a sincerity of expression which is rare in his uneven art.

As Poussin's fame grew Bourdon inevitably followed in his wake. Such a picture as Christ and the Children, Paris, is admirable for its dignity, very ingenious in its juxtaposition of architectural and draped forms. But the scenic and incidental features somewhat overweigh the central motive—"Suffer little children to come unto Me." One's gaze goes to other parts of the picture—to the three apostles draped like Roman senators, to the woman appealing to St. Peter, to the illumined clouds above a skyline broken by citadels and towers. A something theatrical about this really very able picture betrays itself on observation, and places it below the Poussins which it emulates.

He was an excellent portraitist. The portrait of Queen Christina on horseback anticipates much of the candor and freshness of the later English school. His portrait of Descartes may instructively be compared with Frans Hals' more drastic likeness of the philosopher.

In 1657 and 1658 Sébastien Bourdon was working in his native city, where he was naturally much feted. There he painted for the cathedral one of his most elaborate and sensational pictures—the Fall of Simon Magus. His success on his return to Paris was immense. He had many strings to his bow, and as many patronages. Rogier de Piles, who knew him, writes that he bet he would paint a dozen full-sized heads from life in a day. He won the bet, and De Piles adds, "these heads are by no means the least good that his brush produced." He died in 1671, not quite sixty years old.

Among the direct products of Lebrun's teaching are Charles de la Fosse (1636–1716) and Jean Jouvenet (1644–1717). They illustrate the degree of accomplishment that may be expected from Academic training, and their considerable differences in color, for example, seem about as much due to circumstances as to temperament. De la Fosse had the good sense to shorten his stay at Rome in order to study at Venice, and there he had the good taste to analyze the work of Paolo Veronese. Paolo was the most schematizing of great masters, though he had the taste to conceal his schemes. De la Fosse brought everything to formulations, and on his return was ready to make in agreeable blond colors any arrangement of draped or nude figures that might be desired. He had that kind of reliable, showy, intelligent talent which the School of Rome was to foster in abundance—to the despair of slow-moving geniuses. He was soon employed at Versailles, and the color sketch (Fig. 407), at Rouen, for his ceiling in the Hall of Apollo represents his talent admirably. The god with his plunging horses, the attendant hours, are handled with energy and gaiety, and assembled in the medallion with a fine rhythm. In such a picture, essentially superficial as it is, one must, after all, respect its perfect professionalism. It does unfalteringly what it sets out to do. Apart from his painting, Charles de la Fosse played a useful role as a teacher. In his later years he lived with the fine amateur, Crozat, Watteau's patron. It was De la Fosse who insisted that Watteau present himself for membership in the Academy. This was one of the last public acts of a man nearing eighty. It was a gracious and open-minded one.

Every generation usually produces one or two painters who like to construct what the art student mockingly calls "machines"—vast and intricate figure compositions charged with sensational emotion. Such painters generally make their sensation and are soon forgotten. Do such names as Makart, Munkacsy and Rochegrosse mean anything to my younger readers? These were the famous machine makers of my youth. Genealogically the line is respectable, for the first famous machine is Michelangelo's Last Judgment. In Paris, towards the end of the seventeenth century, the approved machine maker was Jean Jouvenet (1644–1717), who multiplied very big and energetically constructed pictures on religious themes. He was a Norman from Rouen, at seventeen came to Paris to study at the Academy, promptly won the favor of Lebrun and was employed in a minor capacity at Versailles. He never went to Italy, and the strong baroque tinge of his work reflects chiefly the influence of Rubens. That a favorite pupil of Lebrun might form himself on Rubens suggests that Academic orthodoxy was all along rather a matter of profession than of practice. Apparently the student who didn't dispute the maxims could do about as he pleased.

Jouvenet's Descent from the Cross (Fig. 410), painted in 1697, for a generation was exhibited among the world's greatest paintings, in the Salon Carré. It is a very able picture. It seeks to give the physical data of the scene with utmost energy, to express the accompanying emotions with dramatic completeness. As compared with its exemplar, Rubens, the picture lacks distinction, both in color and in emotional effect. In the last years of the century Jouvenet painted a number of gigantic oblong stories of Christ, for the Church of St. Martin in the Fields. They are now distributed between Lyons and Paris. The Raising of Lazarus and the Miraculous Draught of Fishes, at Paris, are composed with clarity and energy. In Christ expelling the Money Changers, Lyons, painted in 1706, Jouvenet fairly magnifies the theme into a forced emigration. Yet he keeps the centrality of the motive of Christ with the scourge, while by hints he tells much of the worldly sumptuousness of the profaned temple. He uses the light and dark arbitrarily, and very skillfully, to suppress or emphasize figures of men and beasts in dense groups—it is our modern stage device of the spotlight anticipated by nearly a couple of centuries. The work attests a real sympathy and an imagination and workmanship resolute and masterly, if not very fine. This overcharging of the emotional content is, of course, a baroque characteristic. There is generally some loss involved in these operatic attacks upon the sensibilities. In the Death of St. Francis, Rouen, the dying saint disappears amid the zeal of the officiants administering last rites, and the insipid angel in the air offering a crown. Of a sounder psychology is St. Bruno in Prayer. It is unlike Le Sueur's reading of such themes in the passion of supplication which relaxes the whole body. The emotion is reinforced by the two edified brothers who view the saint with reverence. This is one of the simplest and finest Jouvenets.

Naturally a favorite of Lebrun was asked to do mythologies. At the Invalides and in the Palais de Justice, at Rennes, one finds Jouvenet, vigorous creator of symbols. The big ceiling at Rennes, in the oil sketch at Grenoble, is typical. The theme is the Victory of Faith. Faith, enthroned in the clouds, is attended by the Virtues, a knightly armored archangel drives the Vices out of the picture. It is a thing that had been done and was yet to be done hundreds of times; it has rarely been done with more confidence and real conviction. Jouvenet's allegorical figures have this advantage over those, for example, of De la Fosse, that they seem to be somebody and to mean something, and not merely to be drawn out of a standard repertory.

There are surprises in the work of this very able painter. Who would expect from the pictorial stage manager such an expression of truthfulness and naturalness as the Choir of Notre Dame (Fig. 411),

Paris? An old canon is celebrating his jubilee. The rite is nearly over, he is giving the benediction, piously kneeling men and women and a pair of monks are still bent in prayer. The figures are small in the vast and luminous space of the church, which is realized with the simplicity and fidelity of the Venetian *veduta* painters. It is a pic ture of extraordinary documentary value, and evidence of a versatility which circumstances did not fully allow Jouvenet to develop.

The new painterlike style became more or less standardized in the work of two portraitists, both admirers of Rubens and Van Dyck, Nicolas Largillière and Hyacinthe Rigaud. They were the first Frenchmen since the Clouets to make a great name simply as portraitists.

Largillière was born in Paris, in 1656, but his early education was gained at Antwerp, where at sixteen he was admitted to the painters' guild. His master was a nobody, but his real teachers were the paintings of Rubens and Van Dyck. At eighteen he worked for a time with Sir Peter Lely, Van Dyck's pupil and successor in London. From these studies Largillière made himself a flexible and colorful style. His execution was brilliant, but never obtrusive; his judgment in giving to every element of a picture precisely the emphasis it deserved, was admirable. Because he painted women in decoletée and satins and men in periwigs, one is at times tempted to set him down as a flatterer, a mere fashionable painter. This is an error. To be sure, he fixed the forms which court painting was to follow— fair ladies as Diana or some sylvan nymph—but Largillière never fails to bring out the essential character of his sitter. Like most professional portraitists, he is at his best when painting his intimates or those whom he admires for other than hierarchical reasons.

When he came to Paris, towards 1675, he paid his tribute to Lebrun by painting him in his studio at work on one of the wall panels for Versailles. The picture is in the Louvre, and very well represents the official manner of Largillière. He was skillful in painting groups, such as the votive picture of Magistrates, 1696, in St. Étienne du Mont, and an oil sketch for a similar group, in the Louvre. He takes pains to make his single portraits pictorial by providing suitable accessories. Here his taste is both florid and sure. Perhaps he is really at his best in his simpler portraits: the admirable head of the young Voltaire, Musée Carnavalet; the robust and vital presentment of the Huguenot matron and refugee, Mme. Stephen Benezet, at Princeton. Best known is the family group, at Paris (Fig. 412). The painter sits at ease, with his fowling piece at his knee and partridges before him; his wife, richly dressed, sits opposite. The pretty daughter has just sung her song to her parents, the left hand, with the music sheet, has dropped, the right hand holds its gesture, showing the daintiest of forearms and fingers. There is a hint of trees and of a parklike background. Bring poetry into such a picture and you will have Watteau. A queer world where one shoots in a peruke and wears silks and satins out of doors, but a world that Largillière thoroughly liked and understood.

There are really no poor Largillières, and the reader may study his pictures almost at random. Very characteristic are a Portrait of a Lady, at Rome, and the portrait of the painter Forest, his father-in-law, at Berlin. Largillière lived to be ninety, dying in 1746, twenty-five years later than Watteau. His art is the bridge between Poussin and Lebrun, and Boucher and Nattier. It would be foolish to compare Largillière with the great masters of poetical or psychological portraiture. He deals with face values, but does so with sympathy and with the resources of a fine intelligence and a swift and light and accurate hand. To the art lover who finds something artificial in Largillière, I can only say that such artificiality is in the sitters, and is merely the French precision and self-consciousness, which the non-French rarely like. To appreciate Largillière one will do well now and then to forget his sitters and look at his painting.

Hyacinthe Rigaud finds, I imagine, an even more imperfect sympathy outside of France than Largillière. A democratic taste instinctively resents the exaggerated pompousness of such official full-length portraits as Louis XIV (Fig. 402), Paris, the great orator, Bishop Bossuet, Paris, or the Portrait in Armor of the Prince-Elector of Saxony, Frederick Augustus III, Dresden. Only historical study will cure this natural democratic revulsion. One learns that potentates of state and church were like that, and were expected to look like that. A king, a field marshal or a bishop could hardly strut or pose too much. On the whole, Rigaud merely faces the official facts and gives the true record of them.

He was born in Perpignan, at the roots of the Pyrenees, in 1659. He studied at Montpellier, where he saw Van Dycks and portraits painted under his influence by Sébastien Bourdon. Rigaud by his thirtieth year was the most popular court portrait painter. This involved a quantity production. Portraits of famous people were multiplied and sent about as gifts. So Rigaud organized a small factory. There were assistants who were specialists on textiles, armor, architecture, furniture, hangings. Ordinarily Rigaud merely selected the pose and painted the face. Van Dyck in his latest years had worked in this spirit, with deplorable loss of quality. What is surprising in these composite Rigauds is that they show no feebleness anywhere and hang together consistently.

We have to do with an imposing and brilliant sort of portraiture, entirely forthright and quite without finesse. The merit is rather institutional than personal. Rigaud was really a victim of his popularity. His was a sensitive taste, as his collecting seven Rembrandts and eight Van Dycks suggests. There are intimate portraits, such as that of an officer, at Aix (Fig. 413), there are faces, such as his own self-portrait, Musée Carnavalet, touched in with the most delicate truthfulness and precision. Rigaud lived on into the Regency, times less congenial, certainly less pompous. His art changed little, on the whole went off in his later years. He died in 1743, eighty-four years old, a venerable relic of the Grand Siècle in the Paris of Voltaire, Rousseau, Chardin and Boucher.

Except as an educational gesture, the grand style seemed dead. To be sure, art students still drew from the antique before drawing from life; candidates for the Prix de Rome still nimbly executed their paintings on a theme from Plutarch, Virgil or Ovid. But the temper, even of historical and mythological painting, had completely changed. Nobody sought that tempered delectation which Poussin regarded as the aim of art; instead everybody sought to give pleasure in the everyday sense. It would have seemed safe to bet that the grand style had gone the way of the religious orthodoxies to oblivion. But the fundamentalisms die hard and have an odd way of continuing in suspended animation until they are again wanted. No, it really wasn't safe to bet on the decease of the grand style in Mme. de Pompadour's time. Only two years after Largillière died, Jacques Louis David was born.

# BIBLIOGRAPHY AND NOTES

T HIS brief list of books is made from the point of view of the occasional reader with scholarly instincts. Such a reader will want only leads to further bibliography, and direction to better reproductions of pictures than are possible in this book. Such are the very modest aims of the following bibliographical notes. Many works in foreign languages are cited chiefly for their superior illustrations. These are indicated by an asterisk.

## GENERAL WORKS

*Allgemeines Lexikon der bildenden Künstler*, ed. by U. Thieme and F. Becker. Leipzig, 1907–. In progress, nearly finished. The standard work for biography and bibliography.

Such brilliant and highly subjective books as *The History of Art*, by Élie Faure, available in French and English; *The Arts*, by Hendrik Willem van Loon; and *A World History of Art*, by Sheldon Cheney, will be stimulating and profitable to those who already have considerable direct experience of art; to others, I feel such books will prove merely confusing and misleading.

### CHAPTER II

*Niederländisches Künstlerlexikon*, by Dr. Alfred von Wurzbach. 2 vols., with supplement. Vienna and Leipzig, 1906–1911. Though somewhat dated, still an indispensable aid to bibliography and documentation, location of pictures, etc. Unfortunately, Dr. Wurzbach sometimes introduces unproved theories as facts, notably in his treatment of Rogier van der Weyden. Covers the entire art of the Netherlands, even including Dutch and Flemish painters who made their career abroad.

*The Van Eycks and their Followers*, by Sir Martin Conway. London and New York, 1921. By all means the best general survey in English, but inadequately illustrated. Extends from the immediate predecessors of the Van Eycks to Pieter Bruegel the Elder. Hereafter noted simply as Conway.

*Histoire de la Peinture Flamande*, by Fierens-Gevaert. 3 vols. Paris and Brussels, 1927. An able survey from the beginnings to Pieter Bruegel the Elder. Superior illustrations.

*Hubert and Jan van Eyck*, by W. H. James Weale. London and New York, 1908. Somewhat superseded by the new edition of Brockwell, but still very valuable for fullness of documentation and illustration. Cited as Weale 1.

*The Van Eycks and Their Art*, by W. H. James Weale, with the co-operation of Maurice W. Brockwell, London and New York, 1912. Cited as Weale 2. A corrected and somewhat enlarged edition of Weale 1 in smaller format.

*Die Altniederländische Malerei; vol. 1, Die Van Eyck, Petrus Christus.* By Max J. Friedländer. Berlin, 1924. Cited as A.N.M. Since Dr. Friedländer's studies are conducted in the order of research, they are addressed to the specialist, not the layman. His illustrations are the best generally available and his great work is for that reason cited chapter by chapter. Dr. Friedländer seems to me far too skeptical as regards attributions to Hubert van Eyck.

*The Discoverer of Landscape*, by Bryson Burroughs. *The Arts*, September, 1927. An admirable approach to the problem of Hubert by an accomplished American painter and museum curator.

Perhaps a word of warning is necessary to the credulous reader who falls foul of the thoroughly erratic and quite negligible book, *Hubert van Eyck, Personnage de Legende*, by Émile Renders. Paris and Brussels, 1933. He reduces Hubert to a historic myth, and gives all pictures of an Eyckian sort to Jan.

Friedländer, A.N.M., XIV, p. 75 ff., accepts General Renders' view. But Alan Burroughs, *Art Criticism from a Laboratory*, Boston, 1938, Chap. XII, shows conclusively that two painters worked on the Ghent altarpiece.

Erwin Panofsky, *Art Bulletin*, December, 1935, and Hermann Beenken, *ibid.*, June, 1937, maintain differing opinions as to a complete revamping of the arrangement of the Ghent altarpiece by Jan after Hubert's death. Both arguments are ingenious, but I feel that it is not demonstrated that any such revamping took place. At best their theories represent possibilities.

CHAPTER III

Weale and Friedländer, cited in the preceding section, are really the essential works, and Conway represents the average sensible position of scholars on the problem of the Van Eycks. General Renders, in *Jan van Eyck, Son Œuvre*, Bruges, 1935, with a joyous irresponsibility continues his endeavor to reduce Hubert van Eyck to a historic myth. For its abundant comparative cuts of good scale the book is very valuable to the student. The upshot of General Renders' studies seems to be simply that Jan was more profoundly and permanently influenced by Hubert than we had suspected.

For Petrus Christus the reader need hardly go beyond Conway, and Friedländer, vol. I.

CHAPTER IV

Conway, * Friedländer, A.N.M., vol. II, are the best resources for Robert Campin, Rogier de la Pasture (generally but I think erroneously, since he was a native of French Flanders, called Van der Weyden), and Jacques Daret.

* *Rogier de la Pasture*, by Jules Destrée. 2 vols. Paris and Brussels, 1930.

The various attempts to split Rogier in two—a Rogier of Brussels and a Rogier of Bruges—are elaborately defended in Wurzbach, *Niederländisches Künstlerlexikon*, and, I think rightly, dismissed summarily by Friedländer.

The indomitable General Renders seeks to reduce Robert Campin to the shadow of a name by attributing all the pictures usually ascribed to Campin to the first manner of Rogier. *Solution du Problème Van der Weyden, Flémalle, Campin*, by E. Renders. 2 vols. Bruges, 1931. Very valuable for comparative illustrations of large scale, which seem to prove merely that Campin was a stronger influence on Rogier than we had supposed.

Friedländer, A.N.M., XIV, p. 81 ff., accepts General Renders' view. Again Alan Burroughs, *Art Criticism from a Laboratory*, Boston, 1938, shows that the pictures generally given to Campin are quite different technically from those of Rogier.

* Le Maître de Flémalle et les Frères Van Eyck, by Charles de Tolnay.  Brussels, 1939.  Dates Campin's work somewhat earlier than is usual, and claims for him priority in a tonal and atmospheric manner.  A suggestive essay with admirable illustrations.

Dirck Bouts und seine Schule, by Wolfgang Schoene, Berlin, 1938.

### CHAPTER V

Conway, * Friedländer, A.N.M., vol. III (Bouts); vol. IV (Hugo); vol. V (Geertgen); vol. VI (Memling).

* Hugo van der Goes, by Joseph Destrée.  Paris and Brussels, 1914.

For the Princeton Epiphany, my article in Art in America, April, 1938.  "An Epiphany by Hugo van der Goes Finished by Gerard David."

* Hans Memling (Klassiker der Kunst).  Stuttgart.  No date. Virtually all the pictures in half-tone cuts of fair quality.

Les Maîtres d'Autrefois, by E. Fromentin.  Available in English. Is important for criticism of Memling.

The Masters of Past Time, by E. Fromentin.  London, 1913.

### CHAPTER VI

Conway, * Friedländer, A.N.M., vol. V (Bosch); vol. VI (David); vol. VII (Massys); vol. VIII (Mabuse); vol. IX (Patenier); vol. XI (Antwerp Mannerists).

* Gerard David und seine Schule, by Eberhard Freiher von Bodenhausen, Munich, 1905.  Additions, Bodenhausen and Valentiner, Zeitschrift f. bildende Kunst, May, 1911.

* Quentin Massys, by Harold Brising.  Leipzig, 1908.  Good illustrations of large scale.

* Lucas van Leyden (1494-1533).  Leipzig, 1908.

* Lucas de Leyde, by N. Beets.  Brussels and Paris, 1913.

* Hieronymus Bosch, by Paul Lafond.  Paris and Brussels, 1914.

Hieronymus Bosch, by Walter Schurmeyer.  Munich, 1923.

* *Jerome Bosch. Le Retable de Saint-Antoine du Musée Nationale de Lisbonne.* Brussels and Paris. No date. A portfolio of excellent illustrations with many details.

* *Hieronymus Bosch,* by Charles de Tolnay. Basel, 1937. The best critical survey, well illustrated.

### CHAPTER VII

* *Histoire de la Peinture Française, T. I.,* by Louis Dimier. Paris and Brussels, 1925. A very summary but also excellent survey. Cited as Dimier.

* *Les Peintres Français . . . de la Provence,* by L.-H. Labaud. Marseilles, 1932. Very valuable for illustrations.

* *Catalogue de l'exposition des Primitifs Français,* Paris, 1904. An album of good illustrations of large scale. Very useful for study.

*The French Primitives and Their Forms,* by Albert C. Barnes and Violette de Mazia. Merion, Pa., 1931. A severely technical study.

* *Gothic Painting in France,* by O. A. Lesmoine. New York and Florence.

* *Les Primitifs Français,* by Charles Sterling. Paris, 1939.

### CHAPTER VIII

*German Masters of Art,* by Helen A. Dickinson. New York, 1914. An excellent survey, well illustrated.

* *Die Kölnische Malerschule,* by Heribert Reiners. Cologne, 1925.

* *Die Altdeutsche Malerei,* by Curt Gläser. Munich, 1924.

* *Meister Bertram von Minden,* by Alexander Dorner. Berlin, 1937.

* *Meister Francke,* by Bella Martens. 2 vols. Hamburg, 1926.

* *Stephan Lochner . . . ,* by Otto H. Foerster. Leipzig, 1938.

*Lucas Moser und Hans Multscher,* by Alfred Stang. Leipzig, 1922.

*Konrad Witz, Gemäldestudien,* by Hans Wendeland. Basel, 1924.

*Michael Pacher,* by Eberhard Hempel. Vienna, 1938.

CHAPTER IX

*A History of Spanish Painting*, by Chandler Rathfon Post. Cambridge, Mass. Vols. II-VII, 1930–. Few readers will need to go beyond this standard and richly illustrated work, though for many it will seem prolix. Bermejo, the only one of these painters likely to interest deeply the average art lover, is very fully treated in volume V. Post's work gives the leads to the superabundant Spanish bibliography.

*Jaime Huguet*, by Benjamin Rowland. Cambridge, Mass., 1932. Treats many aspects of Catalan painting.

\* *Spanish Painting*, by E. Harris. Paris, 1937. Perhaps the best resource for illustrations.

*Paintings in the Collection of the Hispanic Society of America.* 2 vols. New York. Many small but clear cuts of paintings not otherwise accessible to American students.

CHAPTER X

*German Masters of Art*, by Helen A. Dickinson. New York, 1914. An excellent survey, well illustrated.

*Albert Dürer*, by T. Sturge Moore. London and New York, 1905. A poet's estimate.

\* *Albrecht Dürer . . .* , by Dr. Friedrich Nüchter (translation). London, 1911. I know of no more helpful guide to the beginner than this concisely composed analysis with its wealth of good illustrations.

\* *Dürer (Klassiker der Kunst)*. Stuttgart. No date. Fair halftone cuts of all the paintings and engravings. Available also with French or English text.

*Albrecht Dürer's Schriftliche Nachlass.* Ed. by E. Heidrich. Berlin, 1910.

*Literary Remains of Albrecht Dürer*, by William Martin Conway. Cambridge, 1889.

*Dürer's Kunsttheorien*, by Erwin Panofsky. Berlin, 1915.

*Matthias Gruenewald . . .* , by Arthur Burkhard. Cambridge, Mass., 1936.

*Matthias Gruenewald*, by Oskar Hagen. Munich, 1919. The best critical treatment.

* *Der historische Grünewald*, by Mathis Gothardt-Neithardt. Munich, 1938.

*Trois Églises et Trois Primitifs*, by J. K. Huysmans. Paris. A somewhat perfervid but also highly suggestive criticism of the Colmar altarpiece.

* *Hans Holbein the Younger*, by Arthur B. Chamberlain. 2 vols. London and New York, 1913. The most comprehensive treatment in English.

*Hans Holbein the Younger*, by Ford Madox Hueffer. London and New York. No date. A brief and good critical essay.

* *Hans Holbein D.J. (Klassiker der Kunst)*. Stuttgart. No date. Complete reproduction in half-tone of all the paintings and copies of lost works.

*Holbein*, by Max Reinhardt. New York and Paris, 1938. Excellent reproductions of most of the works. Reasonably priced.

Holbein's very distinguished designs for woodcutting are perhaps most readily available in *Holbein der Jungerer*, by H. Knackfuss *(Künstler Monographien)*. Bielefeld and Leipzig, 1902.

*Albrecht Altdorfer*, by Georg Jacob Wolf *(Künstler Monographien)*. Bielefeld and Leipzig, 1925.

* *Albrecht Altdorfer*, by Max J. Friedländer. Berlin, 1925.

* *Albrecht Altdorfer*, by Otto Benesch. *Pantheon*, March, 1938. For 400th Anniversary.

* *Die Gemälde von Lucas Cranach*, by Max J. Friedländer and Jakob Rosenberg. Berlin, 1932. Superior illustrations.

*Lucas Cranach the Elder*, by W. L. Burke. *Art Bulletin*, vol. XVIII, 1936, p. 25 ff. An excellent critical and stylistic analysis.

## CHAPTER XI

*Carel van Mander, Dutch and Flemish Painters.* Translated from the Schilderboeck by Constant van de Wall. New York, 1936. While Van Mander is not a meaty author, his pages admirably give the color and suggest the taste of his land and century. On such painters as Massys, Mabuse, Scorel, Frans Floris, Pieter Bruegel and others he may be read with amusement and profit. Dr. van de Wall contributes necessary corrections and valuable bibliographical notes.

Wurzbach, *Niederländisches Künstlerlexicon*, is the best aid on the factual side. See bibliography for Chapter II.

*Jan van Scorel*, by G. J. Hoogewerff. La Haye, 1923. Fully illustrated.

\* Friedländer, A.N.M., vol. XII.

*Pieter Aertsen*, by Johannes Sievers. Leipzig, 1908. Well illustrated.

\* Friedländer, A.N.M., vol. XIII.

*Jan Sanders (van Hemessen)*, by Felix Graefe. Leipzig, 1909.
\* Friedländer, A.N.M., vol. XII.

\* *Bernart van Orley*. Friedländer, A.N.M., vol. VIII.

*Antonio Moro, son Œuvre*, by Henry Hymans. Brussels, 1910.
\* *Antonio Moro und seine Zeitgenossen*. Friedländer, A.N.M., vol. XIII.

\* *Frans Floris*. Friedländer, A.N.M., vol. XIII.

\* *Pieter Bruegel l'Ancien*, by Renée van Bastelaer. Brussels, 1907. The standard work, well and profusely illustrated.

*Pieter Bruegel the Elder*, by Virgil Barker. *The Arts*, September, 1926. An excellent brief survey.

*Die Zeichnungen Pieter Bruegel's*, by Karl Tolnai. Munich, 1928. Good reproductions of virtually all the authentic drawings.

\* *Pierre Bruegel l'Ancien*, by Charles de Tolnay. Brussels, 1935. A brilliant and suggestive essay, but the arguments for Bruegel as a vitalist and systematic moralist seem to me very tenuous. Valuable reproductions of details from the pictures.

\* *Pierre Bruegel l'Ancien*, 37 *Chromotypies*, ed. by Max Dvořák. Vienna. A large portfolio of good color reproductions of the finest Bruegels.

\* *Pieter Bruegel*, by Gotthard Jedlicka. Zurich, 1938. A laboriously elaborate analysis of Bruegel's principal works. Can be conscientiously recommended only to readers with unlimited patience and a complete command of German.

## CHAPTER XII

\* Dimier, *La Peinture Française*, vol. I, treats this period ably and succinctly. See bibliography for Chapter XXII.

*The Renaissance of the Arts in France*, by Mrs. Mark Pattison (Lady Dilke). 2 vols. London, 1879. Dated, and pays relatively little attention to painting. Valuable for historical background.

*Characteristics of French Art*, by Roger Fry. New York and London, 1933. A brief and brilliant survey.


CHAPTER XIII

*The Story of Spanish Painting*, by C. H. Caffin. New York, 1910. Very sketchy for this earlier period.

*Geschichte der Spanischen Malerei*, by A. L. Mayer. 2 vols. Leipzig, 1922. The best popular survey, unfortunately available only in German and Spanish.

*Art in Spain and Portugal*, by N. Dieulafoy. New York, 1913. An excellent but very brief survey.

* *Spanish Painting*, by E. Harris. Paris, 1937. The best single album of illustrations.

*Catalogue of the Hispanic Society of America*. See bibliography for Chapter IX.

*El Greco*, by Manuel D. Cossío. Madrid, 1908. The first thoroughgoing study, and still indispensable for students. Unfortunately the illustrations are very poor.

*El Greco . . .* , by Albert F. Calvert and C. Gasquoine Hartley. London and New York, 1902. The pioneer work in English and still perhaps the best popular treatment.

*El Greco*, by Elizabeth Trapier. The Hispanic Society, New York. An up-to-date study with many small but clear cuts.

* *Domenico Theotocopouli, dit El Greco*, by M. Legendre and A. Hartmann. Paris. Editions Hyperion. All El Greco's pictures in satisfactory reproductions, a few in color.

*Francisco Ribalta and his School*, by Delphine Fritz Darby. Cambridge, Mass., 1938.

*The Painting of Francisco Herrera the Elder*, by John G. Thacher. *Art Bulletin*, September, 1937.


CHAPTER XIV

*Rubens*, by Max Rooses. 2 vols. Philadelphia and London, 1904.

*Rubens, his Life, his Work and his Time*, by Emile Michel. 2 vols. London and New York, 1899. Both, elaborate and encyclopedic.

\* *P. P. Rubens (Klassiker der Kunst)*. Stuttgart. No date. Fair half-tone cuts of virtually all the paintings.

\* *Rubens. Paintings and Drawings.* 245 illustrations. Phaidon Ed. New York: Oxford University Press. Superior reproductions well selected at a most reasonable price. Strong in autographic sketches.

*Great Masters of Dutch and Flemish Painting*, by W. Bode. London and New York, 1909.

*Les Maîtres d'Autrefois*, by E. Fromentin, Paris. A classic critical survey by a painter-critic. Translation, *The Masters of Past Time*, London, 1913.

*Peter Paul Rubens*, by R. A. M. Stevenson. London, 1898. A very workmanlike critical monograph from the painter's point of view.

*Great Masters*, by John La Farge. New York, 1903. The essay on Rubens in this volume is the best available in English.

The adventurous reader will find profit in reading what Sir Joshua Reynolds writes about Rubens in his *Discourses* and *Journey to the Netherlands*.

\* *Jakob Jordaens . . .* , by Max Rooses. London and New York, 1908. The standard work, well and fully illustrated.

\* *Anthony Van Dyck, a Further Study*, by Lionel Cust. With 25 illustrations in colors. New York and London, 1911.

*Van Dyck*, by Lionel Cust. London and New York, 1906. A brief survey.

\* *Anton van Dyck (Klassiker der Kunst)*. Stuttgart. No date. Virtually all the pictures in half-tone cuts.

CHAPTER XV

*Frans Hals*, by Gerald S. Davies. London, 1902. Briefer version, London, 1904.

*Frans Hals*, by E. W. Moes. Brussels, 1909.

\* *Frans Hals, herausgegehen von W. R. Valentiner (Klassiker der Kunst)*. Stuttgart, 1921. Good half-tone cuts of all the pictures.

*Great Masters of Dutch and Flemish Painting*, by W. Bode. London and New York, 1909.

Fromentin offers the best criticism. See bibliography for Chapter XIV.

### CHAPTER XVI

* *Rembrandt, his Life and Works,* by Emile Michel. London and New York, 1903.
* *Rembrandt, Gemälde,* Besorgt von A. Bredius. Vienna. Phaidon Verlag. Excellent reproductions of all the pictures. Very reasonably priced.

For criticism, Fromentin's *Les Maîtres d'Autrefois* is essential. Bibliography for Chapter XIV.

*Rembrandt's Etchings,* by Arthur M. Hind. 2 vols. New York and London, 1912. On the whole the best guide to Rembrandt's prints.

*Les Eauxfortes de Rembrandt,* by André Charles Coppier. Paris, 1917. A searching and instructive technical study.


### CHAPTER XVII

*Great Masters of Dutch and Flemish Painting,* by W. Bode. London and New York. A summary and genial survey of the entire seventeenth-century field by a great expert.

*Old Masters and Modern Art,* by Sir Charles Holmes. Vol. II. London and New York. A searching study, largely technical, by an accomplished painter.

*Adriaen Brouwer et son évolution artistique,* by Frederik Schmidt-Degener. Brussels, 1908.

*Adriaen van Ostade,* by Adolf Rosenberg. (Künstler Monographien) Bielefeld and Leipzig, 1900.

*Jan Steen, Forty Illustrations.* By Frederik Schmidt-Degener, London, 1927.

*Terborch und Jan Steen,* by Adolf Rosenberg. Bielefeld and Leipzig, 1897.

*Teniers der Jungere,* by Adolf Rosenberg. Bielefeld and Leipzig.

* *Die Niederländischen Maler des 17ten Jahrhundert,* by Max J. Friedländer. Berlin, Propyläen Verlag, 1926. Well illustrated, many color cuts. The best brief survey.

Many examples of Dutch painting in American possession are reproduced in *Catalogue of a Collection of Paintings by Dutch Masters of the Seventeenth Century,* by W. R. Valentiner. New York, 1909 (Hudson Fulton Celebration).

Illustration. There is some difficulty in finding adequate illustrations for many of the Dutch and Flemish little masters. Most serviceable to the studious reader will perhaps be the albums of good half-tones published by Hanfstaengl of Munich for the galleries of Amsterdam, Berlin, Cassel, Dresden, The Hague, Leningrad, London and Munich.

### CHAPTER XVIII

*The Great Masters of Dutch and Flemish Painting,* by W. Bode. New York and London, 1909.

*Old Masters and Modern Art,* by Sir Charles Holmes. Vol. II. London and New York.

*Gerard Dou,* by W. Martin. London and New York, 1902.

\* *Gerard Dou (Klassiker der Kunst).* 1913.

*Leonaert Bramer,* by Heinrich Wichmann. Leipzig, 1923.

*Jan Vermeer of Delft and Carel Fabritius,* by C. Hofstede de Groot. Amsterdam, 1909.

*Vermeer de Delft,* by Gustave Vanzype. Brussels, 1908.

*Vermeer of Delft,* by E. V. Lucas. London, 1922.

*Jan Vermeer of Delft,* by Philip L. Hale. Boston, 1913. A painter's searching analysis, better illustrations than the new edition.

*Vermeer,* by Philip L. Hale, completed, etc., by Frederick W. Coburn and Ralph T. Hale. Boston and New York, 1938.

\* *Pieter de Hooch (Klassiker der Kunst).* 1928. All the pictures in half-tone cuts.

*Gerard Terborch,* by Franz Hellens. Brussels, 1911.

*Pots and Pans, or Studies in Still-life Painting,* by Arthur Edwin Bye. Princeton and London, 1921. A readable and perceptive survey of the whole field of still-life painting. Fully illustrated.

See also *A Catalogue of a Collection of Paintings by Dutch Masters of the 17th Century.* Bibliography for Chapter XVII.

### CHAPTER XIX

*Great Masters of Landscape Painting,* by Émile Michel. Philadelphia and London, 1910.

*Great Masters of Dutch and Flemish Painting,* by W. Bode. London and New York, 1909.

Jacob van Ruysdael, by Jakob Rosenberg. Berlin, 1928.
Meindert Hobbema, by Georges Broulhiet. Paris, 1938.


CHAPTER XX

The School of Madrid, by A. de Beruete y Moret. London and
New York, 1911.

The Painters of Seville, by N. Sentenach. New York and London. No date. Mayer, see bibliography for Chapter XIII.

Catalogue of the Hispanic Society of America, see bibliography
for Chapter IX.

Jusepe de Ribera, by August L. Mayer. Leipzig, 1923.

Francisco Zurburán, by Hugo Kehrer. Munich, 1918.

Diego Velasquez und seiner Jahrhundert, by Carl Justi. 2 vols.
Bonn, 1888. After fifty years still the standard work, though many
pictures have turned up since its appearance.

* Velasquez, by A. de Beruete. Paris, 1898. An English translation of the first edition, 1896.

* Velasquez (Klassiker der Kunst). Stuttgart. No date. Good
half-tone cuts of all the paintings.

Velasquez, by R. A. M. Stevenson. London and New York,
1899. A searching analysis of the style by a painter.


CHAPTER XXI

The Painters of Seville, by N. Sentenach. London and New
York.

Murillo, by Albert F. Calvert. New York and London. No
date.

* Murillo (Klassiker der Kunst). Stuttgart, 1913. Good half-
tone cuts of all the pictures.

Biografia de Pintor Sevillano Juan de Valdés Leal, by José Ges-
toso y Peréz. Seville and New York, the Hispanic Society, 1916.

Juan de Valdés Leal, by Paul Lafond. Paris.


CHAPTER XXII

Histoire de la Peinture Française, by Louis Dimier. Paris and
Brussels, 1925. 5 vols., I, II, III.

*Die Französisch Malerei des Siebzenten Jahrhundert*, by Werner Weisbach. Berlin, 1932. Devoted chiefly to the cultural and stylistic aspects of the subject. Well illustrated.

*Characteristics of French Art*, by Roger Fry. New York and London, 1933. A brief but brilliant survey.

*The Renaissance of Art in France*, by Mrs. Mark Pattison (Lady Dilke). 2 vols. London, 1879. Largely devoted to architecture and minor arts and pretty well dated, but still valuable on the historical side.

*Georges de la Tour*, by Hermann Voss, *Art in America*, vol. XVII, pp. 40–48.

New ascriptions to De la Tour, Paul Jamot, *Gazette des Beaux Arts*, May, June, 1939.

*The Les Nain*. The fundamental study is by Paul Jamot, *Gazette des Beaux-Arts*, April and May, 1922, March, 1923.

* *Les Le Nain*, by Paul Fierens. Paris, 1933.

*Entretiens sur les Vies . . . des plus Excellens Peintres*, by C. Félibien. 2nd ed. 3 vols. Paris, 1675 ff. The generally liberal views of a critic fundamentally academic. Interestingly written in dialogue form. Félibien knew many of the painters of whom he writes. I cite the second edition, Paris, 1685, 1688.

*Abregé de la Vie des Peintres*, by M. de Piles. 2nd ed. Paris, 1715. Brief and generally judicious comment on the painters most esteemed in his time. First edition published 1699.

*The Art of Painting, Translated from the French of M. de Piles*. London, about 1720.

These two critics, despite a certain narrowness in taste, reach the high-water mark of art criticism in their time.

CHAPTER XXIII

*Claude Lorrain*, by Walter Friedländer. Berlin, 1931. The only complete critical survey.

*Claude Lorrain*, by George Grahame. London, 1895. A straightforward, factual account.

*Claude*, by Roger Fry. *Burlington Magazine*, August, 1907. A brief but illuminative appreciation with reproductions of some fifteen of Claude's finest drawings.

*Claude Gellée dit le Lorrain*, by Pierre Courthion. Paris. 1932.

A good critical essay. Excellent reproductions of sixty-five paintings and forty drawings.

*Les Dessins de Claude Lorrain*, by Louis Demonts. Paris. No date. Excellent reproductions of the Claude drawings in the Louvre.

*The Drawings of Claude Lorrain*, by Arthur M. Hind. London and New York, 1925. Good reproductions of some seventy of Claude's finest drawings.

For painters influencing Claude:

*Agostino Tassi*, by Jacob Hess. Munich, 1935.

*Adam Elsheimer*, by Heinrich Weizsacher. Berlin, 1938.


CHAPTER XXIV

Dimier, vol. II; Weisbach; Fry and Pattison. See bibliography for Chapter XXII.

* *Nicolas Poussin*, by Émile Magne. Paris and Brussels, 1914. Excellent illustrations, including most of the drawings.

* *Nicolas Poussin, sein Werk und sein Leben*, by Otto Grautoff. 2 vols. Munich, 1914. A searching analysis of Poussin's style and development.

*Nicolas Poussin*, by Elizabeth Denio. London, 1899. A straightforward and readable biography.

Félibien and De Piles. See bibliography for Chapter XXII.


CHAPTER XXV

Dimier, vols. III-V; Weisbach; Félibien; De Piles; Fry and Pattison. See bibliography for Chapter XXII.

*Les Doctrines d'Art en France—de Poussin à Diderot*, by André Fontaine. Paris, 1909. An indispensable guide to the esthetic battlefields of France in Louis XIV's and Louis XV's times.

# PUBLIC COLLECTIONS OF PHOTOGRAPHS

Most of the great American museums have large collections of photographs which are available to the public. Many American universities and colleges have important collections, most notable perhaps those of Harvard and Princeton.

With certain restrictions, the Frick Art Reference Library, New York, offers extraordinary facilities to the student.

The collection of Sir Robert Witt, London, is generously open to all applicants. The Courtauld Institute, London, has large collections.

Similar collections in many of the great cities of Europe cannot be enumerated here. The traveler may easily locate them by applying to his banker or consul.

# REPRODUCTIONS OF PAINTINGS

THE BEST reproductions are none too good for the serious student of painting. The photographs of Hanfstaengl and Bruckmann are available for many of the galleries of northern and western Europe.

Alinari of Florence has partly covered in our field the Italian galleries, the Louvre, and the gallery at Dresden.

Dominic Anderson of Rome has photographed extensively in London and Madrid.

Les Archives Photographiques, Paris, is the official purveyor of photographs of French paintings.

Bulloz of Paris has covered much of the painting of the Low Countries and many important loan exhibitions at Paris. Giraudon of Paris has also a rich series, especially in the French field.

For the Spanish primitives, Arturo Mas of Barcelona was the best resource before the war.

Most European and American art museums sell very reasonably photographs of their pictures.

Color reproductions abound at attractively cheap prices, but since these are copies of copies, I cannot recommend them for study.

# APPENDIX

## Historical Illustrations

Wishing to share with the reader at least a little of the incidental reading—much of it delightful to me—which has accompanied the preparation of this book, I here gather a few historical illustrations which were too bulky to be carried in the text. They are chosen to make concrete certain important aspects of the art and civilization of western Europe in the Renaissance, and also to suggest the vicissitudes of critical opinion.

### CHAPTER II

### *Business and Guild Relations*

Painting till into the seventeenth century was a handicraft and a business rather than a liberal profession, and was conducted, under guild authority, according to strict business principles. The elaborate contract for pictures which is printed in the *Historical Illustrations for Early Spanish Painting*, Chapter IX, is typical for all western Europe up to the foundation of Academies about the middle of the seventeenth century.

The situation may be suggested by Melchoir Broederlam's receipt of December 16, 1401, which may be a last payment for the shutters now at Dijon (Fig. 5):

"16 December 1401. Receipt of Melchoir Broederlam, in the matter of two hundred francs.

Let all know that I, Melchoir, painter and varlet de chambre to Monseigneur the Duke, have had and received the sum of two hundred gold francs, which were due me for several expenses and missions which I have made and undertaken in painting and making very richly two panels, altarpieces to put in and give to the Church of the Carthusians.

Witness my seal, etc." (Dehaisnes. *Documents et Extraits, etc.,* Lille, 1886, T. II, p. 796.)

All painters until towards the middle of the seventeenth century and the foundation of Academies were required to join trade guilds. Since the painters in any city were relatively few, they were often associated in the guild with other fine trades, such as glass making, wood carving, embroidering, and even saddlery. Such a guild was really both a workers' and employers' union. It regulated conditions of apprenticeship and qualifications for membership. In particular it required under penalty high standards of workmanship. A few regulations from the painters' guild of Ghent, 1338 (Dehaisnes. *Documents et extraits divers concernant l'Histoire de l'Art dans la Flandre, etc.* Lille, 1886, T. I, p. 329), will make the matter clear.

1. "No one shall enjoy the privileges of the corporation and will not be accepted as a free master of the trade of the painters or sculptors, unless he has the right of citizenship.

4. Every painter belonging to the corporation will work with good color on stone, canvas, panels with shutters or without; if he violates this regulation, he will be condemned to a fine of ten Paris livres.

5. Every gilded or silvered work, on stone, canvas or panel, in which false gold or silver shall have been used, will be confiscated, and he who is responsible for the offense shall be condemned to a fine of ten Paris livres.

6. The work which, by agreement, should be made of fine azure or red, and for which has been used, in the judgment of the dean and director of the craft, ordinary colors, shall be the occasion for its maker of a fine of ten Paris livres.

7. No sculptor may use in his works poor wood, whether it be sap wood or with rotten knots, under penalty of a fine of four livres, eleven sous, of Paris."

The painters' guilds marched in religious processions sometimes with the subsidy of the city. (See Dehaisnes, T. II, p. 765. 1397–1398. Accounts of the City of Bruges—Painters' Guild.)

"By decree of the burgomaster, Florent de Hamere, the city has given for the benefit of the painters, as a gratuity to aid them to bear the expenses which they have incurred the day of the procession, in marching before the Holy Blood [Corpus Christi] with music. XVIII livres."

## The Problem of the Altarpiece of the Lamb

The inscription runs in one line along the lower frame of the closed altarpiece. It is written in Latin hexameters with inner rhyme divided into verses; punctuated and with necessary readings in square brackets it runs:

[Pictor] Hubertus e eyck.  majorque nemo repertus
Incipit pondus, q[ue] Iohannes arte secondus
Perf[ecit], Iudoci Vyd prece fretus.
VersV seXta MaI Vos CoLLoCat aCta tVerI

The last curiously capitalized line is a chronogram. The date is found by adding the capital letters—MCCCLLXVVVVII = 1432. A rough translation is:

"Hubert van Eyck the painter, than whom no greater is found
Began this task, which John second in the art
Carried through, at the urgent insistence of Jodoc Vyd.
On the sixth of May he calls you together to behold his work."

General Renders, in *Hubert van Eyck, Personnage de Legende*, Paris, 1933, has declared the inscription apocryphal for no other reason than that it is first mentioned nearly two hundred years after its date. He regards it as fraudulent and also the doggerel epitaph of Hubert, known only through sixteenth-century copies, which gives the date of his death.

The argument of General Renders seems to me simply fantastic. Until the seventeenth century, and the beginning of antiquarian research, practically nobody bothered to read signatures and inscriptions. Besides, the inscription strung along the frame at length was visible only when the altarpiece was closed, and then with difficulty. The early visitors who have left records, like travelers generally, observed the open altarpiece with care and the closed altarpiece casually.

Dr. Max J. Friedländer, A.N.M. I, XIV, where he accepts General Renders' vagary, with less than his usual acumen ascribes the whole Hubert group of panels and miniatures to Jan, and very oddly suggests that Jan would have painted over whatever Hubert had painted on the Ghent Altarpiece in order to bring it into harmony with his own work. This is to think in modern terms. The technique of early fifteenth-century painting in Flanders was so standardized that panels by different masters could be brought together without such need of "harmonizing" retouching. The upshot of Dr. Friedländer's argument is that while Hubert van Eyck may have existed, we have no paintings that may reasonably be ascribed to him.

What really emerges from the stylistic analogies collected by Friedländer and Renders is merely the fact that Jan van Eyck must have been Hubert's pupil and much more dependent on him than we have imagined. The opinion given in my list as to the activities of the two brothers is approximately that of nine out of ten competent students of the problem. Nothing is mine except the suggestion that the Eve and the portrait of Jodoc Vyd may be by Hubert. I believe that the whole of the open altarpiece was designed and carried far by Hubert.

The ingenious theories of Beenken and Panofsky that the lower order was planned as a triptych with shutters seem to me unproved. Panofsky's theory that the altarpiece was put together by Jan from three works left in Hubert's shop is enticing, and seems to explain certain anomalies in the layout, but again I feel his very interesting argument falls short of demonstration.

### Literary Sources of the Altarpiece of the Lamb

As Weale 1 has shown, page 37, the text that has influenced the painter of this paradise is Revelation, XXII, 1: "And he showed me a pure river of water of life, clear as crystal, proceeding out of the throne of God and of the Lamb." The motive is used more literally in the curious Paradise of Jan or Hubert van Eyck which is known only from an old Spanish copy at Madrid, cut, Weale 1, p. 162.

But the Adoration of the Lamb is as Weale 1, page 37, has shown, much more specifically derived from a vision told in the *Golden Legend* about the feast of All Saints. We read that the year following, the institution of the feast of Pope Gregory, 605 A.D.:

"When on this day a sacristan of the Church of St. Peter had devoutly made the circuit of all the altars and had implored the good offices of all the saints, and had returned to the altar of St. Peter, there, resting a little, he was taken outside of himself, and behold! he saw the King of Kings sitting on a high throne, and all the angels dwelling about Him. Then came the Virgin of Virgins with a resplendent diadem, whom an innumerable number of virgins and continent men followed. For Her the King promptly arose and made Her sit in a throne by Him. Then came one clad in camel skin, whom a multitude of venerable elders followed; then another arrived adorned with papal robes, whom a chorus of others similarly clothed followed; afterwards proceeded an innumerable multitude of knights." (*Legenda Aurea*, Ed. Graesse, p. 727.)

Most of the elements of the Adoration of the Lamb seem traceable to this passage.

I believe it has escaped notice that the amazing sumptuousness of the setting and costumes of the upper order may have been suggested by the Knight Tyndale's vision of the splendor of the martyrs and celibates in heaven. I translate a few lines from *Visio Tungdali*, hsg. A. Wagner, Erlangen, 1882, p. 47.

"There appeared for them [the martyrs, etc.] a number of seats of gold made with gems and all sorts of precious stones and covered with the rarest silks, in which were seated the elders, men and women, clothed in silk and white stoles and all sorts of ornaments, such as had never been seen before, nor the mind could imagine. The face of each was splendid, like the sun at midday, and they had hair most like to gold, and they had golden crowns on their heads adorned with gems."

It has been suggested that the *Visions of St. Hildegarde* are the main literary source of the Adoration of the Lamb. See *Kunst en Mystick. De Anbidding van het Lambe. door Dr. Lod. Clysters.* Tongerloo, 1935. It seems rather that St. Hildegarde drew heavily on a common stock of Apocalyptic imagery which came to Hubert van Eyck through the Book of Revelation, the vision quoted above from the *Golden Legend*, and through similar features of the liturgy for All Saints.

### CHAPTER III

## Jan van Eyck Confidential Agent

From the abundant documentation in Weale, concerning Jan, a few extracts may be made.

> "To Jan van Eyck, varlet de chambre and painter of my said lord, the sum of ninety-one livres, five sous, at the rate of XI groats, Flanders money, the livre, which at the command and decree of my said lord is to be paid, allotted, and delivered in cash, partly to make a certain pilgrimage which my lord has ordered to be made for himself and in his name, of which he wishes no other mention to be made [why should a pilgrimage by proxy be secret business?] and also against what may be due him [from the duke] because of a certain long secret journey, which also is not otherwise to be mentioned." (Weale I, p. XXXII.)

A considerable journey, for Jan spent almost a year's salary, 100 livres, on it. Date of payment August 16, 1426. Jan apparently set out immediately on a similar secret journey, for on October 17, 1426, he received no less than 360 livres, which must have included payments far beyond his traveling expenses. No mention was to be made of those journeys.

A notice of July 1427 records a bonus of twenty livres "considering good and agreeable services which he has rendered in his calling and otherwise." This shows that Jan had made paintings for the duke which have not come down to us. (Weale 1, p. XXXII.)

It should be clear that by his duties as a confidential agent Jan van Eyck's opportunities for painting were seriously curtailed.

### CHAPTER IV

## Guild Regulations at Tournai

The minimum apprenticeship at Tournai in the fifteenth century was four years, but we have cases of ten years of such training. To become a free master the apprentice had to make a masterpiece on a set theme and under supervision.

"And when they shall have chosen to make their master-piece of portraiture [painting] they will be obliged to make and compose it in paints or stuffs, on such stories or images as the dean and directors of the said trade of painters shall order." (A. de la Grange, *Etudes sur l'Art à Tournai.* Tournai. No date. P. 82.)

The close control of the Tournai corporation of painters over conditions of work is shown in instances cited by De la Grange, p. 83.

Jacob Brevelant of Bruges was admitted to the mastery but "only to paint works in tempera called cloths of Bruges." Michel Vinque was charged with "taking upon himself to make entrées [perhaps pageants] for banquets, which he had been forbidden to do." Apparently Vinque abused an opportunity as a decorator to usurp the functions of a master of ceremonies. Jehan Gourdin, a plumber, was allowed to paint his lead work but "only with black oil color, without the right to use any other color."

Evidently the ideal of jurisdiction so dear to modern trade unionism was already very much alive among the old guilds.

### Painting and the Religious Drama

The considerable influence of devotional literature—especially that of the *Meditations on the Life of Christ* ascribed to St. Bona-ventura—and the religious drama—especially that of the mystery plays—upon the painting of the fifteenth century has been well treated by Émile Mâle in his *L'Art Religieuse de la Fin du Moyen Age,* 3ᵉ Ed., Paris, 1925.

The mysteries, which were devoted to the life of Christ in the broadest sense, were celebrated on great feast days with utmost elabo-ration. The sumptuousness of much Flemish painting—especially in such subjects as the Epiphany—is doubtless due in part to this influ-ence. The Netherlanders were accustomed to seeing the great Bib-lical characters attired in a completely unBiblical richness. The miracle plays, devoted to the deeds of the saints, were also to a certain extent suggestive to the painters. One often feels in the unnatural stiffness, and as well in an occasional exaggeration, the under- or overacting of the solid citizens who took the parts. See Dürer's description of a great religious pageant at Antwerp in 1520, in Illustrations for Chapter VI.

Such influences were in the air, but perhaps because we have only a fraction of the mystery and miracle plays, it is seldom possible to make specific parallels between the pictures and the texts. The compartmented pictures of Memling, at Munich and Turin, for example, representing the Life of Mary and the Passion of Christ, suggest a direct relation with the mysteries, each episode of which had its separate scenery—"habitation." But again Memling may have drawn his groups and arrangement from the miniature painters, who in turn were probably to a considerable extent guided by their visual memories of the mystery plays. We are dealing in short with a widely dispersed and constant possibility of interchange between painting and the religious drama.

### CHAPTER V

## A Great Painter's Odd Jobs

The entirely miscellaneous character of a painter's business in the fifteenth century may be suggested by certain payments to Hugo van der Goes contained in the accounts of Ghent.

"Item. Given by order of the above-mentioned magistrates to Hugo van der Goes because he made in painting a certain number of escutcheons with the blason of our holy father the pope which had been fixed before the gates of that city to announce the pardon proclaimed in the aforenamed city, the 16th of June (1469). VIII sous.

Item. Given to Hugo van der Goes, painter, for pictures made by him and his assistants, serving for the said joyous entrance of our very dreaded lord and prince aforesaid, set up at the level of the aforesaid figures upon cloths at the sides of the streets and otherwise according to the memorandum of the magistrates and the receipt of Hugo himself.

(1468–1469) XIIII livres." (*Hugo van der Goes*, by Joseph Destrée. Brussels and Paris, 1914, p. 246.)

This considerable payment was made for decorative hangings painted in tempera on cloth, to celebrate the duke's visit—in short, for work less permanent than modern stage scenery and in many ways similar thereto.

### CHAPTER VI

## Dürer Describes a Religious Pageant

By reading Dürer's diary one may fairly see the procession, at Antwerp, in honor of the feast of the Assumption, August 19, 1520. Splendidly dressed, the guilds marched in close ranks, with candle bearers and trumpeters in the intervals between the companies. There were also many drummers and fifers in the German style—"Everything blown hard and used to make a racket."

"There I saw spaced far apart but in close order: the goldsmiths, painters, stonemasons, silk embroiderers, sculptors, chest makers, domestic servants, sailors, fishermen, butchers, leather workers, weavers, bakers, tailors, shoemakers. Similarly the shopkeepers, merchants and their helpers. Behind came the shooting companies—with arquebus, bow, or crossbow, and also travelers and wayfarers. Afterwards came a great throng of officials, nobly and richly clothed. But before them the religious orders and their patrons, very piously. Last the canons and priests of Our Lady's Church. . . .

There twenty persons carried the Virgin Mary with the Lord Jesus, most richly adorned, in honor of God the Father. And in this procession many joyous things were done and finely planned. There were many pageant wagons, plays on ships, etc. Among them the throng and sequence of the prophets; then the New Testament, as—the Angelic Greeting (Annunciation), the holy three kings riding on great camels and on other strange beasts, charmingly decorated. Also how Our Lady fled to Egypt, very impressively pious, and much else which for brevity I will omit. . . .

At the end came a great dragon, which St. Margaret and her maidens led on a leash, which was very pretty. St. George followed with his squires, a very pretty knight. There also rode in this company, attractively and richly clothed, boys and girls from many regions, simulating their patron saints. This procession from beginning to end, before it passed our house, lasted more than two hours, so the throng was so big, that I could not describe it in a book, so I let it go at that." (*Albrecht Dürer's Schriftliche Nachlass.* Hsg. Von Ernst Heidrich. Berlin, 1910, p. 41 ff.)

It should be recalled that Dürer, who shows much sympathy both for the religious and spectacular aspect of the ceremony, was a Protestant.

I ask the tolerance of a possible meticulous reader for merely paraphrasing much of the long quotation.

## Hell According to the Monk Tungdalus

Since Jerome Bosch read and apparently enjoyed the *Visio Tungdali,* the reader should be able to bear a little of it. I translate from the chapter devoted to the murderers.

"They came to a gorge very terrible and shadowy and covered with the murk of death. It was very deep and full of burning coals, having an iron cover, which seemed to be six cubits thick and more white hot than blazing coals. The stench of which exceeded every tribulation the soul had so far passed. There descended upon this [white hot] disk a multitude of the most miserable souls and there were reduced to ashes. Then, after the fashion of cooking in a pan, they are liquefied, and what is worse, they run about as grease does over a griddle, and they are renovated amid hot fires for renewed torments." (*Visio Tungdali,* hsg. A. Wagner, Erlangen, 1882, p. 13 f.)

Such a passage tells us what the furnaces which abound in Bosch's hells meant to him and his public.

### CHAPTER VII

## Lost Works on Secular Themes

The surviving pictures of the fourteenth and fifteenth centuries are with a few exceptions on religious subjects. There was, however, a great activity in designing non-religious subjects of which we find the traces chiefly in miniatured manuscripts and tapestries. There is abundant evidence of mural painting on secular themes in France and Flanders. Obviously the potentates who eagerly read the histories—and romances of chivalry, which were probably regarded as history—would have wanted also to see them. The actual situation is suggested in the estate inventory, 1404, of the tapestries of Duke Philip the Bold of Burgundy. More than half of his rich collection of tapestries were on such subjects as follow:

From ancient history—Semiramis, Jason, Hector; from medieval history or legend—Charlemagne, the Twelve Champions of Christianity, King Arthur, Perceval, Tristan, the Queen of Ireland (Iseult); from medieval allegory—Roman de la Rose, the Vices and Virtues; on pastoral themes—the Shepherd's Art, the Twelve Months, a Shepherd's Dance, a Lady between Two Lovers, History of the God of Love and finally a Hunting Scene. (Dehaisnes, T. II, p. 894.)

A year later the estate inventory of the Duchess Marguerite of Flanders adds the following significant items:

The God of Love with Juno, Pallas and Venus, the Vow of the Peacock, Demoiselles defending a Castle, Story of Alexander, Story of Tristan. (Dehaisnes, T. II, p. 907 f.)

Obviously these wall hangings in their castles were more often seen and enjoyed by the Burgundian sovereigns than the miniatures in their manuscripts and the altarpieces in their oratories and chapels. In short, the panel paintings which are necessarily the theme of this book fail to represent the persistence of secular medieval taste deep into the Renaissance. It is well to remember that the romances of chivalry were immensely popular up to the time when Cervantes, possibly with his tongue in his cheek, about the beginning of the seventeenth century, condemned them as a public peril. For that matter the late Gothic painters doubtless made many pictures of a secular sort which have been lost. We know that Cardinal Ottaviani, in 1455, owned a picture by Jan van Eyck representing women of noble form coming out of a warm bath. In a picture of the interior of the Van der Geest Gallery, at Antwerp, painted in 1628, we see a picture of a nude young woman assisted by a maid at her toilet. The original was of the period of Jan van Eyck. It was a rather large picture, the figures perhaps a quarter the scale of life. An illustration is in Weale, T. 1, pp. 173, 176. At Leipzig is an old copy of a very curious picture of a nude girl performing a love charm probably against a faithless lover. Illustration in L. Kaemmerer, *Hubert and Jan van Eyck*, Leipzig, Abb. 88.

Such waifs and strays must represent many lost pictures of the sort.

CHAPTER VIII

## Petrarch Admires the Rhine Maidens

The feminism of the Cologne School and of its ambassador in Flanders, Hans Memling, seems to have rested on the sound and natural basis of the charm and comeliness of the damsels of the lower Rhine. We may see them through the enchanted eyes of the poet Petrarch. He was at Cologne on St. John's Eve of 1333, and a friend took him to the Rhine to witness a remarkable spectacle.

> "The bank was covered with a great and splendid throng of women. I was thunderstruck. Ye Gods! what beauty! What faces! Whoever's heart was not already engaged [Petrarch had already seen Laura] must have fallen in love. I was set on a little elevation which I might grasp what was going on. The crowd was incredibly great but without pushing or violence. Eagerly in turn up to their waists in the fragrant grass, their sleeves rolled beyond their elbows, they washed their white hands and arms in the current, murmuring pleasant things unknown to me in their foreign speech."

Like a good humanist Petrarch turned upon his guide two verses of Virgil:

> "What means this concourse at the stream
> And what seek these souls?"

The answer was that the rite averted evil and brought luck throughout the year. (*Epistolae de Rebus Familiaribus*, Ed. Fracassetti, Vol. I, Lib. I, Ep. 4.)

As usual the poet is the prophet of the painter. It will be a century and more before a Lochner and a Memling will paint what Petrarch saw in the young women of the lower Rhine.

## Painting and Devotional Poetry

That lyrical, not to say sentimental, idealism which prevailed in the lower Rhineland, and in the person of Hans Memling reached Flanders, is perhaps based less on the writing and preaching of the mystics than in its echoes in hymns more accessible to the laity. All the garden and flower lore so lavishly adorning the Blessed Virgin Mary appears earlier in the hymns. I quote a stanza from Mone's great collection *Hymni Medii Aevi, Friburgi Brisgoviae*, 1853–5. Hymn no. 601 is entitled:

### Rose Garden of the Mother of God

| | |
|---|---|
| Tu hortus voluptatis plenissimae | "Thou! Garden of pleasure In fullest measure! |
| Cum stilla suavitatis verissime | With sweetest dew 'Tis ever true. |
| Tu cedrus honestatis altissimae | Thou cedar high Of courtesy |
| Cypressus caritatis fortissime | And cypress strong For loving long." |

The customary symbols for Mary's virginity are nearly all compressed into the four stanzas of Mone's hymn no. 348:

### A Trope for Cockcrow

| | |
|---|---|
| Flos de spina procreatur et per florem decoratur sic Maria fecundata fecundata sublimatur quando parit filium | "The flower is begotten of a thorn and receives a flower's beauty so is Mary made fecund and fecund purified when she bears her son |
| Porta clausa pertransitur neque patens invenitur manna vermis enutritur virga flore redimitur rosa parit lilium | The closed door is crossed nor yet found open manna is grown from worms the rod is redeemed by its flower a rose bears a lily |
| Rore vellus irrigatur rubus ardens non crematur quando verbum incarnatur | The fleece is moistened by the dew the burning bush is not consumed when the Word is incarnated |

et intacto conservartur                     and harbored to become
  puellari in gremio.                    a child in the intact womb."

A hymn in the Low German spoken at Cologne (Mone, II, p. 419) likens Mary to every sort of sweet flower. I translate the initial lines of several of the stanzas.

> "God greet thee noble red rose,
>     Maria full of grace."

> "God greet thee lily, purest flower,
>     Mary mother without man."

> "God greet thee, fair violet,
>     flower which withers not."

> "God greet thee, most sincerely,
>     Marigold delight of all the world."

> "God greet thee, flower which stands in the corn,
>     blue in hue as azure,
> That art thou, Mother elect,
>     Albeit a pure maiden."

> "God greet thee, everlasting flower,
>     First blossom after winter's stress."

> "God greet thee, peony, purple fair."

> "God greet thee, sweet bean blossom."

The hymn closes comprehensively:

> "God greet thee, every sort
>     of flower of the world."

Such informal and popular expressions of worship and adoration were familiar throughout Christendom at the end of the Middle Ages. It was, however, only the painters of the lower Rhine who fully utilized this rich and charming lyrical folk poetry.

CHAPTER IX

## A Contract for a Catalan Retable by Huguet

Until well along in the sixteenth century all painting, throughout Europe, was made in the most businesslike way under specified contract. To represent the situation I translate roughly from the Catalan a contract of March 14, 1457, between Luis Guillem, merchant of Barcelona, and Jaime Huguet, painter. The document has recently been published by Professor Chandler Rathfon Post in *A History of Spanish Painting*, Vol. VII, part 1, p. 49, note:

"In the name of God, Amen."

"A contract, [I abridge the legal locutions] between Luis Guillem del Castell and Jaime Huguet for a retable for the benefit of the Church of the Friars Minor of Berga under the protection of the Saints Anthony of Padua and Anthony of Viana. That is St. Anthony of Egypt.

First the said Jaime Huguet promises to make the retable, which without the base and canopy is to be three palms high and two palms wide, entirely at his own expense, and the said retable is to be according to a drawing made by the said Jaime, except that the lateral parts instead of having two stories each, as shown in the drawing, shall have three stories each. Which drawing remains in the keeping of the said Jaime Huguet and inscribed by the hand of the said Luis Guillem del Castell with the following words: 'Drawing of the retable to be made by Jaime Huguet, painter, except that the lateral panels are to be made with three stories notwithstanding that they are painted [in the model] with two.' And the panel, except the base, is to be divided into three panels and in the central panel are to be painted Saint Anthony of Padua and St. Anthony of Viana. And in each of the side panels shall be three stories [about the contiguous saint]. . . . And in the central pinnacle shall be painted a Crucifixion with the Marys and St. John; and the base is to have five divisions in the middle, the Pietà . . . and in the remaining four divisions images of male and female saints to be chosen by the said Luis Guillem del Castell. . . . And the said Jaime Huguet promises to make the retable at his own costs and charges, of good, seasoned oak well keyed and cleated as befits a good retable, and it shall be gilded with good, fine gold and [painted with] good blue and all other good and fine colors such as the retable may require and as is customary."

### CHAPTER X

## Some Opinions of Dürer on Art

Dürer's very various activities on his Flemish trip may be sug-gested by a page from his diary written at Antwerp:

> "Master Lucas, who engraves on copper, has invited me
> as a guest; he is a little man born at Leyden.  He was at
> Antwerp.  I have eaten with Master Bernard, the engraver.
> I have given a stiver and a half to the agents.  I have made
> four florins and a shilling out of my art.  I have made the
> portrait of Master Lucas van Leyden with the silver point.
> I have lost a florin.  Item.  I have given the doctor six
> stivers.  I have given the manager in the Augustinian mon-
> astery a Life of our Lady, and have given his boy four stivers.
> I have given Master Jacob a copperplate Passion and a
> woodcut Passion and five other pieces, and have given his
> boy four stivers.  I have changed four florins for expenses.
> I have given two Philip's florins for fourteen fish skins,
> etc. . . ."  (*Albrecht Dürer's Schriftliche Nachlass.* Hsg.
> Von Ernst Heidrich.  Berlin, 1910, p. 107 f.)

A passage from a letter which Dürer wrote February 7, 1506 (new style 1507), from Venice to his friend the humanist Pirkheimer at Nuremberg:

> "I have many good friends among the foreigners, who warn
> me not to eat or drink with the painters.  Also there are
> many enemies. . . . They blame my work, and say it is
> not in the antique style, hence no good.  But Giambellino
> has praised me highly before many gentlemen.  He wants
> something of mine, and came in person and begged me to
> paint something for him.  He is willing to pay. . . . He
> is very old and is still the best painter.  And the things
> which eleven years ago so much pleased me no longer
> please me."  (P. 124.)

Dürer's esthetic ideas were intellectualistic and very similar to those of Leonardo da Vinci, which he cannot have known.  But here and there in his scattered writings he also gives a large place to the creative imagination. Remarking on the infinite variety of a good painter's work he writes:

"Such lucky chances are very frequent with artists and their imagination (Gemüt) is full of images which it is possible for them to make. Therefore if such a man should live for many centuries, one who fitly commanded his art, and was trained to it, he through the power which God has given to us men, would day by day pour out new forms of men and beasts, making them so, that no one else had ever seen them or thought of them." (P. 264 f.)

One recalls in reading these proud lines such unique inventions of Dürer's as the Melancholia, Great Fortune; Knight, Death and the Devil, Sea Monster, etc. Together these three extracts may suggest the old blend of the small-town man, genius and thinker in Albrecht Dürer.

CHAPTER XI

## Van Mander on the Italian Style and Scorel

Carel van Mander's praise of the Italian manner and of Scorel as its pioneer in Flanders:

"Later when Rome became less agitated under the peaceful rule of the popes, many beautiful pieces of sculpture in marble and bronze were discovered and delivered from their gray crypts. The statues which came to light out of darkness became a beacon to the art of painting. They opened the eyes of our art students so that they could discriminate between the ugly and the beautiful, and discover the perfection in living human figures and in the limbs of animals, in nature. . . .

Therefore, the Italians, enlightened on this subject, had rendered the true character and poses of the human figure before the painters of the Netherlands were able to do so. The latter had a certain traditional conventional method of working. They persistently and industriously tried to improve by studying ordinary, daily life, but they were in the dark, so to speak, with little light to guide them until the moment that Joan van Schoorel brought to their attention the best artistic methods from Italy. Because he had visited Italy, and come to the Netherlands to enlighten the art of painting, he was called by Frans Floris and other artists the Lantern Bearer and the Paver of the Way." (*Carel van Mander, Dutch and Flemish Painters*, translated by Constant van de Wall. New York, 1936. P. 158.)

Van Mander's partially just but far too sweeping depreciation of the early painting of the Netherlands should be read in view of the circumstances. The iconoclasm of 1566 and the prolonged wars had destroyed most of the older painting, so that his facilities for the study of the native school were far inferior to our own. The amazing disorder of the times may be sensed very vividly by reading Adam van Mander's account of the vicissitudes of his father's life. (*L. C.*, p. XLI-LXIX.)

### Bruegel and the Morality Plays

Proverbs, popular superstition and folklore must have contributed much to the painting of Jerome Bosch and Pieter Bruegel the Elder. The books of Baldass and De Tolnay make good pioneer exploration of this background. Less has been made of what seems to me a strong influence on Bruegel, namely that of the morality plays. These plays, with their allegorical characters, Wealth, Poverty, etc., really have a very long ancestry in the allegorical literature of the Middle Ages. As far back as the Battle of the Soul (Psychomachia) of Prudentius we have the battle of the seven Vices against the seven Virtues. The widely read "Roman de la Rose" did much to popularize allegory in the semidramatic form of dialogue. It is probable that allegory was acted habitually much before the fifteenth century. From then on it was a favorite dramatic genre. Colleges, schools, the numerous chambers of rhetoric in the Low Countries constantly wrote and performed morality plays or their equivalent well into the seventeenth century. In particular the chambers of rhetoric habitually gave table plays, with from three to five characters, which could be staged and rehearsed without elaborate preparations. The painters belonged generally to the chambers of rhetoric, and Old Bruegel may have seen representations of, or heard debates on such themes as Carnival and Lent, the Strong Boxes and Penny Banks, at his club.

It is difficult to make specific links between the pictures and the morality plays, for the reason that very few of the latter are preserved. They went out of fashion early in the seventeenth century, and they had no Biblical or ecclesiastical authority to keep them alive.

### CHAPTER XII

## France, Sixteenth Century

The bankruptcy of the Italianizing movement in French painting in the sixteenth century, as compared with the relative success of Flemish Romanism, indeed in comparison with the beneficent effects of Italianism on the architecture, poetry and sculpture of France itself, invites serious study. Perhaps it may be explained by the fact that, unlike the Flemish painters, the French painters did not go to Italy for more or less independent studies, but succumbed to the authority and prestige of Italian artists who were called to France. Such a succession of Italian masters as Leonardo da Vinci, Andrea del Sarto, Benvenuto Cellini, Primaticcio, Il Rosso, Niccolò Abate must have meant for French painters an appalling and unattainable superiority. Nothing could have seemed possible but servile imitation with its inevitable results in inferiority of expression. Furthermore, through most of the sixteenth century the French painters lacked opportunity to use even such talent as they had. The great public commissions were given to the Italians. There was a formidable group of Flemish Romanists in Paris, who had the preference with patrons. Under these circumstances nothing but the traditional art of portraiture could flourish. Of course if any really great painter talent had then emerged in France, he might have coped with these difficulties. Without bearing too heavily upon what may be coincidence, as soon as the Italian painters were no longer called to France and the French painters went to Italy, early in the seventeenth century, the improvement of the art of painting in France was notable and progressive. With this the shifting of royal patronage from the Italians to Rubens—in every way a better model—may have had something to do, while the simultaneous extension of Caravaggio's naturalism provided a new and potent influence free from mannerism and, so far as it went, sound and constructive.

CHAPTER XIII

## The Fame of El Greco

Italy immediately lost track of El Greco, while in Spain in his own times he was rather notorious than famous. Such Spanish commentators as Jusepe Martinez, Padre Siguenza and Pacheco were clearly as much appalled as impressed by his work. What could be done about a man who had casually told Pacheco that Michelangelo was a great artist but a poor painter? The artist who had failed to please Philip II, whose taste, as a patron of Titian, was well above the average, naturally failed to please aristocratic Spain. To be sure the poets Paravicino and Gongora wrote laudatory sonnets for his tomb, but it is to be feared that these poets merely saw their obvious laudatory duty and did it.

Upon the cultured, not to say pedantic Francisco Pacheco, El Greco made a strong and mixed impression. Pacheco, I cite his *Arte de la Pintura* from the Madrid edition of 1866, was both fascinated and shocked at the paradoxes offered by El Greco's work and character. He was the most careless of painters, and also the most caretaking.

> "In the year 1611 he showed me a cupboard full of clay models made by him to help him in his works, and what surpasses admiration, the originals of everything he had painted in his life, painted in oil on canvas, but of small scale—these in a room which by his command his son showed me— What will the presumptuous and lazy say to that?" (Vol. II, 12.)

In a discussion of the superiority of drawing to color, Vol. II, 318, Pacheco falls foul of "a singular opinion of El Greco."

> "Therefore I greatly marvel (and may I be pardoned for this anecdote not offered for approval) that when I asked El Greco in the year 1611 which was most difficult, drawing or coloring? he answered, coloring. And even this is not so strange as to hear him speak with so little appreciation of Michelangelo (who was the father of painting) saying that he was a good man and didn't know how to paint. So who-

ever has had dealings with this man will not think it odd
that he held himself aloof from the common opinion of his
fellow artists in order to be as singular in everything else as
he was in his painting."

Pacheco even suspects El Greco's direct painting is a conscious
pose, classing him with painters who work carefully but finish sketchily to seem clever. (II, 75.)

> "Therefore some will believe that Domenico Greco went
> over his paintings many times, and finally retouched them
> in order to make the colors distinct and not united, and to
> give cruel brush strokes, to make a show of power. And
> this I call to work in order to become poor."

All the same El Greco is a great painter. We must recall,
Pacheco says, that there are artists who can dispense with beauty,
as Vasari, Michelangelo, Caravaggio and our fellow Spaniard,
Ribera, but have great power of suggesting relief. (I, 393.)

> "And we may include in this number Domenico Greco,
> for though we have elsewhere written against some of his
> opinions and paradoxes, we cannot exclude him from the
> roll of great painters, seeing that some of his handiwork is
> as plastic and vivid (to be sure in his manner) that it equals
> that of the greatest."

After his death, except for a few incorrect factual notices, El
Greco was pretty well ignored for over two centuries.

Apparently the first admiring word about him was written not
by any professional critic but by a wandering captain of the British
navy, named S. S. Cook, who in 1834 published at London two thin
volumes, *Sketches in Spain during the Years 1829–32.*

Captain Cook had his misgivings; his general attitude is about
that of Pacheco.

> "Unfortunately he [Greco] adopted an unique and extraor-
> dinary tone of colour, which destroys all pleasure in exam-
> ining the greater part of his works, but the most masterly
> freedom of design is always to be seen in the worst of his
> productions."

Captain Cook owned two Grecos, being possibly the first foreigner to spend money on this unwanted art.

> "Two specimens are in my possession, which it would seem impossible were the work of the same artist, one in the best Venetian manner, the other in that peculiarly his own, but not the worst of it."

Captain Cook properly thought the Burial of Count Orgaz the most important Greco, but found the upper part to be in "the bad manner." So he consistently declared the Assumption, for Santo Domingo, now at Chicago, to be "in the grand Italian manner, perhaps his finest work." But with all these reservations, Captain Cook's heart was in the right place. He writes of a small color sketch for "the clearing of the temple" that it is "equal to any design by Michelangelo." (*Sketches in Spain*, I, 157 f.)

Carl Justi, the learned and diligent biographer of Velasquez, was the first modern scholar to write with appreciation and knowledge about El Greco, but his two articles were buried from the laity in the pages of the *Zeitschrift für bildende Kunst*, 1897–98.

As usual the artists had anticipated the critics. The brilliant Fortuny owned and treasured a Greco; so did François Millet, whose Greco, a Santo Domingo de Guzman, passed to Degas. (Cossío, p. 329.)

The first adequate essay of a popular kind, and the first considerate criticism of Greco in the English language, was published by an Irish spinster, Hannah Lynch, in her excellent little book *Toledo*, London, 1898. Cossío, p. 643, suggests that Beruete put her up to it, which I doubt. It is difficult to put an Irish woman up to anything. She writes about the group at the foot of the Burial of Count Orgaz:

> "Did ever a canvas before so perfectly gather all the fugitive moods, all the underlying currents, all the grace and charm, the vices and defects of a single race, and give them complete visibility in their wavering expression? This is to carry portraiture to its highest perfection."

A little earlier than 1900, El Greco was beginning to be an esoteric cult among the artists and amateurs of Paris. Within the next three or four years, chiefly under the suggestion of John Sargent, the important Grecos were slowly entering the American museums and more important private collections. But as late as September of 1904, Señor Emile Parés, at Madrid, kindly opened a rude box for me, removed the protective straw, and offered me the superb St. Jerome, now in the Frick Collection, for 100,000 pesetas, about $9,000. For a young newspaperman, it was an astronomical figure.

Cossío's book of 1908 may be said to mark the complete rehabilitation of El Greco. It has become customary to associate the revival with the advent of post-impressionism, which merely accelerated a going movement. Cézanne has been falsely regarded as an early champion of El Greco. He did closely imitate a woman's portrait by El Greco, but under the impression that he was imitating a Tintoretto. For the precise facts see *Paul Cézanne*, by Gerstle Mack. New York, 1935, p. 150 f.

### CHAPTER XIV

How well Rubens' patrons understood his methods of quantity production and the pains they reasonably took to secure the maximum of his personal attention are shown in a contract made with the Jesuits of Antwerp. A few extracts translated from the Flemish follow:

"The 29 March 1620. Father Jacobus Tirinus, prior of the Jesuit House, agrees with Signor Petro Paulo Rubbens.

First, that the aforesaid Signor Rubbens should as quickly as possible deliver the 39 paintings within the year.

Second, that the aforesaid Rubbens shall make the drawings for all the 39 pieces and shall be bound to finish them completely with his own hand, and to have them executed by Van Dyck with others of his own pupils . . . and after they are finished and in place shall perfect them with his own hand.        *        *        *

Fourth, that the aforesaid prior on the day of the delivery of the aforesaid 39 pieces is bound to give the aforesaid Rubbens the sum of 7,000 guilders.

Fifth, that the aforesaid prior is bound to deliver the canvas necessary for the making of the 39 pieces."

Clearly the most any patron could hope from any big job of Rubens was that the design should be wholly his, the execution by good assistants, and a little retouching by Rubens at the end of the work.

This complete decoration for the Jesuit Church is now known only through engravings, since the church was burnt in 1718. It is interesting that Rubens' Christian names are given in the Italian form, as he habitually signed them.

Rubens was so universally popular that criticism pretty well let him alone in his lifetime, taking him for granted. On the whole the best observations on Rubens are those of Félibien and De Piles, written about half a century after his death. Their position was an embarrassing one, for they were both associated with the Academy, both admirers of a painter who had become the very symbol of esthetic unorthodoxy. So they both tempered their praise with reservations which perhaps they did not deeply feel. Félibien, *Entretien VII*, rather overplays the cautious rôle, and I do not quote him. De Piles is more generous.

> "He expresses his subjects with much energy and clarity, he brings into them much grandeur and nobility. His individual expressions are proper to the subject; there are none which fail to interest the spectator, and one will find many which reach the sublime. . . .
>
> His attitudes are simple, natural, without coldness, contrasted and animated without exaggeration, and judiciously varied. . . .
>
> His landscapes are made with the same intelligence as his figures; and when he has wanted to represent views naturally ungrateful and insipid as are those of Flanders, he has rendered them piquant by devices of light and shade, and by the accidental features which he has introduced; the form of his trees is not very elegant, he follows that of his country, and the touch is not as precious as that of Titian. . . .
>
> Whatever depends on color is admirable in Rubens: he has carried the science of chiaroscuro further than any painter. . . .
>
> He has used the brightest colors to draw from them the effect he intended, and he is the only one who could add

to this brilliancy a great character of truthfulness, and could keep amid so much brilliance a surprising harmony and force." (*Abregé de la Vie des Peintres*, 2nd ed. Paris, 1715. P. 394-396.)

Frans Hals had to wait for the dawn of impressionism, about 1860–70, for anything like general fame. Such sensitive and diligent pioneers of taste as Haydon and Hazlitt (active in the 1830's and 1840's) either never saw a good Hals or were unimpressed by what they saw. Meanwhile the geniality and brilliancy of Hals' portraiture had gradually commended his work to gallery directors and private collectors. Even as sensitive a critic as Théophile Gautier, in his *Guide de l'Amateur au Musée du Louvre*, 1882, dispatches Hals, then not well represented at Paris, in these general, if laudatory terms. "Van der Helst and Frans Hals, what admirable portraitists! They hold their own not without honor beside the Rembrandts, Rubenses and Van Dycks." (*Guide*. Paris, 1893. P. 158.)

Dr. Waagen in *Treasures of Art in Great Britain*, London, 1854, lists half a dozen Halses in British collections, and praises each summarily as "animated" or "brilliant in execution." A little later the general histories of art begin to treat Hals with respect. But I do not know of any really searching estimate of his genius until Fromentin's *Les Maîtres d'Autrefois*, 1876.

### Aspects of Dutch Taste in Painting

The consistently native character of Dutch painting rested on conscious and intelligent choice, and not, as some have supposed, on isolation and ignorance. Three generations of Romanists had not merely familiarized the Netherlands with imitations of the Italian manner but had also brought in engraved and painted copies of Italian pictures, some originals and many casts from the antique. The Dutch genre painters, as the lists of their properties show (see A. Bredius, *Künstler Inventäre*, in seven volumes, The Hague, 1915–21), often owned Italianate or Italian pictures. For example as sturdily Dutch a painter as Jan Miense Molenaer of Haarlem, Judith Leyster's spouse, died in 1668 in possession alongside 178 Northern pictures of "A Rape of Proserpine by an Italian gentleman." (*Künstler In.* I, p. 2.)

Rembrandt, as the inventory made for his bankrupt sale in 1656 attests, owned a number of Italian pictures—ascribed to Palma, Giorgione, Raphael and Titian—and took the pains to compile great albums showing in engraving the works of Raphael, Michelangelo and Titian. In short, Rembrandt knew his Italian Renaissance well.

A more instructive instance is that of the art dealer of Amsterdam, Johannes de Renialme, whose stock was inventoried in 1640 and on his death in 1657 (vol. I, p. 228). Presumably his stock, as is always the case with a good dealer, represented a working compromise between his own taste and that of his customers. In 1640 he had no foreign pictures, but had a picture by an Italianate of Utrecht, Poelemburg. His taste must have been pretty good for he had no less than eleven landscapes by Hercules Segers. He had nine paintings by Jan Miense Molenaer, two by Rembrandt, one each of Frans Hals and Van Goyen.

By 1657 his stock was still preponderantly Dutch but contained many Italian and other exotic items. He had sold about half of the Segerses and Molenaers. He now owned twelve Rembrandts. His Italian pictures were all of the Venetian school—two Bassanos, two Palmas, two Titians, two Padavaninos, one Tintoretto. The Flemish school was represented in his shop by four Rubenses and one Van Dyck. His primitives were two Lucas van Leydens, three Cranachs, four Holbeins. He had pictures by such living French artists as Valentin, Bourdon and Claude Lorrain, and as well two canvases by Ribera. Such evidence combined with that of the gallery interiors painted by Teniers and others show that the taste of the Low Countries was quite various and liberal. The Dutch and Flemish merely had the courage to like their own art best, which was a fortunate situation for their artists.

The official appraisals of Renialme's pictures are interesting. Rembrandt's Christ and the Woman of Samaria, now in the National Gallery, London, was appraised at fifteen hundred florins, a Resurrection of Lazarus at six hundred. A Kitchen Maid by Gerard Dou was thought worth the same price, as were two groups by another Rembrandt pupil, S. Koninck. A portrait of a Woman by Titian was worth only four hundred florins, as was a Descent from the Cross (a rather unsalable subject) by Rembrandt. In general the paintings of Rembrandt's pupils are priced as high as those of their master.

The Claude Lorrain, a novelty, was priced high at five hundred florins.

To find modern equivalents for these prices is difficult, but I feel that, multiplying the florin by ten, we shall not be far from the present dollar values.

### CHAPTER XVI

### A Contemporary Opinion of Rembrandt

While Rembrandt's etchings have been continuously valued, his painting has suffered vicissitudes of praise and dispraise. Unluckily there are few contemporary estimates from Holland. The best foreign contemporary appreciation is that of Félibien, the first edition of whose *Entretiens* was published in 1667. I cite the second edition, 1688, Tome II, Entr. VII, p. 238 f. The *Entretiens* take the form of a dialogue between the author and an art-loving novice, Pymandre.

> "Rembrandt . . . was a rather universal painter, who made many portraits. All his pictures are painted in a very special manner, and are very different from that which seems licked smooth, into which most of the Flemish painters fall. For often he merely made big brush strokes, and laid the thick colors one upon the other without fusing or softening them. However, as tastes differ, many people have made much of his works. It is true also that there is much art in them, and that he has made very beautiful heads. Though they do not all have the graces of the brush, they have great power; and when one sees them from a proper distance, they yield a very good effect, and seem to have much [plastic] roundness."

Pymandre is scandalized at this moderate praise of anything so crude and unfinished. Félibien continues:

> "All the works of this painter are not of the sort [you describe]. He has so well placed the tints and half-tints side by side, and has so well understood his lights and shadows, that though he painted in a coarse fashion, which often seems merely blocked in, all the same does not fail to succeed, as I have said, if one is not too near [Félibien had probably never heard Rembrandt's saying that his pictures

were to be seen, not smeit]. For with distance, these
powerfully set brush strokes, and the thickness of paints,
which you have remarked, diminish to the sight, and fuse
and mix together, and give the effect one wants. . . . The
distance which one needs to see a picture well is not only
that the eye may have more space and convenience in
taking the objects in, and seeing them better together, but
also that there may be more air between the eye and the
object."

To appreciate the broadmindedness of this criticism one should
recall that Félibien was the intimate friend of Poussin and official
historian of the French Academy.

See also Charles Coypel's just estimate of Rembrandt in Illustrations for Chapter XXV.


### CHAPTERS XVII AND XVIII

Until well along in the nineteenth century the little Dutch
masters were at best tolerated by those who were supposed to represent good taste. Below that level they were always loved. Indeed
the emperors and minor sovereigns who bought the great Italians as
willingly bought the little Dutchmen. But on the whole the taste
for the Dutch realists was regarded as inferior, and any open cham-
pionship of them was unusual in the seventeenth and eighteenth
century.

As early as 1700 the French critic Rogier de Piles in his *Abregé
de la Vie des Peintres* made a rather casual selection of the Dutch
painters. He wrote admiringly of Rembrandt and Brouwer, but
ignored completely Frans Hals, Metsu, Steen and all the landscapists
except the Italianate, Both.

I. B., who published in 1754 *Lives of the Most Eminent Modern Painters who have lived since or were omitted by Mons. De Piles,*
writes enthusiastically of Hals and Ruysdael, and discriminatingly
concerning Terborch, Ostade, Van Goyen, Paul Potter and others.
On page 101 he gives an interesting hint of the collecting taste of
his time.

"There is a fashion in paintings as well as in cloaths.
Teniers has had a long reign. Polembruck, Wouverman,

Gerrard Dou, Mieris and Schalken succeeded him; at present it is A. Ostade, Metsu, Potter, Vandervelde, Vanhuysum and Vanderwerf. The curious not only set these masters now above the former, but eagerly bid upon one another for them at sales, and run them up to an extravagant price."

Jonathan Richardson, Jr., in his *Works*, 1773, pays in his advice to critics and collectors next to no attention to the Dutch school, but gives the information (page 276 of the edition of 1792) that "Rembrandt has long been a fashionable master [in prints]. The date of Rembrandt is getting over, and other masters are getting into fashion."

The very tolerant Sir Joshua Reynolds here and there patronized the painters of the Low Countries, but rather gingerly. Towards the end of his Sixth Discourse, delivered in 1774 to the students of the Royal Academy, he remarks in "Frank Hals"—"that strong-marked character of individual nature which is so remarkable in his portraits, and is not found in an equal degree in any other painter." But Sir Joshua deplored a lack of "patience in finishing" which left Hals second to Van Dyck. So complete a misunderstanding of Hals' technique by an accomplished painter is deplorable.

As for Jan Steen, whom Sir Joshua evidently regarded as the best of the little masters, "had he lived in Rome instead of Leyden, and been blessed with Michael Angelo and Raffaelle for his masters, instead of Brouwer and Van Goyen . . . he now would have ranged with the great pillars and supporters of our Art."

Such sheer silliness from a really wise person should make us of less wisdom very humble.

Sir Joshua Reynolds in his *A Journey to Flanders and Holland in the year* 1781 takes for an artist of his authority an unusually generous view of the little Dutch masters. Oddly enough his noble patrons in England had bought or inherited hundreds of good Dutch and Flemish pictures. But these were hung in bedroom or corridor, somewhat apologetically, and not in the gallery.

Sir Joshua gives almost all his space to Rubens and Van Dyck, while not neglecting Rembrandt. His list of the best painters of the Low Countries is interesting both for its inclusions and omissions.

"The most considerable of the Dutch school are Rembrandt, Teniers, Jan Steen, Ostade, Brouwer, Gerard Dou, Mieris, Metzu and Terburg: these excel in small conversations. For landscapes and cattle, Wouwermans, P. Potter, Berchem and Ruysdael; and for buildings, Vanderheyden. For sea views, W. Vandervelde jun., and Backhuysen." (*The Works of Sir Joshua Reynolds*, London, 1801. Vol. III, p. 371.)

I omit his list of flower painters, etc.

The list is by no means a bad one, but it is odd that he never thought enough about any Hals he may have seen to write about it specifically, and failed to respond to the Goyens and Hobbemas. Still stranger is the omission of Cuyp, who was admirably represented in English private collections. One hopes he never saw a Vermeer of Delft, and that is probable. His summing up of the matter is a nice blend of personal condescension and professional admiration.

"A market-woman with a hare in her hands, a man blowing a trumpet, or a boy blowing bubbles, a view of the inside of a church, are the subjects of some of their most valuable pictures; but there is still entertainment, even in such pictures: however uninteresting their subjects, there is some pleasure in the contemplation of the truth of the imitation. But to a painter they afford likewise instruction in his profession; here he may learn the art of colouring and composition, a skillful management of light and shade, and indeed all the mechanical parts of the art, as well as in any school whatever. The same skill which is practised by Rubens and Titian in their large works, is here exhibited, though on a smaller scale. Painters should go to the Dutch school to learn the art of painting, as they would go to a grammar school to learn languages. They must go to Italy to learn the higher branches of knowledge." (P. 69 f.)

Despite the disapproval or faint praise of the highbrows, the Dutch masters steadily made their way among the unspoiled citizenry. Even in France academic opinion shifted in their favor (see quotation from Charles Coypel, Director of the Academy, p. 847). In 1771 the print seller and expert Basan published an album of the pictures of the popular Duc de Choiseul, *Recueil d'estampes gravées d'après les tableaux du cabinet de Mgr. le Duc de Choiseul,* Paris, 1775. The Duke owned one hundred twenty-eight pictures of which over a hundred were Dutch and Flemish. He had a Le Nain. The triumph of the little Dutch masters is marked by the criticism of William Hazlitt who in *Painting and the Fine Arts,* Edinburgh, 1838, p. 26 f., wrote the first real appreciation of Rembrandt. To Sir Joshua's "howler" about Jan Steen, Hazlitt furnishes the complete answer. To be sure the Dutch painters copied nature closely,

> "having no preference, or preference of one thing to another, unless that they preferred that which was most obvious and common. We forgive them. They perhaps did better in faithfully and skillfully imitating what they had seen, than in imagining what they had not seen. Their pictures at least show that there is nothing in nature, however mean or trivial, that has not its beauty, and some interest belonging to it, if truly represented. We prefer Vangoyen's views on the borders of a canal, the yellow-tufted bank and passing sail, or Ruysdael's woods and sparkling water-falls, to the most classical composition which they could have invented out of nothing." (*The Fine Arts,* London, 1838. P. 27.)

This prolonged opposition to the most ingratiating of pictures merely shows the folly of seeing pictures through the ears, by formulas, rather than through the eyes. Sir Joshua had handsomely admitted the superiority of the Dutch technique while regretting that it was applied to inferior subject matter. It remained for Hazlitt to vindicate the value of the devotion of the Dutch little masters to the actual scene and to insist that "Whatever is genuine in art must proceed from the impulse of nature and individual genius."

That is a saying to remember in these days when self-elected individual genius is quite ready to go it alone, without nature.

CHAPTER XIX

## Landscape Painters of the Low Countries

With the possible exception of the Italianates and Paul Potter, whose scanty production soon acquired a scarcity value, Dutch land-

scape painting was without honor in its own time and country, and
its ablest practitioners died in poverty. Until early in the nineteenth
century there was no critical writing of any consequence about the
Dutch landscapists. All the same their works were slowly gaining
favor as the love of nature enlisted such writers as James Thomson
and Rousseau. By 1750 most of the great Ruysdaels had been added
to the Dresden Gallery by the King of Saxony. Already the best
Cuyps and Hobbemas were in English hands. By 1800 Dutch landscape painting was a beneficent influence on Old Crome and Georges
Michel, and a little later on Constable and Turner.

I believe the first writer to assert the greatness of Ruysdael was
Goethe, in an essay, "Ruysdael as Poet," published in 1813. He
notes in three notable Ruysdaels at Dresden, Castle Bentheim, the
Old Cloister, and the Jewish Cemetery, a common purpose to show
as compared with the eternal renovation of nature, the transitoriness
of man's most enduring work.

> "The second picture, famous under the name of The
> Cloister, has with a richer, more attractive composition, the
> similar aim: to represent the past in the present, and this is
> achieved in the most admirable manner, what is dead and
> gone being brought into the most clear relation with the
> living. . . .
> The third picture on the contrary is wholly dedicated to
> the past, without granting present life any rights whatever.
> It is known under the name of The Cemetery. The tomb-
> stones indeed, in their ruined condition, point to something
> more than passed away, they have become tombstones of
> tombstones." (Goethe's *Schriften zur Kunst.* Stuttgart und
> Berlin. Part 3, p. 3 ff., Cotta ed. bd. XXXV.)

Of the pictorial accomplishment of these great works Goethe
makes next to nothing, but his reading of their spiritual meaning is
profoundly just.

Pilkington's *General Dictionary of Painters* was widely read in
England in the first quarter of the nineteenth century. His perfunctory articles on "Kuyp," Goyen, Hobbema and Ruysdael show that
their works were eagerly sought and highly paid in England at that
time. A more considerate but on the whole factual treatment of
these painters is offered.

But William Hazlitt, an audacious and felicitous pioneer of taste in many fields, was the first Englishman to write searchingly and specifically about these masters. His "Notes on the Gallery of Dulwich College" contains his most important observations.

> "Cuyp must have possessed incomparably more imagination than any other Flemish landscape-painter, or than all the others united; for though he appears rarely to have strayed beyond the suburbs of his native town of Dort, he has, by the aid of an extremely limited number of objects of study that he met with there, created scenes of the most chaste and exquisite beauty, unlike anything that he could have seen, and yet consistent with nature and with themselves in every particular. He seems to have conceived these scenes in his mind in the first instance, and (so to speak) finished them there, and then as it were *breathed* them on his canvas, almost without the aid of his pencil—so sweetly clear, delicate and ethereal some of them are." (*British Galleries of Art*, London, 1824. P. 170 f.)

Hazlitt cleverly pointed out the thinness of Wouverman's art, and gives guarded praise to Hobbema and Ruysdael.

> "His [Ruysdael's] trees have equal firmness and decision with those of Hobbima, and perhaps even more crispness and spirit; and his waterfalls, and pieces of running water, actually talk and move—you can almost hear them as they go. . . . There is also great force and depth in the foliage, which he always introduces into his scenes in great profusion." (l. c. p. 187.)

In 1843, the youthful and overenthusiastic John Ruskin published the first volume of *Modern Painters*, in order to extol Turner at the expense of all his predecessors. No one has understood landscape beauty more deeply than Ruskin, and, paradoxically, no one has written more foolishly about landscape painting. His slighting paragraph on Ruysdael may instructively be compared with Goethe's noble tribute quoted above.

> "Ruysdael's painting of falling water is also generally agreeable; more than agreeable it can hardly be considered.

There appears no exertion of mind in any of his works; nor are they calculated to produce either harm or good by their feeble influence. They are good furniture pictures, unworthy of praise, and undeserving of blame." (*The Works of John Ruskin*, Library Ed., vol. III, p. 517.)

Such writing in a really great writer is simply infuriating.

Happily nobody believed Ruskin in this matter. Delacroix in his *Journals*, about 1859, mentions Ruysdael among the great painters, and when towards the end of the nineteenth century Fromentin and Bode wrote admiringly about the Dutch landscape painters they merely expressed the general opinion of the judicious.

Modernistic criticism has on the whole ignored these painters, perhaps narrow-mindedly and unfairly.

CHAPTER XX

## The Fame of Velasquez

Velasquez naturally received favorable mention in the *Arte de la Pintura*, of his father-in-law, Pacheco, whose survey covered only his gifted son-in-law's early activity.

But in general, even in Spain, the recognition of Velasquez' supremacy as a portrait painter was strangely retarded. The generally liberal Félibien devotes a slighting and very brief paragraph to Velasquez in the *Entretiens* (T. II, p. 454). The interlocutor, Pymandre, asks what is to be thought of the royal portraits by Velasquez "in the lower apartments of the Louvre," and also if Spain has not produced great painters. Félibien, speaking with authority, answers.

> "I notice here the same qualities which are found in other painters not of the first rank, except it seems in observing the manner of these two Spaniards that they have selected and regard nature in a very peculiar fashion, not giving to their pictures beyond resemblance to nature, that style [*bel air*] which dignifies and lends grace to those of the other painters about whom we have spoken."

They had been speaking about Andrea Sacchi and Pietro da Cortona.

The Venetian painter, critic and poetaster Marco Boschini, in his *La Carta del Navegar Pittoresco*, etc., Venetia, 1660. P. 56 ff., gives considerable and favorable attention to Velasquez chiefly because he had praised the Venetian painters and dispraised the Romans. Boschini even calls Velasquez a "perfect painter," being led, I fear, by the need of a rime for his doggerel, for he does not elaborate the compliment:

> Fu Don Diego Velasquez gran sugeto
> Del Catolico Rè Pitor perfeto.

> "Don Diego Velasquez, a great subject
> Of the Catholic King, was a perfect painter."

About the only kind words the eighteenth century vouchsafed to Velasquez were written by a nameless French captain and by the poet Thomas Gray. The captain, in a very interesting *Voyage d'un Amateur des Arts*, Amsterdam, 1783. T. I, p. 91, advised visitors to the Louvre to ask to be shown the bathroom in the old apartment of the queen—"the paintings are by Velasquez, a painter very little known, whose style has great merit."

The poet Gray in a tabulation of artists which he made for his own convenience wrote opposite Velasquez "great fire and force." (*Literary Works of Sir Joshua Reynolds*, London, 1801. Vol. III, p. 320.)

But Jonathan Richardson, mentor of two generations of British collectors, never even mentions Velasquez in the various editions of his book *On Painting*, last edition, London, 1792.

So far as I know the first sensitive and intelligent criticism of Velasquez is that of the unfortunate painter, R. B. Haydon. It was written for the seventh edition of the Encyclopaedia Britannica, and reprinted in *Painting and the Fine Arts*, London, 1838. P. 195.

> "In masterly execution and life, he surpassed Rubens and Vandyke. Of all the great painters, he seems to have despised the most the vulgar appetite for what is called *finish*, that is, polished smoothness. Every touch of Velasquez is a *thought* calculated to express the points of the *thing* intended to convey it. Masterly beyond description, and delightful beyond belief, he conveyed the impressions of life as exquisitely as if his imitation breathed."

A little earlier a young American naval officer, A. S. Mackenzie, traveled joyously through Spain and published anonymously *A Year in Spain by a Young American*, in 3 vols., London, 1831. Brigands and dancers interested him more than painters, but he wrote concerning Velasquez (vol. I, p. 225):

> "His portraits for furnishing accurate representations of individuals are perhaps superior to those of Titian and Vandyke. They are not, indeed, highly wrought, but have about them the strong strokes of a master."

The English campaigns in Spain during the Napoleonic Wars shook loose many pictures by Velasquez, most of which came to England, and the fame of Velasquez grew as realism and impressionism, of which Velasquez was the supreme exemplar, came to be leading tendencies in Paris and its artistic dependencies. From 1880 to say 1910 and the dawn of post-impressionism, Velasquez was *par excellence*, the painters' painter, the incomparable model. The recent swing towards abstraction and expressionism has somewhat diminished his prestige, I think only temporarily.

CHAPTER XXII

The development of French painting under Louis XIII and XIV is best studied in the writings of Charles Félibien and Rogier de Piles. Both were moderate liberals, both were officially associated with the Royal Academy of Painting. They wrote most judiciously about painters whom they personally knew, and their eyes were open to old and contemporary painting outside of France. They may be regarded as the pioneers of modern art criticism—a criticism which proceeds less from *à priori* principles than from appreciation of personality as expressed in the work of art.

Félibien's most important work was modestly called "Chats." *Entretiens sur les Vies et sur les Ouvrages des plus Excellens Peintres*, Paris, 1677. I cite the second edition in two volumes, Paris, 1685. Writing in dialogue form, Félibien tends to lengthiness, but he is invariably sensitive and interesting.

De Piles' most valuable work was the little handbook *Abregé de la Vie des Peintres*, Paris, 1699. It was the first work of this sort to classify artists by national schools. It proposed a marking system for artistic greatness, which, while a bit pedantic, became popular. De Piles was nevertheless an enlightened and generous spirit. I cite the second edition of the *Abregé*, Paris, 1715. There are old English translations which are here used on occasion.

### Opinions on Vouet

The extreme popularity of Vouet did not blind these generally friendly critics to his flimsiness.

> "I will tell you frankly," writes Félibien, "that, as for invention, he did not have a facile and easy genius [this was attacking Vouet on what was generally regarded as his strong point]. I have even learned from some of his ablest pupils that he could not compose a picture without use of the model. . . . He was ignorant of perspective and knew neither the unity or affinities of color, nor harmony of light and dark. What is most to be esteemed in his pictures is the beauty and freshness of his brush stroke. . . . But what can say most for his fame is that the excellent precepts of that learned man formed able men; and one may admit, as I have said that it was in his time that painting began to appear here with a more beautiful and noble air than formerly it had." (*Entretiens.* T. II. P. 190.)

De Piles raises doubts even as to Vouet's value as a teacher.

> "One may say on the one side that Vouet's manner improved the insipid taste that reigned in France when he arrived; on the other side that it [his manner] was so unnatural, barbarous, yet facile and received with such avidity, that it infected the taste of all his pupils up to the point of making them acquire a habit of which they had painfully to rid themselves; and, as I have said, that expeditious manner was not that of Vouet, but that of his interests." (*Abregé*, p. 457.)

### The Character of Philippe de Champaigne

Our two critics admired Philippe de Champaigne with some reserves because of his austerity, particularly his lack of fine color. Félibien passes on anecdotes which tell about Philippe de Cham-

paigne's most sturdy and serviceable character. Once Cardinal Richelieu offered the painter whatever he might wish for himself or his
family.

> "But Champaigne answered that if the Cardinal could
> make him a better painter than he was, that would be the
> only thing that he had to ask of his eminence; but as that
> was not possible, he asked of the Cardinal only the honor of
> his favor and courtesy." (*Entretiens.* T. II. P. 580.)

The anecdote may suggest the fastidiousness that accompanied
the strength and rectitude of Philippe de Champaigne's portraiture.

> "When appointed a rector of the Academy," writes Félibien,
> "in that position he showed a conduct and disinterested-
> ness almost unexampled, sharing the emoluments of his posi-
> tion with such as had need of them and being willing to
> receive them only to do good to others." (*Ibid.*)

### The Les Nain

The Les Nain, although academicians, got scornful, short shrift
from Félibien, whose tolerance did not reach to genre painting. He
writes:

> "The brothers Le Nain made portraits and narratives, but
> in a manner with little nobility, often representing simple
> subjects without beauty.
> 'I have seen,' Pymandre interrupted, 'some of their pic-
> tures, but I avow that I could not stop to consider these sub-
> jects in actions base and ridiculous.'
> 'The works,' I continued, 'in which intelligence has little
> part soon become boresome. Not but that when there is
> verisimilitude, and the things are expressed with art, these
> things do not surprise at first sight, and do not please us
> for some time before they bore us. Because this sort of
> paintings can divert us only for a moment and at intervals.
> One sees few knowing persons who care much for them.'"
> (*Entretiens.* T. II. P. 487.)

Félibien does give the Les Nain an obscure place in the sun.
De Piles some twenty years later did not find them worth mention-

ing. Recent criticism has perhaps overdone the reparation due for this long neglect, for at their best the Les Nain are hardly second-class painters.

## Claude Lorrain

The German artist and archaeologist Joachim Sandrart was a friend of Claude and is our best witness as to Claude's methods. He writes:

> "Claude lay before daylight and into the night in the fields so that he learned to depict the morning and evening glow with great naturalness, and when he had well observed it in the fields, he mixed his colors accordingly, and ran back to the house with them, and thus he gave to his distinguished work greater naturalness than any before him."
> (J. Sandrart. *Teutsche Academie*, Frankfurt, 1675. P. 332.)

This passage strikingly shows to what extent Claude had systematically memorized natural appearances and their equivalents in paint. His painting in the open air, of which Sandrart, as instigator, makes much, was only a transient and insignificant episode.

Félibien, oddly, ignores Claude completely. De Piles, doubtless attracted by Claude's gift as a colorist, writes a sympathetic notice, mostly out of Sandrart.

> "Sandrart reports that being on the Campagna with him, studying together, the Lorrain made him notice, as a natural scientist would have done, the causes of the diversity of the same view, that is to say that it appears now in one way, now in another, for the one who observes the colors, as it appears in dewy morning or quiet evening.

*   *   *

He was so absorbed in his work that he hardly visited any one. His diversion was the study of his profession, and by cultivating his talent he has made pictures which have gained for him throughout the world an immortal reputation in the kind of painting which he embraced. From this one may gather what persistence in work can effect against a dull spirit. He worked painfully, and his work failed to meet his intention. He sometimes was a week making and unmaking the same thing." (Abregé, p. 522.)

John Ruskin's attempt, in Modern Painters, to bump Claude off in the interest of Turner, has only a remote historic import. Claude's fame has been singularly stable, and recent criticism tends to enhance it.

CHAPTER XXIV

### Nicolas Poussin

Félibien's, after two centuries and a half, is still one of the best estimates of Poussin.

"Whatever work he made, he never proceeded violently; he conducted himself with moderation, without seeming feebler at the end than at the beginning of his work, because that fine fire which ever warmed his imagination had always an equal intensity. The light which illuminated his thoughts was uniform, pure and without smoke. Even when he had to show vehemence in his compositions, sometimes wrath and indignation, whether he was obliged to represent the effect of a just grief, he was never too much carried away, but conducted himself with a constant prudence and a constant wisdom." (Entretiens. T. II. P. 437.)

Rogier de Piles in general shared Félibien's admiration for Poussin, but makes his reservations.

"His nude figures are much like painted stone, and have rather the hardness of marble than the delicacy of flesh alive and full of blood.

\*     \*     \*

His landscapes are admirable for choice of site, for novelty of components, for truthfulness of lay of land, for variety of trees and lightness of touch—in short for the originality of the subjects which he introduces. So that he would have made them perfect if he had strengthened them a little more by local color and by light and shade.

* * *

However great his genius was, it could not reach to every branch of painting; for the love that he had for the antique so bounded his mind that it prevented him from considering his art from every side—I mean that he neglected color.

* * *

Indeed his colors are generalized and not imitation of those of nature which he rarely saw: I speak of his figures and not of his landscapes in which he took more pains to consult nature, the reason of which is palpable, namely not having found landscape in ancient marbles, he was forced to seek it in Nature.

* * *

All in all, Poussin was not only the ablest of his nation, but also the peer of the greatest painters of Italy." (Abregé, pp. 467-470.)

De Piles failed to perceive the sacrifices necessary in an art like Poussin's. Sir Joshua Reynolds, in his rough notes for the "Discourses" makes this point well.

"Poussine('s) manner (supra Grandeur) is simpl(e) accurate determined formal determined with the utmost precision (in) formal measured steps, everything is in order –hard.

* * *

Poussine('s) stile would have suffer'd degradation, had if his pictures had the effect of Titian's, the effect would not have corresponded with the simplicity which Poussin made wished to be his predominant character; it would have been too rich." (The Literary Works of Sir Joshua Reynolds, by Frederick Whiley Hilles. New York, Cambridge [England], 1936. P. 230 f.)

De Piles transmits an anecdote which makes its picture and well suggests the personal probity and independence that underlay Poussin's graciously austere art.

"One day the Prelate Massimi, who later was a cardinal, having gone to see Poussin, the talk lasted insensibly till night, and as the Prelate left, Poussin, lamp in hand, walked before him, lighted him the length of the staircase and so saw him to his carriage. This was so painful to M. Massimi that he could not keep from saying:

'I'm very sorry for you, M. Poussin, that you haven't even one manservant.' 'And I,' replied Poussin, 'am much more sorry for you because you have so many.' " (*Abregé*, p. 463.)

CHAPTER XXV

In May 1681, the Academy made a treaty with the old Maîtrise, but as regards popularization maintained a right of censorship.

"IX. That everyone in these two bodies who shall make designs for engraving or to engrave themselves, shall be obliged to show them to the Academy to have the visa affixed before they are publicly shown, so that nothing unfit shall be exhibited, and in case of failure to do this there shall be a discretionary fine." (*Procès Verbaux de l'Académie Royale*, etc., ed. A. Montaiglon, Paris, 1875. I. P. 46.)

Dec. 6, 1659. M. Pader presented his qualifying picture (Perpetual Peace under Augustus) and was received on condition of continuing his translation [of Lomazzo's *Treatise on Painting*] and to publish nothing that he might write concerning the arts of painting and sculpture without first communicating it to the Academy and receiving its approval." (P. 162.)

The first lecture. May 7, 1667.

"The Academy assembled to hear the lecture which M. Ch. Lebrun had been ordered to make on the St. Michel of Raphael." (P. 319.)

June, 1667. Philippe de Champaigne, Titian's Descent from the Cross. (P. 320.)

July 5, 1670. Sebastian Bourdon read a lecture on the propor-

tions of the Commodus, the Hercules, the Wounded Gladiator, and
the River God [Nile] of the Belvedere. (P. 350.)

The students did not observe academic decorum. November
29, 1670, twelve were expelled.

> "For divers insolences, as they left the school, beating each
> other up, with howls and strange antics, throwing stones
> into the neighboring shops, and for their vileness, in the
> very school itself: they defecated on the duds of the
> model." (P. 353.)

The state of universal tolerance at which French taste arrived
early in the eighteenth century is well expressed by the address which
the first painter of the king, Charles Coypel, delivered on September
7, 1720, before the Académie Royale de Peinture et de Sculpture.
The lecture is in the form of an elaborate commentary on a poem
which he had earlier written for the instruction of his son.

Coypel pokes fun at the old feud of the Poussinists and Rubensists, insists there is no superiority of form over color. He likes, contrary to the royal taste, the little Dutch masters.

> "Imitation is generally pleasing to men, since in the slight-
> est objects exactly imitated, it always yields its effect. Even
> in great things one can hardly prize it too much: it is only
> the prejudiced half-learned, or painters spoiled by routine,
> who are insensible to it.
>
> The little pictures of the Flemish and Dutch are much to
> be recommended on this score, and I am sometimes put
> out that they are banished entirely from the cabinets into
> which are gathered the pictures of the old Italians: I know
> that these [Dutch pictures] lack the selection, nobility and
> elevation which one finds in the Italians; but in the sub-
> jects which suit them they are sometimes perfect, even by
> reason of the naïveté of the expressions.
>
> Kalf [the still-life painter, p. 562], in the objects which he
> has imitated after nature, seems to me to speak the language
> of painting, as well as Giorgione and Titian, with the dif-
> ference that he does not know how to say such grand
> things as these great masters of art." (*Discours Prononcez*

*dans les Conférences de l'Académie Royale de Peinture et Sculpture.* Paris, 1721. P. 21 f.)

Coypel, as director of the Academy, advises the students to study the principles of many good masters, especially Giorgione and Titian for color, Correggio, and Rembrandt, Rubens and Van Dyck for chiaroscuro, Raphael, Annibale Caracci, Domenichino, Guido for drawing and composition. Even such irregulars as Tintoretto and Paolo Veronese are to be consulted with caution. Pains should be taken to avoid a certain monotony of antique sculpture.

> "If Poussin, so profound and to be respected for knowledge of the antique, had been able to combine with the great beauties which he drew from the antique, that naïve imitation of nature, he would have been sometimes less hard in his drawing and painting. His color would have been more true, more strong and more harmonious. His drapery would have been softer, of a greater style, less dry and more varied, as well as the expression of his female heads, which are all the same, and which seem to be taken from antique heads. Variety is necessary in painting as in all the arts." (*Discours*, p. 112.)

Of course the criticism of Poussin is contestable. Its very existence within a generation of Poussin's death is striking evidence of the liberalizing of official and academic doctrine in France.

Finally a very perceptive observation on Rembrandt's technique.

> "The works of Rembrandt which most show the touch, and even the harshest, are really infinitely searched, and are painted with as much suavity and relief as those of Correggio, in which one does not perceive any brush strokes. Such beautiful things as Raphael executed himself are, whatever you may say to the contrary, on the same principles." (*Discours*, p. 42.)

# INDEX *

* See Appendix (pp. 805-848) for incidental historical illustrations relating to the
leading painters discussed in the text.